D1327719

Age of Assassins

by the same author

SAVAGE GIRLS AND WILD BOYS
A History of Feral Children

AGE OF ASSASSINS

A History of Conspiracy and Political Violence
1865–1981

MICHAEL NEWTON

faber and faber

First published in 2012
by Faber and Faber Limited
Bloomsbury House
74–77 Great Russell Street
London WC1B 3DA

Typeset by Donald Sommerville
Printed in England by CPI Group (UK) Ltd, Croydon, CR0 4YY

A CIP record for this book
is available from the British Library

ISBN 978–0–571–22044–1

2 4 6 8 10 9 7 5 3 1

For Lena Müller

Contents

CONCLUSION

Plates

Acknowledgements

I especially thank my editor Julian Loose at Faber and Faber, and my agent Victoria Hobbs at A. M. Heath. Both had good reason to believe that this book would never be finished, and I am grateful for their keeping faith with me, as well as for their encouragement, knowledge and good advice. Thanks are also due to the production team at Faber and especially to Donald Sommerville who skilfully copy-edited and typeset the book. I thank also the very helpful Rebecca Lee, Alex Holroyd, and, for her excellent work on the picture research, Bronagh Woods.

I would like to thank: for access to Lucy Cavendish's manuscripts, Ian Killeen at Special Collections, University of Birmingham Library, and for permission to quote directly from manuscript sources, Mr N. C. Masterman.

For their help and cooperation, I am grateful to the staff of Princeton University Library, the Staatsbibliotek zu Berlin, the library of Leiden University, The British Library, The Newspaper Library at Colindale and The National Archives in London, and particularly to the International Institute of Social History in Amsterdam, Lambeth Palace Library and the Liddell Hart Centre for Military Archives, King's College London.

I thank Lorna Gibb, Christopher Hamilton and Ingrid Horrocks for taking the time to read some of the manuscript, for offering helpful suggestions and sustaining my confidence. Gregory Dart, Richard Hamblyn, Sarah Quigley and Stephen James were also writing seemingly unending books at the same time that I was; their good humour and good sense were invaluable. Lee Sands offered many rewarding suggestions, especially regarding titles. (The clunkier ones are all my own.) And thanks to Richard Allen for Serbian counsel, to Jason Whiston for his friendship and advice, and to Karl Miller for continuing to be concerned.

In the course of writing, I was sometimes very hard-up for cash; for this reason, I especially want to thank Eileen Gunn and the Royal Literary Fund for awarding me a grant which kept me going.

For their support I thank my colleagues at the Universiteit van Leiden: Nadine Akkerman; Sieglinde Bollen; Jan Frans van Dijkhuizen; Joke Kardux; Evert-Jan van Leeuwen; Peter Liebregts; Tessa Obbens; Sara Polak; Richard Todd; Karin van der Zeeuw. Above all, Jenny Weston took time out from her own research to help me by sharing her academic know-how.

My biggest thanks go to my family, especially to my mother and father who have always helped and always listened, and to my daughter Alice, who provided much needed relief. Without the unfailing gentleness, warmth and patience of my wife, Lena Müller, this book would never have progressed beyond endless research. For this and for many other reasons, I am hugely grateful to her, and for that reason this book is dedicated to her.

Preface

'Voici le temps des assassins.'

    ARTHUR RIMBAUD

This book is the history of our love affair with violence. During the seven years in which I was writing it, people would often ask me what prompted me to devote so much time to a subject such as assassination. Though usually embarrassed for an appropriate response, looking back now I would say that it was one representative incident, apparently unconnected to the subject itself, that provoked my curiosity.

Some years ago I was lecturing on a temporary contract in the Department of English at Princeton University. I was supervising one student's junior paper; she was a sweet and amiable young woman, intellectually alert, sensitive and thoughtful, an ideal student of literature. One day she came to my office a little late. I asked her what she had been doing. Without embarrassment or any awkwardness, she promptly explained that she had been watching on the internet the film of the beheading of Nicholas Evan Berg, an American businessman kidnapped by Islamic militants in Iraq. I was taken aback. Why on earth had she watched such a thing? She shrugged, and said that she couldn't really explain it, but that lots of the students on campus had viewed the murder on their laptops. It seemed as though the fact that this man's death was there online as an image had rendered it morally neutral, just an interesting thing to see, a test of courage for the viewer, a boundary challenged, a small thrill.

This book is an attempt to explain my bafflement, my horror really, not just at the fact that she had permitted herself to collude in such a way with an act of political violence, but at the apparent flatness with which she did so. Shock was a kind of stimulant, assassination an entertainment. It was the conjunction of that student's gentleness and her willingness to participate vicariously in cruelty that pulled me up. That complicity is, I believe, at the centre of the story of assassination in the last 150 years. It is this which this book seeks to investigate and unravel.

I should make it plain that I do not see myself as above the connivance at the heart of our fascination with violence, and, in particular, the violence of assassination. On a more intellectual level, it was researching William Shakespeare's *Macbeth*, with its indebtedness to the Gowrie conspiracy, whereby plotters attempted to assassinate King James using witchcraft, that first drew my attention to the subject. Yet I had taught a course on crime movies at a London art school, and been puzzled even then by the voyeuristic glee with which students immersed themselves in murder. On two occasions, to my consternation and bafflement, a young woman student chose Myra Hindley as the subject of her final presentation, in both cases endeavouring to get in touch with her. I was troubled, but, after all, this was my course: it was I who had set up the situation in which such a thing could happen. In teaching the course, it struck me, in particular, how often the assassin was presented as a sensitive and tortured soul, or otherwise a cool embodiment of power. How had this situation arisen? Why did the figure of the assassin invite such equivocal and potent responses? In short, *Age of Assassins* is an attempt to answer these questions and examine those thoughts. It is both a narrative history of modern assassination and an attempt to reflect upon a situation in which such vicious crimes could look at best, heroic, and at worst, grimly fascinating.

Although there are excursions elsewhere and glances backwards and forwards, this book focuses largely on the USA and Europe from Dublin to Moscow during the years from the assassination of Abraham Lincoln to the attempted murder of Ronald Reagan. Even within this framework I had to select. The story of assassination is of course much bigger than this. However, it is one of the arguments of this book that by taking this narrower focus an interconnected narrative of events emerges. Although assassination is by its nature abrupt and shocking, yet within this framework one thing does lead to another. Within the book's limits, there is in any case a plenitude of examples and contexts, from Tsarist Russia to Civil Rights-era America, from Armenia to Berlin, from presidents to industrialists, from monarchs to pop stars. Although some stories are mentioned in passing, my intention has always been not to take history in the gross, but to allow space to explain the political and cultural situation in which such murders have taken place, and to give enough detail to provide a sense of the character and qualities of both assassins and victims.

While I am suspicious of classifications in this area, in writing on this subject nonetheless some kind of working definition has to be made. We can say that assassination is the murder of a powerful or prominent person on account of their power and prominence. This rather minimal description is intended to be as all-embracing as possible. We might add that an assassination is a murder in which the impact is perceived as being, among other effects, political. Yet even a statement asserting that assassination is the killing of a political figure for political and not personal reasons runs into trouble, as it would seem to exclude all such murders committed by the mad, a limit that would rule out the consideration of some of the most significant assassinations.[1]

Such problems of definition are long-standing; the deed lives in its interpretation. Up until the late nineteenth century, political murder manifested an ethical contradiction. On one side, such slayings were the product of Roman virtue and Republican rectitude; in this instance the victims were tyrants and their killers were termed 'tyrannicides'. On the other lay a feudal model of loyalty (perhaps more praised than practised), in which such killing seemed the worst kind of treachery; in this second instance, such murderers were named 'assassins'. Here the word's etymological roots among the Crusaders' wars against Muslims were implicit; such killers were marked out as foreign, as demonic heretics. The sense of 'assassination' as murder by ambush similarly fitted the horror and cunning of such crimes.[2]

If one long-standing distinction separates the tyrannicide from the assassin, another divides the assassin from the terrorist. Though inter-twined, there are crucial differences between a history of assassination and one of terrorism. This is especially true for the post-war period in the USA, as assassinations become the province of the lonely and politically unaffiliated individual. Even before then, while many assassinations were tied to revolutionary movements, it was clear that the crime was very often a freelance effort, an action by an individual against an individual. In the passage from terrorism to assassination, the target moved from society in general to society's identifiable and famous leaders.

From the 1860s to the present day, assassinations have often exerted enormous influence, provoking revolutions, shifting policies, even sparking wars. However, sometimes they produced no major change at all, merely enforcing an adjustment of personnel. The route to success or failure by which individual assassinations provoke a key transformation is a subject that this book consciously does not treat at length. For one of its arguments is that in its 120–year period, assassination shook itself loose from the bonds of political efficacy. Instead, beginning with Lincoln, the sheer fact of having acted at all, and that act's immediate metamorphosis into a portent was all at which the assassin really aimed.

An assassination is always a catastrophe; it is nothing if not dramatic. Sometimes, indeed, it may even subside into melodrama. But, in narrative terms, there must always be a spectacular intrusion into the ordinary process of living, an intervention disrupting the expected. There, at the centre of the thing, is a shot, a stabbing, an explosion, a crime seeming to come out of nowhere. Historians are professionally committed to the notion of sequence, that one thing follows another. And yet of all historical subjects, assassination may leave us most sceptical about this fixation on cause and effect. Such murders can be seen as fractures in the spine of chronology.[3] In this sense, twentieth-century assassination is of a piece with the crisis of storytelling felt by the modernist writers, their sense that a fragmentary and disrupted world cannot be explained in a story. Stories with beginnings, middles, ends, coherent characters, are replaced in assassination, as in modern fiction, by apparently random deeds.

Writing the history of assassination therefore could mean simply to unfold a sequence of sudden killings, without background or context, just a gathering of history's 'greatest hits'. However, such a book would hold little interest. Isolated from the situations that most often gave them purpose, such abrupt happenings lose all significance. Rather the aim has been to write a story that unsettles our belief in story, while also using narrative to frame connections, to find the causes in the apparently causeless. The method of this book depends upon the idea that storytelling embodies a form of understanding. However, in terms of the representation of assassination, such a story must itself have crisis written into it. In so far as they select, shape and fall back upon a rhetoric, all histories necessarily partake of the nature of fictions. And yet the intention remains to preserve fidelity to the truths of an event. Such truths prove elusive, yet of all forms a story may best bear witness to their obscure presence.

Although there is some reference to archival documents, for the most part the book surveys the primary and secondary printed material on the subject. I have relied therefore, I hope judiciously, on the archival research of others. Those looking for new conspiracy theories or the naming of new suspects will be disappointed. My intention was always to present something of the history of this subject from Lincoln to Reagan and to explore its complexities through narrative and reflection. Much of that history seems lost to our ongoing historical memory; my hope was simply to bring it back to light and in the process to illuminate its meanings.

A Justifiable Killing

And not rather, (as we be slanderously reported, and as some affirm that we say,) Let us do evil, that good may come?
ROMANS, 3: 8

He begged Nina not to go. Couldn't she postpone for just a short while her holiday with their children? But then what reasons could Stauffenberg give her? There were none. So Nina bought her train tickets for Lautlingen, and left on 18 July 1944.[1] The next night, perhaps his last night, he tried to ring her, but the lines were down; there had been bombs dropped on Ebingen. He didn't know if he would ever speak to her again. In the morning, Schweizer came in his car to pick up Stauffenberg and his brother. In an early morning fog, they met Werner von Haeften at Rangsdorf airfield. The brothers parted. And so, around eight o'clock, Haeften and Stauffenberg flew out of Berlin, with a bomb concealed in a briefcase.

In July 1944 Claus Schenk Graf von Stauffenberg was in his late thirties, the epitome of the handsome and courageous German military man. Indeed he had, some twelve years earlier, twice served literally as a model for the German soldier, posing for a sculptor's SA monument and for another heroic statue of a German pioneer to adorn the bridge across the Elbe at Magdeburg. Stauffenberg represented all that the Nazis were fighting for, the apotheosis of Teutonic manhood. There was the enchantedly privileged childhood: the velvet suits and long pre-pubescent ringlets; the fearless skiing with his older twin brothers, Berthold and Alexander; the summer house at Lautlingen; the little cart for the brothers led by their very own donkey; the music lessons; the harvests; the unbearable excitement of reading Hölderlin.[2] And then, the long trauma of the Great War, his cousin dying at Verdun, the visits of wounded heroes from the Western Front. Claus too had been a twin

– but his little brother, Konrad, had died a day after their birth. He was a soldier, scholar, horseman. He played the cello feelingly; read Homer in Greek; learnt Russian; became fluent in English; was charming, frank, punctiliously careless in conversation: in short, a Swabian aristocrat.

With such a background, it may not be surprising that Stauffenberg should have been drawn at first to the National Socialists, sharing as he did their sense of a heroic Germany and feeling, too, the wounding indignities of Versailles. In this he resembled many who would later become prominent in the resistance against Hitler; for countless Germans in the early 1930s, Nazism meant the repudiation of Versailles and a return to stability and community after what they perceived as the democratic chaos of the Weimar years.[3] Yet there was always something in the Stauffenbergs that drew back from the abyss of total commitment to Nazism.[4] There were, for instance, the snobberies of his caste; the Jewish friends; the exemplary influence of Catholicism; even the mystical Germanism of Stefan George that so enthralled the three brothers, longing to share in the old poet's *Reich des Geistes* (kingdom of the spirit).[5] Significantly for Stauffenberg's later direction, George never gave his blessing to the Nazi regime, deeming its vulgarities an inadequate embodiment of the true Germany of which he had dreamed.[6] Once war had broken out, Stauffenberg considered Germany's victory the most important thing; no move could be made against the Nazis while the war was yet to be won.[7] However, by the early 1940s, he was disillusioned with the Nazi Party, and long perturbed by their anti-Semitic measures. It was not just the defeats on the Eastern Front but the massacres and atrocities committed against the civilian population there that finally pushed Stauffenberg into the fold of the resistance.[8] Such evil had to be stopped. With his soldier's pragmatism Stauffenberg was unlikely to join in passively with the subtleties of 'inner emigration'. He would simply do something about it. He would kill Hitler.[9]

He was an unlikely assassin. His military code of honour meant that he could not disguise from himself the fact that assassination meant treason; only a few days before the attempt, he declared that if he undertook the killing he would go down in German history as a traitor; but if he didn't kill Hitler, he would be a traitor to his conscience.[10] Either way, the notion of duplicity clung to the deed. After all, Germany was a nation at war; for that reason, back in the winter of 1941, he had refused an offer to join the resistance.[11] Aside from such moral concerns, there were practical problems in claiming the role of assassin. During service in North Africa Stauffenberg had suffered terrible injuries from a bomb blast, losing his right hand, two fingers from his left hand, his right eye, a kneecap, and enduring other head injuries. Despite these handicaps, Stauffenberg enviously longed to be the one to act.

By the time the German resistance came together for one last attempt on Hitler's life, in many respects it was already too late.[12] On 20 July 1944, Stauffenberg acted out of a stoic despair. The killing was bound to be useless: the Allies were uninterested in German internal resistance, and their war aims (unconditional surrender) were such that they were bound to smear the conspirators with the same stab-in-the-back myth that had blemished the image of the 1920s Weimar government. Even succeeding in killing Hitler might not solve the problem of the worst kind of Nazi rule, and the best possible result for the conspirators would be to hasten defeat and so bring disaster to Germany. Yet either they acted and incurred national shame; or they did not act and incurred national shame. Standing against Hitler was already to endure, or be comforted by, a unique kind of loneliness; Stauffenberg had accepted long ago the isolation of moral refusal. When Stauffenberg walked into the Wolf's Lair, he was already certain that the outcome of his actions, if he succeeded or failed, would gain the approval of very few. It would have to be a leap of faith, choosing dishonour to save honour. Given the situation in Nazi Germany, treachery had become true patriotism.[13] Their crime would be an act of expiation for their nation's greater crimes.[14]

Events would realise their foreboding: the plotters would indeed be misunderstood. As might be expected, the immediate reaction to the attempt would be horror at the betrayal of the Führer. Yet this hostile response to the assassins did not vanish with the end of the fighting. Stauffenberg's attempt triggered bitter post-war debates as to whether the conspiracy exemplified heroism or treason. Even after the war many, including churchmen such as Bishop Wurm and Cardinal Faulhaber, condemned the conspirators as traitors.[15] To most people assassination was still just disloyalty.

When Stauffenberg returned to Germany from North Africa, he desired to join the resistance against Hitler. He could have had a

number of conspiracies to choose among; there were several inter-
connected but distinct resistance groups, from those working with
Ernst von Weizsäcker and the Auswärtiges Amt, to Helmuth James von
Moltke and the Kreisau Circle, or the Christian resistance of Dietrich
Bonhoeffer and the Freiburg Circle, the Stuttgart Circle joined around
the industrialist Robert Bosch, or a resistance cell working within
German military intelligence (the Abwehr) overseen by the wily
Admiral Wilhelm Canaris.

From among the options, Stauffenberg joined those led by General
Ludwig Beck and Carl Goerdeler; the young soldier's energy meant that
he was soon in a position of authority within this group. In pressing
so strongly for assassination, Stauffenberg clashed with Goerdeler, who
for a long time had disdained any thought of such a move.[16] Goerdeler
is an equivocal hero, a man suspicious of democracy, a nationalist
and a conservative who in the 1930s had worked, with more or less
enthusiasm, for the Nazis. He disliked assassination, and retained for
a long time the implausible belief that Hitler might be persuaded to
resign for the sake of the country.[17] Despite his antipathy to the deed,
by the summer of 1943, Goerdeler, Beck, Fellgiebel and others among
the resistance were persuaded as to the necessity of a coup.[18]

While Goerdeler might have felt that tyrannicide was a dubious
tactic, others in the wider movement plainly disagreed. The attempt
to kill the Führer in the summer of 1944 was by no means the first
such endeavour. Yet Hitler had proved provokingly lucky in avoiding
death. Several attempts before the war had all ended in failure and retribution. On 9 November 1938 in Munich, during an SA parade commemorating the failed 1923 *Putsch*, a Swiss student named Maurice
Bavaud muffed an attempt on Hitler's life. The night before Bavaud's
attempt a cabinetmaker named Georg Elser had planted a bomb at the
beer hall where Hitler would address the crowd. But Hitler's speech was
briefer than usual, and the bomb exploded after he had left the building,
killing a few Nazis in the process. Both Bavaud and Elser were caught,
tried and killed (in Elser's case right at the end of the war in Dachau).[19]

Thwarted plans and botched attempts proliferated. With shades of
Geoffrey Household's novel *Rogue Male* (1939), the British military
attaché in Berlin, Colonel Mason-Macfarlane, suggested that from his
apartment he could take a pot shot at the Führer. Whitehall demurred.

Later it was mooted that the RAF might bomb Hitler's victory parade in Paris and so dispose of him; again this notion went nowhere, abandoned due to the niceties of military etiquette; it was only sporting to permit the Führer his moment of triumph.[20]

In the months leading up to the bomb plot, the resistance tried on several other occasions to end Hitler's life. There was the time in 1943 when resistance members Colonel Henning von Tresckow and Fabian von Schlabrendorff left two mines (British magnetic devices captured after the assaults on St Nazaire and Dieppe) on Hitler's plane, in the form of a small parcel that Schlabrendorff asked another Wehrmacht officer to deliver (as part of a bet, he said). They had disguised the bomb to look like a bottle of cognac. The fuses were set, but it was too chilly on the plane and they failed to ignite. Schlabrendorff had to set off on the next flight out to retrieve his 'present' and defuse the mines.[21]

Shortly afterwards, convinced that the only way to save Germany was to kill Hitler, with the same two mines, Colonel Rudolph Baron Christoph von Gersdorff agreed to blow himself up taking Hitler with him in the process.[22] The assassination was set to happen at an exhibition of captured booty at the Heroes' Memorial celebrations. But once again luck was on Hitler's side. Gersdorff couldn't make the mines go off simultaneously, so had instead to set ten-minute fuses and then walk around with Hitler, keeping close to him while waiting for the moment of detonation. But Hitler, despite Hermann Göring's feeble efforts to interest him in the treasures on display, raced through the exhibition in two minutes flat. Gersdorff had to hurry into the toilets to defuse the mines still stuffed in his overcoat pockets.

All attempts were limited by the simple difficulty of getting near enough to Hitler to kill him. The resistance needed access if they were to achieve their desires. And then suddenly, when it seemed as if they would never have a chance again, the conspirators' luck changed. In the summer of 1944, Stauffenberg was made deputy to General Friedrich Fromm, the Commander-in-Chief of the Home Army. In this new role, the man who most wanted to be Hitler's assassin was now thrown into a situation where he would have to report regularly to the Führer. The opportunity to kill Hitler had fallen to Stauffenberg.

The plotters had to move quickly too. The war was pressing to its conclusion, with British and American troops in Italy, and the Russians advancing from the east. The resistance movement was beset: General Oster, Dietrich Bonhoeffer and Hans von Dohnanyi had been arrested in April 1943; on 19 January 1944, Moltke was arrested; after a number of wildly risky deeds, Canaris lost his position at the Abwehr. One of the conspirators, Julius Leber, had been arrested more recently and was even now being tortured by the Gestapo. With the Allied invasion of France and the Russians pressing westwards, it became increasingly clear that unconditional surrender was the sole remaining hope for Germany.[23] The chance for negotiations with the foreign powers was over; only the gesture still needed to be made.[24]

On 6 July 1944, Stauffenberg attended a meeting at the Berghof, Hitler's mountain retreat. He had explosives on him, but missed a suitable moment to set them off. On 11 July, Stauffenberg was back at the Berghof, but this time decided to do nothing, as the conspirators still hoped to kill Himmler and Göring too, who were both absent from the meeting. They must wait their moment.

On 14 July, Hitler moved his headquarters back to *die Wolfschanze* ('the Wolf's Lair'). Hitler had once declared that he understood all too well why 90 per cent of assassinations had been successful; the only preventative measure was an irregular existence, one whose habits could not be predicted.[25] Now someone who understood the leader's routines was pursuing his life. The very next day, Stauffenberg attended another briefing with the Führer. Again Himmler and Göring weren't present, but this time Stauffenberg decided to go ahead with the killing anyway, only then to find that no occasion arose to ignite the fuse.

At his home the next evening, 16 July, in the Wannsee area of Berlin (where in 1942, the plans for 'The Final Solution' had first been formalised), Stauffenberg told his fellow conspirators that the next time he was in Hitler's presence he would kill him.

Was it a kind of vanity on Stauffenberg's part that made him grab for himself the role of assassin? Or was it that he wanted himself to bear the burden of treachery and guilt? For whatever reason the decision was reached, it was surely a mistake. Leaving aside the enfeebling effects of his injuries, it was perilous indeed to have Stauffenberg double up as assassin and as one of the coup leaders. After the murder, Stauffenberg was to flee 'the Wolf's Lair' and join the conspirators in Berlin, while General Erich Fellgiebel would remain behind to phone with news of the success or failure of the attempt. With the news, the plotters in Berlin would then initiate the coup. The code word to begin was *Walküre* ('Valkyrie') – in homage to the *Nibelungenlied* and Wagnerian opera, the tales of heroic Germany that both the Nazis and the conspirators loved. The division of roles meant that, if the insurrection were to succeed, Stauffenberg would first have to kill Hitler and then rush back to Berlin to manage the coup itself. The journey would only increase the risks and multiply the chances of failure.

So it was that around 10.45 on the morning of 20 July, Claus Stauffenberg flew into *die Wolfschanze*, with his aide, Lieutenant Werner von Haeften. With them was Generalmajor Hellmuth Stieff.

The headquarters were concealed in the Masurian woods of East Prussia, a short distance from the nearby town of Rastenburg. Hitler had taken to calling himself 'Wolf' in the 1920s; he enjoyed the name's associations of animal vitality and strength. In June 1941, he had moved his headquarters to *die Wolfschanze*, just as the onslaught of the Wehrmacht on the Soviet Union began. The closeness to the Eastern Front made the place ideal for directing the military operations, as Hitler as head of the armed forces was bound to do.

The Wolf's Lair was a dull and forbidding place, surrounded by checkpoints and ringed with wreaths of barbed wire. Hitler's bunker, at the northern end of the complex, was one of ten, each camouflaged and constructed from concrete two metres thick. Both Hitler's bunker and Field Marshal Keitel's had rooms big enough for military briefings. Most rooms were small and sparsely furnished. It was as though they had settled permanently in some place of transit. They ate in a barracks with a dining hall (except for Hitler who as the war reached its end often took his meals alone with his German Shepherd bitch, Blondi). A short distance away the Wehrmacht Operations Staff were housed in another complex – HQ Area 2.

Life in *die Wolfschanze* followed its own accustomed rhythms: the boring, enclosed, habitual life of briefings; the nocturnal Hitlerian monologues that drifted drearily on into the small hours, as his officers and secretaries struggled to keep awake. In the summer months, the swampy woods swarmed with midges under a dreary pervading heat. They lived on in weird isolation, hearing reports from the war, and poring over maps in the military briefings that took place every day before lunch and at 18.00 each evening. The same faces gathered over the same maps; the same view of receding trees; the same soft drone of the midges; the same small talk; the same dismal hopes; the same fantastic plans.

On arrival, that 20 July, Stauffenberg was taken for breakfast with the headquarters commandant's staff at the officers' mess inside security perimeter II. Haeften, still carrying the explosives, went with Hellmuth Stieff to Mauerwald, the Army HQ. Before 11.00, in preparation for the briefing with Hitler at 13.00, Stauffenberg was driven into the main compound for some preliminary meetings with Generalleutnant Buhle and other staff officers. At 11.30, now rejoined by Haeften, Stauffenberg went to Keitel's office for a further meeting. All through the briefing, Haeften waited outside in an empty corridor. The explosives were right by him in a tarpaulin-wrapped parcel. Oberfeldwebel (Sergeant-Major) Werner Vogel, one of the soldiers who worked with Keitel's adjutant, Major Ernest John von Freyend, noticed that Haeften seemed edgy. He became curious and inquisitively asked Haeften if he knew what was in the package. Although nervous as hell, Haeften kept his head. It was only something that was needed for the briefing with the Führer, he explained. Satisfied, Vogel wandered off, leaving Haeften sweating with the bombs.

The final preliminary meeting with Field Marshal Keitel ended early; Mussolini was arriving at *die Wolfschanze* later that day, and the Führer wanted to be ready for him.[26] The main meeting would begin at 12.30. At 12.25, word came through that General Heusinger, the Army General Staff Chief of Operations, had arrived on the train that linked the Army HQ at Mauerwald with *die Wolfschanze*. Keitel wanted to be on time, and so wrapped up the meeting. As the meeting finished, Stauffenberg mentioned to Major von Freyend that he'd like a minute to wash and to change his shirt. The mid-day heat was stifling, and the request was clearly a reasonable one. Haeften went with him; a one-handed man would naturally need his aide's help in changing. The two of them slipped into Freyend's bedroom in Keitel's hut, while Keitel and his men waited outside in the sunshine.[27]

Haeften held the explosives, while Stauffenberg set the fuses. He had to remove each fuse from the primer charge and squeeze it with pliers to break the glass phial inside the copper casing, releasing the acid that would slowly corrode the retaining wire. The instant that the wire was fully corroded, the bomb would explode. As quickly as they could, they began to set the first of the bombs, whispering together, hugger-mugger over the briefcase, careful not to use too much force and simply snap the wire in the fuse. Then all at once the door opened and Vogel, the same inquisitive soldier, stepped in, lingering near the door, blocked by Stauffenberg's back, with news that Fellgiebel had phoned Stauffenberg with orders from Keitel that they should get moving: Keitel was getting anxious that they were going to be late for the Führer. Stauffenberg snapped that they were coming as quickly as they could. The soldier stared and waited, wondering what the two men were doing huddled over together; perhaps he should go and take a closer look? But at that instant, Major Freyend called impatiently into the hut for them to hurry up. Stauffenberg closed the briefcase, and he and Haeften followed Vogel out of the door, to walk across to the Führer's bunker.[28]

Had the hurry spoilt everything? What had Vogel guessed? Stauffenberg could not be sure, and there was no time now to confer with Haeften. But Stauffenberg had made his first slip. Flurried by Keitel's restlessness and made anxious by the inquisitive presence of Vogel at the door, he had abandoned half of the bomb, believing there was no time to set both of the fuses, so leaving the other bomb unset in Haeften's bag: only one of the two bombs was in the briefcase, primed and ready. He had failed to realise that one fuse would have been enough for both bombs: in the force and heat of the blast, all the explosives would undoubtedly have gone off just as they should. Unwittingly, Stauffenberg had already created the possibility of failure. But there was nothing else to be done. They could not turn back now, or start again. They had set out with two kilograms of explosives, more than enough to kill everyone in the briefing room; after the interruption, there was only half that amount. But the glass phial that set the fuse was broken. The attempt to kill Hitler was still on.

They didn't have long, and were uncertain as to just how long they had. It was hard to tell with the British timers they were using – they could go off up to five minutes early. But, whatever happened, before thirty minutes were up, the bomb was going to explode. They were irretrievably launched on an attempt that they knew would either change the course of the war, or end with their futile and perhaps dishonourable deaths.

As they walked to the briefing in the midsummer heat, one of Keitel's adjutants, petulantly annoyed at the delay and perhaps aiming at an irritable and patronising kindness, tried to snatch the briefcase from the one-armed Stauffenberg, who swiftly jerked his hand away.[29]

It took just over four minutes to walk across the compound. The officers talked together as they went. The briefing hut was next to the guest bunker where Hitler had been living for the past week, while his usual bunker was reinforced with more concrete, a necessary precaution as the front edged closer and closer to East Prussia.

The hut was made of stone with steel shutters over the five windows to protect those within from shrapnel and broken glass. Stauffenberg may have reckoned on the shutters trapping the blast in the room and therefore adding to its force. But because of the heat the shutters were up, and every window was open.

The group was late, as Keitel had feared; the briefing had already begun. Haeften waited outside, leaving Stauffenberg with the slowly corroding fuse; it was Haeften's job to prepare the car for their escape. From now on, Stauffenberg was alone.

Stauffenberg and the adjutant went in together. There was an immediate disappointment: neither Göring nor Himmler was there. As the officers stepped into the busy room, Stauffenberg handed his briefcase to the playfully tetchy adjutant, asking if it could be placed with him as near to the Führer as possible. His all too visible injuries, Stauffenberg explained, included some hearing loss (his blown-out eye was covered with a black eye-patch, his missing arm obvious in an empty sleeve sewn across his breast). If he was to hear everything the Führer said, he would need to be close to him. So Stauffenberg was led near to the centre of the table, where Hitler sat on a stool, surrounded by his generals and their adjutants. There were maps spread out on the table. Heusinger was reporting to Hitler, standing as was customary at such a moment just to the Führer's right. Keitel's adjutant put Stauffenberg's briefcase down on the floor, and then left him just between Heusinger and his assistant, no more than a few feet from Hitler himself. Stauffenberg stood there, stiff and self-possessed, looking every inch the proud German soldier; handsome despite his disfiguring injuries. Hitler shook hands with him, the wounded war hero; Heusinger talked on.

A few minutes passed. Maybe a little more. With his foot, Stauffenberg edged the briefcase along the floor as close to Hitler as possible. Stauffenberg murmured to himself – a telephone call; he signalled to Keitel's adjutant. The two men left the room, and Stauffenberg asked if he could call General Fellgiebel. A sergeant placed the call, and the adjutant went back into the room. The briefcase was still there, of course, on the floor just to the left of Heusinger, just now finishing his report. Outside Stauffenberg took the receiver and then put it down. He walked out of the hut across to the adjutants' building, Bunker 88.[30] Haeften, Fellgiebel and an Army driver were waiting for him there. Talking all the time, they walked together to the car. Before they reached it there was an enormous explosion from the direction of the briefing hut.

The bomb had exploded early, the half-hour fuse lasting around fifteen minutes. A slight delay would have been fatal, trapping Stauffenberg himself right next to the source of the blast. Quickly afterwards Fellgiebel spotted a body wrapped in the Führer's cloak being carried out of the hut. The assassins drew their own conclusions. They had done the deed; now they must get out and ensure the coup's success.

They drove to the first checkpoint, and bluffed their way through. It was fairly easy, and the sun was shining as the car drove through the woods in the July heat, on through another checkpoint. At the third, they found obstacles on the road and the officer in charge refused to let them pass. Stauffenberg rang Möllendorf, one of the officers with whom he had eaten breakfast, and persuaded him to countermand the checkpoint's order. Reluctantly the guards waved the car through and the assassins drove back to the airstrip where the plane was waiting for them. They drove within sight of the blasted hut; there was a thick skein of smoke over the compound and debris everywhere. The building was wrecked; they could see that. Soldiers and orderlies were running up to the ruin. They drove on, away from *die Wolfschanze*. As they went Haeften threw the unused one-kilogram bomb away into the woods that bordered the road. The Heinkel He 111 was waiting for them on the runway, ready to take them back to Berlin. Stauffenberg was certain; he had killed Hitler.

But the Führer was still alive. At 15.00, when they landed in Berlin-Rangsdorf, they narrowly escaped arrest, as Heinrich Himmler had ordered for them. A flurry of activity was underfoot as the conspirators sought to capitalise on what they believed to be their success. However, the move against them was also already under way. By late that evening the arrests were in full spate, the conspirators in disarray; the news that Hitler had survived the bomb crippled the coup. Stauffenberg, Haeften and three other leaders of the plot were shot in a Berlin courtyard some time after midnight; Stauffenberg's last words were the cry 'Long live holy Germany.'[31]

The rush with which Stauffenberg had prepared the bomb had meant that only half the explosives they'd intended had been taken into the briefing hut. Nonetheless, when the bomb exploded in the crowded room, the devastation was shocking, wrecking the enclosed space, breaking up the ceiling and bursting the eardrums of everyone there, ripping the clothes from their bodies. Amazingly, only four people were killed: one lost his legs and died that day; another lost an eye and a leg, dying two days later; a third was impaled by a shaft of wood; a fourth died of infections from wounds received in the blast. Yet, for the conspirators, the bomb was a failure: they'd wanted everyone in the room to die.

By late autumn all the remaining conspirators were in prison awaiting their inevitable execution. Although faced by certain, very painful death, some of the plotters came to feel the horror of what they'd done. They accepted the righteousness of the verdict that condemned them. After all, weren't they traitors to their country? While some went to their graves convinced that they had acted for the good of Germany, others admitted their guilt. Hellmuth Stieff realised afterwards that everything they'd done was wrong, a sin against conscience and fidelity. In a letter to his wife written just before his execution, he confessed as much: the verdict was just; he had much for which to atone. Albrecht von Hagen, a young conspirator, wrote to his wife, contrite that his stupidity in getting involved in the treacherous plot would leave her a widow. General Erich Hoepner declared it an act of providence that they hadn't managed to kill their leader as they'd planned. God had been watching over their country, protecting it from the treachery they themselves had foolishly embraced.[32] Such confessions were not merely the product of torture, but were just as much a reversion to a deep-seated code of allegiance and military honour.

Their leader was Adolf Hitler. After the bomb had exploded, he'd been in high spirits, elated and fearless. 'I am invulnerable! I am immortal!' he repeated over and over. The conspirators would be hanged, one by one, using piano wire. Hitler was rumoured to have entertained himself with film of the first two dozen or so killings.[33]

In the aftermath of the explosion, other men were killed who had opposed Hitler, but not even taken part in the conspiracy; it is possible that the Gestapo arrested over 7,000 people; about 200 were tried and convicted.[34] Although for a long time a passionate opponent of Hitler's, in this instance one of the victims, Helmuth James Graf von Moltke had merely conversed with some clergymen about what the church might do if the Führer were assassinated; he was sentenced to death, with four others, for this relatively innocuous deed. But he had never supported assassination as a possibility or as a starting point for a new German government.[35] As he faced the gallows his one consolation was that he hadn't actually sullied himself with action:

We are according to these proceedings, untouched by the Goerdeler muck [aus dem Goerdeler-Mist raus], we are untouched by any practical activity. We are being hanged because we thought together.[36]

While the good man Moltke had agonised, Goerdeler had indeed acted, first as a worker alongside National Socialism, and later as a leader of the resistance. His earlier actions had, it was true, smeared him with muck, and yet he had later, however feebly, in however compromised a way, worked for the end of Hitler. To Goerdeler, after all his culpable work alongside the Nazis, the fact that a few men were prepared to face death for a chance to kill Hitler, the living personification of evil, would be one of the few redeeming features to be drawn from the whole Third Reich.[37]

After the war, to some in Germany and to many elsewhere, Stauffenberg's assassination attempt has proved an oddly equivocal inheritance. Most would see the attempt as a good deed, but one done somehow by the wrong people. Unlike the conspirators of the July bomb plot, the left-wing resistance are naturally untainted by fellow-travelling with the Nazi regime. At best, it might be thought that the unambiguous impact of the bomb at Hitler's feet helped to smooth away the ambiguities in the political beliefs and public lives of the leading men of the resistance on the right. If so, it took a bomb to do it. A comparison might be made with other heroes of the German *Widerstand*, or resistance – a comparison with what has been taken as the simple affirmative heroism of the young anti-Nazi activists Hans and Sophie Scholl. The Scholl siblings hurt no one, their chief action being the distribution of leaflets with other members of their group of student conspirators, *Die Weisse Rose*; their motives were a love of freedom for its own sake and a passionate and political dislike of Nazism. The very ineffectuality of their actions imbues them with greater power; the small gesture that they made was itself cruelly enough to warrant their execution. Both brother and sister were young, attractive, good-hearted, resolute and really wholly admirable. The Nazis executed them and other members of *Die Weisse Rose*, in Munich, in February 1943. Now Sophie Scholl truly is a symbol of human potentiality in the face of tyranny.[38] She is impossible to dislike. Contrariwise Stauffenberg and the other conspirators of the July plot against Hitler seem ambivalent heroes, their deed the product of an exceptional situation (*eine Ausnahmesituation*) that couldn't and shouldn't be repeated.[39] They have been seen as conservative in outlook, and as essentially being 'Junkers', militaristic aristocrats from a class that few post-war historians could bring themselves to love or even admire.[40] Their opposition to Hitler from within a military order that had simultaneously prosecuted a war of conquest further compromised them. Their involvement with the regime they eventually set out to overturn; their failure; their conservative politics and perhaps power-hungry desires: all these things render them shifty and difficult to place.

So it was that the would-be tyrannicides were marked by failings, compromises and collaborations. Yet this was a good conspiracy; these were benevolent assassins. Admittedly, many in the plot had once been enthusiastic Nazis, others were anti-Semites: their motives were confused, complex. Some resented a government that had demoted them; others despaired at the party's incompetent handling of the war; some were disgusted by the massacres in the east. But above all, they knew that they could not succeed; even if they killed Hitler, there was very little chance that they could depose the Nazis themselves. They acted, knowing they would lose their lives, to make a gesture that had to be made if they were to salvage some little honour for Germany.

Yet few of the plotters had the impeccable record of the theologian Dietrich Bonhoeffer, who had always stood against the regime and courageously advocated just violence against it. In 1945 Bonhoeffer was executed as a traitor; now he, like Sophie Scholl, is a hero. Bonhoeffer's combination of faith and resistance characterised the broader non-Communist movement against Hitler. Many of those who resisted Hitler were committed Christians, among them Hans-Bernd von Haeften and Martin Niemöller.[41] Even Stauffenberg had approached Bishop Conrad von Preysing of Berlin, to ask his advice about the ethics of assassination, and was eager to discuss the theology of tyrannicide with his fellow conspirators.[42] Yet, of all the Protestant resisters, it was Bonhoeffer who most unequivocally rejected the Nazi regime.[43] Presented with the opportunity to flee Germany, he had instead decided to return and fight the Nazis at home. He was a unique conspirator. One day after Stauffenberg's assassination attempt had failed, he was writing a letter from prison, talking of the worldliness of Christianity, the humanity of Christ.[44] What is most striking is that his position went beyond intellectual opposition; he was ready to approve conspiracy and assassination.[45] For Dietrich Bonhoeffer, peace had to give way before the demands of truth and justice.[46] In acting responsibly the Christian cannot know the final moral meaning of his or her deed, but must deliver themselves up to the hope of grace.[47] Bonhoeffer did not need to be reminded that those who live by the sword, die by the sword. He understood nonetheless that, in the ethics of a responsible life, success was more than good will, the goodness being something potentially released by action.[48]

The best chance of Bonhoeffer's stance having practical impact came through his friendship with George Bell, the Bishop of Chichester. Through the war years, Bell was both a contentious figure and an immensely appealing man. Bell's friend Basil Liddell Hart described his simple goodness, his intellectual depth, commenting: 'He has been outspoken in advocating what he believes right, however unpopular it may be – outspoken to the hazard of his reputation and prospects.'[49] He had fostered the growth of church drama, encouraging T. S. Eliot's career as a dramatist; he spoke up for refugees, for church unity, for the moral standards of a just war. Though imagined as a man soft on Nazism, in fact Hitler had no more committed enemy.[50] For Bell, the war had to be recognised as a conflict between a Christian order and nihilism, with 'the enterprise of Hitler' being 'the enterprise of an evil spirit'; the Nazis were a spiritual foe.[51] The boundaries of that Christian order were not confined to the British nation; Bell understood that true-hearted opponents to Nazism were similarly to be found in Germany. Christian faith trumped national concerns, linking the individual to a community greater than the nation and to a morality that transcended local convenience. It was in this spirit that Bell so vigorously opposed the area bombing of German cities; if it had been wrong for Hitler to level cities, then it must equally be wrong for the Allies to do the same.[52] To some this position rendered Bell suspect, and he was pictured as an ineffectual liberal, even as a man dangerously duped; it is likely that Bell's stance on saturation bombing cost him promotion to Archbishop of Canterbury; as late as 1967, a radio broadcast described him as 'The Controversial Bishop Bell'.[53]

Nonetheless Bell shared the widespread belief, exemplified by his great opponent, Lord Vansittart, that there was something inherently wrong with German culture, even with the German mind.[54] Yet, unlike many at the time, he was ready to distinguish between the Nazis and the German victims and opponents of Nazism. In Bell's view, lumping together the Nazis and the non-Nazis helped to produce a united front in Germany. Through the 1930s, he had supported the German anti-Nazi church movement and worked on behalf of European refugees, particularly Jews. These interventions had led to many friendships with the leading figures of the German-speaking resistance.[55] In the third year of the war two of these friendships would bear surprising fruit.

In May 1942, Bell seized the opportunity to travel to neutral Sweden. His task was to foster links between the two countries, in his case by meeting with Swedish churchmen. On 13 May, he arrived in Stockholm, and began a tour of the country. The visit was a success, Bell's amiability winning him friends and his sermons attracting impressive numbers of churchgoers. However, the visit would prove productive in other, clandestine ways.

On 26 May, at a Student Movement House in Stockholm, Bell found Dr Hans Schönfeld, an old acquaintance from the struggle of the German churches against Hitler, newly arrived from Geneva.[56] It seems likely that Schönfeld had been instructed by Hans-Bernd von Haeften; others have speculated as to how far he spoke on behalf of the entire Kreisau Circle of resisters against Nazism.[57] Schönfeld told Bell that plans had been laid for the entire Nazi elite to be destroyed; above all, Hitler would be eliminated.[58] The new government would negotiate a peace, halt the persecution of the Jews, end the alliance with Japan, introduce a socialist economic order, and aim for a European federation of nations, one imbued with Christian faith and moral principles.[59] It was a remarkable meeting, one that opened up vistas of the internal opposition to Hitler. However, a meeting would rapidly follow even more remarkable than the first.

On 31 May, Bell travelled to the little town of Sigtuna. And there he received his second visit from the German resistance; entirely unexpectedly, Dietrich Bonhoeffer was there to meet him, similarly bearing news of the plot against Hitler.[60] The two were old friends, having met when the young German was working for a few years as a pastor in London; in his later prison letters, Bonhoeffer would refer to the Bishop as 'Uncle George'.[61] Bonhoeffer knew nothing of Schönfeld's mission; in ignorance, the wider resistance had sent two emissaries to the same man. Hearing of Bell's visit, Bonhoeffer had hurried back to Berlin from Geneva, wangled a courier's pass, and taken the plane to Stockholm.[62] The two men discussed the resistance to Hitler; at Bell's insistence, Bonhoeffer named key figures in the German resistance, including Goerdeler.

Later that day, Schönfeld joined them, and together they discussed possible plans. Bonhoeffer was palpably unhappy about the pass to which Germany had come; he told Bell: 'Oh, we have to be punished.'[63] Yet he appeared to baulk at the 'elimination' of Hitler, or, rather, wanted that elimination to be undertaken in the right spirit. Bell wrote:

The Christian conscience, he said, was not quite at ease with Schönfeld's ideas. 'There must be punishment by God. We should not be worthy of such a solution. We do not want to escape repentance. Our action must be understood as an act of repentance.' I emphasised the need of declaring Germany's repentance, and this was accepted.[64]

To some this may look a fine distinction. Yet Bonhoeffer was more or less obscurely alluding to the necessity of tyrannicide or even to a specific assassination plan. The young pastor's concerns did not alter the fact that he wished Hitler dead:

We know of the despair which seized all those who were engaged in subversive activities in July and August 1940. We know of a meeting held at that time where it was proposed that further action should be postponed, so as to avoid giving Hitler the character of a martyr if he should be killed.

Bonhoeffer's rejoinder was decisive: 'If we claim to be Christians, there is no room for expediency. Hitler is the Anti-Christ. Therefore we must go on with our work and eliminate him whether he be successful or not.'[65]

Both Bonhoeffer and Schönfeld asked Bell to pass on what they had said to the British government, and to endeavour to secure support for the German resistance's plans. It was essential to receive encouragement from abroad, to elicit some sign that an internal coup would be backed by Allied support.[66] There had to be a recognition that the German nation was not synonymous with the Nazis, and that if Hitler were overthrown there would be a readiness from outside to support the anti-Nazi movement.

Bell left convinced that the overthrow of Hitler by his fellow Germans was not only possible, but imminent. In an article named 'A Visit to Sweden', published on 24 June 1942 in the *Christian News-Letter*, Bell writes as though the death of Hitler was at hand; as far as he is concerned, the crux is what the Allies should do in response to that death. There is evidence of the same belief in his letters of that time.[67] A crash seemed imminent, more imminent than most people expected. Would civil war in Germany commence? Would reprisals against the Nazis and collaborators inevitably follow?[68] Both the essay and his letters from the time clearly respond to intimations from Bonhoeffer and Dr Schönfeld that an assassination and coup were being planned.[69]

Back in England, Bell approached Anthony Eden, the British Foreign Secretary. Eden had already received 'peace-feelers' from German opponents to Nazism; however, he was inclined to view these overtures as an attempt by dissident factions in the military to maintain a strong German Army and to hold on to 'as much as possible of Hitler's territorial gains'.[70] On 30 June 1942, Eden and Bell met, and Bell passed on all that he had learnt in Sweden, giving the Foreign Secretary to understand that the assassination of the Nazi leaders was planned. The bishop passed on the thought, given to him by a Norwegian minister, that those in Germany who were against the Nazis nonetheless believed that, in the current wartime situation, the choice was between Hitler and slavery; even so they chose slavery. If only some word could be given which would make the choice less stark for right-minded Germans.[71] Yet Eden thought little of the prospects for revolt and doubted the integrity of the anti-Nazi faction. No direct encouragement would be given; no statement made that could tacitly show British endorsement of their plans. There the matter rested.

In July 1944 Eden was worn out and over-stretched, drained by troubles in Greece and the situation regarding the Jews, beset by worries over Soviet reliability and exhausted by the responsibilities of being Winston Churchill's 'right arm'.[72] Earlier in the war, Eden had suggested that no one would take a German resistance seriously until it did something to get rid of the present regime.[73] Now, with news of Stauffenberg's bomb, they had made such an attempt, and still no one took (or could afford to take) the German resistance seriously. In fact, in his diary, Eden's private secretary, Oliver Harvey, remarked that the failure of the July plot was in Britain's interests.[74] In any case, the Cabinet were instantly dismissive of the plot; Ernest Bevin wrote it off as a Nazi stunt.[75] Later Eden would claim to have taken Stauffenberg's attempt more seriously; yet still nothing was done.

On 11 August 1944, Bell wrote a letter to Lord Halifax, declaring: 'The attempt on Hitler's life came as a rather ironical comment on Vansittart's refusal to see any difference between the Gestapo and the General Staff.'[76] Yet the irony went further, as Vansittart's view of a wholly evil Germany continued to win out. The Allies effectively denigrated the July plot as a 'revolt of the generals', a militaristic internecine palace plot in which the bad attempted to murder the worse, or even as an attempt by a few contaminated men to demonstrate their distance from Nazism in order to save their own skins when the war was over.[77] Nonetheless Bell continued to press for British support for the resistance. He wrote to Eden, requesting that something be done to liberate the captured conspirators, and that an appeal be made to the good Germans. Both requests were ignored.[78] Bell begged Eden to help some of those implicated in the plot; no help was given, and the implicated were murdered. A sense lingers that Eden missed a trick;

two of his biographers (David Carlton and Alan Campbell-Johnson) omit the incident altogether; Robert Rhodes James veers away from the matter with the remark 'On this, controversy continues to this day'.[79]

On 9 April 1945, in the concentration camp at Flossenburg, the SS murdered Bonhoeffer. Bell wrote to Franz Hildebrandt:

I have just returned from the United States, where I heard the grievous news of Dietrich's death. It is a real tragedy. I had so much hoped, with so many others, that he might have been spared to do a wonderful work for the future in Germany: but it was not to be.[80]

In 1957, when Bell announced his retirement, the *Daily Mail* proclaimed him the 'Bishop Who Might Have Stopped The War'.[81] For a brief moment, in order to end wider killing, two eminent men of the church had conspired together in a plot to murder the leader of Germany.

* * *

What kind of an assassination is it when men of the integrity and decency of Dietrich Bonhoeffer or George Bell are prepared to involve themselves in it? Murder becomes a penitential sacrifice, the assumption of sin in order to signal the necessity for repentance. Few would dispute the justice of plotting to kill a Hitler. Yet it is salutary to remember that, for most of the assassins in this book, all their intended victims were Hitlers. When the young Anarchist Alexander Berkman stepped into the office of the industrialist Henry Clay Frick, and tried his best to shoot and stab the man to death, in his own eyes he was doing so not for reasons of perversity or wickedness, but out of rectitude and the desire for justice. Like Hitler, in Berkman's view, Frick was killing people using the weapons of enforced poverty and the machinery of the state; it was only justice to kill him in revenge.

The bomb plot against Hitler is therefore both the starkest and the most equivocal example of the moral paradox of the good assassination. For all the modernity of its setting, it represents a singularly old-fashioned approach to such murders, being one of the last instances of such a crime which could fairly be defined as 'tyrannicide'. Its moral complexities are such as to make us pause in simply denouncing all assassinations as outrages; it invites us to search out complexity where we might have condemned, to find out reasons where we might have rebuked. It seems a good place from which to plot our direction towards the crimes to follow, an ironic beacon of honour to guide us through the mingled idealism and nihilism, passion and madness to come.

In recounting that history, the book will tell of the key Western assassinations: of Abraham Lincoln and Tsar Alexander II; of President Garfield and President McKinley; of the Phoenix Park Murders; of the killing at Sarajevo that sparked the Great War; of the killings that scarred Weimar Germany, and the acts of revenge of Armenians against Turks; of the Kennedys; of Malcolm X and Martin Luther King. It will pay almost as much attention to those failed attempts that nonetheless revealed the way the times were going: the shots fired at Queen Victoria; Vera Zasulich's demonstration against Governor Trepov of St Petersburg; the assault on the American tycoon Henry Clay Frick; the attempts on President Truman and Governor Wallace; the mad attacks on Presidents Ford, Nixon and Reagan. Just as telling as symptoms of the age are acts perhaps only peripherally associated with politics: the shooting of Andy Warhol; the murder of John Lennon.

PART ONE

The Assassination Suite
The Proliferation of Political Murders
1865–1883

A Murder at the Theatre

Here Captain! dear father!
　This arm beneath your head!
　　It is some dream that on the deck,
　　　You've fallen cold and dead.
from WALT WHITMAN, 'O Captain! My Captain!'

He stood in the barn waiting to die. It was still dark. Herold was gone and the soldiers were outside. He leant on his crutch, with Herold's carbine in one hand and the pistol in the other. Suddenly the hay began to blaze and he hobbled towards it. They might as well burn him to death in the barn. But when he reached the fire, he hesitated. It would be over soon anyway. He tottered towards the barn door, a gun in each hand, but as he reached the centre of the barn there was a shot and a bullet passed through his neck. He fell, and the soldiers came in, and tried to lift him; but they could not move him. More came and they carried him out into the pre-dawn half-light, and laid him on the grass close to the barn. They washed his face with icy water, and he came to, and opened his eyes. He was trying to speak. The soldier put his head down close to his lips. 'Tell mother I die for my country,' he said.[1]

The barn was blazing now, and the heat grew strong, so the soldiers lifted him again and carried him a short distance away, and laid him down on the porch of the farmhouse. They sent for a surgeon. While they waited for an hour the officer bathed his head with ice-water and moistened his mouth with a wet cloth, for he could not lift his head to drink from the cup they offered him. Again he spoke of his mother, and then added, 'I did what I thought was for the best.' It hurt to speak. More than once, he asked them to kill him. But they would not. They stood over him, and the officer wet his head and wiped his mouth with the cloth. He longed to cough, and managed to show them so, and he wanted the officer to place his hand on his throat to help him. So the officer placed his hand on his throat, but he could not cough.

Then he said, 'My hands.' They raised one of his hands, and cleansed it with water. He stared at it, as they held it up before him. And then he murmured, 'Useless, useless.' The soldier let his hand fall.

When the surgeon came and examined the wound in his neck, he told the soldiers that the man might live a day more. But just then the wounded man's expression changed, his eyes turned glassy, and he began quickly to die. The pain was terrible. He died at 7.20 in the morning. He had received his death wound some four hours before.[2]

Three things confirmed the identification of the body. First there was the scar on the back of his neck, and in his teeth the fillings he had had done only two weeks before. And on his hand were the initials of his own name, J. W. B., where he had primitively tattooed them when he was a child.[3] He was John Wilkes Booth, and he was the man who had murdered Abraham Lincoln.

* * *

John Wilkes Booth was born near Bel Air in Harford County, Maryland, on 10 May 1838. He grew up at Tudor Hall, its name a tribute to an Elizabethan (and Shakespearean) past, and the suitable home therefore for Booth's father, an English actor in exile. Renowned for his Richard III and other villains, Junius Brutus Booth had been, for a moment or longer, a rival to Edmund Kean on the London stage; he had played Iago to Kean's Othello. Short in stature, he had made up for this deficiency with an acting style formed around 'the sudden and nervous expression of concentrated passion'.[4] Junius Brutus was a patriot's name, and he gave one to two of his sons too – John Wilkes recalling the eighteenth-century British libertarian politician and rogue. The father adhered to a radical tradition of independence and republican rectitude. He loved the notion of American liberty and hated the fact of American slavery. Maryland was a good home for such a man, for while a slave state, the culture of slavery was relatively weak there, and the institution in the slow process of dying.[5]

Junius Brutus Booth did everything very young: marrying, becoming a father, playing the king. In 1821, he abandoned his first wife and son and emigrated to the United States with a new lover, Mary Ann Holmes – a 'flower girl' and a dark and remarkably attractive woman.[6] At Bel Air, Maryland, he headed a new family and tried to become a farmer, tilling a soil replete with mementoes of the Algonquin Indians.

The Booths were a melancholy and brooding family; the 'element of mirth' had been denied to them.[7] Three of the couple's children died. Junius Brutus Booth was particularly given to madness and depression. In 1829, he broke down on stage, howling to the audience, 'Take me to the Lunatic Hospital!'[8] In 1838, the year that John Wilkes was born, his father attempted suicide. In photographs, he assumes a wistful, resigned look, like a moping child. Beyond the depression were other more amiable forms of eccentricity. A Pythagorean and vegetarian, he once attempted to persuade a clergyman to give a decent burial to a flock of pigeons.[9] A student of the occult, the Koran, and Catholicism, he similarly embraced a devout Americanism: 'in his later years he is said to have kept in his drawing-room a picture of George Washington before which he insisted all visitors should bow in reverence'.[10]

Given his theatrical inheritance, it was apt that John Wilkes Booth would also become a performer. Both his brothers were famed on the stage, most notably Edwin Booth. Edwin was the better actor, his presence calm, dignified and measured. Like all in the family, his genius was for tragedy. It was claimed that Edwin gained his air of seriousness by looking after his drunk, mad father.

A younger son, John Wilkes Booth often ran away from home. He was both mischievous and a mother's boy (Edwin called him 'his mother's darling'), and at school showed himself to be an untalented, but dogged student.[11] He had inherited too, as his sister Asia Booth believed, the family despondency:

Yet through all his fitful gaiety there was traceable a taint of melancholy, as if the shadow of his mother's 'vision' or the Gipsey's 'fortune' fell with his sunshine. Perhaps the forecast of his awful doom lay over him.[12]

At the age of seventeen John Wilkes Booth made his debut in *Richard III*, playing Richmond, exactly as his dad and brother had before him.[13]

He was in some ways a bad actor, given to over-doing it, forcing a performance through passion. But he was attractive in his mother's style: dark-haired, dark-eyed. Indeed there was something vague about those eyes, an expression that combined the wistful with a certain coolness. He had a drunk's dreaminess, a drunk's elegance, and a drunk's short temper. There was about him 'an exaggeration of spirit – almost a wildness', something perpetually wound up to the point of striking.[14] And yet he could express too a quality of gentleness allied with indifference. It was a charm that resisted censure, the appeal of a handsome drinker. Women adored him. He could afford to repel their advances by frank admissions of his callous character, knowing full well the erotic allure of such confessions.[15] Few of his pursuers gave up. Yet there was something fatal in his feelings for women. As well as charges of adultery, there was a reported rape when he was nineteen years old. In 1861, one ex-lover (Henrietta Irving) tried to kill him, but only cut him on the arm; she stabbed herself afterwards (almost succeeding in killing herself). He was the languid receiver of daring love letters (up to a hundred per week); lines of his 'widows' importuned the Booth family after his death.[16]

For Booth was a theatrical star, a member of the nation's most prominent acting family. He had appeared only once with his two brothers, in *Julius Caesar* in New York, a performance designed to raise cash for the Shakespeare memorial statue in Central Park. The more talented Edwin played Brutus, Junius Jr. played Caesar and John Wilkes played Antony, crying out for vengeance against the assassins. In 1863, Abraham Lincoln had very likely seen Booth act in a mediocre drama entitled *The Marble Heart*, and may have seen him perform in other plays too.[17]

While Booth had inherited a role in the family business, his politics were determinedly opposed to those of his father. Booth was a racist, believing that America was a country made for whites and that African-Americans should properly be subordinate, looked after paternally by their racial betters. He quit a job at Richmond Theatre so he could witness the execution of the ardent abolitionist John Brown. In 1859, Brown attempted to spark a slave rebellion in the South by seizing the Harper's Ferry arsenal. The plan failed, very likely as Brown himself had known it would, and he was captured and, with six of his fellow conspirators, sentenced to death. Booth later aggrandised this spectatorship at his demise into a role in the man's capture.[18]

Booth may have supported the cause, but he neglected to fight in the war. Late on, when the South was already clearly heading for defeat, he decided to offer his practical help. In early 1865, with two childhood friends – Michael O'Laughlen and Samuel Arnold, both of them former Confederate soldiers – he began planning to kidnap Lincoln.[19] However, their plot required more conspirators. In January, Booth confided his Confederate sympathies to John H. Surratt, a young man who was delivering Southern orders and plans to associates in Canada. Dr Samuel Mudd of Bryanstown, Maryland, a mutual acquaintance, was reportedly the man who introduced them.[20] Booth wooed Surratt, slowly insinuating more details of his plans, without prematurely committing himself. Eventually he confessed all. They would abduct Lincoln, take him to Richmond, and so end the war – or at least create an opportunity for a large-scale exchange of prisoners. Booth and his gang conspired in Washington in John Surratt's home, owned by his mother, Mary Eugenia Surratt.

It was a daring project, but ultimately a botched one as, on the day of the planned kidnapping, the President failed to turn up where he was expected. A letter written some little time before reveals Booth's attitude to the cause he wished to serve:

On the other hand, the South have never bestowed upon me one kind word; a place now where I have no friends, except beneath the sod; a place where I must either become a private soldier or a beggar . . . I have never been upon a battle-field, but oh! my countrymen, could you all but see the reality or effects of this horrid war, as I have seen them in every State save Virginia . . . My love (as things stand to-day) is for the South alone. Nor do I deem it a dishonour in attempting to make for her a prisoner of this man, to whom she owes so much misery. If success attend me I go penniless to her side.[21]

The South was a desire, an ideology, an image; it was the object of his unrequited love, a precious ideal in a tarnished world.

On 9 April 1865, news came of Richmond's fall to the Union forces led by General Grant, and that General Robert E. Lee, the Confederates' military genius, had surrendered; two days later, Lincoln hinted at the coming of limited African-American suffrage. The news threw Booth into despair. On the night of 13 April, Washington celebrated the victory with a 'grand illumination', the streets of the capital lit by candles and gas-lights; fireworks were set off in Lafayette Square.[22] At 2.00 in the morning, a depressed Booth wrote a letter to his mother:

Dearest Mother!

I know you expect a letter from me, and am sure you will hardly forgive me. But indeed I have nothing to write about. Everything is dull; that is, has been till last night. (The illumination.)

Everything was bright and splendid. More so in my eyes if it had been a display in a nobler cause. But so goes the world. Might makes right. I only drop you these few lines to let you know I am well, and to say I have not heard from you. Excuse brevity; am in haste. Had one from Rose [his sister Rosalie Booth]. With best love to you all, I am your affectionate son ever,

John.[23]

The next morning, 14 April, Booth visited Ford's Theatre to pick up his mail. It was a dark day, threatening rain.[24] Harry (Henry Clay) Ford, the theatre-owner's son, told him that the President and General Grant would be coming that evening to watch the play. Booth sat on the steps of the theatre and read his letters. He turned round and asked Ford if he was certain that the two men would be coming.[25] He was very pale. From this unpredictable opportunity, a fresh idea for a conspiracy suddenly emerged, a last throw of the dice against the all but victorious North: he would assassinate Lincoln, and while he was at it organise the simultaneous slaying of William Henry Seward, the Secretary of State, and Andrew Johnson, the Vice President. In a single night, they would incapacitate the enemy government and gain consent to a reprieve for the South. Though General Robert Lee's Confederate forces had already surrendered at Appomattox Court House, General Joseph E. Johnston's forces were still in the field; there are indications that Booth only carried out the assassination in the belief that the war would carry on.[26] (Johnston finally surrendered on 26 April, though it was not until the end of May that the last significant Confederate forces admitted defeat.) In a country still at war, the murder of the ultimate enemy general was not so much a crime as a military duty. War meant the trading of violence; it seemed the nation had become inured to killing. Booth had been there at the hanging of John Brown, the beginning of it all. Now he would be there at the end.

Booth had to call upon some of his Confederate associates: David

Herold ('a feeble minded youth of nineteen'[27]) and George Atzerodt – described as a 29-year-old coach-maker and repairer, German by birth, and an immigrant to the United States. Atzerodt was an old acquaintance of John and Mary Surratt.

Booth's most useful accomplice would be Lewis Payne Powell (aka Lewis Paine), the son of a Florida Baptist minister. He was still a very young man, though a battle-tried one. Another ex-Confederate soldier, he had been wounded at Gettysburg, and he was – in the eyes of some – almost crazy. Paine was indeed unbalanced by grief: his two brothers had been killed in the war, and he had himself toiled through the trauma of the fighting. He later told how he had seen Booth act some years before, and had been forcibly impressed by the older man.[28] It was the first play that Paine had ever seen.[29] He spoke to the actor afterwards and the two men became friendly. They had met again by chance on the streets of Baltimore in 1865, and renewed the friendship. It seems that Paine had been initially drafted into the kidnapping plot. Now he was asked to play a role in a far more deadly endeavour.

By mid-afternoon, a plan had been hatched: Paine would kill Secretary of State Seward; Atzerodt would kill Vice President Andrew Johnson; Booth himself would kill Lincoln. Herold would assist with the escape. There was no intention to involve Surratt, Arnold or O'Laughlen in the assassinations. This was, after all, a more drastic plan than a mere attempt at kidnapping. However, Booth did persuade Mary Surratt to discover what she could about the guard posts manning the routes out of Washington.[30]

The motives for murdering Lincoln were obvious: revenge; provoking fear in the North; rekindling hope for the South. Andrew Johnson was a Southerner (and former slave-owner) who had gone over to the Unionist side. Only a few weeks before, Johnson had disgraced himself by turning up drunk to the Senate to take his oath of office as Vice President. He was another suitable target for the conspirators' act of destabilising revenge. During the afternoon of 14 April, Booth went round to Johnson's residence and left a note for him ('Don't wish to disturb you; are you at home?'), possibly with the intention of learning his movements.[31] Some, however, have seen this message not as part of an attempt to murder the Vice President, but rather as a sinister indication of Johnson's complicity with Booth.[32]

The third target would be William Henry Seward (1801–72), Lincoln's Secretary of State, once his great political rival and now his great friend. Seward was a conviction politician glad to support unpopular causes (including the rights of immigrants) and a Machiavel of goodness, scheming behind the scenes to attain the least bad result.[33] He was charming, cultured and only a little conceited. While Lincoln's poor childhood was notorious, Seward had grown up in patrician comfort in Orange County, New York.[34] Meeting him in 1860, the historian Henry Adams described him in this way:

A slouching, slender figure; a head like a wise macaw; a beaked nose; shaggy eyebrows; unorderly hair and clothes; hoarse voice; offhand manner; free talk, and perpetual cigar, offered a new type – of western New York – to fathom; a type in one way simple because it was double – political and personal; but complex because the political had become mature, and no one could tell which was the mask and which the features.[35]

In the 1840s, as Governor of New York, Seward had been a leader of the anti-slavery Whigs, standing against enslavement as unjust, unnecessary and outmoded. In the South, Seward was a much-hated figure, seen by some as one of the arch-instigators of the war against Southern institutions. Seward was a believer in business, abolition and American expansionism, the author after the Civil War of numerous territorially acquisitive strategies, most of which failed due to a lack of equal interest in Congress. (However, in 1867, he successfully followed through with one scheme, the purchase of Alaska from Russia.)

Seward might justly have believed himself robbed of the Republican candidacy by Lincoln, the largely untried lawyer from Illinois, for in 1860 Seward was a famous man, a spirited opponent of slavery, and an experienced Senator and Governor of New York. However, Lincoln was more likely to carry the Midwestern states and on the subject of slavery appeared the more moderate of the two men, and so duly won the nomination. Lincoln then defused the threat offered by Seward, and other disappointed men, such as Salmon P. Chase, by absorbing them into positions of authority in his Cabinet. Yet, as late as the spring of 1861, Seward was manoeuvring against the newly installed President. Many imagined that Lincoln would be a cipher of a President, while Seward wielded the real power from behind the scenes. In fact, Lincoln had quickly established his authority over Seward, initially through his impressive inauguration speech and then with his skilful handling of the Fort Sumter affair. Moreover, the two men had rapidly formed a deep friendship and community of interest.

* * *

Booth spent the day of 14 April preparing for the murders. At some point he went back into the theatre and bored a peephole into the back of the President's box. The hole would give him a view directly onto the President's back. Then he jammed a bar of wood into the outer door.[36] Afterwards he went to a local livery stable and hired a horse, saying that he would come back for her at 4 p.m. When the hour came, he returned dressed in riding boots. He took the horse, and went to a local hotel, where he tried to gather his thoughts. He slipped, for privacy's sake, into an office there and wrote a letter which he gave to a fellow actor, John Matthews, whom he had bumped into on Pennsylvania Avenue. A group of Confederate prisoners, General Lee's soldiers, had just passed the two men by, and Booth was in lachrymose mood. "'Great God!'" he declared, "'I have no longer a country!'"[37]

The contents of Booth's message remain a matter of speculation. Booth told Matthews to take what he had written to John Coyle, editor of the *National Intelligencer*. However, Matthews forgot about the errand until much later that night. When he finally got home, Matthews opened the letter, and saw that it was a justification for the assassination. Booth had previously tried and failed to recruit Matthews for his conspiracy to kidnap the President. Understandably anxious that he would now be implicated in the deed, Matthews panicked, and burnt the letter. In 1881, with the help of a journalist, Matthews reconstructed its text from memory. Much of the recreated document (apart from its beginning and end) substantially repeats an earlier letter that Booth had written in 1864 for his sister Asia Booth Clarke. As this earlier dispatch had since been widely printed, it is also quite likely that Matthews had read it in the intervening sixteen years between assassination and publication. Only the opening and closing passages of Matthews's version differ markedly from the earlier missive to Asia Booth. However, both the original letter to Asia and Matthews's expanded version offer some insight into Booth's state of mind and his beliefs about the deed.

Booth's letter, or rather letters, display a volatile mixture of doubt and self-justification. 'Many, I know – the vulgar herd – will blame me for what I am about to do, but posterity, I am sure, will justify me,' he wrote on the day of the murder – according to Matthews at least:

Right or wrong, God judge me, not man. Be my motive good or bad, of one thing I am sure, the lasting condemnation of the North . . . In a foreign war I too could say 'country, right or wrong.' But in a struggle such as ours (where the brother tries to pierce the brother's heart) for God's sake choose the right.[38]

The tone here shows itself surprisingly tentative, self-persuading perhaps. He goes on to say how his country's history has taught him to hate tyranny – a tyranny clearly embodied in Lincoln. Yet, in the next sentences, he praises the nobility and the blessings of slavery in a country formed for white men; such a view was a standard defence of the 'peculiar institution' in the South. The moral confusion laid bare here remains the keynote of Booth's justification. For decades, advocates of slavery had re-imagined its evil as a positive good, a civilising influence on both master and slave, a vestige of old-world feudal sensibility in a degraded industrial world of 'free labour'.[39] Their self-imaginings pitted an agricultural order against the coming mechanistic world. Southern gentlemen sensitively guarded their 'honour' with a fineness of feeling that betrayed their underlying discomfort about their situation. Accustomed to defending the indefensible, they were apt to find insults everywhere. It was a fantasy of order, and a hallucination of cruelty, 'haunted by suspicion, by *idées fixes*, by violent morbid excitement'.[40] Booth exhibits the same muddle. For he continues his defence by declaring that perhaps the South was in the wrong:

Even should we allow that they were wrong at the beginning of this contest, cruelty and injustice have made the wrong become the right, and they stand now before the wonder and admiration of the world as a noble band of patriot heroes. Hereafter reading of their deeds Thermopylae would be forgotten.[41]

The South has become classic ground. On the afternoon itself, it seems that Booth wished to place his own deed likewise in terms of ancient probity. His experience of Shakespeare put the deeds of Brutus before him: 'The stroke of his dagger was guided by his love of Rome. It was the spirit and ambition of Caesar that Brutus struck at.' And he goes on to quote those wilfully blind lines of Brutus' when the Roman imagines, as he must know is impossible, that one might kill the pride of Caesar and leave his body intact: 'Oh that we could come by Caesar's spirit, And not dismember Caesar! But, alas! Caesar must bleed for it.'[42] When, on the run from the law, Booth came to write his diary, he marked the opening date as '14 Friday the Ides'.[43]

Using the 'crimes' of John Brown as his text, Booth wonders how what was crime in that man could be seen as righteous in the eyes of the Unionist cause, how vice could become virtue. The unspotted and innocent flag had been tainted. And yet throughout his letter, it is the instability of those categories of good and evil, and, we may assume, his own relationship to them, which is most striking. If Matthews remembered correctly, when much of the letter was written, Booth was no fanatic convinced of his own deed's justice; he was grandiose, self-exculpating, self-pitying and somehow puzzled.

The day wore on. Booth ate, and then met his accomplices, Atzerodt, Herold and Paine, to discuss their plans. It is likely that this is the first moment that Atzerodt heard what Booth had planned for him. Afterwards Booth rode to the theatre, and left his horse with a boy. He went in and out of the theatre several times.[44] Soon he would have to act. Between four and five o'clock, he killed time drinking whiskey in Peter Taltavul's bar, 'The Star', right next door to Ford's Theatre, stoking up some Dutch courage for that evening's deed.[45]

* * *

On the morning of 14 April, Lincoln presided over a Cabinet meeting. Among others, General Grant was there, and Edwin M. Stanton, the War Secretary, Hugh McCulloch, the Treasury Secretary, with Frederick Seward standing in for his incapacitated father, since Seward senior was temporarily laid up in bed with a fractured arm and jaw, following a carriage accident earlier that month. It was Good Friday. Lincoln was in a cheerful mood. They discussed the best way to effect reconciliation with a defeated South. Lincoln brought up a dream he had had. He told his colleagues:

that a peculiar dream of the previous night was one that had occurred several times in his life, – a vague sense of floating – floating away on some vast and indistinct expanse, toward an unknown shore. The dream itself was not so strange as the coincidence that each of its previous recurrences had been followed by some important event or disaster, which he mentioned.

Some of the politicians present were sceptical; the victories and defeats that had followed were surely coincidences. Another pointed out that, as things were, it was unlikely there could now be any more victories or defeats, since the war was over. And the last suggested that perhaps real knowledge of a coming change brought about the dream, rather than the dream itself presaging anything. "'Perhaps,' said Mr. Lincoln, thoughtfully, 'perhaps that is the explanation.'"[46] In the afternoon he pardoned a deserter and a Confederate spy and then went for a short drive with his wife. After dinner, he went back to the War Department and worked some more. It was after eight by the time he finally left.

It had been a busy last month. The toll of the war and its pressures showed in Lincoln's worn features. For years Lincoln had steered a more or less steady course between the radical abolitionists and the ordinarily prejudiced citizen, seeming, in Frederick Douglass's words, tardy, cold, dull and indifferent to the radicals, while being, compared to the average, swift, zealous, radical and determined.[47] Now, at the end of it all, he looked aged and drained. Lincoln's genius had been to combine the brilliance of a pragmatic politician with the force of a moral visionary. Yet, in seeking to accommodate the border states or moderate Southern opinion, he had been obliged to assume positions that in retrospect seem half-hearted. With regards to the issue of slavery, he had passed through many political positions, as gradualist, even as supporter of the establishment of a colony overseas for America's slaves, before reaching abolitionism.[48] However, there is no doubt that he consistently hated slavery, had long hoped for its eventual demise (as he believed the framers of the Constitution likewise had), and had fought to resist the expansion of slavery into the western territories. Nonetheless, his main aim remained the preservation of the Union, and in the end emancipation was largely the lever that would achieve that aim.[49] And Lincoln did put through the proclamation that began the emancipation of the slaves, and he did, as he intended, save the Union.

In late March, following an invitation from General Grant, he had made a visit to the front line before Richmond. His guides had worried about his safety. He travelled south on a steamboat, whose sister ship had recently been blown up by a bomb disguised as a lump of coal, a 'cowardly assault' in Lincoln's view.[50] His wife went with him, an irascible and jealous presence always in need of propitiation. With Grant, he saw wounded men and exhausted Confederate prisoners, and was moved by the suffering, and keyed up by the bustle of it all. On 4 April, he entered the city of Richmond, only hours after the collapse of its defending Southern army. For those in charge of his safety, Lincoln's visit there was an anxious affair, the threat of assassination a real one.[51] However, Lincoln was fearless. His courage was rewarded by a public demonstration of love and respect by the city's liberated blacks and poor whites. To the President's embarrassment, people knelt before him on the street; in a perilously anti-hierarchical gesture, Lincoln responded to one impassioned salute by raising his hat to an old black man. A Southern woman turned her eyes from the moment in disgust.[52]

On the boat journey home, he read *Macbeth*, going over several times the lines where, in guilt and horror at his deed of assassination, Macbeth envies Duncan's sleep.[53] Back in Washington, he visited injured troops in prison, shaking hands, offering compassion. He was fêted by triumphant crowds. On the night of 11 April, he gave a speech from the window of the White House to a waiting mass of people, in which he hinted that he favoured black suffrage. Among the crowd, furious at Lincoln's tentative declaration, was John Wilkes Booth, who on hearing the President's words, reportedly remarked to a friend: 'That means nigger citizenship. Now, by God, I'll put him through! . . . That is the last speech he will ever make.'[54]

It had been announced that the President and General Grant would both attend a performance at Ford's Theatre.[55] The play was to be *Our American Cousin*, starring an English actress, Laura Keene. The President preferred not to go; his wife was feeling poorly, and he had worked hard all day. However, careful not to offend the prickly Mrs Lincoln, General Grant had already cried off, and had boarded instead the late train to New Jersey, where he hoped to see his family. With Grant no longer going, Mrs Lincoln did not want to disappoint the expectant crowd, and so persuaded her husband that, against his own inclinations, he roused himself and with his wife, a little after eight o'clock, they set off for the theatre. As was quite usual, there was little in the way of security, merely one policeman, John F. Parker, and a White House messenger named Charlie Forbes. Lincoln's favoured bodyguard, Ward Hill Lamon – a man given to sleeping before the President's door in the White House, armed to the teeth with guns and knives – was away on a mission in Richmond.[56] It was a misty evening, hazy and dimmed.[57] By the time they arrived, the play had already begun. The President made a bow from the box, as the actors paused, the orchestra played 'Hail to the chief', and the audience rose and applauded enthusiastically.[58] Then with two friends, Major Henry Reed Rathbone and his fiancée (and step-sister), Clara Harris, Lincoln and his wife took their seats in the state box, the President sitting in a large armchair directly overlooking the stage from the level of the dress circle, and the evening continued.

The instant that Lincoln arrived at the theatre, Booth hurried back to Mary Surratt's house. The news about the patrols guarding the capital's roads was favourable. He rode back to Ford's Theatre and tied up his horse by the rear entrance, leaving a boy with her to keep her calm. He went into the theatre and then immediately left and took another whiskey and then some water in Taltavul's saloon bar next door.[59] He then went back into the theatre, going under the stage. During the interval, he fortified himself with a brandy. The play recommenced. The President's guard, John Parker, was engrossed in the performance, and did not notice Booth approaching the box.

The play was going well; the large audience were charmed. References in the play to Lincoln himself were met with cheers by the audience and laughter and bows from the President.[60] Lincoln sat on his cushioned rocking-chair. Mary Lincoln was in high spirits. She leaned against her husband and put her hand on his knee. "'What will Miss Harris think of my hanging on to you so?'" she asked him. "'She won't think anything of it,'" he told her. They were to be his last words.[61] Booth waited. He had a single-barrel Derringer pocket pistol and a dagger. The third act began. Suddenly Booth walked around the aisle of the dress circle, and then up to the door of the President's box. Here he took off his hat, and leant for a while against the wall.[62] During a pause in the play, a change in scene, as an actor prepared to come on, Booth took a bunch of visiting cards from his pocket, and handed a card or note to Forbes, the White House coachman, who was on the seat nearest to the door.[63] Forbes read it, and allowed him past, so Booth stepped through the outer door of the President's box. Lincoln had his back to him, the four friends looking down on the performance below. Booth moved inside. The audience were all laughing at a scene-closing joke. Unseen, Booth raised his Derringer, reached out his arm over Mrs Lincoln's shoulder, until the gun-barrel was close to the President, murmured the word 'freedom', and fired.[64]

The bullet ripped into the back of the President's head and tore inside. When Rathbone rose and tried to stop him, Booth stabbed with a knife at the man's breast, but the stroke was deflected and slashed instead across the Major's upper arm.[65] Then Booth rushed to the front of the box, still holding the knife, cried out, 'Sic semper tyrannis!', and then launched himself forwards over the twelve-foot gap down onto the stage below.[66] The spur on his boot caught on a flag on the box, and he landed awkwardly, breaking a bone. Despite the pain he raced across the stage, then scuttled to the rear of the theatre, attempted to stab the theatre's orchestra leader, dashed out through a side-door into a back alley, and from there hopped and limped to the main Avenue. There his horse was waiting for him; he mounted, and he and Herold sped off into the night, pursued ineffectually by one of the audience, a colonel in the Union Army.[67]

The audience heard the shot, but assumed in the moment it was part of the play. It was only Mrs Lincoln's screams of 'murder' and then Booth's dramatic leap that startled the paralysed audience into active uproar. There were screams of 'kill him' and 'hang him'; men wept. Mrs Lincoln was on her knees, shrieking.[68] People ran to the box; the President was still alive, but quite unconscious. There was blood on the back of the rocking-chair, and some of his brains had leaked out from the wound.

Booth had dropped his gun and his hat on the floor of the box; the spur that had caught on the flag was found on the stage. These clues though were hardly necessary; there had been nothing hidden about the deed. A well-known actor had taken the stage; it was always going to be certain that he would be recognised. Booth had often played at Ford's Theatre; it was his insider knowledge of the building that facilitated his rapid escape. Yet, from this public place, he successfully vanished from view. The roads out of Washington were guarded, the steamboats on the Potomac searched, but no further trace of the assassin could be found.

Meanwhile the other two targets of the conspiracy were meeting their fates. In his bedroom at the Kirkwood Hotel, Vice President Johnson passed the night unscathed. When it came to the moment to strike, Atzerodt, his appointed assassin, flunked it and slunk home. William Henry Seward was not to be so fortunate. Around ten o'clock, just as Booth was firing on Lincoln, Lewis Paine also set to work. He had a dagger and an aged and rusty Navy revolver. Still weak from his carriage accident, Seward was already in bed. (He had impetuously tried to restrain two bolting horses while out on a ride with his family.[69]) His son, Frederick William Seward, who worked for him as Assistant Secretary of State, was staying with him and others of the Seward family in his Washington house. After a better night than he had passed previously, and a solid breakfast of egg, toast, shad and coffee, Seward senior had spent the day in bed, having Tennyson's 'Enoch Arden' read to him by his daughter Fanny.[70]

While Herold waited outside to help with the escape, Paine mounted the steps to the front door, and told the doorman, William Bell, that he had new medicine for Seward. Bell let him into the house, assuming he was a messenger bearing a fresh prescription from Dr Tullio Verdi, one of Seward's three attending physicians. However, having allowed entry, Bell hesitated to let the stranger go further, though Paine insisted in his 'thin', 'tenor' voice that he must administer the medicine himself, as the doctor had given him specific instructions about its use.[71] After arguing a long time with the doorman in the hall, Paine pushed past him and strode heavily up to the third floor, where Seward's room was located.[72] But, alerted by the loudness of Paine's tread, Seward's son, dressed in his underclothes, was there before him.

That evening, Fanny Seward had been reading *Legends of Charlemagne*. After a visit by Dr Norris, her father had fallen into a light sleep. After a while, around ten o'clock, he woke, and smiled at her. Yet, hearing voices outside, Fanny went to the door, and found her brother, talking with a very tall young man. She told her brother that their father had woken up, thereby inadvertently revealing to Paine in which room the

Secretary of State was resting. Paine asked her roughly if Seward was indeed awake; she looked back to her father to hear him say 'Almost'. He was drifting in and out of sleep. Then her brother shut the door, and she went back to the bedside.[73]

Out in the hall, the stranger declared that he had a message from the doctor. But Frederick William Seward was adamant that his father should not be disturbed; the gaslights had already been lowered in the rooms, and the household was preparing for sleep. The two men argued while the younger Seward refused to admit the stranger; his father was too sick to accept any kind of visitor at that hour. Apparently persuaded, Paine feigned to be leaving, walking down the steps with William Bell, who told him 'Don't walk so heavy', when suddenly Paine turned, sprang forwards, and levelled his gun at Fred Seward's head to shoot him.[74] He swore as he pulled the trigger, but there was only a click as the gun misfired. So Paine lunged forward and pistol-whipped Fred Seward, fracturing his skull.

Alarmed by the noise, Fanny Seward opened the door of the sick-room, and saw her brother pale and bloody, and the stranger by him. Paine burst into the room, punching Fanny out of the way, and stabbed with his Bowie knife at the male nurse (an invalid soldier named George Robinson).[75] Fanny pleaded with Paine, 'Don't kill him'; it was these words that again woke her father up. Paine rushed to where William Seward lay on his bed unable to move, and the Secretary of State had one glimpse at his assassin's face, as he desperately struggled to raise himself so as to protect his daughter. The half-light in the room made it hard to see as Paine tore forwards and slashed the Secretary of State several times across his face; he would have cut his throat too, but Seward escaped by flinging himself out of the bed. Fanny looked on, and the thought came to her, 'This must be a fearful dream.' Yet all the ordinary things of the room were still there, the bureau, the book she had been reading: it was no dream.[76] She was pacing up and down the room screaming as Robinson wrestled with Paine; it was her screams that brought Major Augustus Seward, the Secretary's eldest son, hurrying into the room. The dim light in the room confused the Major. He saw one man struggling with another and, imagining at first that it was his father fighting deliriously with his nurse, he moved forward to pull back the striving figure. As he did so, he felt at once the height and strength of the struggling man. It was not his father. He shoved the man forward, and Paine attacked him too, striking the Major five or six times on the head with the butt of his knife. Amazingly Major Seward was apparently little hurt by his onslaught, though he staggered back, and Paine, calling out over and over, 'I'm mad, I'm mad,' turned and hurtled from the room, and fled down the stairs.[77]

* * *

Immediately after the shooting, the President's body had been carried a short distance to a boarding-house opposite Ford's Theatre. As news spread, crowds gathered outside. There was panic on the streets; mounted patrols passed; rumours of the killings spread.[78] The President was taken to a small bedroom decorated with prints; a copy of a Landseer painting of a white horse hung over the bed. He was stripped and laid on the bed, with a coverlet over him. The Cabinet met around the President's bedside. Blood seeped out from the wound in his head, soaking the pillows. His eyes filled with blood; the flesh around them looked heavily bruised. He breathed hard, yet was unconscious. He seemed to be in no obvious pain. During the night, his breath grew feebler and interrupted. Just before the end, his wife was allowed to visit him. She fell crying on his body, and then after a few moments was led back out from the room. At 7.22 in the morning, Lincoln died. His mouth hung open afterwards, so they closed it by tying a handkerchief around the head. The face looked contented in death, almost smiling. They closed his eyes, and placed nickels on them; later these were replaced with silver half-dollars.

Although on the Saturday rumours spread of the Secretary of State's death or of that of his son, in fact all those wounded at the Sewards' house survived. Seward was left with wounds to his face and neck.[79] These were staunched, and cooled with ice; when one of his doctors visited him the next day, he looked at the bloody mess, and remarked, 'Assassination in the vilest form'.[80] It was Seward's son Frederick who was most badly injured, his skull fractured in several places and the brain exposed. On the day of the President's funeral, Seward watched from his sick-bed as his friend's coffin passed:

He used at a subsequent period to tell of his vague and dreamy memory of being propped up with pillows, and drawn to the window, to witness the passing funeral pageant of the President. The great black catafalque, with its nodding sable plumes, caught his eye, but he was physically too weak to grasp its full significance.[81]

* * *

The assassins themselves had become fugitives. Hearing the commotion inside the Seward house and the shouting of servants, Herold had fled. Believing Paine had been caught, he rushed to tell Booth the news. They met on F Street and then rode out together to the Navy Yard Bridge. They were stopped there by sentries who were enforcing the nine o'clock curfew. The two men bluffed their way through, and were allowed to pass.

On leaving Seward's house and finding Herold gone, Paine clambered onto his horse, a bay mare, and rode off, with William Bell, the doorman from the Seward house, right behind him until he reached I Street.[82] Paine hid out for three days in a cemetery, and then on 17 April, around midnight, moved on to Mary Surratt's house, the one place (he ought to have guessed) where he was most likely to be detected. Sure enough it was a particularly bad moment to break cover, for federal agents were in the house in the process of arresting Mary Surratt herself.[83] When he came into the room and found Mrs Surratt and her daughter surrounded by Union officers, Paine supposedly remarked, 'I guess I've made a mistake.' He was identified by William Bell, and was clapped in heavy irons and taken in too.[84] To confirm his identity, Major Seward made the experiment of holding Paine as he had held him on the night of the assault, and making the young man repeat the phrase 'I'm mad, I'm mad.' The re-enactment worked; at the end of it, the Major was sure they had found the right man.[85]

After impulsively deciding not to kill Johnson, Atzerodt had been without a plan. The police soon caught up with him in his bed at the house of Ernst Hartman Richter, his cousin.

Yet the chief culprits remained at large. A $50,000 reward was offered for the capture of Booth; John Surratt and Herold both had $25,000 on their heads. Troops scoured the countryside of Maryland; various men were mistaken for Booth and arrested.

Meanwhile the real Booth was on the run. His ankle was broken and he was pale from the pain of it.[86] Around midnight on the night of the murder, he and Herold arrived at Surratt's Tavern for whiskeys and to pick up guns.[87] From there the two men kept on south through Maryland. But Booth needed medical help. They decided to call at the house of Dr Samuel Mudd, by some accounts the man who had introduced Booth to Surratt in the first place. Herold and Dr Mudd had to help Booth off his horse, and take him into the house, his shoulders draped with a shawl.[88] There the doctor cut the boot from Booth's leg and set the limb with plaster. Booth asked for a razor, and with it he shaved off his moustache. Then Mudd made up a crutch, and Booth and Herold rode on to hide in the woods.

They kept heading south. They went to Samuel Cox's house in Maryland, where they hid out in a thicket. From 16 to 21 April, they were fed by a man named Thomas Jones, while they waited to cross the Potomac River.[89] Once again they had found a person willing to protect them.

Booth wondered about how the killing had been received, and was somewhat relieved at first by the admiration of some among the defeated Confederates. As time went on, he began to realise how much his deed might have compromised the South, learning from newspapers shown to him by Jones how they had reacted to his heroism with horror.[90] Booth was a disappointed man. In a brief diary he made while a fugitive, he told of his losses. On Saturday 22 April, Booth wrote out the following:

After being hunted like a dog through swamps, woods, and last night being chased by gun boats till I was forced to return wet cold and starving, with every mans hand against me, I am here in despair. And why; For doing what Brutus was honoured for, what made Tell a Hero. And yet I for striking down a greater tyrant than they ever knew am looked upon as a common cutthroat. My action was purer than either of theirs. One, hoped to be great himself. The other had not his countrys but his own wrongs to avenge. I hoped for no gain. I knew no private wrong. I struck for my country and that alone. A country groaned beneath this tyranny and prayed for this end. Yet now behold the cold hand they extend to me.

God *cannot* pardon me if I have done wrong. Yet I cannot see any wrong except in serving a degenerate people. The little, the very little I left behind to clear my name, the Govmt will not allow to be printed. So ends all. For my country I have given up all that makes life sweet and Holy, brought misery on my family, and am sure there is no pardon in Heaven for me since man condemns me so. I have only *heard* what has been done (except what I did myself) and it fills me with horror. God try and forgive me and bless my mother. To night I will once try the river with the intent to cross, though I have a greater desire to return to Washington and in a measure clear my name which I feel I can do. I do not repent the blow I struck. I may before God but not before man.

I think I have done well, though I am abandoned, with the curse of Cain upon me. When if the world knew my heart, *that one* blow would have me great, though I did desire no greatness.

To night I try to escape these blood hounds once more. Who can read his fate, God's will be done.

I have too great a soul to die like a criminal. Oh may he, may he spare me that and let me die bravely.

I bless the entire world. Have never hated or wronged anyone. This last was not a wrong, unless God deems it so. And its with him, to damn or bless me. And for this brave boy with me who often prays (yes before and since) with a true and sincere heart, was it a crime in him, if so why can he pray the same I do not wish to shed a drop of blood, but 'I must fight the course' Tis all thats left me.[91]

The doubts of the letter written before the deed are here both deepened and resisted. At times Booth's wounded ego predominates. The discrepancy between his self-image and his rewards lacerates him. He takes refuge in grandiosity, his act too great to be understood by the others for whom he performed it. There is something of the petulance felt by the badly reviewed in his self-justification, his aggression, his baffled sadness. It is a paradox of this story that Booth is the only assassin to be discussed in this book who already enjoyed fame, and yet is one of those assassins for whom the idea of fame might well have proved a spur to commit the crime. Measuring himself against his more famous and talented father and brother, John Wilkes Booth had pressing personal reasons for making his name.

And still, beneath all, runs his fear of God's judgement of the deed. An image printed in Philadelphia in 1865 depicts a handsome and thoughtful Booth, a gun in his right hand, tempted by the hideous figure of Satan; behind them both Lincoln innocently watches a play.[92] This diabolical version of Booth's motivation bears, of course, little relationship to his self-image as tyrannicide. A tyrannicide acts within a political frame; the virtues of men are all that concern him. And yet, the fugitive knows, God has other concerns. Booth longs for greatness and despises it. Only God and his own conscience see his heart. After all, it seems that he had the actor's weakness for publicity. He undertook to kill in a spirit of absolute independence, but the theatrical shout, the leap to the stage are just as truly expressive of his character. His letter burned by Matthews deprived him of a scaffold speech, a moment of Shakespearean persuasion. Silenced, fugitive, his outcast state signalled itself in a terrifying solitude. He was alone with his deed. He would not be understood.

Around the time that he wrote this diary entry, on Friday 21 April, the fugitives crossed the Potomac on a boat given to them by Thomas Jones. Yet, on Sunday 23 April, Booth was to endure another instance of the cold hand of ingratitude that his country offered him in recompense for his noble act of tyrannicide. Following the advice of Dr Mudd, Booth and Herold sought medical attention from Dr Richard H. Stewart in King George County, Virginia. To Booth's chagrin, Dr Stewart turned them away with only a contemptuously provided meal, and no medical attention. Angered, Booth wrote a resentful letter in which he rebuked Stewart's lack of hospitality and offered $5 for the meal they had been ungraciously given. On second thoughts, with cash running low, Booth rewrote the letter enclosing the more modest sum of $2.50. He could no longer afford his own indignation.

Usually they were luckier. Time after time, they received food and help from the people they met. Some have argued that this had little to do with luck, but was because they were knowingly following a Confederate 'underground railroad' of safe houses from North to South.[93] Once they came upon a straggling group of Confederate troops. Herold was agitated and quickly confessed, without consulting with Booth, that they were the 'assassinators' of Lincoln. Sympathetic, the soldiers took the two runaways to Richard H. Garrett's farm in Caroline County, a little south of Port Royal, Virginia, on the Rappahannock. The troops asked if the farmer and his family would put up a couple of injured Confederate soldiers, meaning Booth and Herold. Booth was still on crutches. The Garretts agreed and took the two men in, hiding them in a tobacco barn.[94]

The pursuing Union troops heard news that two men answering to the descriptions of Booth and Herold had been seen crossing the river from Maryland to Virginia. There had as yet been no search in Virginia. A party of cavalry were sent to investigate under the command of Lieutenant Colonel Everton J. Conger and Lieutenant Baker. They were to intercept Booth at Port Royal. It was known that Booth's leg was broken, and estimated that he would have gone no further than that point. The cavalrymen took a steamboat and travelled downriver as far as Port Royal. At the ferry stop there, they interrogated the ferryman. He told them he had seen no one. At this point, Baker put his hands around the man's throat and pressed the fingers tight. Still the man pleaded that no one had come through there. Baker brought out some pictures of Booth and Herold, and the ferryman's black assistant instantly identified the men. They had come through yesterday. At this point, the ferryman confessed everything. He had rowed two men across some time before.

It was 25 April. With a clearer sense of Booth's progress, the cavalry set off, and rode about fourteen miles or so. In a hotel bed in Bowling Green, they found eighteen-year-old Willie Jett, one of the soldiers who had come upon Booth and Herold. Jett told them where the assassins were hiding, and led the cavalry to the farm.[95] It was the middle of the night when the soldiers reached the farm. They surrounded the place and then began to move in. Garrett came out of the house onto the porch and called out, 'What's this?' They said they would tell him everything, if he lit a candle. So he went back inside to fetch a candle, and Baker followed him into the house, put a gun against his head and demanded to know who those men were who'd been sitting on his porch.[96] The old man told him that the men had gone, and Baker threatened that he would blow his brains out. Garrett's son came in. He was dressed in Confederate uniform. He pleaded with them not to hurt the old man, and said that he would tell everything. Baker put the gun to the son's temple, and told him that if he lied he would kill him. The son said he would lead them to the men.

They went back outside and over to the barn. Another son of Richard Garrett's joined them, also in Confederate uniform. Baker ordered the first son to go into the barn, get the weapons from the two men, and bring them out. So he took out his keys, unlocked the barn doors, and passed inside. It was just about 3.00 in the morning. After a while, Garrett came back out, locked the door, and passed the keys to Baker.

They had refused, he told him; had offered to shoot him too; they would not come out.

The soldiers conferred. They decided to give the criminals a choice. They could give their guns to Garrett's son, and face a fair trial; or they could burn to death in the barn. Baker was sent forward to make the proposition. They parleyed a while, Baker calling into the barn, and Booth from within calling out. Booth asked for a fair chance. He had only one good leg. Would they withdraw and let him come out, and fight them fairly? They would not. Their aim was to capture him, not kill him in a fight. Meanwhile the soldiers led their horses away. If there was to be shooting, they would not want the horses harmed, or for them to bolt.[97]

Herold wanted to surrender. The soldiers could hear Booth arguing with him, calling him a damned coward who wanted to give in, his actor's voice sharp and clear in the stillness, while Herold's words were muffled, indistinct.[98]

Then they had the following exchange. Booth called out:

'Captain, who are you? I could have picked off half a dozen of your men while we were talking, and could have had half a dozen good shots at you.'

Baker replied by calling for him to surrender. 'We have come here to take you, not to fight you.'[99]

But Booth had determined to die. His sense of himself required it. The artistic possibilities of the scene were immense. He would die a publicly heroic death. The soldiers could hear voices in the barn. Then Booth called out that Herold wanted to surrender. He would come out with his hands up. The soldiers were wary lest it was a ruse, and the two runaways had much to do to persuade them that Herold had given his rifle to Booth, and now had no gun. Booth did his best to exonerate Herold from the crime, crying out that only he was guilty. At last, Herold emerged nervously from the barn into the pre-dawn gloom, with his hands up, and was taken by the waiting Baker.

They decided to smoke Booth out. Lieutenant Colonel Conger crept up and pulled some straw out through the slats of the barn's walls, lit it, and then pushed it back in, onto the pile of straw inside. The fire soon took. Conger watched through the wooden slats as Booth came forward, perhaps with the intention of throwing himself into the flames, perhaps only to put the fire out.[100] And for a moment by the light of the blaze Conger could see Booth's face wracked by despair. Then, with a sudden resolve, Booth moved towards the door with his two weapons, Herold's rifle and his pistol. It was then that a gunshot struck the assassin, and blew into and then out of his neck, and he dropped to the floor. There was initially a confused sense that Booth had shot himself, but the possibility was quickly dismissed. The bullet had been fired by Sergeant Boston Corbett. Originally an Englishman, Corbett was a fanatically pious young man; in 1858 he had castrated himself after he spoke to a prostitute on the street in Boston. He was eventually committed to an asylum.[101]

The soldiers carried Booth to the porch. He managed his dying words, a message to his mother. He begged Conger several times, 'Kill me, kill me.' He was in much pain. They did not kill him, but let him go on, tending him as best they could, and by the time he died, four long hours later, it was daylight and all was over. He was dressed in a Confederate uniform. He told them to tell his mother that he died for his country. In his pockets were his diary and photographs of five beautiful women – one of them his upright Unionist fiancée, Lucy Hambert Hale.[102] His hair and moustache had been cut off roughly by way of disguise, and his hair was matted and dirty. There cannot have been many chances to wash since he had killed the President. The mouth hung open, so, just as had been done with Lincoln, they took a handkerchief and tied it around his head. He looked more dignified that way. Then the physician closed his eyes, and they put him in a horse blanket, and sewed him up.[103]

* * *

Fully to grasp Booth's murder of Lincoln, his act must be placed in a wider context of American political violence. Some years before, in June 1862, Seward had been warned of the dangers of assassination. On 15 July 1862, he wrote the following answer:

There is no doubt that from a period anterior to the breaking out of the insurrection, plots and conspiracies for purposes of assassination have been frequently formed and organized. And it is not unlikely that such an one as has been reported to you is now in agitation among the insurgents. If it be so it need furnish no ground for anxiety. Assassination is not an American practice or habit, and one so vicious and desperate cannot be engrafted into our political system.

 This conviction of mine has steadily gained strength since the Civil War began. Every day's experience confirms it. The President, during the heated season, occupies a country-house near the Soldiers' Home, two or three miles from the city. He goes to and comes from that place on horseback, night and morning, unguarded. I go there unattended at all hours, by daylight and moonlight, by starlight and without any light.[104]

 Seward's conviction that assassination was un-American was widely shared.[105] Such murders were the product of court intrigues, palace coups, or the conspiracies of oppressed and disgruntled subjects. American democracy and political openness ensured that such machinations could not flourish. One element of the psychic shock induced by the events of Good Friday 1865 in Washington was the feeling that America's exceptional status had been compromised, its republican virtue tarnished. It was kings who caused assassination, just as they were its victims. The republican integrity of the United States should have rendered an assassination an impossibility. Soon the grotesque anomaly of Lincoln's murder would be marked down as the consequence of the equally grotesque exception of the war and its violence; moreover the essential nobility of the aims of the war itself helped to ameliorate the impact of the President's murder and the attack on Seward. America's sense of itself could be retained. There was, as yet, insufficient reason to forfeit the assurance of uniqueness.

 Booth's attack stunned America; yet there had been precedents and forewarnings. The Abraham Lincoln Papers deposited in the Library of Congress preserve around a dozen warnings of assassination plots sent to the President by anxious citizens. Such people wrote to Lincoln, reporting conspiracies they had overheard.[106] Some were plainly cranks, or making an implicit threat on their own account – one correspondent even suggested darkly that both Presidents Zachary Taylor and William Henry Harrison had already met 'violent deaths' (the first had died of gastroenteritis, the second of a cold).[107] Other messages were more serious.[108] Many of these belong to the months when Lincoln was still President-Elect. He appears to have taken such threats philosophically, and remained careless of danger; the warning missives themselves he had filed in a folder marked 'assassination letters'. As Seward had done, in August 1863 Walt Whitman wrote of seeing Lincoln almost every day, riding to and fro from the White House to the Soldier's Home (his residence in Washington), guarded by a troop of soldiers, sometimes sitting in his open two-horse barouche, but always quite visible:

I see very plainly ABRAHAM LINCOLN'S dark brown face, with the deep-cut lines, the eyes, always to me with a deep latent sadness in the expression. We have got so that we exchange bows, and very cordial ones.[109]

Others also knew of this daily routine. Once, on a summer night in 1864, a sniper shot Lincoln's hat off as he rode back home from the White House.[110] Though that lucky escape forced a more serious approach to his security, Lincoln continued to resist advice to protect himself better, arguing that such precautions might provoke the very deed they were designed to prevent.[111]

On his election in 1860, Lincoln had been far from a universally popular choice; Whitman had also recorded the silent reception the President-Elect had been awarded on his passing through the streets of New York on his tour preceding the first inauguration.[112] There had also been assassination threats during Lincoln's triumphal post-election journey around America. Both Allan Pinkerton, a detective employed to guard Lincoln, and Frederick Seward passed word to Lincoln of conspiracies. As a result of their information, the President-Elect had been forced to cancel a proposed stop in Baltimore, as strong evidence had emerged of plots against his life hatched in secret meetings of 'banded rowdies'.[113] The plan was for a mob to surround and kill Lincoln while he was changing trains. Baltimore's reputation as a centre for violence meant that such hints were bound to be taken seriously.[114] Instead Lincoln passed through the city by a night train, without previous warning, travelling on straight to Washington, DC – though as it turned out there were suggestions of death threats in the capital itself.[115] It was the knowledge that Lincoln's life could not be secured against the intentions of his would-be killers that prompted the change in itinerary. However, when news of his aborted visit reached the newspapers, some were publicly dismayed by Lincoln's timidity. Edwin Stanton, the Attorney General at the time, and no ally of the new President, sneered that he had 'crept into Washington'.[116]

However, it was no moment for quixotic acts of valour. In Baltimore and elsewhere, the sense of 'personal hostility' towards Lincoln was palpable. Despite the cat-calls of some, most could accept that Lincoln was no coward, and was fully prepared to brave the risks; it was simply that the consequences of his murder would be fatal for the country. Lincoln had had to bow to the pressure of well-wishers and adopt a policy of circumspection.[117]

From his first election to the end of the war, there were calls for Lincoln's assassination in some Southern newspapers, including the Richmond *Dispatch* ('to slay a tyrant is no more assassination than war is murder. Who speaks of Brutus as an assassin?').[118] In such tirades against tyranny, the South's own tyranny against the slaves was happily forgotten; 'How is it,' Samuel Johnson had remarked, 'that we hear the loudest yelps for liberty among the drivers of negroes?' Sometimes such bloodthirsty calls were not limited to the South, but were repeated in the border states: the *Exchange*, a Baltimore newspaper edited by the son of Mr Howard, a pro-Southern police commissioner for the town, did not 'hesitate to recommend assassination as a remedy for the obstacles the secessionists encounter in their work. "It is difficult to determine", his paper wrote the other day, "whether the country most needs a Brutus or a Washington."'[119] Such rhetoric recalled the casting of Andrew Jackson as Caesar, and his would-be assassin, the mad Richard Lawrence, as his Brutus.[120]

But it was more than a matter of rhetoric. There were wartime conspiracies against Lincoln, most notably the work of the so-called 'Sons of Liberty', or the 'Knights of the Golden Circle', a pro-slavery secret society, that was rumoured to have plotted Lincoln's murder.[121] An image from the period shows a triptych of 'Theory' (a Knight of the Golden Circle), 'Practice' (John Wilkes Booth) and 'Effect' ('The Martyr President').[122] This was of a piece with the Northern sense that the crime represented the spiteful impotence of newspaper invective actualised as a deed. As would happen after both William McKinley's and John F. Kennedy's deaths, the intemperate nature of press reporting would attract some blame for Lincoln's murder.[123]

Though some have doubted the story, the most startling wartime plot against the President was very likely a wild scheme envisioned by William Clarke Quantrill, a former schoolteacher who had become a grimly murderous or patriotically heroic (depending on your point of view) pro-slavery partisan active on the Kansas–Missouri border.[124] True or not, the assassination would have been entirely within the spirit of Quantrill's bushwhacking attacks. It was Quantrill who led the infamous punitive raid against the town of Lawrence, Kansas, where he and his men put to death 182 men and boys.[125] Lincoln remarked, with curious prescience, that the attack on Lawrence was something 'that could no more be guarded against than assassination'.[126] Soon after the assault on Lawrence, Quantrill set out eastwards from Missouri, perhaps hoping to murder Lincoln too, but stumbled upon a Union patrol in Kentucky and was himself shot, dying nearly a month later in a military prison.[127]

These assassination threats should be understood within the context of a long-standing potential for violence in American political life. In May 1856, a Southern-born Democrat politician, Philemon T. Herbert, shot dead a waiter in a hotel restaurant.[128] Later that same month, Southern statesmen reacted with threats of violence when Charles Sumner delivered a scathing two-day speech in the Senate attacking pro-slavery violence in Kansas, in the process defaming a South Carolina Senator, Andrew P. Butler. A couple of days after the speech, these threats were realised when, on the floor of the Senate chamber, Butler's nephew, South Carolina Congressman Preston Brooks, beat Sumner repeatedly on the head with a gold-tipped cane.[129] Sumner was pinned down by the desk he was sitting at, and was unable either to resist or to evade the blows. For four years, Sumner's health was ruined by the attack. By fellow Southerners, Brooks was lauded for his bravery and his upholding of Southern dignity; he was reputed to have been given presents of new canes by women of the South.[130] His punishment was a $300 fine.[131]

In 1859, this volatility in Senate and Congress flashed into life again over the distribution of Hinton Rowan Helper's provocative book *The Impending Crisis*. As anger increased, politicians took to wearing guns in the Senate and the House for purposes of protection or intimidation.[132] Northern dismay at such action reflected its distance from the frontier violence that still characterised 'long-settled' parts of the South.[133] Moreover, there was the brutalising effect of the violence of slavery itself, a system that habituated white masters and their families to the beating of their slaves.

Yet such readiness for bloodshed was not confined to the South. John Brown's commitment to political violence belonged to the same process. In 1856, three years before the Harper's Ferry raid, he had already perpetrated one massacre in Kansas. His turn to violence, his belief that American guilt had to be purged by blood, was of a piece with yearnings elsewhere.[134] Although Brown's passionate endorsement of action over mere talk found its context within purely American frustrations, it also echoed similar statements among the revolutionaries of Europe.[135] Unlike his Old World counterparts, Brown had Christian martyrdom in mind, yet he showed the same Romantic attachment to the politics of gesture and of passion, of doing deeds rather than persuading. Brown's rebellious venture was quixotic, an action defined by the prospect of its own failure. Dying for a cause could be as useful as killing for it. Others were willing to accept Brown's performance as martyr, and his turn to force was matched by others in America among the anti-slavery movement, some of them formerly pacifist: Ralph Waldo Emerson affirmed that Brown made the gallows holy; Frederick Douglass declared that slave-holders and tyrants equally deserved death.[136] This readiness to accept killing as necessary would prove an element in the drift towards war, as small-scale acts of violence pulled the nation towards the great blood-letting to come.

Lincoln's death can be viewed as the last atrocity of the Civil War. Equally reasonably, we may place it as the first act of violence of the period of post-war Reconstruction, unusual only (though far from unique) in the victim being white. In the years after the war, lynchings, burnings, beatings, whippings, mob violence and murders proliferated, in a wave of political violence aimed at suppressing newly won black freedoms and restoring the power of the displaced Southern elite. And in one sense any white person in the South was a member of the 'elite'. The heyday of Klan violence lasted for several years before being finally ended by the Ku Klux Klan Act of 1871. Both leading black politicians and white 'scalawags' (supporters of Reconstruction) were assassinated, but the violence extended downwards to schoolteachers (both male and female), noted Unionists, mere private individuals and Republican voters.[137] The violence was perpetrated in great part by loosely organised conspiratorial groups and secret societies such as the Ku Klux Klan and the White League, as well as by more open groups such as the Red Shirts or the Knights of the White Camellia. Such fraternities both resembled other secret societies formed at the time in Europe and, unlike them, operated within a particular paradoxical position: the killings and acts of intimidation were fundamentally conservative, a series of actions designed to retain the position of power held by the dominant whites. On the other hand, officially at least, they were working outside the law of the land, and in this way could resemble other revolutionaries of the period, were it not for the fact that their vicious acts were perpetrated against the poorest and most oppressed. Their hostility to the government in Washington was a given, and their counter-revolutionary work was at heart intended to thwart post-war Radical Reconstruction. In one sense, the terrorist violence of the Reconstruction period was a form of sullen partisan warfare, turning Southern defeat into the Democrats' victory. However, among their international contemporaries, the Ku Klux Klan and other similar groups most resembled the perpetrators of ethnic violence in the Balkans and Asia Minor, not least in the fact that victims and attackers were often neighbours. The secret societies treated their black American neighbours as something between a subject people and a territorial rival. As we shall see, the violence also resembled the later smaller-scale wave of assassinations in Weimar Germany, in so far as the courts were often either complicit in the violence or were prepared to find mitigating circumstances for right-wing killing.[138]

* * *

Had they succeeded in their aim and killed the President, Vice President and Secretary of State in one swoop, Booth and his accomplices would have left the USA leaderless. The next President would have had to be chosen by a vote of Congress. In fact, some have suggested that, in view of his ruinously wasted Presidency, if the conspirators had succeeded in murdering the self-assured but ultimately disappointing Johnson, they might have done the nation a favour. Whatever the case, and though the consequences of such a triple murder are incalculable, one thing remains clear: the Confederates would still have lost the war.

In April 1865, the Union was strong with the joy of victory, and it was easy therefore to nourish a hope for reconciliation. As it was, the assassination undoubtedly altered the tenor of the years to come. Booth's murder of Lincoln crushed that hope and tarnished the peace. It was a vivid restating of the cause of hostilities, and hammered home a feeling that the South had been treacherous. Those, like Joseph Holt, who were already in favour of revenge against the South's leaders were confirmed in their desire for retribution.[139]

Some have felt that Booth's death deprived the public of a trial that might have explained the reasons behind the terrible event. The evidence from the trial that did take place suggests otherwise. Shamefully, the prosecutors set out to present a version of events, not to establish the truth behind the assassination. Although they were aware that the conspirators had first planned merely to kidnap Lincoln, this information was deliberately suppressed in order to blacken the accused men and woman.[140] In Washington, the other conspirators had their spell in court, but little was decided except their punishments. John Surratt escaped to Canada, and on to Rome, where, under an assumed name, he joined the Papal Zouaves, was recognised, caught and brought back to the USA. There he was tried but released, after the trial against him ended in a hung jury. His mother, Mary Surratt, proved less fortunate.[141] The facts against her were that she was a Confederate sympathiser (she had been upset by the fall of Richmond), that Paine had gone to her house to hide out, that her son had been involved, that the conspirators had made their plans in her house, that she had reconnoitred the routes out of Washington on the day of the murder and made enquiries as to the pickets that guarded them, that she had delivered Booth's field glasses, that she had been involved with Confederate ·blockade-runners, and that she was intimate with Booth, and perhaps knew of (or helped him find) a supply of guns.[142] Although some have argued for her innocence, the array of proofs regarding her involvement was formidable, and enough to secure the death sentence, despite the promised efforts of her distinguished lawyer, Reverdy Johnson, Senator from Maryland.

Similarly Dr Samuel Mudd's arrest and imprisonment remains controversial. Some see him as an innocent and aggrieved doctor doing his duty, others as a central part of the conspiracy to kill Lincoln, Seward and Johnson. For a brief while, Mudd's reputation was ruined; his name was literally Mudd. Escaping the death penalty, he was sentenced to prison, and then in 1869 was pardoned by President Johnson.[143]

Other than Mary Surratt and Mudd, the accused were Herold, Paine, Atzerodt (all three of whom were condemned to hanging) and Arnold and O'Laughlen, who were sentenced to life in prison. The court was a military tribunal, a matter of controversy for those who see the proceedings as a miscarriage of justice, though probably no more than a mark of the continuing influence of the war, and possibly of an acknowledged sense that the assassinations had been its last blow. There may also have been anxieties that a civil trial, by jury, would have led to even worse injustices.[144] Though they have been much derided, there is evidence that at least some in the commission approached the trial with an open mind, and were ready, if properly convinced, to find at least some of the accused innocent.[145]

The tacit aim of the trial was to prove that Booth had not acted alone, and that his little privatised conspiracy was an intricate part of a larger Confederate plot. This conspiracy theory was commonly believed at the time. The prosecution were not framing the accused, but acting on a broadly shared assumption: suspicions that the murder was a Confederate conspiracy formed almost immediately on the hearing of the dreadful news.[146]

The head of the Bureau of Military Justice, Joseph Holt, was disposed to be convinced of the Richmond government's involvement. It was imagined that the assassination plot had been organised in Canada by Confederate agents, with the encouragement of the Southern government. Northern spies confirmed these suspicions with fanciful stories of overhearing murderous Southern intentions. President Johnson issued a $100,000 bounty for the Confederate President Jefferson Davis's apprehension.[147] A popular song printed in 1865, 'Jeff's Last Proclamation' contains the following stanza:

> I thought that friend Booth sure would help me away
> By murdering President Lincoln for me
> But I find it has only hastened the day
> That will see me hang high on that sour apple tree.

The title page to the song indeed depicts Davis hanging from a tree.[148]

The initial enthusiasm for the conspiracy theory waned as high-ranking figures such as Secretary of War Edwin Stanton began to have second thoughts about the veracity of some of the accusations in

play. Meanwhile, on 10 May 1865, the former Confederate leader had
been captured in Georgia. However, Davis was tried for treason, not
for assassination, and in a civil, not a military court; these were clear
indications that the government was losing faith in its own conspiracy
theory. While President Johnson and Stanton doubted the accusations,
Holt and others were pressing for the cases to come to trial. Nonetheless
the charges against Confederates such as Clement Clay and Davis
began to disintegrate on closer examination, and one chief prosecution
'witness' to the supposed conspiracy, 'William Campbell' (actually
Joseph A. Hoare), admitted to fabricating his story. Soon even Holt
had to confess that the charges based on the testimony of his current
informers and spies would not stand; however, he was still convinced
of Davis's guilt, and continued to press for him to face a military trial.
Likewise the House Judiciary Committee clung vindictively to the
myth of the Confederate President's involvement.[149]

For a long time after the trial's conclusion, the idea of a conspiracy
was dismissed, yet it has been voiced again more recently by some
historians, as, in the post-Kennedy era, the taste for conspiracy theories
has returned. Other versions of the intrigue exist, the most popular,
long-standing (there were many who voiced suspicion back in 1865),
and apparently unlikely alternative view being that the plot was led
by Andrew Johnson, the succeeding President.[150] An Assassination
Committee was established soon after Lincoln's death with the aim of
ascertaining the level of Johnson's connivance in the killing. On closer
examination belief in his complicity faltered, and the Committee never
even bothered to submit a report.[151] These conspiracy theories are now
largely unprovable, one way or the other. Nevertheless, there remain
major flaws in the idea that Booth and the others were agents of a
wider Confederate secret service scheme. There is every indication that
the Good Friday plan to murder Lincoln and the others was a largely
improvised and indeed rather amateurish affair, thought up on the hoof
and without a great deal of foresight. No proper measures had been
put in place to help Paine escape, and therefore it was pure fluke that
(for a time) he did so. The plotters panicked, backed out, ran off, and
generally behaved in such a way as hardly suggests a well-organised and
thought-through conspiracy. On the other hand, there were indeed,
as we have seen, other Confederate plots against the President's life,

and Booth appears to have known people in the 'Confederate railroad', unless his escape route was either judiciously chosen, or very fortunately stumbled upon.

On balance it seems much more likely that Booth was a freelancer – an egoist with a penchant for command and a great deal of megalomaniac charisma – who persuaded a number of not particularly well-placed individuals to take part in a hare-brained scheme. The only conspirator who proved at all adept or useful was Paine. Atzerodt, a famous coward who fled at the sight of a pistol, was put in charge of a murder. If this was the key Confederate secret service operation of the last stages of the war, why was it entrusted to a womanising, near-alcoholic thespian who had never seen military service, a taciturn and possibly lunatic soldier, a cowardly German, a middle-aged woman, and a light-witted pharmacy clerk?

At the trial, Paine's counsel tried to prove a defence of insanity, using Paine's carelessness in failing to conceal his identity and the very ferocity of the attack as indications of mental illness.[152] An expert witness was called who argued that Paine suffered from 'moral insanity', that is, 'when the moral or affective faculties seem to be exclusively affected by disease of the brain'.[153] Paine's illness, it was argued, feasibly enough, was the product of the rigours and horrors that he had experienced in the war. Where this defence became improbable was in the suggestion that the attack itself, on a sick man whom Paine had never met before, was evidence of insanity. This required draining the act of all political significance, imagining the country was in a normal condition itself, or that Seward was a private individual just like any other. The defence went so far as to suggest that a belief that the Civil War had been fought against slavery was itself a delusion, at which point the expert witness demurred and the judge intervened.[154] Throughout the trial Paine remained silent, keeping his own counsel. He said nothing; he looked around the courtroom, with his fierce, uninterpretable stare. When asked how he could think his attack on Seward justified, he merely answered that in war a person was entitled to take the life of another. The defence failed, and Paine was sentenced with the rest of them.

There is a photograph of Paine taken in the days leading up to his execution. His hands are clamped together in rigid metal handcuffs. (In the wanted posters, these hands are described as 'soft' and 'small'.[155])

He had been chained ever since he had tried to kill himself by bashing his head against the metal walls of the prison ship where for a time he had been incarcerated.[156] In photographs, he wears a long-sleeved pullover, the neck cut square against his muscular body. He looks, above all, young; his hair tousled and unwashed, and swept off his forehead; leaning back against the wall; handsome. He gazes towards the camera, his expression more thoughtful than defiant, his puzzled eyes keeping quiet. There are images too of his death, as he and three other of the conspirators were hanged in a prison yard at the Arsenal on 7 July 1865. Hanged with him were Mary Surratt, George Atzerodt and David Herold. Right up to the last minute, there were hopes of a reprieve for Mary Surratt; but, to the disgust of many, none came. A series of photographs preserves the event. The first presents a crowded wooden platform and behind it a prison wall lined with soldiers. A second photograph shows the platform crowded with men with hats and umbrellas shading themselves from the sun; the condemned sit on chairs and listen to their death sentences. They stand up. The nooses are placed around their necks, and white hoods placed over their heads.[157] And then at last the crowd stand around or look down beneath their feet at the swinging bodies of the three men and one woman, the motion blurring their form in the long exposure, with ropes tied to keep their arms close to their sides, over what must be a fifteen-foot drop.[158]

*   *   *

When Lincoln was assassinated, America had already been for four years a nation immersed in killing and grief. Some have viewed the war as the first truly modern industrial conflict, a foretaste of the Great War to come; others have argued that it was 'the last merchant-agrarian war', a conflict that created the conditions for the true American industrial revolution.[159] Recently historians such as Mark Neely have downplayed the extent of the violence of the Civil War. Neely argues that a conflict long understood to have been marked by a ravenous ferocity, where men died in huge numbers, and entire areas of the country were devastated, was in fact an affair marked by chivalry and restraint on both sides. Others, such as Drew Gilpin Faust, would disagree, showing how, as the public awareness of death assumed mythic proportions, suffering became a unifying factor for the nation. Without accurate figures it is difficult to assess the impact of the war, but even conservative estimates suggest a level of destruction, of lives, of livestock, of property, that would have left few untouched. Around 620,000 American soldiers died, in battle, or from the effects of disease; the number of civilian deaths is unreckoned.[160]

However, the nation was far from inured to bloodshed. It was precisely the shock of Lincoln's murder coming just as the fighting had ceased and peace had been attained that so disturbed people.[161] Mourning requires meaning; it expresses the effort to comprehend and to salve, to give meaning to a lost life, and to the lives of survivors. An American culture that found such value in individual life had been suddenly faced with death on a mass scale. The dead had dwindled into numbers; as a nation, Americans sought meaning for the individuals concealed in those numbers. Lincoln's greatness and death was on one level just another war death, but also something profoundly more. The loss of the President was the loss of an individual life, one that stood for the life of the nation as a whole.

The impact of the crime hit home sooner and perhaps with more force due to the new possibilities of the penny press and the haste permitted by the telegraph.[162] Although by our standards it seems a primitive technology, actually the modern rapid diffusion of information was already in place. Within hours of the shooting, several reports had been sent; even while the President was dying, the newspapers knew of the event. This was a crime of which everyone instantly felt the impact. All of America's cities woke up to the same news. America was the stage on which Booth had performed:

A thousand American cities, linked together by a network of lightning, have this morning awakened to the simultaneous knowledge that he who 12 hours ago was their first citizen, the chief architect of their fabric of a resuscitated Union, the figure-head round which clustered their hopes and pride, is numbered with the dead. Already over hundreds of thousands of square miles is every particular and detail of the rash and bloody deed of last night scrutinized by millions of eager eyes.[163]

The deed itself was drawn and re-drawn by dozens of artists. Two moments caught the eye: Booth firing into the back of the President's head, an image of subterfuge and perfidy, and Booth's leap from the box onto the stage, a demonic plunge. Illustrations also circulated of the scene when Booth himself was shot in the Virginia barn. The imagination lingered on these moments, picturing the violence. The degradation of Booth's death was felt in such illustrations to be a fitting doom, an act of poetic justice. Clearly the public were hungry for such images. In June 1866, 'Dashiell's Western Panarama and Moving Mirror' [*sic*] used the latest technology to exhibit a view of the President's assassination, his funeral, and Booth's flight, capture and death.[164] The Library of Congress's online catalogue entry wrongly records that the poster advertising the event marks in pencil that the panorama would be presented at the 'Union Hell'.[165]

Rather than a sense of unreality, it is grief that marks the response to the killing. In a supplement to the poems in his book *Drum Taps*, a sequence of reflections on the war and elegies for the dead, Walt Whitman added one more short group of funeral songs. Among these was 'When Lilacs Last in the Dooryard Bloom'd', Whitman's monumental, elusive threnody – his lament for the dead – that sweeps around the fact of Lincoln's passing, without ever settling down into a statement of the loss. It comes as a surprise to learn that Whitman later considered renaming the poem 'President Lincoln's Funeral Hymn', so public and concrete does that title seem in comparison to the indirectness of his method.[166] The subject may be thought to be Lincoln's assassination, but rather the verse enacts an oblique flirtation with death. As contemporary reviewers noted, there is no loss, no melancholy, but rather a sense of grandeur.[167] Walt Whitman imagined the scene of Lincoln's murder as a 'great death', an act that condensed a nationality, the secession period's 'highest poetic, single, central, pictorial dénouement . . . How the imagination – how the student loves these things!'[168] Lincoln's death here seems august, a happening from classical history, altogether Greek. His death marked the maturity of America. It was a death for the Union and also a union with death. More even than the horror of the war, Lincoln's assassination was a symbolic drawing-in of death itself into the understanding of America. Whitman felt Lincoln's murder as 'tragic', but also saw that America, the Union, transcended any mere individual fate.[169]

The small-town life of Washington, DC, and the opportunities for casual meeting had made Lincoln a familiar figure for Whitman. As we have seen, they were on bowing terms, and, on 4 March 1865, Whitman had been present at the inauguration, where he had seen the President 'looking very disconsolate, and as if he would give anything to be somewhere else'.[170] This sense of acquaintance was easily imagined as a kind of intimacy by Whitman, the bard of street-glances and casual pick-ups. This closeness gives Whitman's elegy a force beyond that of the mere 'public poem'; for Whitman, as for many Americans of the time, the political was embodied in persons – and Lincoln's history, his words, his very presence, vivified the notion of his public office. This sense of Lincoln's presence was intensified by his practice of meeting with visitors at the White House, and his communicating his ideas through letters printed in the nation's newspapers.[171] Disturbed by the way that the Civil War had rendered the dead anonymous, with its battlefields thick with unknown corpses, Whitman's – and the public's – relation to Lincoln graced death again with dignity.[172]

Lincoln's funeral took place on 19 April, the anniversary of the first fighting in both the Revolutionary and the Civil Wars.[173] It is reckoned that at least one million, and perhaps as many as seven million Americans saw the passing of his coffin as it made the long journey by rail from Washington back to Springfield, Illinois. This was Lincoln's apogee, the moment when he came closest to pulling the whole nation into one entity. The murder on Good Friday suggested parallels with the sacrifice of Christ. To many, Lincoln's death seemed like that of a father.[174] In May, Whitman met with a sick Union soldier. The soldier spoke of Lincoln: 'Take him altogether, he was the best man this country ever produced. It was quite a while I thought very different; but some time before the murder, that's the way I have seen it.'[175] Lincoln would come to appear, in time, what Grant had called him, 'the conspicuous figure of the war', and the most successful and important of American Presidents. In 1909, Leo Tolstoy described him as 'the greatest general and greatest ruler of the world'.[176]

Yet many passionately hated Lincoln, for his pursuance of the war, his emancipation of the slaves, his love of 'niggers'.[177] Even in the Northern states, there were some who were content to see that Lincoln had been killed. The same mixture of feelings appeared in the South: some abhorred the deed; others celebrated it.[178] We know that there had been death threats made against the President before, and the possibility of assassination had long existed. Lincoln was loathed by many – in the North as in the South – and there were many who felt that, as Booth claimed, Lincoln really was a tyrant.[179]

And indeed Lincoln might well be considered a dictator. With the emergency of secession as the instigating factor, he enlarged Presidential power in an unprecedented way, introducing such drastic unconstitutional acts as the suspension of *habeas corpus*, martial law, the emancipation of the slaves, and the introduction of conscription. These powers were largely assumed by proclamation, and first promulgated without the sanction of Congress (though Congress later ratified Lincoln's choices).[180] The three Constitutional amendments introduced because of the war all expanded the state's power; the first ten amendments had all had the purpose of limiting that power.[181] Moreover, for his first term, Lincoln was a minority President, with just under 40 per cent of the vote, the lowest figure for a winning candidate in the nation's history, the lack of a substantial mandate making his sweeping actions seem all the more autocratic.[182] In Britain, the 'coarse cruelty of Lincoln and his hirelings was notorious'.[183] John Ruskin's splenetic outpouring to his American friend, Charles Eliot Norton, that the war was 'the most insolent and tyrannical – and the worst conducted – in all history' was idiosyncratically forthright, but voiced a common sentiment.[184]

While Lincoln assumed extraordinary powers, he exercised them with caution. This use of executive power was exceptional; the circumstances were exceptional too. Lincoln worked pragmatically, and with the intention of ultimately preserving the Constitution and the Union. As James G. Randall argued, it is as though, in Lincoln's own mind, the honesty of his actions excused their illegality; as the same writer went on to remark, American government had hitherto been based on 'legal guarantees and limitations, not upon the variable factor of a ruler's personality'.[185] In any case, the gains in the authority of the President initiated by Lincoln were quickly forgone after his assassination. He was the first President to be re-elected since Andrew Jackson, and the second time around received 55 per cent of the vote, a clear endorsement of his policy of emancipation for the slaves and of his prosecution of the war. The very fact that he allowed the usual four-year election to take place in wartime signals his adherence to democratic principles.

Nonetheless, since the beginning of the conflict, many in the South had imagined Lincoln as the 'Abolition tyrant' and 'the tyrant at Washington', and seen the Yankee North as despotic. The fight against 'tyranny' was of course formative in America's understanding of itself, since the Declaration of Independence had been forged in order to fight against George III's 'establishment of an absolute Tyranny over these States'. Such images drew upon the deep resources of classical literature, and the implicit comparison of modern America with the ancient Roman Republic.[186] In the eyes of some Democrats, Lincoln's success as a wartime leader itself laid him open to charges of 'Cæsarism'.[187] Clement L. Vallandigham's wartime political campaign against Lincoln was based on the belief that the government was a despotism, aiming at destroying fundamental American freedoms. Until Lincoln mitigated the severity of the response, the government's treatment of Vallandigham himself (arrested, refused a trial, and condemned to prison) appeared to bear out his accusations.[188] Yet ultimately Lincoln's tolerant treatment of this prominent opponent belies his image as tyrant. Nonetheless 'Peace Democrats' in the Northern states condemned Republicans as 'tyrants'.[189] Abolitionists felt the same way about slave-masters in the South. Both sides appealed to an image of American freedom, the South in particular clinging to a Jeffersonian image of individual liberty, including the liberty to own slaves.

Even as Lincoln was decried by many as a usurping tyrant, there were simultaneously odd yearnings for the suspension of democracy and the establishment of dictatorship. The mysteriously beloved Union General George B. McClellan definitely flirted with the thought of becoming a dictator.[190] General Joseph Hooker was known to have advocated the rule of a dictator, and at the end of the war some in the South suggested that General Lee might seize ultimate power.[191]

When, at the crucial moment, Booth cried out the Latin motto of the state of Virginia, '*Sic semper tyrannis*' (thus always to tyrants), that shout was both ludicrous and momentous. Two years after the murder, an article in *The Times* placed the origin of modern assassination in the years that were then supposed to have brought the revival of classical learning in Europe. The rediscovery of Greek and Roman models meant a new return to the authority of the classics, and with it a revival of the idea of certain political murders as noble and virtuous, not assassination but tyrannicide:

The origin of modern political assassination must be sought in a period somewhat anterior to the Protestant Reformation . . . In Italy, especially, where the reproduction of Republican forms and terms in the free cities encouraged the spread of Pagan maxims, regicide, under the specious name of tyrannicide, was exalted into the grandest achievement.[192]

To this British commentator, tyrannicide appeared Italian, Roman Catholic, foreign. You can praise the fortitude of such men or their courage awaiting death, he suggests, but to applaud the murder itself is entirely wrong:

It is this trifling with sacred principle, this halo of romantic and dramatic interest awakened in favour of virtues out of date, this perpetual relapse into Paganism, which heats the imagination of crack-brained wretches like Booth, and brings them to their deaths in uncertainty whether they deserve God and man's curses, or their blessings.[193]

This article is itself interestingly unclear as to whether Booth is all bad. Others saw the deed as badness without precedent – there was at least misguided nobility in the example of a would-be tyrannicide such as Ravaillac or Felice Orsini.[194]

Similarly an article by Gustave Janicot in the *Gazette de France*, 28 April 1865, made the comparison clear:

Booth had to speak Latin to make himself recognised in the land of liberty, where he accomplished his crime. He had to speak the language of Brutus to reveal his origin, and to show plainly that he belonged, by the nature of the deed, to the Old World.[195]

A letter a few days later in the same paper remarked:

The assassin, a comedian, jumping on to the stage, and brandishing the classic dagger, exclaiming to the affrighted public the stupid phrase, *Sic semper tyrannis!* No, really – and you are right in saying so – that is not American.[196]

Even to Europeans, the murder seemed a betrayal of the American ideal.

Yet Americans did not have to wait for European commentators for the connection between Roman virtue, or Italian Renaissance corruption, and Booth's exploit to become clear. In a speech delivered within a year of the event, Frederick Douglass named the killing, the inauguration of a new crime – a stranger to our latitude. We had heard of it among the monarchs of Europe, where men were goaded to desperation by tyranny, but had never dreamed that in this land of free ballots, a crime so monstrous as the assassination of our Chief Magistrate could be possible.[197]

Booth's act signalled the last collapse of the myth of Southern chivalry; rather than a deed from medieval romance or the novels of Sir Walter Scott, its precedents lay with Caligula, the Borgias or Charlotte Corday. As we have seen, Booth himself cast his role as that of the noble Republican tyrannicide. A poem praising Booth, entitled 'Our Brutus', was printed and proved popular.[198] When Henry Adams, the American novelist and historian, heard the news, he was in Rome: 'where it seemed singularly fitting to that nursery of murderers and murdered, as though America were also getting educated'.[199] Getting educated, getting corrupt.

Somehow, in reading the material related to the Lincoln assassination, it proves hard to dodge an overpowering sense of the ludicrous. Everything regarding the conspirators happens in stark and lurid colours. The gestures are grandiose, the participants melodramatic. Perhaps it comes from Booth's theatrical milieu; he aimed at great tragedy, and achieved *grand guignol*. Ford's Theatre appears like a toy theatre, the actors brilliantly coloured, though smudged, their outlines too clear for reality. When Booth leapt on to the stage, he was throwing himself onto the one place where he felt truly comfortable. Booth's mad energy and his bustle make him resemble Richard III, more than Brutus. From the moment he began his conspiracy, he forsook dignity, though he sought it over and over, that part of him he had misplaced. Only Lewis Paine comes over across the years as noble, as understandable, though at the time his dogged and glaring silence was the most mystifying thing of all. Now it appears existential, the possibly deranged young man a Meursault, Albert Camus's 'Stranger', before the fact.

Yet, compared with later American assassinations, as we shall learn, there is a quality in this crime that does not deprive the event of meaning. The biography of both assassin and victim make sense; there is madness, but even the madness adds meaning to the event. It was the last act of a war, but one that though dreadful was hardly senseless. There is passionate significance here, and not just futility. Lincoln's killing was a tragedy, even though it was a stagey one. The murder both took place in a theatre and also possesses some of the atmosphere of a theatrical event; the shot itself was thought by many in the audience to be a theatrical dénouement, an element in the comedy. Yet, if the murder was a performance, it was one motivated by ardent energy and political fervour. Behind it lay images of greatness and classical virtue, and of American independence.

In the late 1880s, the commander of the troops who had caught up with Booth, Lieutenant Baker, went on the lecture circuit, offering anecdotes of the assassin's death.[200] Unable to stage any more plays there, Ford sold his theatre soon afterwards, clearing a good profit. At the house opposite, where the President had died, they were busy asking for compensation of up to $550 for the cleaning of carpets and bedclothes. In any case, they'd been making money out of it all – reportedly charging admission fifty cents a time to the lines of curious citizens.[201]

Enemies of This World

His only excuse is his fanaticism.
MIKHAIL BAKUNIN ON NECHAEV

I: Bazarov's Children

In January 1878, a young woman called Vera Zasulich stood in line among the petitioners waiting to see Fedor Trepov, the Governor-General of St Petersburg. The petitioners edged closer, and she moved with them. No one seems to have picked her out, no one remarked on her, she was just another of the anonymous crowd of the importunate. Yet under her cloak was a revolver, for she had determined to perform a deed of justice, to mark herself out for an instant as that most remarkable of beings, the blameless assassin. Any second now, she would open fire on Trepov.

In retrospect it seems an extraordinary moment, the shuffling throng, and one among them ready not to plead, but to shoot. Yet in the Russia of that time, such deeds had precedents, and Zasulich had more than her share of exemplars. She herself would soon become a role-model for others, an illustration of revolutionary virtue. To understand how this came to be it is necessary first to trace the arrival of Nihilism in Russia, and in particular the career of that archetypal terrorist, Zasulich's one-time lover, Sergey Gennadevich Nechaev.

* * *

Lincoln's murder shocked Europe. Having applauded such actions as Felice Orsini's attempt to kill Louis Napoleon, many of the continent's political radicals now lamented this new assassination. However, in one country, Booth's deed excited revolutionaries eager for extreme measures. These were Russia's Nihilists; it would in turn be the imitation of Russian tactics by Irish Nationalists and international Anarchists that would drag Europe and America into an era of 'terrorism' and assassination. Through the example of the Nihilists and in particular the character of Nechaev, Russia graced the world with a new persona, one that would be donned over the next century by the West's righteous assassins.

Russia's exceptional political situation created a uniquely amorphous and vicious opposition. At the head of the state stood the divinely sanctioned figure of Alexander II, Tsar of Russia. He proved an unlikely reformer, making changes so as to prevent change; he would do anything but limit his own power. Although fundamentally conservative, in February 1861 he nonetheless oversaw the central liberal reform of the period: the emancipation of the serfs. There were good reasons to push emancipation through. The military defeat of the Crimean War exposed Russia as under-developed and ineffectual; many believed that the poor quality of the peasant recruits was responsible for the Army's flaws. Some argued that serfdom prevented capitalist growth in the country; there were also clear moral concerns; and, beneath all, the fear that if they did not purge the system from above the serfs would in time destroy it from below.[1]

However, emancipation was not the unalloyed improvement that it had promised to be, and its botched provisions inaugurated a period of political unease. Although the peasants were now nominally free, in practice nothing much had changed. While no longer their masters' property, they had the use of less land (and less good land) after emancipation, remained impoverished and economically constricted, subject to corporal punishment, compelled to endure military conscription, and bound to repay (at 6 per cent interest) the debt incurred by the 'gift' of freedom for another forty-nine years. Far from the Tsar appearing the saviour of the Russian people, there were many radicals who considered the emancipation to be a confidence-trick that conceded little.

The resulting bathos produced Nihilism. As they never pursued one coherent project or stood as a single party, it proves hard to define who the 'Nihilists' were or what 'Nihilism' was. Rather Nihilism denoted both a loose political programme and an attempt to recreate the self.

Nihilists identified themselves by their unconventional dress: short hair
for women; long hair for men; workers' clothes; blue-tinted glasses.[2]
Denial of convention easily formed its own conventions. Social niceties
were dropped; Nihilists were studiedly brusque. Adherence to the
rational allowed little room for politeness. They were curt; they said
what ought to be said and no more. According to the Anarchist Prince
Peter Kropotkin, a Nihilist's abiding principle was 'absolute sincerity'.[3]
Behind this style of revolt lay a medley of interests, attitudes and beliefs.
Above all, the Nihilists sought to be 'new', the bearers of an authentic
future.

The Nihilists were disparate in their social origins. Yet patterns
emerged. They came from among the varied and ambiguous ranks of
the *raznochintsy* (men of mixed background) – a set of unplaceable
individuals bound to no one traditional class. They were educated, but
belonged neither to the peasantry, nor to the merchant class, nor to
the gentry. They were intellectuals, journalists, the children of priests,
doctors, perpetual students, lawyers, and teachers. In some cases, an act
of refusal turned someone into a *raznochinet*; these had denied their
class or refused their social inheritance. Their careers blocked, shut
out from the machinery of the state, many were poor and frustrated
by the existing social order.[4] Nevertheless they sought a public role.
Initially at least, the Nihilists were supposed to be utilitarian, scientific
and rational; they took nothing on trust and sceptically probed the
mystique of authority; they were nothing, if not critical. If a belief or
a moral value shattered in the process then that merely demonstrated
its reprehensible fragility.[5] The only absolute was the good of the
Russian people. The movement in Russia was only a manifestation of
a wider European phenomenon, rendered extreme by Russian political
conditions. Behind it lay the influence of J. S. Mill, the anti-Christian
scepticism of Ludwig Feuerbach, the Positivism of August Comte. If
she had been Russian, George Eliot would have counted as a Nihilist.

For a while, the movement remained nameless. Then, with his
portrait of Bazarov in his novel *Fathers and Sons* (1862), Ivan Turgenev
coined both the word 'Nihilist' and the character-type. For Turgenev, the
epithet carried a trace of his ambivalence: it was a means of designating
a younger generation that he simultaneously admired and suspected.
Yet the ageing novelist was famously to declare that he was perhaps

a bit of a Nihilist himself, a pronouncement that outraged politically conservative writers such as Fyodor Dostoevsky.

Meanwhile, in a familiar move (the same process can be traced in the history of such words as 'punk', 'queer' and 'puritan'), Dimitri Ivanovich Pisarev, one of the editors of the radical journal *Russkoe Slovo*, proudly claimed the word. Definition by others became an act of self-definition. Originally 'nihilist' had meant a 'person lacking in education and cultural refinement'; Turgenev had altered its meaning, but the original connotation persisted.[6] By declaring that he too was a Nihilist, Pisarev embraced the term's equivocal implications: perhaps what was needed was a generation who would bluntly criticise and attack. Soon the word caught on, even though it was misleading: it clearly implied the refusal to believe in anything, when in fact the 'Nihilists' themselves were fervent believers in their own brands of positivism and materialism.[7] There was nothing dry in such enthusiasms; they loved 'the people', and beneath their rationalism glowed an unscientific compassion.

As a movement, Nihilism's early origins belonged to the mid-to-late 1850s, in the ferment created by the defeat of the Crimean War and the hopes produced by the accession of the new Tsar. But though born in optimism, it came to public attention in the moment of disappointment. Following the emancipation, a plethora of pamphlets circulated, calling for all kinds of radical destruction. Soon there was destruction in fact, as St Petersburg suffered a spate of anonymous arson attacks. The government and the conservatives scented a budding revolution.

The career of Nikolay Andreyevich Ishutin best manifests the transition between the essentially benign Nihilism of the early 1860s and the violence that was to follow. Only in his twenties, Ishutin set about living out the life of the Nihilist as found in literature, although he chose as his model not Turgenev's tragic Bazarov, but rather the free-thinking, sexually experimental revolutionaries of Chernyshevsky's 1863 novel *What Is To Be Done?*[8] Ishutin practised the pieties of the rebel. He looked down on culture, despised art, and programmatically neglected his own education.[9] His group of fellow revolutionaries, named 'The Organisation', meditated a number of gratuitously appalling crimes in order to further the cause and demonstrate their impeccable distance from bourgeois morality. One considered poisoning his father so the revolutionaries could inherit the old man's money. They laid plans to steal from a merchant and to ransack the postal system. However, plans were precisely what their transgressions remained.

From within the Organisation emerged another smaller and even more secret group, melodramatically designated 'Hell'. The members of Hell were mostly of comfortable middle-class origin or the children of country priests. They pledged themselves to terror. They sought a full-scale peasant revolution and scorned reform as a sop to prevent real change. The ultimate aim was to assassinate the Tsar himself, with the hope that this extreme act would incite the revolution they craved.

Lincoln's murder inspired Hell. Less than a year afterwards, someone affiliated with the group would attempt his own tyrannicide. The time for making plans was over. Dmitry Karakozov indeed looked the part of the romantic killer: of noble blood, he was long-haired, young, carelessly dressed, interestingly pale. Dismissed from university in 1864 for not paying taxes, he became a schoolmaster in a free school organised by Ishutin.[10] In early February 1866, he vanished for a couple of days, leaving a suicide note behind him. In fact, he had visited a nearby monastery. When he returned, he told Ishutin and the other members of Hell that he had decided that he was the one who would kill the Tsar. Their bluff called perhaps, the others tried to dissuade him from such a dangerous scheme. But Karakozov was adamant; he would become an assassin.

On 4 April 1866, after a walk in St Petersburg's Summer Garden the Tsar was pulling on his cloak just prior to climbing into his carriage, when Karakozov stepped up from the crowd that had gathered to watch, fired a shot and missed.[11] Karakozov ran for it, but was quickly caught, and brought before the Tsar who asked the young man whether he was a Pole. Given the vicious repression there following the 1863 revolt it must have seemed a safe bet. 'Pure Russian,' Karakozov told him. Why then had he done it? 'Look at the freedom you give the peasants,' he said.[12]

The Tsar panicked. The time of great liberal reforms ended; the White Terror began. Alarmed, vulnerable, and anxious that its vulnerability had been laid bare, the government lost its nerve. The Emancipator Tsar initiated a period of reaction that would last to his death, and indeed beyond. Count Pavel Pavlovich Shuvalov took charge of the Third Section, the country's secret police; a special protection service bolstered security around the Tsar.[13] Having helped to break the Polish rebellion with a violence that had shocked Europe, Nikolai Muravev was brought in to crush insurrection at home. Ishutin and the others were soon hauled in. So it was that the Tsar learned from them of a mythical international group of revolutionaries, a compound of Ishutin's myth-making, legends of Freemasonry and misinterpreted rumours of Karl Marx's International. In any case, the Tsar swallowed the story, and contacted Bismarck, the Prussian Minister-President, to warn him of the danger. Otherwise retribution was complete. Members of Hell were transported to Siberia; Karakozov was hanged – the first Russian revolutionary to be executed since the revolt of the Decembrists in the 1820s.

To one young radical in particular, this abortive act showed the way to the future: 'the foundations of our sacred cause were laid by Karakozov on the morning of 4th April 1866 . . . His action must be regarded as a prologue. Let us act, my friends, in such a way that the play will soon begin.'[14] These were the words of Sergey Gennadevich Nechaev. At the time of the attempted assassination, Nechaev was eighteen years old, living in Moscow, taking exams that were meant to enable him to work as a schoolmaster. He failed them. Within four years he would be the most famous revolutionary and advocate of assassination in Europe.

II: A Stranger to Us

Though without physical charm or intellectual distinction Nechaev imposed his will on others. He was different. Even to his fellow revolutionaries, he seemed to come from an elsewhere. Another would-be assassin, Vera Zasulich, remarked of him: 'He was not a product of our world, of the intelligentsia; he was a stranger to us.'[15]

Sergey Gennadevich Nechaev was born on 20 September 1847 in Ivanovo, a village he later described as the 'devil's swamp'.[16] On its muddy streets, among the puddles and the piles of manure, pigs, chickens and packs of dogs wandered. His father, who was born illegitimate, was a gilder, house-painter and, on special occasions, a waiter. His mother, a daughter of a successful master painter, died when Nechaev was seven or eight years old. He was brought up by his father, very strictly. Life was not all hardship: as a child he once performed in a theatre. Apparently, he was rather a good actor.[17]

As a schoolboy, Nechaev began a pattern of looking for mentors among older men. He became almost a disciple of his schoolmaster Dementev, and a little later corresponded with and so befriended a radical writer, F. D. Nefedov. These men, only ten years or so older than the teenage Nechaev, were not only father figures, they were routes for escape from the village dullness. Nechaev's complaints about the boredom of life in dreary Ivanovo catch the familiar note of adolescent angst. He was small and suffered from acne. He wrote out Gatsbyesque lists for self-improvement and dreamed of freedom.[18] Given his infatuation with Dementev, it was probably in the spirit of emulation that these dreams coalesced into a plan to become a teacher. Aged seventeen, he moved to Moscow in order to study for the requisite exams, eking out an impoverished existence in digs. It was here that he heard of Karakozov's failed assassination attempt against the Tsar. Shortly afterwards he moved to St Petersburg. Here he took the rest of his teaching exams, this time passing successfully in the summer. In the autumn, he began work at Andreevskij Parochial School in St Petersburg, in the weeks just after the trial of Ishutin and his group.

For a while, he took little part in radical activity. In 1867, after a year at his first school, Nechaev transferred to another, also a primary school. He was in a strangely mixed position. He had escaped from home, but his flight had gone no further than the teaching of ten-year-olds.[19] He found his way into the revolutionary underground through an introduction provided by a student named Orlov, whom he befriended on a trip back to Ivanovo in July 1868. Having met Orlov, Nechaev both began to frequent radical groups, and also to put into action a new style of being. For, by that summer, the deferential and bookish youth had remoulded himself. From all accounts, Nechaev up to this point in his life was a fairly ordinary and even likeable lad, sympathetic, affectionate and diligent. Now he made himself tough. The new Nechaev talked for victory. His manner became unbearably proud; he was severe with his friends and haughty with equals. With those from a class above himself, 'he kept a strict silence and tried to cast his shadow over them'. He concealed the facts of his past, creating an air of mystery.[20] It was a role, and one intended to make an impact. In practice, it repelled and impressed in equal measure.

At first, as Nechaev entered the revolutionary world, in meetings he was noted merely as a silent man. With Orlov's introduction, he attended gatherings of the Smorgon Academy, a radical student group. In order to get closer to the students, he began sitting in on classes at the university, even as he continued his job at the primary school. Although disliked by many, soon he was a conspicuous and energetic figure in the movement. He created a small revolutionary committee of his own, and wrote with fellow members Orlov and Petr Nikitich Tkachev *A Programme of Revolutionary Action*.[21] The programme was to end the existing social order, and so establish a world with 'complete freedom of the renewed personality'.[22] In the meantime, Nechaev's concern was the creation of 'revolutionary prototypes'.[23] Following Ishutin's lead, he imagined the new man as ascetic, ready to give up everything for the revolution. While most students were moderate, Nechaev also began advocating violence. He would operate within the tradition of Karakozov's gesture. Nechaev was firmly convinced of the relativism of moral rules. He argued for the efficacy both of Jacobin tactics and also of deliberate deceit. Nechaev's aggressive manner meant that he was never going to establish a large group, but by agitating at the University and the Forestry Institute, he did create a small circle of friends.[24]

Nechaev had formed a cabal, but he had also isolated himself within the broader movement. He had alienated moderates but, with the help of his friends, had begun to forge a legend around himself. He stage-managed a fake arrest, and let it be known that he had alerted the cause with a note thrown out from a railway carriage. The note found its way to the willing eighteen-year-old revolutionary Vera Zasulich, who was to circulate the gripping news of his apprehension to the students. He made a mysterious trip to Odessa; there were further rumours of his being twice arrested, and twice escaping. A message that he had actually broken out from St Petersburg's Peter and Paul fortress also reached Zasulich. Somehow the undersized schoolmaster had begun to seem like a larger-than-life hero of conspiracy. In March 1869, he quit Russia, travelling to Brussels, and then down to Geneva. He had gone looking for Bakunin.

* * *

It is an indication of the extent of Nechaev's ambition that he should immediately have set out to woo such a man. Mikhail Bakunin was the pre-eminent figure among the Russian revolutionary exiles, a founder of anarchism, a force of nature, and just the type to develop a crush on a killer. Violence electrified Bakunin. He was somehow benevolently violent himself, impulsive and exaggerated. In his writing he over-used the italic; he was always hammering home his point. It was not only the fact that he was prodigiously tall and grossly obese (twenty stone at least) that gave him always the attitude of a large man in a small room. He glimpsed in the Russian peasant a picture of himself as he would ideally be: a natural rebel, a pirate, a brigand. His image of revolution became, characteristically enough, a matter of provoking the deceptively stodgy masses into revealing their concealed but genuine desire for revolt. Alexander Herzen considered him a kind of mastodon, Karl Marx thought him like a bull. He was a frontal assault of a man, silly, but on fire.

Bakunin was born in Tver, north-west of Moscow, in 1814, the third of ten children and the eldest son of a retired diplomat and noble. Family life was a beautiful protection. Surrounded by loving sisters and admiring younger brothers, young Mikhail Bakunin was the adored despot of the family. He plunged into philosophy, first Fichte and then Hegel, and emerged from this soggy Germanic element committed to revolution; for him, utopia became a practical solution.

At the end of the 1840s, Bakunin's great moment arrived. In September 1847, he wrote a letter to Georg Herwegh, announcing, 'I await my . . . fiancée, revolution. We will be really happy – that is, we will become ourselves, only when the whole world is engulfed in fire.'[25] He did not have to wait long. 1848 came, the year of revolutions. He rushed back to Paris to be in the thick of things, and then swept off to foment revolt in Poland. He hoped that a war might start there, and bring about the anarchy that he desired with all his heart.

But the revolutions petered out. He was sentenced to eight years in prison in Russia. There he wrote his *Confession* and lost his teeth. In 1855, on the accession of Alexander II, he was released into exile in Siberia. In 1857, he married there an eighteen-year-old Polish girl, Antonia Kiriatkowska. Though apparently an unstoppable force, Bakunin was sexually impotent; while Antonia bore him two children, these were in fact fathered by a mutual friend, one Carlo Gambuzzi. In 1861, Bakunin escaped from Siberian exile, travelled to San Francisco and then sped across America to Boston, and so on to England, where he stormed into Alexander Herzen's London drawing-room, fat, flustered and ready for action: 'the latent power of a colossal activity for which there was no demand'.[26]

Herzen represented a paradox to match Bakunin's single vision, both in love with European culture, with its art, music and literature, and also convinced that it was dead and rotting. Herzen had inherited something of Peter Chaadaev's notion of Russia as a cultural blank. Yet the very rawness of the nation, its place closer to the beginning of things, gave it the prospect of a future.[27] Meanwhile, like many, Herzen believed that the history of Europe was over, or close to its end. The old society was exhausted, and a new one must come. Europe's very prosperity provided evidence for its sickness. Everything was comfortable; everything was moribund. A conflagration was called for, the birth pangs of a new world. The violence that Bakunin offered was distasteful, but also an indication of hope. Things would have to be cleared away before the new order began. Years before, Herzen had excitedly discovered an article by Bakunin that ended with the fervent declaration: 'The passion for destruction is at the same time a creative passion.' In their different ways, both men understood the deep appeal of such a thought.

After travels in Sweden and Italy, Bakunin ended up in Geneva, broke. He lobbied successfully for the job of translating Marx's *Das Kapital* into Russian. The publisher would pay 1,200 roubles for the translation, 300 of them in advance. Herzen was taken aback when he heard the news: he knew Marx and Bakunin were not exactly on friendly terms. In any case Bakunin had taken up a task that by temperament he was bound to shirk. He gave up the dull bookish work of translation after a few pages.[28] There he was in Geneva, living the life of the penniless émigré, plotting his takeover of the International. He appeared relentless, in control of his destiny, and perhaps the force that would tip the balance of the destiny of whole nations. But very soon an unexpected event would change all that. He was about to meet Nechaev.

* * * *

When Nechaev found him in Geneva, Bakunin was living in the city, longing for a student movement to emerge. Youth would spark the revolution. His desire, as expressed in his *Confession*, was to send out the 'young men' ('and any others of use') fitted by capability, character and manner to do revolutionary work. In his eyes, the new army should also be led by 'the young and anyone capable of carrying arms'.[29] It was a note that was to sound over the next hundred years and beyond: youth was pure, inspired and filled with the wisdom of impulsive action. Both Bakunin's values and his methods were those traditionally associated with adolescence. So it was that Nechaev's unexpected arrival appeared a portent to him.

Nechaev was only twenty-one, but he could tell Bakunin a whole history of adventures. He mystified his own past, making up a better one. The new Nechaev was the creation of a few books and articles, by Chernyshevsky, Turgenev, Bakunin himself, some histories of the French Revolution, and maybe the newspaper accounts of the trials of the leaders of Hell. He was a passionate actor; Bakunin was at once convinced. They soon became an incongruous couple: Bakunin, looking older even than his years, obese and wildly bearded; and Nechaev a rather dapper man in worn-out clothes, neat with his black hair swept back from his crooked face and his trimmed black beard that covered only some of the scars left by his disfiguring acne.[30]

Bakunin considered Nechaev an *abrek*, 'a pitiless warrior of the Caucasian peoples', such as those that the Russians were fighting on their southern borders.[31] He saw in the young man the incarnation of an ideal of activity without debilitating reflection, someone who by instinct had embraced action over thought, much as Bakunin himself had some twenty-five years before. However, Bakunin's anti-intellectualism was a genuinely intellectual stance; Nechaev was anti-intellectual out of contempt. Nechaev therefore embodied something that Bakunin coveted yet was too clever to possess. Both men agreed that liberal prattle went nowhere; but only Nechaev was genuinely indifferent to the appeal of such chatter.

For Nechaev, Bakunin was another father figure to woo and exploit. Also, by associating with Bakunin he was bound to acquire some of the great man's prestige. Bakunin undoubtedly had a crush on him. There would indeed be unverifiable rumours that the relationship between the two men was precisely that of lovers.[32] Bakunin wrote to a friend on 13 April 1869: 'They are charming, these young fanatics, believers without God, heroes without rhetoric.'[33] Nechaev informed Bakunin that he was in charge of a huge revolutionary organisation and had escaped from the Peter and Paul fortress. It was impressive and precisely what Bakunin wanted to hear. Bakunin told Nechaev in turn of his own 'World Revolutionary Alliance'. Both men's secret societies were at bottom fictions; each hoped to enlist the other for revolutionary organisations that did not in fact exist. They were locked together in the peculiar intimacy of two penniless pickpockets busy robbing each other. There is about their relationship something of the atmosphere of an adolescent game: as evidence of his membership of the 'Russian Section of the World Revolutionary Alliance', Bakunin presented young Nechaev with a membership card. Wonderfully, it was numbered 2,771, although in fact it was the first and only one ever issued.

Meanwhile Nechaev let Bakunin know that his organisation in Russia needed cash. Some years before a Russian named Bakhmetev had given 20,000 French francs to Herzen for the financing of revolution. Bakunin set about relieving Herzen of half this sum in order to pass it on to Nechaev for propaganda purposes.[34] Herzen was sceptical of his old friend's new protégé, but nonetheless surrendered the money.[35] Nechaev at once launched a propaganda campaign based on the writing and distribution of pamphlets. His first aim was revolution. His second was convincing the Westerners that he had a huge following in Russia, and the Russians that he had a huge following in the West.

One of the key pamphlets of this propaganda campaign, and a central text of the advocacy of political violence for its own sake, was the infamous *Catechism of a Revolutionary*.[36] This is a short pamphlet organised into twenty-six numbered paragraphs. The work describes the 'revolutionary type', the kind of person required to push through the revolution. Although the object of much scholarly debate concerning its authorship, this work is almost certainly a collaboration between Bakunin and Nechaev, with Nechaev as main author and Bakunin as editor and writer of a few of the document's injunctions.[37] Hating autocracy and its repressions (which were indeed extreme), they respond with rigour. Ideas are pushed to the limit; the revolutionary pursues without pity a single aim. The word 'Catechism' was a joke invoking the creation of a new church, conjuring up the commitment of the Christian monk pushed towards amoral violence in the service of revolution.

The revolutionary was 'a lost man', 'an implacable enemy of the world', committed to destruction, indifferent to others, revolution his only good, obdurate, prepared to be tortured, primed to kill.[38] The *Catechism* drew on radical tradition, from the memory of the Jacobins to the Romantic glorification of the bandit. It set out concrete plans: the killing of intelligent representatives of the state; the blackmail of functionaries; conspiracy with ambitious liberals, while preparing the ground to blackmail them too; the driving of armchair radicals into the performance of actual deeds. It offered a conspiratorial model for revolution, dependent neither on agitation nor on propaganda, but on hard action. It was not Nihilism; it was beyond that. The revolutionary was in the world, but not of it. Pity was dead, both for yourself and for others, even though pity for 'the people' might still lurk some distance behind its declarations. Revolution inspired by compassion for the miserable has here become a cold activity. It was a text that set a moral standard, while delineating morality as so far understood as merely bourgeois obfuscation. The Anarchists embraced its rigours; Lenin admired it and plagiarised its ideas; a hundred years after it was written it became a central text for Eldridge Cleaver and the Black Panthers.[39] It offered a vision to live up to.

Such propaganda awarded Bakunin and Nechaev the initiative against their more circumspect colleagues. Praise of violence for its own sake was a new thing, and, while morally worrying, rather thrilling. In his journal, the organ of the *Narodnaya Rasprava* (The People's Retribution), Nechaev went to the lengths of listing potential victims, including high-ranking officials like General Mezentsev and Trepov and writers such as the conservative journalist Mikhail Katkov. In fact, the *Catechism* and the other pamphlets that Nechaev was printing were altogether too outrageous even for those within the movement. Some wondered if Nechaev might be a double agent, deliberately creating compromising documents to discredit the revolution. Some were so furious that they contemplated sending assassins to Geneva to murder him.

Nechaev might have been unpopular at home, but he still knew that he must return to Russia. Central to his timetable for revolution was the prospect of a peasant uprising. He believed that the peasants would undoubtedly rebel at the next legal stage of the emancipation of the serfs in February 1870, when the legislation would impel them to accept either a smaller allocation of land or a lifetime of debt.[40] The unfairness of this provision looked certain to trigger rebellion. Nechaev decided that he had to be in Russia, to build on the propaganda that he had produced with Bakunin and to rouse this imminent revolution.

It is one of the paradoxes of Nechaev's career that, for all his words, the only assassination he would commit would be of one of his fellow conspirators. He returned home in August 1869, via Odessa. He travelled on to Moscow and immediately began creating a new revolutionary cell. He made contact with Uspensky (born of noble family in 1847), who worked at Cherkesov's bookshop, a centre for the radical underground.[41] Uspensky introduced Nechaev to Dolgov, who likewise joined the gang. Then there was Ivan Ivanovich Ivanov and some other students from the School of Agriculture. Another new recruit was Ivan Gavrilovich Pryzhov, a heavy drinker a good twenty years older than the rest. Having been refused permission to attend university, Pryzhov had lived for years as a struggling writer, recording the facts of peasant life. His ultimate aim was to produce a history of destitution in Russia, a subject he was well equipped to explore. Pryzhov, who had seen everything and met every kind of person, had never met anyone like Nechaev. He was immediately convinced and ready to join the conspiracy. Nechaev also brought in the Likhutin brothers, two young nobles. To prove his zeal, one of the brothers disguised himself as a policeman and extorted 6,000 roubles from a fellow student.[42]

Over these disparate men, Nechaev exerted the domination of personal allegiance. All of them shared their leader's sense that the revolution was only a few months away. They were living in the pause before the apocalypse. Nechaev let his disciples believe that behind him was a vast international organisation of revolutionaries – a version of Ishutin's boast to the Tsar. Nechaev's influence was everything; the others were ready to follow him unthinkingly. Yet suddenly at one of their meetings, Ivanov, one of the agriculture students, criticised Nechaev's orders and dictatorial manner. Perhaps enraged by the insubordination, or ready to bind his group together with an irreversible transgression, or genuinely anxious that Ivanov might go to the authorities, Nechaev reached his conclusion: Ivanov should die. On 20 November 1869, a meeting was held and Nechaev notified those others that he could definitely trust, that the Central Committee (a body that did not in fact exist) had warned him that Ivanov was about to denounce their society to the political police of the Third Section. Their lives and the revolution itself were at stake. All at the meeting agreed that Ivanov must be prevented.

The next day Ivanov was told that he should join the others that night in the gardens of the School of Agriculture. A typewriter that Ivanov had stashed there was required for propaganda purposes; they needed him to show them where he had hidden the machine, so they could dig it up. Nechaev, Pryzhov and two others met Ivanov there.[43] It was a cold night and the pond beside them was thickly frozen over. There was a struggle; Nechaev's hands were badly bitten; but in the end they succeeded in murdering Ivanov. He was shot in the back of the neck. They weighed down his body with bricks and dropped it into the water through a hole in the ice. Later, back in the rooms of one of the gang, as Nechaev was handling the gun it again went off and the bullet nearly struck Pryzhov. It was an accident, of course. Yet, later still, the gang would wonder if Nechaev had not intended to kill Pryzhov too, and pin the blame for the murder on him.[44]

Within twenty-four hours, Nechaev departed for St Petersburg, on his way back out of Russia. He fled the country accompanied by a female disciple. She was arrested at the border, but Nechaev himself escaped the police. He had left just in time. The killers had concealed the corpse ineptly; Nechaev had even left his hat at the scene of the crime. Ivanov's body was discovered on 25 November 1869; the police hunt began. A general round-up of radicals was carried out, many of them actually hostile to Nechaev. By the end of the following year seventy-nine 'nihilists', students and young revolutionaries were facing trial. But the prize suspect, Nechaev, remained on the loose.

* * *

In January 1870, Nechaev fled back to Geneva, where he promptly wrote another manifesto. There was a price on his head but he seemed indifferent to the dangers. He had become notorious, as he had desired.

That summer, while Nechaev schemed and wrote articles, his co-conspirators and others only tangentially connected to him, including downright enemies such as Felix Volkhovsky, were being put on trial in St Petersburg. Although, despite opposition from the government, the courts discharged many, for the members of Nechaev's inner circle their fates were sealed.[45] To take only one example, Uspensky was sentenced to fifteen years; in 1875, he tried unsuccessfully to kill himself, but survived only to be hanged by his cell-mates in 1881 due to the ungrounded suspicion that he was a spy.

Nechaev was the absent centre of the trial. At the tribunal, Pryzhov affirmed:

The first reason for which I became an ally of Nechaev is that he, like me, came from the people. Anyone who comes from the masses, however little he thinks, is faced with two possibilities: he can either die on the high road . . . or become an agitator. However strange or paradoxical this idea may seem, it is absolutely true. And so I joined Nechaev. I have lived for forty years and I have met many people, but I have never met anyone with Nechaev's energy, nor can I imagine that anyone like him exists.[46]

It was a telling testament to Nechaev's charisma.

Bakunin was still immensely impressed by 'Boy', as he had come to call him. Bakunin wrote to a friend:

You remember my young barbarian? Well, he has returned. He has performed feats such as you and your people will not even believe. He has borne terrible torments: captured, beaten half to death, then freed, he is resuming his old tasks with redoubled energy.[47]

Did those incredible feats include Ivanov's murder? It is unclear at what point Nechaev enlightened Bakunin about the killing, or how he presented the murder to his collaborator.

It is possible that at first Bakunin accepted Nechaev's version of events that Ivanov was a police spy, or even that he admired the killing's rigour. Yet, by the summer, something had changed. On 2 June 1870 he wrote a letter in which he demanded that Nechaev repudiate the use of violence against fellow revolutionaries.[48] Implicitly he does not renege against the *Catechism*'s commitment to the use of violence against those outside the revolutionary circle. He insists that Nechaev accept the values of brotherhood and renounce plans for dictatorship to follow the revolution. The letter was an accurate reading of Nechaev's character, but it represented an insight gained too late.

Do you remember how angry you were when I called you an *Abrek* and your catechism a catechism of *Abreks*? You said that all men should be such, that a complete renunciation of self, of all personal wishes, pleasures, sentiments, affections and ties should be a normal, natural, everyday condition for everyone without exception. You wished and still wish to make your own selfless cruelty, your own truly extreme fanaticism a rule of common life. You wish for an absurdity, an impossibility, a negation of nature, man and society . . . You are a fanatic – and therein lies your enormous characteristic strength; but at the same time this is your blindness . . .[49]

Bakunin was ready to break with Nechaev, but in the end he did so not on abstract grounds, but because the younger man had turned his hitherto laudably amoral tactics against him. Having bullied many others with Bakunin's willing consent, Nechaev made the grievous error of bullying Bakunin. Bakunin too late realised that this noble brigand, this boyish embodiment of all he had always believed in, really was outside the law, even with respect to their own relationship. Nechaev's energetic brutality also entailed the full use of his tactics, the plans to blackmail, counterfeit and even murder. Even now, Bakunin was outraged by Nechaev's behaviour while continuing to see such actions as legitimate when used against the established order.[50] Only his discovery that he himself might prove a necessary victim of the revolution was disturbing. Bakunin, the apostle of destruction, was shocked.

In July 1870, he wrote a letter to friends. Previously he had sent them a letter of introduction for Nechaev, asking them to help look after the young man in his attempts to dodge the police. Now he was writing again, but this time it was a letter of warning. Nechaev would lie, win their confidence, while all the time plotting against them, spying, stealing letters, sowing discord between friends, seducing a wife or a daughter. He had identified the revolution with himself.[51] The letter presents a fascinating portrayal of Nechaev's methods. There is a note of panic, a genuine bewilderment, and behind it the sense that, while admiration remains, he at last recoils from Nechaev as from something sinister.

Following the break with Bakunin, Nechaev left Switzerland for London, and after a brief stay there, went on to Paris just at the height of the Commune and the Franco-Prussian War. He was on the run, but he nonetheless kept writing and proclaiming the coming revolution, satirising the aristocracy, inciting the students, and even describing in print his own death. He was truly living like the hero of a novel. A consummate propagandist, he wrote a series of letters to left-wing newspapers across Europe, defending himself and pleading his innocence of Ivanov's murder.[52] He went back to London, then down to Switzerland where he was concealed by Mazzinians at St Moritz. Everywhere he went the police pursued him with spies, double agents and infiltrators. In the pursuit of authenticity one of these hapless disguised policemen was forced to join a rebellion staged by Bakunin in Lyons in 1871, and ended up being arrested by the French police; he even became quite friendly with Bakunin.[53]

Switzerland, like Britain, had long been a safe haven for political refugees. However, the Russian government had declared that Nechaev was merely a common criminal. On this basis, the Swiss police were also persuaded to join in the hunt, and began searching the houses of émigrés in Geneva. The elusive Nechaev was finally run to earth in Zurich, where his arrest by Pfenniger, the Chief of Police, had the flavour of an official kidnapping (Pfenniger was rumoured to have been given 20,000 francs to ease the extradition process). The runaway terrorist was handed over to the tsarist police, and taken back for trial in St Petersburg. Despite everything that had passed between them, Bakunin could not help but feel sadness at Nechaev's arrest. He wrote:

I don't know how you feel, but as for me, I feel very sorry for him . . . He was a man of rare energy; and when you and I first met him, there burned in him a clear flame of love for our poor and downtrodden people, he had a genuine ache for the people's age-long suffering.[54]

Nechaev was tried in January 1873, found guilty of common murder (all his attempts to turn the trial into a political one were suppressed by the court), and sentenced to twenty years' hard labour in Siberia. If he survived, at the end of that time he would remain there in exile until his death.

Without Nechaev at his side, Bakunin carried on his advocacy of terrorism as a necessary catalyst for revolution. Having been obsessed with an *abrek*, he continued to celebrate banditry, brigandage and guerrilla warfare. When the Commune was overturned, and Paris was in flames, Bakunin praised the violent chaos. At last the world really was engulfed in fire. In his statements, it is often hard not to jumble those moments when he is speaking of anarchy as turmoil and those when he is writing of anarchy as social model. The muddle is a telling one.

Meanwhile Bakunin carried on his feeble plots to take over the International, but was outwitted by Marx who destroyed the organisation rather than let it fall into Bakunin's hands. In struggling against Marx, Bakunin believed that he was beset by a Jewish plot; in resisting Bakunin (a 'Mahomet without a Koran'), Marx and Engels felt that they were fighting against a Russian conspiracy, behind which were the nihilist Russian students, of whom Nechaev was the 'ideal type'.[55] In 1877, Marx dismissed the actions of the Russian students as a mere 'symptom of the disintegration of Russian society'.[56] Their idealism was all too likely to end in suicidal terrorist missions, designed to prove their adherence to the cause and their distance from bourgeois conventions. Marx and Engels were not impressed. "'These all-destroying anarchists," they wrote sententiously, "who wish to reduce everything to amorphousness in order to replace morality by anarchy, carry bourgeois immorality to its final extreme."'[57] In a few years, one of these young Russian revolutionaries would be writing to Marx, and instigating a reversal of his views that left him admiring the young killers both of Ireland and of Russia. Her name was Vera Zasulich, and she was first going to become the most famous female assassin of Europe since Charlotte Corday had stabbed Marat in his bath.

III: Vera, or a Nihilist

Ever since she was a young teenager, Vera Zasulich had been involved with revolutionary politics.[58] She was born in 1849 into the indigent gentry, the daughter of a military officer. When her father died three years later she was sent to live with rich relatives on their estate in Biakolovo. She seems at that moment, at this distance, like a young Jane Eyre. Here she felt alienated from her adoptive family, an outsider to their wealth. A dreary future as a governess awaited her; yet she had in her that which would kick over the traces: a compassion for suffering (aroused by a childhood infatuation with Christ) and her hunger for a greatness equal to that possible for a boy. The cause of revolution, with its principles of free comradeship between men and women, enticed her. Here was the liberty for which she yearned.

In 1869, she was arrested in connection to the Nechaev plot. Unlike many who were picked up by the police, as we have seen she had a genuine link to the outlaw. Two of her sisters married members of the Nechaev circle; it was probably her sister Ekaterina who introduced Vera to these radicals.[59] (Her other sister, Alexandra, was married to Uspensky, one of Nechaev's chief comrades.) Zasulich met Nechaev at teacher-training college in St Petersburg, and was impressed by his practical hunger for revolution.[60] It seems that soon after their first meeting, he announced that he was in love with her. She promptly rebuffed him, and later suspected (probably rightly) that such statements were merely a technique he had, and that his 'loves' were mere necessities for the cause.[61] However, despite her doubts, it is possible that later on in the night that this declaration was made Nechaev and Zasulich slept together as lovers. A few weeks afterwards, Nechaev went to her room very early one morning, and while she lay in bed shoved a package into her hands. From then on Zasulich, aged eighteen, unwittingly connived in Nechaev's fantastic plots, providing a forwarding address for his revolutionary letters.[62] For this involvement with the great man, she paid the price of two years in prison. On release in 1871, she was banished to Kharkov, where she remained, continually harassed by the police, until 1875.

She then moved to Kiev, where she joined a revolutionary circle named the Iuzhnye Buntari (Southern Rebels). In a reworking of Nechaev's murder of Ivanov, suspicion fell on one of the group, who it was decided was an informer. His outraged comrades attempted to kill him by beating him with chains and then pouring acid onto his face. Unfortunately for him perhaps, the man survived, though horribly mutilated and blinded, and, understandably enough, sought revenge on his comrades by indeed informing the police of all he knew. There is no evidence whether Zasulich condemned or condoned this appalling attack.[63] With the break-up of the Iuzhnye Buntari (Southern Rebels), she became involved with the Zemlya I Volya (Land and Freedom) group, for whom she began work as a typesetter. So she proceeded with her career as a revolutionary foot-soldier, until, in 1878, one impetuous act made her instantly famous. She was then twenty-eight years old.

On 6 December 1876, in front of the Cathedral of Our Lady of Kazan, facing the Nevsky Prospect, supporters of a new version of the Land and Freedom movement were offering prayers for Nicholas Chernyshevsky, the imprisoned author of *What Is To Be Done?*, when for the first time they publicly unveiled their flag. (They had formed their new grouping earlier that year.[64]) In a speech, the leader of the group praised the Decembrists who had rebelled against Nicholas I, Karakozov who had tried to kill the Tsar, and even Nechaev himself.[65] This impetuous demonstration in broad daylight in the centre of fashionable St Petersburg was swiftly and brutally broken up by General Fedor Trepov, the city governor, and a gang of policemen. Thirty-two people were arrested, among them one Alexey Stepanovich Bogoliubov (also known as Emelyanov). He was not a member of Land and Freedom, and not even a particularly committed agitator, merely someone sympathetic to the cause who had found himself caught up in events. It seemed to eye-witnesses that the police were simply arresting anyone who had the long hair of a student.[66]

Bogoliubov was sentenced to fifteen years in jail. They took him to the St Petersburg House of Detention from where he was to be moved to the prison where he would serve out his term. However, while there, Bogoliubov perhaps unwittingly performed a trivial act of insubordination that aroused the fury of the Governor-General. Trepov was there to inspect the prison, just then home to 193 political prisoners awaiting trial. Arrested *en masse* on trumped-up conspiracy charges, these captives were the cost of a failed attempt by the young *narodniks* to 'go to the people'. Trepov was notorious as an uneducated brute; his involvement in the putting down of the Polish rebellion was infamous. As the Governor-General passed, Bogoliubov attempted to speak to him. The young man was reprimanded for this impertinence. When Trepov came back that way, it appears that Bogoliubov refused to remove his cap in the presence of his superior. Enraged by this rudeness, Trepov went to hit the prisoner and knocked the cap off; as some witnesses declared, the young man then hit him back. Trepov furiously ordered that the prisoner be flogged with a birch whip. Such a punishment was illegal; since 1863 corporal punishment against convicts was permitted only in special cases. It was clearly an act of personal vengeance. Bogoliubov was beaten in a place where Trepov knew that his cries would be heard by the other prisoners; an example was being made of him. The young man was whipped so badly that he went mad; he died two years later in prison.[67] Other prisoners protested, and were beaten as a result.

The event was a scandal, but, unless something positive was done, like most scandals it would soon be forgotten. The revolutionaries agreed that they in turn would make an example of Trepov. Land and Freedom made plans to murder him after the trial of the 193; meanwhile they did not want to prejudice the cases of these radicals and republicans.[68] However, before their scheme could swing into action, Vera Zasulich decided to commit her own freelance assassination.[69] The cruel injustice of the deed had so enraged her that she decided something must be done quickly. It was nothing personal; she had never met Bogoliubov or seen Trepov (though she had once been arrested at a demonstration that Trepov had broken up). She would defend human dignity against the embodiment of malice. She thought of her strategy in this way:

On me [Trepov's act] made the impression, not of a punishment, but of an insult inflicted from personal enmity. It seemed to me that such a thing could not and ought not to pass unnoticed. I waited to see whether some one would take the matter in hand, but all were silent, and nothing prevented Trepov or any other influential official from repeating such arbitrary acts. Seeing no other means of directing public attention to the affair, I determined, at the price of my own ruin, to prove that a human being may not be insulted in that way with impunity. It is a terrible thing to raise one's hand against a fellow creature, but I could find no other means . . .[70]

She would shoot Trepov. It was all the same to her whether she killed or only injured him; her own fate was similarly a matter of indifference. Later she wrote of her feelings then: 'It seemed to me that I was calm and totally unafraid of losing my free life; I had finished with that a long time ago. It was not even a life anymore, but some kind of limbo, which I wanted to end as soon as possible.'[71] She made a pact with a friend, Maria Kolenkina, that on 24 January, while Kolenkina assassinated Vladislav Zhelekhovskii, the prosecutor in the trial of the 193, she herself would kill Trepov. As it turned out, Kolenkina would prove unsuccessful in even approaching her target; Zasulich had better luck.[72]

On the day after the trial of the 193 concluded, a grey day, Zasulich made the short journey to Trepov's office. Here the general listened to petitions and examined complaints. A crowd of people had gathered in the January cold. Zasulich waited in line for her turn to approach the great man. At last they spoke, and just as Trepov turned from her to deal with the next supplicant, she pulled a gun from under her cloak, and fired at him at point-blank range, the bullet entering his pelvis, wounding and not killing him. She then threw down the gun, stood quite still, and waited to be arrested. They beat her, of course, and then bundled her into a room, and then wondered a little feebly what to do with her next. Meanwhile, as they deliberated, in the immediate aftermath of her deed Zasulich moved from moments of dissociation and strangeness to an honest desire to advise her nonplussed captors.

My foresight, and consequently my precise plan of action, did not extend beyond the moment of attack. But every minute my joy increased – not because I was in full control of myself . . . but rather because I found myself in an extraordinary state of the most complete invulnerability, such as I had never before experienced. Nothing at all could confuse me, annoy me, or tire me. Whatever was being thought up by those men, at that time conversing animatedly in another corner of the room, I would regard them calmly, from a distance they could not cross.[73]

This mingled feeling of elation and satisfaction appears often in the personal accounts of assassins from those years. The work has been done, and their own lives in the process thrown away. A sudden liberation from the burden of self fills them; they ascend to a height above life.

Vera Zasulich's trial took place in March 1878. Since the Tsar's emancipation of the serfs, there had been other significant and welcome reforms. The best of these was the much-needed overhauling of the criminal justice system. In 1864, judicial reforms were enacted that really did form the framework of an equitable and workable legal system.[74] One of the provisions in these reforms was the right to trial by jury for criminal cases, as opposed to political crimes. Although

Zasulich's motives were palpably political, the government decided unusually to treat the case as an ordinary crime and run the risk of a jury trial. Count Pahlen, the Minister of Justice, calculated that under those circumstances a conviction would carry more force and demonstrate the disgust that the Russian public felt for such acts of terrorism. He attempted to persuade the judge to weight things against Zasulich. A conviction must be secured. To his credit, the judge, the hugely admirable Anatolii Koni, would not listen to a word of these approaches.[75]

If at this point Pahlen deduced that he might have made a colossal misjudgement, the trial itself would only confirm his worst fears. The prosecution, led by the lacklustre K. I. Kessel, was almost farcical; Vera's ferocity was ludicrously exaggerated, Kessel saying for instance, quite untruly, that she had had to be wrestled to the ground to be prevented from firing again. The jury were unimpressed. Only Zasulich herself seemed moved by Kessel's tedious speech, and when he declared that even Trepov had a right to live, she hung her head in shame.[76] On the other hand, the defence led by P. A. Alexandrov was stirring. The courthouse, which was packed with St Petersburg's leading citizens, was visibly moved. Even Zasulich shed a tear to hear herself and her crime so movingly eulogised. Koni provided a well-balanced summing-up. All was in the hands of the jury. What would have seemed impossible at the beginning of the trial, by its close looked inevitable. Indignation against Trepov and sympathy for Zasulich's courage meant only one possible end, despite the weight of evidence against her. People were applauding even before the verdict of not guilty was announced. And at the point when the words that meant freedom were spoken, the crowd went wild; Zasulich's triumph had come; she was the heroine who had attacked illicit autocracy in the spirit of righteousness. In her case, justice had assumed the mask of terror. Even the Foreign Minister, Prince Gorchakov, an emissary of autocracy, cheered; even that great supporter of tsarism and Russian religious destiny, Fyodor Dostoevsky – who, having satirically immortalised Nechaev in *The Devils*, was to use elements of Zasulich's trial in *The Brothers Karamazov* – turned to his companion and declared that to punish Zasulich would have been wrong.[77] Almost everyone was elated; only Koni and Zasulich were suitably sober. The result depressed the judge, who knew that an acquittal made nonsense of the law, and disheartened Zasulich, who had been deprived of her death.[78] Both the upholder of the law and its breaker understood the impossibility of the situation; only the euphoria of the crowd was fully, irresponsibly unreasonable.

Zasulich herself was confronted by the terrible responsibility of living on; her freedom had been returned to her. There were of course those who wished immediately to snatch it back. The Tsar promptly ordered her re-arrest, and Trepov and his supporters prepared to grab the would-be assassin from the courthouse crowd. Fortunately Zasulich was spirited away; the police pursued, but were prevented by the mob. In the mêlée that followed, many were injured, and one person killed. The crowd believed that the police had opened fire; more likely, it seems, a student had let off his gun, and, mistakenly believing he had murdered a policeman (the shot glanced off the lucky man's helmet), had shot himself.[79] Vera herself headed for exile in Switzerland.

Zasulich's significance lies not so much in her deed, as in her getting away with it. Russia had reached a point where even those who went to the lengths of violence to defend the regime could not wholeheartedly believe in the rights of their own cause. A shamefaced authority faced a dedicated rebellion. Her acquittal signalled the public's moral revulsion with the authorities and sympathy with the radicals. But, more than this, it showed the failure of civilised values in Russia. The tensions between an autocratic state and an independent legal system burst out here with unusual force.[80] Bogoliubov's imprisonment, Trepov's brutality, Vera's vengeance, the jury's defiance: each spelt contempt for the rule of law. It was not a miscarriage of justice, but rather a miscarriage of the law. Zasulich was morally justified, there was little doubt of that, but both Trepov's cruelty and her passionate response demonstrated that legal norms did not operate in Russia. There should have been no room for a tyrant like Trepov, and no need for an avenger like Zasulich. Oppressor and assassin were placed in an intimate relationship; each called forth the other. As long as such beautiful moments as Vera's exoneration could happen, there was truly no hope for Russia.

There is an intriguing account of Zasulich's character in Stepniak's *Underground Russia* (1883). Stepniak sets out to provide an honest appraisal of a real person (a friend of his), distinct from the hagiographies and illusions of those who do not know her. The resulting image is itself, despite his protestations, a kind of ideal. He paints her as a Hamlet of the revolution, a saint of modesty, a shy heroine, humbly evading her notoriety. Zasulich comes across as an upright character, a noble soul, and a gallant assassin. She was black-haired, vigorous, physically striking, though dowdy and careless of her appearance (as expected of a young revolutionary woman). She could be melancholy, or mercurial; given to jokes and thoughtfulness, acclamation and depression.[81] Later she confided to Stepniak her feeling on hearing the jury's verdict:

> I remember that one day, in relating to me how she felt when she received from the President of the Court the announcement of her acquittal, she said it was not joy she experienced, but extreme astonishment, immediately followed by a feeling of sadness.
>
> 'I could not explain this feeling then,' she added, 'but I have understood it since. Had I been convicted, I should have been prevented by main force from doing anything, and should have been tranquil, and the thought of having done all I was able to do for the cause would have been a consolation to me.'[82]

Zasulich had prepared herself for a harsh sentence. Liberty left her with the surprising task of having to live. After her deed, her life seemed in abeyance, as though waiting for its main event, when all guessed that event was already behind her. A friend remarked: 'Vera would like to shoot Trepoffs every day, or at least once a week. And, as this cannot be done, she frets.'[83]

Her life after the assassination attempt was an improvised and frustrating affair. She was effectively still on the run, living in tedious Switzerland, refusing attempts by the Anarchists to appropriate her deed, making do with working for the Marxist Liberation of Labour Group.[84] She wrote to a friend: 'I don't talk for months on end (or only to myself, in whispers) except in shops "Give me a pound of this". I go to Geneva once a month, sometimes less: I'd go more if I had to. So there is my life! I see no one, read no papers, and never think about myself.'[85] She worked for the revolution; she never married. Inevitably, when 1917 came and the Revolution arrived, like many of the radicals of the generation of the 1870s and 1880s, she was utterly dismayed by the shape taken by the course of events. She saw quickly that in practice the dictatorship of the proletariat was merely just another dictatorship.[86]

The propaganda success of Zasulich's attempt inspired others in Land and Freedom to endorse a policy of assassination. When she fired her gun impotently at Trepov, Zasulich launched a new phase in the 'Nihilist' project. It would end only with the death of the Tsar. The Russian conspirators began to cling more fervently to a belief in assassination's absolute efficacy. Such murders were the ultimate political tool; they exposed the weakness of the government and announced the irrepressibility of the opposition. Behind such noble aims were other less lofty motives. Police and 'terrorists' grew locked together in a war of revenge. Both sides seemed bound to an endless vendetta: the repression swayed the rebels to violence; the violence pushed the government into acts of repression; these in turn worsened the terrorism, which led to further extreme governmental measures; and so on. Both descended to violence and became the mirror image of their enemy.

Throughout 1878, 1879 and 1880, the chaos increased.[87] Whatever happened, the revolutionaries won. If they failed, they still left their target feeling exposed; if they succeeded, they demonstrated their power. If they were repressed, they unmasked the government as repressive, and so demonstrated the need for their own violent and subversive practices. Many police spies and informers were executed; policemen were killed. The ultimate target was to be the Tsar himself. The secret police could not cope with the problem. There were too few of them and their surveillance techniques were too rudimentary. The commitment of the terrorists to their single aim and their anonymity made the work of the security forces arduous. All the terrorists had to do was to keep trying. In April 1879, shots were fired at Alexander II. The incident inspired repressive measures by the government, and these hardened the Nihilists in their acceptance of terrorism's legitimacy. They began to lay concrete plans for the Tsar's assassination. The Bakunist left of the movement refused to endorse the idea, and thereby lost all influence. Power moved to the supposedly more 'moderate' group who sponsored the murder plot. The plan was a bold one; it excited émigrés; if they could achieve their aim, that truly would be genuine action.

Zasulich's example was crucial in this swing towards the practice of terror. She was an inspiration to crime. A police official was murdered in Kiev, in the spirit of emulation. When, that August of 1878, a young man, Sergei Kravchinskii, executed General Mezentsev on the public street, he was consciously following the example of the courageous Zasulich.[88]

For most within the movement, the heightening of the stakes seemed inevitable and just. And yet for Zasulich herself, there was no such easy acceptance of the killings. Soloviev's infamous attempt to assassinate the Tsar with a bomb at the Winter Palace merely depressed her. As years went by, Zasulich's position grew clearer. The assassin's deed was really prompted by a psychological weakness and was without revolutionary merit. It led not to great social changes, but only to an ineffectual puff of violence. It exhilarated other revolutionaries, who sensed vicariously and inappropriately the retort of power. But it merely dismayed and sickened potential supporters among the masses, or rendered them passive spectators of outrage. The people were not roused to rebel by such deeds, but became mere witnesses to others' glorious, or infamous, violence. Worst of all was terror's dependence upon a sickly illusion in the mind of the assassin herself. Zasulich knew this at first hand. The assassin worked in a spirit of vanity or of anomie, either conceited by an impression of their own potency, or buoyed up by the awareness of their own insignificance. The assassin embraced the victim's death and their own, and both inspirited them with the weightless emancipation from the burden of having to live at all. Zasulich's act of terror had sought to publicise another's brutality; the danger was that such acts would only advertise their own horror. The injustice that prompted them would be forgotten in the simple impact of the assassin's bullet. It was, she might have realised, only her own incompetence in merely hitting Trepov in the hip that had permitted her deed to appear noble.

IV: The People's Will

While a new generation acted, Nechaev brooded in prison. He never went to Siberia. By express order of Alexander II, he was put instead in the Peter and Paul fortress in St Petersburg, the prison for political prisoners. From his cell, Nechaev continued to exert influence on the political scene. It is said that various high-ranking officials visited him in his dungeon. Nechaev even succeeded, it was rumoured, in getting a message to Alexander II, informing him that absolutism would no longer do. On another legendary occasion, General Potapov, a high-

ranking officer in the Third Section, visited him, and the two men fell
to arguing. Potapov suggested that Nechaev might write an excellent
report on the organisation of revolutionary committees. The rebel
refused, Potapov threatened him with violence, and Nechaev responded
by slapping the venerable General so hard that the old man's nose began
to bleed. After that, Nechaev was safely secured in chains and tied to a
rod in the wall, in a half-crouching position, in which he could listen
to the shrieks of the madman in the next cell, the only other prisoner in
the dungeons. He was kept in solitary confinement and never allowed
to speak.[89]

Undefeated, Nechaev nevertheless successfully worked his charms
on his guards, managed to break the silence rule and soon had them
believing that he was still an important figure in a secret organisation,
even with connections to the Tsar. Soon Nechaev had assumed the
status of a martyr in the eyes of his captors. His life improved. He was
allowed to read and, it was rumoured, wrote a novel. In 1879, hearing of
the new revolutionary organisation, People's Will (Narodnaya Volya),
Nechaev got in touch with the executive committee. The students and
other radicals were amazed that Nechaev was still alive and so close.
Plans to help him escape were laid, though they fell through. Meanwhile Nechaev offered advice on spreading confusion when they should
finally manage to kill Alexander II.[90]

A member of People's Will named Soloviev found a job as a carpenter
at the Winter Palace and smuggled in dynamite, which he left under
the dining room. The bomber estimated the time at which the Tsar and
his dinner guests would eat, lit a slow fuse and left the building. A delay
caused by the late entrance of a guest of honour saved the Tsar's life. On
5 February 1880, the bomb exploded, too soon, killing eleven people,
and injuring over fifty. The Tsar had escaped.

But the attempts kept coming, with increasing daring. There was
a plan to murder all the Governor-Generals one by one, and so end
that office. The father of Sophia Perovskaia, one of the plotters, had
himself been a civilian Governor-General. (Women played a crucial
role in People's Will.) But the over-riding priority was murdering the
Tsar. There was a sequence of attacks. A campaign was organised to
blow up the imperial train. Groups of agents in Moscow, Kharkov and
Odessa worked independently as part of the grand conspiracy. Their

local plans were submitted to a committee who oversaw the operation. They would explode dynamite on the railway tracks and so destroy the train that carried the Tsar. They dug under the rails and planted the bombs. The explosive material in Odessa was suddenly demanded by the agents in Moscow. At Kharkov, the detonator failed, and the Tsar passed over the dynamite safely. On 19 November, the Tsar arrived in Moscow. The would-be assassins had bought a house by the railway line. They would blow it up as the train passed. It was around ten o'clock. They let the first train through, assuming that it was there to pre-empt attack, and as the second train in the entourage passed, they detonated the explosives. The train was derailed and smashed. But the Tsar had been on the first train after all. Once again, he had eluded their grasp.[91]

Rumours reached the underground of a trip that the Tsar was planning from Odessa. The terrorists rented a shop that would stand by the Tsar's route through Odessa to the ship. Two of them, Nikolai Sablin and Sophia Perovskaia, would live there, pretending to be man and wife. Meanwhile they would lay a mine for the Tsar's carriage under the pavement outside, by drilling a tunnel from the shop out to the street. The work was laborious and dangerous: one of the terrorists lost three fingers in a botched experiment with fulminate of mercury. But the Tsar's trip was cancelled, and the tunnel had to be filled in.

The assassination attempts began to restrict the Tsar's freedom of movement. For a brief time, it seemed that the only safe way to quit his home in the suburbs would be by boat.[92] The Tsar at this time sought the 'dictatorship of the heart'; he would secure his position by loving the people and so winning the people's love. He was beleaguered and vulnerable. In the midst of the turmoil, he took refuge in a private affair. In the aftermath of the Karakozov shooting, the Tsar had fallen in love with a teenage girl, Catherine Dolgorukova. She became his mistress, and he, to the contempt of the court, devoted himself to her. She was everything to him. He was feeble, romantically duplicitous and vague. And around him, his assassins were drawing in.

The conspirators seem to have suffered from few doubts as to the rectitude of their actions. Russian political thought had long been concerned with the question of loyalty to the throne. For 'conservative' thinkers, the tension lay between submission to authority and the right to rebel. Should a subject be constant to a bad king? If a king were a tyrant, was it legitimate to rise against him, or even to assassinate him? In this sense, Russian thought mirrored concerns from the era of absolutism in Europe. However, with its commitment to the Orthodox Church and its link to Byzantium rather than Rome, Russian ideas developed quite differently. There was no particular cultural allegiance to a Roman classical model of tyrannicide. In the Muscovite period, some had argued that it was lawful to murder an unchristian tsar. These beliefs led to conspiracies against Peter the Great. Peter's supporters argued that such tactics were Ottoman in origin, a foreign import onto Russian soil.[93] By the period of the French Revolution, historians were praising the essentially Russian quality of patience in suffering; faced with a tyrant like Ivan the Terrible, the people merely bowed their heads and bided their time. Unlike those in France, Russians exercised humility in the face of tyranny.

The motivations behind the new terror were manifold. In 1879, in an open letter sent to the Tsar, as in other texts, the members of People's Will set out their reasons. The state itself ruled through arbitrary violence. Terroristic activity would include the murder of government officials and vengeance for instances of official lawlessness. They would 'break the spell of governmental power', their success shattering authority's mystique. They would prove that it was possible to fight against the powers that be. In doing so, they would 'strengthen the revolutionary spirit of the people'. The fight itself would produce trained forces capable of struggling against the government.[94]

The historian Alexander Chubarov has described the relationship between People's Will and the Tsar as resembling a duel.[95] Both sides were locked together in a struggle that increasingly began to look like the pursuit of vengeance, the satisfaction of honour. In the meantime a new police department replaced the old Third Section.[96] As Richard Pipes puts it: 'Before the First World War no other country in the world had two kinds of police, one to protect the state and another to protect its citizens.'[97] Count Michael Loris-Melikov took control of the effort to crush the rebels, using both repressive tactics and liberal concessions. His ultimate aim was to return to the normal rule of law, once the terrorists were defeated. Meanwhile he acted on the understanding that simple repression pushed the liberals towards the radicals. His hope was to isolate and split the revolutionary party, but instead he was, in due course, effectively to be sacked by his own side.

In any case, the conspirators were not to be taken in by concessions. They were buoyed up by their smaller successes, encouraged in their chief ambition. In January 1881, another shop was rented, this time in St Petersburg, and again a plan was hatched to lay a mine outside it. The shop lay on one of the Tsar's routes for his Sunday trip to the Michael Riding School. He actually passed the shop one Sunday in February, but the mine was not yet ready and the opportunity was missed. The committee agreed that March would be the month for their next attempt. Every Sunday they would lie in wait at the shop. The mine would go off and, if the Tsar survived the explosion, they would finish the job by throwing hand-held bombs at his carriage.

At the very end of February the mine was charged. There were rumours that the police were on the verge of great discoveries. Was the plot about to be unearthed? It seemed possible that, just as they were closest to success, all would be ruined. Sophia Perovskaia urged that on the first Sunday, 1 March, if the Tsar did not go over the mine, they should in any case attack his carriage with the hand-held explosives. The bombs were untried, and there was a risk that they wouldn't go off, but despite these worries, the committee approved the plan. On the Saturday night, the group spent their time preparing the bombs, trimming the shell-cases, filling them with detonating jelly.[98]

The next day, the Tsar took a different route back from the Riding School. His assassins were forced to adopt the fall-back plan. At the place by the Catherine Canal that they had appointed to execute the second plan, the group waited. As the Tsar approached, the first assassin threw his bomb. It exploded beneath the Tsar's carriage, wounding the horses and killing a Cossack outrider. The carriage came to a stop, and amazingly the Tsar stepped out unhurt. He was eager to help attend to the wounded. But then another of the gang threw a bomb too, and in the resulting carnage the Tsar was fatally wounded – his legs broken, his left eye gone, and his abdomen torn. Within a few hours he died in the Winter Palace.

The assassins had won. Their chilling persistence in achieving their aim would inspire many later assassinations. Simply by their doggedness and narrow idealism a small group of men and women had destroyed

the emperor of a large and powerful nation. They were not the leaders
of a larger movement; they did not act for any general will. They were
a tiny conspiracy, but they were undaunted. Nonetheless their deed led
to their own destruction, set back the possibility of the constitution for
which they were fighting for over twenty years, and ultimately gained
precisely nothing. It was a triumph and a precedent, a disaster and an
imbecility. On the very day he was murdered, Alexander II had signed
a document that signalled, in his own words, a 'first step towards the
constitution'.[99]

Some days after the killing, the Revolutionary Executive Committee
of the People's Will wrote to the new Tsar, Alexander III. The letter
sympathised with the loss of his father (while pointing out that many
others in Russia had had loved ones taken from them). Both sides had
suffered, and were suffering now. But now was not a time for sympathy.
The assassination, they declared, was an inevitability, a fate, that had
gifted the new ruler with an occasion for genuine change. If the
opportunity were missed, then a bloody revolution would necessarily
follow. Old things would be swept away; the existing order would
be smashed. The people wanted change. The rulers must reflect that
any government was only a manifestation of the will of the people.
They could kill a few revolutionaries, hang a few assassins, but the
coming change was unstoppable. The new Tsar had the opportunity
to co-operate with history. If he flunked it, there would soon be no
more Tsars. They called for an amnesty for all political prisoners, an
examination of social and political life by representatives of all the
people, leading to free elections. There should be freedom of the press,
freedom of speech, the freedom to assemble, and the freedom to put
forward whatever election programme they cared to.[100]

But the revolutionaries were in no position to negotiate. Many
peasants assumed that the assassination attempts were committed by
wicked landlords angry with the Tsar for carrying through their emancipation.[101] Alexander III was intent on vengeance. With the exception
of one pregnant woman, the six conspirators, including Sophia
Perovskaia, who were caught and found to be directly involved were
hanged. The assassination ended the possibility of progress towards
a constitution. The killing was a victory that the movement itself
could not survive. The subsequent trial and backlash meant the end

for the movement – for the moment. The assassins handed on only an inspiration, a precedent. And for autocracy too, the moment lived on best as a symbol, though one of disorder, of suffering, almost of honour. On the site of the Tsar's murder, on the Catherine Canal, the Church of the Resurrection of the Saviour on Spilled Blood was built.

The success of People's Will in killing the Tsar provoked an appalling worsening in Nechaev's prison conditions. He died of scurvy on 21 November 1882. He was thirty-five years old, and had spent eight of those years in close confinement, darkness and chains. Nechaev had achieved little, and all that his advocacy of terror and violence amounted to was a spiteful murder of one of his fellow revolutionaries. Yet, he bequeathed to the world the image of a life, one that could exist for others, much as it had existed for him, as a role – one that many others after him would also play.

3
The Praise of Murder

Im Anfang war die Tat! [In the beginning was the deed!]
GOETHE

I: Consecrating the Dagger

On 2 June 1878, while Kaiser Wilhelm I was riding down Unter den Linden in Berlin, an assassin fired a shotgun twice from an upstairs window. The Kaiser was injured, pellets peppering his head, back and shoulders. The assassin then shot himself in the head and was left dangerously wounded. The would-be killer was no maddened thug, but a highly educated man, Dr Karl Eduard Nobiling. His deed took place less than a month after another attempt on the Kaiser's life, also on Unter den Linden, though on that occasion, in May 1878, Emil Heinrich Max Hödel had altogether missed his target. It seems Vera Zasulich's assault influenced both attempts.[1] Zasulich had become a model assassin with an international reputation. The impact of such deeds as hers was growing obvious, their gruesome and shocking effectiveness as propaganda beguiling. They seemed a ready way to act out a deep hostility towards things as they were. As such, assassinations and acts of terror would now be endorsed and celebrated by European intellectuals jaded with thinking and writing, and eager for action. Assassination's extremity enchanted the most radical of Europe's thinkers.

* * *

In 1888, while living in Turin, the philosopher Friedrich Nietzsche wrote his personal testament, *Ecce Homo*. Buoyed up by knowledge of his greatness, indulged by waiters, favoured by the women in the market and adored by passers-by, he luxuriated in the autumnal Italian light and triumphed over the harvest of his life's labours.[2] The madness that would mask his last years had come to him gently as elation; forty-four years old, he was life's spoiled child, a genius, a destiny. In *Ecce Homo*, in this spirit he looked back on his first major book, *The Birth of Tragedy*, as 'my attentat on two millennia of anti-nature and the violation of man'.[3] In both German and French, '*attentat*' means assassination or violent deed; the philosopher's chosen victim was Europe's Christian inheritance and the anti-nature that Christianity defended. Nietzsche used the same term of his next book, the *Untimely Meditations*, four linked essays he now glorified as 'four attentats'.[4] In choosing this word, Nietzsche adopted the language of that decade's Nihilist and Anarchist assassins; its resonances affirm that his revaluation of all values falls in with a wider project of obliteration, in which revolutionary ethics battle against bourgeois complacency. For all his contempt for the Anarchists, he rallies to their destructive work. He poses as a man pleased to draw his rapier; he remarks of himself, 'I am not a human being, I am dynamite.'[5] When megalomania finally enshrouded him, he wrote to August Strindberg, 'I want to have the young Kaiser shot.'[6]

Why should Nietzsche express his desire for innovation in terms of political murder? Most obviously, he is simply playing tough, the thinker striking a pose of violence. He is cool; he is a killer; he will astonish us. He plays out the allure of the man of action, anxious that being a mere philosopher is hardly dangerous enough. He suggests that to murder religion would be a political act. At the end of a decade of violence, when others before him embraced violence and especially assassination, Nietzsche claimed the glamour of outrage.[7]

In March 1881, responding to the Tsar's murder, a leading article in *The Times* asserted that the 'political assassin is one of the powers of the world':

He has no place in an almanac, or a year-book, or a political survey, but his spirit is there, and hovers over the pages as we turn them. There are good governments and bad governments, there are republics and monarchies constitutional or despotic, and there is assassination, menacing and, to some extent, modifying all . . . The paganism and the political fanaticism of all ages have consecrated the dagger or the bullet of the assassin, and ranked him amongst the demigods, the saints, and the martyrs.[8]

The assassin moves mysteriously, strikes suddenly. The contexts that create such violence drift from view, for all forms of government produce him. The article closed with the thought that the 'sword of Damocles' still hung over the thrones of the world.

Only two days later another London-based newspaper proclaimed the figure of the assassin, but with quite different intentions. Printed with a sanguinary red border ostensibly to mark the anniversary of the revolution of 1848, the edition of the German-language Anarchist newspaper *Freiheit*, Saturday 19 March 1881, openly applauded the Tsar's murder and called for the assassination of other 'tyrants', as well as other 'representatives of State and social order'. The blow was a 'Brutus-deed'; the paper lamented that a monarch was not assassinated every month.[9] The title of the article was, in English, 'At Last'. Such articles were hardly a novelty for *Freiheit*; it had been extolling bloodshed for months. Nonetheless this copy of the paper proved especially popular, selling out across London; enough so that a second edition was printed.[10] Less than a week had passed since the Tsar's killing.

The man who wrote the inflammatory article was Johann Most. He was born, illegitimate, in 1846 in Bavaria, though his parents married after his birth. He was a mother's boy, cosseted and soothed. Then in quick succession came the two great tragedies of his early life. At the age of seven, an infection following a small operation hideously disfigured his face. Then, two years later, his mother died of cholera. His father soon remarried; young Most loathed his step-mother. Johann dreamed of escape, longing to be an actor (his father had once been a zither player in the theatre), though his twisted face prevented him from having such a career.[11] Only when he was old enough to grow a beard could he begin to mask his disfigurement, saving himself a little from his crippling self-consciousness. He turned to other means to liberty besides the stage, joining the labour movement in the Jura, becoming involved with the area's Anarchists and Socialists. He began to pursue a life of protest, and so inevitably a life of conflict with authority. He would spend years moving in and out of jail, always ready on release again to goad the government. In 1869, he was imprisoned in Vienna for making a speech critical of the German regime. A little later, he was sent to prison for five years for organising a march for manhood suffrage in Vienna, but only served a few months of that sentence. In

1871, on his release, he left for Germany. Here he began publishing a radical newspaper. The talent for rhetoric and declamation denied the stage would find another forum in writing. Almost weekly, Most was summoned to court on account of his publications. He was elected to the Reichstag in 1874, but it took a mere three months before he was arrested for making a speech in praise of the Paris Commune. He passed another two years in prison.

A couple of years after his release, Most was triumphantly re-elected to the Reichstag. In 1878, having grasped the opportunity provided by one of the failed assassination attempts on Kaiser Wilhelm, Bismarck's government launched a raft of anti-socialist legislation.[12] Most had recently spoken of Hödel's assassination attempt at a public meeting attended by police spies. For this offence, he went to prison for six weeks; on his release he was sentenced to a further five months.[13] The atmosphere of constraint drove many radicals out of the country, Most among them. Like many of the others, he travelled to that common refuge for all political exiles, London. There, in January 1879, he started publishing *Freiheit*, the paper of the German Communistic Workingmen's Club.[14] Despite its association, the paper was Anarchist in outlook. From October 1880, Most's home and the newspaper's offices were a few blocks north of Oxford Street at 101 Great Titchfield Street. Although it was based in London, the paper's print run of 1,200 copies was distributed covertly across the whole of Europe, where it found a ready audience among German-speaking radicals in exile and at home.[15] He may have resided in London, but Most's world was still that of German left-wing politics; he learnt little English and rarely mixed with the locals. The tone of *Freiheit* was starkly revolutionary, in fact, far too revolutionary for some: he was expelled from the German Social Democratic Party (SPD) in August 1880.[16] Especially inflammatory was the fact that Most championed terror.[17]

Until the March 1881 article on the murder of the Tsar came to their attention, the British police had been content to ignore Most's ineffectual radicalism, since its impact was limited to German-speakers in Britain and abroad. But this was a provocation too far. Charles Edward Marr, a teacher of languages, read the article, was disgusted, and promptly posted a copy to a member of Parliament, Lord Hamilton, who in his turn passed it on to Sir William Harcourt, the Home Secretary. Harcourt ordered immediate action. On 29 March, Police Constable Henry Ward visited *Freiheit*'s offices at Great Titchfield Street, disguised as a German. Here he found the newspaper sold out, but, having 'put on a regretful countenance', was given a printed copy of the offending article itself.[18] The next day, Inspector Charles Hagan, a native German, likewise paid a visit to *Freiheit*, and arrested Most.

Most was tried for seditious libel and soliciting or encouraging murder.[19] Meetings of support were held on Most's behalf and the assassins of the Tsar compared to William Tell.[20] Yet such backing would prove fruitless.

In May 1881, at the Central Criminal Court in London, Most's case went to trial. The Offences against the Person Act, 1861, had made it a punishable offence to solicit the murder of another; the Most trial applied that legislation to the publication of an inflammatory newspaper article.[21] Sir Henry James, Attorney General of England, prosecuted; A. M. Sullivan, an expert in criminal libel, acted in Most's defence. The transcripts of the trial record the scrupulous fairness with which the prosecution dealt with Most. He was treated with consideration and his political views, other than his encouragement of assassination, were not allowed to form an element in the trial. Sullivan's eloquent defence declared that 'murder' meant killing someone within 'the King's peace', and that as Russia was not within the King's peace, the prisoner had not incited to murder within British jurisdiction. He defended the liberties of British journalism; had not *The Times* written just as Most had done? He invoked Shakespeare and Milton, Byron and Shelley, Disraeli and even Gladstone, as all, at one time or another, damning tyranny and (in one way or another) lauding tyrannicide.[22] But eloquence was in vain. Most had gone a little beyond merely celebrating assassination in general terms. He had implicitly and in 'unpersonal' terms suggested that specific people be killed, namely the new Tsar and (less clearly) the Kaiser.[23] This was not a general encomium, but an encouragement to particular murder. After a little less than twenty-five minutes, the jury came to its decision. On 26 May, Most was sentenced to eighteen months in prison, the sentence dating back to his arrest in March 1881. An attempt to appeal against the sentence was made, on the grounds that the statute under which Most had been sentenced was designed not for libels, but for actual conspiracy to commit murder abroad. Most, it was argued, had never so conspired. But the appeal failed: it was enough to 'solicit or persuade'.[24] Most remained in prison. Meanwhile, at 'a shop in Foley Street, sales of *Freiheit* jumped from 3 to 100 per week'.[25]

II: Advocating Violence: The Anarchists

Within four weeks of Most's imprisonment, London witnessed a decisive turn in the history of our subject: the Anarchist movement endorsed assassination. The Anarchists were about to outstrip the Nihilists as the archetypal bomb-throwers and assassins.

How did Anarchism come to be born? In one version, the movement emerged through Bakunin's influence, with a base in Switzerland.[26] In this model of things, in 1864 the tenets of Anarchism were formed at the first International, then nourished within the Jurassian Federation following the schism within the International held in 1872. The Anarchists proceeded at first in a state of uneasy parasitism, sharing a revolutionary agenda with the Communists, but distinct from them in the methods they advocated and in the nature of the society they fought for. The Anarchists suspected Marx of authoritarianism; Marx derided the Anarchists as romantic simpletons. When, in June 1876, Bakunin died in Bern, the movement was strong enough to continue without him.

Such a tidy account of the development of the movement ignores the wide variety of Anarchisms on offer in the late nineteenth century. There was Max Stirner's extreme individualism; William Godwin's rational benevolence; Proudhon's near-socialist mutualism; Bakunin's collectivism; Kropotkin's Anarchist communism; even Tolstoy's pacifistic Anarchism. Then in the 1880s and 1890s, inspired by these myriad philosophies, 'a group of crazy fanatics then came forward, in whom the merely destructive spirit develops itself'.[27] One Anarchist mode was indeed love for obliteration for its own sake. Some in the ranks had inherited Bakunin's longing for ruin, 'the eternal spirit which destroys and annihilates'.[28]

Yet the spectrum of beliefs meant that the hackneyed image of the frenzied, conspiring Anarchist could not fit the multitudinous reality. They were anti-utopians who were themselves utopian, idealists committed to the establishment of the ideal on earth here and now. The romance of Anarchism grew from the creation of unreal spaces – both the shining future, and meanwhile the contemporary underground of conspiracy. These threatening anti-heroes were simultaneously ridiculed and admired. If the Anarchists' public image took on the quality of caricature that was because they were felt to be impotent and unlikely to spark a genuine revolution. Yet in some moods many who ostensibly despised Anarchism also secretly longed for a new order of things.

The belief that all law is coercion bound together all shades of Anarchist. This idea that government is violence allowed Anarchist terrorism and assassination to seem to its perpetrators a logical quid pro quo. Governments enacted violence through the waging of wars, state control, the legal system, the institution of the prison. The individual response of freelance violence offered by solitary assassins or isolated bomb-throwers merely repaid such aggression in kind.

Ultimately the many Anarchist assassins who terrified the rulers of Europe and America from the 1880s to the 1920s shared one common aim: simply to change the world by undoing all established social modes and conventions. An undemanding sadness touches the student of past utopianism. These revolutionaries lectured; they wrote; they passed resolutions; they struggled. All that activity, all that hope, and yet we, their descendants, know the futility of all they planned. Contemplating the failures of the past might lead to a quietist belief in the life of private virtue. But what if that quiet life is not one of virtue, but rather of ambiguous goodness at best, a life that holds itself together through the consciously suppressed knowledge of a necessary violence, happening out of sight?

There is, of course, no necessary relationship between Anarchism and violence. The majority of Anarchists have been, and continue to be, admirable and peaceable individuals, and, in some cases, people whose lives attain uncommon nobility. The beliefs of Anarchists may bear a visionary beauty and a wild hope that appeal to the free spirit in all of us. Nonetheless, it is the essentially idealistic impulse in Anarchism that throws into starkest relief its troubled relationship to killing. This paradox is present in a great deal of political violence, particularly when performed on behalf of the oppressed. Yet in the history of Anarchist violence the contrast and confusion are stronger, and more intrinsic.

Anarchists were model revolutionaries. No matter how visionary they were, they believed passionately in their own ideal, and imagined they could reach it by the strength of their own actions. They felt that their actions had effects in the world (and the bigger and more extreme the action, the better the effect). Violence merely cleared the path to a secular New Jerusalem, one that would be achieved by personal heroism. Even as it preached the sacrifice of the individual, Anarchism therefore was a hero-worshipping and individualist creed. The revolutionary was merely a foot-soldier and an instrument of history. They could lay down the burden of self within the revolution, declaring their own unimportance in order to try to bring themselves into existence. They could kill for freedom, and believe the killing had meaning. Maybe the deaths of a few thousand were all that separated the world from the future paradise.[29]

* * *

The decision to turn to violence came in mid-July 1881, when international Anarchists met in London for a conference. London was the natural venue for the event; it was, after all, the bolthole for political refugees. At the London conference, there were Anarchists present from France, Belgium, Italy, Russia, Austria, Germany, Spain, Switzerland and America. Many of these cosmopolitans were already resident as immigrants in London. The city's status as an international metropolis without parallel fitted the Anarchist agenda; Anarchism was a movement that despised frontiers; Bakunin, the movement's spiritual head, had advocated the destruction of nation states. Only six Britons took part, all socialists, and none possessing any significant influence.[30]

For national police forces Anarchism's internationalism rendered it especially slippery. It was created by people who yearned for statelessness, unaware of the terrors that condition would come to hold in the twentieth century. They wished to cast themselves free from the context of tradition, not to know where they came from, to reject the weight of the past and make instead pure existential actions. Such deeds would guarantee their own meaning. Blowing up others was a symptom of their weightlessness: the bomb was not an aberration, but a symbol of their condition. They would live beyond law, beyond tradition, beyond others. There they could make the authentic gesture. Whatever else throwing a bomb is, it is not bourgeois.

Earlier in 1881 the Anarchists had attended a congress for socialists in Paris, but had been expelled.[31] In March, an organising committee had begun to set up the London congress, with support from a number of revolutionary newspapers: Johann Most's *Freiheit*; Kropotkin's Geneva-based *Le Révolté*; a Chicago-based German-language paper, *Vorbote*; and 'a French paper published by a police spy, *La Révolution sociale* (which was so convincing that it attracted contributions from leading revolutionaries)'.[32]

While the public events of the July Congress occurred at Cleveland Hall, most sessions were held surreptitiously in a pub on Charrington Street, off the Euston Road.[33] It had been urged that the congress would create two bodies, operating simultaneously: one to present the public face of the movement, and a secret one of small conspiratorial groups to determine on action. It was tricky to manoeuvre such organisational matters – there was never any possibility of the assembled Anarchists agreeing on the creation of a central organisation, their creed prohibited it. However, the agenda of the Congress rendered secrecy desirable. For the Anarchists were ready to endorse murder as a political weapon.[34]

Though the direction of the next four decades was decided that summer in London, the resolution was of course the culmination of a longer process. For several years, the movement had been edging towards violence. In 1877, the burning of the Benevento archives by activists signalled the potential of such revolutionary deeds. In 1879, the Jurassian congress voted for revolution by the deed; in December 1880, Carlo Cafiero wrote an article in *Le Révolté* declaring his support for 'permanent revolt, by spoken and written words, by the dagger, the gun, dynamite'.[35]

As the 1870s came to a close, assassination attempts were proliferating: in 1878 there were the two against the Kaiser; later that same year came Juan Oliva Moncasi's attempt on the King of Spain. In the summer of 1881 there were several different igniting factors: attempted insurrections in Italy; the ongoing violence in Ireland; the success of the Nihilists in killing the Tsar; even the very recent shooting in Washington, DC, of President Garfield.

The desire to forgo speech for violence was everywhere. Many looked to Russia: some breathed in the influence of Bakunin's endorsement of action; Jean Grave commented that the Russian Nihilists made him prefer dynamite to the bulletin.[36] The brilliant success of the Russian assassins inspired Anarchists everywhere. Beside the Nihilists' sacrificial (and murderous) methods, passing resolutions and writing exhortatory pamphlets looked anaemic and inane.

Excluding Russia and Ireland, Italy was the nation that witnessed the strongest sweep towards violence. The Italian Anarchist movement had emerged from the independence movements led by Mazzini and Garibaldi, and the country had in any case an established national tradition of insurrection. Perhaps the idea of 'propaganda by the deed' (*propaganda dei fatti*) originated in Italy with Carlo Pisacane (1815–57), Duke of San Giovanni, former chief of staff for Mazzini and a disciple of Proudhon and Fourier.[37] In 1857, Pisacane wrote:

propaganda by the idea is a chimera, the education of the people is an absurdity. Ideas result from deeds, not the latter from the former, and the people will not be free when they are educated, but will be educated when they are free. The only work a citizen can undertake for the good of the country is that of cooperating with the material revolution; therefore conspiracies, plots, attempts, etc., are that series of deeds by which Italy proceeds to her goal.[38]

This Italian influence on the idea and practice of violence was to continue until the years following the end of the First World War. As well as home-based violence (including in 1900 the disposal by Gaetano Bresci of their King Umberto), Italians operated as freelance assassins in other European countries. They were responsible in 1894 for the murder of President Sadi Carnot in France, in 1897 for the assassination of the Spanish Prime Minister Antonio Cánovas, and for the killing in 1898 of the Austrian Empress Elisabeth.[39] The Italian Anarchist taste for terror would also come to bear fruit nearly forty years after the London conference in a wave of violence in the USA.

Outside Italy, the views of the Frenchman Paul Brousse were symptomatic of the shift towards favouring assassination. In August 1877 in Brussels, he wrote an article for *Le Bulletin* declaring his support for '*La propaganda par le fait*'.[40] The next summer, an essay by Brousse appeared in *Avant-Garde*, praising the two attempts on the life of the

German Kaiser. Consequently the authorities suppressed *Avant-Garde* and in April 1879, in Switzerland, Brousse was sentenced for having incited the murder of 'monarchs and magistrates', and for detailing the most effective methods for killing such 'tyrants'. It was declared that Brousse was one of a group who sought a 'new social organization' that 'would have revolution for its starting point, murder for its means, and anarchy for its ideal'.[41]

Brousse's yen for violence was symptomatic. He and his fellow Anarchists were activists for revolution and theorists of murder. The admirable Elisée Reclus was another such long-term fighter for Anarchist ideals: a romantic figure, during the days of the Paris Commune he had enlisted as a military balloonist.[42] Kropotkin wrote, 'He knew how to die poor, after having written wonderful books.'[43] Reclus was a brilliant writer and geographer, the author of a major work, the popularising *Nouvelle Géographie universelle: la terre et les hommes*, published between 1876 and 1894 in nineteen volumes.[44] His ideals remain those of the radical left today: peace-loving, feminist, anti-racist, scientific, a free-thinking vegetarian (even vegan) anarchist. He also supported violence.[45] In December 1879, he wrote in Kropotkin's journal, *Le Révolté*, the following salute to the assassin:

Either you are a robber, assassin and firebrand with the oppressors, the happy, and potbellied, or you are a robber, an assassin and a firebrand with the oppressed, the exploited, the suffering and the underfed.[46]

Such invigorating calls to arms influenced many. The notion was wide-spread that the Anarchists must either seize the day or allow the oppressors to win. From this feeling of urgency sprang the coming carnage.

However, the single most significant delegate in London was the leading Russian Anarchist, Prince Peter Kropotkin (1842–1921), the founder of *Le Révolté* (1879) and, since the stepping-down of James Guillaume, the unofficial head of the movement.[47] Kropotkin repre-sented the benevolent face of Anarchism. Some sixteen years after the London Congress met, Oscar Wilde could describe him as 'a man with the soul of that beautiful white Christ that seems coming out of Russia'.[48] George Bernard Shaw similarly thought him 'amiable to the point of saintliness, and with his full red beard and lovable expression [he] might have been a shepherd from the Delectable Mountains'.[49]

He was angelic, clubbable, a good friend to many prominent members of literary London. Yet, although he did not like the phrase itself, Kropotkin in 1881 was, for the moment, also an equivocal believer in the necessity for 'propaganda by the deed'.[50]

He may have been influenced by Brousse's pronouncements on the topic, and the views of his fellow geographer Reclus forcefully impressed him.[51] There is no doubt that Bakunin's ideas on revolt had similarly moved him.[52] Moreover the repeated efforts to murder the Tsar and the government's harsh response to those attempts could not help but fire up so ardent a Russian as Kropotkin. What he rejected about the concept of the deed was the thought that such exploits would limit themselves to propaganda; he preferred to think that preliminary, and even failed, acts of revolt might in due course spark revolution.[53] Regarding the violence itself, he was relatively untroubled.

Kropotkin's career was one likely to inspire a romantic fascination. He was a revolutionary who had been a page to the Tsar; a dreamy and idealistic youth, in 1862 he joined the Cossacks; ten years later, he went to Siberia as a geographer. In 1874, he became an Anarchist; shortly afterwards he was arrested and put in the Peter and Paul prison, from which he escaped. Short, balding, stocky and toothless (as had happened with Bakunin, his teeth had all fallen out in prison), he was an unlikely-looking hero.[54] Yet his history exuded an impeccable glamour.

His tentative belief in violence sits oddly with his genuinely beneficent philosophy of life. A man of science, he rejected the harsh lessons of the social Darwinists, preferring to find in nature the validation for his belief in co-operation, solidarity and peaceful care. In his view, laws are a useless and positively harmful intervention in the processes by which we should regulate the world according to our reason and morality.[55] Law is static, while life is in motion. There was also a vein of pity in him – though a pity reserved for the noble and suffering assassin, rather than his victim.[56] In the early 1880s, these admirable, if idealistic, predilections could co-exist with his judgement concerning the necessity for acts of violence. Though indeed, although he accepted the need for violence, he did so with far less enthusiasm than most of his fellows in the movement (including those he published in Le Révolté).

Given the tastes of the assembled Anarchists, it was therefore no surprise that the single most striking measure approved at the London

Congress was the adoption of 'propaganda by the deed' as a revolutionary method, including the use of bombs and assassination. After decades of philosophising and refining, of pamphlets and editorials, European revolutionaries were ready to embrace instead the redemptive efficacy of the act. The 'practical lesson' provided by a deed would reach the people more effectively and more emphatically than the less direct exhortations of literature.

The belief in direct action arose from a new sense that politics concerned the masses, and therefore had to be understandable by them. There was a new audience for political deeds, and to reach an illiterate peasantry, actions were infinitely preferable to words. The revolutionaries sought therefore a public arena other than print. Paradoxically, however, the force of their deeds was in fact made to be mediated through print media: through books, pamphlets, newspapers, slogans and posters. They celebrated the directness of action, yet word of their actions spread as stories, narratives or even only images.

In part these ideas of engagement emerged from the experience of defeat. Yet, oddly, the Anarchists persisted with the tactics of violence even though the deeds themselves were soon shown to be as ineffectual as writing. In Spain, Italy, Ireland and Russia, assassinations resounded in a vast complacency. The long-awaited revolution was perpetually delayed. Men were shot, bombs exploded and bodies were torn; nothing changed. Where the stasis might have induced despair in the radicals and Anarchists, they instead transformed the futility of these gestures into acts bearing the seed of a better world. Defeat itself was dreamt of as inspiration; the impotence of the violence ceased to matter. They flung their dynamite at a structure that seemed impregnable. An act of faith was required in which they promised themselves that what appeared most useless in their actions would bear fruit later. It no longer mattered that a bombing or an assassination changed nothing immediately. They were breaking up the edifice; they were awakening the slumbering people. The sudden and paltry violence of an event drew the future closer. The fleetingness of political murders assumed the dignity of a tradition that was coming into being.

The deed was for the mass, and against it; it was the act of an individual, but one whose individuality was subsumed in their relationship to the people. It might seem that there were three requirements for the new violence to flourish: nationalism, industrialism and a revolutionary tradition. Yet in practice the appeal of assassination diffused itself everywhere.

The London Congress had begun with a dispute over the adoption of the following statute: 'The Congress . . . declares that this association, like all the societies and individuals adhering to it, recognises that *truth*, *justice* and *morality*, without distinction of colour, belief or nationality, must be the basis of our behaviour to all men.'[57] Serreaux, one of the foremost advocates of the new mayhem, and (according to George Woodcock, the great historian of the Anarchist movement) a police spy, moved that the word 'morality' be struck from the resolution; Kropotkin fought to retain it – and won.[58] There were moves to promote the study of chemistry and military sciences – Gérard Gérombou, a Belgian anarchist, had been sent to stress the importance of technical knowledge; clearly the aim of such studies would be the production of bombs and weapons. Again Kropotkin demurred, feeling that such efforts would squander the movement's revolutionary energy in pursuit of something that required years of effort in order to make gestures that would change little.

The most strident voices wanted dynamite; Kropotkin still hoped that their priority would be the peaceful dissemination of ideas among the peasants.[59] But the more extreme delegates to the Congress were to carry the day. Deeds of violence and other kinds of illegality were the direct route to revolution. Such acts spoke with more force than any publication could hope to do.[60] Kropotkin was disappointed by the move. He feared that an absolute acceptance of the idea of 'propaganda by the deed' would reduce legitimate violence, including assassination, to the paltry level of 'a publicity stunt'.[61]

One appeal of the act of violence was that it forced the Anarchists to remain revolutionary; there was no danger of being ushered into the polite dead-end of parliamentary agitation. Illegal and extreme methods allowed no compromise with the authorities. The Anarchists symbolically – and literally – were expressing their contempt for law and their repudiation of conventional politics.

There were distinctive features to the new brutality. It possessed much that is expressed in the more recent concept of terrorism as 'asymmetrical' action: the small was pitched against the great. Yet contained within the Anarchist version is the thought that such action is on the part of the great against the small – of the masses against the propagators of the system. The world of the conspirator was contracted; it fed upon the pathos of the tiny band. Yet the conspiracy was strong. It demonstrated that it had the power to destroy what it wished to destroy. This power was seen as the expression of the huge constituency for whom this tiny group fought; representative violence faced the stultifying lie of representative government. There would be acts of vengeance and acts of education that would terrify the rulers and instruct the people.

In the decades following the London Congress, there were few explicit defences of dynamite. It would be stupid to court arrest. Nonetheless the Anarchists' papers would be imbued with the spirit of the new doctrine. But this was nothing to its ubiquitous presence in the mainstream press. Out of the approval for violence agreed on in London that summer sprang an international bogeyman – the bomb-throwing, dagger-wielding Anarchist:

If the madmen who threw bombs in theatres and Parliaments have no object, but to spread terror, their deeds are at any rate crowned with a partial success. Crime for crime's sake, for the mere purpose of creating a feeling of fear, can only be the produce of a diseased brain. We can understand that the Greeks, who had grown up in the admiration of Democratic freedom, celebrated the memory of tyrannicides, because they liberated the country from men who had lawlessly and violently usurped arbitrary power . . . This explanation, however, fails in the presence of Anarchism. For who can believe that by destroying the State, and by indiscriminately annihilating human life, happiness and bliss will be brought to mankind?[62]

For the next forty years, this incomprehensible figure would be synonymous with the assassin. We will see later its ideal type personified in Alexander Berkman and Leon Czolgosz, two young idealists in America, ready to kill a 'robber baron' or a President.

4

Insanity Rules

Murder is negative creation, and every murderer is therefore the rebel who claims the right to be omnipotent. His pathos is his refusal to suffer.

W. H. AUDEN, 'THE GUILTY VICARAGE', MAY 1948

I: To Kill the Queen

In Britain as in America, assassination trials provided the test cases that transformed the legal treatment of insanity.[1] In America, the key events would be the assassination of President Garfield, and, a hundred years later, the attempted murder of Ronald Reagan. In Britain, the legal changes coalesced around three attempts to kill the sovereign and one botched endeavour to murder the Prime Minister. Taken together, the cases of James Hadfield, Edward Oxford, Roderick Maclean and Daniel M'Naughton can be seen as bringing a new clarity and humanity into the law regarding the insanity defence.[2]

The story properly begins with James Hadfield, the would-be assassin of King George III. There had been previous attempts to kill the king, notably in 1786, when Margaret Nicholson had a stab at doing so with a foiled thrust of a penknife. She was examined by the Privy Council on the charge of treason and found to be insane.[3] However, the key case in the history both of assassination and of mental illness is Hadfield's. Though the idea that the Hadfield trial created a defence based on insanity has been overstated, it is undoubtedly true that the case registered a new sensitivity to the nuances of madness.[4]

In 1794, James Hadfield had been severely wounded while fighting against the French, receiving eight sabre cuts to his head. Following his discharge from the Army, he was taken in by a millennial cult, and persuaded to assassinate King George III. He was set on by one Bannister Truelock, an Islington shoemaker and prophet.[5] Hadfield believed himself in 'constant intercourse with our Saviour; that the world was coming to a conclusion; and that it was necessary that he should sacrifice himself for its salvation'.[6] However, he positively understood that what he was planning was against the law; indeed he was tired of life and hoped to be executed for his deed, especially as his death would hasten the Second Coming.[7] On 15 May 1800, at the Drury Lane Theatre, while the monarch was standing for the national anthem, Hadfield fired a pistol at him; fortunately George had chosen that very moment to bow to the audience, and the shot missed. The bullet was found buried in the pilaster next to where the King had stood.[8] The King immediately called Hadfield to his presence, and the ex-soldier cheerfully greeted his monarch with the words 'God bless your royal highness; I like you very well; you are a good fellow.'[9] Hadfield clearly bore his king no ill will.

They charged Hadfield with treason, thus allowing him the luxury of being defended by the highly eloquent lawyer (and later Lord Chancellor) Thomas Erskine.[10] For the prosecution, Sir John Mitford, the Attorney General, attempted to distinguish between general and partial insanity, though in his view the partially insane should not be excused from criminal responsibility.[11] 'General insanity' entailed a total deprivation of memory and understanding. For the defence, Erskine maintained that there was no such insanity as general insanity, and that the test should rather be whether a defendant had acted under a 'delusion', and if this delusion had informed the criminal act.[12] On examination, Hadfield was found to be perfectly coherent on most matters, but completely irrational regarding others.[13] Erskine's eloquence succeeded in making 'partial insanity' a mitigating factor in dealing with a crime. In court, Hadfield's ghastly war wounds (which were plainly visible) also spoke for him, arousing sympathy and patriotic sentiments that may have influenced the decision to acquit. Indeed Hadfield was found not guilty, on the grounds that he was insane at the time the act was committed; he spent the next decades in Bethlem (where his co-conspirator, Bannister Truelock, would also be confined).[14] Hadfield's acquittal led to the passing of the Criminal Lunatics Act of 1800 which permitted automatic confinement of the insane after a successful plea of insanity.[15]

Until then the prevailing view had been that to be acquitted on grounds of insanity, the accused must be completely crazy, on the intellectual level of an infant or an animal. Judicial mercy would be applied only to those who were idiots from birth, or to someone who, congenitally or at the crucial moment, had no memory or understanding.

If the Hadfield judgment represented something of an advance in the humane understanding of such matters, the next major case was a set-back, the trial of John Bellingham, Britain's last successful high-level assassin, being a lamentable miscarriage of justice. From St Neots in Huntingdonshire, Bellingham had endured a hard and unforgiving life: his land-surveyor father had died insane, and he himself endured shipwreck, bankruptcy and his house burning down.[16] He was maddened by trading losses in Russia, where he was arrested for debt and imprisoned for five years. The British ambassador, Lord Granville Leveson-Gower felt that he was unable to intervene in the affair, since Bellingham had been quite legally sentenced. Bellingham, however, felt betrayed; the experience marked him, and he descended into a paranoid state, obsessed by the injustice of his misfortunes. On his release he persistently lobbied the British government for recognition and compensation; having approached everyone else, in May 1810, at 10 Downing Street, he attempted to hand Prime Minister Spencer Perceval a petition, but Perceval's secretary passed on the information that Perceval refused to present it to Parliament.[17] Failing to find redress, on 5 May 1812, he started haunting the House of Commons' gallery; early that same month he began practising with his pistols on Primrose Hill.[18] On 11 May 1812, he entered the House of Commons and lay in wait in the lobby for Granville Leveson-Gower. However, this intended victim failed to appear, but Perceval arrived, and was hurrying towards the entrance door to the House when Bellingham, feeling that he must nonetheless murder someone, stepped forward and at close range shot him right in the heart.[19] Some have believed that his choice of targets (the Prime Minister over the King) perhaps marked the shift of power from the monarch to parliament; in fact it just seems to have been bad luck.[20] Bellingham made no attempt to flee; when the cry went up to find the rascal who had fired, he stepped forward and said, 'I am the unfortunate man.'[21]

In the wake of the Luddite riots, many believed the deed was part of a conspiracy, perhaps the start of a British revolution. People gathered ominously in Parliament Square; at Newgate Prison a crowd attempted to free Bellingham.[22] A poem called 'Bellingham' compared Perceval to Caesar, and was ready to pity the noble killer; a letter was sent to the government claiming to be from an accomplice, and signed 'One of the fifty, Brutus'![23] Although clearly many were furious with the government, and in despair about the inequality of British society, Perceval himself may seem an unlikely target for an assassin, being, it was true, a reactionary and mediocre politician, more diligent than charismatic, but also a notably generous and decent man, a devout Evangelical and a dutiful fellow. However, he had fought the militants hard, imprisoning Sir Francis Burdett in the Tower, and forcing a stand-off between the government and radical factions, and had blocked all prospect of Catholic Emancipation; for all his private virtue, he was not short of political enemies.

Later there would be worries about the conduct of the Bellingham trial, as the process was pushed through before witnesses could arrive who could have reflected on the perpetrator's sanity. At the Old Bailey Bellingham himself complained about the hurry in which he was being tried, and that 'my prosecutors are actually the witnesses against me'.[24] There was something in this; one of the three judges, Sir John Mansfield, wept on the bench as he remembered Perceval. Despite the precedent of the Hadfield trial, he directed the jury that if someone should commit a crime while labouring under a delusion, but was otherwise fully sane and aware of the difference between right and wrong, then they could not be accounted as insane.[25] Bellingham was accordingly judged responsible for his actions, and was hanged a week after he had committed the murder. There were many who cheered him at the execution and who called out in his last moments, 'God bless you!', though for Bellingham, his face covered in a cap, the cries were likely so muffled he could not hear what was said. When the rope dropped, out of sight men pulled on his legs to hasten his death.[26] The law was left in a state of confusion. It was in the context of this unsettled response that the courts and the general public reacted to the series of assaults on Queen Victoria.

* * *

On 27 April 1865, on hearing the news of Lincoln's murder, Queen Victoria wrote a letter to King Leopold of the Belgians: 'These American news are most dreadful and awful! One never heard of such a thing! I only hope that it will not be catching elsewhere.'[27] Following the suggestion of Earl Russell, the Queen privately sent her condolences to Mrs Lincoln.

No one can better appreciate than I can, who am myself utterly broken-hearted by the loss of my own beloved husband, who was the light of my life, my stay, my all, what your sufferings must be; and I earnestly pray that you may be supported by Him to Whom alone the sorely stricken can look for comfort, in this hour of heavy affliction![28]

In her journal, she reflected on the terrible events in America. She indulged in the democracy of the emotions, and seemed joined more closely to any common grieving widow than to another queen like herself. The humility was sweet to her, at a moment when the vulnerability of the great had been made so apparent.

Though she dreamed herself an ordinary woman, Victoria had already suffered from the assassination attempts that were the occupational hazard of high rank in the nineteenth century. In 1837, soon after her coronation, a German named Stüber was incarcerated in Hoxton Lunatic Asylum after having threatened the murder of the new Queen.[29] Later, in the November of that same year, a captain of hussars menaced her; he, it turned out, was similarly insane.[30] However the first serious attempt on her life would be a case that would, like Hadfield's, also have ramifications for the Anglo-American understanding of insanity.

On Wednesday 10 June 1840, preceded by outriders and followed by two equerries, Victoria and Albert drove out in a low four-horse droshky through the garden-gate entrance of Buckingham Palace on Constitution Hill, and set out on the short journey to visit the Duchess of Kent at Belgrave Square.[31] Very soon after they had left the Palace, it happened. A man was waiting, with his back to the railings of Green Park, his arms folded under his coat so as to conceal the pistols he held in each hand. He pulled out both his guns, fired once and missed; before he let off his second shot, Albert had shielded his pregnant wife.[32] On the royal couple's return journey, an impromptu escort of gentlemen on horseback formed a guard around the carriage, cheering the Queen and waving their hats as they rode. Reports reached the press that the moment she returned to her private apartments, Victoria 'burst into a flood of tears'.[33]

The assailant had been brought down by bystanders. (These perhaps included John William Millais, who was there with his eleven-year-old son, John Everett Millais, later to become one of the Victorian period's greatest artists.[34]) The would-be assassin was taken to Queen's Square Police Station, followed by an angry crowd who surrounded the building.[35] His name was Edward Oxford, and he was a fair-complexioned, dark-eyed youth, only eighteen years old, though looking much younger.[36] He seemed unperturbed by his arrest, and indeed rather amused by it all. He still had time for a little snobbery: he gave his profession as barman, and when the policeman asked him if he meant 'pot boy' Oxford replied, 'no something higher than that'.[37] The police searched his rooms at West Street, and found papers apparently belonging to a secret society, 'Young England'. This clandestine band of brothers surely had no existence outside Oxford's romantic fancy, being just a wistfully deranged gesture towards a larger life.[38] Even now an atmosphere of unreality hung over the event; in a letter, he described the shooting as 'this bit of a scrape that I have got into'.[39]

Detective work proceeded. At the scene of the crime, where thousands came to gawp and speculate, a search was conducted for the fired bullets. To help with the hunt, one man wrote to the police suggesting that an experienced archer should shoot arrows experimentally from where Oxford fired his gun – where the arrows landed would provide the most likely spot for the missing bullets.[40]

The police investigations soon revealed much of Oxford's life. Born in Birmingham, he had left for Hounslow at the age of three. At the age of sixteen, he moved to London where he began work as a barman at the Shepherd and Flock on the High Street, Marylebone. A letter to the police from Oxford's fellow barman there revealed a dangerously erratic character. The assassin was always laughing or crying; he drank too much. He was constantly quarrelling with the writer, and had threatened another barman with a knife.[41]

Oxford was charged with 'high treason'; when he was brought to court, he laughed hilariously with pleasure at receiving so much welcome attention.[42] The trial was postponed so statements could be gathered and witnesses subpoenaed who would prove his insanity. When the case finally came to trial, early in July 1840, much evidence was presented as to the madness of Edward Oxford's father.[43] Oxford's mother, Hannah, who had run a coffee-shop on Waterloo Road, had a dark view of her family's history. She revealed that Oxford *père* had been subject to bouts of lunacy. He suffered from rages, eccentricities, suicidal impulses; he had once ridden a horse around the parlour, and another time sliced up his own sheets and blankets. The mother had herself suffered from delusions. It was not surprising therefore that her son should himself be strange.[44] There were also indications that his grandfather, a sailor, had been similarly crazed. This hereditary taint being firmly established, it was a simple matter to prove the son's share of the disease. There were also the tell-tale circumstances of the crime: that he had made no attempt to secure his own safety, and had incriminated himself by his open and unprompted confession. All this pointed towards someone not of sound mind; one expert witness suggested that Oxford suffered from a lesion of the will, making him susceptible to a 'morbid propensity' to commit eccentric or criminal acts.[45] Examined by John Conolly, the physician at Hanwell Lunatic Asylum, Oxford had appeared vague as to why or when he would be put on trial. When asked if he knew how wrong it was to shoot at the Queen, he calmly replied, 'Oh, I might as well shoot at her as anybody else.'[46]

After some deliberation, the jury found him 'guilty of discharging the contents of two pistols at Her Majesty', though they voiced their doubt (in the absence of any bullets being found) that the pistols were properly loaded, and also recorded their belief that 'the prisoner was of unsound mind at the time of committing the offence'.[47] As this verdict left it unclear whether Oxford was guilty or not, the jury were asked to reconsider and returned with the clear verdict of 'not guilty, he being at the time insane'. Oxford was confined as a lunatic for thirty-five years, first in Bedlam and then at Dartmoor. On release he set sail for Australia where he found work as a house-painter.[48]

Nearly two years later, almost on the very spot where Oxford had made his gesture, another young would-be assassin fired at the Queen. It was Sunday 29 May 1842, when Victoria and Albert were once again shot at in their open carriage. The gunman somehow escaped, and the next day made a second attempt. As on the previous day the assassin missed, but this time he was seized by a soldier and a policeman – the lucky constable was standing only three feet away from the assailant at the moment he fired.[49] The shooter's name was John Francis, and he was a florid, plump, unprepossessing youth, with a 'rolling eye'.[50] He had worked, like his father, as a carpenter in the theatre. Like Oxford, shortly after his apprehension he had his moment of *hauteur*, when he reacted sniffily to the suggestion that his father was a mere 'scene-shifter'.

To the Queen's relief, he was found to be without accomplices and merely, as she put it, 'a mauvais sujet'.[51] Strangely this left the matter of Francis's motivation puzzlingly open. Why had he wanted to kill the Queen? No answer was ever provided. Francis's defence – in the absence of any bullet being found – was that there had been no bullet in the gun that he had fired, and therefore no intention of murdering the Queen. His plan was merely to frighten. In his mind, the whole incident was a 'frolic'.[52] On 1 July 1842, he was sentenced to death, but then reprieved following the intervention of the Queen, much to the dismay of Lord Melbourne, her former Prime Minister, who considered that such crimes against the monarch demanded the strongest penalties.[53]

In early June 1842, Victoria was fired on again in St James's Park by a John William Bean, a youth 'deformed in body', very short and hunchbacked. He evaded arrest for a while, with the result that all the hunchbacks of London were harassed by the police. Bean's father informed the police that the boy had been inspired by Oxford and that his chief motive was the hope of fame. He was found to be insane and given a brief eighteen months in prison.[54]

Any assault on the monarch was by definition treason, yet that name seemed too weighty for the flimsy deeds of Oxford or Bean. An attempt to allow room for manoeuvre in such matters prompted the introduction of an act whereby serious assassination attempts could be distinguished from the mere desire to frighten.[55] Yet dissatisfaction about the outcome of these cases persisted. Sadly an opportunity soon arose to clarify the law. It would occur in respect to yet another act of assassination, though this time a fatal one.

The murder in question took place on 20 January 1843, when Edward Drummond, Private Secretary to Robert Peel, was shot near the Salopian Coffee House just north of Trafalgar Square. It was the middle of Friday afternoon. Drummond was walking back from a visit to his bank on Charing Cross Road, when a man came up behind him, quickly drew a pistol and fired it at close range into the left side of his back. The assailant hoped to fire twice – he had already pulled a second loaded pistol from his jacket pocket, cocked and aimed it – but before he could fire, a policeman knocked him down. The two men fought violently, but the policeman proved the stronger. (The second gun went off during their struggle.) As the policeman led the assailant away, the gunman remarked, 'He shall not disturb my peace of mind any longer.' Meanwhile, wounded, Drummond staggered back to the bank. But there was little that could be done: he died five days later.

In the police station, among the attacker's possessions was found a label with his name and address: 'Daniel M'Naughton, 7 Poplar Row, New Kent Road'. Interrogation quickly discovered that the murder was a case of mistaken identity: M'Naughton believed he had killed the Prime Minister, Robert Peel. Peel was the kind of politician who might indeed attract an assassination attempt: high-handed, earnest, and divisive, he possessed the will to go his own way at whatever the cost. In the eyes of some, he had already betrayed his own Conservative Party by supporting Catholic Emancipation and not long after Drummond's murder his stance over the Corn Laws would split and damage the party for years.[56] In mistaking Drummond for Peel, M'Naughton had made an understandable mistake: Drummond lived in 10 Downing Street, the Prime Minister's official residence, and, the two men being good friends, would often stroll over to Peel's private home at 4 Whitehall Gardens. M'Naughton had long spied out Drummond's movements, lingering and watching in the area of Whitehall; one recruiting sergeant saw M'Naughton there so often that he assumed he wished to join the Horse Guards.[57]

On 3 March 1843, the case went to trial. The prosecution's case was on the face of it irrefutable. There was no doubt that M'Naughton had shot and killed Drummond. The fact that he wrongly imagined that his victim had been the Prime Minister was no mitigation to the charge of murder. However, a postponement of the trial to allow the defence counsel to gather information regarding M'Naughton's state of mind gave away the nature of the defence.

For the prosecution, Sir William Webb Follett, the Solicitor-General, laid out his rebuttal and the problem inherent in the insanity defence.

Naturally it would be wrong to punish an 'unconscious being'. But were not all crimes 'committed by persons labouring under some morbid affection of the mind'?[58] Assassins in particular were subject to such delusions. The jury were invited to look across the Channel to France. There had been attempts, like that of Fieschi on the life of King Louis Philippe, using bombs or 'infernal machines' that had caused death and injury to ordinary bystanders: 'What motive had they? We know of none but that of an ill-regulated mind, worked upon by morbid political feeling.'[59] Was there not some kind of madness at work in all such assassins: shooting at the monarch with no hope of escape, planting bombs that would kill many others as well as their intended target?[60]

The defence would have to prove, the Solicitor-General argued, that M'Naughton was incapable of knowing right from wrong, and was therefore wholly unaware that he was committing a crime. It would not be enough to show that he was insane on some subjects only, prone to delusions that could co-exist with a rational state of mind. He quoted the authority of Lord Hale, who had determined that only a total want of reason, either chronic or temporary, could acquit a prisoner.[61] But if insanity co-existed with rational thought, intention, even discrimination, then the criminal was punishable. The Solicitor-General cast doubt on Lord Erskine's skilful defence of Hadfield over forty years before: the defence counsel's insistence in that case on the 'innocence' of anyone who committed a crime due to their suffering from an irrational delusion was in fact far from being legally the case. Citing Lord Justice Mansfield's summing-up in the Bellingham case, he spelt out three kinds of insanity: that which was tantamount to idiocy from birth; those lunatics subject periodically to a complete loss of reason; and those, otherwise rational, who were subject to delusions of persecution. The last group could not excuse any crime they had committed on the grounds of insanity.[62] What mattered was a complete inability to tell right from wrong and not to know the laws of God and nature.

Coming to the description of M'Naughton's life, the prosecution took the jury through a series of choices and events that all seemed to bear the stamp of a rational man. M'Naughton had worked competently as a wood-turner, had opened bank accounts, saved money, speculated on investments, and indulged in the study of science as an after-hours hobby. He had moved from Glasgow, travelled to London, found lodgings and lived peaceably enough. It was all plausibly quite sane. Various witnesses were called who strengthened this image of M'Naughton as a competent and even canny young man.

For the defence, Alexander Cockburn began with a speech outlining his own horror at the crime of assassination, and the weight of responsibility upon him in defending that assassin's life. The Solicitor-General had guessed correctly: M'Naughton's defence would turn on the question of his sanity. The Solicitor-General had cited the authority of Lord Hale. In contradiction, Cockburn quoted the American physician and author Dr Isaac Ray, the foremost expert on mental illness and crime. Ray affirmed that when Hale had suggested that a partial insanity was no grounds for acquittal, he had formed his judgment during a time when few were insane, and those few were consigned to public asylums. There the mad could be observed by visitors, the reasonable confronting the raving and the chained. Now insanity was more widespread, more subtle, and its treatment more humane, it appeared in quite another guise: preoccupied, distracted, quiet.

Writing in the 1830s, Ray noted that the civil treatment of insanity allowed for an individual being *non compos mentis*, while in criminal cases responsibility for a crime was said to exist if even 'the slightest vestige of rationality' remained.[63] Ray believed that the key test should be whether the criminal act occurred due to the individual's 'mental unsoundness'.[64] A criminal might know that murder was wrong as such, but believe insanely that the particular murder they committed was a different matter and to be judged by other standards.[65] In Ray's opinion, very few are so mad as to be unable to distinguish right from wrong. Rather the mad have partial possession of that power, being rational in some areas of life, while on the subject on which they are deluded, they lose hold of the common moral view of things.[66]

Cockburn then turned to the authority of Erskine in his speech at the Hadfield trial: the madman was one 'whose whole reasoning and conduct, though governed by the ordinary dictates of reason, proceed upon something which has no foundation or existence'.[67] A delusion was a defect of the imagination, 'a false case or conjuration of his own fancy'.[68] He would show that M'Naughton suffered from such a delusion, and that the murder he had committed had sprung from this source. A man could be perfectly sane in some regards and a functioning member of society, while mad on that one point. It was on this definition of insanity that he would defend the prisoner.

There was one last element of the Solicitor-General's argument to counter. The prosecution had raised the spectacle of fanaticism. Yes, argued Cockburn, there were religious enthusiasts who murdered in the name of God. And there were political fanatics who slew in the name of the public good, acting 'under the belief that in some great emergency, while they were sacrificing the moral law, they were ensuring the welfare of their country'.[69] But though M'Naughton had picked out the Prime Minister as his victim, there was nothing political in his deed.

The opening speeches complete, Cockburn went on to call a succession of witnesses bearing testimony regarding M'Naughton's state of mind. M'Naughton's Glaswegian father spoke first; Daniel was his 'natural son'. He had first been apprenticed into his father's shop, and then had worked for himself as a journeyman wood-turner. It seemed that, though a man who craved affection, Daniel had felt himself unloved. He was fond of children and small animals, carrying crumbs in his pockets for the birds. It was a life of frustration: working hard in the day, then studying hard at night; complaining of incessant pain in his head; sitting with his face in his hands. The young man had considered throwing himself into the Clyde to end the agony, harassed as he was by 'the fearful phantasms of his own imagination'.[70] Slowly overwhelmed by the images in his head, he gave up his job.[71] He travelled to France, but could not escape from himself. At first he believed he was persecuted by the Jesuits, and then by the police, and then by all the world – and, finally, by the Tories.

Witness after witness gave testimony regarding M'Naughton's persecution fantasies. A number of expert medical men were called, among them Forbes Winslow, author of *The Plea of Insanity in Criminal Cases*, Sir A. Morrison, and Drs Sutherland, Monro and Bright. Monro spelt out the prisoner's state of mind: 'the prisoner said he was persecuted by a system, or crew, at Glasgow, Edinburgh, Liverpool, London, and Boulogne. That this crew preceded or followed him wherever he went; that he had no peace of mind, and he was sure it would kill him; that it was grinding of the mind.'[72] Winslow's testimony was rather unwarranted, as he had not examined M'Naughton himself, but merely gave an 'expert' opinion based on what he had seen of the accused during the trial. In his view M'Naughton should be diagnosed as suffering from 'monomania', a condition named by the French psychiatrist J. E. D. Esquirol in which the intellect is unimpaired, but the affections and natural feelings are aberrant.[73]

Swayed by the weight of such evidence, the jury found M'Naughton not guilty, on the ground of insanity.[74] In view of this verdict, on 26 May, the House of Lords asked a group of four judges (including the three who had presided at M'Naughton's case – Chief Justice Tindal, Justices Coleridge and Williams) to give answers to five questions, designed to clarify the law. A fourth judge, Justice Maule, who had not been present at the original trial, was also consulted. They sought to determine what should be done with those suffering from delusions, in what circumstances should someone be declared unpunishable due to insanity, and what should be done regarding the legitimacy of supposedly expert testimony, when the expert forms his judgement in court and not on the basis of a proper examination.

On 19 June 1843, the judges gave their answers to the questions in the House of Lords. Maule could not come to an agreement with his fellow judges, in part because in his view the abstract nature of the questions did not admit an all-purpose response. He preferred to leave such matters to judges in individual cases and not to pin them down with rules that might become inapplicable.

The other three judges – while sharing Maule's objections – were prepared to give more definitive answers. They came up with the following guidelines, summarised here, the so-called 'M'Naghten Rules'.[75] Firstly, someone labouring under a delusion who commits a crime connected to that delusion is punishable, if at the time of committing the offence he knew it to be contrary to the law. If someone suffering from an insane delusion regarding one thing, but not otherwise insane, commits an offence, 'he must be considered in the same situation as if the facts in respect to which the delusion exists were real'.[76] In other words, just as it would be punishable to kill a man who really was persecuting you, it should be punishable to kill a man who you only imagine is doing so, provided you know that murder is a crime according to the law of the land.

Secondly, 'to establish a defence on the ground of insanity it must be clearly proved that, at the time of committing the act, the party accused was labouring under such a defect of reason, from disease of the mind, as not to know the nature and quality of the act he was doing, or if he did know it, that he did not know that what he was doing was wrong'.[77] Rather than a generalised knowledge of right and wrong, the jury should be directed more specifically regarding the act with which the defendant was charged.[78] If the accused knew that that act was one he ought not do, and the act was in fact illegal, then he was punishable.

Thirdly, if they are to give an expert opinion on whether an accused person is insane, medical witnesses should have examined the prisoner and not simply rely on an impression gathered from attending the trial.

The M'Naghten Rules asked if the accused was suffering from a disease of the mind, and, if so, could know the nature of their act at the time he or she committed it, and whether that act was right or wrong. Therefore the rules focused on the defendant's knowledge, the question of how much he or she knew concerning the act that they had committed. In time, questions arose as to the subtleties of the word 'know' – should it register a mere cognitive knowledge, or a finer 'affective' understanding of the crime? The idea of 'right and wrong' also proved more slippery than might be thought: was the crime 'wrong' in society's eyes, but 'right' in the disturbed vision of the perpetrator?[79] The rules dominated the law in the UK and USA for well over a century, yet in two respects they were found inadequate and other guidelines were followed. Firstly was added the idea of 'irresistible impulse', by which a sudden mad urge could overthrow the understanding and force the individual to perform the dreadful act. Secondly, under the influence of Isaac Ray, some courts (most notably in the District of Columbia) adopted the 'product' test, whereby, as we have seen, the issue was whether or not the criminal deed had emerged from the defendant's mental disease.[80]

Ever since their creation the Rules have been a subject for controversy, often unmasked as vague, confused or self-refuting. Some have argued that McNaughton should have been found guilty under the terms of the rules established by his trial.[81] The Rules were never meant to be a binding, 'sacred' text – yet they became so, even though in practice what the judges had meant in the writing of the rules was unclear and a matter of debate.[82] One difficulty lay in defining madness itself, helpless before the shifting variety of the disease and the rapid progress in scientific development regarding its understanding. By its very nature mental illness came to appear protean. In dealing with the legal response to such complexity, the Rules could not do much to maintain clarity.

Though the Rules had set out a working solution to the problem, the British press remained sceptical about such verdicts as had been given in the M'Naughton case: the *Illustrated London News* decried the failure to consider assassinations in 'any other light than as acts of madness'; even *The Lancet* dissented regarding the verdict on M'Naughton.[83] Such rules as the judges set out, it was supposed, did little to protect the Queen from further attack, though for thirty years there was no serious attempt to harm her. In May 1849, Victoria was fired at by an Irishman named William Hamilton, but there were only blanks in the gun, and so this was clearly only another 'wanton and wicked wish merely to *frighten*'.[84] Then, on 27 June 1850, one Robert Pate, a former lieutenant in the 10th Hussars, struck the Queen on the forehead with the brass top of his cane, crushing her bonnet. By far the least serious of all the acts of violence, it seems to have been the deed that aroused most indignation. *The Times* expressed a kind of weariness about the predictability of the insanity defence that would presumably secure Pate's acquittal: 'we trust that this slipshod method of sacrificing the interests of society to a whiff of maudlin sympathy for the fate of a ruffian will not be permitted to influence the decision upon this case'.[85] However, contrary to these fears, Pate was not proved to be insane and was sentenced to seven years' transportation to Australia.

In Britain and America growing irritation about miscreants 'getting off' with an insanity plea was plainly voiced. In the UK this annoyance finally spilt over into contradiction. On Thursday 2 March 1882, one Roderick Maclean fired at the Queen, as she sat in a railway carriage at Windsor Station. The assassin was seized at once by the police, just in time to save him from being beaten by the crowd (including a couple of over-zealous Eton schoolboys wielding umbrellas). Even as it was, he was manhandled before they could get him away to Windsor police station. The next day the revolver was shown to Victoria. It could be fired rapidly, and one bullet had indeed been fired. She was pleased at this: it showed there had really been an attempt on her life, and not just another shot at intimidating her.[86]

Maclean's attempt brought out the usual speculations. The *Daily Telegraph* declared: 'He may prove the first of the English nihilists.'[87] The link between assassination and Nihilism was now so strong that one appears to have necessarily evoked the other. While Oxford's and Hamilton's efforts had seemed isolated incidents, now with Russian, Irish and Anarchist violence at work, this shooting took its place among a plethora of assassinations and attempts. As such the usual anxieties about a conspiracy seemed more pointed than usual.

But Maclean was no wicked conspirator. He was yet another pitiful fellow, poorly dressed, hungry and mad. In order to carry out his scheme to murder the Queen, he had walked from Southsea to Windsor; he was too hard up to pay the rail fare. Born in 1854 on Oxford Street in London, oppressed by hallucinations and delusions, he had passed a melancholy life of grocer's shops, provincial journalism and workhouses. As a child, he had attempted to persuade another boy to derail a train; later he mused about the possibility of blowing up St Paul's. He had fixed and irrational beliefs about the colour blue, the number four, people dressed in mourning, and his own potential for immortality (he was an amateur poet). He clung to the notion that the British people had formed a conspiracy in order to 'annoy' him. For most there was ample proof of Maclean's insanity: he was 'epileptic' and subject to fits (sadly, in the 1880s this was considered substantial evidence of madness); in 1874, Henry Maudsley, an eminent British psychologist, had declared him 'not of perfectly sound mind'; he had passed a year or so from July 1880 onwards in the Bath and Somerset Lunatic Asylum at Wells.[88] At Maclean's court appearance, Maudsley himself was called as a witness. There were also clinical examinations at the time of the trial: all four doctors affirmed that Maclean was indeed mad and when tried for high treason at the Reading Assizes, Maclean was found 'not guilty on the ground of insanity'.[89]

Nonetheless there was intense public scepticism about the validity of the plea, and a corresponding sense that such assassins should all rightly be put to death.[90] One executed assassin would have deterred all the others, and so spared everyone the long parade of the Queen's would-be killers. Oddly this was a view that the first of the aspiring assassins, Edward Oxford, himself shared: if only they had hanged him, he mused, 'there would have been no more shooting at the Queen'.[91]

The Queen herself disapproved of the verdict.[92] She wrote: 'The bullet found – and *yet* he is only to be shut up. It is Oxford's case over again . . . And this always happens when a Liberal Government is in!'[93] Her anxieties initially prompted a letter from her Prime Minister, William Gladstone, humbly agreeing that there was a contradiction when a man who had plainly committed a deed should be found 'not guilty' regarding it.[94] She was not placated. After all, though Maclean was insane, there was no doubt that he had shot at the Queen with the intention of murdering her. How could he be considered 'not guilty'?[95] The Queen's scepticism was to alter the law, with the wording of such verdicts changing to a special verdict of 'guilty but insane'.[96] In trials this new distinction led to a double duty for the jury, who had to decide both whether the defendant had really committed the act for which he or she was being tried and also whether they were sane. (Although the subject of expert testimony, in Britain as in America the final decision as to the defendant's sanity rested with the jury.) It was an interesting distinction regarding the nature of guilt: with the old wording, the subject was irresponsible, while with the new form, there was guilt, but of a diminished or modified kind. (It should be remembered here that in legal terms 'responsible' means punishable.) The Queen had insisted not so much on the matter of individual responsibility, as on the guilt implied in the act itself: assassination was a guilty act, whatever the state of mind of the assassin.

II: Going to Lordy

Mörder sind leicht einzusehen. [Murderers are easy to understand.]
RAINER MARIA RILKE, FROM *DUINO ELEGIES*

In early 1881, capitalising on the interest piqued by the murder of the Tsar, Wirt Sikes, a diplomat at the American consulate in Cardiff and previously the author of a volume on British goblins, wrote a book on assassination. His intention was to expose the futility of such deeds.[97] Assassinations, he declared, both failed to accomplish their purpose and inevitably rebounded on the killer. Sikes had once glimpsed John Wilkes Booth; characteristically enough the young actor had been boozing. Only a few months before he would kill Lincoln, he was 'standing up at the public bar of a drinking-saloon, through whose wide open doors any passer-by in the street could see him, drinking a glass of toddy with the spoon against his cheek'.[98] If the writer hoped to discourage further additions to the illustrious list of victims, he was to be disappointed. When Sikes published his book, Booth's murder was still the only American assassination, and something of an anomaly in the history of the subject. Within a few months of publication, another American President was to fall victim to another assassin.

After the shameless favouritism of Ulysses S. Grant (President 1869–77) and the confrontational stance of President Rutherford Hayes, James A. Garfield entered the political field as a mere compromise candidate, designed to smooth over rifts between opposing wings of the Republican party. It was James Gillespie Blaine who eased Garfield into the Presidency. Blaine was a kingmaker who had spirit and dash enough to be king himself, though the taint of louche dealings kept him from the top job. Twice he was a candidate for the highest office, and twice he failed. In 1880, when Blaine helped Garfield to the White House, he sacrificed his own hopes of obtaining the Republican candidacy. He knew that Garfield's bid was on surer ground. In recompense, the new President would make Blaine Secretary of State, for though the Republicans won the election, it was by the slimmest of margins, only a matter of some few thousand votes.[99]

Blaine and Garfield were strikingly different. Blaine was a man about town, patrician by birth, whereas Garfield really did take the path from log-cabin to the White House. Garfield's physique, tall and broad-shouldered, manifested reassurance. His father died young, when James was only two years old, and he was brought up by his mother alone. Despite a background of rural poverty, Garfield sought out education, and became enough of a classical scholar to work for a while as a professor of ancient languages. He married his 'childhood sweetheart', Lucretia Randolph. A pious Christian, he became a minister and (despite the disapproval of his church) a conviction politician. He was a passionate abolitionist. When the Civil War came Garfield formed a company of volunteers, while Blaine dodged the draft by hiring a substitute to go in his place – a standard practice for those rich enough to pursue it. Garfield was made colonel of the regiment, and went on to fight a 'good war', becoming, at the age of thirty, one of the Union

Army's youngest generals. His success as a soldier pushed him to the centre of the political stage. Soon he was combining a career in the House of Representatives with military campaigns, before resigning his commission to be a full-time Congressman.

Garfield rose through the Republican ranks, propelled by his educated articulacy and his good nature. He seems, at this distance, a wholly admirable man: gentle, intellectually curious, kindly – too straightforward a fellow, one might think, ever to become President. He might have liked to be above the game, but events made him a player. When he won the candidacy against Grant, he had not even put his hat into the ring. For once, the old ruse of *nolo episcopari* appears to have been literally the case. This embodiment of the American Dream won the election. Soon he faced a spat in government with the 'Stalwarts' over Cabinet appointments. The Stalwarts were a faction among the Republicans who had begun as proselytes for Reconstruction in the defeated South and were staunch supporters of the system of patronage in their own party. Initially this second stance set them in opposition to the plans of President Grant. However, after the 1872 election Grant embraced the Stalwarts; later, out of disgust at the reforming zeal of President Hayes, they returned the compliment by campaigning for their man to stand for an unconventional third term.[100] Grant was the Stalwarts' man, and they were not pleased when Garfield won the day. In his battle against entrenched interests, Garfield fought his way ably. In the end, despite his enemies' tactics, he successfully asserted the rights of the President over the power of the Senate. A good man was in the White House.

Yet this serious and amiable character was soon to be struck down by a clown of the absurd. There was nothing noble about Garfield's nemesis, just a harebrained hobo, a brilliant buffoon. Garfield would not find the decent death that he deserved.

On the morning of 2 July 1881, President Garfield was due to go on a welcome summer holiday. He would travel first by rail to New Jersey then on by yacht to New England, and then make a tour of the South. The past two months had been a time both of political struggle and of personal anxiety. His wife, Lucretia, had been seriously ill, even close to death. Now she was better. They had taken one short holiday already, but it had been interrupted by the death in a railway accident of Garfield's uncle and a cousin. So now Garfield would join his family again and take the long break they all needed. He planned to leave in good time that morning. Although he was not an early riser, Blaine had promised the President the night before that he would come and see him off on his holiday. Garfield was pleased; he suggested that he would in that case have a parting word for him.[101] So that morning, a little after nine o'clock, Blaine met the President at the White House as arranged. They chatted in the Cabinet Room and the Library and then they rode together to the depot of the Baltimore & Potomac Railroad.[102] Garfield conversed freely; he was in an especially good mood. When they arrived at the depot, on the B-Street side, there were still fifteen minutes before the train would depart. The two men went to pass the time inside, walking arm in arm through the ladies' waiting room into the main hall. And there Charles Julius Guiteau found them.

From childhood Guiteau had been given to moods, veering from agitated egotism to a suppressed sulkiness. He reportedly did not speak until he was six years old.[103] Something was always thrusting him into activity. Perhaps he was already a little mad; there was lunacy in the family, after all: three of his aunts and uncles died in the asylum; several cousins and his sister ended up in the same place.[104] He had been born into a fairly comfortable bourgeois home in Illinois in September 1841. His mother died young and he was left, aged seven, to get by with his father, Luther Guiteau, a businessman and follower of the Perfectionists. Guiteau's mother appears to have constrained her husband's interest in this cult; after her death, he was as free to practise his beliefs as he wished. The Perfectionists considered sin and death to be illusions. It was an appealing belief, and for a time it enticed the young Guiteau as much as it did his father. The son was drawn too, no doubt, by the most obvious manifestation of Perfectionism: that is, the free love practised at the cult's base in Oneida, New York.

So it was that young Guiteau joined his father in the community. However, he didn't get on with his fellow utopians. At first, he enjoyed the favours of three Perfectionist women, but as soon as the inhabitants of Oneida grew better acquainted with his character, it became clear he was unlikely to bed a fourth. To know Guiteau was to dislike him. So the young man departed the Happy Valley for an improbable life of upright Christian devotions and gleeful naughtiness. While the piety enticed a similarly upright wife, Annie Bunn, a harmless librarian, the debaucheries helped him to lose her. After nursing him through a syphilitic attack, she left him. That was inconvenient, of course, but meanwhile he had big plans. He would become the leader of the Perfectionists, a newspaper proprietor, a lawyer, even the President. His egotism was unabashed, his spirits rampant. All the anecdotes concerning him reveal a weird frenzy; once he chased his sister around her farm waving an axe.

He pursued his goal of fame. Yet nothing quite worked. He travelled the country as an itinerant preacher; but there wasn't enough money in it. Then he earned his living as a debt-collector, siphoning off the cream of the money he gathered for his own glorious schemes. Whenever his own rent was due, he slipped out with his bags in the night and sloped off to a new part of town or a new city altogether.

As the 1880 Presidential campaign opened, Guiteau frequently pretended to be on intimate terms with both Blaine and Garfield. He had even given both their names as references to Mrs Ellen Grant, his landlady.[105] Such grandiose claims to connection were natural to him. He wrote a bad speech for Garfield's campaign (which was never delivered), and thereafter dawdled around the party offices. Throughout the early spring of 1881, on the basis of his one speech, he nagged at Garfield and Blaine for an ambassadorship.[106] His preference was for Paris. In his own mind, he deserved no less. Later, when Paris seemed out of the question, he decided he might settle for Austria. His would-be sponsors were less convinced. He hounded them as best he could, even buttonholing Blaine in the State Department's elevator. Rebuffed, his importunity became threatening.[107] This was not the first time that Guiteau had sought advancement in this way. He had previously made a speech for Horace Greeley's 1872 Presidential campaign, and had then promptly resolved to become minister to Chile. Why he should have picked on Chile remains unclear; perhaps he liked the way it looked on the map.

Guiteau belonged in the realm of magnificence. His flamboyant nature pleasantly concealed from view the drab beneath the splendour. He was a man of myriad opinions. He wrote reams, most of it un-readable; he hired halls and declaimed his lengthy speeches, mostly unheard. His fellow boarders declared that he had a 'cat-like tread' and a disconcerting habit of silently creeping up on people.[108] His whole life was performed at the frantic pace of an under-rehearsed but over-confident tragedian. He bustled from one government building to another, waiting for his big moment. When it came, it turned out to be quite different from what he had expected. It wasn't to be Garfield or Blaine who gave him a job, but God himself. And the job was to murder the President.

Why Guiteau conceived the idea that the President must die is unknown. There was perhaps the motivation prompted by the cumulative impact of his failures. Vitriolic newspaper attacks on the Presidency by the Stalwart press may also have been partly responsible. After the shooting, Guiteau on several occasions claimed to be a Stalwart, including in comments to the officer who arrested him and in a letter to General Sherman.[109] In the speech he wrote supporting Garfield's campaign, Guiteau describes himself as having once been a Grant man, though that in itself would not necessarily entail being a Stalwart, or even a continued supporter of Grant. Some 'Stalwarts' supported Garfield, once he had won the nomination. However, a significant number of them (and this was the problem) persisted in backing Grant, even after Garfield's election.[110] If Guiteau were a Stalwart that would provide a motive for disliking Garfield, but an improbable one for wanting actually to kill him. In any case, the fact that Guiteau had worked on Garfield's presidential campaign suggests that his 'Stalwartism' was an opportunistic affair prompted by pique at not receiving a sinecure equal to his self-conceit.

In any case, on the evening of 18 May 1881, the thought of murdering Grant came to Guiteau suddenly, with all the force of an inspiration. The Lord instructed him to dispose of the President. Guiteau comprehended his duty; everything pointed towards the 'removal' of Garfield. Afterwards life would go much better for everyone. Since God had marked him out for the irksome task he was honour-bound to murder him. He would in this way avert another Civil War. With a sense of patriotic duty, and a comforting belief in the pettiness of all human endeavour, Guiteau resolved to act.

He borrowed some cash and bought a pistol.[111] He wrote long justifications of his deed; he experimented with shooting his gun. Throughout June, Guiteau looked for a suitable occasion for the killing.

Things appeared reassuringly easy. Garfield eschewed bodyguards and security measures; his attitude to assassination was fatalistic. Besides, in Garfield's view, excessive anxiety about such matters would militate against the democratic nature of American political life. The President was a man among other men. He made himself ostentatiously vulnerable.

In June, Guiteau read in the papers of the President's plan for a brief holiday. The railway station depot struck him as the ideal place for a shooting. But the President's holiday came and went, and Guiteau missed his chance. For, when Garfield left, the sight of the President's convalescing wife looking so thin and holding her husband's arm so tenderly had given Guiteau a pang of sympathy, and he went home without killing anybody.[112] On the day of the President's return, Guiteau simply could not be bothered to kill him. It was too hot and he was not in the mood. But then a new opportunity arose. News came that Garfield would be passing through the station again, on his way to leaving the capital for the whole summer.

On 2 July Guiteau awoke early, ate a decent breakfast, put on a slouch hat, and caught a cab to the station. Before the President's arrival, Guiteau wandered in and out of the depot several times. He asked someone in the ticket office what train the President would be taking, and the man helpfully told him.[113] On Guiteau's last entrance, he deposited two thick packages of papers by a news stand. He had addressed these to the press; he was already thinking ahead as to how he would portray his deed to the public. In the men's lavatories, to the satisfaction of Freudians, he took out his pistol and examined it. He then skulked by the door of the ladies' waiting room, mooching and killing time. In his pocket was his five-chamber British Bulldog 44-calibre pistol. There seemed nothing remarkable about him, not even his restlessness. That was, after all, a usual state for people waiting to make a journey. Yet the ladies' waiting room attendant did take notice of him: he was always passing the door of the room, and looking inside, a little too intently. It was her job to keep an eye on men who did that.[114]

And then Guiteau's moment came. As the President and Secretary Blaine sauntered into the ladies' waiting room, Guiteau passed inside and came up behind them, so that he was close to the President, then he pulled out his gun, took aim and let off a shot, striking Garfield on the edge of the right arm. Garfield fell forward, his legs folding under him, looking around to his right as he did so to see who had shot him.[115] As he fell, Guiteau moved in close and, pointing the gun slightly downwards, squeezed the trigger again. If the first shot had merely winged his target, the second was an unequivocal hit. Having fired, Guiteau made a dash for it, barging past the stricken President and on outside, straight into the arms of Officer Kearney, a startled policeman who was running into the building to see what had happened. Guiteau bellowed that he had an important letter to take to General Sherman and 'that would explain it', but, unperturbed, Kearney kept hold of him.[116] No one was going anywhere, until he knew what had happened inside the building. Just then bystanders rushed out and identified Guiteau as having shot the President. At first, Kearney thought this must be a joke. But Guiteau promptly confessed. Only then did they take his pistol from him.

Blaine had impulsively begun to run after the gunman himself, but was recalled by the President's groan. He turned back and saw Garfield lying on the ground, bleeding from his arm and his groin. He had vomited and was lying unconscious in the mess. Only then did the Secretary take in what had happened.

After the wounds had been examined, they laid the President on a mattress and he was carried out. The police cleared an exit through the crowd, and bore the President down to a waiting ambulance. The doctors all considered that he would die that day.

The letter explaining the deed was found in Guiteau's pocket. It announced:

The President's tragic death was a sad necessity, but it will unite the Republican party and save the Republic. Life is a flimsy dream, and it matters little when one goes. A human life is of small value. During the war thousands of brave boys went down without a tear. I presume the President was a Christian, and that he will be happier in Paradise than here. It will be no worse for Mrs Garfield, dear soul, to part with her husband this way than by natural death. He is liable to go at any time, anyway. I had no ill will toward the President. His death was a political necessity. I am a lawyer, a theologian and a politician. I am a Stalwart of the Stalwarts. I was with Gen. Grant and the rest of our men in New York during the canvass. I have some papers for the press which I shall leave with Byron Andrewes and his cojournalists, at 1420 New York Avenue, where all the reporters can see them. I am going to the jail.

· Charles Guiteau.[117]

The letter's queasy combination of self-aggrandisement, opaque political purpose and the 'all is vanity' note strikes all the key elements of Guiteau's pose. If Guiteau was indeed a Stalwart, then assassination was a canny act, as it would propel the Stalwart Vice President Chester A. Arthur into the White House. (In a move typical of Garfield's political instinct for compromise, Arthur had been given the Vice Presidency in a gesture of rapprochement with the Stalwarts.) Despite his professed Stalwartism, as far as his politics were concerned, the *Washington Post* was clear about one thing: 'Guiteau may not be a Nihilist, but that he is the next thing to nothing, is self-evident.'[118]

Lincoln had been shot at the close of a war, with scenes of horrible violence fresh in the minds of many. Garfield was struck down in a time of peace. The blow appeared to come from nowhere. As had happened with Lincoln, first thoughts were of a conspiracy. Guiteau's unconvincing political affiliations with the Stalwarts were nonetheless scrutinised suspiciously. However, Blaine condemned attempts to place Guiteau at the centre of a wider plot. Party unity – national unity – was what was needed now. But such denials of others' complicity were more than expedient; they were true.

For now, the President did not die. He was sick, and the wound was a horrendous one, but somehow he rallied. He made jokes about his condition, telling his son not to worry since 'the upper story is alright, it is only the hull that is a little damaged'.[119] The doctors, his family, Blaine, the nation itself, all began to hope. It seemed that he might after all pull through.

* * *

In 1881 in Washington, DC, it was a cicada summer. Every seventeen years, the creatures burrow out of the ground and in vast numbers swarm in the June and July heat along the Eastern Seaboard from New Jersey down to the capital. Their shrill, indifferent scream and the stifling air formed the background for those early July days. In the

President's apartments, new carpets were laid to muffle sounds; thick calico curtains were hung to keep out the brightness.[120] He sweated in the Washington heat.

It was the summer of his dying. Reports were given to the press of the rapid changes in Garfield's condition: a rise in temperature; incoherence in his speech; his pulse; his sleeps. His condition fluctuated. The surgeons fingered the groin wound, and prodded it with instruments. They made incisions into his body and oozed out the pus, and all without anaesthetics. On a clipboard, Garfield wrote, 'Strangulatus pro Republica' – 'tortured for the Republic'.[121] It was a bitter joke, and a last gleam of the liberal education and the ancient language that had first helped to lift him from obscurity. He grew thinner. His thighs were so wasted that it was said one could circle them with the fingers of one hand.[122]

At the end of the summer, when September came, they moved Garfield from the continuing humidity of the capital to the cool air of Elberon, near Long Branch on the New Jersey shore. They travelled by train past the silent crowds. He rallied for a while. There was a colder spell forecast, some days away. And the sea breeze revived him, blowing over the balconies through the open windows to his bed. But it was a false hope. When the long-expected death came, it came suddenly. He died on the night of 19 September, having awoken from a sleep with complaints of a terrible pain about his heart. They put his body in ice, and prepared it for embalming.

For Queen Victoria, President Garfield's death provoked thoughts of Mrs Garfield's loss and again prompted memories of her own lost husband, Prince Albert. In her Balmoral journal she wrote: 'Heard that poor President Garfield had at last sunk under the long and cruel suffering which he had struggled against since the 2nd July. Terribly sad – such a loss and such a grief for his poor wife. Telegraphed to her and to Mr. Lowell.'[123] For the first time on such an occasion, as a mark of respect the Court went into mourning for a week.[124]

* * *

Guiteau passed the summer in prison. On arriving there, he had refused to walk barefoot across the cold stone floor lest he catch his 'death of cold'. The jailer informed him that he would be catching his death another way quickly enough.[125] Yet he soon settled in. He was fairly comfortable and ate well, expressing a particular fondness for fish. By the autumn, he was even growing somewhat fat.

The only interruption to trouble him came just as the President was moved to the coast. On 11 September, a detachment of troops arrived at the prison to guard him. But some of the men were weary of protecting a man who would be better dead. So it was that one of them, an artillery sergeant named John A. Mason, calmly jumped out of his wagon, aimed his gun up at a window from which Guiteau was often glimpsed, and fired. The shot grazed the assassin's head and struck his coat, which was hanging on a hook behind him, ripping through a picture he had left in the pocket. Then just as calmly, Mason surrendered himself and awaited justice. There was no doubt that the sympathies of the public and the common soldiers were with him.

On the day the President died, there was a large mob outside the prison. There were rumours that Guiteau would be dragged out and lynched. Journalists stood among the throng. When Guiteau heard the news of the President's death, he remarked simply, 'Is that so?' He went on to say that he was glad the man's sufferings were over. The whole thing was in the Lord's hands. And outside the crowd waited.

On 19 November, while in the prison wagon en route from the courthouse to the jail, Guiteau was again shot at, on this occasion by one Bill Jones, a self-styled 'Avenger' of Garfield on horseback. Guiteau saw Jones coming and dodged the bullet. Thinking he had succeeded in killing the assassin, Jones fled the scene. He was soon caught, tried, but acquitted. (Nearly thirty years later, Jones, by then a farmer, was arrested for the murder of a neighbour.)[126]

But all these attempts at wild justice came to nothing. Guiteau had his trial. He pleaded not guilty. His case as he presented it rested on three basic points. Firstly, he had shot the President but not murdered him: his death had come much later and from other causes. (In fact, the criminally bad care provided by the doctors, who had probed Garfield's wounds with unsterilised and even unwashed hands, was indeed in part responsible for the death. Though of course without the shooting there would have been no defective treatment.) The second strand to his defence was that the shooting was no murder at all, but resembled rather the shooting of someone in a war. So many courageous young men had died in the Civil War, what was different about his firing a gun at Garfield? He himself was a 'peace man', cowardly and not given to violence.[127] Thirdly, and most crucially, he had only acted with such mental determination because the Lord was behind him. Responsibility for the crime lay with God, who had suggested it, and not with him, who was the mere actor of a divine command. There was no suggestion of murder. He had merely sought to 'remove' the President.[128]

Such a case would require the most skilful of advocates; Guiteau nominated himself for the task. Having rejected the services of one Leigh Robinson, Guiteau found himself nonetheless lumbered with a defence counsel in the form of his brother-in-law, George M. Scoville (Robinson's colleague). With eye-witnesses to the shooting, and Guiteau's own confession in writing, there was never any possibility of an ordinary acquittal. Nonetheless Scoville (who had also been a Stalwart) provided a workmanlike job and really did the best he could for his errant brother-in-law.[129] However, Guiteau still more or less sought to conduct his own defence, spending a great deal of the trial goading and insulting his own advocate.

In fact the outrageousness of this behaviour was typical. The efforts of the judge and district attorney to attain a proper solemnity foundered before the accused's pugnacious impishness. The trial swayed on the edge of farce. Guiteau's absurdity threatened at every moment to tarnish the solemnity of Garfield's death. It was not even actual ridicule; it was more manic and unstoppable cheek. The trial allowed the man to shine in the limelight; it was an opportunity that he would not pass over. He played up and he played the fool. He mimicked the judge, and mocked his own lawyer; he lamented the quality of his handcuffs. Yet an odd indifference went with this mischief. He could appear insensible; he hardly noticed the many beautiful women in court who came daily to observe him. Yet always he threatened to explode into another harangue. His antics provoked laughter, and the laughter encouraged him. He triumphed in one-liners; reputedly he was too mentally disturbed to make longer forays and had not the power to connect his thoughts.[130] He began to humour the crowd, and more people flocked to the courtroom just to witness his foolery. There was little that could be done about it. A charge of contempt would only delay the main trial, and could be used by an accused man as a means for prolonging life by delaying a capital judgment.[131] Speculation grew that he might even be gagged.

So it was that, despite the seriousness of his crime, Guiteau became for the press a figure of fun. The *Globe* termed the trial 'one of the most successful judicial comedies that has been seen in this undignified age'.[132] *Funny Folks* printed caricatures of 'Guiteau's Mirthful Matinées'; *Judy* unveiled 'The Larking Murderer'.[133] Guiteau's madness was not just a subject for psychological and legal investigation; it was theatre. His outbursts in court, his heckling, his comic asides, all were somehow a role he was playing. His madness was a performance, and one, perhaps, manipulated for effect. He played to the gallery, setting off his staccato interjections or his brief rolling periods, basking in the attention. His own view of insanity was that it was best understood by the words 'divine pressure'.[134] And he also evoked the figure of Abraham, the father of faith, who, on the order of God was ready to murder his own child.

Yet one more factor contributing to the mayhem was Guiteau's firmly held belief that someone would assassinate him. Given the recent attempts by Sergeant Mason and Bill Jones, this was not a mere paranoid fancy. Arriving at and leaving the courtroom involved a daily run through a jeering crowd. Mounted police guarded him. He refused to stand in court, convinced that it would make him a better target.[135] He gave his testimony sitting, rambling on for a week, glad of the audience no doubt, and apparently impenitent about the means by which he had obtained it. He regretted the personal side of things, of course, but his duty forced him to rise above such weakness.

Guiteau's ex-wife, Annie Bunn – now Mrs Dunmire – was called as a witness. She was petite, slender, dark-haired, and just thirty-two years old. Her second husband, Theodore Dunmire, was reportedly excited by the idea that his wife's new-found fame meant that he might sell her photograph and be entitled to the royalties.[136] But Annie Bunn sought rather to diminish her notoriety. Neither she nor Guiteau were eager to reveal the sordid details of their marriage. He wished to conceal his sexual transgressions and his syphilis, and she hoped to cover up the shameful fact that she had had a child by him – a child that had been given away. She testified cautiously concerning their itinerant married life in New York, moving from apartment to apartment. Their time together had been unsteady, but she stated that she considered her ex-husband to be perfectly sane.

But even Annie Bunn could not conceal her husband's extreme eccentricity. Guiteau's brother-in-law, Scoville, naturally enough chose the route of arguing that his client was a crazy idiot.[137] Guiteau, likewise naturally, bristled at this characterisation. Guiteau's own view was not so much that he was insane, as that he was a man under the pressure of a guiding (and in his own eyes true) belief – that God had demanded Garfield's removal. To the assassin's chagrin, the decision that the court faced turned on the question of his sanity and therefore his ability to understand at the moment that he was firing the pistol that he was committing a crime.

Often in the case of an assassination, the discovery of the assassin's insanity disappoints. It is startling how often public opinion has transformed mere madness into political motivation. As we have seen, in Bellingham's case, there were people ready to claim his murder of the Prime Minister as a genuine tyrannicide. One expert on the M'Naughton case has suggested that M'Naughton was by no means mentally ill at the time of the shooting, that M'Naughton cleverly feigned madness, and that the diagnosis was intended to downplay the political context of his act.[138] In the case of Maclean, in early April 1882, questions were asked in the House of Commons as to whether the assailant were an Irishman, and this despite the attempt by Sir William Harcourt and the Home Office to calm national anxiety over the matter.[139]

Such a reimagining of events took place similarly with Guiteau. Perhaps because civil service reform had been a major theme of the previous ten years of political life, in popular legend and in a continuing tradition of American historical writing, Guiteau was remoulded as a disappointed 'office-seeker'; in this view his failed attempts to find a job in the administration triggered the assassination.[140] As such there were some who lamented the crime and the sentence, while there were also those clear-sighted enough to gain political capital out of Guiteau's megalomaniac frustrations. These saw the murder as the regrettable product of a failure to have a civil service open to all the talents. The only flaw in this vision of events is Guiteau's utter lack of talent. Nonetheless, a couple of years after the assassination, in 1883, the Pendleton Civil Service Reform Act was passed easing entrance to the profession. Attempts to understand Garfield's murder in this way are symptomatic of the desire to draw the craziness and abruptness of assassination into the frame of coherent political history.[141]

Without such political motives, the necessity for understanding the mad assassin's motivation seemingly ends. The crime safely joins the class of the incomprehensible; when it is so consigned we feel that we can place the deed. Yet there remains the force of strangeness, both of the act and the person. Both evil and madness contain an element of the unintelligible; something in them resists explanation.

In 1835, Richard Lawrence had attempted to assassinate President Andrew Jackson; luckily his pistols had misfired. The jury on that occasion 'took five minutes to return a verdict of not guilty by reason of insanity before sending Lawrence to confinement for life'.[142] In Guiteau's case, things would not be so simple. As we have learned, the insanity plea was a controversial one at the time, many seeing it as an underhand means of dodging justice.[143] One doctor involved in the medical examination recalled some twenty years later 'the pressure, direct and indirect, exerted by the force of public opinion' that they should find Guiteau sane.[144] The *New York Herald* affirmed: 'Our civilisation is, however, so very refined that the plea of emotional insanity is almost omnipotent, and a man can be forgiven for any crime if it can only be proved that he was greatly excited when he committed it.'[145] In fact, as this quote itself demonstrates, legal and public attitudes to insanity were in a period of transformation.

During the nineteenth century and indeed some decades later, in cases involving insanity most American courts followed the English common law, tracing their attitudes back to precedents forged in English courts and statutes passed in the British parliament.[146] When Richard Lawrence had been found not guilty by reason of insanity, the prosecution itself had recommended the test that the deed should be the 'unqualified offspring of the disease', even if the perpetrator still understood the difference between right and wrong.[147] In the nineteenth century's later decades, it became necessary in some states to enter a special plea of insanity, but even then the British M'Naghten Rules were followed.[148] Certainly, in trying Guiteau, the Washington court adhered to the British formulation in judging insanity by the measure of those rules.[149]

As we have seen, the M'Naghten Rules declared that a defendant was understood as responsible if he comprehended 'the nature and consequences of his act and knew it to be forbidden by law'.[150] The law required an absolute dividing line between responsibility and irresponsibility. Yet Guiteau's insanity was not so simple a matter.

The defence called twenty-three expert psychological witnesses who declared Guiteau mad; the prosecution supplied thirteen doctors who asserted he was sane. The defence's most impressive expert was Charles Spitzka, a young American neuroanatomist who had trained in Germany. Guiteau's moral monstrosity, his imperfect brain, the doctor argued, could be adduced from the unavoidable stigmata of his condition: the nature of his face, the shape of his skull.

The prosecution experts disagreed. Dr Allan McLane Hamilton affirmed that the shape of Guiteau's head did not indicate insanity; it only appeared flat due to his haircut.[151] In December, Guiteau allowed his beard to be shaved and a cast of his head to be moulded to aid with the phrenological and physiognomical analysis of his character.[152] Anything which served the understanding of the man was considered pertinent.

In his study of the subject, Charles Rosenberg shows that the debate in court as to Guiteau's madness was a battlefield in a larger conflict over the nature of mental illness, a division between asylum superintendents (provincial, religious and intellectually conservative) and a younger generation of New York-based neurologists (cosmopolitan, agnostic and in touch with the latest ideas from Europe).[153]

The debate came down to the double problem of motivation and responsibility. Central to the arguments of some who gave evidence at the trial was the much-disputed thesis of 'moral insanity', which the progressives accepted as a condition in which a person could be intellectually 'normal' and so understand the likely practical consequence of bad actions, while being unable to understand the moral nature of their choices. Though sometimes highly intelligent, such people lacked a moral sense. As for the conservatives, they considered the new-fangled term as simply another name for 'wickedness'.[154] George H. Savage, the Medical Superintendent of Bethlem Hospital, wrote:

Undoubtedly if the person knows the evil of his crime, knows also the tendency to commit that crime, and yet, with all his education and endeavours, cannot prevent himself from committing it, he is scarcely to be considered morally responsible; but at the same time it is going rather far to consider such patients morally insane.[155]

Some years later, at a meeting of the Medico-Psychological Association, Savage argued that these deadly impulses were on a spectrum that included such common tendencies as the inability to look down from a height or the urge to throw oneself in front of a train.[156]

The idea of compulsion lay at the centre of the dilemma – could one be compelled to commit a crime? The psychologist George M. Beard was clear about the contradictions of the case. Guiteau was a classic example of a religious monomaniac. The law could not hope to deter such figures with the threat of distant punishment. Guiteau was prompted to his crime, it would seem, by the belief that he would receive both an earthly and a heavenly reward. In Beard's view, the insane committed a crime *because* they knew it was wrong. The mad were impelled to carry out acts the most shocking, the most invidious, the most taboo; punishment itself might act as an inspiring factor. It was not in knowledge that the insane were weak, but in power – especially the power to resist their own impulses.[157]

Yet who could say if someone were so mad as to be unable to prevent themselves from killing? Clearly Guiteau had used rational methods to commit his crime, such as planning, foresight, guile, organisation; a madman could hardly be both so considered and so cunning.[158] Yet he acted under a confused will. Madness entailed such incoherence of character. The mad person's act, to be defensible, should be an abrupt break in the patterns that a person creates for themselves, an aberrant fall from yourself. Stranger still was when fixity of delusion sustained a mad coherence; the self constituted according to a folly.[159] In such circumstances, the division between responsibility and madness would hardly be an absolute one.[160]

What this debate showed most clearly was the difficulty of defining insanity at all. The human mind could not be accurately measured or understood, and definitions of normality proved slippery. In these circumstances the likelihood of determining the nature or extent of deviation from the normal was, technically at least, remote. Rigorous medical intervention into the area of mental illness was expanding, pathologising behaviour that would have seemed merely bad or odd a few decades before. The frontiers of insanity were spreading; *The Lancet* declared:

At the present moment, insanity would seem to be anything experts choose to make it. There is no clearly formulated ideal of sanity, and the least 'strangeness' or weakness is held to be, if the general circumstances appear to render the assumption convenient, a sufficient proof of insanity to deprive an individual of his liberty and social privileges.[161]

In understanding insanity the law struggled to make distinctions about states of mind that were in flux. Social views of such states were similarly unstable. At times, eccentric behaviour (such as that of one of the Queen's assailants, Robert Pate, who bathed in whisky and water) accumulated as evidence of deeper madness. These propensities suggested a character formed in madness; committing a vicious crime might be seen as all of a piece with such habits. In these conclusions, the insane appeared as a class of persons, different from us, their criminal actions emerging naturally from their otherness.[162]

If the M'Naghten Rules stated that to be innocent such assassins must not know that they commit wrongful murder, then assassination in general seems peculiarly imbued with this cleansing innocence. For most assassins, the idea of their act being unlawful loses itself in the idealism or unworldliness of the deed, whether that be accounted the political motivation, or the mad compulsion. In Isaac Ray's consideration of insane murder, he remarks on those who are quite sane but feel themselves compelled to kill, to outrage the moral order that they otherwise adhere to, 'and thus have acted the part, if the expression may be allowed, of an insane Abraham or Brutus'.[163] It is a strong clue to the understanding of the subject, as Ray links the father of faith and the archetypal tyrannicide.

Insanity might appear as a dissension from the majority view of things, a way of not sharing in the 'basic concepts, perceptions, values, skills, and attitudes common to members of the community'.[164] In this it might be thought to resemble the minority insights of Anarchism, a species of politics that at the time itself could seem insane. On 17 February 1894, after an Anarchist bomb exploded futilely in London's Greenwich Park, the *Evening News* enquired, 'Are Anarchists Lunatics?', and then obligingly answered its own question with a 'Yes'. One retired police detective wrote in his memoirs: 'anarchism is undoubtedly a form of mental derangement, one must not look for reason on the part of those who espouse it'.[165]

In Guiteau's case, the idea of moral insanity depended on an ordinary understanding of right and wrong. The mad criminal falls outside that understanding; but what of criminals whose sense of right and wrong is coherent, ideological, but antagonistic to that of his victim and his accusers? What of a Nechaev who rejects the bourgeois ethics of ordinary life, in favour of revolutionary ethics? Just as the insanity defence was being put to question, another category of assassins had emerged who likewise tested the concept of shared understanding that underpins all criminal trials. The revolutionary's sense of right and wrong was pitched quite differently from that of the majority. Were they too insane? As the century ended, assassination, whether by the insane or the idealistic, necessarily cast society's moral categories into doubt. The insane person finds a home in those categories as an exception – either as an idiot who does not understand, or as one marked out as simply depraved. The assassin who kills from an outraged conscience can likewise be comprehended as tyrannicide or assassin, noble Brutus or primal betrayer. Such killers question the entire moral scale and tear a gap in our understanding of the world.

The poor aspirants to assassination examined in this chapter were largely troubled by persecution mania, or what we would call paranoia. Insignificant in themselves, they invented a plot for their lives in which the most prominent people in the land were their enemies, casting themselves as the doomed but plucky heroes of a dark drama. The assassinations that they hoped to carry out were meant to end their oppression and lift them into the realms of the recognised. Firing a gun at a monarch or a politician proved an excellent means of attracting attention, even for those paranoiacs who believed themselves already too much attended to.

The conjunction of the private and the public proves central in the case of the mad assassin. Such criminals imagine that their own life has significance on the national scale, though their grievance remains something personal. To them, the political seems a matter of persons, their personal sphere of public significance. The public realm was important in this way to all nineteenth-century assassins: to the 'Fenians' and Nihilists through the notion of vendetta; to the Anarchists, through the idea that the individual target embodied an institution.

* * *

At the close of the trial, Guiteau made a speech in his own defence. He declared that he had been insane on the day of the shooting, and that he would not do the same thing again for a million dollars. For a man so money-obsessed as Guiteau that was something. On 25 January, as the verdict approached, and the summing-up began, Guiteau became ever more agitated and spiteful in his interruptions. He grimaced; he fidgeted; he flinched; he roared. When Porter, the counsel for the prosecution, had finished, the judge summed up. At 4.40, the jury retired to consider their decision. They returned just under an hour later, finding him guilty.

There was little to be done. Guiteau's sister, Mrs Scoville, visited Mrs Garfield in order to plead for clemency. But the President's wife refused to see her. Garfield himself seemed already forgotten, the press of politics swirling on past the vacancy his death had made. He had been in office 200 days; now Chester Arthur was President, deep in the process of getting civil service reforms passed, the chief focus of his time in office – in the eyes of some, these were reforms in part prompted by Guiteau's absurd career frustrations. In this sense, Guiteau was more influential on Arthur's presidency than Garfield himself.

The date of the execution was set for 30 June 1882. Guiteau prepared himself for his end. He was quieter now, almost subdued, though still visited by his fits of rage and mirth. A belief that he would still find a reprieve was responsible for his serenity. But when the final day came, Guiteau gave up all hope of a pardon and reconciled himself, as best as he was able, to his death. His spiritual advisers came and told him there was no more hope. Guiteau dismissed the revelation. His only concern was that the execution should be punctual and that it should not be botched. When a bouquet from his sister arrived, for the first time since the assassination he was moved and he kissed the flowers and wept. He made a will but he had only two things to dispose of: his story and his body. The first he gave to his priest, with an injunction to publish it and so set the record straight. His body he left to the state, to do with as they would, though not for any mercenary purposes. He still imagined that they would raise a statue honouring him as a patriot and Christian. Fantasy was his element to the end: with less than a day to go before the hanging, a washer-woman came to collect a debt for 60 cents; he handed her 50 cents and announced that he would pay the balance on the following Monday. Later this transaction was on his mind. After he had kissed his sister, he passed one last dime to his brother, and told him to pay the washer-woman; perhaps after all it would be better to settle the account today.[166]

Before the day itself Guiteau passed a sleepless night, but as the morning approached finally dropped into unconsciousness from sheer exhaustion. He ate the traditional hearty breakfast, and seemed unaffected by the thought it would be his last. He would be hanged at noon; he told the chef to get dinner for him at eleven sharp. He worried only that something would go wrong on the gallows. While he bathed inside, out by the scaffold the spectators and those who hoped to make money out of them were gathering. Someone set up a cake stall.

Fresh from his bath, Guiteau wrote out the 'last words' he would speak from the scaffold. It was good to have something prepared. His second dinner was brought in around 11.30 a.m.; like his breakfast it consisted of steak, fried potatoes and eggs. He ate it and drank an enormous quantity of coffee. The police guarded the building. One hundred and fifty spectators were admitted; they took their seats before the scaffold. As the soldiers lined up and paraded in the courtyard, Guiteau heard the rattling of their muskets and wept bitterly. They pinioned his arms and led him out. He had brushed his hair and was as cool as he could be. He delivered his prayer. It consisted of a spiel of self-exoneration and rage against his blind and misguided executioners. He was quite certain that God was on his side. They put the rope around his neck. He then declared to the crowd that he would recite some verses. He took out a piece of paper on which his poem was written. 'The idea,' he informed them, 'is that of a child babbling to his mama and papa.' He then intoned the verses: 'I am going to Lordy; I am so glad that I am going to Lordy; I am so glad I am going to Lordy; glory hallelujah! glory hallelujah!' There was much more in the same vein. As he recited, he began to break down; but then he rallied and went on again with his poem. 'I saved my party and my land; glory hallelujah! but they have murdered me for it, and that is the reason I am going to Lordy; glory hallelujah! glory hallelujah! I am going to Lordy.'[167] Then he dropped the paper and cried out, 'Glory, ready, go!' And with the idiocy of those last words still ringing in the air, the doors beneath his feet opened and he plummeted through them. In the instant his neck broke and he died at once.

They exhibited his skull to interested spectators in Washington's Army Medical Museum. But then, that October, someone stole the thing. Such was the end of Guiteau.

A Killing in the Park

I: Murderers Among Us

In 1867, just as the Nihilists endorsed extreme measures in Russia, Irish political violence was launched in Britain, as nationalists struggled against colonial rule. That autumn at Balmoral there were rumours of 'Fenian' attacks planned on the Queen herself. A detachment from the 93rd Highlanders was dispatched to protect her.[1] Then, in Manchester, a policeman guarding a prison van was shot and a bomb exploded at London's Clerkenwell prison causing horrendous damage. However, both events were planned, not as terrorist outrages or as assassinations, but as prison breaks.[2] In London, they simply used too much explosive; had the convicts who were hoping to escape been exercising in the prison yard, they would unquestionably have died. The destruction was extensive: sixty feet of prison wall was blown down, along with the tightly packed houses opposite; the blast killed seventeen people and many more were blinded or maimed. Children were among the dead and wounded. The city was alarmed; as many as 5,000 special constables enlisted in London alone.[3] Such violence was foreign to British experience; for analogies, people had to look to France.[4]

Only days after the explosion, fears increased that the Fenians were plotting to kidnap the Queen, or even perhaps carry out the 'graver design of assassination'.[5] The danger, it was suggested, was greatest at Osborne House on the Isle of Wight; she would certainly be safer in London. Behind the government's anxiety for the Queen were traces of their desire to draw her out of her self-imposed isolation. Victoria undoubtedly sensed this, as she replied to the request with a firm assurance that she would be quite as safe at Osborne as anywhere else, had no intention of moving, and advocated the suspension of Habeas Corpus as a way of dealing with the Fenian outrages.[6] The Earl of

Derby wrote back that they would prefer not to cause 'so serious an infraction of the liberty of a whole people for the sake of punishing a few desperate conspirators'.[7] A story reached the Queen's ears of two ships loaded with Fenians sailing from New York with the intention of coming to Britain and murdering her. Victoria understandably 'could not help feeling nervous and upset'.[8] Yet the precautions taken to increase her safety were themselves such as seemed to render her 'little better than a *State prisoner*'.[9] It was proving difficult to balance the need for protection and the individual's freedom.

Three of the group responsible for the failed escape and the killing of the policeman in Manchester were publicly hanged. The Queen approved of the sentences, but in Ireland there were many who abhorred the punishment. None of the three who died had deliberately murdered anyone; the policeman was killed accidentally, and two of the condemned men were to be hanged for no greater crimes than wounding and the shooting of horses. Other luckier men involved in the incidents were released early, in 1877. In the Parliamentary debate concerning these releases both Isaac Butt and Gladstone himself remarked that it would be wrong to take the deaths resulting from the bomb itself as being deliberate murder. Set free with them was Michael Davitt. Davitt (1846–1906) was a one-armed old campaigner with the Irish Republican Brotherhood (the IRB). He had been imprisoned in 1870 when implicated in a planned assassination of an informer, although in the incriminating letter Davitt had only attempted to dissuade the assassin from striking.

On his release Davitt made contact with another prominent Irish political figure, Charles Stewart Parnell (1846–91). Parnell was an unlikely partner for the Fenian revolutionary and despiser of landlords. He was himself a landlord, aristocratic in origin, Protestant in religion, a shy and apparently ineffectual chap who loved cricket and hunting. He was a poor orator and a plodding thinker. From this unlikely chrysalis would emerge the most significant and improbably charismatic Irish politician of the later nineteenth century; unselfconscious himself, he was fated to become an emblem for others. While at Cambridge University, Parnell had perceived the political rewards of violence; later, in a speech given at Manchester in July 1877, he argued that the concession of the disestablishment of the Church of Ireland had been won by the bomb

in Clerkenwell and the shooting in Manchester.[10] Yet Parnell's aim was
to achieve Irish Home Rule through constitutional means, even though
those means often entailed obstructionist and delaying tactics in the
House of Commons. Davitt was more sympathetic to the violence,
believing that its roots grew from the injustices of the political order.[11]
He was prepared to work with Parnell, but he would not relinquish the
possibility of the necessity for armed struggle.

Meanwhile the Royal Family's exposure to Irish violence had
not ended with the events of 1867. On 12 March 1868, there was an
assassination attempt on Prince Alfred, Duke of Edinburgh, while he
was visiting the Australian colonies; news didn't reach England until
mid-May. The incident took place at a fête in Sydney, a day of crowds
and a display by around 300 aborigines. The Prince was wandering
close to the fringe of gum trees, when he was shot in the back at close
quarters by an Irishman, Henry James O'Farrell, the bullet striking his
body below the chest, only half an inch from the spine. O'Farrell shot
again, but the bullet went wide, and he was preparing to fire for the
third time, in order to shoot himself, when he was brought down by a
bystander. The shot instead hit someone running up to help the Prince,
passing through the man's foot. At the trial, it was hard to determine
whether the motivation for the assault was insanity or Fenianism,
though in the end it was agreed (or found expedient to agree) that the
man was simply crazed. The prospect of a disloyal colony was a hard
one to contemplate. Nonetheless the Prince did not go on to visit New
Zealand as planned, a decision partly motivated by news of Fenian
sympathy on the islands. (This included a 'funeral' for effigies of the
Manchester Martyrs at Hokitika.[12]) O'Farrell was found guilty, and
sentenced to be hanged.

In 1872, the murder of Lord Mayo in India seemed to offer a
promising precedent to the Irish people. The *Leinster Independent*
carried an article inciting, or at least endorsing, assassination:

Its purport is that a vanquished people, like the Poles, the Irish, or the Hindoos,
inevitably have recourse to what is termed the wild justice of revenge. They
become assassins. The sense of justice is outraged by the subjugation of a nation
. . . Hence justice stimulates slaves into homicide, but there is this difference, that
while the Irishman invariably strikes down the agent, the Hindoo aims at the
principal. The Irishman imitates the dog which runs after the stone and foolishly

bites the missile. The Hindoo flies at the throat of the stone-thrower and rends out his vitals.

The Times was outraged: the 'effect of such teaching as this is not neutralized by a few cold words which follow, deprecating assassination'.[13]

On 29 February 1872, just a few weeks after the assassination of Lord Mayo, there was another embarrassing attack on the Queen. Only a couple of days earlier Victoria had been greatly moved by the celebrations for the Prince of Wales's recovery from illness. The Queen was in the inner courtyard of Buckingham Palace, returning from a drive around London's parks, when a boy ran up and endeavoured to catch her attention. In one hand he held a sheet of paper, and in the other a pistol. He apparently tried to assault the Queen, but was prevented from getting to her by John Brown, her faithful Scottish manservant. The boy's name was Arthur O'Connor, and he was the great-nephew of Feargus O'Connor, the Chartist agitator. He was seventeen years old, tall and slim. Prolonged ill health accounted for the slenderness: he had been a patient in Great Ormond Street Hospital and King's College Hospital.[14] He had clambered over the Palace walls, and then made his way through the gardens to the courtyard. The gun turned out to be unloaded, and of such bad quality that even if loaded it could not have been fired. Distress at Irish grievances had prompted the episode. The boy's paper was a petition regarding Fenian prisoners, which he had wanted Victoria to sign. Many in Ireland who disapproved of the attempt were quick to point out that O'Connor was by birth a Londoner.

The Queen had panicked. Victoria's gratitude to her servant Brown was immense. And though scared by what might have happened if the gun had been loaded, the next day she felt enough pity for O'Connor to refer to him in her journal as 'the wretched boy'.[15] Flogging was one possible punishment for his crime – something at which, understandably enough, O'Connor appeared terrified.[16] After the Queen's intervention, O'Connor was spared corporal punishment, though he lost his freedom.

Young O'Connor's dejected attempt at violence was a presage of things to come. The end of the 1870s brought an agricultural depression in both Britain and Ireland. Everywhere relations between landlord and tenant soured.[17] In Ireland poor conditions and hostilities were pressed to the limit. In 1879, rain ruined the Irish harvest, aggravating the already poor condition of peasant tenants. While Ulster landlords introduced measures of rent relief, in the rest of Ireland there was to be no remission. Memories of the terrible famine of the late 1840s revived; the overhanging shame and anxiety produced by those memories coloured the violence that was to come. Landowners seized the opportunity to create unpayable rent arrears, and so evict troublesome tenants. In 1879, evictions doubled, and the next year they doubled again.[18] The government failed to ease the situation. Yet distress created a political opportunity; the Land League seized it.

Established in Ireland in 1879, the Land League helped to organise what amounted to a social revolution. The League's development owed much to Davitt and Parnell's leadership. Its origins lay in economic distress; its ostensible object was the betterment of tenant rights. Yet it remains a matter of historical debate whether ordinary people joined the League for political or economic reasons. The leadership certainly had political aims, and saw the League as a means to bind together palpable grievance and a nationalist agenda. It seems likely that tenants were most anxious about their livelihoods. Since his release from prison, Michael Davitt had thrown himself into the land agitation, seeking the end of landlordism, which he wanted replaced by land nationalisation. As chief of the movement, in a series of incendiary speeches across Ireland Parnell declared that tenants should resist eviction, be free to sell their own properties, pay less rent or even pay no rent at all. The other leading figures were prepared to go as far or even further than Parnell. Davitt and others were arrested for seditious speech, but the cases were dropped before they could go to court.

As conditions worsened, agrarian violence increased. Such militant action had a long-standing tradition in Ireland, going back at least as far as the Whiteboys and Ribbonmen of the 1830s. The land system's injustices and the coercion used to protect that injustice fostered violence. The rebels' techniques followed traditional patterns: 'the arms-raid, the threatening letter, the disguised visit at midnight, the mutilation of animals as well as people'.[19] Yet there is evidence that the revival of violence in the few years beginning in 1879 was more apparent than real. Whatever the case, there is no doubt that it was precisely the appearance of violence that mattered. The press reported murders, assaults and threats; an atmosphere of orchestrated outrage formed. Most particularly some victims' high social status exacerbated the impression of a state of emergency.

A General Election in 1880 ousted Benjamin Disraeli's Tories, and brought in a Liberal government headed by William Gladstone. The new Chief Secretary for Ireland was W. E. Forster. Forster was a wealthy businessman and a bluff, no-nonsense and somewhat radical politician; his nickname (suggested by his ungainly physique and hairiness) was the 'Gorilla'. He counted Thomas Carlyle and the Christian socialist F. D. Maurice among his friends; Matthew Arnold, the poet and critic, was his brother-in-law. As a private citizen, Forster had visited Ireland during the famine, and had done his bit to alleviate conditions there. Forster was an able and civilised man, but a disastrous choice. He failed to change anything and refused to deal with Parnell, despising the Irish leader as no better than a thug.

Meanwhile the number of evictions escalated. But the resistance offered by the Land League made the evictors' work more perilous. Forster reported to Parliament that in some instances as many as a hundred policemen were required to protect one process-server, and two hundred to manage an actual eviction.[20] The government-sponsored Bessborough Commission called for support for the tenants' demands. Attempts to ameliorate the condition of evicted tenants in Ireland with a Compensation Bill merely aroused the consternation of the landed interest in Parliament; Lord Lansdowne resigned over the issue. Where aristocratic power depended upon property rights, there could be little room for leeway: the House of Lords voted against the proposed bill by 282 votes to 51.[21]

The government's failure created a power vacuum. Something had to be done, and the Land League was there to do it. With the support of tenants and the priesthood, the weight of public opinion was behind them. Following the defeat of the Compensation Bill, Parnell initiated a campaign of shunning those who profited from the land crisis. In Mayo, the 'sending to Coventry' of a Captain Boycott introduced a new word to the English language. The inventive tactic of boycotting existed in parallel with more traditional methods; murders and other acts of violence also increased. Forster attempted to prosecute Parnell and thirteen other leading figures in the Land League, but the trial came to nothing and the violence continued. Symbolically, the key murder – among the spate of killings – was that of an aristocrat and landlord, one Lord Mountmorres.

The blow fell in September 1880. Mountmorres was a signally unpopular landlord on the borders of Mayo and Galway. A dispute had arisen over lambs that he considered some malefactor had wilfully drowned. Recently an escort of policemen had guarded him, but growing tired of their presence, he decided to trust instead to a revolver he kept in his pocket.[22] On Saturday 25 September, Mountmorres drove into Clonbur, a village of some twenty houses. The next day, a Land League meeting was to be held; he made enquiries about what was expected.

It was mid-afternoon. He mounted his single-horse open carriage and set off on the road between the village and his home at Ebor Hall on the northern shore of Lough Corrib. There was plenty of cover for his murderer among the broken stone walls and the scattered rocks that lined the road. When the assault came, Mountmorres was only half a mile from home.[23] The attack must have been swift and unexpected: he had had no time to pull his gun from his breast-pocket and defend himself. There was very likely only one assailant. The gunman came close enough for black traces of gunpowder to be clearly visible around the wound in Mountmorres's head, even dusted across his eyebrows; it seems the killer administered a *coup de grâce*. All six of the gunman's bullets had found their target. After the shooting, when Mountmorres had fallen to the earth, the horse trotted away, taking the carriage on down to the lodge-house. The lord lay there bleeding. A villager came by, saw the body, but believing it was a drunk left him there.

For a while, Mountmorres's men waited for him, thinking he had chosen to walk the rest of the journey home. But he never came. They searched for him, until they found his body lying in his blood on the road. Amazingly some signs of life still lingered, and they took his body to a local farm, attempting to revive the dying man. But Hugh Flanagan, the farmer, would not allow them to cross the threshold; he was too scared of what the consequences might be for himself and his family. Mountmorres died in the open ground of the yard.

Many supposed that Mountmorres had been assassinated because he was a lord; it was more likely merely the death of another landlord. Yet an attack directly on the Irish aristocracy raised spectres of revolution that unnerved the government. The policy of coercion would continue, and ultimately under its remit assassinations took place that would render Mountmorres's murder insignificant indeed. Four men were arrested, but released without charge, due to lack of sufficient evidence.[24] Meanwhile the Land League denied all charges of involvement. A bad landlord had been killed in hard times; there was little reason to suppose that such a deed required an organised body to have arranged it. On the Sunday when the people gathered for the promised Land League meeting, one of the bands sarcastically played the Dead March from *Saul* as they passed the courthouse where Mountmorres's body lay.[25]

II: Advocating Violence: The Fenians

Queen Victoria was fretting about events in Ireland and, more significantly, about the Irish in America: from Balmoral Castle, on 15 June 1881, in response to specific threats, she wrote the following letter:

The Queen thanks Mr. Gladstone for his letters of yesterday and the day before. She is glad that measures are being taken to bring this monstrous language of the Irish Rebel Fenians before the United States Government, as it is *not* right, to say the very least, to allow such things to be published in a country professing friendship for Great Britain and on friendly terms with her. It is worse than the *Freiheit*; as the incitement to assassination is more *positively* directed against *persons whose names are given*. Why should the Prince of Wales be pointedly pointed out and not herself, or is the Queen also condemned? In *America generally* she is a *great favourite*, she knows. The Prince of Wales' people should be warned and he himself to be careful (which he is not) into what company he gets. Mr. Gladstone, the Queen trusts, will also be careful. The doubts about the *Dotterel* and the boast of O'Donovan Rossa, as well as the tacit agreement of Mr. Parnell in their horrible ideas and practices, taken together with what happened at Liverpool [a cache of dynamite had been discovered], are very disagreeable circumstances; as even if they are *not* true they will keep us in constant anxiety.[26]

The Queen's disquiet concerning Jeremiah O'Donovan Rossa was not misplaced; nor was 1881 the last time he would personally threaten the Prince of Wales. In 1887, after an assassination attempt on the

Prince by a crazed Englishwoman, O'Donovan Rossa responded by broadcasting a $10,000 reward for the first person to take him, dead or alive. Since 1875, lately in his journal *The United Irishman*, he had been publicly advocating violent measures against Britain, including dynamite attacks on public buildings and the assassination of public figures. In his view the Irish should 'Burn everything English, except her coals'.[27] He later announced that '"a verdict of murder" had been returned against Mr. Gladstone and that "four Irishmen had volunteered to carry out the verdict"'; Ireland would be freed by the 'sword alone'.[28] These ideas were still unpopular with the majority of nationalists and republicans, though the suppression of the peasantry during the Land War would soon cause many to adopt his views.[29] In 1880, O'Donovan Rossa formed the 'United Irishmen of America', an incendiary organisation, though in fact a rather negligible group of about a couple of hundred adherents.[30]

To the British, O'Donovan Rossa stood out as the epitome of Irish bloodthirstiness, the embodiment of the 'Fenian' desire for vengeance. The Fenian Brotherhood had been founded in New York in 1858, as an American organisation intended to work in tandem with the Ireland-based IRB (variously Irish Republican or Irish Revolutionary Brotherhood).[31] 'Fenian' was therefore initially a term coined in America, and a concept dependent upon an American distance from Irish affairs.[32] The Irish in America, displaced by famine or poverty, had been cut free from the chains of expedient acquiescence with British rule; as such they were ideally placed to resist that rule.[33] In 1866 and 1870, there were a pair of feeble invasions of British-ruled Canada, quixotic adventures designed to spark a greater war between the USA and Britain (a war which would enable, it was hoped, open rebellion in Ireland). During the 1870s, the Fenians had been replaced by Clan na Gael, an equally hardline outfit similarly hoping to pursue liberty by violent means. Although, by the late 1870s, the Fenian movement had been largely superseded, the word 'Fenian' continued to be applied indiscriminately to the Invincibles, the United Irishmen, Clan na Gael and IRB men well into the next decade (and indeed beyond).

The conjunction of Irish violence at home and Nihilist violence in Russia meant that 'Fenians' and Nihilists could easily be seen as parallel cases. From the late 1870s, 'Fenians' and Nihilists began to be grouped together by journalists. In September 1881, it was reported, with perhaps questionable accuracy, that throughout Castlebar in Ireland a placard had been distributed calling on the 'Nihilists of Castlebar!', declaring 'Nihilism is not confined to Russia' and signed by 'CAPTAIN (on behalf of the Irish Nihilists)'. The same placard promised 'Perdition to Victoria', a clear incitement to assassination, and an obvious reference to the recent murder of the Tsar.[34] In the autumn of 1881 newspapers carried the story that the 'Irish Nihilists' had vowed to embark on a programme of assassination and bombings.[35]

At the trial of Parnell in January 1881, the defence counsel had specifically to deny that there was anything resembling the Nihilist in the Land League.[36] The IRB may have seen themselves as adopting Nihilist tactics; in a report by Sir Robert Anderson, the head of the Criminal Investigation Department (CID), a source is quoted saying that they intended to adopt 'a system of warfare characterized by all the rigours of Nihilism'.[37]

Nihilists resembled 'Fenians' above all in the fact that each were committed to a project whose limits were circumscribed by the idea of the nation. However, the international basis of Irish identity in the later nineteenth century – the product of over seventy years of emigration – also lent to the 'Fenians' something of the Anarchist and Communist cosmopolitanism. The fact of the Irish diaspora internationalised the movement. There were Irish nationalists at work in most of the English-speaking colonies, and particularly in the USA, as well as in Paris and the islands of Britain itself. International in scope and organisation, nonetheless in practice the 'Fenians' were very different from their Anarchist counterparts. Although widely dispersed, they all looked towards a nationalist idea of home: their own beleaguered and suffering island. The exile of Russian political refugees had a similar effect on the Nihilist movement; a national struggle planted adherents across the globe.

It was the extremity of men such as O'Donovan Rossa that laid the Irish nationalists open to the charge of being 'Nihilists'. Though his views were apparently minority ones within the nationalist movement, there was in fact in those years, 1878–82, a pronounced shift towards physical force. In August 1881, less than two months after the Anarchists in London opted for propaganda by the deed as a political tactic, at 'the Great Dynamite Convention' in Chicago, the Irish nationalist republicans in America apparently followed suit. Angered by news of British brutality in Ireland, the mood at the conference was strongly in favour of a show of direct action. Once again the influence of the Russians' extreme tactics was felt: 'It was to be a warfare characterised by all the rigours of Nihilism.'[38] There were direct calls for assassination. Terence Powderly, the usually circumspect President of the Knights of Labor (the workers' organisation), proclaimed:

The killing of English robbers and tyrants in Ireland, and the destruction by any and all means of their capital and resources, which enables them to carry on their robberies and tyrannies, is not a needless act. Hence I am in favour of the torch for their cities and the knife for their tyrants till they agree to let Ireland severely alone.[39]

The convention was choosing the methods of warfare, both open and clandestine, bomb plots and tyrannicides. Though no explicit resolution was passed, there was no doubt that the movement was ready for the adoption of direct – in other words, violent – action.

However, this was one moment where broad American support for Irish rebellion was at its weakest. Guiteau's shooting of President Garfield had sickened the nation, and compromised support for political violence. The discovery that a shipment of weapons and explosives had been intended to leave the USA for Liverpool dismayed many: the American correspondent for *The Times* (of course, hardly a neutral witness) reported: 'Guiteau's pistol had made the American nation keenly alive to the enormity of the crime of assassination and this dynamite plot, coming on top of the other, meets the sternest rebuke.'[40]

The American involvement in Irish violence was part of the very cosmopolitanism of assassination that Americans themselves most feared. Just as in time the nation was to terrify itself with the bogeyman of the immigrant assassin, Irish Americans were quite openly working for international political violence. Yet when, within a year, the most stunning act of political violence struck, it would emerge from a revolutionary group almost unheard of in America – the Invincibles.

III: Phoenix Park

Brought unexpectedly back from retirement by the election victory of 1880, Gladstone was looking for a suitable opportunity to step down. But the right moment was forever postponed.[41] Events constantly bustled the government onwards into scenarios of desperation, and Gladstone's chance of a withdrawal from public life likewise receded. Ireland overtook him; the situation there was hardly one where he could afford to take his hands from the reins. His instincts were divided between a sense of the landlord's sacred duties (his holding the land in trust, a place maintained jointly by landlord and tenant) and a belief in the efficacy of the free market. For once, the tension between these views ceased to work productively. The British government's tactic was to marginalise the political leaders of the Land League, while trying to better the situation through well-meaning reform. Parnell seemed the chief enemy, and inevitably they began to move against him.

As far as Forster was concerned, the disturbances in Ireland were something that simply called for stricter policing and harsher measures against a few bad apples and 'village ruffians'.[42] Gladstone considered this naïve. The agitation of the Land League amounted to a social revolution; it was hardly a problem that the suspension of Habeas Corpus would solve. For a while, the government battled on, mingling repression with reform. But the situation was not improving. A Coercion Act was brought in that promoted injustice while failing to impede the violence; and then a Land Act was passed in 1881, apparently radical in its measures, full of good intentions, and yet that, in the short term at least, pleased few.[43]

Then Michael Davitt was arrested again for breach of terms of his 'ticket-of-leave', or, in other words, his parole. The move was unjustified, and a Commons protest against it led to the suspension of thirty-six Irish MPs. Forster opted to lock up the political leaders of the League, believing that without their control the violence would decrease; this merely revealed his fundamental misunderstanding of the grass-roots nature of the disturbances.[44] Nonetheless, on 13 October 1881, under the terms of the recently introduced Coercion Act, Parnell was arrested. At least the action pleased Queen Victoria: she wrote to Gladstone declaring the move was a 'great thing'.[45] Three other Land

League leaders were apprehended: John Dillon, Thomas J. Sexton and James Joseph O'Kelly. The arrests provoked immediate strife: battles with the police and riots in Dublin followed. Probably without the active support of Parnell, though he signed his name to the deed, the leaders in jail in Kilmainham issued a proclamation that tenants should pay no rent (the 'No Rent Manifesto'). As a policy this was a failure; the priests preached against it and the tenants paid their rents. Yet the main force of the Land League's stance held. The tenacity and courage of local associations to stand both against the demands of obdurate landlords and the tyrannous tactics of the police led many in government to realise that nothing would come except through negotiation.

During 1881, a still more radical group emerged from among the ranks of the Irish Republican Brotherhood. They would call themselves 'The Invincibles', and they would push the project of political violence in directions that the wider movement abhorred.[46] It is possible that through an agent named Timothy Brennan there was some influence from the American 'Fenians', with their recent commitment to violence.[47] According to the historian Owen McGee, it seems that the group may likewise have been indirectly advised by John McCafferty, who had been a member of a Confederate Army unit that had planned to kidnap Abraham Lincoln. The links are speculative. McCafferty had since advocated the kidnapping of British public officials, and with the imprisonment of the Land League leaders may have done so again, on this occasion in the USA to P. J. (Patrick Joseph) Sheridan and Patrick Tynan. Sheridan and Tynan may well have passed on McCafferty's ideas when they visited Dublin in late 1881, bringing funds to help the 'no-rent' movement – funds that the Invincibles would appropriate for ends of their own, though it is possible, of course, that Sheridan and Tynan were fully in the know that the cash would in fact be used to bank-roll an assassination.[48]

The Invincibles hoped to dispense with the tyrants of the country; from among these tyrants, Earl Cowper, the Viceroy of Ireland, and Forster would be the first to be removed. Later the name of Thomas Henry Burke, the Under-Secretary, and a hated figure among nationalists since he began his work for Dublin Castle in the late 1840s, was added to the list.[49] In ways remarkably similar to the Anarchists' faith in 'propaganda by the deed', the Invincibles' policy was to pursue 'perpetual action'.

They also followed the example of Mazzini, the Italian republican conspirator, in so far as they believed that conspiracy itself might liberate Ireland.[50] The Invincibles included an initial core of John Walsh, James Mullett, Daniel Curley, Edward McCaffrey and James Carey. Carey was a prominent citizen, a member of committees and a respectable and solvent landlord. Later, other nationalists were recruited from the solid and respectable working class: Peter Doyle, for instance, was a coach-builder. Among the other foot-soldiers were a publican, a shoemaker, a number of carpenters and a minor clerk. (McCaffrey himself drove a mineral-water van.) Another recruit, Joe Brady, was something different – a stonecutter by profession, but also a young man who had come out of the Dublin tenements, one of a family of twenty-five children.[51] Patrick Tynan may have joined, though if he did, it was probably merely in the role of go-between; P. J. Sheridan perhaps also signed up with Carey, meeting him incognito as a priest (a favourite disguise) and advising him of plans to murder government officials.[52]

Altogether there were fifty men in the organisation in Dublin. Soon they set to work. They murdered a police informer, named Bernard Bailey, then shot another innocent man, and botched the bombing of Dublin Castle.[53] They thought of buying a house on Cork Hill in order to give themselves a clean shot at Earl Cowper. They scouted the grounds of Phoenix Park. The park was a product of Restoration Ireland and the return of royalist exiles from Paris, Brussels and Amsterdam, invigorated by their spell abroad and determined to turn Dublin into a real capital city.[54] On one side of the park was the Viceroy's residence; it was bordered to the south by the road that ran along the north bank of the Liffey from Dublin to Chapelizod. It seemed an ideal venue for a murder.

Ignorant as it was of these conspiratorial developments, the government finally recognised that the policy of imprisonment had failed. By early 1882 about a thousand Irishmen had been arrested, many of them imprisoned without trial.[55] The policy had enraged Irish popular opinion, while removing from the situation those responsible leaders who had acted as a brake on the movement's potential for violence. The result was rather an increase in disorder than its lessening. As Parnell put it, his absence left 'Captain Moonlight' in command.[56] Moreover, while intended to eradicate violence, coercion was itself violent. To take only one example, in October 1881, a demonstration at Belmullet by Land League supporters, consisting mostly of women and children, was savagely suppressed; as well as many who were severely wounded, one woman, Mary Deane, was shot down and another, Ellen McDonagh, stabbed to death from behind.[57]

The coercion had an air of fluster and cruelty. One Major Clifford Lloyd circulated a document which exonerated in advance anyone who killed a potential assassin. It was an extraordinary gesture, and one in obvious breach of the law. The government stepped in and repudiated the letter.[58] Meanwhile some ostentatiously bellicose men such as Major Traill (a Resident Magistrate) were arming themselves in preparation to repel attack; Forster approved such freelance methods of self-defence.[59] A letter bomb was sent to Forster, but discovered in good time.[60] The violence also threatened to migrate to Britain itself. In March 1881, there was an attempt to blow up the Mansion House in London, apparently only foiled by a policeman noticing the burning package which contained the bomb a few moments before the flame ignited the fuse. The mayhem was getting out of control. Gladstone even wrote to Cardinal Newman, requesting that he use his influence to persuade the Pope to condemn priestly involvement with the land agitation.

In prison, Parnell was made as comfortable as possible, but his frustration was obvious. He was being outflanked by more radical men and women. Meanwhile the government was ready to talk. From his prison cell, and with Captain William Henry O'Shea acting as go-between, Parnell opened negotiations with the Cabinet on the hope of reconciliation over the Land League issue. At one time a hussar, O'Shea was now more prosaically an Irish Home Rule MP, though one who still summoned up the madcap possibility of a cavalry charge.[61] Unknown to most, that February the Captain's wife, Katharine O'Shea, had given birth to Parnell's daughter. The two had been having an affair since the late summer of 1880. Now her husband was acting as a clandestine emissary for the imprisoned Irish leader. (There are doubts as to how much Captain O'Shea knew of the affair at this stage.) The message that O'Shea brought from Parnell was clear: if something could be done over the issue of rent arrears, then Parnell would do all he could to bring about peace.

And then a murder occurred that shocked everyone. W. Barlow Smythe was a landlord of West Meath, though his character in that position is hard to determine: according to some he was a paragon, while others declared that Smythe had become a hated figure among his tenants, and knew that there was a threat to his life.[62] On Sunday 2 April 1882 Smythe was on his way home from church; with him in the carriage were Mrs Henry Smythe his sister-in-law, and Lady Harriet Monck. The presence of women was supposed to render a potential male victim safe, as it was understood that no agitator would endanger a woman's life. (This very taboo was soon to save the life of Forster himself.) But on this occasion, the assassins had no such compunction. Three masked men came up to the carriage, their faces blackened, and fired inside before running off. The shots missed their intended target, but Mrs Smythe was struck horribly on the left side of her head and died in the instant. She was a gracious and popular figure in Dublin society, and a mother of a young family too.[63] The landowning class in Ireland was horrified. And many were clear as to who was ultimately responsible for the murder. On 3 April, W. B. Smythe wrote a public letter to Gladstone himself: 'I lay the guilt of the deed of blood at your door in the face of the whole country.'[64] In his view, the supposed policy of appeasing the tenants while coercing the Land League's leaders was demonstrably failing. The Prime Minister appears to have learnt a different lesson from the killing, and from the string of agrarian murders committed since April 1881: the legislation so far passed had done nothing to reduce the death toll.[65] Something new had to be brought forward.

Following Parnell's approaches, Gladstone and his Cabinet colleague Joseph Chamberlain saw a way forward. They would move towards a rapprochement with the Irish leader. It is hard to characterise Gladstone's policy at this moment, and to do so may necessarily involve taking sides. One image of Gladstone is that of a man of deep conscience and religious convictions, slow to come to views, but tenacious in holding them. Another is that he was a political opportunist – putting his weight behind whatever seemed popular or ripe as a means to earn more power.[66] It is likely that he believed the situation one that could be remedied, without recourse to harsh repression.[67] Opportunist or idealist, the crucial thing is that there seemed an opening to create a workable compromise.

But Forster demanded more assurances. The murder of Mrs Smythe had deeply shocked him; she had been a friend. There must be a new and tougher Coercion Act to instil order when the ringleaders were released; in any case there should first be order now in Ireland. There ought also to be guarantees that Parnell and the others would not continue to act illegally. However, unknown to Forster, Parnell had pressing personal, as well as political reasons to seek a rapid compromise. On 10 April, Parnell was released from prison so that he could go to his nephew's funeral in Paris. He took the opportunity to visit Mrs O'Shea at her home in Eltham to see their daughter. While he was in Paris the baby – Claude Sophie – fell seriously ill. On 19 April Parnell returned from Paris to Eltham, and with an extension to his parole, began to press for a break in the deadlock. Kitty O'Shea tended the dying girl. His lover's unhappiness was one more reason for Parnell to secure his release from prison.[68] In the meantime, there was nothing else to be done but to return the next day to Kilmainham jail.

On 22 April, a Cabinet meeting was to be held to discuss the issue of Parnell's release. Forster had to cross over from Ireland for the discussion. As he did so, a plot to assassinate him sprang into action. The Invincibles had chosen their target. For days they had stalked him, looking for an opportunity. One time Forster brushed against one of his would-be assassins in the open street. On his last night in Ireland, a group of fifteen men gathered at Dublin's railway station, and, with full knowledge of Forster's movements, waited to commit their murder. They were to shoot the horses and then the occupants of the carriage.[69] Fortunately for Forster, a last-minute change of plan had him taking the earlier train. They waited until midnight; when the carriage did come, they stopped it, but Forster was apparently not inside; only his wife and daughter were there. The would-be killers moved off, unwilling on moral grounds to risk killing a woman. The assassination attempt therefore passed without the authorities learning of it until several months later, after another more successful effort had been carried to its conclusion.

Knowing nothing of his recent brush with death, at the meeting on the 22nd Forster voiced his opposition to reconciliation with the Land League's leaders; he disliked the surreptitious dealings with O'Shea, and the prospects of negotiating with a scoundrel like Parnell. Forster suspected, probably rightly, that Parnell was not opposed to a bit of righteous brutality. Where Forster was most likely wrong was in believing that Parnell was directly involved in the violence himself. But it was clear in which direction the government was moving. On 28 April, via Captain O'Shea, Parnell passed on a letter to Gladstone declaring that if the Land League leaders were released, an act were passed clearing rent arrears, and the Land Act amended, a way could be found out of the crisis: the violence would cease.[70] On 30 April, Forster met with O'Shea in London.[71] As far as Forster was concerned, Parnell had declared that, having organised outrage, he would now prevent it, if he were set free and this concession made. The Chief Secretary for Ireland set himself against the release. But the rest of the Cabinet were determined to break the deadlock. Another Irish nationalist, John Redmond, had suggested bringing in a bill to deal with rent arrears, a move that would tacitly recognise the Land Act. Joseph Chamberlain was entrusted with the charge of negotiating with Parnell through the mediation of O'Shea.[72] On 2 May 1882, Gladstone announced the release of Parnell and other imprisoned Irish MPs. The release of Davitt (to the horror of the Queen) was announced soon afterwards.[73]

Paul Bew, an authority on Parnell and Irish history, has argued that between the Irish leader's release and his leaving for London, there occurred a highly significant set of meetings in Dublin.[74] Possibly Parnell bumped into P. J. Sheridan, who may or may not have had first-hand knowledge of the Invincibles' assassination plans. The two men wandered into Trinity College Library, where according to T. J. Quinn, who said that he had heard it from Sheridan himself, the 'conversation turned to physical force methods of freeing Ireland'. This could have included, if the meeting indeed occurred and Sheridan was in fact in the know, intimations of the plan to murder Burke. Sheridan may even have inducted Parnell into the IRB.[75] Following Patrick Maume, Bew speculates that, if this swearing-in happened, Parnell may have done so in order 'to control the hard men'.[76] Bew also reports an impassioned outburst by Mr Brady, father of Joe Brady, one of the Invincibles:

It was they [Parnell and the Parnellites] who misled my brave boy. Joe had as good a right to kill Cavendish as others to kill Lord Mountmorres. And Parnell knew

well what was being done, *though all the bridges were cut that might lead up to him.*
Do ye think there could be 500 Land Leaguers in Kilmainham, with everybody
free to see his friends, and not one of them to tell Parnell that brave men had their
knives waiting to kill Forster and coercion?[77]

The moment unveils all the difficulty of writing about such matters.
Mr Brady, the confidential informer, was speaking to the historian
and former politician Frank Hugh O'Donnell, more popularly known
as 'Crank' Hugh O'Donnell, a long-standing enemy of Gladstone.
O'Donnell also despised Parnell. His was hardly a neutral voice. Moreover, setting aside questions of partiality, a conspiracy was being set up
to murder high-ranking officials in the British government in Ireland.
By its very nature this conspiracy was secretive. No one was to know
anything. Is it so persuasive to imagine that such a secret conspiracy
would inevitably be shared with a top-ranking politician who was not
necessarily in favour of such extreme actions? The Invincibles were
a new group, whose vicious tactics would wrong-foot many in the
nationalist movement. It is a measure of the success of their conspiracy
that their plans evaded informers and nay-sayers.

If Forster had known about these putative meetings between Parnell
and the conspirators, he would have felt entirely vindicated. Over
the previous days there had been one last concerted effort to make
the Chief Secretary give in over the matter of the prisoners. On 30
April Gladstone wrote a letter to him, in which he disclosed his own
wonderment about Parnell's overtures.[78] Forster and Gladstone met
again late on May Day night. However, Forster refused to grant any
concession to Parnell; as Gladstone put it, he refused to share 'collective
responsibility' for the Irish leader's release.[79] Visibly deserted by his
colleagues in the House of Commons, who, without intervening,
watched him baited by the Irish MPs, Forster appeared to be an isolated
figure.[80] On 3 May, he resigned as Chief Secretary for Ireland. The next
day, cheered from the Conservative benches, he defended his decision
before a crowded House of Commons; the Prince of Wales sat watching
from among the peers. While he was speaking, Parnell, the man he had
put in prison, walked into the Commons to listen to his declaration.
With him in the chamber were the other two released prisoners, Dillon
and O'Kelly. O'Kelly in particular repeatedly demanded to know – to

the amusement of the House – why Forster had had him put in jail. Forster declined to reply.

The Viceroy of Ireland, Earl Cowper, had been as horrified by the turn of events as Forster was. He had told Gladstone that to release the three prisoners was tantamount to a declaration that the British government could not maintain the rule of law in Ireland without them. He promptly resigned.[81] John Poyntz Spencer succeeded him as Viceroy of Ireland, and on 4 May, a new Chief Secretary for Ireland was appointed. While many expected that Joseph Chamberlain or Sir Charles Dilke would receive the task, the choice instead first fell on Sir Andrew Marshall Porter, the Solicitor-General for Ireland. But Porter refused the job.[82] By 3 May, thoughts had turned to Lord Frederick Cavendish, the husband of Mrs Gladstone's favourite niece, Lucy. It was a family appointment, but without a stain of nepotism. Cavendish was a promising and admirable young man, with an interest in Irish affairs, and already some success as Secretary to the Treasury. He was also the brother of Gladstone's old rival, Lord Hartington; the appointment would have the collateral benefit of healing that breach too.[83] Cavendish was in two minds about accepting. He preferred really to stay with the Treasury. On Horse Guards Parade, Cavendish met by chance Lord Eversley and, voicing his doubts, asked him if he wouldn't rather take the job. Eversley declared that his disapproval of the policy of coercion would require him to know beforehand precisely what the new policy would be before committing himself to such a role.[84] Eversley's scruples left Cavendish still considering his position.

Cavendish had married Lucy Caroline Lyttleton in 1864. She was then a young maid of honour to Queen Victoria and a daughter of a solidly aristocratic and jolly family mostly occupied with county society, Christianity and cricket. She was spirited and chatty, while her husband was silent and dignifiedly morose. Though apparently, therefore, badly matched, in fact they were a notably happy couple. They walked and rode together, and recited poetry to each other; when they were courting Frederick told her how he had shot two buffaloes in America, which made her proud of him.[85] She was gentle and sweet and they lived a life of small excitements: meeting famous writers such as Robert Browning and Thomas Carlyle; waltzing at a ball; taking a trip to the zoo; wondering at the arrival of a telephone at Hawarden Castle.

The only lingering sadnesses were the absence of children of their own and the suicide of Lucy's father during one of the fits of melancholy that darkened his later life.

At the age of forty-six, Lord Frederick Cavendish's career was, as has been said, promising, but it was as yet hardly glittering. He was a mediocre public speaker, suffering as he did from the family lisp; he lacked both the ability and the desire to get the newspapers behind him. He was a quiet, but efficient worker, a man of solid abilities, but hardly a political star. Photographs present a dreamy-eyed chap, the lower half of his face vanishing in a cloud of beard. The younger son of the Duke of Devonshire, there remained over him the unplaced extraneousness of one who does not expect to inherit.

On Saturday 29 April, Lucy met Frederick at the Treasury, and they went away for a few days to Warlies, near Epping Forest. Frederick was worried over events in Ireland. On the Saturday, a gale blew all afternoon and night, but on the Sunday the weather was lovely, and they walked together through the forest.[86] When they arrived back in London, the political establishment were in ferment over events in Ireland. That Tuesday 2 May, Lucy saw nothing of her husband until dinner time. Then he told her that his name was one of those that had been put forward to be the new Chief Secretary. After dinner, Frederick went back to the House of Commons. The next morning, he went to speak to Lord Granville, and put forward the stronger claims of his brother, Lord Hartington, to the post. 'I told him I had no tact, no real knowledge of Ireland, no powers of speaking.'[87] He heard that the post had been offered to Porter, the Irish Solicitor-General. It seemed that he was out of danger. But Porter declined the job. When Frederick came home, he told Lucy, 'Well, I am in for it.'[88]

There was a dinner that night at Sir John Lubbock's. Nothing could be said of the appointment before the Queen had confirmed it. So Lucy studiously talked of other things – in particular of Charles Darwin who had recently been buried in Westminster Abbey. Afterwards there was a party at Downing Street. Here Frederick could feel freer and mentioned the news to some colleagues. Knowing already of the appointment, Lord Rosebery enquired of him, 'Are you going to your martyrdom?'[89]

At the party, Lucy talked to Forster's wife, and found she knew nothing concerning the identity of his successor. Afterwards she chatted with her uncle. Gladstone was sheepish; he felt that she would dislike the move. So she reassured him, and told the old man that they were both very flattered. He was relieved, and in turn sought to please her, saying that she would see no less of her husband. Afterwards Frederick went on talking a long time outside on the street of Carlton House Terrace. All that night he did not sleep.

His father 'hated' the appointment, so much so that Frederick regretted taking it. That night of Thursday 4 May the family all dined together. Frederick himself was worried about Gladstone – Uncle William. The old man had had a great deal to cope with this week. The next morning he walked over to Downing Street with Lucy. They talked about Ireland as they went. He said, 'The more I think of this business, the more sickening it is; to have to go at new Coercion.' Lucy told him, 'If you really do think yourself incompetent for it, you ought to refuse; but if you can't say that, then it must be your duty to accept.' For a moment she almost feared that he would indeed refuse; but instead he merely said, 'Well, as to that, I must let the others judge for me.' It was a beautiful spring day. Together they made plans. Perhaps he might take the night boat-train to Dublin; he could not be sure. Lucy would have to order dinner early just in case.[90] They talked of what it would mean to live in Ireland, and of how their plans must change. In Downing Street they parted. She went visiting, and then popped over to the Treasury to give up the key Frederick had arranged for her.

News of Cavendish's appointment amused or infuriated many. In Ireland, it was greeted with rage and incredulity. Cavendish seemed too insubstantial for such an important job. Rumours began to circulate that he was merely to take the position on a temporary basis, and soon an Irishman would fill the post.[91] In Britain, the appointment was seen as risible. One journal reported the following comments from the lobby of the Houses of Parliament:

'Absolutely absurd!' 'The only reason I can see is that he always speaks as if he had a hot potato in his mouth.' 'No political reputation to lose,' &c. &c. In fact, a broad smile overspread everyone's countenance at the mention of this subject, and it may be that after all the Government are heading for a fall.[92]

Early on the Friday evening, Frederick and Lucy ate together. There was a flurry of packing and finding clean shirts and arranging things.

There was very little time. The train for Ireland left at 8.20 p.m. They kissed each other goodbye. There was nothing particular said. She stood on the doorstep and watched him go in the brougham. He very nearly missed the train.[93]

At 6.00 that same evening, Gladstone met with Captain O'Shea. O'Shea said that all was now on track for putting down the land agitation in Ireland. From the conversation, Gladstone gathered that Parnell had been instrumental in the campaign of violence but was now sincere in the desire of calling a halt to it. The Irish leader's only anxiety appeared to be that he might be ousted by men more violent than himself.[94]

That night, the new Viceroy, Lord Spencer, and Cavendish sailed across to Ireland, and in Dublin the Invincibles gathered at King's Bridge. They had spent part of the day in Phoenix Park waiting to kill Burke. With Forster gone, he was to be the new target. However Burke wasn't at the Lodge in the park; he had gone into town. So it was that evening that there were twenty or so men scattered about the bridge. But Burke did not pass by that night. The men agreed to meet at 10.00 the following morning. And then that Saturday morning, James Carey, one of the Invincibles, thought he saw Burke walk by him on Usher's Quay. But he could not be sure it was the man. Only one of the tyrannicides – Joseph (Joe) Smith who worked at the Castle – knew exactly what Burke looked like. So the two men simply passed each other on the Quay; could it have been Burke?[95]

The murder was already planned, but events at Ballina, County Mayo, that same Friday might well have added to the assassins' determination. Police had fired on a demonstration in celebration of Parnell's release. Many were injured, all of them children, and one twelve-year-old boy, Patrick Melody, was stabbed, and died on his own doorstep.[96]

On Saturday 6 May, Parnell, Dillon and O'Kelly met Michael Davitt at the gates of his prison in Portland, and travelled with him by train back to London. Davitt was furious at the state of Ireland; Parnell thought Home Rule imminent, or at least very likely, and the men laughed and talked about the jobs they would have in a Home Rule government: Davitt would be Inspector of Irish Prisons.[97] By nightfall, the jokes would turn sour.

On the Saturday, Spencer and Cavendish arrived in Dublin, and were greeted by a great pageant. There were flags, parades of soldiers, streamers, a band to play the National Anthem and cheering crowds. It was a beautiful May morning. The Mayor gave the keys of the city to Spencer. That afternoon, in the Privy Council Chamber at Dublin Castle, they swore their new oaths of office. Rockets were fired to signal the close of the ceremony. Then they spent the afternoon in the Viceroy's private apartments in the castle enduring the smiling obstructions of its civil servants. Thomas Henry Burke, now a marked man, worked with them.

While they were signing, James Carey met Joe Smith in Wrenn's public house on Parliament Street. Some of the would-be killers were there too: Joseph Brady, Timothy Kelly, Thomas Caffrey, and Patrick Delaney. They drank very little. There were two cabs for the gang; John Fitzharris, also known as 'Skin the Goat', was driving one, and Michael Kavanagh was driving the other. They put on slouch hats so as to conceal their identities a little. And then they got in – Carey too and Joe Smith – and they passed along the quays and crossed Kingsbridge to the north side of Dublin, and then they drove into Phoenix Park. This was where they had decided to kill Burke; Smith was to point him out to the others. Smith and Carey got out and waited. The park was busy with people strolling in the late May afternoon. Carey went over to watch a game of polo; he had never seen anyone play polo before. Somewhere else, at another part of the pitch, Lord Spencer, the new Viceroy, was likewise pausing to watch the game.[98] The other Invicibles waited some way away. A carriage came for Smith and Carey; its driver, Michael Kavanagh, was 'right enough' at first, but then grew increasingly agitated. Only afterwards did Carey realise it was because he was frightened.[99]

It was 7.05 and still there was no sign of Burke. Joe Smith checked his watch; 'He's not coming,' he said. Then Smith walked up to the turn of the road; there were two men on the path ahead. '"Here's some one; here he is," he said, and he made towards the road.'[100] Carey told Kavanagh to look sharp, and then Smith and Carey got into the car; Kavanagh slipped the nosebag from the horse. They rode through the park; Carey had a white handkerchief in his hand. That was the signal. There were seven men there on the footway: Joseph Brady, Timothy Kelly, Patrick Delaney, Thomas Caffrey, Michael Fagan, Daniel Curley and Joseph Hanlon. They had seen the handkerchief and knew Burke was coming. There were two men walking down the path, one much taller than the other. It was Burke, the tall man, they wanted. 'Curley asked, "Well, is he coming?"' and Carey told him, 'Yes, the man in the grey suit.' Smith had no idea what was happening, and unsure of what he should be doing had stayed in the car. Carey told Smith to go home, and so he left at once. Burke and the man with him were still about 200 yards away. Carey left too, walking over towards Island Bridge. When he was some distance away, Carey turned to watch. The two men walked down the path, until they came to where the seven were waiting for them. The seven opened ranks, and the two passed through. There were three in front, and then four men closed in from behind. Carey saw Joseph Brady bump into Burke, and then raise his left hand and with it strike him in his grey suit. With that Carey had seen enough, and he turned and went.[101]

Tempted by the beauty of the spring evening, at the end of the day's long work, Cavendish had decided to take a walk. So when Spencer left for the Viceroy's Lodge by carriage, Cavendish set off on the same route by foot. Burke left Dublin Castle a little after the others. The three men had planned to eat their evening meal together. The staff at Dublin Castle knew that plots were rife against any high-ranking official, but no guard accompanied them; no watch was kept. Tired out, Burke hailed a cab at the park gate, but he had only gone a little way when he caught up with Cavendish strolling along the wide road in the park.[102] He stopped the carriage, climbed down, and the two men walked on together, arm in arm, conversing companionably.[103] Statues of English statesmen were scattered around the park. The lawns spread out beside them, or sometimes they strolled under trees. Two men on tricycles passed them, heading in the direction of the Phoenix monument. It was by all accounts a lovely, bright spring evening.

A boy named Samuel Jacob out bird-nesting saw the scuffle, and thought it was ruffians wrestling. He watched two of the men fall to the ground, and then three of the others scrambled into a carriage. But a fourth man went up to one of the men lying on the ground, and struck him again.[104] Jacob, who was some distance away, thought he had only hit him with his hand. Then the last man ran and clambered with difficulty into the carriage as it quickly drove off in the direction of Chapelizod. Another man, walking his dogs, likewise saw what he took to be a group of drunks fighting; those people who were gazing from the windows of the Viceregal Lodge thought the men were only playing.

Having completed a circuit of the park, the tricyclists came back and found Cavendish lying bloody on the main road, and Burke a little way off down on the pathway. They cycled as fast as they could to fetch the police from the park gate. It was too late; both men were dead. Burke had received several thrusts in the chest, one from behind into the heart and a savage one into his neck. After death, his throat had been cut deep enough to sever the windpipe. Although he was wearing gloves, his hands were much cut too. Cavendish had several wounds to his torso, most likely the fatal one being a cut under his arm that had pierced into his lungs. Brady's rage and strength must have been considerable; his first slash with the dagger had fractured the bone in Cavendish's arm. Cavendish's face in death looked like one sleeping; only Burke 'showed the agony of a struggle'.[105]

After reaching the Lodge, Lord Spencer had gone out for a brief canter around the park, paused to watch the polo match, and then headed home.[106] He was just then sitting in the Lodge reading newspapers, when repeated shrieks from the park distracted him. The cries cannot have been those of Burke and Cavendish, who had been murdered in an eerie quiet, but rather the shouts of the men who had discovered the bodies. He got up and went outside into the garden, and saw a man leap over the palings that separated the Lodge from the Park. The man shouted that Cavendish and Burke had been killed. Spencer instinctively began to move outside, when one of his household warned him that it might be a ruse to get him into the Park.[107] He himself speculated if the site of the murder had been chosen as 'the only part of the main drive of the park which was within view of the windows of his private sitting-room'.[108]

As Brady had struck Burke, Cavendish had called him a ruffian and hit him with his umbrella. This gentlemanly action was to prove fatal. Brady was angered, and had stabbed him in the arm. Burke had fallen to the ground. They set upon Cavendish, killing him. Brady walked over to where Cavendish was lying, and stabbed him once again. Then he strode over and calmly slit Burke's throat. He wiped the blade on the grass, threw the knife into the carriage and climbed inside. They had not planned to kill Cavendish; it was a sheer fluke.

IV: The Hand of the Assassin

Sir William Harcourt, the Home Secretary, was the first in the government
to hear the news, receiving two telegrams. The first declared that Burke
had died, and Cavendish was seriously wounded; the second carried news
of Cavendish's death. Harcourt dispatched Gladstone's private secretary
to break the news to the Prime Minister.[109] Gladstone and his wife
had been at a dinner at the Austrian Embassy. They had left separately.
Mrs Gladstone took the carriage home, her husband choosing to walk.
According to London gossip, he was accompanied by, was indeed arm-
in-arm with, a pretty woman he had met at the Embassy.[110] When he
came back home, in the hall, his secretary, Edward Walter Hamilton,
told him the intelligence from Dublin.

Gladstone and his wife left at once for Carlton House Terrace to see
their niece. But she had already learned everything.[111] Lucy Cavendish
had offered a prayer for Fred that morning that he might find good
guidance. There had been visitors, people to talk over the new
appointment and all that it might mean for them both. In the afternoon, she had gone to Westminster Abbey; again she had knelt down
and prayed for her husband. From her carriage, she saw a newspaper
placard with a notice of some boys killed by the police in Ireland. The
news upset her. Freddy was going to have a lot to deal with in his new
job. She had met Forster's wife again, and they had talked of the duties
of a Chief Secretary and a Chief Secretary's wife. That night she stayed
at home. She read a letter from an uncle in which he extravagantly
praised his own children. And she thought how sad it was that Fred had
never had children, and that all his good qualities had not passed down
to them. At midnight her sister-in-law, Louisa Egerton, came in, and
Lucy looked up and as soon as she saw her face, fear seized her. There
was very bad news. Freddy was dangerously wounded. There was still
hope then, but then her sister, Meriel Talbot, came, with more word,
and there was no more hope.

When Uncle William arrived:

[She] saw his face, pale, sorrow-stricken, but like a prophet's in its look of faith
and strength. He came up and almost took me in his arms, and his first words
were, 'Father, forgive them, for they know not what they do.' Then he said to me,
'Be assured it will not be in vain,' and across all my agony there fell a bright ray of

hope, and I saw in a vision Ireland at peace, and my darling's life-blood accepted as a sacrifice for Christ's sake, to help to bring this to pass.[112]

She insisted that no one should feel that it was wrong for Freddy to have been sent to Ireland.

Well did Dean Church say that no Roman or Florentine lady ever uttered a more heroic thing than was said by this English lady when on first seeing Mr. Gladstone that terrible midnight she said, 'You did right to send him to Ireland.'[113]

Her religion sustained her; she had the feeling of 'falling down a precipice of grief, but with the feeling of *falling soft*'.[114]

Although 'this grief lay heavy & stunning upon us', Gladstone had too much to do to dwell upon Freddy's death. All Sunday he worked on Irish affairs. Forster apparently offered his services as Chief Secretary, but unsurprisingly was passed over in favour of Sir George Otto Trevelyan.[115] In the evening, Gladstone met Lucy again, and found her 'marvellous in the armour of a Christian heroism'. Last thing at night, he read a book on the prophets of Israel.[116]

On the Monday afternoon, the House of Commons was packed. Most MPs, including Parnell and the other Irish members, were dressed in mourning. When Gladstone addressed the House, he was pale, and his voice faltering and so slow that it seemed that he would at any moment fall silent.[117] He spoke first of the loss of Burke. And then, he turned to the murder of Frederick Cavendish.

The hand of the assassin has come nearer home; and though I feel it difficult to say a word, yet I must say that one of the very noblest hearts in England has ceased to beat, and has ceased at the very moment when it was just devoted to the service of Ireland, full of love for that country, full of hopes for her future, full of capacity to render her service.[118]

He had died a noble death. It was reported that some 500 years before an ancestor of Lord Cavendish's had been murdered by another set of rebels led by Wat Tyler.[119]

The House was adjourned out of respect for the two dead men. Perhaps 30,000 people, including 300 MPs, attended Cavendish's funeral at Edensor, in Derbyshire, the family's ancestral burial-place. Meanwhile the press squirmed over the flippant comments they had made about Cavendish only the day before the killing (many of these appearing in print on the very day he was murdered). *Punch* issued the following apology, bordered by black mourning lines: 'Something was written on this page of the Diary about Lord Frederick Cavendish's appointment to the Chief Secretaryship. But the friendly jest is blotted out by the bloody hands that struck down this blameless, kindly gentleman, even as he touched the shores of Ireland, bearer of the olive branch of peace.'[120] Cavendish had metamorphosed from a joke into a martyr.

Parnell was distraught. He had been outflanked, and in a way he could not have predicted. He even considered, it would appear, resigning from public life.[121] He was persuaded to stay on by Chamberlain and Dilke, and by Gladstone himself. After all, Gladstone's Irish policy depended on him. Parnell had met that Saturday night with Davitt and Dillon, and they talked about what they might do. Together they wrote a manifesto condemning the killings.[122]

The murders had exposed the impossibility of Parnell's position. Some years later, in 1887, Parnell would be framed by forged documents and openly accused of complicity in the Phoenix Park killings – an accusation without basis in fact.[123] For unionists, Parnell was the enemy – a tacit supporter and probable front for terrorism; for the Invincibles, Parnell was the problem, a provincialist unable properly to cut ties with Great Britain. But for now there was nothing for Parnell to do but to press on. As the immediate horror of the event receded, Parnell appears to have felt the British response to the killings in Ireland to be symptoms of hypocrisy. At a time when British rule around the world sustained itself through oppression, war, execution and theft, the uproar over the death of a few landlords and government figures in Ireland looked sentimental.[124]

The sense of their exceptionality conditioned the response to the assassinations. This remains a major part of the impact of all such killings: the massacre of the anonymous moves few; the murder of one gifted with fame stirs all those who touch the flow of reputation, through the press most particularly. Assassination is a parasite of renown.

In America, the news produced a commotion.[125] There was horror in Ireland too; letters of commiseration and indignation were sent to the Queen, and to Lucy Cavendish. For a little time, a cross cut into the ground of Phoenix Park marked the spot of the murder, but Dubliners soon erased it.[126] Yet it seems that the majority feeling in Ireland,

and abroad, was that of sorrow at Cavendish's death as a stranger to Ireland. This generosity did not extend to Burke, who some at least, and perhaps many, seem to have regarded as fair game.[127] The shops kept their shutters half-closed in respect, and many fixed black crape to the shutters as sign of mourning. James Carey, who had planned the killings and given the signal that initiated them, coolly joined in the mood of mourning, and proposed a motion of condolence with the unfortunate widow.[128] Divers plunged into the waters of the canal dock searching for the assassins' knives.

Though, as we have seen, an explicit link between the Nihilists and the Land-Leaguers or 'Fenians' had been forged since 1879, it was in 1882, in the immediate aftermath of the Phoenix Park murders, that the connection became most insisted upon. The *Belfast News-Letter* reported a Unitarian minister who described the killings as the 'answer of Irish Nihilism to Mr. Gladstone's statement'.[129] The subject seems to have remained a pulpit favourite. In a sermon of July 1882, an East Anglian vicar connected 'the American rowdy, the French Communist, the Russian Nihilist, the Irish Fenian and the English rough' in a union of perfidy.[130] An editorial in the *Birmingham Daily Post and Journal* pilloried 'Irish Nihilists'; the London newspaper the *Daily News* spoke of the murder as 'a last convulsive effort of Irish Nihilism'.[131] Outside Britain and Ireland, the link between Nihilism and 'Fenianism' was similarly commented upon. There were reports in Britain that the Austrian press were speculating 'that it is the Nihilist–Fenian combination in America which has organized the Moonlighters' bands and provides dynamite and infernal machines'.[132] In both the Hungarian and Spanish press, similar links were suggested.[133] Irish bombers were rumoured to have been trained by Professor Mezeroff, a 'Russian Nihilist' and 'the dynamite apostle'.[134]

On Sunday 14 May 1882, the sermon at Hawarden Parish Church explored the question of the meaning of suffering and the apparent triumph of evil in the world. A man sent out on a task of conciliation had been cruelly killed, and the good Christian must resist the first instinct for revenge.[135] This was to be the keynote of Lucy Cavendish's response to the murder. Lucy sent a letter to the Viceroy asking that there should be no 'panic and vindictive vengeance'; the letter was read out in Irish churches, and her gesture much admired.[136] Her attitude moved many. Gladstone wrote to Lady Cavendish: 'You have made a mark deeper than any wound.'[137] She rose above vindictiveness, while being inwardly devastated; for two years, every night she wept as she went to sleep. Yet she wanted to be good. In a note sent to an Irish well-wisher, she insisted that she did not condemn the Irish nation for the deed, or believe that they had sought her husband's death.[138]

The Phoenix Park assassinations were no worse than other crimes: the killing of Mountmorres or of Mrs Smythe, or indeed of Mary Deane and Patrick Melody. Ireland had suffered a sequence of such violent deaths, followed in their turn by reprisals or the violence of the state. Yet to few did it seem a murder like any other. Its distinction lay in three directions: one of the victims was British, not Irish; it was a direct strike against the 'governing class of the kingdom'; and it was even, for Gladstone, a familial blow.[139]

After the killing, the gang delivered cards to the newspaper offices of the city, marked with the words 'Executed by order of the Irish Invincibles'. The assassins were as taken aback as everyone else to learn that they had killed Cavendish. There was nothing personal in the deed; Burke and Cavendish were eliminated merely as symbols of British rule. In the next months, the Invincibles toughed out the initial revulsion at the murders. They began to provide reasons for the act of violence. They pointed to the killings at Belmullet; they retold Burke's tarnished career; they compared British rule to Russian or Turkish oppression; they brought up the taint of Cavendish's antecedents, his position as landlord, and blamed him for the murders at Ballina the night before.

Historians disagree on the impact that the murders produced. For some the event was a disaster with no discernible effect; a tragedy, but one that lay outside the broad course of policy.[140] In 1980, Paul Bew wrote: 'the appalling crime wrecked the emerging Parnell–Gladstone consensus'; in 2007, the same author affirmed that the 'Phoenix Park assassinations, which at first glance seemed likely to blow away the Gladstone–Parnell new departure, actually strengthened it ... the popular disapproval of the murder in Ireland gave Parnell the necessary accretion of political strength he required to follow the Kilmainham strategy'.[141] Perhaps the effect was mixed: the government passed the Arrears Act as they had planned, but they brought in further acts of coercion, though those included elements that had been planned for a while.[142] The Habeas Corpus Act was temporarily suspended in Ireland and the Prevention of Crimes Act introduced. For a while the British flirted with the possibility of trial without jury, but moved away from so extreme a measure. On the other hand, with Cavendish still alive, the government could have continued with the practice of reform; the murders derailed them. Everything had been thrown out by a chance event – especially the chance of Cavendish being killed too.

That the assassins had gone to work with knives deepened the event's horror. Their use was imagined as an Irish-American innovation.[143] Guns could easily have been employed: the Invincibles had access to firearms, and trained regularly in their use. But the knife brought killer and victim close together. The assassins leapt the distance accorded to respect, and with each blow struck at the deference established in class relations. Therefore the shocking intimacy of the murders meant more than the exposure of the weakness of British security. It brought the ruling class face to face with the mob that threatened it. The witnesses' impression that the aristocratic Lord Cavendish was just a rough fighting or playing in the park intensified the moment's squalor. Two worlds had collided, and the brute power of the lower of those worlds had degraded as well as destroyed the higher. After the murder, the way in which both Frederick Cavendish and his suffering wife were elevated into noble and gentle figures formed in part a counter-response to the humiliation of the killings. Gladstone reported to the Queen: 'Though he was slaughtered by a dagger or cutting instrument, it appears that the expression of the countenance is not altered.'[144] Aristocratic privilege and grace, that had been so shamefully mortified, was reasserted; the indignity of the street brawl rose up into a vision of sacrifice.

In one way there is no doubt as to the effect of the killings. The murders exposed in one stroke the impotence of the administration to prevent them. The very site of the murders was an insolent affront to British authority – right there in plain view before the Viceroy's residence. It was a jolt, as Davitt said, to Britain's 'pride and power'.[145] As Lady Ferguson put it, 'four ruffians armed with knives . . . shocked not only Dublin, but the empire'.[146] The previous failures and misses counted for nothing; and indeed their gradual revelation only deepened the impression of a sinister shadow behind colonial rule. The mere fact of violence both called out the desire for firmer and more coercive rule, while instilling the belief that no amount of firmness or coercion could succeed in these circumstances. The Irish seemed ungovernable; the British appeared inept.

Yet no one had planned to kill Cavendish. His death was unforeseen, a pitiless gift that surprised everyone. The timing of the killing looked like a deliberate rebuke for British attempts to offer concessions to Ireland. And clearly that was one intention behind the timing of the deed. Contempt for Parnell undoubtedly motivated the assassins, as they repudiated efforts to solve the problem of British rule by constitutional means. Yet they themselves had not anticipated the force of that rebuke. Not for the last time, the unpredictability produced by violence was to push events in startling directions.

So though the murder was a mistake, the assassination worked. By bringing violence to the very centre of power, the Invincibles wrecked the prospect of conciliation. The worse, the better. As John Morley remarked: 'It has been said that the nineteenth century had seen the course of its history twenty-five times diverted by actual or attempted crime. In that sinister list the murders in the Phoenix Park have a tragic place.'[147] Though some have doubted the impact of the murders, there is no doubt that, at the time, they seemed to have 'suddenly shattered all those fair hopes, and made the dark history darker'.[148] To some British observers, the killings showed the futility of reconciliation with the Irish, the impossibility of compromise. There would either have to be direct, authoritarian rule, or the surrender of Ireland to the Irish. As the last choice seemed an impossibility, they could do nothing but pursue the first.

V: Advocating Violence: Phoenix Park

Meanwhile Johann Most languished in prison; yet *Freiheit*, his paper, thundered on. For many in the radical community, Most's imprisonment seemed a gross injustice; William Morris, for one, was infuriated by the verdict. But there was no help for it. Most went first to Newgate and then on to Cold Bath Fields Prison, the House of Correction at Clerkenwell.[149] In prison, Most made his mark as a complainer; various petitions (that he should be allowed newspapers, books, writing materials, extra milk, and the chance to learn English) wended their way to the Home Secretary. He worked the system well and seems to have been treated fairly leniently. On the advice of the prison medical officer, he was allowed a bed or hammock (rather than the usual plank) and given only light labour, on account of his delicacy and deformed mouth.[150] And he had known worse than the privations of jail, remarking, 'Since childhood, life has been so vile I can bear anything.'[151]

The police continued to monitor *Freiheit* after Most's conviction, most likely with the aim of intelligence gathering, but perhaps also seeking a reason to close the paper down. If they required a pretext for action, the editors were not slow in providing one. In May 1882, *Freiheit* very visibly flashed forth the old revolutionary fire. When news reached England of the murders of Cavendish and Burke, *Freiheit* was unique in openly applauding the deed. The murders, it declared, were an act of 'popular justice'.[152] It was blatant provocation, and the authorities acted precisely as anyone would have expected. Warrants were issued for the acting editors, John [Johann] Neve and Karl Schneidt. They narrowly escaped arrest after a raid on the paper's offices. A fellow German, William Mertens, though merely a compositor for the paper, was caught, and following trial was sentenced to three months.

While Mertens was still in the hands of the police, *Freiheit* appeared again, this time praising Most, assassination in general, and declaring its solidarity with the Phoenix Park murderers in particular. The police launched another raid and once more failed to apprehend Neve and Schneidt, though they seized as much as they could of the publication's portable assets. Another young worker for the paper, Frederick Schwelm, was captured. Like Mertens, he was by his own account a hapless typesetter. This lowly role did not prevent his imprisonment for seventeen months, the severe sentence the result of his angry reaction to his conviction. These events could only add to the suspicion directed against Most. Following a letter sent to Scotland Yard by Charles Edward Marr, a witness at the original *Freiheit* trial, Most had already been briefly, but implausibly suspected of involvement in Roderick Maclean's shooting at the Queen.[153]

Although unable to catch the producers of the newspaper in action, police action of an efficient or repressive kind (depending on your point of view) led to a situation in which no printer would print it, and no bookseller sell it. Neve and Schneidt fled the country.[154] Publication continued ineptly in Switzerland, but on Most's release in October 1882 he determined to re-establish the paper. He would do so, but not in Britain; soon he was bound for America, where, as we shall see, his connections to assassination would remain close.

VI: Carey's Justice

In 1882, Ireland appeared to be a society on the verge of dissolution. The first six months of 1882 were savage indeed: bailiffs were killed, informers gunned down in Dublin, there had been the shooting of Mrs Smythe. Then in August, while the government hunted down the Phoenix Park assassins, another murder shocked Ireland. On this occasion, the Joyces, an entire family – father, mother and three young children – were killed in their own home at Maamtrasna in Connemara. It was supposed they had known something of the killing of two bailiffs, grandfather and grandson, named Huddy. The killings revealed a shameful squalor of life; Lord Spencer visiting the victims' house remarked that in England such a building would be considered too fetid to be used for pigs. There were other killings, and other attempted killings: even as the Maamtrasna trial was in progress, Patrick Delaney (one of the Phoenix Park killers) was arrested that November for conspiring to murder Justice Lawson.[155] One of the judge's bodyguards saved him by felling Delaney as he pulled out a revolver and prepared to fire.

The government knew that it must reimpose the rule of law, and that the legal system should be seen to operate with faultless success. The first step was to track down and convict the killers of Cavendish and Burke. There were arrests on suspicion in July 1882, but everyone was released without charge. Carey, the man who had pointed out Burke to the assassins, was among this group. His impeccable image as a victim of imperialist bullying helped his election to a place on Dublin City Council in November of that year. However, in the early hours of 13 January 1883, the façade of innocence crumbled. The police, aided by the Marines, made a series of night raids on houses across Dublin. Carey found himself re-arrested on charges of conspiracy to murder. There were seventeen arrests in total on that night. On the 15th, three more arrests followed. When the prisoners were arraigned on 20 January, Carey seemed the most cool and unconcerned; he was even puffing on a cigar as he strolled from the prison van to the courthouse. He protested his own innocence vigorously and denounced the inconvenience of being arrested. There were attempts to pull in more suspects. Another suspected killer, O'Brien, shipped as a sailor at Swansea under the name William Westgate. 'Mental anxiety caused him to confess' to the ship's captain – and he was arrested at Puerto Cabello, before ending up being held at Caracas.[156]

Twenty men stood trial for the Phoenix Park killings, and for the attempted murder of an informer named Field. Four of the accused men were to turn informer. First, there was Robert Farrell, a Dublin labourer, who knew little, but had been involved in the planned but abortive attacks on Forster. Then there came Michael Kavanagh, twenty-eight years old, who had driven a carriage bearing four assassins to the Park on the evening of the murders. Another, William Lamie, also turned Queen's evidence. But beginning on 17 February, the last informer was to give the most spectacular evidence of all. It was James Carey himself, one of the principal leaders of the Invincibles and the man who had actually planned the murders in Phoenix Park. He was clearly one of the guiltiest of the detainees, and had been marked out as the leader by the testimony of both Farrell and Kavanagh. He would, in exchange for his own freedom, give Queen's evidence against his former friends. It is possible that, with the exception of Joe Brady and Timothy Kelly, all the accused men offered to inform on the others.[157] The danger of their predicament and anxieties about their families made such collaboration understandably attractive; Carey is likely to have been motivated in part at least by family feeling. Individually, they had been honourable conspirators; now placed under extreme duress, some of them chose to blemish their own reputations. Because Carey's evidence was the best, he gained his life and the reputation of a traitor; the others went to their deaths as martyrs.

The trial of the Phoenix Park murderers in Dublin was a national event; ticket-holders crowded Kilmainham Court House, eager to hear the revelations concerning the assassins. The three main informers stayed together in Rosemount Cottage in Kilmainham, under close police protection. There were doubts of course about the value of information given by former members of the same conspiracy, but there was enough corroborative evidence from others to add crucial weight to the informers' accusations.

On Carey's evidence, in the early summer of 1883, Michael Fagan, Joseph Brady, Daniel Curley, Timothy Kelly and Thomas Caffrey were hanged. Brady was the godfather of Carey's youngest child. Others, including Edward McCaffrey, were sentenced to long terms in jail. Some were acquitted, including Fitzharris, or 'Skin the Goat', the cab driver. While Carey had gone to lengths to exonerate certain of the accused men, especially James Mullett and Joe Smith, he had also accused the wife of Frank Byrne, a prominent Land Leaguer, of bringing the murder weapons from London to Dublin; however, when she was presented to him, he failed to identify her.[158]

Behind everything lurked a mysterious 'No. 1', the ultimate leader of the organisation: was it one of the men they had failed to extradite from abroad, John Walsh, P. J. Sheridan or Patrick Tynan? In absentia, these three additional men were charged; all three would eventually manage to flee to the USA. A letter to the Home Office had suggested John Walsh as a possible suspect.[159] In February 1883, an attempt to repatriate Walsh from Paris failed: a man could not be extradited simply on suspicion of having committed a crime. After his release Walsh visited the British Consulate in Le Havre to enquire after some missing banknotes, and said, while chatting, that Carey was the real 'No. 1' and that the murders were 'a very great calamity' for Ireland. Even a trusting mind might find such casual information disingenuous; yet it might also be true.[160] Six years later, Walsh was still trying to get his banknotes back. In America similar extradition procedures were set in motion to secure the arrest of P. J. Sheridan.[161] The fact that the crimes were political in nature complicated the extradition process. Similarly there were attempts to extradite Tynan, 'No. 1', the head of the 'Irish Assassination Committee' from France, then Mexico and then the United States – though proceedings had to be dropped due to lack of evidence.[162]

As mentioned above, in 1887 *The Times* sought to smear Parnell with complicity in the Phoenix Park murders, printing letters forged by one Richard Pigott that blamed the Irish leader. As part of their campaign, P. J. Sheridan (who was then living on a ranch in Colorado) looked set to offer incriminating evidence (either true or untrue) to the newspaper in exchange for cash. However, Sheridan's information, or misinformation, never reached the paper, as the man was simply milking *The Times* for funds; he would likewise sidestep attempts to get him to testify at the Special Commission that looked into the matter.[163]

Ten years after Phoenix Park, Sir Robert Anderson initiated new moves to extradite Tynan. Once again these floundered due to a lack of convincing evidence.[164] Yet in the early 1890s, while nursing these suspicions against Tynan, the Home Office was secretly financing the same man to write his memoirs.[165] So it was that he went at this time from financial desperation to being 'in funds'.[166] In September 1896, while starting a European tour, Tynan would be followed by British detectives and arrested again in Boulogne regarding a suspected dynamite plot; however, following an appeal by Tynan to President Cleveland, the accusation came to nothing and he was released and expelled back to America.[167] Around this time Arthur James Balfour was in possession of evidence that suggested Tynan had only claimed the credit of being 'No. 1' – while the real 'No. 1' had been Walsh, who was now dead.[168] While Anderson pursued Tynan, there were many in government who considered the police chief 'a most unscrupulous fellow', and therefore resisted following his lead.[169] They were probably right to have qualms: the involvement of Tynan, Walsh or Sheridan in the killings remains doubtful.

The executions of the Phoenix Park killers weakened the feelings of pity for the victims first evoked after Cavendish's death. Justice had been done, but to many it seemed like vengeance. Even in the fierce round of retribution, there was still room for one small and profound gesture of forgiveness. A nun visited the men awaiting execution in Kilmainham, offering spiritual succour particularly to Brady, who had at first been an unwilling participant in the murders and had been a good son to his mother. The nun was Burke's cousin.[170]

Still the Irish nationalists were not above wanting some vengeance of their own. Naturally, there were bitter, indeed murderous thoughts against Carey. In his own mind, he justified his co-operation to himself on the basis that no one was arrested on his testimony. Others did not take this view. His wife, Margaret, and their seven children had to be protected by armed guards; at his house windows were smashed. His tenants took the opportunity of refusing to pay rent to such a scoundrel. It was clear that he could not remain in Ireland, and live.

An arrangement was struck with the government. That same summer of 1883, with his family, Carey secretly travelled, via London, to South Africa. After everyone else, Carey himself boarded ship, the *Kinfauns Castle*, from a small boat off Dartmouth. He and his family were travelling steerage under the assumed name of Power.[171] Carey brought a Bulldog revolver with him, in case of danger.

There was another Irish couple on the boat, and in the course of things they became friendly with the 'Power' family. Although Irish by birth, Patrick O'Donnell had lived for years as a cowboy in the west of the USA. A tall and slender man, he had been employed for a while as a booking agent for lecture tours, and had even worked for Mark Twain.[172] O'Donnell had deserted a wife in America, and was now travelling to South Africa with his young lover, Mary Gallagher, with whom he had been living above a London coffee-house. (On board, she would be known as his 'wife'.[173]) In the initial newspaper reports on the events that followed, she was coyly described as his 'niece'. As the ship travelled south, Carey (using the alias 'Power') and O'Donnell formed the habit of drinking together every night. Everything went on amiably, and the two couples became chums. They got on so well in fact that O'Donnell declared that he would travel with the 'Power' family to Natal.[174] The night before they reached their destination at Cape Town, however, the two men argued drunkenly, but hardly seriously over a card game. The next morning they reached land.

There on 27 July they disembarked, and boarded the *Melrose* going on to Natal. While they were waiting to change ships, one of the other passengers, Cubitt, an Englishman, went ashore early and found a bar in which to have a drink and read a newspaper. It was in the paper that he discovered something startling.[175] Their fellow passenger, James Power, was revealed to be James Carey, the infamous approver. Helpfully there was even an illustration of the man. Cubitt met O'Donnell on the quay, and asked him who he thought James Power really was. Then he showed O'Donnell the illustration, and told him what he had read.[176]

When O'Donnell learnt the news and recognised the face, he said simply, 'I will shoot him.' O'Donnell went back to the ship, and they set sail. The next day, Sunday 29 July, O'Donnell found Margaret Carey in the second class saloon.[177] He suggested that they all have a drink together, and one of Carey's children went to fetch his dad from up on deck. They went into the saloon. Soon it was busy; Carey's fifteen-year-old son, Thomas, was there, and Maggie, one of his younger daughters, O'Donnell's girlfriend Mary Gallagher, and two of the crew. Only Margaret Carey retired to her berth with their baby. All appears to have been quite affable. They sat around and talked and laughed and drank ale. Carey was smiling. On the settee Mary Gallagher had her arm around O'Donnell's shoulders. Carey was standing only a few feet across from him. They drank each other's health. O'Donnell's American experiences had made him a fast shot. Suddenly he pulled out his gun and fired.[178] Carey writhed in pain, slewed around and tried to stagger to refuge in his wife's cabin. Margaret Carey had heard the shot and made for the saloon; Carey's fifteen-year-old son rushed past her into the cabin and tried to find the revolver the family owned (it was kept there in a portmanteau), but the bag was locked, and he could do nothing in time. By the time he managed to force the lock and produce the gun, it was all over, and he simply tucked it away in his pocket.[179] Meanwhile O'Donnell had held out his hand and fired twice more, hitting Carey in the shoulder and near the spine. Carey called to his wife, 'O Maggie, I'm shot.' He stumbled forwards onto her, and they both fell to the deck. He would take fifteen minutes to die. O'Donnell put the pistol back in his inside coat pocket. Then Carey's wife struggled up, with blood on her chest, and went over to the killer, and said, 'O'Donnell, did you shoot my husband?'[180] Mary Gallagher's arm was still around her lover's shoulders. And O'Donnell replied, 'Shake hands, Mrs Carey. Don't blame me.' In using her real name, he was letting her know why her husband was dying. O'Donnell then added either 'I had to do it', 'I didn't do it', or 'I was sent to do it' – a crucial distinction. Mrs Carey did not shake his hand. 'No matter, O'Donnell, you are no informer,' Mary Gallagher said.[181]

O'Donnell was a simple man, completely illiterate, with a withered (or at least incapacitated) left arm.[182] He was therefore hardly material for a professional assassin. On the other hand, newspaper reports concerning Carey were found in O'Donnell's trunk, though whether these were those that he had read in Cape Town is unclear.[183] The dispute over the words O'Donnell said to Margaret Carey meant the difference between imagining him as an assassin hunting down his prey, and a hot-blooded Irishman acting on a sudden impulse. Though rumours spread that O'Donnell had followed the Careys from England, it is more likely that he committed his murder spontaneously on learning that he had shared his journey with a scoundrel and traitor like Carey. Such impromptu violence need not surprise us: when word reached Dublin of Carey's murder, bonfires were lit in celebration.[184]

In December, O'Donnell was tried at the Old Bailey in London. Throughout the trial, the Carey family remained in hiding, under police protection; Mrs Carey came daily to the court disguised as a female prison warder.[185] O'Donnell offered a story of self-defence, in which Carey and he had quarrelled, and both had gone for their guns, but O'Donnell had been quicker. It was later rumoured that Scotland Yard itself had given credence to this story.[186] However, only Thomas Carey's confused testimony about the family pistol lent credence to this account; otherwise all the evidence was against it. O'Donnell was sentenced to be hanged and, on Monday 17 December 1883 in Newgate Prison, he was executed. An American newspaper lamented his death as an 'assassination'.[187] His brother, who was outside with the watching crowd, saw the black flag raised, and declared to the other watchers that his brother had died as bravely as any man had.

One cycle of violence had been completed. But of course the troubles between Britain and Ireland were far from over. One immediate development was the beginning of a dynamite campaign, the fruit of the movement's step towards 'propaganda by the deed' and 'Nihilist' tactics. The bombings began during the trial of the Invincibles, with the discovery of caches of explosives in Birmingham, Leicester and Fife and an explosion at Whitehall on 16 March 1883. A sequence of bomb outrages, or at least intended outrages, followed in London: attempts to blow up Mansion House and Scotland Yard, to bring down London Bridge, and even to topple Nelson's Column. The concept of 'the spectacular' was clearly already present in these plots. Later there were bombs in the House of Commons (Gladstone's usual seat was exploded), in the Underground, the chief railway stations, even the Tower of London.[188] They were attacking the symbols of Britishness, the elements of the popular perception of order and power. There were even false rumours, leading to the arrest at Cowes of one Mademoiselle

Drouin, a hapless and entirely innocent French invalid, of a planned dynamite assassination of the Queen at Osborne House.[189]

Though not as dangerous as gunpowder, and soon apparently to be superseded by gelignite, the Irish use of dynamite itself appeared ominous and unnerving, this new benefit to humanity having quickly metamorphosed into a curse.[190] Though the bombs had failed to produce terror in London, it was the indiscriminate nature of such devices that most shocked; at least the Russian Nihilists had aimed at the assassination of individuals.[191] Sir William Harcourt, the Home Secretary, responded with the passing of the Explosive Substances Act in 1883, making it illegal to possess explosives without a licence, or to plot an explosion. In addition, the bombing brought the Special Branch into existence.[192] Therefore, in the mid-1880s it looked as though the most telling political violence was set to be a product of Irish nationalism. However, in the next thirty years, across Europe and the United States, it would instead be the Anarchist killer who would strike the darkest blows in the history of assassination.

PART TWO

Ragtime Assassins
A Case Study of Emma Goldman,
Alexander Berkman and Leon Czolgosz

6

Frick's Gallery

He has simplified the world like an assassin.
Where his barrel points is where evil is.
IAIN CRICHTON SMITH

Even then society was dividing between banker and Anarchist.
HENRY ADAMS, *THE EDUCATION OF HENRY ADAMS*

I: The Tycoon

All day the stranger had been waiting to see him. He had come, gone away, and then returned several times. He was not to be refused; he had come for Mr Frick, and he would meet with him. A card had been sent inside to Frick's office, with the following message: 'Dear Sir, I would like to see you at your earliest opportunity. Alex. Berkman.' So, that was the stranger's name. The clerks in the lobby had looked him over as he sat outside in the waiting room: pale, dark-haired, clearly foreign. He was young, even boyish, surprisingly so for a representative of a New York employment agency. He was ready, they informed Mr Frick, to supply 'blackleg' labour to the mill.

At work in the office on the summer Saturday morning, Frick was finding it hard to make space for such a distraction, but the young stranger's insistence persuaded him. An arrangement was made: if the stranger was there at 2 p.m., then Frick would spare the time to see him. He was busy, but he admired perseverance. And if they were to break the strike, as they must, the mills could certainly use outside workers.

Maybe it was unusual to receive visitors in this way, but Frick prided himself on his freedom from conventions. He had insisted, for instance, despite the worries of his friends, that he should still travel around Pittsburgh without a guard and be available for callers at the office too.

These were gestures of patrician unconcern, the kind of thing that gave the right impression: calmly heroic, ostentatiously democratic, rising above the unpleasant atmosphere of the strike.

At the appointed time, the stranger came. Frick was there with John Leishman, the Vice President of Carnegie Steel, working together at the long table in the private office. From the far end of the room, the door opened and the stranger walked in. He looked nervous, and Frick rose from his armchair to meet him. Just then the stranger raised his hand and an instant afterwards the bullet struck Frick's neck. There was the sound of the shot in the room and in the same instant the odd sound of its thick slap as it tore into his flesh. Without warning, Frick felt, rather than pain, the presence beside him of someone both lost and immeasurably consoling. Then he sank to the floor. The stranger came and stood over him, quite close. He fired again, and again the same sound, too close, and another bullet burst into Frick's neck. He was slumped on the floor, waiting for the next shot. But Leishman saved him: moving as quickly as he could around the office furniture, he reached the stranger and clutched at his arm and the third bullet vanished instead up into the ceiling. They struggled, Leishman and the stranger, fighting for the gun in the stranger's hand. Frick rose to his feet somehow and joined the mêlée, the three men tussling over the pistol, each one desperate to seize hold. For all that he seemed immature and frail the stranger was astonishingly strong, and Frick was so bloody, and then all at once the stranger took a knife with his one free hand and slashed Frick several times on the leg. Men rushed in from the outer office, the clerks and a visiting carpenter, and brought the stranger down. They pinioned the young man to the floor; the carpenter beat him on the head with a hammer. Then, while the stranger tried to speak, Frick watched from below the long table.

They took the stranger out of the room. He had gone without saying anything. Once he had left the room, Leishman passed out. Frick struggled to his feet and leant on the table, and then said, after some little time, 'Well, I believe I feel like fainting.' He was helped onto a comfortable chair, where, feeling strangely at ease, he dictated a telegram. One copy was to be sent to his mother, one to his wife, and one to Andrew Carnegie. It read: 'Was shot twice but not dangerously'. For Carnegie's message, he also added: 'There is no necessity for you to come home. I am still in shape to fight the battle out.' He wouldn't have wanted to disappoint Carnegie or betray his trust; the strike was still under control after all, despite this palaver.

He remained in the office, desperate to get back to work. When the surgeons came, they had to probe by hand the wounds in his neck to feel for the bullets; there were no exit wounds – it was this, no doubt, which had saved him. Frick told them that he would not need an anaesthetic; if he were fully conscious he'd be better able to guide the surgeons' fingers. While the search for the bullets still continued, Frick returned to his desk. Though blood was spattered around the office, there was still business to be done. He must sign some letters, and help in the negotiation of a loan. Also there was the matter of issuing a statement to the public. It would be wrong to let the unpleasantness affect morale or the image of the firm. The statement promised: 'This incident will not change the attitude of the Carnegie Steel Company toward the Amalgamated Association. I do not think I shall die, but, if I do or not, the company will pursue the same policy and it will win.'[1]

Finally, at 7.30 p.m. that night, the operation to remove the bullets from his flesh was over. Now that everything was complete for the day, and the work properly done, Frick was carried off home in a stretcher. The family had kept the news from Adelaide, Frick's wife, who was frail after recently giving birth. But she knew something was wrong, and when her husband returned, and was being carried up the stair-case, she came out from her bedroom to see him. He asked her how their child was, for their new son was very ill. She was shocked. Her husband was pale, weak and heavily bandaged. The doctors calmed Adelaide, and Frick was taken to bed. He stayed there for the next two weeks. It was a fiercely hot summer. All through his recovery he remained hard at work. The bedroom made a more admirable office than a bedroom: it had always been a sombre and chilly place. He lay with a telephone by the bed, and several secretaries on hand. With over-excited stoicism he fought the strike, his head and neck swathed in bandages. There he heard the news of his wife, also fighting for her life just some doors away, with only his dressing-room between them. And there too he heard the funeral service for his 28-day-old son, his namesake, born and died during the strike, perhaps the victim of an attempt to poison the entire family.[2] When his convalescence was over, he went back to work as usual, a little paler, a little thinner, but the same indomitable man.

There was one positive result: the attack had restored a little of Frick's lost popularity. Not that he wanted particularly to be popular. More gratifyingly the attack sullied the strike, even though the stranger was not a striker at all, but an outsider, a foreigner and an Anarchist. The workers began to capitulate; while public opinion turned, money was growing scarcer and scarcer. Replacement workers flooded into the town, taking the jobs of those few unrepentant strikers. On 18 November 1892, the strike ended. Frick had broken the unions at the Carnegie steel works. He wrote to Carnegie, 'We had to teach our employees a lesson, and we have taught them one they will never forget.'[3] While Carnegie advocated reconciliation with those they had destroyed, Frick was more unsparing. Not a single striker regained his job at the plant. Everything was working out very happily. It was, however scary, a good job well done, good for the mills, good for business, good for Carnegie, and good for America. It was also good for Frick. He was the victor of the struggle after all.

Yet he didn't seem much like a victor. He had lost his son, the second of his children to have died within a year. The loss of his daughter, Martha Frick, had been even harder to bear. The couple's middle child, she had been only six years old.[4] During her final illness, a strike at the mines in Morewood had proved for Frick an agonising distraction from caring for his daughter. Martha died in July 1891. He would never recover from the loss, though he had little time to mourn her; the plans for his coming battle with the recalcitrant union at Homestead were already in place.

The son of a well-to-do farmer and his wife, Frick had been born on 19 December 1849 in the springhouse at Westmoreland County, Pennsylvania. He spent his childhood and youth in the Mennonite village of West Overton. It was the era of self-help and Frick was gifted with the industrious virtues. Undistracted by friends (the delicate youth had none), he worked his way up, as a good millionaire should, clerking in a downtown store in Pittsburgh.[5] Then he moved from West Overton to Broad Ford, and became bookkeeper for the Overholt distillery, named after and owned by Frick's family on his maternal grandfather's side. Loans from Judge Mellon (the Mellons were family friends) helped the young man to build his first coke ovens and expand his mining concerns. Like most businessmen, he suffered in the financial panic of 1873, though he also managed to profit a little from it too. He worked hard through the difficult years of recession, acting as his own sales agent. He speculated and bought competing coke plants. When the economic recovery came in 1879, it made him rich; he became the Coke King, a millionaire before his thirtieth birthday.

The industrialist and would-be philanthropist Andrew Carnegie bought the majority shareholding of Frick's Coke Company, thereby ensuring a ready supply of coke for Carnegie's steel factories, and giving Frick an instant return.[6] This left Frick even wealthier and with something that, compared to the struggle of the previous years, looked like leisure.

Like a youthful hero from a Henry James novel, Frick looked up from his labours and left for Europe. He had always had a bent for art, investing as a youth in so many paintings that it even aroused the inquisitively puritanical attention of Judge Mellon. The judge inspected the young man's passion, and decided that, though regrettable, it was 'not enough to hurt'.[7] Frick left for Europe with the judge's son, Andrew Mellon, now the head of the family bank, and received his aesthetic *coup de foudre* among the pink-cheeked Bouchers and flirtatious Fragonards of London's Wallace Collection. Here was something beautifully beyond the business grime. More than most such men, Frick needed a private realm where he might escape. He was clumsy with others, efficient but remote. In public display his frustrated inwardness manifested itself as reserve with his equals or hauteur with subordinates. With children and paintings, he could unbend. But he was not ready yet to withdraw from the business life where he did so well and showed so badly.

He returned to prosaic America, but held on to romance as best he could by falling in love with and then marrying, in December 1881, Adelaide Howard Childs, daughter of the Pittsburgh boot-making family. Though it may sound like a business merger, they shared genuine affection and desire. In photographs, Adelaide Frick looks striking, with her strong fair face, her dark hair and blue eyes. The newly married couple went to live at Monongahela House, a swish hotel in Pittsburgh, elegant enough for an interlude but hardly the place to begin family life. On 15 August 1882, with Adelaide already pregnant, the couple moved into an expensive new building in the Point Breeze neighbourhood of Pittsburgh.

After London and Paris, Pittsburgh was miserable: a city of factories and darkness. Point Breeze offered a little respite. Located in the chic East End of the city, it was a posh suburb and the home of many of Andrew Carnegie's business associates, including Henry John Heinz, the canning and food-processing tycoon, and Richard Beatty Mellon, the brother of Andrew Mellon. By the end of the decade, Frick was one of Carnegie's partners, replacing Henry Phipps as chairman of Carnegie Brothers and Company in January 1889. Meanwhile the house was to be the Frick family's refuge from sordid things. A black iron fence decorated with gold-leaf fleur-de-lis surrounded it, a pretty fence, but a fence nonetheless, designed to hold the unattractive at bay. Frick renamed the property Clayton, after himself. An American pseudo-château, shielded by trees, the house was fine, but not everything Frick with his eye for elegance could desire. So, from 1891 until spring 1892, Frick had the place renovated by Frederick J. Osterling, a 25-year-old local architect. While the work was being done the young family lived in another house in the area. It was in the summer of 1891 that little Martha died. When the Fricks moved back in, with Adelaide pregnant again, and preparations under way for the Homestead strike, the place was sumptuous but, more important, fashionably so, filled with 'porcelain, sculpture, silver, glass, ornaments, souvenirs from trips, and family photographs'.[8] It was a dream home. It had everything: the stained glass window by A. Goodwin & Company of Philadelphia, showing 'Love in the Tower'; the spires; the gazebo; the porch at the front, not enclosed until 1899; the parlour, the breakfast room, the orchestrion; the gold, the marble; the chintz, the marvellous pictures; the main entrance to the house at the front, the children's entrance at the side and rear – the entrance that two of their children would now never pass through.

There he was, a hard man, or at least a man with a reputation for hardness, engulfed in art and opulence, peering out at a world that seemed to besiege him just at those moments when life snatched what he most valued away. It was the same: the strikers at Morewood who poisoned his last moments with Martha; the strikers at Homestead who worried his son into the grave. How beautiful and orderly was the life at Clayton. How unsightly and strange, the strangers from outside who encroached on its graceful tidiness. Of those incursions from the ugly world, the Anarchist with his dagger and gun was the strangest of all.

II: The New Woman

While Frick gazed from American realities towards the deep beauty of Europe, many Europeans oppressed by poverty and political repression yearned for American liberty. It was two of these aspiring migrants from far away who were to prove Frick's nemesis.

Emma Goldman opens her autobiography with her arrival in New York City on 15 August 1889, a symbolic moment of regeneration in the drama of an immigrant. It is a moment of expectations, for Goldman had no place to stay and no work to do, but also an artful beginning, signalling the instant in which the twenty-year-old Goldman can at last immerse herself in the promised opportunity of urban America.

Goldman's childhood offered little in the way of freedom. On 27 June 1869, she was born in Kovno, in what was then part of Russia but is now in Lithuania, the child of Abraham and Taube Goldman. Abraham was an abusive and distant father, handsome but indifferent to his daughter, whom he wished were a boy. She suffered many beatings.[9] It was a childhood without much play, in a culture split between German and Russian. At the age of seven, she was sent to school in Königsberg in East Prussia, where she remained until she was thirteen. While she was there she lived with her maternal grandmother in a flat too small for the family; Emma shared a bed with her youngest aunt. She seems to have enjoyed school, and to have had a good relationship with her teacher, who impressed her with stories of Vera Zasulich, the would-be assassin of Trepov. At first her mother's hatred of the Nihilists dampened the spark struck by these accounts. For a while, her daughter loyally shared her mother's dislike. However, in 1881, hearing that the Tsar's young assassins had been hanged, she experienced an unexpected compassion for them. The injustices perpetrated in Russia moved her. Her turning towards Anarchism began with this instinctive capacity for sympathy – a characteristic cause for a person always deeply swayed by her feelings. Young Emma was an emotional girl, readily moved by literature, almost overwhelmed by a trip with her teacher to the Königsberg Opera House to see Verdi's suitably gloomy Il Trovatore.

In 1882, Goldman rejoined the family in their new home in St Petersburg. The passage to Russia from Germany was not an easy one, and in
mid-winter Goldman and her mother and two brothers had to be smuggled
across the border, the path of their secret journey forcing them to wade
through a brook whose icy waters left the young girl ill for weeks. Her
father had lost his job, and was beginning his precipitous slide away from
the comfortable middle class. Yet it was a propitious moment to arrive in
Russia, in the aftermath of the turmoil produced by the assassination of
Tsar Alexander II, and a time when, despite the realities of the situation,
it seemed as though the revolutionary students had the future in their
grasp. After Prussia's conservatism, Russia thrust Emma back into a radical
milieu. As she explained nearly twenty years later:

I am a Russian through and through, although little of my life was spent there.
I was born in Russia, but was brought up in Germany and graduated from a
German school. All that didn't make a German of me. I went back to Russia
when I was 13 years old, and felt that I was returning to my home. My family
was orthodox. None of my revolutionary tendencies was inherited – at least my
parents were not responsible for them and were horrified by them.

While I was in Germany I did not think much about anarchy, but when I went
back to St Petersburg my whole attitude toward life changed, and I went into
radicalism with all my heart and soul. You see, things are different in Russia from
what they are here or anywhere else. One breathes a revolutionary thought with
the air, and without being definitely interested in anarchy one learns its principles.
There was discussion and thought and enthusiasm all around me, and something
within me responded to it all.[10]

As well as the atmosphere of rebellion, there were Nihilists in her
extended family, there to offer an alternative model for adulthood to
that provided by her conservative parents. Turgenev's *Fathers and Sons*
had already impressed her. Now she read and adored Chernyshevsky's
What Is To Be Done? – an act that all but amounted to an initiation
rite for a young revolutionary – and went to work in a factory, making
corsets and, later, gloves, a move which was both a financial necessity
and, in hindsight at least, also a reprise of the Russian radicals' impulse
to 'go to the people'. She adopted the style of the Nihilist women, with
short hair and practical clothes.

Her father tried to marry her off when she was only fifteen. Her
unwomanly desire to study infuriated him; on one occasion he flung a

French grammar book she was reading into the fire. Goldman resisted the plan to marry. She had better things planned. Her beloved sister Helena was to emigrate to the USA. Goldman could not bear the thought of separation from her, and persuaded her parents to let her go too. In late December 1885, they sailed, steerage class, to America, under the names Emma and Helene Binowitz.[11] Her father paid the passage.[12] They stayed in Rochester, New York, with Lena, another more unsympathetic sister, who had travelled to America some years before. The two sisters settled down to earning enough money to bring their parents over to America.[13] Emma was well thought of within the Jewish community.[14] She began factory work at the Garson Company in Rochester, finding it airier than the Petersburg factories she already knew, though after the Russians' shabby bonhomie, the American system felt dreary and constricted. Rochester too was lacklustre, a boring place for a young woman with a hankering after adventures.

Given the small scope of her life, it is not surprising that she should have grabbed at the first chance to shatter the alienating monotony. Early in 1887, she met Jacob Kershner, a ladies' tailor and a fellow Russian, and in a fit of homesickness for the language and life they had both left behind, she married him. Such an early marriage is of course a well-worn strategy for a free-spirited person still unsure of how radically they may defy convention: to the young, marriage may assume the guise of escape.

However, more fruitful diversions were opening up for her. With her sister Helena she began attending meetings of a German socialist group in Rochester. At one meeting, Johanna Greie came to talk on recent events in Chicago. The lecture was crowded, with policemen lining the walls of the hall. Goldman was swept away by the woman's speech. When Greie finished her talk, she went to speak to Goldman; she had never seen someone so obviously moved. Goldman was always clear about why she had to become an Anarchist. 'No I am not of peasant blood. I came from the middle class. I am not an Anarchist because I had nothing to eat,' she concluded. 'The Haymarket riot and the judicial murders that followed made an Anarchist of me.'[15] More than any other event in the American political history of the 1880s, it was the aftermath of the Haymarket riot that did most to radicalise Goldman and with her a generation of socialists and Anarchists.

On 3 May 1886, during agitation for a statutory eight-hour day, police attacked strikers at the McCormick Harvester Company in Chicago. A worker was killed and several wounded. Anarchists called for a protest meeting the next evening in the vicinity of Haymarket Square. The meeting took place at Des Plaines, north of Randolph Street. Although posters had been produced calling for the workers to arm themselves, it was a rather unspectacular and quiet affair. Only between 800 and 1,000 people attended, not including a large police contingent who stood looking on at the speeches being delivered from a wagon at the side of the road. Chicago's Mayor, Carter Harrison, was there to see if there would be any trouble, but he left near the end, convinced that the protest had passed off peaceably. At 10 p.m. the meeting concluded and the police began to move towards the crowd to disperse them. Just then some unseen assailant lobbed a bomb into the ranks of the police. The explosion killed one policeman instantly; a further six would die of their wounds.

The police swiftly arrested the leading Anarchists at the meeting; eight were charged with murder. Of the eight, six were German immigrants. The trial took place in June 1886. All eight were found guilty and seven were sentenced to death. The following November, the sentence of two of the men was commuted to life imprisonment. On 10 November 1887, the day before their execution, one of the men, Louis Lingg, anticipated the sentence by exploding a charge of dynamite between his teeth. The explosion ripped away half of his face; several hours later, in utter extremity of pain, he died. He was only twenty-two years old. Next day the remaining four men, including the leading Anarchist agitators August Spies and Albert Parsons, were hanged. They were buried at Waldheim Cemetery in Forest Park, Illinois, a site that would become a place of pilgrimage for many in the Anarchist movement. Nearly six years after the executions, a judicial review of the case carried out by Judge John Altgeld found what Anarchists and socialists had long known. All eight of the 'Haymarket Martyrs' had been entirely innocent of the charge of murder.[16] Judge Altgeld concluded that the trial had been a gross miscarriage of justice. The jury had been packed, the offence had not been proved, and the judge had prejudiced the chances of a fair hearing. In any case, the men had been unfairly declared guilty by the newspapers long before they came to trial.

Memories of Haymarket and the example of the men who had been unjustly killed in its wake drew Goldman, and many others, into the ranks of the Anarchists. Young Louis Lingg, in particular, seemed a figure of romance and beauty: 'He became the beacon of our lives.'[17] When Goldman heard the news that the Haymarket Anarchists had been executed, she was so emotionally overwhelmed that she dropped to the floor in a fit of weeping, and had to be put to bed.

She began reading Johann Most's *Freiheit*, and through that paper, other works of Anarchist literature. Jacob Kershner, her husband, shared nothing of her new interests. Once his bookishness had impressed her, but his work now left him too tired to read. Always frankly sexual, Goldman was dismayed to discover on her wedding night that Kershner was impotent. When this condition persisted, the couple visited the local doctor. Apparently Kershner would require some more time to 'build up his manhood'. They grew further apart, and soon Goldman determined to leave. The marriage that had been meant to liberate her from dullness had rendered life even duller than before. Her separation from Kershner caused a family scandal – her parents had now joined their children in Rochester – but she was determined. Anarchism would be her escape. She decided to go to New York, the centre of American Anarchism, and in August 1889 she arrived in the city, alone. There she would live as an early example of the 'new woman', claiming the metropolis as her own space and enacting her own sense of freedom – an easier task in New York than in Rochester. It was a bold step, and one that immediately plunged Goldman into the centre of revolutionary politics in America.

III: The Rebels

Late on her very first day in New York, an auspicious moment to begin any relationship, Goldman met Alexander Berkman. She had gone with a young Anarchist acquaintance, Solotaroff, to Sachs's café on Suffolk Street. There she met Anna and Helen Minkin, two young sisters of her own age, and Russian and Jewish like her. After a short conversation, the girls agreed that Goldman should live with them. At least, she would not be homeless. Just then a youth loudly ordering food stole her attention. Solotaroff introduced them. It was Berkman.

He was younger than her, only eighteen, but strong; his face was stern. 'A determined youngster', she thought.[18]

Berkman too was impressed. He had been sitting in the chilly café for a couple of hours, watching the regulars arrive. He had got himself into a debate with a couple of Russians, when a young woman had walked in, diffusing 'an atmosphere of strength and vitality'. She intrigued him; he knew most of the city's Anarchists, but this woman was a stranger to him. When they were introduced, they talked at once like old friends. She called him 'comrade'; on her lips, the word was thrilling. Berkman immediately invited her to go to hear Johann Most lecture, and together with the Minkin sisters, they went to see the great Anarchist speak. Goldman could not believe her luck. As they crossed Delancey Street, Goldman slipped, but Berkman caught her, saving her from cracking her head on the sidewalk. 'You have saved my life,' she told him.[19]

On release from jail in Britain, Most had left for America, and on arrival in Manhattan continued publication of *Freiheit* there. He soon established himself as a leading figure among American Anarchists and an object of hate and ridicule for the mainstream press. In 1883, he had been largely responsible for the Pittsburgh Manifesto, the first major American statement of Anarchist aims. Two years later, with knowledge gained from a spell working in an explosives factory in Jersey City Heights, he published *Revolutionäre Kriegswissenschaft* ('The Science of Revolutionary Warfare'), more poetically known afterwards as 'The Anarchist Cook Book', a 'how to' book for terrorists and assassins.[20] He had strengthened his reputation as a firebrand of the left, praising the murderous violence in Austria perpetrated by Herman Stellmacher and Anton Kammerer, the latter having participated in a sequence of killings, including those of a soldier and a pharmacist. When in 1884 the young Anarchists were caught and executed, a large demonstration was staged in New York, at which Most declared 'that if he had one thousand Stellmachers the social revolution would be accomplished in three months'.[21]

After the excitement of anticipation, Goldman's first impression on seeing Most in the flesh was one of pure disgust. The man was sickeningly ugly. 'He was of medium height, with a large head crowned with greyish bushy hair; but his face was twisted out of form by an apparent dislocation of the left jaw. Only his eyes were soothing; they were blue and sympathetic.'[22] However, she soon outsoared this first impression. Goldman was always apt to be seduced by the power of rhetoric. As she listened to Most's speech, she lost all sense of his disfigurement. As had happened when she had listened to Verdi, or heard Johanna Greie lecture about Haymarket, she was again transported to a pitch of pure sympathetic passion.

The next day, Berkman called on her at the Minkins' apartment. They spent hours talking, and soon discovered that they had much in common. They both came from the same town, Kovno, both could take an oath on Chernyshevsky's novel, and both could claim a family connection to prominent Nihilists.

Berkman's real name was Alexander Schmidt Bergmann; his friends called him Sasha. He was born in Vilnius, in what was then west Russia, in November 1870. He came from a family of respectable middle-class Jews: his father, Joseph Bergmann, owned a large business selling leather in St Petersburg. However, his maternal uncle was Mark Andreyevich Natanson, a founder member of the Chaikovsky Circle which with its broad revolutionary sympathies and advocacy of the policy of 'going to the people' was in the 1870s a benevolent counter-balance to the pure negativism of Nechaev's violence. This uncle – known to Berkman as 'Maxim' – was to prove an inspiration to the young boy. The rumours about the political beliefs of both his mother and uncle were thrilling. As he grew up in St Petersburg in the 1870s and early 1880s, the country seemed in turmoil. There were stories of bombs exploding while he was at school, and then the news that his uncle Maxim had been sentenced to death following the assassination of Alexander II.[23] Years later, Berkman would excitedly discover that his uncle was in fact alive and well, and living in exile in Siberia, but the fact of living for years with the image of a dead Nihilist hero in the family inevitably fired Berkman's imagination.[24]

Berkman's father was proud to be giving his children a first-class Russian education with private tutors and some years in the gymnasium. However, when Berkman was twelve years old, his father died and the family were forced to move in with their uncle Nathan in Kovno, Goldman's home town.[25] Young Berkman continued his studies there, but was to prove a free-thinking, politicised teenager. His father gone, he was anxious to prove himself a *man*. Rebellion was one means of doing so. Jewish children were obliged to take religious instruction. Young Berkman, however, informed his teachers that there was no God, and then wrote an essay to prove it. He was kept back a year as punishment. He was expelled from college and put on a black list that meant he could not hope to be accepted at any college in Russia.[26] He may have been politically resolute but he was a socially clumsy adolescent. Encased in his pious Nihilism, he could declaim his radical sympathies freely and be the man he wanted to be. Yet he was too shy to speak to girls. At the age of fifteen, he followed two girls from school, Masha and Lena, but turned out to be too awkward to take his hat off to them, and so missed his chance to be introduced.[27]

He was particularly distant from his mother. Although it seems she was something of a Nihilist, she was also a snob. Unlike her brother, she had no intention of going to the people and refused to permit her children to associate with 'menials'. On one occasion, young Berkman was struck when he witnessed her slapping a servant. He felt instinctively that she was in the wrong. He once fought with her physically: she cut his hand with a ladle, and he threw a salt-cellar that shattered a mirror. There was, it seemed, so much anger in him. Even when he was sixteen years old and she was dying, he could feel the tenderness in him estranged.[28]

Her death in 1887 precipitated his departure for America. As a Jew, his elder brother, Max, had been refused admission to a Russian university, and so had gone to study instead at Leipzig. With all possibility of education at a university or college denied him in Russia, Berkman decided to follow in his brother's footsteps. However, he ended up merely passing through Germany and travelling steerage to the USA. In February 1888 he arrived in New York. America offered some immediate liberty. In Eldridge Street, a few months after his seventeenth birthday, he had sex for the first time, although the girl refused to kiss him.[29] He could read and study Anarchism without anxiety about state censorship. With such freedoms came the responsibility to earn his living. Unused to physical labour, he found life in the United States precarious, living for over a year on only 5 to 7 cents a day.[30] Eventually he found work as a cigar maker and then a tailor. He called upon Johann Most, and learnt typesetting so that he could work on *Freiheit*. Striving for Anarchism was his life, but he still had to earn money; so he worked as a tailor at Zimmerman's shirt factory at East 11th Street.

It was partly through Most's influence that Berkman had become an Anarchist at all. Long afterwards, he recalled how he had first heard Most's name:

A plank in the bridge . . . In the *most* [Russian for 'bridge']. What a significant name! How it impressed me the first time I heard it! No, I saw it in print, I remember quite clearly. Mother had just died. I was dreaming of the New World, the Land of Freedom. Eagerly I read every line of 'American news.' One day, in the little Kovno library – how distinctly it all comes back to me – I can see myself sitting there, perusing the papers. Must get acquainted with the country. What is this? 'Anarchists hanged in Chicago.' There are many names – one is 'Most.' 'What is an Anarchist?' I whisper to the student near by. He is from Peter, he will know. 'S–sh! Same as Nihilists.' 'In free America?' I wondered.[31]

Moreover, just as for Goldman, it was news of the Haymarket riots and the judicial executions that followed that brought Berkman to Anarchism.

On Goldman's second day in New York City, Berkman introduced her to Most. After she had been so swept away by his passionate declamation the night before, the meeting began disappointingly. Most was irascible and self-pitying. However, he took an interest in the young woman Anarchist, questioned her about herself, and suggested that they should meet again.

Goldman saw a lot of Berkman in those next few weeks. Berkman soon introduced her to his cousin and schoolfriend Modest Aronstam. Aronstam had emigrated to America with Berkman. They were so much together that people nicknamed them the Twins. An easy patronage characterised Berkman's relationship with Aronstam, or 'Fedya' as he called him. Berkman knew himself to be the real radical thing: committed, tough on himself and others, as close as he could mould himself to Nechaev's image of the committed revolutionary.[32] All this vigour impressed Goldman deeply:

Alex Berkman, was such an enthusiast, that he could go without proper food for days and give his earnings for the cause, he was an Nihilist of the Bakunin type, he did [not? – an interesting Freudian slip] acknowledge friendship love or any other feeling, save the cause . . .[33]

In contrast, in Berkman's opinion, Fedya was spoilt, self-indulgent and criminally artistic. Fedya's weakness was a taste for beauty, something which could only be an unnecessary luxury until the revolution had relieved the world of poverty. Goldman was not so sure. She felt split between the two friends' attitudes, admiring Berkman's consistency and fire, but sharing Fedya's love for art. She also became quickly aware that Fedya's interest in her was something more than comradely.

Her sympathy with Fedya revealed the fundamental difference between her nature and Berkman's. Berkman was willing himself to play the part of the ascetic. He was putting himself through a more benign version of the transformation performed by Nechaev: he was becoming hard. However, Goldman possessed then, as through all her life, an instinct for pleasure. For all her moral seriousness, her Anarchism was the manifestation of a deep desire for self-expression without constraint. Once during a party she had declared to her husband that she wanted to dance until she died. The rebellious and even self-destructive ardour of that romantic request forms the keynote for her life. Goldman was never adept at following rules, even the rules that the Anarchists had newly prescribed for themselves.

This capacity to ignore prescriptions was going to be handy in her present situation. Very soon after her arrival in New York, Goldman found herself the object of sexual and romantic interest for Berkman, Fedya and, strangest of all, Johann Most. She was an unlikely *femme fatale*. She was short, not quite five feet tall, large-hipped, with curly blond hair. Her lower lip jutted forward a little, but clearly she was an attractive woman, affectionate, intelligent and committed. It seems she was even sexy – judging by the ways that men and, on occasion, women reacted to her over the next forty years. Goldman and Most began to pass time together in a passionate friendship, talking in cafés, going on walks. Most adopted the tutorial position, recommending books, telling the young woman the history of Anarchism. Goldman was charmed and a little impressed at her own power to grant happiness to such an illustrious figure. Without yet revealing his feelings, Berkman was plainly jealous, and avoided Goldman for a while. When they did meet again, their relationship quickly deepened, even as she continued her relationship with Most.

Disliking life at the Minkins' apartment, where the father of the sisters seemed to have an unhealthy interest in one of his daughters, Goldman found an apartment of her own on Suffolk Street. There, in the narrow room, she consummated her affair with Berkman, doing so a few hours after having heard Most give a speech, at which she had been so stirred that her 'very soul' was 'contracting and expanding in the rise and fall of his voice'.[34] Now that she and Berkman were lovers, they rented a place together, forming a small commune with Fedya Aronstam and Helen Minkin in a four-room flat on 42nd Street. Soon after moving in, a quarrel with Fedya kept Berkman away from the apartment for a few days. While he was away, Fedya and Goldman became intimate. Feeling that they were in love, the two of them resolved to confront Berkman with the situation when he returned. However, the moment did not feel favourable, and they kept their secret. Away from the erotic possibilities of the apartment, Most suggested that Goldman, with her eloquence and convincing passion, should speak for the cause. A lecture was arranged at Rochester, and on the way to Grand Central Station to see her off, Most started passionately kissing her in the cab. Berkman was waiting for her at the station with an American Beauty rose.

The Rochester lecture was a success; Goldman had found her public voice, and discovered that she could now move others, as she herself had been so often moved. However, although Most had created the opportunity for Goldman's success, on her return it was clear that he resented it. He required her to be a ministering angel, a helpmeet, a devoted Desdemona to his Othello. Despite her enormous capacity for kindness, Goldman had no interest in performing this role. The two quarrelled, and though they made up soon afterwards, the shadow of an impending break was already over them.

Goldman and Fedya made love. She told Berkman about what had happened, and he responded in full accordance with the revolutionary ideals of the household. She was at liberty to do whatever she wanted. He would triumph over his own latent bourgeois jealousy and celebrate her freedom to love. He was even glad that the two people he loved most should also love each other. That night, when Fedya returned, the three revolutionaries embraced and promised to dedicate themselves to the Cause, even at the cost of their own deaths if that were required of them.

To complicate matters still further, it seems that Berkman also had a crush on one of the Minkin sisters, most probably Anna. Once he had visited, and finding her sick, had been directed to her bedside by her father. He had sat beside her, talking to her softly. He saw that the pillows had slipped, and leant over to straighten them, and so involuntarily touched her hair. For a moment, he was intoxicated and leant forward and kissed her hair. Another time, coming back from seeing Sarah Bernhardt in *Tosca*, he had sat by her bed and talked with her about the play and about Bernhardt's décolleté. The conversation turned to her own bosom, and Berkman persuaded her to allow him to touch her. "'You – like them, really, Sasha?" The large eyes looked lustrous and happy. "They are Greek, dear",' Berkman replied before kissing her between her breasts.[35]

Goldman now left on a lecture tour with Most. The old Anarchist told her the story of his adventures and sufferings. She loved him for the dangers he had passed, and he loved her that she pitied them. He was living in the shadow of an imminent prison sentence. He told her of his fears of going back to prison: the last time on Blackwell's Island penitentiary, they had shaved his beard and so laid bare the disfigurement that he had so long concealed. All his life, he had been tortured by the self-consciousness created in him by his mutilation. She was stirred by compassion for him and the two became lovers.

There were serious questions before Goldman and Berkman. The dilemma of how they would best serve the revolution was pressing. News of terrible conditions in Russia weighed on them. Was their place in the struggle back at home? Or should they stay and fight there in America? A tad disingenuously Most advised that Berkman ought to go to Russia and conspire, while Goldman's talents would be better used propagandising in America. They both began thinking of a return home. Whatever the two young radicals would do would prove a culturally significant choice. In one sense, Berkman and Goldman's collision with American history and the violence they brought with them were the consequence of importing Russian political hopes and methods to the USA. Certainly this was how Berkman himself saw the deed that was to come. Despite the murders of Lincoln and Garfield, Berkman believed firmly that his was the first *attentat* in the USA. In the USA, conservative commentators at the time, and since, also put down the revolutionary politics and violence from the 1890s to the end of the First World War as a consequence of immigration. Terrorists were a virus from abroad;

socialism and Anarchism being responses to European tyranny could not flourish on American soil.[36] Stressing the Russianness of Berkman and Goldman and of their hopes and aims may repeat the burden of such an analysis. However, this view of things is not the whole story; the reality is more complex. The anti-immigrationists were wrong in denying the presence of many second- and third-generation American radicals, as well as others of even older 'stock'. Moreover, they forgot, as Goldman never did, that America itself was founded in a revolutionary act. In 1908, while being questioned by a Board of Special Inquiry, Goldman was asked whether she believed in the violent ousting of a government. She replied:

I believe in the method laid down by the Constitution of the United States, that when the Government becomes despotic and irksome the people have the right to overthrow. You will have to hold the Government of the United States responsible for that.[37]

And, finally, these critics of the Anarchists misunderstood in its deeper sense what an 'American' is. All 'Americans' were immigrants once. Another way of putting it is that the end of the century saw the infusion of radical thought from Germany and greater Russia, an infusion that expanded the notion of Americanism, and became not an externally alien pressure, but joined a native impulse.

In 1890, preparatory to their prospective move back to Russia, Berkman, Goldman, Helen Minkin and Fedya all went to live in New Haven, Connecticut. Berkman was to work in a print shop, while the women would open a dress-making co-operative, modelled on the one initiated by Chernyshevsky's character Vera in the novel *What Is To Be Done?* At this time, there was little contact between Most and Goldman, and what there was tended to end in argument, as she refused to have sex with him. Most accused her of preferring 'that Russian Jew', Berkman, no doubt forgetting in his fury that Goldman was also both Russian and Jewish. As if the situation were not complicated enough, Helen Minkin now revealed that she was desperately in love with Most, and left New Haven to be closer to him.

The New Haven co-operative did not last long. Fedya was unable to find work; Berkman and Goldman returned to New York. Both the young revolutionaries were moving away from Most's brand of

Anarchism to embrace that propounded in *Die Autonomie*, a journal run by a German Anarchist, Joseph Peukert. Most and Peukert were old enemies. Most held him responsible for the arrest of one of his friends and colleagues, Joseph Neve. It is unlikely that Peukert was involved intentionally in Neve's arrest, but he was certainly a good friend of Karl Theodor Reuss, a figure in the Anarchist movement who would much later be unmasked as a member of the Berlin Political Police. It is possible that Peukert inadvertently gave information to Reuss that proved compromising for Neve.

Peukert had been a delegate at the July 1881 Anarchist Conference in London, and then had been again active in that city from 1884, where he founded Gruppe Autonomie and began printing the journal *Die Autonomie*. He was an advocate of Kropotkin's Anarchism, which meant, at this time, a belief in the efficacy of self-government by decentralised small groups, faith in individual action, and, therefore, support for propaganda by the deed. Such beliefs were all favourably received by Goldman and Berkman, who were also getting tired of Most's dictatorial manner and growing increasingly interested in Kropotkin.[38] In 1890, Peukert had arrived in America, where he founded *Der Anarchist* and tried to clear his name of the accusations regarding Neve. In his support, Berkman advocated in December 1890 that an investigation into the Neve affair be conducted by members of the movement. Most was furious. Goldman found herself between the two men, still drawn by Most's passion and need for sympathy, but strongly attracted to Berkman's youthful zeal.

The need for a final choice was delayed for a while by Most's imprisonment. In 1887, on the day after the execution of the Haymarket Martyrs, Most had delivered a provocative and rabble-rousing speech, one which led to a conviction for incitement to riot. Most appealed against the sentence, and managed to delay his incarceration, but in June 1891, he was finally returned to the penitentiary on Blackwell's Island. He would remain there until April the following year.

The young Anarchists' wandering life continued. Fedya had gone to work in Springfield, Massachusetts, as a photographer, a suitable profession for a failed painter. Goldman joined him, and soon afterwards Berkman came too. The three of them invested the last of their money in an ice-cream parlour in Worcester, Massachusetts. They were

there when news reached them of Homestead. It was the moment that
endowed their chaotic lives with the grace of a single purpose: the
assassination of Henry Clay Frick.

IV: Homestead

The only cure for terrorism is justice.
   TERRY EAGLETON

Born out of the economics of laissez-faire, a new American plutocracy
dominated America's 'Gilded Age'. Though the majority of the new
tycoons were born into money, a small group of the first generation
of these new 'captains of industry' started off in poverty.[39] All were
expansive dreamers, believers in progress – the country's and their
own – seeking their fortunes like poor Jacks, sloughing off in the
process their impoverished origins: John D. Rockefeller's dad was a
purveyor of supposedly medicinal potions; Jay Gould had tended
cattle; Andrew Carnegie laboured as a bobbin-boy in a factory
cellar.[40] These self-made men struggled, speculated, and, by force of
will, out of the harshness of their lives found enrichment. Many were
'Yankees' who, with a trusty paid substitute, had sidestepped service
in the Civil War.[41] They profited by the war in other ways, making
money from the economic opportunities; New York's population of
millionaires tripled during the war years.[42] As much as the President
themselves, they embodied the great American promise. They may
have started with good, and limited intentions – Carnegie swore
that he would never, should never earn more than $50,000 per year,
and was ashamed of the great disparity in fortune between the rich
and poor – but they had tied themselves to a force greater than their
own.[43] Incrementally these great men, these industrious personalities,
transformed into automata of acquisition.

There were ironies at play in an Anarchist setting out to murder
an industrialist. Both sides would have laid claim to the word
'individualism' – though the prophets of industrialism preached the
potency of the individual within a world of unfettered competition,
while Berkman's particular brand of Anarchism was as much interested in social co-operation as in individual freedom. For the big

industrial companies, a relatively recent arrival on the American scene, a language had evolved in which the corporation was modelled on the legal fiction of being an 'artificial individual'.[44] As such they staked a claim to an American tradition of individualism and personal liberty, attached to a free-market economic philosophy. The fact that very recognisable individuals headed such companies, from Carnegie through Rockefeller to Frick, fostered this illusion; something of a press-created personality cult based on a Horatio Alger-style rhetoric of self-help had grown up around those men. Each in turn stood for a particular industry: Carnegie for iron and steel; Rockefeller for oil; John Pierpont Morgan for banking.[45] The workers were anonymous members of a mass; their bosses owned famous names and faces, and the public institutions they endowed advertised their social aims while exalting their individual success. Not everyone, of course, shared this rosy view of the magnates, and indeed they were often viewed as being as lawless and criminal as the Anarchists themselves. It was in this spirit that Jay Gould was nicknamed 'The Spider'.[46] Still the official view, at least, was that such billionaires manifested all the sweet nobility of life. Ranged against these rugged American individualists, living embodiments of the spirit of self-reliance and of success, were the European diseases of paternalism and socialism, the two things being closely allied in popular representation. That the socialists reputedly came from abroad, from the old dead world of Europe, the discarded father of the nation, was itself witnessed in their adherence to un-American beliefs in social planning and intrusive laws. The Anarchists were more difficult to pin down. Their hostility to government brought them uneasily into the shade cast by the supposedly 'individualist' corporations. The fact that corporations relied on government support in the form of preferential treatment, contracts and tailor-made laws was only the first of many paradoxes in the situation. That many 'native-born' Americans were supporters of labour rights or, indeed, of Anarchism was just one other.[47]

Andrew Carnegie was impressed by Frick's firm handling of his own labour disputes. Particularly interesting was the incident at Morewood, where Frick had worked constantly to wrong-foot the union, turning an amicable dispute into a confrontation, one which ended with striking miners being fired at by Pinkerton detectives. Eight men were killed. The criminal investigation that followed led to the conviction of ten of the miners and the acquittal of all the detectives. It was a grand achievement. Carnegie was keen to bring the younger man in as his partner, and, more vitally, to have him push through drastic changes in the running of the steel company. Meanwhile Carnegie would vanish to the hygienic remoteness of the Scottish Highlands, and sample the fishing at Cluny Castle.[48] A notable philanthropist such as himself could not dirty his hands with such squabbles. In April 1892, he set sail for Scotland and Frick went to work.

Homestead was the prize of all Carnegie and Frick's steel plants. The dreary factory spread alongside a bend in the Monongahela River. The most modern, the most efficient of all the company's plants, it turned out steel for bridges, buildings and American warships.[49] Yet the unions there were also especially troublesome. They had defeated the bosses on two previous occasions (in 1882 and 1889), gaining union recognition at the mill, and had stooped before to violence and intimidation.

The battle of Homestead was really to be about who had the power to run the mill, and about the values of the bosses who chose to run it. A paternalistic relationship between workers and employers had led to a situation where the union exerted a great deal of control on working hours and even the quality of the pig iron. Like most capitalists of his era, Frick was ready to ditch the old connection. What mattered was not the worker, but efficiency, mechanisation and the smooth running of the business according to market dictates.[50] The pretext for the conflict would be the end of a three-year contract regarding a sliding wage scale that would come at the end of June 1892.

With Carnegie's cognisance, Frick decided to pick a fight and break the union. Negotiations about pay and conditions were essential, as Frick insisted, at a time of recession in the steel industry. But soon after they had begun, they broke down. Frick had a fence built around the plant, separating the factory from the town with a twelve-foot-high wooden stockade. The fence was punctuated with regular holes suitable for firing a rifle from. Platforms were built within the plant for searchlights and guards. On 25 June 1892, Frick announced that, from now on, the company would deal with workers on an individual basis when agreeing pay, hours and working conditions. On 30 June, a 'lock-out' was initiated. On 1 July 1892 the existing contract with the Amalgamated Association of Iron and Steel Workers expired, and Frick launched his attempt to break the union and run the plant on 'blackleg' labour.

Frick had contacted the Pinkerton agency and ordered 300 guards for the first week in July. The Pinkerton National Detective Agency was established by Allan Pinkerton in 1850; at one point in the late nineteenth century its employees outnumbered the regular Army. Pinkerton had worked for Abraham Lincoln (he was one of the men who warned the President of the assassination plot in Baltimore) and had been the head of General McClellan's secret service.[51] The Pinkerton men were the original 'private eyes' and also a repressive force used regularly by bosses against unionised labour. Frick had already used Pinkerton agents at Morewood, where, as now, their presence had served to antagonise striking workers. It is said that Frick had insisted that the Pinkertons should not use their guns. But he had the example of Morewood behind him. He knew what these men would do, if pushed into a corner. Such a violent confrontation was by no means a new thing in American life. In 1873, a series of coal strikes had left many murdered. In 1877, a railway strike led to vicious riots, the worst of which occurred in Pittsburgh.

As Independence Day 1892 drew near, the workers began to organise their own campaign. They constructed a barricade of their own, designed to lock out Frick and the bosses from the plant. Workers patrolled the Monongahela River on the look-out for blacklegs; a cordon of striking men manned the waterfront; roads were blockaded; and guards were posted at the railway station and the gates to the mill.

On the morning of 5 July, the local police tried to post a guard of their own at the site. The eleven officers arrived by train to be greeted by several thousand angry workers and their families. Appraising the situation, the officers quickly came to a decision that they would not after all guard the works, preferring to leave that job in the hands of the strikers. Surrounded by cheering crowds, the police left peaceably by the next available train.

A more forcible attempt to regain control of the plant, masterminded by Frick, began in earnest later that day. Three hundred Pinkerton men would try to enter the Homestead plant, coming by train from Ashtabula in Ohio. On the train with them were unmarked crates of rifles and ammunition. At nearby Bellevue, around midnight, they disembarked and stepped into two barges. Two small tugs began to drag the barges upriver to Homestead. It was a foggy night and hard to see anything clearly, but some of the strikers spotted the Pinkerton men two miles short of the factory. Word was sent back to the strikers at the plant by telephone and a message brought by a mounted courier. The workers poured out, and soon a thousand men were waiting on the riverside for the barges' landfall. It was now early morning, and the dawn was fast coming. As the Pinkerton agents approached, the workers reportedly opened fire. Strangely, not one of the detectives was hit by these volleys, and the boats continued onwards, aiming to land inside the plant itself. It was 4.30 a.m. The workers tore through the fence to get to where the Pinkertons were landing, and immediately warned the invading detectives not to occupy the plant. The leader of the agents responded by saying that they were there legally and that the men should depart at once or risk injury. At this point, apparently, the strikers again opened fire, and with surprising ineptness again failed to hit a single Pinkerton man. The Pinkertons certainly returned fire, and with greater accuracy it would seem, for all at once thirty strikers were shot. Enraged, the strikers charged the detectives and drove them back. The Pinkertons re-boarded their barge and withdrew to the river, where they bided their time, looking for another opportunity to land.

The courageous Pinkertons continued in their lawful activities, floating opposite the works on the Monongahela, hampered only by the ineffectual sallies of the strikers, who fired aged cannons at them (one shot blowing a hole through the roof of one of the barges), and attempted by foul means to set fire to one of the barges by igniting oil spread on the water. There was another attempt to land, again seen off by the strikers. The battle raged for fourteen hours, until, at last, around 5.00 in the afternoon, overwhelmed by superior numbers, the Pinkertons capitulated. Their guns were thrown in the river, and the hapless men, running the gauntlet of an irate crowd, were marched to the local skating rink (the jail was too small to hold them), where they were mistreated and badly beaten up. Estimates vary as to the fatalities that day. A likely number is that three Pinkertons and seven strikers had been killed. At the time, the number of dead was rumoured to be far higher, from twenty-five to thirty-eight, with the weight of the casualties falling on the side the reporter happened to favour.[52] It is even harder to estimate the number of the wounded.

The workers were, for the moment, victorious. On 8 July, Adelaide Frick gave birth to a son, though he did not look likely to live long. Adelaide too was very sick. On 12 July 1892, eight and a half thousand of the Pennsylvania militia swept into Homestead, dislodged the workers, and allowed Frick and his men to regain access to the plant. From here, he continued to oversee the battle with the unions, with his mind always returning to Adelaide and their new child. A congressional committee investigating the riot questioned Frick on 13 July. He told them that he had employed Pinkerton detectives for a week before the strike began, and had ordered that they should be armed. On 14 July martial law was declared. Frick settled himself down to a long battle.

However, events were about to take an unprecedented turn: Berkman had decided on his intervention. At the very beginning of July news reached Berkman, Goldman and Fedya of the confrontation with Frick. They decided to write and distribute an Anarchist manifesto among the striking workers at Homestead. They were still busy with the process of composition when, on 6 July 1892, Goldman came home to their little flat in Worcester, Massachusetts, excited with news of the battle of Homestead.[53] The workers' success thrilled all of them. They saw it not as a spontaneous act of defiance, but as evidence of the tactical skill that would be needed to defeat Carnegie and Co.[54] Early reports, at least as Goldman and Berkman understood them, suggested that the Pinkertons had opened fire without warning at the workers on the bank, killing many. The time for words alone was surely over. The trio immediately knew that their revolutionary destinies were linked from henceforth to America and not Russia. They quit Worcester and ice cream and returned to New York.

Initially, the plan was to go and give the fighters (*Kämpfer*) of Homestead some good advice. Berkman was worried that the strikers, having found the right tone 'by setting power against power', would become 'half-frightened about their courageous deed'. It seemed the right moment 'to propagandise sensible points of view'.[55] But more was required than just the dissemination of a printed appeal:

I wanted to use the opportunity to show – for the first time in this country the solidarity of the Anarchists with the working people by one unyielding *deed*, and by this to gain the sympathies of the people for the Anarchists and their goals. My decision was soon made: I go to Pittsburgh, I spread a revolutionary appeal among the 'strikers' of Homestead and I clear out of the way the monomaniacal Atilla [*sic*] H. C. Frick, head of the Carnegie Works, – as a lesson for the oppressed, a warning of what will come for the oppressors, – 'a blow like Brutus" [*ein Brutus-Stoss*] for the tormented, the murdered, the martyred, – a propaganda deed for the social revolution.[56]

Berkman was already convinced of the rectitude and justice of such propaganda. He had quoted approvingly to Goldman only a few days after their first meeting, the words of the Haymarket Martyr Louis Lingg: 'If you attack us with cannon, we will reply with dynamite', adding that he intended one day to avenge the Anarchist dead.[57] He had already mastered the basic fact of 'revolutionary ethics': only that which was good for the revolution was good at all. Goldman too was ready to embrace positive action. A few years before, outraged by the caricatures of Most printed in the press, she suggested to Berkman that they should dynamite a newspaper office. However, Berkman had his sights set higher, and thought they should wait for a more suitable target. The three of them, Fedya, Goldman and Berkman, all believed that there had been women and children killed at Homestead. The man in charge of the whole operation bore the ultimate responsibility for that. Moreover murdering Frick would put Carnegie back in charge of the strike; it seemed very likely that the munificent industrialist would be forced to give in to the workers rather than compromise his public image. The moment had come. Frick was to be the ideal victim of the first American *attentat*.

Goldman was 'spellbound' by Berkman's calm daring. He refused all offers of Fedya and Goldman's help. He would go to Pittsburgh alone and blow up Frick. Using Most's *The Science of Revolutionary Warfare*, Berkman set about trying to make a bomb, but the experiments did not work (they included an abortive attempt to create a practice explosion on Staten Island), and instead they opted for simply shooting the man. Goldman was to propagandise after the event, showing the workers that Frick had to be killed, not because of who he was, but because of what he stood for. There was no grudge against Frick the man, who was, after all, merely a man like other men. Berkman was to murder a symbol.

Berkman, Goldman and Fedya needed help in performing the assassination, but who could they ask? Most was out of the question. He had been released from prison a couple of months before, but since being free had kept aloof from his former protégés. There was the additional problem that they could hardly tell their friends what they were planning. They wished to finance both a pamphlet explaining Anarchist solidarity with the workers, and the murder itself. Berkman reckoned they would need around $100. Arriving in New York, he spread word that he was unemployed and looking to borrow money so he could go west and start again. On this premise, he tried to cadge some cash from friends, but failed: they were either too poor themselves, or, taking his story too seriously, advised Berkman to wait in New York until he found some work there. However, they could not afford to wait. Goldman approached Peukert, and told him in vague terms, without naming names, what was required, but, as they had feared, he wanted nothing to do with whatever Berkman was up to. While doctrinally sound, Peukert lacked the stuff of genuine martyrs and still confused the end with the means. There was nothing else for it but to pool their resources, which altogether amounted to a paltry fifteen dollars. They simply couldn't afford the expense of an explanatory leaflet, and this idea was dropped. Still it was enough to get Berkman to Pittsburgh, and provide him with a night's lodging there, before he was able to move in with some Anarchist acquaintances, Carl Nold and Henry Bauer. Neither of these men was to be informed about the true nature of Berkman's visit.

On Tuesday 12 July 1892, the time came for Berkman to go. Sasha, the familiar name by which Goldman and the others knew Berkman, said goodbye to his 'sailor girl' at the Baltimore and Ohio Station. Both knew that they would never see each other alive again.

V: The Pittsburgh Raskolnikov

With his suitcase in his hand Berkman felt happy, in a good mood about things. Alone, he sat up for a while, thinking over the glorious deed to come. Then, lulled by the motion of the train, he fell asleep.

When he woke up, he was anxious that he had lost his wallet, but when he checked it was still there, with everything intact: the addresses of his comrades, Nold and Bauer, a dollar bill and a small picture of Frick cut out from a newspaper. There was a six-hour stopover in Washington, and he decided to take a look around the city, and was distracted for a while from his dismal thoughts by the white imposing beauty of Capitol Hill.

Berkman arrived in Pittsburgh on 13 July 1892. It was 11.00 p.m., too late to go to Nold and Bauer, so he checked in at Merchants Hotel. He gave his name as Rakhmetov, in honour of the hero of Chernyshevsky's *What Is To Be Done?* He would also use another alias during the next few weeks, Bachman, but Rakhmetov was the one with most personal significance, amounting to something between a grim joke and an honouring allusion – one that both honoured the book, and honoured him. Yet the use of the alias possessed another personal significance to Berkman. It made his deed generic. He was stealing his own name from himself, and performing his action simply as an instrument of the revolution; he was not himself any longer, he was merely a 'Rakhmetov'.[58]

The next morning, early, he went to Nold's house. Carl Nold was only a year older than Berkman himself, a love child from Weingarten in Germany, whose father had 'died slowly from wounds sustained in the Franco-Prussian war'; he had come to America when he was fourteen. He now had a wife with whom he had 'a free union' and a baby son. He was a supporter of Most. In the next two weeks, the very tall Henry Bauer, another German, would stay alongside Berkman at Nold's. Some nine years older than Berkman, Bauer had come to America to avoid the army, and was then converted to Anarchism by the events at Haymarket.[59] Berkman was entirely unaware that his hosts were suspicious of him, and that they had sent an enquiry to Most concerning his reliability. Most had replied by warning Nold and Bauer against him. Each night, while Berkman slept, Bauer lay awake beside him, his hand on a cocked pistol, ready to shoot Berkman at the first sign of treachery.[60]

All the evidence suggests that, as he waited for a favourable opportunity to do the killing, Berkman was working himself up into a dark and elevated determination – one that he would himself satirise afterwards. Frick was simply a 'bloody villain' and a construct of economic oppression, not at all another human being. Similarly de-humanised were the workers themselves, whom Berkman aggrandised into what he was happy to term 'the People', the 'grand, mysterious, yet so near and real, People'.[61] He was caught between two abstractions: the amorphous aggregate of the People and Frick, the equally vague symbol of their enemy. He had no doubt that the modern capitalist was a contemporary form of the tyrant.[62] He walked the streets feverishly buoyant, unaware of everything but his own mood of exultation. The place receded, leaving only an unreal sense of his purpose. The mission was suicidal, he knew, and this very fact contributed to his euphoria. Soon he too would be a martyr like those murdered by the state after Haymarket. The moral question was an irrelevancy. He had already solved the problem some time before:

The question of moral right in such matters often agitated the revolutionary circles I used to frequent. I had always taken the extreme view. The more radical the treatment, I held, the quicker the cure. Society is a patient, sick constitutionally and functionally. Surgical treatment is often imperative. The removal of a tyrant is not merely justifiable; it is the highest duty of every true revolutionist. Human life is, indeed, sacred and inviolate. But the killing of a tyrant, of an enemy of the People, is in no way to be considered as the taking of a life.[63]

He was ready to take the ultimate step and so prove himself 'a *man*, a complete MAN'.[64] It was the old anxiety all over again, but now within reach of its solution. He was about to prove himself exceptional, and gain meaning, even a sense of his own existence, through martyr-dom and, incidentally, murder. The arrogant assertion of self-denial sustained him. He was twenty-one years old.

He had agreed with Goldman that he would carry out the assassination on Saturday 23 July. He laid plans. He had his first sight of 'Fort Frick', as the Homestead plant had been named after the building of the stockade. There it was, a watch-towered fortress on the opposing bank of the Monongahela River. Striking men with rifles were crossing a ground of ashes and cinders. He walked around Pittsburgh, and the place struck him as an industrial hell of stench and furnaces, smoke and smog.[65] It was oppressive to consider all those of the People who were forced to live here, while industrialists like Frick and Carnegie lived in luxury. And indeed just then, Frick was only a few miles away in his beautiful and newly renovated house, worrying over his sick wife and dying son. Berkman wandered down to Frick's neighbourhood, the fashionable, tree-lined East End, the 'Iron City', where the rich lived.

He had heard that Frick had made a point of the fact that he would still receive callers at the works. He came up with a simple expedient for gaining access to Frick. He would approach him in the guise of an employment agent from New York willing to supply blackleg labour to the mill. The reprehensible nature of his supposed business would be itself a moral comment on the man he was about to sacrifice. On the Saturday morning, he went to the works and was admitted. He wrote out a note on a small card, and had it sent into Frick's office: 'Dear Sir,' he wrote, 'I would like to see you at your earliest opportunity. Alex. Berkman.' For some reason – perhaps he forgot, or panicked, or felt that concealing his identity didn't matter any more – he used not his alias, but his real name.

Frick could not see him now – perhaps later. Berkman left, returned, persisted, pestered the reception clerk. A time was set: 2 p.m. At the appointed hour, Berkman came back. From the reception room, as the door to Frick's office closed, he caught a glimpse of Frick himself, sitting at a table in the back of the room. The clerk came back with Berkman's card. Frick was busy; he would not see Berkman now. What happened next is the scene that began this chapter, but this time it is best described in Berkman's own words:

I take the pasteboard, return it to my case, and walk slowly out of the reception-room. But quickly retracing my steps, I pass through the gate separating the clerks from the visitors, and, brushing the astounded attendant aside, I step into the office on the left, and find myself facing Frick.

For an instant the sunlight, streaming through the windows, dazzles me. I discern two men at the further end of the long table.

'Fr—,' I begin. The look of terror on his face strikes me speechless. It is the dread of the conscious presence of death. 'He understands,' it flashes through my mind. With a quick motion I draw the revolver. As I raise the weapon, I see Frick clutch with both hands the arm of the chair, and attempt to rise. I aim at his head . . . I hear a sharp, piercing cry, and see Frick on his knees, his head against the arm of the chair. I feel calm and possessed, intent upon every movement of the man . . . About twenty-five feet separate us. I take a few steps toward him, when

suddenly the other man, whose presence I had quite forgotten, leaps upon me . . .
Suddenly I hear the cry, 'Murder! Help!' My heart stands still as I realize that it is
Frick shouting. 'Alive?' I wonder. I hurl the stranger aside and fire at the crawling
figure of Frick. The man struck my hand, – I have missed! He grapples with me,
and we wrestle across the room . . . By the throat I catch the stranger, still clinging
to me, when suddenly something heavy strikes me on the back of the head. Sharp
pains shoot through my eyes. I sink to the floor, vaguely conscious of the weapon
slipping from my hands.

'Where is the hammer? Hit him, carpenter!' . . . The weight of many bodies is
pressing on me. Now – it's Frick's voice! Not dead? . . . I must get the dagger from
my pocket – I have it! Repeatedly I strike with it at the legs of the man near the
window . . .

Police, clerks, workmen in overalls, surround me. An officer pulls my head
back by the hair, and my eyes meet Frick's. He stands in front of me, supported by
several men. His face is ashen gray; the black beard is streaked with red, and blood
is oozing from his neck. For an instant a strange feeling, as of shame, comes over
me; but the next moment I am filled with anger at the sentiment, so unworthy of
a revolutionist. With defiant hatred I look him full in the face.[66]

Weak from the blows sustained from the carpenter's hammer,
Berkman was dragged from the room. A police wagon was called for,
and by the time it had come a crowd had gathered on the street outside,
calling to lynch him. Berkman was bleeding, and anxious: he had lost
his glasses in the struggle. He could not stop himself from trembling.
When they reached the Central Police Station in Oak Alley, the police
had to help him out of the wagon, and, once inside, had to give him
whiskey before he was fit to speak.[67]

Chief O'Mara questioned him, and then the police took the requisite
mug-shot, by which point they seem to have found the missing glasses.
In the picture, Berkman looks remarkably composed, even sleepy,
possibly the effect of the whiskey; he's rather handsome, his black hair
ruffled, in a shirt with no tie and an open jacket. Though the half-smile
he appears to be giving may have had another secret cause, one that was
soon to be revealed. They took him to a cell; Berkman was twitchy and
excitable. Suddenly Chief O'Mara spotted Berkman twisting something
inside his mouth, and so quickly gripped him by the throat and with
his other hand prised his jaw open. A cartridge of dynamite rolled out
into the policeman's fist. Berkman had planned to blow himself up like

the heroic Louis Lingg.[68] Asked what the cartridge was, Berkman, still playing the role of tough guy, replied 'Candy.'[69]

Left alone, he no longer felt so tough. The cell made him claustrophobic. He had been questioned rather gently, but they had given him salty food, and now he was thirsty and called for water; none was brought to him. He started to run through events in his mind. What distressed him most was that he had been prevented from killing Frick by a carpenter, one of the People. He was puzzled. Why would the man have done this? He could not sleep from thirst.

He was taken to the local jail. Fashionable ladies visited, but were more eager to stare at a newspaper artist who had murdered a young girl than take a look at Frick's would-be assassin.[70] At night, the guards kept an eye on him to prevent another suicide attempt – the death watch, it was called. All the immigrant nationalities that formed America were in the jail. Berkman set about trying to learn the rules of the place. After one conversation with a black prisoner, another white inmate let him know that it was not done for a white man to talk with the 'niggers'. The conversation was anyhow a rare example of amiability in Berkman just then. He felt removed from the others, set apart in his revolutionary dignity. It was hard not to think that his noble act was somewhat tainted by his being lodged with common criminals. When one of the other prisoners shortened his name to 'Aleck', Berkman sneered at the attempted intimacy.[71] Above all, he was irritated to discover that none of his fellow prisoners could be made to understand why he had felt it necessary to kill Frick at all. In their political naïveté they believed that unless the reason was some personal grudge, it was just the steelworkers' affair, not his. Otherwise it was pure madness. Berkman was dismayed. Was this an indication of how the People would judge his *attentat*? Fortunately, on reflection, Berkman concluded that his fellow prisoners were not a part of the People as such, and therefore their insensitive views could be safely dismissed.

Yet when he finally met an imprisoned striking worker, the experience was similarly disillusioning. Even the worker assumed the attempted murder was the outcome of some failed business deal. It seemed as though the Americans were incapable of understanding a murder on anything other than personal terms. This was intensely disappointing. He had no interest in Frick as a person; he had struck not at a man, but at a symbol. Why could they not grasp this? The Americans had proved small-minded; he missed Russian idealism. If only he could die on the barricades like 'a real man'![72]

His mind turned to the forthcoming trial. He decided that he would not present a defence but rather offer an explanation. Given the obvious misunderstanding of his deed, it was necessary that he should bring the People to a deeper comprehension of the value of its 'terroristic effect'.[73] More importantly, it was vital that the People felt 'the depth of a love that will give its own life for their cause. To give a young life, full of health and vitality, to give all, without a thought of self; to give all, voluntarily, cheerfully; nay, enthusiastically – could any one fail to understand such a love?'[74] Such a feeling was not sentimentality; it was the sacrifice of the individual for the mass. These were soothing reflections. He believed himself innocent, and in any case refused to acknowledge the moral force of an oppressive state's legal codes.

It was then that Berkman received terrible news. Frick had survived. A prisoner gave him a newspaper clipping all about it during exercise. 'You're a poor shot,' he teased him.[75] In the next weeks this taunt became a familiar one. He did his best to maintain his revolutionary dignity, and not brood on ignorant slurs. He waited for the trial, feeling that his life was already over. After the trial would come prison. He was sure of that. He was like a dead man. Everything would have been bearable if only he could know how his deed had been received in the world outside. He longed for news, not for personal reasons of course, merely in his function as a revolutionist. A note was dropped for him, and he discovered that Nold and Bauer were both in the prison too, both charged with conspiracy to kill Frick. This was a terrible blow, but a worse one quickly followed: Most had repudiated the attempted assassination. It seemed impossible. Could the defiant man who had been Berkman's hero, who had gone to prison several times for praising violence and celebrating assassination, now surrender all principle? Was it cowardice, dislike, or even jealousy? Emma Goldman would know. He longed for a letter from her. She was the only one he could trust. But what had she been doing since they had said their farewells that night in a New York railway station?

VI: The Trial

While Berkman, her 'Sasha', had been in Pittsburgh preparing for the event, Goldman had been waiting in New York. She was distraught and without a cent. Recollections of Dostoevsky's *Crime and Punishment* prompted her to model herself on the character of Sonya, the pious prostitute. She decided that the only way for her to earn money was to go out on to the streets and entice men. Sasha would approve, she was sure. It was revolutionary, after all, to gain the end by any means, and there could be no question of bourgeois morality. She borrowed five dollars for some suitable clothes and on the Saturday night, 16 July, she walked up and down 14th Street in her new dress and high heels looking for business. None came. She walked until her feet ached. When she finally did pick up a punter, a kindly man in late middle age, he took her for a beer, and told her that she was quite unsuited to her new profession, and advised that she find a new one. They debated the matter for a while, then he presented her with ten dollars and they parted.[76]

On Monday a note came from Sasha, telling her that he was staying with Nold and Bauer but required more money. Goldman wrote to her sister asking for fifteen dollars, adding to it five of those she had received from the kindly stranger. With the other five she repaid the money she had used to buy the streetwalker clothes.

The next Saturday, she received the news of Sasha's attempt. Frick was fatally wounded, it seemed, and Sasha . . . well, Sasha too would soon be killed. That night, she went with Fedya to hear Most lecture, eager to hear what he would say about Sasha's *attentat*. Most was dismissive, declaring that he considered the story of the assault a put-up job. Goldman was horrified. Was Most drunk, or merely terrified of the detectives undoubtedly present at the meeting? Actually this apparent act of betrayal represented rather the public expression of Most's disillusionment with 'propaganda by the deed'; since 1885 he had been privately moving away from the firebrandism of the early 1880s.[77]

More news was coming in of the assassination. The police were looking for 'Bakhmetov'. On the Monday word reached them of Nold being apprehended by the police; Bauer's arrest followed the next day. That same Tuesday an article appeared in the *New York World*, in which

Most publicly criticised Berkman's deed. Goldman was furious. But the worst news of all was that of Frick's recovery. Goldman resentfully viewed his survival as another instance of social injustice. It was the money to pay the finest doctors that had saved his life. Some desperate measures would be needed. Fedya travelled to Pittsburgh with a stash of dynamite with the intention of completing the job, but somehow the police received news of his presence in the city, and the second *attentat* was called off. Meanwhile Goldman was in hiding with her friends Peppie and Frank (Fritz) Mollock in their apartment in New York. Secrecy was vital. A police hunt was under way. So far they had avoided the attention of the law. By the time the police did finally raid Goldman's old apartment, she had already disposed of all the incriminating evidence of Berkman's preparations.

Goldman could avoid the police, but it was harder to escape from the journalists. A reporter from the *World* was on her trail. On 27 July, this journalist interviewed Claus Timmermann, a member of Die Gruppe Autonomie, then went to 310 5th Street, looking for Goldman. The janitor, Mrs Walsh, told him that Goldman had gone. She'd only been living in the rooms for a fortnight or so, and had been sharing them with the Mollocks. By chance just then Friedrich Oerter, also in Peukert's Autonomie group, called round.[78] Oerter could only speak German, so a neighbour interpreted. Though still a young man in his very early twenties, Oerter was short, stocky and indefinably oppressed-looking with his hunched shoulders and hangdog head. At one point, while they were talking, Oerter put his hand to his hip, and the interpreter jumped back, afraid of being shot. 'Like Timmermann, Oerter seemed to consider Emma Goldman as a superior being. They spoke of her with respect, even with a sort of petty awe,' the reporter wrote later. Also like Timmermann, Oerter was taciturn and monosyllabic in his replies. He wouldn't say too much, except, when asked directly, he drew himself up and declared, that, yes, he was an Anarchist.

The *World* reporter loitered outside. After twenty minutes, Oerter left the building and went off and the reporter followed, walking down 5th Street towards Third Avenue, watching as Oerter kept 'putting his hand to his hip as if feeling for or adjusting a weapon'. On Third Avenue, Oerter walked only a little way before he found himself among a crowd, hesitated and then doubled back to the corner of 5th Street.

There he crossed the street and hurried into a German basement bar, run by Justus Schwab, Zum Großen Michel, 209 East 5th Street, a notorious haunt, the reporter suspected, of Anarchists.

The reporter followed him down. It was dark in there after the brightness on the street; the only light came from the door at the front and a second door on a long hall. The bar, a small one, was beneath the covered window. The saloon was crowded for 5 p.m. There were forty men or so in their undershirts, trying to keep cool on the New York July day, drinking beers and smoking, sitting in the brewed shadow of its two dirty rooms, front and back. There were Anarchist posters on the walls and the low ceiling was stained with tobacco smoke. It was a man's bar, dark and smoky, and it was natural that such men as they were – rough, foreign, daytime drinkers – should have removed their jackets, and unbuttoned themselves. Yet among all the men, unchaperoned in the back room, by a basement window opaque with dust and cobwebs, leaning back in her chair reading, was a woman. Her straw summer hat rested on the table beside her. The reporter thought the woman quite pretty at first, with her shapely head, her chestnut-brown hair falling over her pale forehead, and her insouciant pose. And she was young, no more than twenty-three. Yet her blue-grey eyes were partly hidden by her glasses; her lips were too full; her small nose a little too wide at the nostrils for his taste. Her once fleshy cheeks had hollowed slightly, her once rounded neck grown scrawny. Yes, her face might seem pretty, but on inspection her body was disappointing; his discriminating regard summed her up as 'pinched'.

He went up to the woman. It wasn't a bar, after all, where one stood on ceremonies. 'You are Miss Emma Goldman?'

'I am,' she said.

He made a barroom joke, and she smiled, and the smile too he found ugly. He observed a prominent gap between her two front teeth, and the teeth either side of them were missing. Her mouth was better, he decided, in repose.

They talked. Yes, she knew Berkman. Was she an Anarchist? She was, and proud of it. When did she last see Berkman? She couldn't be sure: a week ago, perhaps ten days. When she last saw him, did she know where he was going? Berkman, she told him, was not someone who would make confidences in such a matter. 'But you are his wife?' She couldn't help but laugh. Yes, she told him, they were 'married' – in the Anarchistic way.

She made some furious remarks about Most: 'The old fraud! I only wish that when I had a chance to do it, I had made him give me some of his money. He is a coward, and an Anarchist for revenue only.'

'Were you his Anarchistic wife before he took up with Lena Fischer and you met Berkman?'

Again she had to laugh. She didn't like reporters, she told him. She didn't like any kind of inquisitor.

The men in the bar had begun to gather round the table, ten or twelve of them listening to the strange conversation. Just then another reporter came into the bar, and now moved forward from the crowd and in a pause also asked Goldman a question. 'I have nothing to say,' she declared loudly, so the whole group could hear her. 'Will you not let me alone?' The words seemed a signal. The Anarchists began to edge closer to the two reporters, jostling them and swearing in Russian and German. One of the men standing at a nearby table appeared to be holding an ice-pick. To the man from the *World*, the Anarchists looked like wild beasts, with their heavy beards and their hairy chests showing over the unbuttoned tops of their shirts. The *World* journalist made a bow to the gang. He was a big man, and besides he was carrying a heavy walking-stick. And with this walking-stick and his air of unconcern no harm came to the *World* reporter, as he sauntered out from among them; the other, however, a stripling from the *Tribune*, was struck on the back and neck as he was manhandled out of the bar by the crowd. Goldman was triumphant for the moment, the man from the *World* reflected, but he happened to know that the police were keeping a close watch on her. If there was a way of finding a link between her and the attack on Frick, one would be found.[79]

That evening Peppie Mollock, Goldman's protector, went to Long Island to see her husband, Frank, who was in custody there under suspicion of connection with the plot against Frick. Just after her visit, Frank Mollock was kidnapped, while still in custody, by the Pittsburgh police and bundled off to Chief O'Mara in Pittsburgh. For his part in the fiasco a Long Branch police captain was even arrested by his own police force, outraged by the loss of their very own suspect.[80]

The talk in the papers was of conspiracy. There were strange reports of suspicious foreigners talking at Grand Central Station. A list of millionaires and their addresses had been found in Bauer's possession, a clear sign of a larger plot against America's great and good. The police kept the Fifth Avenue offices of the Carnegie Company under constant guard; a similar watch on Frick's offices was only removed at Frick's own request. Rumours arose of a plot to dynamite the boiler and engine departments of the Carnegie mills. Berkman was clearly only a tool, a foot-soldier, and not the lone assassin he had appeared to be. There were reports of Berkman's Russian past: that he had always been an agitator, and a Nihilist, even at school, and had been a member of Narodnaya Volya, the group behind the Tsar's assassination. The Inspector of Police especially regretted the laxity of the law regarding Anarchists. As it was, apart from the indictments against Berkman, they only really had the charge of 'conspiracy' against the others. Somehow it didn't seem enough.[81]

Thursday 28 July was another hot day. In the rooms they shared with Emma Goldman, Peppie Mollock's children lay on the floor sucking on lumps of ice as big as their own heads. Mrs Walsh, the janitor, read the article in the *World*, in which she herself featured, and was terrified. The neighbourhood had come out to see the Anarchists, and to chat openly in the sun with the policemen watching the house. The landlord must have read the article too: Peppie and Emma Goldman had both been given notice to quit the rooms by 1 August.[82] Peppie was distraught; her husband had been seized by the police; her life seemed to be falling apart around her. When Goldman came home, she found the door locked against her. When Peppie finally let her in, she said she had only secured the door because she was afraid the detectives might scare her children. The two women fought, and Goldman left to stay at her grandmother's at 10th Street and Avenue B.

If Most had failed to grasp the significance of the *attentat*, Peukert and the others at Gruppe Autonomie were thrilled at the deed. Goldman was invited to write a piece for *Der Anarchist* celebrating Berkman; it appeared on 30 July. When Most read it, he responded angrily with an article of his own. A war of words began between the two sides. On 1 August, a meeting was held at the Military Hall, down on the Bowery, where Goldman, Peukert and an Italian Anarchist, Saverio Merlino, all spoke in Berkman's defence. The *New York Times* was there:

The crazy utterances of Anarchy were howled forth for three hours at a public meeting held in a hall at 193 Bowery last evening. More than 300 wild eyed, unshaven, unclean, and foul-mouthed men, and about a score of hard-featured, cigarette-smoking young women, crowded the hall, and though the smoke-burdened air was so nauseating as almost to stupefy those unaccustomed to it, the people stood there and shrieked with delight that was only measured by the violence of the speeches made.

Speeches were given in praise of assassination and crime. Joseph Peukert asserted:

Berkman's heart . . . was in the right spot. His example will be followed by hundreds . . . We fully endorse his deed. They say that Anarchists are bloodthirsty. We are not. It is the bloody barbarism of capitalism that we fight.

He talked of the martyrs of Chicago and of France. (The flamboyant criminal and *soi-disant* Anarchist Ravachol had been executed in Paris only the day before Berkman had set out for Pittsburgh.) Merlino was in fact fresh from Paris and followed Peukert 'with a speech of the most incendiary character in which he frankly confessed that the acts of Anarchists were crimes, but said that they were crimes that it was necessary to commit in the present state of society'.[83] Then Emma Goldman, 'in a cheap blue and white striped dress', her hair tousled, got to the platform, and immediately declared that the room was packed with detectives ready to murder the speakers. 'She didn't look a bit frightened. She seemed rather to court being slaughtered, and the way she clenched her left fist and pounded the hot air was enough to make any policeman think twice before he arrested her.'[84] She spoke in German, declaring: 'We must make the most of this deed of Berkman's . . . and follow it with other similar deeds until there are no more despots in America.'[85]

Besides dividing the Anarchist community, other reactions to the attempted assassination began to emerge. In England, the Anarchist journal *The Commonweal* considered that Berkman's deed should serve as a warning to the skulking Carnegie, a veiled threat to the millionaire currently fishing in Scotland and promoting the electoral prospects of labour candidates.[86] While individual strikers applauded Berkman's act, mostly out of personal dislike of Frick, the union leaders themselves were horrified at a deed that seemed a propaganda coup not for their cause, but for Frick's. It has even been claimed that it was Berkman's 'misguided' assassination attempt that won the strike for Frick.[87] The aggressor had become a victim, and as such was open to the sympathy of the public. They at once condemned Berkman's action, 'and sent condolences to Frick with the message that they prayed for his speedy recovery'.[88] There were more positive responses, such as the soldier who offered three cheers for the man who shot Frick, and ended up being court-martialled, but mostly the deed's effect dissipated and nothing seemed achieved.[89]

Of course, the mainstream press straightforwardly condemned the outrage, though *The Nation* declared that, while Berkman was probably a 'crank', it was more sensible to attempt to kill Frick than a Pinkerton detective.[90] In the main, though, the newspapers were clamouring for the arrest of Most and Goldman and other Anarchist activists. Goldman had risen from obscurity in order to be condemned as a hate-figure. Shoved into the limelight, she did her best to avoid the provocations of the press and the attention of the police.

It was now that she received Sasha's letter. It asked nothing about her life without him, but only worried about Nold and Bauer's arrest and about Most (or 'Wurst' ['sausage'] as they had decided unflatteringly to call him so as to conceal his identity in their letters). She wrote back, downplaying Most's treachery so as not to distress Sasha, and playing up the enthusiasm of Peukert and the Autonomie group. She also wondered how it was that Frick had managed to survive the attack. Her questions hurt Berkman (perhaps he felt his manhood impugned), and he replied with a letter letting her know that the act mattered more than its success.

Goldman was wandering New York, avoiding notice. She found a room in a brothel on 4th Street, near Third Avenue, and waited for Sasha's trial. Then a further blow came from Most. On 27 August, in *Freiheit*, Most published 'Attentats-Reflexionen', an article that praised Berkman's courage but criticised his deed's efficacy. He argued that, given American conditions, an *attentat* in this country would be useless. In terms of their consciousness of themselves as a distinct social class, the American proletariat were too immature to understand the meaning of such deeds. Revolutionary efforts were therefore better placed in pursuing propaganda by the word. It is not hard to supply reasons for Most's distancing himself from Berkman's deed. He was just out of jail, and didn't want to go straight back in. There was also the danger of deportation, which would entail returning to Germany where he would also certainly be put on trial and end up once again in prison. In any case, Most felt that Berkman had betrayed him in joining Peukert's circle. Berkman was the prodigal son, and one who moreover had stolen away from him a woman whom he had strongly desired. It may even have been the case that he believed what he said regarding the inefficiency of Berkman's attack to be true. Whatever the reason, Goldman was horrified. She bought a horsewhip and at Most's next lecture rushed up on to the stage and attacked him, lashing his face and neck, only escaping the angry crowd by being pulled out of the hall by Fedya and Claus Timmermann.[91]

Over the next month, as the date fixed for the trial grew nearer, Goldman continued to propagandise for Berkman and his *attentat*. On 19 September 1892, she spoke at a meeting in Baltimore. She was just ascending the platform when a telegram arrived. The trial had begun and finished in a day. The maximum sentence for the crime was seven years; they had sentenced Sasha to serve twenty-two. He was twenty-one years old now. If he should ever get out, his youth would be lost. She rushed forward and began a passionate speech that drove the crowd to shouts of vengeance. Hearing the disturbance, the police broke in and arrested her, dragging her off to the cells. As we will see, she would be back in police cells many times, ending up, just short of a decade later, under suspicion for involvement in the assassination of an American President.

In Berkman's eyes, his trial had been a farce. He was accused falsely of assaulting Leishman, a downright lie. Frick was there, but would not meet his gaze. Berkman was permitted to make his grand speech, but had to speak in German. The translator was unable to keep up with the flow of his eloquence. Berkman suggested that the translator simply read his speech, at which point he realised that the man was blind. Meanwhile the judge grew bored, and forbade Berkman from saying any more. The opportunity was lost. Sentence was passed, and Berkman was led from the court.

That evening, in despair, he took a tin prison spoon and sharpened it into a blade on the stone floor of his cell. He passed it across his finger and it easily drew blood. Then he got into bed, and thought about how he was about to kill himself. If only Frick had died; if only Most had been more courageous. He thought of how much blood there would be in him, after he had slashed at his wrists, and of how the guards would find his body in the morning and the mattress all soaked with it. He was still dreaming of it when the guards came in. As a reflex he jumped to attention, and the improvised knife clattered to the floor.[92] It seemed he would have to live after all.

7

The Years Between

Q. What is your name?
A. Mrs Jacob Kersner.
Q. What is your maiden name?
A. Well, I am Emma Goldman. I don't go by the name of my husband,
   I always have my own name, and I use it.[1]

I: The Dilemma of Hyacinth Robinson

Walking beside Central Park on the Upper East Side in Manhattan, you come to No. 1, East 70th Street, the home of the Frick Gallery. Frick bought the land here in 1906. The ostentatious gesture was a small revenge against the slights of his former partner, Andrew Carnegie, relations between the two men having soured in the years since their shared victory at Homestead.[2] In 1911, Frick set about turning the site into a home for his private art collection. The building work began in 1913, and was completed a year later. Andrew Mellon, the friend with whom he had discovered Europe all those years before, was the first overnight guest at the new house. Now a public gallery, it is a quietly lovely place, a serene bolthole for the city-sick. Compared to New York's other great museums, it offers a small collection, but a perfect one, replete with treasures. And yet one may feel a slight discomfort there; the art works somehow feel like acquisitions, an airlessness pressing upon the calm. It was here, among the paintings and sculptures that he bought up in Europe, that Frick spent the last years of his life.

In mid-summer 1892, an investigation had been launched into Frick's and the Pinkertons' activities during the Homestead strike. It was possible that this could have ended in a charge of murder. But by November, the threat of legal action against Frick had evaporated. He had come out of the business rather well, were it not for the fact that some people seemed to feel there was a stain on his record: that he had been too harsh with the strikers.

Homestead was grim before Frick's victory; after it, the place became notorious for its ugliness and horror. It sprawled beyond its old confines into a network of smoking chimneys and blunt barrack-like buildings, smearing the area with its greyness. In 1894, fifteen months after the end of the strike, Theodore Dreiser, the American novelist, was sitting in a Pittsburgh library founded by Andrew Carnegie. Here he read the works of Herbert Spencer and Charles Darwin, and contemplated the misery he had just discovered as a reporter in Homestead. It seemed to him a lively image of perdition. Hamlin Garland thought the place squalid and inhuman; the Fabian Beatrice Webb called it 'a veritable Hell of a place' and another English observer, Arthur Shadwell, found it 'hell with the hatches on . . . nothing but unrelieved gloom and grind'.[3]

It is a paradox hardly new that such loveliness as is felt in the Frick Gallery should have its source in the hell of Homestead and the exploitation there, that its beauty should be founded in ugliness, its peace in uproar, and its order in chaos. Yet, as you stroll among the Claudes, the Turners and Vermeers, among all the serenity that endures, it can prove difficult to shake the impression that the paintings there, with their pleasures and their wisdom, are somehow chained as Frick was to the violence of the Homestead strike and the quotidian brutality of industrial life that was its long aftermath.

This sense is close to the questions raised by Henry James in his somewhat undervalued novel of 1886, *The Princess Casamassima*. The book portrays a young orphan, Hyacinth Robinson, torn between revolution and the beauty of art. Robinson makes a pledge to commit an assassination if required, but then afterwards finds himself falling for the gracious allure of aristocratic living. For a book about Anarchism that sounds as though it might owe something to the emerging genre of the thriller, James's novel is a curiously unexcitable and orderly work. Yet it confronts a question also central to Frick's story, and Berkman's and Goldman's. How can we love art, others, the world itself, when there is so much injustice, pain and suffering in it? To some, such a dilemma may seem irredeemably adolescent. Indeed it is an adolescent's question, one posed at the moment in which we become responsible for the place that we are taking in the world. Perhaps only to those who refuse adulthood's compromises does such a question remain a vital one. Of course, Hyacinth Robinson, and also Berkman, Zasulich and Goldman, and indeed many other assassins and advocates of violence that we will encounter in this book, were youths themselves. The merging of youth and political violence is an interesting one: taking only the last two centuries, it is difficult to think of many middle-aged assassins who killed out of their own idealism. Around this time, Ernest Alfred Vizetelly would ponder the strange link between a general upsurge in adolescent crime and the rise of the Anarchist outrage.[4] Political murder is a pursuit for the young.

Somehow the relationship between the assassin and art proves crucial. In his fiction, Henry James commits himself to the insights of a central consciousness, an 'individual sensitive nature or fine mind' upon whom perception would press more deeply.[5] The more thoughtful of the Anarchists – Emma Goldman among them – were also enthusiasts for the idea of 'the beautiful soul', a good, imaginative and curious person alive to the world and to others. This ideal was thrown into the balance between fineness of understanding and the desiccated partiality of political fanaticism. For writers like James and Yeats, the assassin stood for the fanatic personified. It is odd therefore to discover how closely an ideal of courtesy and sensibility informed such violence. Such an understanding was a stumbling block to the conventional idea of the assassin, just as the brutal Ravachol found his counterpart in the gentle killer Caserio.

It is easy to contrast placid Frick gazing on Giovanni Bellini's *St Francis in the Desert* from his seat in the 'Living Hall' with narrow-minded Berkman squatting in a prison cell fixated on some abstract utopia. Yet, as we have seen, both men were involved in the enactment of violence. And as we shall discover, both were open to the complicated joy to be found both in art and in other people. Through life in an American penitentiary, Berkman would find a way out from his own constriction. As he later acknowledged, it was prison that truly made him an Anarchist, a man 'who seeks a more humane form of social life based on brotherhood'.[6] Suffering does not necessarily 'humanise' anyone. But it certainly gave Berkman the prize of connection to others, a human solidarity in pain and pleasure. It may even be said that it gave him wisdom, though, as we shall see, this wisdom did not entail, in the long term, a repudiation of violence and assassination.

Frick suffered too. He became a serious collector of Old Masters from 1899 onwards. He dedicated himself to making a collection to rival, and indeed surpass, the sugared prettiness of London's Wallace Collection. He travelled often to Europe. On a voyage out, he met Elsie de Wolfe, once an actress, now hoping to be an interior decorator. He was just out of Pittsburgh; she was lightly beautiful and incorrigibly charming; and it was to be a long voyage. They came to a business arrangement. Frick required pictures, and the charming Miss de Wolfe would help him choose them.

At night, he would sit contemplating his paintings in the semi-darkness. He could seem unreachably remote, a corporate man, grimly mute or melancholy hushed, not giving much of himself away, unsure if there were much there anyway to distribute. There was something irascible in him. In her adoring biography of her dead grandfather, Martha Frick Symington Sanger, the namesake of Frick's dead daughter, affirms that Frick saw himself in the angry Christ in El Greco's *Purification of the Temple*. Just as Christ purges the Temple of buyers and sellers, so Frick cleansed his factory of rebellious employees. It is possible that Frick's self-deception extended so far, though some may prefer to hope that he was wise enough to see himself, the triumphant capitalist, among the wailing merchants that Christ reproaches.

He was enviably wealthy, the epitome of capitalist success. Yet few would want to be Henry Clay Frick. He had mislaid happiness some-where, perhaps with the death of his young daughter, Martha. Until his own death he carried her image with him at all times. He bought a strange painting in the vein of commercial symbolist art, *Consolatrix Afflictorum* by Pascal-Adolphe-Jean Dagnan-Bouveret, depicting a mother with a child, angels behind playing music, and a mourning man at the mother's feet. He placed the picture in the family dining room, a representation of a comforted grief to be present with the family always. In 1912, Frick confided to a journalist a secret that he had been keeping for twenty years. Just in the moment after Berkman had fired the first shot, he had turned and seen Martha right there beside him, so tangible and real that even in the midst of the violence he had time to think that he must reach out his arms to hold her. Perhaps it was Martha who had saved his life. Berkman had complained that the sun had blinded him as he fired his shots, but Frick believed that he had been 'dazzled' by the spiritual light surrounding Martha's apparition, not by the sun. Frick's office window faced due north.[7] Her ghostly likeness was there reminding him always of his salvation and his loss.

He had her image printed on his cheques.

II: Prison Years

At the Western Penitentiary, Pennsylvania, Berkman began his long prison life. His presence there was pure injustice, the criminal state declaring him to be a criminal simply because it had the power to do so. He had failed to wield his own more limited power. Now he must endure their penalty. He had often talked with Fedya and Goldman about how well they could cope with prison life. A spell in jail was a requisite for a revolutionary, a necessary proving of credentials. The three rebels' image of prison was based on the worst Russian models, but the American reality turned out differently repressive. His cell was not the worm-infested dungeon of legend, but rather a poorly lit narrow room, damp and foul-smelling.[8] In a notebook, he recorded his impressions of that first day in prison, 19 September 1892.[9] He felt indifferent to his own fate, almost oblivious of his surroundings, yet still preoccupied with thoughts of suicide.

The prison itself resembled a model factory, though with its concealed chaos and official violence the reality behind this façade was far grimmer. There was the prison hospital with its blank windows; stacks of high chimneys; the ordered lines of tables in the school room, and over the blackboard the picture of the two unfurled Stars and Stripes. The place was a compound of muddled dirt and mechanical order. Nevertheless there was room for compassion. A guard handed Berkman a towel and soap, and a note of comfort from a mysterious 'friend', promising to include him in a coming jail break – one that never came. The promise may have been illusory, but it sustained him at this bleak moment. Such help was needed because his communications with the outside world were proving frustrating. Letters arrived from Goldman, but they were full of sullen disillusionment about Berkman's failure and Most's treachery. Worst of all, it seemed that both Fedya and Goldman were encouraging him to kill himself, purely for the action's propaganda value.[10] His feeling that Goldman was backsliding did not lessen his increasing need for her. He was in the Bastille of American life; the prison made manifest the nation's desire to sweep suffering out of sight. The institutions of the world could not help but oppress the defiant individual, for that was their secret purpose. Only Goldman remained, strong and free.

But his need for Goldman only further brought home to him the fact that she was outside, while for years he must stay alone without her. At first, his fellow prisoners alienated him. Once seeing the criminals in their striped clothes had pressed on him their utter difference. Now he too wore prison uniform. Yet still the others seemed remote and strange. Then he began to strike up a friendship with Wingie, a rangeman. It was odd and somehow unideological to feel a need for companionship with this rough man. Berkman was still enclosed within his political prejudices:

I shrink from the uninvited familiarity of these men . . . They are not of *my* world. I would aid them, as in duty bound to the victims of social injustice. But I cannot be friends with them: they do not belong to the People, to whose service my life is consecrated.[11]

Still it was good to feel close to someone, even Wingie, but then one day Wingie stroked his new friend's cheek, and Berkman guessed the gesture's intention and recoiled. Berkman soon realised desire between men was common in the prison, which contained many male prostitutes. The discovery disgusted him; he could hardly believe such things were possible. A little later Wingie was put in solitary for an offence that was not his fault. There he lost his mind.

In November 1892, Goldman was allowed to visit Berkman in jail. It seems that Berkman was still hoping for a dynamite cartridge from Goldman, to be passed into his mouth during a kiss, so he might commit suicide in the style of Louis Lingg. The fantasy failed (perhaps Goldman knew nothing of his hopes), and so did the meeting. They were constrained with each other, and distant. Even though it seems to have been his plan, Berkman resented the idea that Goldman had come to hasten his death. But then, just as she was leaving, Berkman felt a sudden rush of pity for Emma, as much a prisoner as he was, and silently he took her hand.

Berkman was put to work making mats, a job that was close to a special punishment, for the dust from the matting fibres worked its way into the prisoners' lungs and left them with infections or even consumption. It was not unusual for a prisoner to collapse spitting blood. A doctor who came to tend one such victim noticed Berkman standing nearby. 'Presently he asked my name. "Oh, the celebrated case," he smiled. "I know Mr. Frick quite well. Not such a bad man, at all. But you'll be treated well here, Mr. Berkman. This is a democratic institution, you know. By the way, what is the matter with your eyes? They are inflamed. Always that way?"'[12] Berkman explained that the soreness had begun with his working in the matting shop. The doctor examined him, and found him easier work making hosiery.

Time was passing. Berkman was enduring, but hardly living. New hope arose when, following a peremptory trial, Carl Nold and Henry Bauer, the Anarchists who had put him up in Pittsburgh while he prepared to assassinate Frick, joined him in the Western Penitentiary. Berkman had left the jail to be a witness at the trial. This brief absence from prison turned out to be another disappointment. Goldman was not in the courtroom as he had hoped. He looked all the time for an opportunity to escape, but he was too closely watched. Yet now came a recompense; the arrival of true comrades changed everything. Life returned. They begin to produce together a magazine – *Zuchthausblüthen* ('Prison Blossoms'), later simply *Blüthen*. They used what paper they could find, even flyleaf pages ripped from library books. The language of choice was German. Berkman had arrived in prison still thinking in German, and when, three years later in July 1895, he came to write some autobiographical sketches, German was still his natural language of self-expression. However, around the same time, Berkman started, through communication with two other prisoners, Hugh F. Dempsey and Robert J. Beatty, both active in the Knights of Labor, to write an English version of *Prison Blossoms*. These new collaborators were also alleged practitioners of 'propaganda by the deed': they were accused of poisoning some 'scab' workers during a strike. To Berkman, such an activity (whether they were guilty of it or not) seemed entirely laudable: 'Morally certain of their guilt, I respect them the more for it, though I am saddened by their denial of complicity in the scheme of wholesale extermination of the scabs.'[13] The individual must sacrifice himself (and others) for the sake of humanity. In consequence Berkman was learning English; prison was turning him slowly into a true Anarchist and a true American. The transition brought subtle estrangements: he borrowed Russian books translated into English from the prison library, and saw the familiar books of his adolescence metamorphosed into the foreign tongue that was becoming his own: 'It is like meeting an old friend in a strange land to find our own Bazarov discoursing – in English.'[14]

He wrote constantly, turning out strident defences of his attempt to murder Frick, the 'act of '92'.[15] Reading these documents, hand-written in prison notebooks, one makes contact with Berkman's desperate pomposity. In those years, he justified himself to an audience that would not listen, making a stand against those who believe that whatever is, is right ('*was ist, ist wert*').[16] He answered the accusations of imaginary adversaries, and in private writings that he could hardly hope would ever become public documents played the articulate advocate that the court had not allowed him to be. Over and over he refuted the indictment of fanaticism, the charge of failure.

Pressure from the authorities led to the closing down of *Prison Blossoms*. After an altercation with a guard Berkman was put in solitary confinement, there living for a while on a 'Pennsylvania diet', or starvation rations. In solitary, he continued his process of self-education. It was all he could do to stop himself from going mad. The heat in the long summer days was stifling. Often he was insomniac. He calculated how many seconds he must spend alone to get through one year: 700,000,000.[17] He spent four hours a day exercising, four practising English, four reading, two eating and cleaning up. He was getting through. By the light of prison candles, he worked his way through an edition of Shakespeare lent by Mr Milligan, the Chaplain, analysing sentences, puzzling out etymologies.[18] There was time to think of the past too, of Emma Goldman, and the other women he had briefly known. He thought of the little commune they had had together, and of his first sweetheart in America, and the girls from his adolescence in Russia, pert, enticing, unreachable.

After a long year he returned from solitary to the main life of the prison, the endless prison days, always the same cycle, and always beneath it all the 'swelling undercurrent of frank and irrepressible sex desire'.[19] And increasingly he found that he was beginning to discover the humanity of his fellow prisoners. Rather than mere instantiations of the criminal class, they were becoming people with names and stories: Jim Grant, put in the reformatory for stealing fruit; young Rush, the descendant of a famous family of physicians, wrongly accused of drowning his girlfriend; 'Reddie' Butch sentenced for three years for stealing a rig for a few hours so he could take his sweetheart for a ride. The guards too were becoming distinguishable, those who had fought in the Civil War tending to be more humane than the others.

These varied and complicated individuals, both prisoners and guards, had found themselves caught in a mechanism that brutalised everyone. There were beatings, false imprisonments, bullying, the random withdrawal of privileges, the hell of solitary confinement. The thing was to try to save your self in the midst of this process. The only way Berkman could do so was to open himself to compassion and connection with others. Using the newspapers, released prisoners revealed the horror inside the penitentiary. An investigation was ordered, but the Warden ensured that during the inspection everything ran at its very best. The result was an inevitable whitewash.

* * *

In a notebook, he kept a record of his vital statistics. There are other notebooks too. Berkman recorded all he could, with the embroiled impartiality of someone trying to keep himself interested, trying to keep sane. There are address books, lists of accounts, lists of prisoners, with dates by their name – of release, or of arrival, it's hard to tell. There are diary entries in miniature, written in an obsessively tiny hand, marking dates, noting things for the unimaginable freedom when release will come. And not just for when you'll be released, for now too; to save something from the repetition of prison time. Who passes a note; who falls sick and goes to the hospital; who you meet, and who you don't. Phrases in German, phrases that raise unanswerable questions: 'last time Oct. 9. 04. nass bei nacht [wet at night] Nov. 27.' And sometimes a glimpse of settled sense: 'Law of 1883 – pay to prisons for more – absolutely wasted.'[20]

In these neat notebooks Berkman wrote out all the knowledge he could gather. Its objective nature belonged with a world beyond the penitentiary walls, facts shared by the world out there just as much as the world inside. There are entries on telepathy, records of a detailed interest in Indian and Tibetan religion. There are lists of the melting points of various metals: gold 2,160°, silver 1,850°, lead 590°; there are lists of apothecaries' weights and measures; there are lists of antidotes for various poisons. There are curious and incontrovertible facts: '*Bible*, Ezra, 7th Chapt. 21st v. contains all the letters of the alphabet, except J.' They are like the records of a strange protracted boyhood, an autodidact's treasure-trove. There's an air of self-reliance too: recipes for home-made mouthwash, directions for making tablets for the most varied ailments. And, among the popular science and the practicalities, suggestions of unexpected longings for beauty: how to mix colours when oil-painting; hints for how to preserve cut flowers; instructions on how to make potpourri, aftershave, and even nail polish.

There are relics of the prison magazine: poems cut out from magazines and stuck into the little notebooks, poems of longing, poems consoling the 'vanquished'; a poem in a prisoner's handwriting, beginning 'Here's to them who lose!'; and then among them, the brief newspaper notice of the death of a prisoner, and in Berkman's handwriting above it, 'Died apr. 24 9.33pm 1901.'[21]

Among a strange list of typed aphorisms produced in jail, Berkman wrote: 'There is a retributive justice implanted in our very acts, as a conscience more sacred than the fatalism of the ancients'.[22] Did his attempted assassination of Frick still trouble him? Had a justice been planted in the deed, or did he invoke merely the justice still awaiting the capitalists and the governments? Another aphorism declares: 'Nothing more dangerous than for a sensitive man to know those against whom he contends. Hatred against the cause shrinks before the feelings for the persons. We become partial unwittingly.'[23] Did he realise that this could mean choosing not to know or understand Frick?

He read in the evenings, composed a novella (since lost) on revolutionary conspirators, and wrote long letters. Those men who loved other men, or took young boys as their lovers, like apprentices of desire, were no longer disgusting or strange to him. That too was love; that too was human. One night, locked in a dark cell with another prisoner, Berkman also found that he could express an intimate tenderness with another man. Prison was forcing him to grow, but still his greatest desire was to escape its horrors. His year in solitary had left him with an unshakeable depression: 'All my heart is dark.'[24] He looked for an appeal against his sentence, but found that because he had represented himself at his trial, and therefore failed to 'take exceptions', an appeal would prove impossible. He began instead to hope for a reprieve. The pardon for the Haymarket Martyrs had aided the Anarchist cause; perhaps a pardon for him would have a similar value. The United Labor League of Pennsylvania passed a resolution in favour of his release, and news reached him that his case would go before the Pardon Board. But the Warden objected to the pardon, and it failed. There was no chance of freedom.

His relationship with Warden Wright had always been tempestuous. In 1895, news came that Kropotkin was in America. Berkman was on fire to see him, to be face to face with the father of Anarchism. Word reached him that Kropotkin was intending to visit soon. But the visit never took place. Kropotkin had sent him a letter, marked 'Political Prisoner', and Warden Wright was in a fury about it. Berkman was sent to his office, and watched as the Warden ripped the letter to pieces. Berkman argued fiercely with the Warden, and so ended up spending seven days in 'the dungeon', a cell two feet by four, and fifteen feet underground, as punishment.[25]

He received word from Goldman that his friends outside were hoping to obtain Carnegie's signature on a petition for a pardon. The scheme fell through, and Carnegie was never approached. Without hope of release, Berkman began thinking of building an escape tunnel. He met up with other convicts and they began digging. Then came a new element to their plan: a tunnel would be dug into the prison from beyond its walls to meet theirs. Through Carl Nold, long since released, and another newly released prisoner named 'Tony', Berkman made contact with Goldman, telling her of his plan. The plot was set in motion. Once freed, Berkman would have to be smuggled out of the country, perhaps to Canada, or Mexico, and then on to Europe. Anarchists on the outside began scouring out a tunnel from a derelict building opposite the prison. They would meet halfway. The prisoners' hopes were raised. There was a close shave when Berkman's cell was investigated in a general search of the prison. Nothing was found that time. But soon afterwards playing children stumbled on the entrance to the tunnel in the derelict house. Berkman was put back in solitary in the August heat, even though the Warden failed to find out whoever it was that had planned the escape.

Berkman spent almost another year in solitary. It was 1900, a new century, and still there were years of prison life ahead. Just before his commitment to solitary confinement, Berkman received news from Goldman of Bresci's assassination of the King of Italy. The news failed to rouse him. Above all, he found that he could no longer believe in the virtue of an individual sacrificing himself for the cause. What after all was the cause compared to the immense value of a single man?

Bresci avenged the peasants and the women and children shot before the palace for humbly begging bread . . . And Bresci will perish in prison, but the comrades will eulogize him and his act, and continue their efforts to regenerate the world. Yet I feel that the individual, in certain cases, is of more direct and immediate consequence than humanity. What is the latter but the aggregate of individual existences – and shall these, the best of them, forever be sacrificed for the metaphysical collectivity?[26]

Berkman had come full circle. Now it seemed that the abstraction of 'the People' was worth less than a present individual. It is hard to know whether these reflections express a change of heart, or a plunge into melancholy. In July 1901, he re-emerged from solitary confinement. It had been hell, often straitjacketed, in terror of going mad. Soon afterwards Berkman tried and failed to kill himself. Cut off from the living, life receded. Only the prison was true. Those outside seemed impersonal and distant. Emma Goldman was so far away, and her life had gone so differently. Yet her steadfastness seemed to hold him together. Of everyone outside, only she had been completely loyal. He thought of Russell Schroyer, a fellow prisoner and his friend, paralysed by a bad injection given by an incompetent prisoner-nurse, a man who had found his post through being a crony of the Warden. Schroyer lay for a long time in a prison hospital bed, though the doctor was convinced the boy was shamming. He stayed there, immobile, his back an agonising patchwork of bedsores, and died with Berkman's name on his lips. Everything seemed senseless.

III: Goldman's Wanderings

In November 1892, Goldman went to the Western Penitentiary to visit 'Sasha' Berkman. She arrived in Pittsburgh on Thanksgiving morning, and that afternoon went out to the jail. 'The grey stone building, the high forbidding walls, the armed guards, the oppressive hush in the hall where she was told to wait', all weighed on her.[27] She was there under a false name – Mrs Niedermann – posing as Berkman's married sister. They were tongue-tied with each other, forced to speak in unfamiliar English. As they kissed in parting, Berkman passed a note to her mouth. She opened it outside. She was to go to a jewellery shop owned by an Inspector Reed the next day; as a prison official Reed had promised Sasha a second visit. She went, but Reed quickly saw through the disguise, and recognised her as Goldman. Goldman flew into a rage, chucked trays of jewellery around, and threatened to kill Reed if Berkman was harmed. Tact was never to be Goldman's strong point.

Throughout the 1890s Emma Goldman lived on a sustaining belief: Berkman was a noble youth who had taken on the troubles of others:

Today, while Frick, in perfect health, lives to enjoy his ill-gotten wealth, poor Berkman is languishing in a dark, musty cell, shut away from his friends and from the world, never enjoying a stray beam of sunshine; still dreaming of a dawn of perfect freedom, and a day when labor will no longer be crushed under the iron heel of wealth. For behind his prison bars his big warm heart still throbs with the hopes and fears of the downtrodden . . .[28]

It was true, but in ways that she could not imagine. Berkman's abstract love of humanity was turning into a particular love for certain individuals, those fellow prisoners who shared with him the hell of the Western Penitentiary. Goldman was better able to uphold the pure meaning of a murder attempted in the hard fervour of the sentimental.

Yet Goldman was learning from life too. Throughout the 1890s, she developed an Anarchism of her own, fusing the aristocratic ideals of Nietzsche with the anarcho-communism of Kropotkin, balancing a belief that the masses are a dead loss against an intense pity for their sufferings. Intellectually unsustainable, through the force and warmth of her character Goldman somehow pulled these opposites in her together, presenting to others over time an impressive consistency. In

the end, she was an Anarchist because she believed in freedom, first
of all for herself, of course, but genuinely for others too. She came to
these views through the promptings of her character and engagement
with her own experience. In September 1893, the press interviewed
Goldman in 'The Tombs', the Manhattan House of Detention at 100
Centre Street. She was awaiting trial for 'incendiary speaking'. She laid
out her beliefs as they stood at that time:

I am an Anarchist, because I am an egotist. It pains me to see others suffer. I
cannot bear it. I never hurt a man in my life, and I don't think I could. So, because
what others suffer makes me suffer, I am an Anarchist and give my life to the
cause, for only through it can be ended all suffering and want and unhappiness.[29]

This was Goldman explaining herself to a sympathetic journalist.
However, her compassion clearly could not embrace Frick. At her trial,
a few weeks later, she was equally forthright (although also properly
circumspect) setting out her views for a judge.

Cross-examination of 'Miss Goldman' revealed that she was in fact married,
but separated. Her childhood in Russia was briefly discussed, as was her living
arrangements at the time of the shooting of Frick. She told the court that while
she could not approve Berkman's deed, she had sympathy and respect for him.
[This, of course, was not the place to mention that she had also helped to plan
the murder.] Yes, she was an Anarchist, but that did not mean she believed in
perpetual disorder. The laws of state oppressed the poor; the only true law was
the moral law. 'I mean,' said she, 'that there is a moral law that indicates every
one not to misuse the liberty of the next one, not to do any harm to them, not
to hurt him; or at least not to do any whatever to the next persons and to try all
possible to love the next one and help as much as possible for the benefit of the
other.' Disentangled from Miss Goldman's quaint English, this looks very like
the Golden Rule. And yet the inconsistent little person was a few minutes later
talking about stuffing bombs with dynamite in as calm and matter of fact a way as
a housewife talks of stuffing a turkey.[30]

Even here her sassiness got the better of her. She told the court that she
would appeal to 'the American workers to live long enough to see the
time come for the use of bombs'.[31]

Then her cross-examination ended with the following exchange:

'What do Anarchists want with dynamite bombs?' the Assistant District-Attorney
asked her. 'To use in the great social revolution that is pending.' And would she

use bombs? 'I cannot tell what I would do. I may not live to the day of the battle,' replied Goldman.[32]

Ten days later, on 17 October 1893, she was sentenced to a year in Blackwell's Island Penitentiary.

Goldman responded to prison with typical resilience. Where Berkman's acts of defiance provoked severe retribution, Goldman out-faced threats of punishments that somehow failed to be used against her. She was put in charge of a group of women workers, but refused to force them to work harder. Her stand made the previously unpopular and misunderstood Anarchist a hero to her fellow inmates. She was given a job in the prison hospital, and took to the work with enthusiasm: in Goldman's character there was much of the born nurse. Another act of disobedience resulted in Goldman's being sent, like Berkman before her, into the prison's dungeon, though her stay lasted only a single day and night. Goldman suffered in prison, as she would suffer anywhere where her liberty was confined. Yet she thrived there too. The prison was a true world, and its interest for her was the interest of life itself, its strangeness and surprise. She befriended the prostitutes, the black prisoners, even the prison chaplain – 'Our fervour was our meeting ground.'[33]

After prison, she campaigned in America, propagandising in English. The next years were chaotic and in some ways incoherent, but never dull: a web of affairs and lectures, of careers picked up and dropped, of journeys and improvised domesticity. She travelled – to Britain, and Vienna, where she thought about attending Sigmund Freud's classes but went instead to hear about sexology from Professor Bruhl; she worked as a midwife; she lectured; she lived. Through it all, she nurtured one consistent hope: Berkman would be free again.

Goldman's life was entwined with Berkman's, united around the unifying pledge of their crime. They had plotted Frick's death together, but only Berkman bore the punishment. Ties of guilt and conspiracy held them. So it was that she spent the 1890s fighting for Berkman's release. Romantically, however, she was not so single-minded. Soon after Sasha's imprisonment, she began a passionate friendship with Ed Brady, a tall, athletic and scholarly young man, just arrived in America after serving ten years in an Austrian prison for publishing Anarchist literature. Yet this relationship too created emotional difficulty – as

Goldman struggled with her desire for the man, while resisting his attempts to compromise her independence. Ed developed her mind, and opened her up to the pleasures of sex. Later, there were other lovers. Yet always there was in her that part of herself that owed allegiance to Berkman, and to Homestead, and, beyond all that, her will to be unconstrained by any man. Her desire for love battled her instinct for liberty; she never found a sustainable and simple resolution.

Above all, Goldman was honest in ways that very few can be. It was the noblest thing about her, and also the most terrifying. There was something unsparing and hard in such clarity. She showed all her feelings, inconsistent as they might be, and owned them all. Yet somehow her honesty did not add up to self-knowledge; she knew each motive, but failed to find herself. Even her unwavering commitment to the cause of Anarchism was tempered by her desire to be free even of that involvement. She knew as well as anyone the costs of activism: the loneliness, the instability, the constant reiteration of defeat. Life came with a price.

From Berkman's imprisonment until the beginning of the new century, Goldman proselytised for violence. This was her public role, the major source of her fame and influence. She would not condemn assassination or deny the value of propaganda by the deed. She was a woman modelled on Vera Zasulich and the other women Nihilists, but transferred from the heart of Russian autocracy to the United States.

In particular she became Berkman's apologist. In 1895, speaking in London, she declared:

What she asked was Berkman's crime? Had he stolen the wealth labor had created? . . . Had he built factories, where men women and half grown children, were slowly tortured to death? . . . Berkman was in prison, because he hated and opposed all this, because he attempted to destroy the life of a man, who had brought disaster and privation upon thousands of people . . . Alexander Berkman decided to strike the blow at the cause of the evil . . . The Brutus of the 19th Century was languishing in one of [the] prisons of America, but was dreaming of the dawn, of a day of perfect liberty when labor would no more be crushed beneath the iron heel of Capitalism.[34]

At a meeting in Pittsburgh, the next year, she referred to the attempted murder of Frick as 'a small crime'.[35]

However, her celebration of assassination did not end with her personal connection to Berkman. In 1897, she expressed her delight at the death of Cánovas del Castillo, the recently 'removed' Premier of Spain, and declaimed against the execution by garrotte of Angiolillo, his assassin.[36] Cánovas could be taken by some to be a special case. Angiolillo was a sensitive young man, Cánovas an authoritarian brute. That May a bomb had been thrown at a Corpus Christi feast killing many bystanders. Cánovas clamped down hard on Anarchists, and many were tortured and executed. Angiolillo's murder of Cánovas was counter-retribution; certainly many glorified the killing as an instance of vengeance's reach. The assassin had killed Cánovas in the presence of his wife, who afterwards ran up to him and slapped him in the face. "'I did not mean to kill your husband," Angiolillo apologised to her, "I aimed only at the official responsible for the Montjuich tortures."'[37] Here the Anarchists and authorities, as had happened earlier in Russia and France, had fallen into a politicised version of vendetta. The country seemed to have returned to a pre-legal way of settling disputes, an eye for an eye, violence matched by violence. The Anarchists, and in America Goldman prominent among them, saw themselves as avengers practising a kind of wild justice. Such a cycle of killings only proved their contempt for law as such. In this way revenge became intrinsic to Anarchism. For the authorities, this lapse into terror carried a far greater risk, the violence of the state apparently exposed and democratic safeguards undone.

This was far away in Europe, of course, but Goldman's strength was her constant linking of European and Russian events to American experience. She even declared that William McKinley, President of the United States, himself had cause to worry, and was already thinking he could be next:

I do not advise anybody to kill, but whether I advise it . . . fortuitously makes no difference. Heroes like Golli [i.e. Angiolillo] do not seek permission of me or of anybody else to do their duty as they see it. So long as tyrants oppress mankind Gollis will be found to execute them. We are not enemies of society. We are enemies of government, for government is tyranny.[38]

That autumn, aware perhaps of how inflammatory her stance could be, she declared that all rulers should be 'removed', with the single exception of President McKinley: he was too insignificant to be killed.[39]

Her praise of violence sat awkwardly with her capacity for pity. In 1898, in San Francisco, she declared 'the world is my country; to do good my only religion'.[40] This was true, but doing good included the slaying of tyrants. She drew the line in some very few instances: for example, she regretted Luccheni's stabbing of the Empress of Austria in September 1898, mostly as she considered that the man had picked the wrong target. In any case, this act of violence directed by a man against a woman found little support among even the most extreme circles. (Luccheni's crime helped to further international governmental co-operation against Anarchists.[41]) Yet even then, she refused to condemn Luccheni outright:

In my opinions, Lucchesi [sic] was an individual who saw that life had nothing in store for him and having nothing to lose he destroyed life. Yet I would not consider him a crank or insane. Rather say that he is a product of present economic political and social injustices.[42]

Such views were undoubtedly controversial, and Goldman was criticised on each occasion she aired them, as for example when, early in 1900, she refused to condemn the assassination of King Umberto of Italy by the Anarchist Gaetano Bresci.

What may strike us as strange was the readiness of newspapers to print her apologies for assassination. Often her views were aired only for the press to condemn them, but the fact remained that a great deal of space was allotted both to her arguments and to her personality. Goldman was already becoming a figure caricaturable by the press, the little sensible woman with a penchant for political violence. It was to prove an irritating but useful relationship. The newspapers hated her in so far as she symbolised a genuinely different approach to social life. However, they found her 'good copy', someone able to provide startling quotes and provocative ideas. The danger was that she would become merely a 'media creature', a cartoon version of herself standing in for a whole movement with her homely figure and her dangerous thoughts. Two things saved Goldman from such a fate. Firstly, there was the incompetent and confused attitude of the press towards her. The media machine was not as yet powerful enough to enclose the freedom of her life. Secondly, she used that freedom genuinely to live.

By the end of the 1890s Goldman was perhaps both the most famous Anarchist in America and, now that Most had apparently reneged on his old ideas, the most notorious advocate for political violence. Her position helped the press to suggest that all Anarchists were simply murderers in waiting. In fact, this was far from the case. Other Anarchists reprimanded her for glorifying murder; no killing could be a good thing, they argued, even if the victim was a despot.[43] The praise of assassination sparked a debate within the movement. At the time, when Goldman and others were petitioning Andrew Carnegie to support Berkman's pardon, her views regarding the use of terror were ripe for satire by her fellow Anarchists.[44] There was, after all, something risible in shooting a man and then inviting the victim and his friends publicly to absolve the assailant. Such ridicule unmasked some of the contradictions in Goldman's position, the knots her compassion tied. She was a public figure and yet also an advocate of violence that threatened to undo the public realm. As she worked through the 1890s and on into the twentieth century, Goldman was entangled in ambiguities that would soon create an incident that changed American history.

8

Shooting the President

Miss Emma Goldman, selon moi; est une – et comment dites-vous cela en français? – une apôtre – oui, une apôtre.[1]

I

On 5 May 1901, in the afternoon, at 170 Superior Street, Cleveland, where the Anarchists of that city usually met, Emma Goldman gave another lecture. Her audience were the radicals of the Franklin Liberal Club. She was talking all over the country, and the event seemed an ordinary one. There were the usual policemen in the audience, forced, as every town's policemen were, to listen placidly to her routine sardonic *bon mots* directed against policemen as such. Patrolman Gibbons was spared the witticisms, for he was waiting on the sidewalk in front, in case of trouble; as usual there wasn't any. The hall was busy, but not crowded. There was the usual collection for Berkman, and the usual disappointing sum was taken. As always she spoke without notes, in her clear English, still with the same faint German accent. As ever, the audience applauded enthusiastically and often. But that was no surprise; Goldman was accustomed to such successes.

She spoke twice on that day, once on Anarchism in general, and once on vice. The speech on vice is, by our contemporary standards, a mild and unexceptionable one. She said simply that whatever people do in private shouldn't be considered vice: homosexuality and masturbation were matters for science not public morals. Some of the audience then were a little shocked, considering discussion of such matters a pity. And we might now be a little shocked at them, at their Puritanism, and their criminal coyness, if their reaction wasn't somehow so quaint.

The first speech was a little different.

In that first address, having outlined the principles of Anarchism,

Goldman spoke, as she often did, in ambiguous defence of political violence:

The speaker deprecated the idea that all Anarchists were in favor of violence and bomb throwing. She declared that nothing was further from the principles which they support. She then went on, however, into a detailed explanation of the different crimes committed by Anarchists lately, declaring that the motive was good in each case, and that these acts were merely a matter of temperament. Some men were so constituted, she said, that they were unable to stand idly by and see the wrongs that were being endured by their fellow mortals. She herself did not believe in these methods, but she did not think that they should be too severely condemned in view of the high and noble motives which prompted their perpetration.[2]

This much was clear: the assassin is in fact the best of men, the one most pledged to action, the one least able to live a life of hypocritical acquiescence in the ills of society.

In the audience at the hall was Leon Czolgosz. Four months later he would kill the President of the United States of America.

During the intermission, the young man approached her, asking for suggestions for books to read. Goldman was struck by his youth, his good looks, his curly blond hair, but more by the combined strength and sensitivity in his face. He never mentioned his name. They talked a little about books that he might read, and then he left, compelled to miss the second half by his job in Akron, Ohio.

That summer, the heat was too strong to continue with her usual lecture tour, so Goldman spent time instead with the Izaaks in Chicago. Abraham ('Abe') and Mary Izaak and their three children were lapsed Mennonites who had converted to Anarchism. The whole family were dedicated to the cause, to sex-equality, free-thinking and the poetry of Walt Whitman. Together all five of them produced an Anarchist journal, *Free Society*. Family life was based on an easy-going egalitarianism that had long impressed Goldman, who had herself experienced paternal despotism. The lull in Goldman's schedule of demagoguery presented an opportunity to visit her beloved sister, Helena, who was once more back in Rochester; the Izaaks' fourteen-year-old daughter, Mary, was to accompany her. On the day she was to leave, the Izaaks prepared a farewell lunch for Goldman and then, as she was packing, Mrs Izaak came in to tell her that an unexpected visitor had arrived. His name was Nieman, and he wished to see Emma Goldman. But Goldman was running late and had no desire for interruptions. Nieman was sent off, but as he left Goldman herself stole a glance at the caller. It was the same curly-haired youth she had met briefly at the lecture in Cleveland. She caught up with him. Together they took the Chicago elevated train to the station. Nieman told her that he had left Cleveland – the comrades were too uninspired there – and had come to live in Chicago. At the station, others were waiting to see her off. She entrusted Nieman to the anarchistic care of Hippolyte Havel, a former lover, and left for Rochester.[3]

Goldman's stay was idyllic. Her brother Yegor was also there with his children, and young Mary Izaak too; the summer was beautifully boisterous. Childless herself, Goldman was the perfect aunt. Although Goldman was now a matronly and bespectacled figure, for her nephews and nieces she could still easily represent the free, the independent, a compelling alternative to their parents' stable virtues. Even young Harry, a ten-year-old Republican and staunch supporter of President McKinley, felt the same truant admiration. Only a printed warning in *Free Society* by Abe Izaak regarding Nieman troubled the idyll; there were worries in Chicago that the newcomer was a spy. Goldman was furious, and contacted Izaak at once. He told her that Nieman kept speaking of acts of violence, and had all the signs of being an *agent provocateur*. Goldman thought this very flimsy evidence on which to condemn a man, and, on her insistence, Izaak printed a retraction in *Free Society's* following issue.[4]

Soon it was time to go back on the road. Goldman flirted briefly with the thought of going to the Pan-American Exposition, which was being held in Buffalo, New York; she could take a look at Niagara Falls while she was there. But there was no money for another holiday and the idea was due to be dropped, when a friend in Buffalo, hearing of Goldman's wish to go, offered money and a place to stay so the whole family could travel there. So Goldman went to Buffalo with young Mary Izaak and her older nieces and nephews. They saw the Falls and did the Exposition, and met with Anarchist comrades in the city.[5] It was a jolly end to the summer.

Returning to Rochester, Goldman found two letters from Sasha.[6] In one, he described his appalling time in solitary, including eight days spent in a straitjacket. He had come very close to losing his mind. Goldman was incensed, and guilty. While she had played with the children, Berkman was far away in the Western Penitentiary, suffering torments. And then she read the second letter and everything was restored. A new Inspector had come and had granted Berkman his old privileges and, for reasons of propaganda or kindness, was ensuring that he was receiving proper medical attention. More vitally, a commutation law had been passed; he would be free in only five years. Overjoyed, Goldman travelled once again to visit him. It was the second time she had seen Berkman in nine years. Their meeting lasted moments. He had been brought out to her, a grey man in a grey prison suit, and for a moment he had seemed a frightening stranger to her. Then she saw in the drawn figure Sasha's familiar eyes. They looked at each other for a moment, both unable to speak. And then the guard called a sudden end to the encounter, and Berkman was led away.[7]

She went from the prison to St Louis where she stayed with Carl Nold. She told him of her terrible meeting with Sasha, and he explained to her that solitary left a man all but mute, speech frozen, and numb. The next day she spent going round the stores of St Louis touting for business on behalf of her lover, Ed Brady, and a new stationery concern he had set up. It was there that she heard – a newsboy was crying out the headline on the street corner – that President McKinley had been shot.

II

Goldman had declared that President McKinley was too insignificant a figure to deserve killing. He was, she asserted, merely a tool of the millionaire Mark Hanna. For once, there is something impoverished in these statements of Goldman's: a flippant joke, and a facile analysis. Henry Adams apparently more or less concurred, describing the McKinley era as the most profoundly ordinary period known in American politics since Christopher Columbus.[8] But Adams understood the value of ordinariness, and if McKinley seemed 'insignificant' to Goldman that was only a mean interpretation of his kindliness and his willingness to waive decision in favour of his party's wishes. Adams also extolled McKinley's 'practical and American' approach to the problems of politics, seeking consensus, pooling interests, managing a common solution.[9] And if McKinley seemed Hanna's stooge, that was only the most obvious explanation for the complexities of the two men's relationship.[10]

William McKinley was born in Niles, Ohio, in January 1843, the seventh of nine children, sickly and small. His father was a small-scale and not-altogether-successful foundryman. McKinley worked for a while as a teacher before enlisting as a soldier in the Civil War, entering the ranks as a private and leaving as a major. Each promotion on the way was the reward for a courageous deed. With the end of the war, he attended law school at Albany, New York. McKinley began professional life as a labour lawyer, and had a stint working on behalf of the miners' union.[11] One significant, if unexpected, part of his Republican political credo was to be his support for the unions and the 'working man'.

He worked his way up through the legal and then the political world, enduring a precarious electoral existence as Congressman for the 17th Ohio district. He began his Washington career and was soon a prominent member of the House Ways and Means Committee. His support for protectionism and the imposition of tariffs favourable to big business lost him his seat in 1890 (after the Republicans had pressed through with his 'McKinley Tariff'), but more importantly it gained him the full attention of Marcus Alonso Hanna.

Mark Hanna was a Republican operator, a plump, dumpy citizen of Ohio, a wealthy businessman, oilman and banker, looking for a politician to boost. His reputation then and since was that of a defender of corporate interests and of the rich. This contained some truth, though Hanna's position was actually a more nuanced one. Dismayed by the confrontational practices employed by the big corporations, he sought a new kind of politics.[12] It was clear that capitalists and politicians must co-operate, and Hanna saw no reason why they shouldn't do so on his terms. Having recently fallen out with Joseph ('Fire Alarm Joe') Foraker, the Governor of Ohio, he alighted on McKinley.[13] Hanna and McKinley had first met in the 1870s when McKinley was fighting the cause of striking workers accused of setting fire to one of Hanna's coal mines.[14] A first liking seeded, but it was later that the two men were drawn to each other. Soon Hanna had an opportunity to show the depth of his liking by helping McKinley out of a personal financial crisis in the midst of the general collapse of 1893.[15] McKinley had nearly bankrupted both himself and his wife through, characteristically enough, being too generous to a wayward friend. Having saved him from ruin, Hanna set about making McKinley President. He was just the man to defeat the perilously radical 'inflationist Democrat' candidate, William Jennings Bryan. Hanna orchestrated McKinley's nomination, bankrolled his campaign, and stage-managed his publicity. Together the two men were invincible. The public perception of Hanna was that of a money-obsessed monster, the brutal face of capitalism.[16] Contrariwise McKinley was gentle, sociable, and gifted with the capacity for being loved. On the surface Hanna was none of those things; his money had stolen them from him. Yet through McKinley, like-minded about protectionism, sympathetic to the unions, and both committed to the nation, he could attain the influence that he craved.

The 1896 election was fought on the issue of the coinage. While Bryan stormed about the country speechifying and drumming up support, McKinley stayed at home and provided daily talks at his door to delegations from across America. It was the whistle-stop whirlwind versus the 'front-porch campaign'; Bryan's untried hope of silver confronted McKinley's steadfast, immemorial 'gold standard'.[17] Although the word did not yet exist in this sense, Hanna was moulding McKinley's 'image'. In doing so, he was only rounding off a process that McKinley himself had begun: 'He staged himself elaborately, remained always in character. He was a man who looked learned, yet who possessed very limited information on history or economics or law.'[18] His very absence of strong views rendered him ideal. A politician was no longer merely a person of integrity or duplicity, a spokesman for a set of beliefs, or the embodiment of a particular class. McKinley was to be a symbol, and one easily read and easily lovable. William Allen White wrote of his 'strength and physical pride, for he was a handsome man with a matinee idol's virility, though not at all sex-conscious'.[19] The quiet approach worked: as an image of domesticated stasis it provided everything an electorate could want. He was both in the old and the new sense of the word, bland: at once unruffled and unstimulating. Where Bryan roared against dark injustice, McKinley painted a rosy picture of American prosperity; it was the sunny version that America wanted. In 1897, McKinley became the twenty-fifth President of the United States.

Neither Hanna nor McKinley appears to have harboured imperialist ambitions for America. For both men, their primary concern was the domestic agenda. Yet foreign policy and imperial adventure dominated McKinley's first presidency. America was drawn into war with Spain on the matter of Cuban independence, and then drawn into assuming tacit dominance over the island. The USA similarly snaffled up Puerto Rico, gobbled up Guam, and then blundered into an annexation of the Philippines, purely as a consequence of defeating feckless Spain. Having assumed control, they naturally put down a native insurrection; after all, the Filipinos themselves were hardly ready to manage their own affairs. Until such time as they were politically mature, America would have to assume the burden of rule.[20] It was in the same spirit of righteous munificence that the USA had acquired Guam, Puerto Rico and Hawaii.

To conservative minds, it was an age of confidence, and McKinley personified the temper of those times: substantial, efficient and naïve. His project was national; he toured the country, presenting himself to America, the accepted symbol of an unarticulated cohesion. He was known as a skilful manager, a practised manipulator of men. To McKinley's supporters, even the disgrace of the Philippines seemed evidence of executive solidity. It was an enviable success; a strategic move swifter than the annexations undertaken by the European powers. For McKinley's critics, the resemblance to the imperial expansions of old Europe precisely indicated the nature of the betrayal. Yet on the domestic stage, the war had played out as a success, and success vindicated everything.

McKinley rewarded Hanna by helping him get into the Senate. To do so, the aged Joseph Sherman was shunted across to the position of Secretary of State, a move that disquieted many by its combination of incompetence and sleaze.[21] Often weakened by chronic rheumatism, Hanna was prone to irritation; his relationship to McKinley could be touchy. McKinley was sensitive to accusations of being Hanna's man; Hanna bristled at real or imagined slights. They offended just as much as they relied on each other, and were enmeshed in a relationship between influence and dependence. However, behind their cosy sharing of power, other newer political stars were emerging, and none was so bright as that of Teddy Roosevelt.

Theodore Roosevelt (1858–1919) could not help but make other men seem tepid. He stands, with Robert Louis Stevenson, Cecil Rhodes and Rudyard Kipling, at the cultural moment that rediscovered the boyish appeal of manly romance. An asthmatic and short-sighted child born to the brownstone houses of aristocratic Manhattan, Roosevelt made himself strong. He boxed, he rode and he shot. Once, when he was in his fifties, the Army complained about a new regulation enforcing a higher level of physical fitness for its soldiers. Roosevelt responded by riding 'one hundred miles over rough Virginia roads' to shame them.[22] In 1884, when his young wife died in childbirth, within hours of the death of his mother, he went out west to a ranch in Dakota to recover from the blow. He stayed there for a couple of years, and, on the model of frontier self-reliance, Americanised himself. When he returned to Washington and political life, he found there were many who could now trust his flamboyance. He married again, and under McKinley became Under-Secretary of the Navy (Kipling remarked, 'I never caught the name of the Upper').[23] While McKinley allowed America to drift into conflict with Spain, Roosevelt enthusiastically embraced the war. He immediately resigned his government post and formed a company of cavalry, the Rough Riders. They fought with distinction in the battle before Santiago; Roosevelt returned to America a colonel and a war-hero.[24]

At the Republican convention in Philadelphia in 1900, despite Hanna's tart resentment (he is said to have protested, 'Don't you realize that there's only one life between that madman and the White House?'), the force of popular enthusiasm swept Roosevelt into the Vice Presidency.[25] Beside the euphoria over Roosevelt, McKinley's endorsement as Presidential candidate seemed an uninspiring formality. The election itself was becalmed. Everyone knew McKinley would win, flushed on to further success on a little wave of imperturbable prosperity. The mood was apathetic, but contented, and McKinley was the figurehead of that mood. The country wanted more of the same; McKinley would be the first President to win immediate re-election since Ulysses Grant. After petty wars and imperial adventures, he ambled back into another four years of power, Roosevelt striding in behind him.

In the spring of 1901, Ida McKinley was perilously ill; only her stubborn refusal to die kept the end at bay. That summer, she recuperated with her husband at their cosy house on Market Street in Canton, Ohio. McKinley wanted to spend some quiet months, free of public engagements, before going to the Pan-American Exposition in Buffalo in September. It was to be a glorious show of American wealth and industrial possibility. He had a speech to write for the crowd there; the idea for it came to him with an after-dinner cigar.[26]

On 4 September 1901, the President left for the Exposition. He was light-hearted, given over, in accord with his mercurial nature, to high spirits.[27] It was not a divisive party political event, but a celebratory holiday. The organisers hoped that the President's attendance would draw in the public, whose attendance so far had been disappointing. Although still somewhat ill, Ida made the journey with him.

That same day, at 6.00 p.m., the President arrived at Buffalo in a specially commissioned train. There were some anxieties that the European mania for assassination might cross the Atlantic to America. In an article in *Outlook*, published in August 1901, a journalist suggested that the Anarchists might endanger McKinley too.[28] So it was that a very public display of the President's security was organised. He was met at the station by a brigade of mounted National Guard and a group of detectives was assigned to his protection.[29] They escorted him the short distance to Delaware Avenue and the home of John G. Milburn, the president of the Exposition. He planned to stay there throughout his time in Buffalo.[30] It was a lovely house, with its balconies and its garden, an unassuming but indisputably comfortable bourgeois residence.

Thursday 5 September was a public holiday in the city.[31] Once again flanked by mounted soldiers, McKinley visited the Exposition. Sure enough the President brought in the crowds. The numbers that day broke the record: more than 100,000 people came to see the President and the Exposition. McKinley enjoyed the public's attention, welcoming such opportunities for ordinary folk to come into contact with the central symbol of American identity. In morning coat and shiny top hat, he was led around the Exposition. There was the Horticulture Building with the lake outside, like a baroque pagoda at a Buffalo Versailles; inside were tables laden with fruits and flowers; enormous jars of preserves; square towers of bottles of champagne; implausible palm trees and trellises of vines. A massive sculpture of frenzied horses shone dazzlingly white in the sunlight. There were Arab chiefs from Cairo and an entrance to the Beautiful Orient (a house of Egyptian wonders) on the Midway.[32] You could take a 'Trip to the Moon' too, in a building where small children and dark-haired adolescent girls played at being moon-dwellers among grotesque artificial caves.

On a large outside stage draped with many flags and crowded with dignitaries, McKinley delivered his oration. He stood with one hand in his pocket, the other holding his speech, his spectacles resting professorially on the bridge of his nose. His thin dark hair was oiled back; the temples were grey; the flesh beneath his chin sank down into the white upturned collar.[33] Afterwards there was an inspection of the soldiers and then that same afternoon a large reception at the New York State Building; McKinley had to greet and shake hands with all 1,500 of Buffalo's notables. Understandably enough, some people detected signs of concealed fatigue in the President. The day ended with a drive back to the Exposition, illuminated for the night, and a firework display. On a request from Mrs McKinley, the mounted guard was reduced in numbers; it hardly seemed worth while having quite so many soldiers on hand.

The Friday was another humid day, the New York state late summer heat draining. By mid-afternoon three people had passed out with heat exhaustion.[34] Before the sun took hold, McKinley made his habitual early morning walk, going out before breakfast to stroll the streets around Milburn's house. Later that morning, McKinley made an excursion to Niagara Falls with his secretary, George B. Cortelyou and others of his retinue. Before going out he slipped three handkerchiefs into a pocket: the heat meant he was likely to need them.[35] He was relieved that he was now done with the speech and was free to enjoy himself. However, his freedom was still set to a schedule. Noon came languidly. The party returned from the Falls to the site of the Exposition.

That afternoon he was to be present at a public reception in the Temple of Music. The building was a rococo fantasy, a gorgeously tasteless dome cornered by flags and topped with statuary, a colonnade setting out uncertainly behind it. It was a quieter day; only 60,000 visitors after yesterday's turmoil. The President made the journey to the Temple, still escorted by mounted guards, and with Secret Service men keeping pace with him. Seated beside Milburn in a carriage, McKinley raised his top hat to a photographer just at the moment of the exposure.

When they arrived, someone took another photograph, the President smiling, and a woman in a white dress and hat smiling beside him; only the detectives' faces were serious and watchful.

Inside the Temple, it was cool, a respite from the sultry day. The building was so far empty. It was around four o'clock. Where two aisles came together, the President took his place with his retinue. Behind them were two bay trees surrounded by potted plants, and behind that hung the Stars and Stripes.[36] Mr Milburn stood at the President's left, Mr Cortelyou to the right.[37] Milburn had been granted this proximity to the President in deference to his importance at the Exposition. Normally in that position a Secret Service man would be at attention. Nonetheless, the President was well guarded. Police were scattered among the hall, ready to scan faces.[38] Detectives grouped themselves around him. On the President's word, the doors were opened and the public began to stream in. The Temple would hold about 20,000 people that day. A packed line of visitors formed to greet the President, trailing out of the building where they lingered beside the Court of Fountains. McKinley stood with his men around him, courteously accepting the good wishes of each of the crowd. He shook each visitor's hand in turn, one after the other. The organist began a Bach sonata. Mr Cortelyou checked his watch. It was time to move things along a little.[39]

A detective saw a man in line with a handkerchief bandaged around his fist, and thought that the fellow must have a sore hand. The man was next in line, and he approached, and reached out with his hand towards McKinley, just like the others, as though to shake hands with him. McKinley too moved towards him, towards the meeting. There was hardly time to gauge the oddity that the offered hand was wrapped in a white handkerchief before the man pushed away the President's hand with his left hand and then the gun hidden in the handkerchief fired and a bullet struck the President's chest on the right-hand side.[40] The sound of the shot was surprisingly muted. Very quickly, no more than an instant later, the man fired again and a second bullet ripped into McKinley's abdomen. Things paused, long enough for the onlookers to watch the smoke rise from the barrel of the gun and from the handkerchief itself which had begun to burn.[41]

And then they tumbled into a chaos of events. There was no third bullet. The men around the President leapt forward to grab the attacker; 'Big Jim' Parker, an ex-slave, who was the next in line to meet the President, pulled the assailant down, and a detective punched the man full in the face – blood sprayed from his nose – a policeman hit the floor and they piled on top of the assassin, desperate to get the revolver – someone kicked the gun from the attacker's hand.[42] Other men in the crowd set on the stranger, and in a free-for-all they all tried their best to strike him; there were six or eight or even more men on top of the assailant, pulling at his arms, his face, his coat.[43] By the time the police had bundled him away he was dishevelled, staggering and bleeding from a tear across his face. And no sooner had he stood up than another policeman punched him in the face and he went sprawling back to the floor again.[44]

With the first shot, McKinley staggered back against one of the bay trees, and then with the second shot he straightened up.[45] He was very pale. He remained standing for an instant and then fell backwards, to be caught by Detective Geary, one of the Presidential entourage.[46] 'Am I shot?' he asked him. Geary opened the President's waistcoat and saw the blood soaking his shirt. 'Yes, I am afraid you are, Mr. President,' he told him.[47] Cortelyou and Milburn helped the President to a bench. Cortelyou bent over McKinley where he sat bleeding; the President probed the wound on his breast experimentally, and then drew his hand away covered in blood. 'This pains me,' he said.[48] He looked down where they were roughing up his attacker, and found it in himself to pity the young man. 'Be easy with him, boys,' he said.[49] Then he told them not to let his wife know that he was shot. The police were clearing the hall, calling for everyone to get out.[50] Afterwards there was silence, as outside people hurried to find a doctor and fetch an ambulance. When the director-general of the Exposition arrived, McKinley expressed his regret that it should have happened here at the Exposition.

They rushed him to the emergency hospital, the ambulance driven at speed through the crowds by a young medical student. A doctor and a medical student attended the President in the back.[51] Someone gave the President a little opium to ease the pain.[52] With them was a Secret Service agent named Penney. McKinley suddenly remarked to Penney, 'I believe that is a bullet' and rummaged inside his shirt and pulled out one of the two bullets that had been fired at him.[53] This first bullet, which had lodged against his breastbone, seems to have simply fallen out and dropped into his shirt.[54] It had broken the skin and destroyed a little of the fat beneath, but had gone no further.[55]

On his arrival at the hospital, it was clear that an operation must immediately take place. McKinley told the physicians: 'Gentlemen, I am in your hands.'[56] The eminent surgeon Dr Russell Roswell Park arrived, back from Niagara Falls where he had been operating on a patient with a lymphoma.[57] Three other doctors also attended. McKinley was stripped for the operating table.

Having anaesthetised the President, they began probing in the abdomen for the second bullet.[58] The daylight was fading, and there was not much light to see by, for though the sunset cast its light into the room, it did not fall into the President's wound.[59] There was a layer of fat to cut through, almost two inches thick.[60] The bullet had missed the intestines, though it had passed through the front of the stomach wall; some food matter had escaped from the stomach, and needed to be cleaned up. They stitched up the front wound, and then making a second incision (around 15 centimetres long) they went deeper into the body. They found another wound at the back of the stomach, and they stitched that up too.[61] An electric light was brought in to improve visibility in the room.[62] The search for the bullet, however, proved fruitless, and after some time, Park called a halt, cleaned the wound as could best be done, and sewed the President up. The hope was that the bullet had lodged in the muscles of the back. They did manage to remove some pieces of coat and skin that the bullet had blasted inwards.

A large crowd gathered before the doors of the hospital. An automobile ambulance carried the President back to Milburn's home. The crowds watched noiselessly, expectantly, their hats in their hands. Many wept. Two Secret Service men rode behind the ambulance on bicycles. A surgical bed and some nurses had already been sent on ahead in a police patrol wagon so that the President would be comfortable when he arrived.[63] The President's wounds were serious, but not likely to prove fatal. The greatest dangers were peritonitis or septicaemia, but as yet there was no sign of these.[64]

Mark Hanna collapsed when they gave him the news. Theodore Roosevelt heard over the telephone at his house in Vermont. The instant they told him, Roosevelt cried out, 'My God!', and the vivid energy of that single, startled and ambiguous shout was just as fatal as the assassin's bullet to McKinley's place in history. He promptly found a carriage, hurried to the train and sped to Buffalo to be near the wounded President.[65]

III

Having sealed the Temple of Music, the police decided to bundle the assassin out. He sat with his bloody nose in an ante-room, surrounded by police. They cleaned him up a little and, despite the threatenings of the crowd that had gathered outside, took him out into a pair-horse carriage. The crowd surrounded the carriage with its prisoner, eager to see the would-be murderer killed. However, the driver managed to force his way through, and headed off with the mob in pursuit.

They brought him to Buffalo's police headquarters. Here they photographed him for the police file. His collar had been torn off in the struggle, and his best clothes no longer looked so good. In the picture, his hair, reputedly blond, looks darker. He was handsome, tousled, his clear eyes looking with disinterested curiosity back into the camera. His pockets were emptied out. He had just $1.51, a teat from a baby's bottle, a pencil and a subscription to a workers' fraternity – The Knights of the Golden Eagle.[66] It will be noted that this list does not contain the speech Goldman had given at Cleveland in May, even though, perhaps with suspicious convenience, the police declared in due course that they had in fact found a copy of that lecture in his pocket.[67]

A Secret Service detective sat beside the assassin on the bed in his cell. He gave the young man a cigar. The assassin was perfectly placid. He told him that he was called Fred Nieman. This name was passed outside to the waiting journalists. He was twenty-eight years old and came from Detroit.[68] He was Polish-German, he told him. (Sometimes his interrogators heard him speak with a slight foreign accent, but mostly not.) Asked why he had shot the President, he replied, 'I only done my duty.' The detective asked him if he was an Anarchist, and the young man replied, 'Yes sir.'[69]

Around 11.00, Thomas Penney, the English-born District Attorney for Buffalo, arrived with James Quackenbush, attorney-at-law, and took over the questioning.[70] The assassin appeared calm, almost thoughtful, though in some pain from the beating he had received. He was sitting

at the table 'with his head somewhat bowed and resting it on his right
. . . hand, in which he held the handkerchief, and rubbed the right
side of his face. At first he did not look up promptly but after a little
he looked up and soon took a lively interest in what was going on.'[71]
He answered all questions quite readily. They asked him to prepare a
written statement, and so he wrote out and then signed the following
message: 'I killed President McKinley because I have done my duty. I do
not believe that one man should have so much service and that another
man should have none.' He showed no sign of remorse. He knew the
end that was coming for him. Afterwards he gave a statement that lasted
two hours.[72] Frank Haggerty (a court stenographer) and John Martin,
Chief of Police, were among those present when the assassin signed his
statement.[73] Here he gave his real name – Leon Czolgosz – and told
them something of his family history. He also apparently mentioned
that he had been influenced by Emma Goldman.[74]

Outside the police station, a crowd had gathered. The mood was
angry, murderous. Many wanted to break in, take the assassin and lynch
him. Police patrolled the streets, trying to keep order. On a couple
of occasions, the crowd tried to breach police lines and storm the
building; but though the policemen shared the crowd's retributive fury,
they repulsed the attacks and kept the assassin safe for formal justice.[75]
For the next days, the danger of potential violence against Czolgosz
increased or lessened as the news of the President's condition worsened
or improved. The police maintained a strict guard and watched for
signs of an attack.

On that first evening, thoughts already turned to the question of
Czolgosz's sanity. Joseph Fowler, the police surgeon, ordered that a
close eye be kept on the prisoner with the intention of ascertaining his
mental state. His quietness, his air of contained resignation added to the
horror of the deed. On Monday 9 September, Czolgosz was moved to
a deeper dungeon, the transfer ostensibly performed for his own safety.
But on 13 September the growing danger of an assault on the building
led to his removal. The prisoner was taken (disguised as a police officer,
it was rumoured) to Erie County Penitentiary, where he was placed
under the charge of Alexander Sloan, Keeper of the Penitentiary. He
was put in the women's dungeon, his whereabouts known only to a very
few policemen, the District Attorney and Sloan.

Medical experts and psychologists examined Czolgosz and found him sane. He was of average height (5 foot, 7½ inches), rather handsome, though his teeth were bad. He did not really drink, refrained from masturbation, though he had had sex with women on occasion; he had had no venereal disease – except gonorrhœa.[76] (More romantically, he informed the Buffalo police chief that he had once loved a girl, but she had left him, 'since which time he had had nothing to do with women'.[77]) He was decent and self-contained. There was nothing ostensibly abnormal about him. The reason he gave for shooting the President was simple: 'McKinley was going round the country shouting about prosperity when there was no prosperity for the poor man. I am not afraid to die. We all have to die sometime.'[78]

As far as the Buffalo Superintendent of Police, William S. Bull, was concerned, Czolgosz was clearly in love with Goldman.[79] As had happened following Berkman's arrest for the attempted murder of Frick, the police and the government jumped to the conclusion that there was a larger conspiracy on hand. Goldman's notoriety made her the centre of this imagined plot. Evidence of a larger conspiracy would mean that Czolgosz could be tried in a federal court. Investigations began into Czolgosz's history. One of the police detectives in Buffalo was sent to Cleveland to investigate the assassin's past.[80] The Secret Service agents were gathering information. They uncovered a great deal of his true history and movements, but also stumbled upon, or cooked up, much false information. Fake or merely misleading reports were submitted, stating that he had been seen talking to two men, one dark with an 'ugly scowl on his face and treacherous looking eye'.[81] On 20 September the Secret Service files noted information from the *New York Herald* that Czolgosz was picked to kill McKinley after the drawing of lots, and that the Izaaks and Goldman were in on the crime.

Statements from Czolgosz's confession began to leak out. Much of it incriminated Goldman. It appeared that her speech at Cleveland had fired him up into a frenzied ache, anxious to kill McKinley: 'Her doctrine that all rulers should be exterminated was what set me thinking so that my head nearly split with pain.'[82] The sheer suddenness of the deed, and the inability to perceive any sane motive for the attack, helped to direct the desire for vengeance towards Goldman. Czolgosz was unpronounceable, unfamiliar, a nobody. Goldman was famous, an equivocal darling of the press, a hate-figure and a celebrity, and therefore entirely apt as the repository of America's anger. The aim of the police and Department of Justice was to present Czolgosz's crime as the work of a conspiracy; one of the chief conspirators must have been Goldman.

In mentioning Goldman, Czolgosz had probably made a mistake, not thinking through the consequences. Perhaps he didn't realise his statements would endanger her, after all it was only a matter of being inspired. Goldman was clearly nowhere near Buffalo, and could hardly be blamed for another man's crime. However, this was not going to stop the authorities from attempting to do so.

IV

The police cordoned off the streets in one block in each direction around Milburn's house.[83] On Saturday 7 September, the day after the shooting, McKinley's wife was allowed to visit him. Once again, the weather was oppressively hot. During the day, Hanna and Roosevelt went to the house too, and Hanna issued a statement declaring the President to be in cheerful spirits.[84] There were, in all, seven eminent doctors working on the case. McKinley slept well that night, though his pulse remained constant at 132, and his temperature uncomfortably high at 102.5. A tent was set up on a vacant lot across the street where the male nurses could sleep. (It was felt that for some duties women nurses would not befit the Presidential dignity.) In the same lot, soldiers encamped to keep guard.[85]

Messages from the governments of Europe and the British Empire were conveyed to the President's bedside, expressing their horror at the deed and their sympathy. On the Sunday, prayers were said for the wounded man in America's churches. The heat appeared to be dropping, and there was a little relief in the humid sick room. That Sunday night, he was restless, but slept well.

On Monday 9 September, the doctors issued a statement declaring that the President's condition was improving. During the morning, he managed to change position in bed without help. He was cheerful and even attempted to chat with the nurses and physicians, although silence was considered the healthiest option. There was a feeling of expectant relief. Mrs McKinley went for a drive. Outside in the slightly cooler

day, the newspaper men waited. They had a large tent of their own to
rest in. Cortelyou was doing his usual job of managing the President's
'image'; in his bowler hat and spectacles, he would go outside to where
the waiting journalists lined up against the rope-barrier, and pass them
carefully chosen bulletins regarding the patient's progress. Crowds of
local people had gathered too, but were kept from the house by armed
guards. Roosevelt was there at Milburn's house, and most of the rest of
the Cabinet. Another bulletin was issued. Temperature and pulse had
both dropped a little. There were rumours that the President's condition
was being presented in a falsely favourable light, and the doctors came
out to talk to the press and denied it. Both Roosevelt and Hanna stressed
that things would soon be all right; the President was on the mend. For
the first time, McKinley spoke of his assassin. 'He must have been crazy.
I never saw the man until he approached me,' he said. 'On being told
that he was an Anarchist, the President responded, "Too bad, too bad: I
trust, though, that he will be treated with all fairness."'[86]

McKinley spent his fourth night since the shooting in the Milburn
house. The pulse and temperature continued to drop. Tuesday began hot
again, but the uncomfortable temperatures of the Friday and Saturday
were no longer a trouble. One of the physicians, Dr Charles McBurney,
who had been called in from New York, considered the recovery to be
going well enough for him to start thinking of going back home. The
President was told of the messages of sympathy he had received and of
the heartfelt response of the American people. He was moved, and said
that he hoped he would recover so he could show everyone how much
he appreciated their trust in him. He slept for most of the day.

Although the second bullet was still lodged in his body, nonetheless,
four days after the shooting, the doctors were confident: a steady
recovery was expected. Yet his pulse was fast, moving between 115 and
104 on Tuesday 10 September, while his temperature hovered around
100. Later on the same day there was a brief scare, but the President
quickly recovered from the crisis. The renewed worry was considerable
enough to keep Dr McBurney in Buffalo. The pieces of coat and flesh
that had penetrated into his body, though removed, had irritated the
tissues. The stitches had to be cut and the wound re-treated. But the
anxiety passed. McKinley slept well again, and was able to drink beef
tea. The next morning he was better. He continued to take some

nourishment, and was only troubled from soreness in his back from lying so long. His wife visited him again after the operation, but was not allowed to stay with him. They were doing their best to spare her any unnecessary alarm; she herself was not well, having been a semi-invalid since the illness she had contracted in California. Though she should naturally see her husband, nothing could be permitted to jeopardise the President's safe recovery.

On the Thursday again all was set fair for a swift return to health. He slept well the night before, was eating solid food, and even began the day with toast and a cup of tea, and later had coffee and chicken broth. The President was out of danger. Dr McBurney finally was able to make his trip back home to New York. And over the last days the attention of the nation began to move from the President himself to the punishment of the treacherous Anarchists behind the foiled attempt.

V

Within hours of the shooting, the police and the government had already begun hunting for Goldman. A Secret Service agent travelled to St Louis, where she had recently stayed with Carl Nold. He discovered that she had ordered her mail to be forwarded to an address in Chicago. Although there were suspicions that the forwarding address was merely a ruse, nonetheless at once the investigation moved northwards.[87] Private detectives were engaged to infiltrate the Anarchist community. The address in Chicago turned out to be that of the offices of the *Arbeiter Leitung*, a radical newspaper. The Chicago operative learnt that Goldman had received mail also from 'the office of the Anarchist's dirty sheet known as "Free Society"'.[88] They pursued leads over the city; they persuaded 'good people' to inform on the fugitive. With the help of local postmasters, the Secret Service arranged for Goldman's mail to be intercepted and copied. The police were slowly closing in.

As soon as she heard the news of McKinley's shooting, Goldman had hurried back to the house. Carl Nold was already there. It seemed that the assassin's name was Czolgosz; the name meant nothing to either of them. Nold at once warned her that the press would connect her to the attempted killing. Goldman was dismissive. What did she have to do with this Czolgosz? The next day, she visited a stationery store on behalf of Ed Brady. She was just closing a deal on a $1,000 order, when she saw the headlines. Czolgosz had confessed that Emma Goldman had incited him to commit the murder. She did her best to remain unruffled, left the store, and went to buy some newspapers. There Goldman learnt that Hippolyte Havel and all the Izaaks had been arrested, and would be held until she was found. Even their children had been taken to the cells. Or, as the Secret Service operative put it: '*Izaak* and several of his under devils are in jail.'[89] A news photo of Czolgosz on an inside page solved the mystery of why she was being connected to the crime, for at once she recognised Nieman from their two brief meetings in Cleveland and Chicago.

Goldman felt her duty was clear. She would have to go to Chicago and surrender herself to the police in order to secure the Izaaks' release. Despite the protestations of Carl Nold, who thought the plan ludicrous, the next day she took a train to Chicago. In the carriage, unaware of who was travelling with them, her fellow passengers angrily debated the event, some declaring that both Czolgosz and Goldman should be hanged. As the train pulled in, she took off her glasses and put on a white sailor hat with a bright blue veil.[90] In this disguise, she negotiated her way, presumably a little short-sightedly, through the crowd. She met with two other European Anarchists, an old flame Max Baginski and his partner, Millie, or Puck. Max told her she was mad to come to Chicago. The mood of the people was just as it had been when the Haymarket Anarchists had been martyred. The police and the press were after her blood.

Sensitive to the fact that, as immigrants, Max and Millie would be in a bad position if she was discovered with them, Goldman stayed in the house of a wealthy American sympathiser, one Charles G. Norris, a 29-year-old Canadian, but now a naturalised American citizen, an ex-insurance clerk, amateur sociologist, and by his own profession, a cool character. He lived in rooms on the third floor of a downtown apartment block, McNulty Flats. Rather thrilled to be sheltering a fugitive from justice, Norris quickly settled into his new role as amateur conspirator. He heard that $5,000 was being offered by the *Chicago Tribune* for an exclusive interview with Goldman. Considering the money would be useful, Goldman and her host arranged that he should bring a reporter to her and claim the money for the cause. After the interview, all three of them would go to the police together. That night Max and Millie visited, desperate that Goldman should escape as soon as possible to safety in Canada. She humoured Max by telling him that she would indeed flee, and then spent the night ripping up letters and other incriminating evidence.[91]

The next morning, Tuesday 10 September, Norris left for the newspaper offices, and Goldman stayed at home. If anyone called, it was agreed that she would pretend to be the maid. She took a bath. While soaking, she heard what sounded like scratching at the bathroom window. Unimpressed, she finished her bath, and was slipping on a kimono, when there was a sudden crash of glass from the dining-room. She went in and found a policeman hanging precariously from the windowsill with a gun in his hand.

The police had been tipped off as to Goldman's presence in the building and had come in force to arrest her. It was 11.00 in the morning when the police arrived, led by Captain Herman Schuettler, and began beating on the door.[92] But Goldman, apparently deep in thought in the bathtub, failed to open it for them, so one of them, Detective Charles K. Herts, decided to climb in to the apartment through the window. Now there he was, with his gun, three floors up. Ignominiously enough, Goldman had to help him clamber into the room. The police waiting at the door were let in and began questioning her. Goldman decided to have a little fun. She pretended to be the Swedish maid. According to her, the police were easily fooled and searched the apartment for evidence of the missing woman. Only when a pen was found with Goldman's name on it did she grow bored of the ruse, and confessed her name to the detectives.[93] According to the police, who had a different version of the story, when she told them that she was Swedish, Schuettler promptly spoke to her in that language. Unable to reply, she laconically declared that 'The game was up', and offered herself to the police.[94] In either case, she was instantly arrested and would have been taken to the police station as she was, had she not insisted that she be allowed to put on some clothes first. She dressed in the white sailor hat, added a white shirt, blue skirt and necktie, and was taken downtown.[95] As she left the building, she caught sight of Norris arriving with the reporter from the *Tribune*. Not wanting Norris to be arrested too, she feigned not to recognise him.[96]

In Chief O'Neill's office, they subjected her to the third degree.[97]
The room was hot, airless. From mid-morning until 7.00 p.m., they
questioned her without a break, shaking their fists at her, a succession
of around fifty raging policemen all repeating the same questions, the
same accusations. A pitcher of water stood close by in the room, but
she was not allowed to take a single drink. The police's object was to
prove she had been in Buffalo the previous week; they were looking for
a direct link to the crime.[98] She declared that she couldn't remember
Czolgosz from Cleveland – though she could remember meeting him at
the Izaaks' in Chicago. (She was most probably lying about Cleveland.
In her autobiography, *Living My Life*, she describes their first meeting,
though it is possible that this may also be the distortion of a romantic
memory.)

Photographs very likely taken by the Chicago Police Department
show a serious figure, white-bloused, a pince-nez settled quizzically on
her nose, a scarf knotted around her neck.[99] Her details were filled out:
her height measured at just over an inch under five feet; her occupation
given as 'dressmaker'. Her complexion was recorded as 'fair', her hair as
blonde, and her nationality as German. It was noted that her eyes were
weak. The crime on the statistics card read: 'fugitive Anarchist'.[100]

Given the oppressive circumstances and the grim possibilities
awaiting her – the police continually threatened her with the electric
chair – she seems to have characteristically remained both calm and
provocative. The interrogation continued, apparently led, improbably
enough, not by a policeman but by Walter Nowak, an acquaintance
of Czolgosz's from Cleveland, who had identified the assassin in
Buffalo.[101] Goldman refused to say if she admired the young assassin,
refused to agree that McKinley was a victim unlike any other, refused
to accept any responsibility for Czolgosz's deed.[102] She didn't help her
case by attacking the wounded President, calling him a tool of Mark
Hanna, untalented, unintelligent, and, as she had said before, too
insignificant to be worth murdering. She decried living and working
conditions in America, the self-proclaimed 'land of the free'; she could
understand how someone might be driven there to political violence.
But violence itself was the speciality of governments, not anarchists.
She was specifically charged with inciting striking building workers in
Chicago to attack workmen.

'That's as true as these stories of the present,' she replied quietly. 'I was in Paris at that time. I never said anything of the kind. I was not here.'

'While there did you see Bresci, the murderer of King Humbert?'

'I did not. I never knew him.'

(She was lying: she had met Bresci when he was an activist in a group in Paterson, New Jersey, and been struck by his difference from the average Italian Anarchist.[103])

'Did you know any of the men who sought to take the lives of rulers?'

'I knew one man, Alexander Berkman, the man who tried to kill H. C. Frick during the Homestead strike. No other.'[104]

It was a brave move to bring up the attempt to kill Frick at this point. But of course, no one there had forgotten what had happened to him or Goldman's likely involvement in the attack.

She was taken to a barred cell, exposed to view on all sides. A nurse gave her some lukewarm water in a tin cup. She promptly fell asleep, but was woken in the night by interrogators shining a reflector into her eyes. The questioning went on for five days.

A warrant charging her with conspiracy to murder the President was issued; she went to the magistrate's court and heard the charges. She would be remanded until 19 September; there was no chance of bail. Inevitably Norris was arrested too. Norris was unimpressed by the police and untroubled at being arrested by them: '"All men are types, and you are a rather peculiar and interesting one," he said, turning to Chief O'Neill.'[105] His defence was clear: Goldman had told him that she was going to hand herself over to the police later that morning, and so he could hardly be seen as aiding a refugee from justice.

The Secret Service were busy gathering any information they could find to secure Goldman's conviction, and were forced to delve into the – to them – highly unsavoury circles of radical America. Sometimes in reading their reports one can still feel their shudder of genuine disgust, as when a Secret Service operative in San Francisco was forced to let an Anarchist named Harry Culman go free, despite his having insulted the country's noble President. He had apparently remarked, among other things, that the President's assassination was 'a lesson'.[106] Unfortunately, there appeared to be no law against such foulness. The police agents found a witness who claimed to know that Czolgosz had visited the offices of *Free Society* where Goldman had also been seen. But as they investigated, voices within their own ranks, even the District Attorney of Chicago, were starting to accept that Goldman might have had no direct part in the shooting.[107] Yet there were other reports, including rumours that the same New Jersey Anarchists who had sheltered Bresci, and were recognised as being friendly with Goldman, had known of the assassination beforehand.[108] The St Louis agent suggested that Czolgosz had travelled to Buffalo with Robert Weinberg, Goldman's agent.[109] Yet the rumours remained unsubstantiated; the leads went nowhere.

A letter of support from Ed Brady freed Goldman to talk about that element of her movements over the last days. The arrest of Havel and the Izaaks meant that there was nothing to conceal there either, so Goldman was able to present to the police a more or less full account of her activities since she had met Czolgosz. She omitted only her visit to Berkman and the names of her hosts in Chicago. Her account was convincing enough to persuade Chief O'Neill that they probably had the wrong woman. He even confessed as much to her while visiting her cell.[110] Following this admission, Goldman's treatment noticeably improved. Her cell was left unlocked, the interrogations faltered. She was able to receive visitors, including sympathetic or merely curious journalists. Randolph Hearst, previously a critic of McKinley's presidency, offered $20,000 for an exclusive interview.[111] It would be a genuine scoop, and would perhaps get him off the hook regarding what some saw as complicity in the crime. It was better for Hearst to line up with the anti-Anarchists, and to give Goldman a platform and then deride her for her views. For Goldman, this was merely a continuation of her usual relations with the press. What was new was the virulent hatred of Anarchists displayed everywhere.

In interviews, Goldman was ready to display a level of humane consideration that she could never have expressed at the time of the attempt on Frick. She baffled one reporter by declaring that, although her sympathies were with Czolgosz, she would nonetheless happily tend McKinley if she were called upon to nurse him.

'You're a puzzle, Emma Goldman,' he said, 'I can't understand you. You sympathize with Czolgosz, yet you would nurse the man he tried to kill.' 'As a reporter you aren't expected to understand human complexities,' I informed him. 'Now listen and see if you can get it. The boy in Buffalo is a creature at bay. Millions of people are ready to spring on him and tear him limb from limb. He committed the act for no personal reasons or gain. He did it for what is his ideal: the good of the people. That is why my sympathies are with him. On the other hand,' I continued, 'William McKinley, suffering and probably near death, is merely a human being to me now. That is why I should nurse him.'[112]

Despite these human complexities, Goldman was now notorious as the 'apostle of aggressive anarchy'.[113] She was the object of national detestation. Patriotic Americans posted letters to the Attorney General and others demanding Goldman's prosecution and, preferably, execution. She herself received an influx of hate mail, some of it describing sexual punishments that the writers hoped would be inflicted upon her. Goldman herself felt their fervid imaginations would fascinate the psychologists.[114] But many took Goldman as merely the most visible representative of a foreign scourge in America's midst. The Department of Justice was determined to arrest and imprison as many Anarchists as possible. As happened when Berkman attacked Frick, they were convinced that the deed must be the consequence of a large and secret conspiracy. Eight detectives were employed to protect the financier Pierpont Morgan; Attorney General Philander C. Knox, McKinley's fellow Ohioan, had it in mind to round up the 'Reds'.[115] An Anarchist named Antonio Maggio arrested in Santa Rita threatened the police with the spectre of 100,000 Anarchists in America.[116] In Pittsburgh, Nold was arrested. There too Goldman's friend Harry Gordon was nearly lynched by a mob; the rope was already around his neck and he was only saved through the intervention of some bystanders.[117]

Czolgosz's crime seemed even more outrageous and incomprehensible than the attacks on Presidents Lincoln and Garfield.[118] In the aftermath of the attack, McKinley seemed a man so inoffensive and good that only insanity or the diabolism of anarchy could be offered as motives for it. So it was that Roosevelt declared the crime to be especially heinous, since:

the President represents the class that constitutes the backbone of the American nation. Among all the rulers of the world and among all the Presidents of our nation there was no opportunity for the Anarchists to select an object for attack whose life, character and works would put them more conspicuous in the wrong than when they assailed President McKinley.[119]

Not all responses were so predictable. Mark Twain's reaction to the event struck a note that would prove truer for the crimes of the future than it would regarding Czolgosz's attempt. Twain had seen the invasion of the Philippines earlier that year as a big crime, and now stood out against this little crime of individual murder by 'this ass with the unpronounceable name'. Writing to Joseph H. Twichell on 10 September 1901, with McKinley still lying wounded, he recalled how he once travelled 1,200 miles to kill a man, found him away from home, and in the gap caused by waiting for his return, had thought the whole thing through, become ashamed, and decided to call the murder off. The problem now would be the publicity that would surround the event, earning the killer notoriety:

his picture printed everywhere, the trivialest details of his movements, what he eats, what he drinks; how he sleeps, what he says, cabled abroad over the whole globe at cost of fifty thousand dollars a day – and he only a lowly shoemaker yesterday . . . Nothing will check the lynchings and ruler-murder but absolute silence – the absence of pow-pow about them. How are you going to manage that? By gagging every witness and jamming him into a dungeon for life; by abolishing all newspapers; by exterminating all newspaper men; and by extinguishing God's most elegant invention, the Human Race. It is quite simple, quite easy, and I hope you will take a day off and attend to it, Joe.[120]

The implication that Czolgosz had murdered for fame was certainly wrong, but regarding the future of American assassination was prescient.

If Twain's response was a relatively nuanced one, most followed the Roosevelt line of outrage and vengeance. Anarchists across America endured public opprobrium. The Anarchist colony at Home, in Pierce County, Washington, was harassed and subjected to violence.[121] Even Czolgosz's family suffered in the backlash. 'The Cleveland *Leader* demanded that Czolgosz's father, a city ditchdigger, be fired; the landlord ordered the Czolgoszes out; and Los Angeles police kept Czolgosz's brother in custody during President Roosevelt's visit.'[122] Goldman's family too were victimised, taken before a Grand Jury and questioned.[123] The police hounded them; her nieces and nephews

were bullied at school; they were evicted from their flat; her father was
forbidden to enter his synagogue.

VI

On the night of Thursday 12 September, the President's recovery
unexpectedly faltered. The solidity was breaking up. He was dying too
soon. Not yet a symbol of anything much, he was slipping back into a
historical vacuum. Soon he would be only a prelude to a politician truly
symbolic; his death was Roosevelt's opportunity. As he slipped out of
life, Roosevelt would come into his own.

Since Wednesday there had been problems giving the President
proper nourishment. Food injected straight into his stomach was almost
instantly expelled. There seemed no alternative but for McKinley to eat
in the normal way. Perhaps the solid food had come too soon; his body
could not assimilate it. He grew tired. Then he was suddenly unwell, his
heart not functioning properly, his skin warm, the pulse fast and weak.
The great man was unbearably vulnerable. The doctors monitored his
bowel movements, and one that he performed at midnight gave them
hope once again.[124] But the reprieve was brief. The end was coming fast.
More nurses were called, and messages were dispatched to Roosevelt
and the rest of the Cabinet, calling them to Buffalo.[125] (Encouraged by
the President's apparent recovery, Roosevelt had set out on a tramping
expedition in the Adirondacks.[126]) On his journey to New York, Dr
McBurney had got as far as Stockbridge, Massachusetts; as soon as he
heard the news, he hastened back. McKinley's heart was slowly giving
up. The day wore on and the physicians struggled; the press waiting on
the street outside received constant messages: he was asleep; the family
were with him; he grew weaker still. He died finally in the early hours
of Saturday 14 September 1901, at around 2.15 a.m.[127]

The journalist William Allen White, always a sceptic on the subject
of McKinley, gazed askance at the great man's passing:

the newspapers carrying the story of his death described it as curiously like a stage
deathbed. They said that as he sank out of consciousness, he was humming 'Nearer,
My God, To Thee,' and that he reached an affectionate hand to Mark Hanna and
parted with him in a well set, school reader deathbed scene. I wondered then if
that was the truth – if the tremendous force of a lifetime of conscious dramatics,

stage-play and character-acting had really persisted thus in death – or whether the power of his life's drama had written the story, as the reporters unconsciously tried to round out the heroic figure that he had envisaged in his heart, and carried into his career. Certainly McKinley died – in truth or in accepted fiction – in character; the statue in the park was expiring.[128]

It's a witty line, one that referred to a man alone with his mortality. The cause of death was gangrene in the wound.[129]

When Roosevelt heard the news, he was at North Creek Station, about to take the train to Buffalo; twelve hours after McKinley's passing, he was sworn in as President.[130] It was to prove a fortuitous change for America, insipidly magisterial McKinley, the man of his party and of Mark Hanna's ambitions, replaced by the impulsive and charismatic Teddy Roosevelt, a mere forty-two years old and a source of some anxiety for some older and more staid Republicans. He is still the youngest American to become President. Hanna was disgusted; he grumbled, 'Anything can happen now that damn cowboy is in the White House.'[131] Ironically, though McKinley was murdered for the sake of action itself, in Henry Adams's eyes it was Theodore Roosevelt who was 'pure act', immeasurable energy exemplified, the creator of political motion.[132] Whatever Czolgosz's aim in killing McKinley, it only possessed a symbolic function. Czolgosz struck not at the man, but at the office, but Roosevelt's immediate accession to power showed that the office itself was unkillable. In fact, the presence of such a dynamic character could make it seem even more resilient than it had before. Czolgosz had struck at the very concept of authority. And now, a man was dead, and authority was intact. All that had emerged in the process was the realisation of the vulnerability of the person who played the role. McKinley's implacable dignity, his pompous suits, his air of gravity, his pince-nez and his paunch, all had been brought down to the suffering and fragility of a man in the late summer swelter on a hospital bed, poisoned from the inside by the bullet from Czolgosz's gun.

On Sunday 15 September, following a funeral service at Milburn's house, the President was moved to the City Hall. A huge crowd had come to see. As they took the body from the hearse, a rain storm broke, and a fierce wind swept the town. The next day, the corpse went by railway to Washington, DC. He lay in state, and the crowds came.

On 19 September 1901, McKinley was buried at Canton, Ohio. The police guard was forced to remain outside Milburn's house until 1 December, warding off curious sightseers, 'the camera and Kodak crowd'. 'Pebbles from the driveway were picked up, leaves that dropped from the tree taken, and one souvenir hunter with more nerve than the others appeared with a mallet and chisel and requested the officer on duty that he be allowed to remove a few bricks from the building.'[133]

VII

Nearly forty years after he had heard the news of Lincoln's death in Rome, Henry Adams could look back on that crisis with ironic nostalgia:

the world of 1860 stood already on a distant horizon somewhere on the same plane with the republic of Brutus and Cato, while schoolboys read of Abraham Lincoln as they did of Julius Caesar. Vast swarms of Americans knew the Civil War only by school history, as they knew the story of Cromwell or Cicero, and were as familiar with political assassination as though they had lived under Nero. The climax of empire could be seen approaching, year after year, as though Sulla were a President or McKinley a consul.[134]

In this initially wistful vision of American history, the remoteness of Lincoln suddenly collapses with the present's absorption into the life of the past. Modern America too appears like ancient Rome, but now it is no longer the world of republican virtue, but the Rome of the emperors, the Rome of palace plots and mad violence.

Czolgosz belonged to nobody; both he and his crime were alien and incomprehensible. Old laments sounded. His deed placed 'America side by side with the slimy insecurity of the Old World. There the dirks have long been brandished, the staccato pistols have long reeked hot with murderous smoke, and behind slashed broadcloth imperial breasts have long beat wildly in anticipatory fear. But that is not America.'[135] To many ordinary Americans, even Czolgosz's 'unpronounceable name' signalled him to be suspiciously foreign. (It is in fact roughly pronounced 'Tcholgosch'.) Perhaps rightly, even the Anarchists would not claim him as one of their own.[136] In questioning by the police, although Czolgosz certainly mentioned the impact of Goldman, it is unclear whether he ever unprompted used the word 'Anarchy'. He killed McKinley not from allegiance to a group, but on the grounds of a personal belief.[137]

No one would claim him, yet there was nothing un-American about Czolgosz. Born in Michigan in May 1873, he was a first-generation citizen, the child of immigrants from Prussia on his mother's side, and on his father's from the partitioned territories of what is now Poland.[138] His father only mastered a few words of English.[139] With five brothers and two sisters he spent an unremarkable working-class childhood of ordinary privations. His mother died in childbirth when he was only twelve years old. His father (who subsequently remarried) was a labourer and the family led an itinerant life as they moved to follow the work, shifting from Detroit to the vicinity of Pittsburgh, and then ending up in Warrensville near Cleveland.[140]

His youth was solitary but stable. He worked as a mill-hand in Cleveland, keeping himself to himself, but attending meetings of the Order of Knights of the Golden Eagle Society, a respectably benevolent Christian mutual aid group. He appears also to have associated with the socialists. In 1898, suffering some kind of collapse, he left work to live on the family farm. Here he let time slip by. He lay in, or went off on solitary rambles, hunting rabbits with a shotgun and a revolver. He was rather a good shot.[141] He was removing himself from the social world; he ate alone, and slept long. A newspaper account of King Umberto of Italy's assassination was his bedtime companion for weeks.[142]

In spring 1901, a new sense of purpose suddenly brought him back to life. He borrowed money from his brother Waldeck. His brother asked him what he wanted the money for: 'They were standing on the street near a tree that was dying, and Leon said, "look, it is just the same as a tree that commences dying; you can see it isn't going to live long."'[143] He made trips back to Cleveland; it was on one such excursion that he heard Emma Goldman speak. He began to move in Anarchist circles. He followed Goldman to Chicago, and tried to join the Anarchists there, but was greeted by hostility and suspicion. He then travelled to the outskirts of Buffalo, where he took lodgings at the nearby town of West Seneca. In August, he abandoned his apartment and went back to Cleveland, and then returned fairly promptly to Buffalo.

He took a room at $5 per month in John Nowak's saloon, a hotel by the city centre, an impoverished area on the east side of town.[144]

He gave his name as Frank Nieman, though he more often adopted the first name 'Fred'; apparently Nieman was his mother's maiden name, though perhaps a pun on being candidly *niemand* (nobody) was intended.[145] He said he came from Cleveland, but also on occasion from Toledo, Ohio. Many of the other guests, as well as John Nowak himself, were Polish or of Polish descent. He seemed poor, and stayed home most evenings. Another of the residents, one Kaernarek, 'offered to find work for him to do, but he said it was too hot to work'. As yet, Czolgosz had no definite plan. He wandered the city.[146]

On Saturday 31 August, Czolgosz went out with Kaernarek and bought himself a gun. It seems that he had come to his decision. From now on, he only had to wait.

On Friday 6 September, Czolgosz woke early. Today he would kill the President. He dressed in his best suit, and ate a solitary breakfast in a café near his hotel. He arrived early at the Exposition. It was just 8.00. He saw the President's train leave for the Falls. He might have shot him then, but there was too big a crowd and he could not draw close enough. He went to the Falls, but again could not get near the President. He did not want to shoot him there anyway. So he took a streetcar back to Buffalo.[147] There were reports in the Buffalo newspapers that the President would be in the Temple of Music at 4 p.m. He decided he would do it there. Afterwards they would kill him. He knew that. He waited around all day, and then he took his handkerchief and wrapped it around his hand, with the revolver clutched in it. Normally, no one would be permitted to approach the President without his hands being fully exposed; but today, in the scorching heat, handkerchiefs were everywhere and the rule was waived.[148] He joined the crowd waiting outside the Temple, and went in with them. The Temple was crowded, but cooler than the streets outside. He was there and could see the President. Suddenly an impulse to give the whole thing up struck him, and he would have left there and then had not the crowd blocked his path out. There was no way to get through. So he decided that he would do it after all.

The man with him in the line to meet the President tried several times to start up a conversation, but each time Czolgosz rebuffed him.[149] Once Czolgosz strayed out of the line – was he attempting again to leave? – but a guard forced him back into place.[150] He met the eyes of another of the Secret Service guards, but the guard saw nothing unusual, just a mechanic wanting to shake hands with the President.[151] When he reached the head of the line, and the President went to take his hand, he shot him. Then he shot him again. He was taking aim for the third bullet, when they knocked him down. He was beaten up, and dragged off for his interrogation. But there was little to tell. He had merely done what he ought. When the President died, Czolgosz was stashed in the dungeon of Erie County Penitentiary. On the Monday morning, 16 September 1901, he was taken via an underground tunnel to the City and County Hall, and indicted with the President's murder.

VIII

The authorities in Buffalo were struggling vainly to secure Goldman's extradition. Meanwhile, she waited in her Chicago cell, guarded by one of the men who had watched over the Haymarket Martyrs some fifteen years before. She was taken to Cook County Jail; on the way one of the guards punched her, knocking out a tooth in the process.[152] A court hearing followed and no evidence having been found to connect her to the crime, she was released. She went to the Izaaks, who also had been released without charge. There she began her desperate attempt to explain Czolgosz's actions to the world and to secure mercy for him.

Goldman's immediate thoughts about Czolgosz were expressed with typical recklessness. In writing about 'The Tragedy at Buffalo' for *Free Society* soon after the event, Goldman was unrepentant in her support of the assassin. Like Berkman before him, he was a Brutus and McKinley a tyrant Caesar, merely the 'president of the money kings and trust magnates of this country'.[153] The opinions articulated were so incendiary that Abe Izaak, the journal's editor, attempted unsuccessfully to tone it down for publication; he feared retaliation from the police. Goldman was livid, and the article was printed as written.[154] She reiterated also her low opinion of McKinley's intellectual prowess; he was still for her the dull nullity he had always been. The horror expressed at the assassination was merely the outrage of the plutocrats at the first sign of the loosening of their power. The popular patriotic support for McKinley was itself an indication of how oppressed Americans really were: they had absorbed the lessons of their masters and parroted them as though they were their own beliefs. She was contemptuous of the attempt to suggest Czolgosz was merely a foreigner, a European blight, when he was in fact 'the child of Columbia . . . Who can tell how many times this American child has gloried in the celebration of the 4th of July, or on Decoration Day, when he faithfully honoured the nation's dead?'[155]

Above all, in Goldman's account, Czolgosz's actions become a force of nature, an inevitable consequence of the way things are, and moreover the way that Czolgosz is:

We might as well ask ourselves of the usefulness of a cyclone, tornado, a violent thunderstorm, or the ceaseless fall of the Niagara waters. All these forces are the natural results of natural causes, which we may not yet have been able to explain, but which are nevertheless a part of nature, just as all force is natural and part of man and beast, developed or checked, according to the pressure of conditions and man's understanding. An act of violence is therefore not only the result of conditions, but also of man's psychical and physical nature, and his susceptibility to the world around him.[156]

It is a curious feature of Goldman's response to the killing, and to other earlier assassinations, that she returns over and over to the idea that assassination is a response to stimuli, and a noble response at that. It seems to her the expression of a nature, a revolt of the person against injustice. There is fatalism here, and a recognition of the mystery of identity. This is in some ways more perceptive than the attitudes of her opponents, who wish to imagine that violence arises from conspiracy or from influence. Her opponents fantasise a self as moulded by others, and therefore meaningful; she sees the individual responding in his natural way to the world in which he lives, making his own actions, and his own destiny.

She was moving away from a Marxist or Kropotkinian view to a Nietzschean one. In imbibing Nietzsche she picked up the idea that there was no objective meaning, only the perspective favoured by an individual: no one path, only the healthy or the sickly. In her view one becomes a killer because that's the kind of person that one is. She throws in the paradox that one becomes a killer because one is so good. Such a belief places the individual beyond law and beyond ordinary moral codes. There is just character in action, like a force of nature, not even choosing itself, but just being.

Yet the individual does not operate entirely alone. Rather his violence mirrors the violence directed against him, a natural retort to the force implicit in government as such: 'Government as present consists of force, and force is now on top, and so long as there is force on top we must have force on the bottom.'[157] Again she finds the conjunction of an inner prompting and a response to outer force. For Goldman, such force was implicit in the very structure of capitalist society. On a more immediate political level this meant seeing the killing as a response to the American invasion of the Philippines, and to clashes against labour at Hazleton, Virden and in Idaho.[158] The good man, enraged by these injustices and feeling them more than others, turns to violence:

It is, therefore, not cruelty, or a thirst for blood, or any other criminal tendency, that induces such a man to strike a blow at organized power. On the contrary, it is mostly because of a strong social instinct, because of an abundance of love and sorrow around us, a love which seeks refuge in the embrace of mankind . . .

The cause for such an act lies . . . too deep for the shallow multitude to comprehend. It lies in the fact that the world within the individual, and the world around him, are two antagonistic forces, and, therefore, must clash.[159]

Pressed down upon by the institutions of the state, the individual strikes back with a counter-force that is an act of love. Czolgosz was a beautiful soul. Almost against his will, his sensitivity had led him to lash out. It was not his fault, but rather those of the social conditions that goaded him.[160]

Such attitudes were highly unlikely to take off the pressure that Goldman was under. Her fate was entwined with Czolgosz's; like Berkman might have done before him, he could lose his life due to an involvement with her. Still she preserved, in the midst of her passions, an insouciance regarding her own fate or her place in popular opinion. Her compassion for Czolgosz, this beautiful, sensitive and impressionable boy, required an equally strong rejoinder from her comrades.

Among her fellow American Anarchists, there was no doubt that the two most significant voices were still those of Most and Berkman. As far as the public were concerned, Johann Most changed tack yet again, and nearly ten years after deriding Berkman for trying to kill Frick, he celebrated Czolgosz. In fact, things were more complicated. Events had manoeuvred Most into once again celebrating an assassination. An issue of *Freiheit* appeared on the day of the assassination, containing an article in praise of tyrannicide by Karl Heinzen. The piece was over fifty years old, a relic of the 1848 revolutions, but Most prefaced it with the statement that it was still true today. When word reached him that an attempt had been made on McKinley, realising that he was in deep trouble, Most tried to withdraw the issue. He was too late. The edition was already in the hands of the police; in fact a rumour exists that the only issue of the paper sold was to a policeman, who promptly initiated the prosecution against Most.[161] In the midst of the angry reaction against Anarchists, *Freiheit*'s readers panicked. Sales plummeted; some people actually moved apartment in order to avoid delivery of the magazine. Most himself was arrested on Thursday 12 September, then released on bail. While making a speech at Frick's Hall, Corona, Long Island, he was re-arrested by police and charged with 'suspicious behaviour'. He was acquitted on this charge, but arrested again following another speech in Manhattan.[162] Most was in a bind. He made his living by giving speeches; the police harassment would prevent him from making enough money to live. Finally put on trial for the publication of 'Murder Against Murder' in *Freiheit*, Most was convicted, inevitably perhaps, given the anti-Anarchist feeling following McKinley's death. After what had begun by looking like a promising appeal, the conviction was upheld and Most went back to Blackwell's Island.

In Berkman's case, things were rather different. In the immediate aftermath of the McKinley shooting, while the wounded President lay in hospital, a new line of enquiry opened up regarding the attempted tunnel escape from the Western Penitentiary. The police, especially Police Superintendent Henry Muth, were now convinced that the tunnel on Sterling Street was the work of Goldman, Nold and Bauer, and designed purely for Berkman. There wasn't enough evidence to charge anybody, of course, but the police remained adamant in their suspicions. Muth also believed that Most was involved with the tunnel, which, in view of the break between the young Anarchists and their former mentor, seems highly unlikely. Even the press seemed sceptical, thinking the whole story a ruse to connect a failed investigation with the attempt on the President's life.[163]

This investigation was one more trouble for Berkman, who of course knew of his real involvement in the tunnel plot. He had been in solitary for over a year, straitjacketed for long periods, mourning prison friends. He was approaching madness, dependent on the kindness of the authorities.

Like Most, Berkman had much to lose from publicly supporting Czolgosz. As he had told Goldman already, Warden Wright was sick, and a new Inspector in the penitentiary had taken on his work and much eased his conditions there. Then there was the commutation law that had reduced his sentence. He could now expect to be free in four or five years' time. This relative liberty was immediately threatened by Czolgosz's attack. A Dr Rubin, a Russian-born physician working in Michigan, had spoken to Berkman at the time of his trial. He now wrote a letter that was passed on to the Department of Justice, suggesting that they go to the jail, get on the right side of Berkman, extract some useful information and so snare Goldman.[164] Whatever came of this helpful proposal, for a brief time Berkman was once again locked up in solitary.

He attended to the news about Czolgosz, and received several letters from Goldman detailing her involvement in the boy's fate and the strains of the investigations and interrogations regarding her own part in the deed. On 20 December 1901, he wrote a letter to Goldman setting out his views. It amounted to a testament of all that prison had taught him:

And you, dear friend? In your letters I feel how terribly torn you are by the events of the recent months. I lived in great fear for your safety, and I can barely credit the good news that you are at liberty. It seems almost a miracle.

I followed the newspapers with great anxiety. The whole country seemed to be swept with the fury of revenge . . . You were splendid, dear; and I was especially moved by your remark that you would faithfully nurse the wounded man, if he required your services, but that the poor boy, condemned and deserted by all, needed and deserved your sympathy and aid more than the president. More strikingly than your letters, that remark discovered to me the great change wrought in us by the ripening years. Yes, in us, in both, for my heart echoed your beautiful sentiment. How impossible such a thought would have been to us in the days of a decade ago! We should have considered it treason to the spirit of revolution; it would have outraged all our traditions even to admit the humanity of an official representative of capitalism. Is it not very significant that we two – you living in the very heart of Anarchist thought and activity, and I in the atmosphere of absolute suppression and solitude – should have arrived at the same evolutionary point after a decade of divergent paths? . . .

We grow broader, but too often the heart contracts as the mind expands, and the fires are burning down while we are learning ... And you, my dear friend, with the deeper insight of time, you have yet happily kept your heart young. I have rejoiced at it in your letters of recent years, and it is especially evident from the sentiments you have expressed regarding the happening at Buffalo. I share your view entirely; for that very reason, it is the more distressing to disagree with you in one very important particular: the value of Leon's act ...

I have read of the beautiful personality of the youth, of his inability to adapt himself to brutal conditions, and the rebellion of his soul. It throws a significant light upon the cause of the *Attentat*. Indeed, it is at once the greatest tragedy of martyrdom, and the most terrible indictment of society, that it forces the noblest men and women to shed human blood, though their souls shrink from it. But the more imperative it is that drastic methods of this character be resorted to only as a last extremity ...

Now I do not believe that this deed was terroristic; and I doubt whether it was educational, because the social necessity for its performance was not manifest. That you may not misunderstand, I repeat: as an expression of personal revolt it was inevitable, and in itself an indictment of existing conditions. But the background of social necessity was lacking, and therefore the value of the act was to a great extent nullified.

In Russia, where political oppression is popularly felt, such a deed would be of great value. But the scheme of political subjection is more subtle in America ... The real despotism of republican institutions is far deeper, more insidious, because it rests on the popular delusion of self-government and independence. That is the subtle source of democratic tyranny, and, as such, it cannot be reached with a bullet.[165]

Goldman's response proved Berkman's sentiments regarding the closeness of their mutual development to be misplaced. He spoke from the heart as well as the head, but Goldman only heard what she believed to be an insensitive dismissal of Czolgosz's suffering. Berkman was faced with a dilemma. Czolgosz's act was a beautiful folly, a sign of an inward refusal to accept life's injustices. Yet it made no sense to kill McKinley, who was no more than a cipher for a system of power that ran through everything. Moreover, Anarchism would always find it hard to root itself in the USA, as its doctrine of self-government mirrors all too closely the mainstream American ideology of self-reliance. Here assassination could not make sense to the public. Without obvious autocrats, there were no suitable victims. The myth that the poor may become the rich through hard work, like the idea that anyone might become President, masked a democratic tyranny that concealed itself behind a myth of self-government, freedom and opportunity. Where everyone already believes they have the freedom of self-governance, why should they require Anarchism? Berkman still believed in the power of violence, only believing that it should match itself to 'historical necessity', a neo-Marxist interpretation which suggested that America was not yet closely bound by such a necessity.[166] Goldman saw none of this. The letter was a blow. She could not believe what she was reading. Could Sasha really be advancing the same arguments that Most had used against his own attempt on Frick? Could he be so inconsistent, so heartless? The letter made her weep, made her ill. She saw only the cowardly hypocrisy of the man who would have killed Frick turning against the lonely and suffering boy who had killed McKinley. She was distraught and she was furious. She broke off all contact with Berkman; his one rock of loyalty was gone.

IX

One week after his arraignment, on Monday 23 September 1901, at 10.00 in the morning, Czolgosz's trial began in the Supreme Court of Erie County. He pleaded guilty, but his defence counsel was bound to refuse to accept this plea, and instead a not guilty plea was entered.[167] As the trial progressed, Czolgosz appeared distracted and absent. He almost never spoke, but looked ahead, absorbed it seemed in thoughts of his own.

The trial went quickly. Almost the first thing the defence team did was to point out that they were unhappy in their allotted task of having to protect Czolgosz's interests. This was hardly a promising beginning. The doctors who had operated on the President presented medical evidence concerning the cause of death. There followed eye-witness evidence given regarding the shooting itself, otiose perhaps given the account of Czolgosz's direct and self-incriminating statements regarding the murder, drawn from the police interrogations. They reported that Czolgosz did not believe that the President should receive services, while others only felt glad to render service to him. They told how the young Anarchist did not believe in church, state, or the marriage relation. He was a Free Lover.[168] At this point, without warning the prosecution closed its case.

As Czolgosz had resolutely refused to co-operate in his own defence, his counsel fell back on the rather desperate measure of pleading with the jury to recognise the assassin as not responsible for his own actions. Despite the defence team's stated reluctance to represent Czolgosz, they nonetheless did their best to present a rhetorically effective defence. They presented the young man as someone driven to the edge of sanity by industrial conditions; the murder of McKinley by an insane man was much like that of a death caused by a force of nature – an accident that none could prevent.

The court still relied on the M'Naghten Rules, as enshrined in the Code of Criminal Procedure of the State of New York, Section 21. Czolgosz's avowal that he knew that he would be 'hung' for the murder indicated that he certainly knew the legal consequences of his deed. The doctors who examined Czolgosz had followed a simpler criterion: 'was Czolgosz at the time he committed the act a victim of mental disease or mental unsoundness?'[169] For several weeks Czolgosz had been examined with reference to his sanity by three doctors. He was also examined by Dr Carlos MacDonald, Professor of Mental Diseases and Medical Jurisprudence at Bellevue Hospital; after two private examinations, the Professor found him to be sane. There was no evidence of delusions, no hallucinations, no morbidity, no mental gloom, no marks of degeneracy. 'On the contrary, everything in his history as shown by his conduct and declarations, points to the existence in him of the social disease, Anarchy, of which he was a victim.'[170]

In the light of this medical evidence, the prosecution argued that Czolgosz was responsible for his own actions in so far as he had willingly exposed himself to the dark ideas of Anarchism.[171] The District Attorney argued for the full rigour of justice to be brought down on Czolgosz. The Anarchists had to be made to understand that law was supreme. The judge, Justice Truman C. White, pointed out that the question of guilt depended upon Czolgosz being considered responsible for his actions at the time of the murder. On Tuesday 24 September, the jury retired at 3.51 p.m, and at 4.23 p.m. returned with their verdict. They had already made their minds up as to his guilt, but wanted to give a show at least of deliberating on the matter. In any case the trial had lasted altogether just eight and a half hours.[172] Czolgosz was found guilty of murder in the first degree. The verdict appeared not to move him. He was led from the court and taken back to his cell.

The next day, Czolgosz's family visited him in jail. His sister wept and his brother was sympathetic, only his father would not speak. Leon told them, 'I was alone in this.' Afterwards they travelled back home to Cleveland.[173] On Thursday, Czolgosz was back in court to hear his sentence. Unusually Penney, the English-born District Attorney, took this opportunity to question him about his background. What schools had he gone to? Did he attend Catholic church? No, he did not often drink alcohol. No, he had never committed another crime. Clerk Fisher asked him if there was any legal cause why sentence should not be pronounced against him. The court was hoping for a final statement perhaps, some speech that would settle the reasons for it all. But Czolgosz had apparently nothing to say. He merely remarked, 'I would like to say this much: that the crime was committed by no one else but me; no one told me to do it and I never told anybody to do it.' He was asked if his mother and father had any connection to the crime. 'No sir; not only my father and mother, but there hasn't anybody else had nothing to do with it.'[174] Clearly Czolgosz was not just trying to exonerate his family. While Czolgosz's initial statements had implicated Goldman in his crime, since before the President's death he had constantly asserted that she had taken no part in his assassination of McKinley. On this public occasion Czolgosz was again setting the record straight.

And then as Justice White pronounced sentence, Czolgosz stood with his lips set, gazing straight ahead. He would be electrocuted. The prisoner remained steady, and showed as before no emotion. The judge 'omitted the usual commiserative evocation, "May God have mercy on your soul!"'[175]

There was contentment in most quarters that justice had been done with such prompt efficiency. Unfortunately, the attempt to discover a conspiracy in the case had broken down for lack of evidence, and Goldman and the others had walked free. But there was still hope that the plot would be uncovered, and the other Anarchists might share Czolgosz's fate. The execution was set for six weeks ahead. That at least was satisfactory.

X

Within days of the assassination, psychologists were presenting their own position as to the reasons for the young 'Anarchist's' crime. One prominent 'alienist', Dr Allan M. Hamilton, declared that Czolgosz was probably driven to the crime by the rhetoric of the yellow press.[176] Thinking of Czolgosz now, one soon halts before a mystifying opacity. His confessions render his crime only more obscure. At the time, his deed hardly seemed to belong to him; it was as though he were Goldman's creature, the murder one committed by proxy. If one discounts this version of events, then there remains only the unsettling brevity of his few statements regarding the crime. Into this gap in our understanding, the psychologists strode. They had the tools to explain everything.

Caught up as they were with the attempt to medicalise crime, Czolgosz fascinated the psychologists of the day. Many were followers of Cesare Lombroso, the hugely influential 'criminal anthropologist' and professor of legal medicine and psychiatry at Turin. During the international Anarchist violence of the 1890s, Lombroso had begun to examine the figure of the assassin. He believed that all criminals were victims of evolutionary regression, displaying signs of their 'degeneration' in physical 'stigmata', marks which the careful criminal anthropologist could detect and decode. 'In assassins we have prominent jaws, widely separated cheek bones, thick, dark hair, scanty beard, and a pallid face,' he declared in 1897.[177]

Lombroso revealed a marked ambivalence towards Anarchism. Unlike many conservatives, he acknowledged some good in its theories and found certain Anarchists heroic – even among the assassins of the movement. For him, Anarchism is even an inevitable development in nations where justice does not exist for the poor. Yet as a political philosophy, he considered, it stumbles on the rock of greed and selfishness; without restraint, society would become a mob preying on one another. Anarchists themselves, however, were rather more astounding:

And when one comes to examine personally, not the theorists of anarchy, but its soldiers – not to say its executioners – one is confronted by a number of the wildest anomalies. In order to have reached this militant stage a tremendous degeneration must have taken place, not merely of the intelligence, but also of the moral sense . . . the persuasion must have been reached that, as in the beginning of the race, crime and action are the same thing, that human life is not a sacred thing, nor murder the greatest of crimes.[178]

The Anarchist represents a puzzling contradiction. He straddles at once the extreme of innovation and the abyss of our primitive origins. The Anarchist's crimes are vestiges not just of a utopian lawless future but of a pre-social, pre-legal past. Their crimes are as much the product of impulse as of conviction; murder comes from an inspiration at once bewilderingly modern and terrifyingly barbaric.

By a similar paradox, though some assassins came from the ranks of the degenerate, many were idealists driven by the desire to ameliorate social life. To Lombroso, criminals, but especially assassins, displayed a perplexing moral complexity, their undoubtedly good actions oddly separated from their blatantly vicious deeds: 'Lacenaire on the same day that he killed Chardon, risked his life to save a cat which was about to fall from a roof.'[179] Lombroso attempted to get around the problem by pathologising the instinct to rebel. He relates revolutions to temperature curves and to topography – for instance, he maintained that the republicans in France tended to live among hills and mountains.[180] The impulses behind assassination dwindle to physical causes; the complexity that had initially troubled Lombroso resolves into observable simplicities.

Some years after his murder of McKinley, Czolgosz remained a test case for medical opinion about the nature of the criminal. In 1910, Havelock Ellis, the noted sexologist and a disciple of Lombroso, wrote a monograph on the criminal which uses Czolgosz as one of its key examples. He begins his book by enumerating the varieties of criminal. The first listed is the *'political criminal'*:

By this term is meant the victim of an attempt by a more or less despotic Government to preserve its own stability . . . Consequently the 'political criminal' of our time or place may be the hero, martyr, saint, of another land or age. The political criminal is, as Lombroso calls him, 'the true precursor of the progressive movement of humanity'; or, as Benedikt calls him, the *homo nobilis* of whom the highest type is Christ.[181]

Ellis clearly favours the idealistic conspirator. Inspired as much by Nietzsche and classical models of tyrannicide as by Lombroso and Darwin, Ellis appears intriguingly baffled by the advent of the modern assassin: '*The Regenticide* – During recent years a particular variety of political offender has in all civilised countries acquired peculiar importance: the Anarchist who kills a king, governor, or political leader, and is termed a regicide, or, more comprehensively, a magnicide or regenticide.' But experts cannot agree as to what causes such killings.[182] He argues that political murder is a product of Western civilisation, as the Greek and Roman roots of theories of tyrannicide suggest. Political murder takes place where there is a vision of political freedom. A pure despotism need fear no assassin. Yet the modern version of the tyrannicide marks himself out by the very ineffectuality of his deed. To kill a tyrant in an age where countries were ruled by absolutist personalities made absolute sense; expunging the despot ends the despotism. However, in a modern state, where rulers, whether monarchs or elected, are mere figureheads, it is known in advance that the crime will change nothing. This is to say more than that kings die, yet monarchy survives. Rather monarchy itself is only a product of a system still greater – the whole complex multitudinous, international, Western world.

Ellis argues that such quixotic assassins are not always insane, though they may in worldly terms appear foolish. Unlike an ordinary criminal, he is not motivated by self-interest; he sacrifices his own life, and that of his victim, for an ideal – in particular, the ideal of anarchy:

This has been the case ever since in 1876 Cafiero and Malatesta proclaimed the desirability of *propaganda by act*, in order to affirm the principle of Anarchism and to spread abroad a knowledge of the natural laws of social life ... It was inevitable that ignorant and hot-headed youths – often of abnormal temperament to start with, and roused to feverish enthusiasm by the spectacle of social misery and contact with an environment of revolt – should be fatally driven to acts of violence, which seems to them likely to speed on the regeneration of the world as well as to ensure a martyr's crown.[183]

Ellis offers two examples of this ideal kind of killer: Caserio, the assassin of President Carnot of France; and Czolgosz. Czolgosz was a good man, he says, attractive and open. A Lombrosian examination of his body found him devoid of the stigmata of degeneration. Clearly the standard models for understanding the young man's motives would not do:

The investigation of two such typical and yet unlike regenticides as Caserio and Czolgosz clearly shows that they are absolutely distinct alike from the insane group of criminals and from ordinary criminals against the common law ... It is the very excess of his sympathetic sensibilities that impels him to his deed of violence. He execrates the few because he loves the many ... He is, as Bourdeau puts it ... a 'philanthropic assassin'. ... This attitude ... most easily arises in young, narrow, and ill-trained minds ... if these regenticidal youths could be preserved from violence for a few years longer, until their knowledge increased and their vision of life widened, they would become respectable and even estimable members of the social state they once wished to destroy.[184]

Here Ellis shares in a different vein the attitudes of the Anarchists themselves; both imagine youth as in a war with age. The idealism of adolescence has become for Ellis potentially and indeed even nobly murderous.

Ellis and the others were merely endeavouring to account for the assassin's deed. The psychological interest in Czolgosz both replicates Goldman's view (he killed because that was his character) and denies it – character being subsumed within biology. Again the idea that an individual might pursue a course through his own will falters, and finds itself replaced by a determinism that removes responsibility or shifts it elsewhere.

XI

But for Goldman the question of Czolgosz's motives struck deeper and more personally. She did her best to be active in Czolgosz's cause. Yet, while she fought on his behalf, doubt remained. First, it was unclear why Czolgosz had initially declared that Goldman had inspired him, or even whether he had really done so. Goldman disbelieved the charge, and appeared to think it a slight on Czolgosz's loyalty. But this left the deeper issue untouched: had Goldman influenced Czolgosz to kill McKinley? She responded to this charge variously. In 1909, in reaction to criticism from a fellow Anarchist, she wrote:

For the enlightenment of T. T. H. permit me to say that the state of New York employed 200 detectives and spent $30,000 to connect me with the 'assassin.' Evidently, they were leaving nothing undone to get sufficient evidence ...

Leon Czolgosz made one statement when he was placed in the electric chair, and the good Christian Brothers, in their great Christian love attempted to draw a confession from their helpless victim.

They told him that Emma Goldman had denounced him as a worthless beggar, or something to that effect. 'It makes no difference what she says, she knew nothing of the act,' was the 'assassin's' reply.

As to what else that boy may or may not have said, only his warders and the prison walls know.[185]

In this way, Goldman often spoke as though the idea of influence were a newspaper concoction or police ruse. Actually this idea went to the heart of her beliefs and the ambiguities of those beliefs.

Goldman's Anarchism celebrated the autonomous individual, yet remained intensely conscious of the power of others to move us – through love, art, oratory, or compassion. The notion of influence is somehow central to her life, and yet the suspicion that a person's action might derive from another threatened her. What if words of hers really had sent that man out to be executed?

In the aftermath of the McKinley murder, the press made a move that would become standard in the aftermath of an apparently senseless crime. The individual killer appears insignificant, his actions ultimately banal, the drama of responsibility and will played out by him being invisible and therefore uninteresting. On the other hand, it is compelling to trace the impulse to action to a relationship to something beyond the self – a conspiracy, a film, a computer game, something that shifts responsibility elsewhere, to some cultural presence we really dislike, or to a more interesting other.

To Goldman, such speculations were a way of avoiding what was unprecedented about the murder of McKinley. Czolgosz's act was a new thing, a social phenomenon. An American had killed a President, but 'neither sectional feeling nor personal interest played any part in the act'.[186] His was a disinterested act. Actually it was precisely this quality of Czolgosz's deed that made it Anarchist, that made it modern. Czolgosz killed McKinley out of idealism, or in fact, as Goldman would argue, out of goodness. At times, Goldman could even make it seem as though assassination were the product of youthful high spirits.[187]

Goldman employed a fine, and perhaps slippery distinction when it came to her endorsement of assassination. She presented herself as sympathising with the killer rather than with the killing. Even within the movement some were confused by this contrast. Here she responds to one such criticism, levelled at her by E. C. Walker for apologising for Czolgosz:

We are open and avowed Revolutionists; but we defy any one to produce a single line from any English Anarchist paper or magazine published in this country within the last twenty-five years where assassination is advocated or even implied. And if this be true, can a just and honest man maintain that the followers of the Communist-Anarchist school of Thought should be treated as criminals?

Yes, literary honesty is a rare jewel, Mr. Walker. If you read in an article in 'Mother Earth' that 'Czolgocz [sic] was a soul in pain,' you immediately declare the writer to be an apologist for Czolgocz. Is sympathy for an unfortunate man identical with justification of or apology for the man's act? As real Anarchists we neither condemn nor justify; our business is to try to understand, understand, understand, Mr. Walker . . .[188]

These were later self-exculpations. In the immediate wake of her release, Goldman was engaged in more practical worries. She did her best to secure a lawyer for Czolgosz at the trial. No one would accept the defence. She travelled to New York, convinced that she could do more good there. She struggled to find a flat in a city where no land-lord would have her for a tenant. There was little she could achieve. She found most of her Anarchist comrades to be lily-livered or self-protecting. Few would speak for Czolgosz; some even stood against his deed and her supposed involvement in it for nuanced and, to her, convenient reasons of doctrine. She was without hope.

XII

On the morning of Tuesday 29 October 1901, just after 7.00, they killed Leon Czolgosz. He had slept well on his final night. 'Almost his last words were: "I am not sorry."' He sat in the electric chair and spoke, incomprehensibly at first, but then with greater clarity. 'I shot the President. I did it because I thought it would benefit the people, the good working people.' They strapped him in, fixing the binding straps to his arms and legs, and placed the mask over his face. He said that he wished he had seen his father. The current was switched on; his body jerked and then froze rigid. For a few moments, he was held there by the current, then the force was reduced, and his body relaxed, and then all at once it was put on again with full force, and again his body spasmed. Again the current was turned down. A doctor stepped forward and examined him. He said that they should turn it on again, and again the force went through him. After that he was dead. It was 7.15.[189]

The autopsy followed; it was over by 12.30 p.m., his body cooling from the electrical charge as the surgeons proceeded.[190] His hair was first rubbed with Vaseline and then flattened so that plaster-casts of the head could be moulded.[191] The brain was cut into its natural sections; no abnormalities were discovered. He was found to have been in excellent health when they killed him.[192] Then Czolgosz's corpse was destroyed using acid; quicklime had been dismissed as not thorough enough.[193] In the prison yard they burnt his clothes and all the letters he had received in prison. All trace of him was to be erased. In the summer of 1907, a McKinley statue was raised in Buffalo.

XIII

Berkman had been dispatched to prison as an alien immigrant; he walked out of it an American. In the 1920s and 1930s, despite working as a translator from the German, he would answer letters from his German publishers in English, declaring that it was easier for him. Around the same time, he stated in an interview that, although he had never been naturalised as a citizen of the United States, he still felt himself to be an American: fourteen years in the penitentiary had made him one.

A newspaper interview with a still imprisoned Berkman appeared on 2 July 1905, describing: 'Grim, silent and cynical Berkman . . . not a man of inviting personality'. The reporter declares that Berkman is more famous than Lincoln on the Lower East Side; he's clearly struck by the apparently unsympathetic character.

'I am an anarchist,' he says, 'but not the kind of an anarchist the newspaper artists picture, with a bomb in one hand and a knife in the other. The men who make such pictures exhibit their ignorance of what anarchy is or what it stands for.' This is a picture of Berkman as he is today . . . He is a serious man and looks upon life seriously.[194]

It's curious that Berkman does not connect the popular image of anarchism to the impact of his own 'attentat'.

Release from jail brought a kind of breakdown. For a time he vanished; there was even a rumour that he'd been kidnapped by Frick.[195] Unable to bear his freedom, for a few months he retreated from Goldman, from the cause, before accepting again a place in the struggle. His friend and fellow Anarchist Voltairine de Cleyre wrote to him: 'And you have conquered Alex; you won out against Death in a slow fight.'[196]

No longer lovers, but comrades in the struggle, Berkman and Goldman spent the years after his release on the periphery of American political violence, or perhaps somewhat closer. In July 1914, he praised the radicals on Lexington Avenue, blown up by their own bomb, one very likely intended for the Rockefellers as revenge for the massacre in Ludlow of striking coal miners. There was the bombing of the *LA Times* offices too; Berkman would later hint that he knew 'the inside story of some explosions'.[197] In 1916, Goldman would also have a similar close encounter; she was in San Francisco when a bomb was thrown at a Preparedness Day parade.

Berkman now declared that he believed in 'defensive violence':

But, if a man ties me down, starves me, and keeps me in subjection, even though he does not raise his hand against me to beat or physically injure me, would you consider it offensive violence if I were to break loose and beat him up, in order to keep my own life?[198]

He was shifting ground from the position he had assumed during Czolgosz's trial, returning to a more emphatic endorsement of revolutionary violence. Goldman likewise continued to hold fast to the necessity of 'the deed'. In 1908, she wrote:

I believe that Anarchism is the only philosophy of peace, the only theory of the social relationship that values human life above everything else. I know that some Anarchists have committed acts of violence, but it is the terrible economic inequality and great political injustice that prompts such acts, not Anarchism. Every institution to-day rests on violence; our very atmosphere is saturated with it. So long as such a state exists we might as well strive to stop the rush of Niagara as hope to do away with violence . . .[199]

For her examples of kindly killers, all motivated by injustice, she presents Caserio, Bresci, 'Angelino' (Angiolillo, the killer of Cánovas)

– and Berkman. Such statements epitomise what Goldman herself understood to be the problem of writing about violence: to understand the act is apparently to eulogise; to sympathise is to seem an accomplice.[200]

In 1912 when Berkman published a memoir of his early life and years in prison, Goldman wrote a blurb for the book: 'Do you want to know the story of Alexander Berkman's life, his development, struggle for the ideal, the Homestead strike, the blow at the tyrant, the first trial, fourteen years in the Pennsylvania penitentiary, and the resurrection?' The terms seem pitiably naïve, Frick still a tyrant, Berkman's quest still 'a struggle for the ideal'; it might almost be a document of adolescence. For Goldman clung to that image, unwilling to let go of her vision of Berkman as a noble sufferer, a killer with heart:

A youth with a vision of a grand and beautiful world based upon freedom and harmony, and with boundless sympathy for the suffering of the masses. One whose deep, sensitive nature could not endure the barbarisms of our times. Such was the personality of the man who staked his life as a protest against tyranny and iniquity; and such has Alexander Berkman remained all these long, dreary fourteen years.[201]

Berkman's book prompted many similar letters. One from Harry Boland is a gush of outraged sentiment, swooning over the pitiful image of Berkman, 'that slim ashen figure beaten into a corner like a lion at bay', recounting how he also once wrote to Oscar Wilde, and ending with the rousing encomium: 'To me the Prison Memoirs of an Anarchist is not a book but a vital real living being that I love, that I love.'[202] To another correspondent, the book was 'grand, as great as the "deed", and greater'. The book was a compensation for the deed's failure: 'it is a monument to you high up to the skies of civilisation'.[203] There were, it seems, still those who would have liked to have seen Frick murdered, still those who believed that such a killing would have been an essentially civilised act.

Berkman himself was reported in the press (who knows with how much accuracy) as looking back on his deed with some complacency. He had been, he suggested, a kind of Nihilist; he had nobly refrained from trying to shoot Leishman; he had only shot at 'Frick's thick neck'. And afterwards?

No, I have now not the slightest bitterness against judge, jury, district attorney, or the men who were the cause of the monstrous injustice to the workmen of the vast steel works. They would not try to see our point of view. We tried diligently to see theirs, and conceded much. But we cannot have Utopia, I suppose, all at once.[204]

A few years later, in 1919, in a statement he gave to the press having just been released from prison again, he declared that he had been sentenced to fourteen years in prison in 'connection with the Homestead strike'.[205] Facing deportation as he was, there were no doubt tactical reasons for this peculiar coyness. Perhaps he suggests that the deed is so famous, he need not mention it. Or maybe he was in fact wary of mentioning it, the proud *attentat* dwindling into a 'connection'?

The circumspection failed. In December 1919, during a post-war crackdown against American radicals, Goldman and Berkman were two of 249 Anarchists and Communists deported to Russia. To their eternal credit, Berkman and Goldman, those two old revolutionary hands, were even more dismayed by Bolshevik tyranny than they had been by capitalist oppression. They met Kropotkin; they met Lenin; they noted the differences between the condition of the two men – one charismatic, poor and suffering; the other, a Nechaev possessing power without grace. In March 1921, the crushing of the Anarchist-inspired Kronstadt rebellion rendered their disillusionment final. In November of that year, they both fled Russia, travelling through Kovno, the town where both of them had spent part of their youth.[206] Years of wandering followed, together or separate: in Berlin, in London, in St Tropez. In February 1928, with money from Howard Young, W. S. Van Valkenburgh and Peggy Guggenheim, and with Emily Holmes Coleman ('Demi') as live-in editor, secretary and companion, Goldman began a two-year project of writing her autobiography.

Berkman and Goldman, those two old friends, devotedly cut clippings from newspapers: injustices; debates on the leisured woman; the story of a murder by a Soviet Raskolnikov; an essay on human monogamy; prison reform; notices of the deaths of friends. Berkman wrote letters to prisoners, mindful of the loneliness of jail. They petitioned publishers with schemes for books, such as a biography of their friend Frank Harris, or, more often, for translations, and nearly always the publishers deferred or delayed, expressing faint interest, but always giving them too little work. There was praise for Goldman's memoir, *Living My Life*, and the praise was a comfort, even if it did not 'cover the material needs of life'.[207] By March 1932, only 1,805 copies of the book had been sold in America; of European and Canadian sales Goldman had heard nothing.[208]

She was soon touring the USA again. Going by Pittsburgh in early April 1934, she felt the stirring of ghosts. It was here that Sasha had tried to kill Frick, all those years before. She went to hideous Homestead, even to the Western Penitentiary, though she could not bear to go inside.

In a synopsis for a radio talk from the early 1930s, 'The Disenchanted Radical', she started off with this: 'A striking example of the disenchanted radical – myself'. It was a startling and surprising statement. She listed the reasons for her disenchantment: the state of America, the failure of the revolution in Russia, fascism in Italy, Germany, and America itself ('the Ku Klux spirit'). And then came this:

The tragedy of the disenchanted radical is the tragedy of our entire civilisation.

Our machine age ruled by the mob-spirit of quantity and vulgar success. The idealist in life, art and letters is doomed to be an exile.

My personal position and experience: a woman without a country.

My experience in America: prison, deportation and exile.

The destructive spirit of our age: the Frankenstein of militarism devouring Europe; American industrialism breaking down under its own weight.

The break-down of our civilisation. The failure of all Socialist experiments.

The last hope of the disenchanted radical and – of the world: the cooperative world commonwealth.[209]

Apart from the promised solution, this could be a Yeatsian lament. Yet Goldman's zest ultimately trumped such dirges. There were consolations: new friendships, with men like Paul Robeson; and young lovers too. On 14 March 1934 she wrote to Berkman from New York: 'You have always found me like a cat. Thrown down some height she falls on her paws. I am starting West with new hope . . .'[210] For, above all, the old friendship with Berkman had outlasted all other connections, running like a golden thread through her life:

My friendship with Sasha is of a rare nature, such which the poets sang about but which one meets perhaps once in a life time. Perhaps it is due to our lives . . . and our love beyond anything else. No matter who has been in my life and there have been many men as well as women, Sasha was uppermost in my thoughts and my heart.[211]

While Goldman ripened and persevered, Berkman suffered. He was living out old age with a troubled younger lover, Emmy Eckstein, in the South of France. He was weary; he had prostate problems, and then was hospitalised with colitis. After initial treatment, he went home, to the Boulevard de Cassole, in Nice, and on 26 June 1936, in the midst of a painful relapse, shot himself in the abdomen, firing at the source of the pain. Better a sudden death than have to go through the agonising, and probably futile operation. But the wound was not immediately fatal; both Emmy and Emma Goldman were there with him as he took his time to die.[212]

The British Library copy of Berkman's *Prison Memoirs*, signed by 'Emma Goldman, London Jan 22 [19]36', ends with a handwritten note, not apparently written by Goldman:

Berkman committed suicide in Nice (I do not know the date). He did this clumsily – just as he attempted Frick's life. He missed the vital organs & died after some time in great pain. His 'wife' was even arrested for some hours for his murder –

The muddle was coloured by French policemen, neighbours &c. and the strange presence of Emma Goldman – & it ended on a note of tragic vulgarity reminiscent of Swift but supplied by the world.

Vindictive to the end, US Steel executives circulated his obituaries and neatly filed them for posterity.[213] One of these obituaries, from the *Weirton, West Virginia Times*, begins with the headline 'The World Better Off'. The writer in this paper has no doubts: Berkman was an assassin who had tried to kill Frick, and had probably been involved in the bombing of the *LA Times* and the Preparedness Day march, as well as other unspecified planned atrocities.[214] Another clipping kept on their file announces that Berkman had directed the activities of hundreds of anarchists from his prison cell.[215] The *Sandusky Register* had the last word, as obituarists tend to do:

The trouble with Berkman and his crowd was not so much their ideals as their methods. They resorted to violence. Anyone who abjures violence has a right to dream pleasantly of 'philosophic anarchism,' as Shelley and Lincoln Steffens did

– a state of life in which every individual would be wholly himself and completely free. But this is merely 'wishful thinking'.[216]

On 12 April 2004 a documentary film, *Emma Goldman: An Exceedingly Dangerous Woman*, was broadcast on PBS in the USA. In a review in the *New York Times*, Virginia Heffernan criticised the programme for not recognising that Goldman was more than just the unobjectionable purveyor of ideas that many now share: 'free speech, free thought and free love'. She goes on to suggest that, more than this cosy forerunner, Goldman, being Russian, had no idea what capitalism was, and that she fantasised 'about an egalitarian world without fathers, kings, religion, factories or marriage'.[217]

In this version of her life, Goldman falls between being just like us and being nothing like us, both reassuringly modern and irrelevantly idealistic. With their vengeful disdain, Berkman's crowing obituaries were closer to the mark. The two old friends had lived lives committed to an idea, committed to the possible justice of political violence. Neither trendy nor outmoded, rather they present to our gaze a possible life: out of kilter, fanatical and strikingly flawed.

PART THREE

The Strange Death of Liberal Europe
From Sarajevo to the Nazis

9

Choosing the Most Terrible

I: Extinguishing the Lights

We were bound to die. We were at liberty to choose the manner of our
death, and we chose the most terrible.
COUNT OTTOKAR VON CZERNIN, 1920

The American Anarchist assassinations were spectacular events. Yet their
historical impact was limited; historically speaking McKinley's death
merely ushers in the Presidency of Theodore Roosevelt. The shooting
of Frick and a farcical threat by Marie Ganz against John D. Rockefeller
were events that disseminated unease, but their practical influence
proved negligible. The Anarchist unrest strained American democracy,
but ultimately the strength of the governmental system absorbed the
effects of the violence, and the American experiment continued.

Similarly Luigi Luccheni's assassination of Elisabeth, Empress of
Austria, horrified the world, being by far the most condemned of
all the Anarchist assassinations; yet the event led nowhere. It was an
accident: Luccheni's intended target had been the Duke of Orleans,
and he had only murdered the Empress on the principle that as he was
there anyway he might as well assassinate someone.[1] The act began with
contingency, and then exploded into insignificance. No retaliation,
beyond the trial and conviction of Luccheni himself, was possible. (In
1910, Luccheni killed himself in prison.) The Anarchist attacks were
merely atrocities, just gestures. The cosmopolitanism that made them
terrifying also made them impotent.

Yet some sixteen years later in south-eastern Europe, in the context
of aspirant nationalisms and failing former 'Great Powers', one
assassination would help bring down an empire.

The region known as the Balkans was in the late nineteenth century
wedged between two disintegrating empires: the Habsburgs and the

Ottomans. In 1867, the Habsburg Empire had redefined itself as a Dual Monarchy – Hungarian Magyars and Austrian Habsburgs – ruling over myriad ethnic and linguistic groups. It might have seemed an impossibility to separate states based on 'nationality' out of the muddle; yet this would not prevent nationalist groups from trying. Acting as a beacon to Slavs within the Empire, independent Serbia's drive for territorial expansion fuelled Balkan instability. Such ambitions relied on 'Pan-Slavism' and the growing belief that a nation ideally represented a single ethnic identity, a single history and a single language. All Serbs everywhere were imagined as belonging to one nation; though such resolute belief denied the basic fact of the region's ethnic and religious diversity. Many individuals did not see themselves as part of a 'people' at all; religion and custom defined them, and even then in a remarkably fluid and shifting manner.[2] Nonetheless, there were those in Serbia who sought the 'liberation' of Serbs everywhere. Northwards, the unwieldy power of the Austro-Hungarian Empire blocked their ambitions. They were countered to the east by similar expansionist aspirations among the Bulgarians, and to the south by the Greeks.

It was Bosnia-Herzegovina that would spark the explosion. In the 1900s, Austria had begun to see the South Slavs as the chief worry, with Serbia the embodiment of that threat. Austria had earlier considered its southern neighbour a chaotic, weak and therefore dependent power.[3] Now, however, Serbia was gaining a certain swaggering strength. The great fear was that Serbia might act as a base for Slav nationalism throughout the Empire's southern territories, as Piedmont had previously focused such ambitions for Italians. Austria wished to act tough and assert itself, rescuing its prestige in the process. In 1878, it had occupied Bosnia and Herzegovina. Now, given confidence by a secret deal with the Russians, Austria formally annexed the two provinces in October 1908. In absorbing a large Serbian minority into its empire, Austria at a stroke created its own Serbian problem.[4] Moreover Alexander Izvolski, the Russian foreign minister, had winked at the deed while not expecting the Austrians to move so promptly, or that outraged Russian public opinion would fall so squarely behind the annexed fellow Slavs of Bosnia; he was wrong-footed, and put out. Since 1906 there had already been a couple of years of economic tension between Serbia and Austria, with punishing tariffs imposed on

Serbian produce. Enraged by the absorption of Serbs into the Austro-Hungarian Empire, the Serbians now looked to Russia for support. So it was that Austria's step nearly provoked a European war; only Germany's backing of Austria forced the Serbians and Russians to back down. Yet what looked like a triumph for Austrian supremacy would provide the impetus for their coming collapse. Henceforward it was clear that Austria could only act with German aid; Russia now suspected Austria, and began actively to promote the Balkan nations' goals to offset Habsburg potency; Serbia was permanently placed in a position of hostility to its powerful neighbour. All the pre-conditions for a great war in the region were in place.

Perturbed by Austrian power, the Russians persuaded Serbia and Bulgaria to co-operate so as to form a regional counterweight. In 1912, the countries duly formed a series of Balkan alliances with Montenegro and Greece, but, to Russia's dismay, rather than uniting against Austria, they turned their attention eastward and set about clearing the Turks from what had long been known as 'Turkey-in-Europe'. The Russians had blundered. Their interests required an Ottoman Empire strong enough to keep Russia's access to the Dardanelles Straits open: Russian trade depended on the Straits; if the Ottomans failed, there would be no guaranteeing the region's future, especially as German ambitions increasingly looked south-eastwards. However, the small states had their own agenda. They aggressively united against the Turks, whom they defeated in a startling series of skirmishes and battles. Out-fought everywhere, the Turks were driven back to Constantinople.[5] On 3 December 1912, an armistice ended the First Balkan War; Turkish power had effectively collapsed in Europe. However, the area's various nationalistic fervours did not translate into mutual respect for each other's nationalism. Success brought dissension among the erstwhile partners, and in the summer of 1913, a Second Balkan War promptly followed, in which the former Balkan allies fought each other, mostly in a gang against Bulgaria, with Romania and Turkey joining the mêlée. The chief losers of the conflict were apparently the Bulgarians, who were forced to give land back to Turkey that they had gained in the previous war, as well as seeing Greece and Serbia divide up Macedonia. However, more vitally, the resulting strengthening of Serbia (it had more or less doubled its territory) did little to ease Austrian alarm about its southern neighbour. As 1914 arrived, the Balkan nations now stood in uneasy relation, each with territorial ambitions unsatisfied or national prestige to regain or bolster.

It was one of the clichés of writing on the Balkans that the region was then a backward place, geographically connected to the European continent, but in fact representing a medieval incursion into the modern world. Entwined with this perception was the belief that the area was particularly prone to violence. Such notions form the context for Bram Stoker's *Dracula* (1897), Anthony Hope's *The Prisoner of Zenda* (1894) or Eric Ambler's *The Mask of Dimitrios* (1939). The Balkans imaginatively became the zone of conspiracy, intrigue and secret murder. Marked by a brutality imagined as alien to the countries to the north and west, the peoples of the region were supposed to practise forms of violence that had become outmoded in the refined world. This accusation conveniently buried any thought of the larger nations' atrocities, the imperialist wars and annexations. It also betrayed the prejudices of its own cultural context, classifying certain kinds of violence as beyond the pale of civilisation, while condoning other more familiar forms.

Nonetheless, atrocities, massacres and assassinations did in fact pro-liferate in the region at the turn of the century. In Serbia, in 1903, an especially horrific assassination took place. King Alexander Obrenović, a man overly impressed by Austrian power, had married an unsuitable and infertile young woman, the shady widow Draga Mašin. His Interior Minister had begged the King not to marry her; 'Sire,' he reportedly told him, 'you cannot marry her. She has been everyone's mistress – mine included!'[6] Unpopular with the majority of Serbs, the new Queen faked a pregnancy, raising fears that she intended to palm off some strange foundling child as heir; when the ruse collapsed, rumours spread that her brother might take the throne. Moreover the King appeared to be moving towards a dictatorship, suspending the constitution and bringing troops onto the streets. A group of military conspirators intervened, entering the royal palace in Belgrade, hunting down the hiding couple, murdering them, mutilating their bodies, and then hurling the corpses out of a second-floor window.[7] Alexander was replaced by King Peter from the Karadjordjević dynasty, one less enamoured of the Habsburgs. More than the fact of the assassination, it was its manner that disgusted the rest of Europe. Killing a king and queen was one thing, desecrating their bodies quite another; worse still, the assassins went unpunished and in Belgrade Cathedral were even publicly blessed.

There were further Balkan political murders and assassination attempts, most of them in Croatia, a place under Austro-Hungarian rule, with a mixed population of Catholic Croats and Orthodox Serbs.[8] While many in the country looked to the Habsburgs as their rightful rulers, there were elements here who temporarily ignored ethnic and religious differences in their combined hostility to the Hungarians.[9] In the years before 1914, there were several attempts at shooting two successive Magyar governors. One particular failed assassination was to prove an inspiration to others. Having decided not to kill Emperor Franz Joseph, during the opening of parliament one young Serb (Bogdan Žerajić) instead fired five rounds at General Marian Varešanin, the Austrian administrator of Bosnia-Herzegovina.[10] The attempt failed and the would-be assassin fired the last round into his own brain.

Within Bosnia, many in the Serbian majority envisioned smashing up the rule of the Austro-Hungarian Empire, and merging themselves into a greater Serbia. To this end Serbian nationalist societies formed: Narodna Obrana (National Defence, 1908) ostensibly relied on cultural activities; while the secret Uyedinyenye ili Smrt (Union or Death, 1911), more popularly known as the Black Hand, dreamt of achieving union through intrigue and assassination.[11]

The Black Hand was a conspiratorial organisation with a deliberately limited membership, but it embodied the dreams of substantial elements in the population at large. As Narodna Obrana gave up on the prospect of armed action, the Black Hand was formed to maintain the pressure for the vigorous and violent pursuit of pan-Serb aims.[12] With its endorsement of the asceticism of revolution, the Black Hand's constitution clearly owed much to Nechaev's 'Catechism of a Revolutionary'.[13] Members of the Serbian government, the police and the army actively supported its aims. However, these officials belonged to a larger network of individual conspirators; the government as a whole had no interest in supporting Bosnia's extreme nationalists. Enfeebled by the two Balkan Wars, the Serbian military needed time to recoup; the country was simply at present too exhausted to risk a clash with Austria. In any case, most hoped to avoid outright conflict; there was no widespread desire to take on the Habsburgs, rather the Serbs coveted the old territories of the Ottoman Empire. It was largely Austria's unrequited hatred that forced them to switch attention northwards. In the autumn of 1913, the Serbians reluctantly adhered to an Austrian ultimatum that they should withdraw from Albania. It was a sign of the times, and a heartening omen for Austrian prestige. For the Habsburgs, war against Serbia became a tempting prospect, an easy way to reassert imperial authority among the southern Slavs.

A sense of the sacred still clung to the old Emperor, Franz Joseph; this holy glow does not seem to have passed on to his nephew and heir. Archduke Franz Ferdinand was a man typical of his time and position; he loved tennis, jousting, his family and shooting things: indeed he shot the big game of the world, blasting his way through (among other beasts) chamois deer, bears, tigers, emus and kangaroos. He was given to extremes, both socially chilly and hot-tempered, disdainful and susceptible; though hardly an intellectual, he could be incisive. As the Emperor's nephew, he might never have expected to become heir-apparent to one of the great European dynasties; perhaps the conditions under which he did so aggravated his already prickly character.

In January 1889, the young man had been propelled into the limelight by the mysterious suicide at a Mayerling hunting lodge of his cousin, Archduke Rudolf, the Emperor's only son. The Emperor loathed Franz Ferdinand, though the old man consoled himself with the belief that the new heir, being consumptive, would not last long enough to inherit. His uncle long ignored Franz Ferdinand's annoying recovery from this sickness, persisting in treating him as an invalid, too weak to play a part in the business of government. Nonetheless, in a spirit of zeal, as well as of opposition, Franz Ferdinand threw himself into politics, eager to be an active heir.

For obvious reasons it is impossible to know for certain how Franz Ferdinand would have attempted to solve his Empire's problems, had he in fact ascended to the throne. With neat dramatic irony, it has generally been believed that Franz Ferdinand was conciliatory towards the Serbs, backed as they were by Russia. Partly out of hostility to the Hungarians, Franz Ferdinand had for a while at least favoured a 'triple monarchy', with the Slavs joining the Austrians and Hungarians as partners, the so-called 'trialist' solution. Such an arrangement would have diluted Magyar influence, as the newly united Southern Slavs (consisting of Dalmatia, Croatia, Bosnia-Herzegovina and Slovenia) would share equal say with the Austrians and Hungarians, while remaining under Habsburg rule. This would weaken Hungary, and contain Slav nationalist aspirations within the Habsburg empire. How seriously Franz Ferdinand entertained this possibility remains a subject for debate.[14] For example, it also appears that the Archduke was liable to have been tougher on minorities within the Empire, and might even have pressed for a return to centralised power in Vienna.[15]

Franz Ferdinand's romantic and inconvenient marriage further complicated his position as heir. While apparently courting Archduchess Isabella of Pressburg, Franz Ferdinand instead fell for the attractive Sophie Chotek, one of her ladies-in-waiting. He dared to request permission to marry the young woman; the stiff-necked Franz Joseph reluctantly acquiesced, borne down by the entreaties of the young man's powerful supporters, but only agreed on the condition that the marriage should be considered morganatic: that is, as a lower-caste woman marrying above her station, neither Sophie nor her children could lay claim to Franz Ferdinand's title or possessions. So it was that Sophie remained a lowly duchess (of Hohenberg). The penalties meted out for their marriage were many and petty; the niceties of court ceremony would be rigidly observed. Inhibited by pompous etiquette, they had to sit apart at the theatre; she could not join her husband for official state dinners.[16] Such treatment perplexed Sophie and pricked Franz Ferdinand's pride; he was understandably touchy about her, mortified that she should be so looked down upon.

In part, in the early summer of 1914, it was the embarrassments produced by their unconventional marriage that would inspire the visit to Sarajevo, and so bring about their deaths. The visit was something of a wedding anniversary present: in provincial Bosnia, Sophie might enjoy the rare delight of receiving all the due of a proper archduchess.

In Bosnia, that June of 1914, the Habsburg armies undertook their yearly military manoeuvres.[17] There were probably unfounded rumours that these were a dress rehearsal for a planned Austrian attack on Serbia.[18] Franz Ferdinand was there to oversee the operation, and inspect the troops. There were various attempts to dissuade the Archduke from making the trip to Bosnia. He was ostentatiously careless of his own safety, indifferent to the many threats against his life.[19] His attitude was fatalistic: 'We are all constantly in danger of death. One must simply trust in God,' he remarked.[20] He arrived on 25 June; over the next two days, he was present at the manoeuvres; and then, on the 28th, he paid an official visit to Sarajevo. Whether deliberate or accidental, it was an inauspicious day to pick. The 28th of June – the feast of St Vitus – is a holy day for Serbian nationalists, as it commemorates the nation's defeat by Muslim forces at the Battle of Kosovo. The nationalists saw their proudest moment in this downfall, the greatest expression of Serbian identity being the sacrificial moment of its loss. For the Austrian heir to visit Sarajevo on this anniversary was bound to inflame memories of the rout, and to inspire the passion to resist. However, the assassination would in fact have been attempted on any day that Franz Ferdinand chose to visit; it was simply an opportunity that was too good to miss.

Only fifty miles from the Serbian border, Sarajevo was a town of minarets and gardens, the Miljacka river running through it, with Turkish and Serbian houses clustered together on its hillsides.[21] The royal couple were to stay in a hotel at Ilidža, a beautiful spa town just a few miles outside Sarajevo. In an attempt to forestall criticism on over-spending, Oskar Potiorek, the governor of Bosnia-Herzegovina, skimped on the security arrangements. He might have applied for more police, but the bill would have been high, and with Bosnia strapped for cash, he decided to make do with the men they already had.[22] It was to prove a very costly saving: in Sarajevo a group of young men were waiting to murder Franz Ferdinand.

The apparent leader of the Sarajevo conspirators was one Gavrilo Princip, a dreamy adolescent, nineteen years old. The pan-Serb movement attracted the young; schoolboys formed secret societies, studied revolutionary texts and yearned for rebellion: 'The young dreamed of nothing but bombs, assassinations, explosives to blow up and destroy everything.'[23] They longed to emulate the example of the Russian terrorists.[24] One of the lawyers at Princip's trial expressed shock that boys so young should have committed the deed; Princip shrugged the question off.[25] The youths were politicised by reveries, and together fantasised a Serbian state, daring, passionate and free. In such a vision, suffering was converted into the noble birthpangs of a cultural metamorphosis.

Princip's father was a *kmet* (peasant), a quiet, unpolitical man, a carter and postman in a village near Bosansko Grahovo.[26] The Bosnian peasantry had suffered, or considered themselves to have suffered, under Muslim landlords, racked by high rents and consigned to social neglect.[27] The Austrians were resented for having allowed such a situation to persist.

Princip had attended high school in Belgrade, where he associated with nationalist groups. By his own report, he had been a quiet, serious, sentimental child.[28] In adolescence, he was a loner, a taciturn, reserved young man.[29] Photographs reveal Princip as a dark-eyed youth, somewhere between a slight Clark Gable and the young Django Reinhardt. As a student he haunted the library, amassing for himself a beautiful collection of books. Troubled as he was by a Hardyesque view that existence was tragic, reading or action offered the only escapes from life's dark insipidity. A passionate reader, he consumed Bakunin, Kropotkin and Herbert Spencer, another step in his radicalisation. Indeed he seems to have been somewhat enamoured with the prospect of an anarchistic social revolution.[30]

Princip was a 'soulful' killer. He was obsessed by the example of Žerajić, the would-be assassin of General Varešanin, by his own report haunting the dead patriot's grave.[31] Considered unfit to fight in the Balkan Wars, he felt that he had been denied the chance to serve his country.[32] This failure wounded his self-conceit. He was convinced that he had it in him to perform a great task for the Serbian cause; assassination was indeed the greatest of tasks: 'For all the young generation, assassins were heroes.'[33] Ultimately, Princip expected to die for his ideas; he would be a sacrifice for his people.[34] The Archduke embodied the powers that oppressed the Serbs; Princip's motive was revenge for all the indignities visited on the Serbs by Austria, his ultimate political aim the union of *les Yougoslaves*.[35] Franz Ferdinand's murder was therefore an entirely legitimate act.

From May 1912 Princip was living in Belgrade on credit, and loans from his brother.[36] He then travelled to Hadjice to finish his exams, before in early 1914 going back once more to Belgrade. During these travels, he gathered together the friends who would strike a blow with him for their great ideal.

Nedeljko Čabrinović and Princip had known each other for four or five years, and been intimate friends for two or three.[37] Described in the press as a 'compositor from Trebinje', Čabrinović had worked for two

months at a printing press in Sarajevo, before finding employment with
'a firm specialising in anarchist literature'.[38] He had led a life of fits and
starts, moving between Belgrade and Sarajevo, holding down a job for
a little while, but without direction. He was full of himself, convinced
of his more-than-human courage and prowess; he had once dreamed of
throwing a bomb into the chamber of the Bosnian Diet.[39] Like Princip,
Čabrinović had consumption; their lives were theirs to give away.

Their original target was to have been Potiorek, the Governor of
Bosnia, but soon the Black Hand raised their sights to Archduke
Franz Ferdinand, the heir to the Austrian throne. Having read in
the newspapers of the Archduke's imminent visit to Sarajevo, in the
Žirovni Vijenac café in Belgrade Čabrinović and Princip hatched a plan
to murder him.[40] (This was at Princip's suggestion; he would always
insist that the murder was initially his idea.)[41]

The next conspirator to be involved was Trifko Grabež, a fellow
lodger of Princip's from Belgrade. Grabež was the son of an Orthodox
priest; uniquely among the conspirators, he had a police record (he had
struck a teacher). Like the others, he had studied at Belgrade; in early
1914, he shared a room with Princip.[42]

Princip then recruited Danilo Ilić, his best friend from school and
a fellow pan-Serb nationalist, asking him in his turn to find more
conspirators.[43] Ilić met with one Mohamed Mehmedbašić and initiated
him into the plot. Mehmedbašić had already attended a mysterious
meeting in Toulouse, at which, perhaps, plans for an assassination
attempt against Potiorek had been discussed. It was expected that such
bloody deeds would vivify Serbian nationalism.[44] This putative meeting
in France is the first indication that the conspirators were working in
connection with the Black Hand.

It remains an open question as to whether these young men were
recruited by the leadership of the Black Hand (possibly by Major Voja
Tankosić), or if the leadership responded to the young men's initiative. It
is also possible that the Black Hand discouraged the attempt, fearing the
murder's consequences. In any case, it is highly likely that these young
conspirators were somehow connected to the Serbian secret service. In
particular, their plot may have been approved by the Black Hand's 'Apis'
('The Bee'), that is, Colonel Dragutin Dimitrijević; certainly one of
the conspirators, Ilić, was in touch with him. Dimitrijević had been a

leading member among the officers who had murdered King Alexander and his wife back in 1903.[45] (Three bullets shot by the palace guards on the night of the coup would still be in his body when he was finally executed, some fourteen years later.)[46] Dimitrijević was, no word is more fit, dashing; magnetically attractive, he was a suave, talented man unscrupulous in the pursuit of his aims, yet another 'beautiful soul'.[47] Even before he met with these teenage hotheads, he had already sent an assassin to Vienna to kill the Archduke, though this would-be killer had vanished and the plot came to nothing.

Perhaps Dimitrijević only helped the conspirators to find weapons; yet it is also plausible that he altered the direction of the conspiracy, and ordered that the Archduke be murdered, rather than the original target, Potiorek.[48] Killing the Archduke would abort the trialist solution, one meant to empower Serbs within the Austro-Hungarian Empire; killing trialism at one stroke kept up the pressure for an independent Greater Serbia.[49]

Whatever the links with Dimitrijević, Princip and the others now made one definite contact with a Black Hand operative. According to Princip at least, they contacted one Milan Ciganović, a Bosnian Serb worker for the railways in his late twenties and a shady figure with connections both to the Black Hand and to the Serbian Prime Minister Nikola Pašić. (As we shall see later, at this distance it is impossible to determine how high up knowledge of the assassination plans went.) Ciganović told Princip that he would give him some bombs, and then brought in Major Tankosić, an Army officer and Black Hand member.[50] The young lads waited for Ciganović to deliver. He finally gave them around a dozen bombs (purloined before the war against Bulgaria), revolvers and cyanide capsules. With Ciganović's help, they were very briefly trained, practising firing their guns in a wood outside Belgrade.[51]

A photograph from that spring of 1914 shows Čabrinović, Ciganović and Princip relaxing in a Belgrade park. Flanked by the two young men, only Ciganović looks at the camera, confident, moustachioed, sporting a rakish fez. Čabrinović moodily gazes to the right, while Princip is lost with his own thoughts, his eyes abstracted and something like the approach of a smile flitting across his face.[52]

With the help of their Black Hand connections, Princip and the others made their way across the border into Bosnia and on to Sarajevo.

Two seventeen-year-old schoolboys new to Princip were recruited, Čubrilović and Popović. Princip did not really trust Čubrilović and decided to do his best to intimidate the boy into loyalty by threatening to kill him and all his family if he let slip their plans.[53]

The night before the assassination, Mohamed Mehmedbašić and Princip met for the first time in a Sarajevo café.[54] They were all armed with bombs and revolvers, and carried capsules of potassium cyanide to bite into once they had succeeded; it was always intended to be a suicide mission. They were doomed men. Later Popović remembered: 'Convinced that I had only until June 28th to live, Vivodan – St Vitus Day – I looked at everything from a different angle. I left my school books. I hardly glanced at the newspapers . . . I failed to react to the jokes of my friends.'[55]

The sun shone that Sunday. There were crowds on Appel Quay on the northern bank of the River Miljacka. Franz Ferdinand had banned the army from the city for the day. There were therefore only 120 policemen on duty. Sophie wore a white dress, while Franz Ferdinand was resplendent in his official costume: his plumed helmet, his dress uniform. A pennant fluttered on the bonnet of the car. Dignitaries in fezzes gathered around. At 10.00, the royal entourage drove out from the Philipovic army camp.

Along the Quay, the assassins were lined up at intervals among the crowd. Positioned along the riverside by the Čumuria Bridge, Mohamed Mehmedbašić and Čabrinović would be the first to take a shot; then Čubrilović, then Popović, then Princip, and finally Ilić and Grabež. Princip himself took up a position by the Lateiner Bridge.

The car approached. And then a series of misadventures started, a textbook example of the contingency and caprice of historical events. Mohamed Mehmedbašić failed to act as a policeman took up a position near him as the entourage were passing.[56] More fortunate, at ten minutes past the hour, Nedeljko Čabrinović threw his bomb, one packed with nails. Count Waldeck described seeing a black package falling on the opened bonnet of the car. The Archduke swiftly scooped it up and threw it back onto the road, where it exploded as it hit the ground.[57] Lieutenant-Colonel Merizzi was injured by the blast; seventy holes were punctured into the car.

Immediately after he had thrown the bomb, Čabrinović bit into his cyanide pill. But the poison was too old and its potency was gone. Baffled, he pushed through the bystanders and leapt over the wall into the river, hoping to drown himself. But the summer heat had shrunk the river, and it was too shallow to drown. Vomiting from the unstable pill, he was pulled down by a throng of people and manhandled into the custody of the police. When the police asked him if he were a Serb, he replied, 'Yes, I am a Serb hero.'[58]

Shaken by the blast, but determined to go on, the royal couple switched cars, driving on in one belonging to Count Harrach. The Archduke tried to persuade the Duchess to return to safety, but she insisted on staying with her husband. The car drove on past the waiting assassins.

Yet it seemed that luck was on the couple's side. Moved by pity for the royal pair, Čubrilović failed to fire his gun – though later he boasted to his comrades that he had let off two rounds.[59] Popović's nerve simply failed him; scared by the explosion, he neglected to take a shot. Having flunked it, Popović ran off home; Mehmedbašić had already done the same.

Down the Quay Princip had heard the explosion, but did not know who had thrown the bomb. The crowd ran, and he ran with them. Perhaps it was all over. Then he saw that Čabrinović had been taken. It crossed his mind to kill Čabrinović and then himself, and then put an end to the affair. But then he saw the cars continuing on their way, and he knew that Čabrinović had failed.[60] The Archduke's car sped by, but it moved too quickly for Princip to do anything more than catch a glimpse of the Duchess. His purpose gone, he wandered over to the Lateiner Bridge, and there he heard that indeed the bomb had proved ineffectual and the assassination was still all to do.

Meanwhile Franz Ferdinand and Sophie drove on to the City Hall, passing the other assassins helpless in the crowd. The Archduke was in a filthy temper. He poured out his rage on the hapless Mayor, who replied by going into his prepared speech of welcome. The politeness defused Franz Ferdinand's wrath, and he answered the speech as graciously as he could. The business of the day continued; the throwing of the bomb began to seem a regrettable but surmounted incident. They debated whether the itinerary for the rest of the morning should be altered. The Archduke expected to continue with the prearranged schedule – the museum trip, followed by a lunch with the mayor – but he was also eager to visit those who had been injured by the bomb. There were worries, dismissed by Potiorek as scaremongering, that such a visit might prove dangerous; it was advised that Sophie should not travel with her husband. However, once again she insisted on remaining at his side.

For the moment, the one remaining assassin waited. Princip had chatted suspiciously with a certain Pušara, someone he suspected of being a police spy.[61] Then, hungry, Princip crossed the Quay and ambled to the entrance of Franz Joseph Street. At Moritz Schiller's food store, he stepped in and bought a sandwich.

At 11.10, the royal entourage drove off from the City Hall. Potiorek had decided that, for safety's sake, they should change the planned route, and go directly back down Appel Quay towards the hospital. However, with Merizzi injured, there was no one officially responsible for passing on this information to the drivers. In the Archduke's car were Franz Ferdinand and Sophie, Potiorek, and (standing on the running board, on the left-hand side of the car) the Count von Harrach, as well as Franz Urban, the driver.

At the corner of Franz Joseph Street, Urban turned right towards the museum. Taken aback, Potiorek ordered him to stop; they should be going straight on. Urban pulled up outside Moritz Schiller's food store. Princip was sitting right there, unobtrusively eating his sandwich. The Archduke's luck had changed. As Urban tried turning the car – there was too little room in the narrow street – Princip stood up, strode over to the right side of the car, opposite to where Harrach was standing, pulling out his pistol as he did so, and from a distance of four or five paces fired two shots directly at Franz Ferdinand; the second shot was intended for Potiorek.[62] Franz Ferdinand moved to shield Sophie from the attack. But the first bullet struck the Archduke in the neck; the second shot hit Sophie in the abdomen. Her death was one final instance of the haphazard arbitrariness of the events. Too late, the car sped off. For an instant it looked as though the royal couple had escaped any serious injury. But as Franz Ferdinand opened his mouth, the blood flowed out of it, welling up out of the bullet-hole in his neck. The shot had sliced through the jugular vein. Blood gushed from the Archduke's mouth onto Harrach's cheek. And then, in Harrach's words:

While with one hand I drew out my handkerchief to wipe the blood from the Archduke's lips, Her Highness cried: 'For God's sake! What has happened to you?' Then she sank down from her seat with her face between the Archduke's knees. I had no idea that she had been hit and thought that she had fainted from shock. Then his Royal Highness said: 'Soferl, Soferl! Don't die. Live for my children!' Thereupon I seized the Archduke by the coat-collar to prevent his head from sinking forwards and asked him: 'Is your Royal Highness in great pain?' To which he clearly replied: 'It is nothing.' Now his expression changed and he repeated six or seven times: 'It is nothing', more and more losing consciousness and with a fading voice. Then came a brief pause followed by a convulsive rattle in the throat, caused by the loss of blood, which ceased on the arrival at the Konak. The two unconscious forms were carried into the Konak where death soon intervened.[63]

They drove to Potiorek's house, but by the time they arrived Sophie was dead. Within ten minutes Franz Ferdinand followed her.

Princip had no time to see if he had struck home, for the crowd had already pulled him off and begun to beat him. He also swallowed his cyanide pill, but it did no more than make him nauseous. He was swiftly arrested, quickly enough to have saved his life, for he might easily have been killed by the mob. He was taken bleeding and puking to the police station.

In the aftermath of the killings, Croats in Sarajevo unleashed anti-Serb riots, smashing the windows of the mostly Serb-owned hotels. Martial law had to be introduced to restore order. With the exception of Mehmedbašić, all the conspirators were arrested within a couple of days. On his arrest, Ilić promised to tell all, if he were spared execution.[64] In fact, he was anyway to be one of those hanged for the crime. Mehmedbašić himself fled to Montenegro only to be arrested there. However, he managed to escape from police custody, and eventually made his way back into Serbia where he joined a group of partisans headed by Major Tankosić.[65]

Princip was unrepentant. He had eliminated a blight from the earth, a man who had done nothing but evil for the Serbian people.[66] Princip and his companions were taken to Theresienstadt.[67] There, in solitary confinement, for Princip the hardest thing to bear was the absence of books.[68] Though he was visited by a psychiatrist, one Dr Martin Pappenheim, Princip was not mad; rather he belonged to a cultural moment and a set of young people where to be an assassin was the highest destiny. The fact that while he was a young child the assassins of King Alexander and his wife had been exonerated, indeed celebrated, might have helped him to receive that impression.

Too young to face the death penalty and in ill-health, Princip and Čabrinović both died in prison before the war was over. The youngest conspirators were released following the Armistice and the demise of the Habsburg Empire. For though the killing of Franz Ferdinand in Sarajevo in June 1914 may not have been the actual cause of the First World War, and therefore indirectly the origin of over forty years of crisis, it was certainly the precipitating factor that destroyed Austrian power and unleashed the slaughter of the following years.

Nothing about the Sarajevo murder makes sense. Its origins remain mysterious, its motivation obscure. The deed takes place in a cloud of conflicting accounts. All the practical reasons for the assassination were in fact self-defeating. If the aim was to prevent a trialist absorption of the Serbs into a newly configured Habsburg Empire, well that was indeed a success, but at a cost that would mean the bleeding of the Serbian nation. Serbia would suffer proportionately the worst casualties of the war, losing 15 per cent of its population to disease or violence.[69] It is true that something vaguely resembling a pan-Serb state was set up in the Treaty of Versailles's creation of a Kingdom of Yugoslavia. However, that state would itself be so anomalous, and so racked by internal divisions, that its King (Alexander I) would himself be assassinated while on a state visit to Marseilles in 1934. (His shooting was recorded on film.) If the conspirators feared that Austria would invade Serbia, the killing merely hastened that invasion. If they hoped for a Serbian revolt, none came; if they sought honour and nobility, they merely found infamy. Out of the deed's meaningless impulse bursts a war of a horror that none could have predicted. Some schoolboys playing the role of doomed heroes helped topple a civilisation.

It seems that none of the conspirators imagined that the assassination would provoke immediate war between Serbia and Austria, and as for their deed sparking a Europe-wide conflagration such an outcome was beyond their conceiving. Čabrinović lamented that 'if I had foreseen what was to happen I should myself have sat down on the bombs so as to blow myself to bits'.[70] Though he toughed it out in court, in private Princip was devastated by reports of the war.[71] Yet, later, he could hardly believe that a world war could have followed on from their choices; he couldn't really feel guilty for that bit of bad luck.[72] They aimed at an individual, the embodiment of all their frustrations. They were too young and too naïve to grasp fully the potential consequences of their actions; they were in love with the heroic deed, and their bloodily rose-tinted imaginations could not picture anything beyond that fair vision: at the trial, Ĉabrinović remarked, 'We thought that only noble characters are capable of committing assassinations.'[73] Their most pressing motive in murdering the Archduke and his wife was the desire to share in that nobility.

There had been brutal assassinations before. Such murders usually occurred within the body politic of a sovereign state, as an element in a coup, or an outcome of insanity. By their trans-national nature, the Anarchist murders of the previous thirty-five years offered no foreign country as suitable target for retaliation; like the pirate, the Anarchist was equally an enemy everywhere. Since they operated outside the boundaries of the nation-state, the vengeance of armed conflict was meaningless in relation to their horrors. The murders in Sarajevo were entirely different in nature. They occurred on Habsburg soil, but could easily seem to have their origin in the very existence of the Serbian state. For once, the response to an assassination could potentially involve war. Yet such a confrontation was of course always avoidable, as long as everyone wanted peace.

However, far from aspiring to avert a war, the Austrians did all they could to invite it. For once, the Austrians were prompt to act, though even this promptness was laggard. The foreign minister, Count Berchtold, believed, or chose to believe, that the murders in Sarajevo had been carried out with the connivance of the Serbian government. He had been, in any case, preparing himself for renewed conflict with Serbia; the struggle was bound to come, and the present crisis gifted Austria with a pretext whose legitimacy could hardly be doubted. With German backing, Austria made the war; they were, in simple terms, disposed to pick a fight. They could bully the Serbs with impunity: if the Serbs acquiesced then Austria had won a diplomatic victory; better still if they resisted then Austria could crush them militarily. The intention was to show themselves a Great Power again. The murders were a cause, but they were also an excuse. Austria would defy its own weakness, and attack.

The Austrians wrongly assumed that Narodna Obrana were behind the killings. Almost at once, a campaign began in the Austrian press blaming the organisation and behind it, members of the Serbian government.[74] In the international press, within hours of the murders, there were rumours of involvement with Belgrade.[75] This accusation against Narodna Obrana may have been deliberately obfuscatory, a way of shifting blame to an organisation more linked to the Serbian political hierarchy; the Black Hand's conflict with Prime Minister Pašić might have acted as evidence for the innocence of the Serbian government and so have removed the excuse for war.[76] The Austrians probably did believe in Serbian complicity; the question was how high up such involvement went. It seems possible that a warning of a likely attack was passed on by the Serbian government to the Austrian Foreign Ministry, though if this was done it was not treated seriously.[77] Pašić was indeed aware of the Black Hand, but was actively antagonistic to them; on the other hand while Colonel Dimitrijević was an enemy of the Pašić government, his possible participation proves nothing either way about their involvement.

In 1917, in Salonika, Dimitrijević would be tried and put to death for his supposed part in the attempted murder of the Serbian King Alexander. Plausibly the trial was arranged in order to appease Austria and so smooth the path to peace negotiations.[78] One certain effect of that trial was the destruction of the Black Hand.[79]

According to the detective work carried out after the war by Seton-Watson, the Sarajevo conspirators almost certainly went about their plot without government help, except for the peripheral and attenuated involvement of three maverick politicians who were secretly also members of the Black Hand.[80] Yet the government's exoneration meant little in the onward flow of events, where the mere suspicion of connivance sufficed.

The Austrians sent a list of ultimatums to the Serbians, including one that was hardly possible to be met if the integrity of Serbia was to be preserved: that is, that the Austrian authorities would supervise the prosecution of Serbian accomplices on Serbian soil. The Serbs agreed to all the conditions, except this one, but were then, by a sign of

Russian support, emboldened to resist more of the demands.[81] In fact, neither their compliance nor their resistance counted. Like others in the Austrian administration, Berchtold had decided that in any case the time was right for a war.

If Austria wanted conflict, the Germans were equally inclined to wage war. Feeling themselves denied the great empires open to Great Britain, France and others, and hemmed in within Europe between France and Russia, Germany had longed for an opportunity to expand its territory as a complement to its own power. The military believed themselves at the peak of their effectiveness; Russia was a waking giant: in a few years, Germany might find itself crushed between its two potent neighbours. It was better to act now than linger and so invite a long decline. By a swift attack, they could still defeat France in the time it took for Russia to mobilise. This one over-arching military plan, the basis of German military thinking in the period, was risky and inflexible.[82] Yet, as circumstances changed, no other plan could be thought of that would save Germany from attack from both sides. It seemed as though there might never again be so convenient a moment to throw the dice.

However, this assumption of German and Austrian aggression, though not incorrect, smudges the complexity of the situation. The alliances that bound the nations together, committing them to war, had been sidestepped in the past, and could have been again. A combination of contingency, accident and choice was at play. Austria and Germany were also swept up into the war, not whole-heartedly, but with regrets and attempts to halt the flood of events. Influential figures were at odds; some faltered, or sleepwalked, or dragged their heels, while others attempted to rush on. For purely military reasons connected to the timetables for mobilisation and the peremptory quality of their own plans, the generals on all sides pressed for war; the diplomats clung to diplomacy; for the most part the monarchs fumbled towards gestures of peace. The Austrians pressed for war, but only meant to settle scores with Serbia, a smaller enemy whose certain defeat would bolster the Empire; they never intended the general European conflagration that would burn down their power. Above all, there is the startling fact of the enthusiasm for war among the populations of Europe, from Britain to Russia. This was, of course, a matter of idealistic ignorance concerning what war means, and understandable short-sightedness about how this particular war would turn out. Misled by the speed of battle in the two Balkan wars, people expected a fast and glorious set of military clashes that would decide questions of European prestige, and, for some, settle the ultimate matter of power between the 'German' ideal and the Slavic spirit. There was even a naïve relish for conflict, the spoiling for a fight, that had seen internal disputes across the continent grow hysterical in the previous three or four years. However, this blood-lust was not shared by all; a yearning for peace remained strong, and, backed by the political will of one remarkable individual – Jean Jaurès – received a last idealistic expression just before the fighting began. However, this reaching for peace would itself be beaten down by yet another assassination.

II: Revolvers aux Poings

Before the killings at Sarajevo, for the first time in years France had a President who was in a bellicose mood. Appointed in 1913, Raymond Poincaré of the Alliance républicaine démocratique was a go-getting, aggressive leader, eager for war and convinced that France could beat Germany. Neither his mood nor his centre-rightist politics were shared by the ruling administration. A recent election had produced a predominantly left-leaning legislature; 20 per cent of the Chamber were Socialists.[83] In June 1914, Poincaré therefore appointed a largely left-wing government led by René Viviani; he might have been forced to pick the technocratic Radical Joseph Caillaux for his Prime Minister, if it had not been for the recent scandal whereby Madame Henriette Caillaux had shot Gaston Calmette, the Parisian editor of Le Figaro, who was threatening to expose the couple's love-letters, written when Caillaux was still married to his first wife. Following the murder, Caillaux had resigned, dashing the prospects that the Socialist Jean Jaurès had set up for a coalition. Jaurès stood as the benign and rational patriarch of the movement in France, the Santa Claus of socialism. He strove, he sometimes compromised, and he flourished; Georges Clemenceau declared that one could spot an article by Jaurès by the fact that all his verbs were in the future tense.[84] Sharing their belief in the power of the state, Jaurès was happy to ally himself with the centre against the right.[85] If Jaurès and Caillaux had come to power, it is possible that some form of reconciliation with Germany might have occurred; like many others in France, Jaurès disliked autocratic Russia, and looked sympathetically towards his fellow socialists in Germany.

Even without Caillaux, however, Jaurès attempted to block the rush to war. He mooted the idea of a general strike in France and other European nations as a means of halting the charge towards combat; Europe's working peoples would prevent the continent slipping into the barbarism of war.[86] The French Socialists backed the audacious and quixotic plan. Yet, despite a large-scale show of public support (in Paris over 100,000 people demonstrated), within days the initiative was dead in the water; there was simply too little international enthusiasm for peace.[87] Nonetheless Jaurès continued to press for negotiation; on 29 July at Brussels' Maison du Peuple he met with German and Austrian socialists (including Rosa Luxemburg); they impractically expected the next Congress of the International to be held on 9 August to salve the conflict.[88] However, Jaurès's heroic pacifism would cost him dearly, for then, as François Mauriac put it, the right assassinated him.[89] On 30 July, at the end of a long day in Paris labouring to maintain the peace, Jaurès stopped for a beer at the Café du Croissant, at the corner of the Rue Montmartre; in the café there with him was the man who, next day, would gun him down.[90]

On that evening the aptly named Raoul Villain, a young French nationalist, was too nervous to kill his man. Though he had never seen Jaurès before, and had pictured a much older chap, he found his target easily; it was well known that Jaurès habitually sauntered home this way from his newspaper office.[91] Villain was enraged at anti-patriotism, and convinced that Jaurès was its source. He would murder Jaurès for his socialism, his pacifism, his betrayal of France. Yet by the time he plucked up his courage to kill the good man, Jaurès's effort towards peace was already dead. On 31 July, it became obvious that the nation was ready to match the Germans and Austrians and to pitch into the war. There would be no more time for peace-making. Nonetheless Jaurès kept fighting; his aim was apparently to appeal to the USA's President Woodrow Wilson. That evening, he would compose one last trumpet-blast of a leading article, one that would rally the people against the lunacy.

Before going to write, he joined some friends and colleagues again at the Café du Croissant. Although the rich bourgeoisie had already left the capital for their summer holidays, the café was teeming with customers. Jaurès and his companions sat at a shared table by the open window, in the close Parisian night; the waiter placed a screen between them and the street. Jaurès had his back to the passers-by. One of his companions showed him a photograph of his daughter; Jaurès asked how old the girl was.[92] For some time Villain watched from outside, and then marched up, pulled the screen out of the way, and fired twice at Jaurès's back. One bullet struck home, at the nape of the neck.[93] Jaurès died there at the café; his funeral took place on 4 August 1914, one day after France and Germany declared war. In the Chamber of Deputies, Paul Deschanel declared that there were no more adversaries, there were only Frenchmen, a claim that time would belie.[94]

Throughout the course of the war Villain awaited trial, a patriot denied the right to lose his life in the trenches of Verdun. When, in March 1919, his case finally did go to court, he was acquitted on the basis of hereditary mental instability. All but the followers of the royalist newspaper *Action Française* were indignant; it had seemed as though the trial had weighed up Jaurès's patriotism as much as it judged Villain's madness.[95] Then on Ibiza in 1936, as the final act in this cycle of imbecility, Villain was himself assassinated by Spanish Republicans.

Jaurès's murder was not only the last blow of the pre-war conflict over socialism, but a portent of things to come. The fact that Jaurès's assassin came from the right might have appeared unusual in 1914; soon it would be established as a norm. As the European right became itself a revolutionary movement, not conservative and reasonable, but radical and irrational, it adopted gleefully the Anarchist and Nihilist tactics of assassination. Both left and right cherished the romantic outlaw figure, the left seeing him as someone fighting for a utopian future, the right seeing him as a partisan for a lost, though once-known world. In reality, this Eden was just as illusory as the revolutionary's shining future.

A mood of blasé bloodthirstiness had set in, contaminating even the world of art. In an anonymous interview conducted in 1930, the Catalan artist Joan Miró remarked of painting, 'I want to assassinate it.'[96] In 1931, Miró clarified this pronouncement: 'The only thing that's clear to me is that I intend to destroy, destroy everything that exists in painting'; he went on to add, 'Painting revolts me.'[97] Looking at Miró's work now, it proves difficult to regain the affront it once provoked;

scandal has dwindled into official art. Yet then his paintings expressed a common longing to destroy the status quo.

Miró's desire to assassinate painting arose from the belief that the old modes tyrannised through convention. The pre-Romantic artists had aimed at honing their mimetic skill, their craft being an act of attention; the Romantic artists justified their work in terms of authenticity, as passionate creation. The focus had moved from the fabricated object to the self's right to expression.[98] Having killed off the decrepit past, art had to begin again; Miró longed to free himself from 'any sort of pictorial influence and any contact with realism . . . I was painting with an absolute contempt for painting.'[99] His art had to be alive for the moment only, avoiding deathliness by its violence, an expression of turbulence and revolt. He wanted his work to show 'all the formal innovations and aggressiveness I had inside me'; elsewhere he described how he aimed at 'plastic aggressiveness'.[100] Miró once implicitly described his own personality as 'strong or excessive, unhealthy perhaps, deadly if you like'.[101]

In the artistic circles of Paris or Barcelona, Miró's pose matched a similar appetite for turmoil among his peers. Traces of its original military meaning still lingered around the term 'avant-garde'. For the painters and poets of Montmartre, the belief that art might itself be revolutionary inspirited their marginal lives. Although never a card-carrying member of the group himself, Miró's views were particularly close to those of the Surrealists. André Masson remarked that 'violence needs artistic expression because, along with hunger and love, it is "at the root of all human beings"'.[102] André Breton affirmed that the purest surrealist act would be to fire a pistol at random into a crowd. He graced his words with mitigations; nonetheless his statement still shocks.[103]

The Surrealists' taste for crime found its most intriguing expression in their celebration of one youthfully attractive assassin. On 22 January 1923, in the offices of the royalist journal *Action Française*, Germaine Berton murdered the journalist Marius Plateau. Plateau's killing was an afterthought; her main target had been the paper's right-wing editor, Léon Daudet. She had earlier prepared to shoot Daudet at a mass for the soul of Louis XVI at St Germain l'Auxerrois, but her target had failed to show up.[104] After firing at Plateau, Berton shot herself, though she survived to face trial. There she presented the shooting as a delayed act of justice for the murder of Jean Jaurès. In July 1914, Léon Daudet had published an article in *Action Française* that hinted at the desirability of assassinating Jaurès, one of several such articles in the French press at that time.[105] In killing Plateau, Berton assailed a scurrilous press. To murder the individual reporter or editor demolished the institutional and apparently impersonal face of a newspaper, returning affairs to the matter of personalities.

That November of 1923 during the court proceedings, Daudet's sixteen-year-old son, Philippe, committed suicide; according to those in the Anarchist newspaper *Le Libertaire*, he dedicated his immolation to Germaine Berton, with whom he was besotted.[106] In December, to complete the bizarre sequence of events, Berton was acquitted, despite being patently guilty of the crime. In this way, those in the French court tacitly expressed their approval of her deed's retributive violence. The French-German writer, Ivan (Ywan) Goll depicted her as possessed by her abhorrence for Daudet, like a medium, walking the streets of Paris in a trance, taking hate like others take cocaine. France, he implied, shared her fever.[107]

André Breton and his wife, Louis Aragon and Max Morise jointly sent the freshly released Berton a bunch of flowers (with the note 'For Germaine Berton, who did what we did not know how to do'). Despite this sweet gesture, Berton's acquittal had rendered her instantly uninteresting. She had ceased to be a symbol of revolt and was in 'accord' with society.[108] The Surrealists' fascination with Berton depended upon an appreciation of the erotics of killing; the murder rendered the murderess attractive. In *La Révolution Surréaliste* (1924) there appeared a famous image of Germaine Berton, her face surrounded by individual photographs of the (entirely male) Surrealist group. The following text from Charles Baudelaire's preface to *Les paradis artificiels* (1860) rests at the foot of the picture: 'La femme est l'être qui projecte la plus grande ombre ou la plus grande lumière dans nos rêves' – 'Woman is the being who throws the greatest shadow or the greatest light on our dreams'.[109] To the Surrealists, Berton was manifestly all woman.

Celebrating Berton offered a marvellous opportunity to irritate the middle classes. The Surrealists could thereby demonstrate their rejection of 'conventional' moral responses to crime and violence, replacing such outmoded reactions with a revolutionary aesthetic enjoyment; following

Thomas De Quincey's provocative essay 'On Murder Considered as One of the Fine Arts', the quality of an assassination could now be understood as a question of taste.

Like much in the movement, the Surrealist celebration of action nostalgically restated nineteenth-century notions. They looked back to the Anarchists of the 1890s, to Ravachol, Émile Henry (who in February 1894 in Paris, tossed a bomb in the Café Terminus) and, above all, to Félix Fénéon.

Ravachol had been the Germaine Berton of his day, a killer for the connoisseur. His real name was François Königstein, and he was a 'scoundrel, an idler and a profligate . . . who . . . lived a roving life for many years'.[110] During a burglary he murdered an elderly man and his maid with an axe; later he robbed a recently buried corpse of its jewels, strangled another old man, and, very likely, killed another old lady. Only then did he become involved in the Anarchist movement, playing a small part in the French Anarchist bombing campaign of the early 1890s, most notably by depositing explosive devices at the houses of a judge and a public prosecutor. His boastfulness led to his arrest; a waiter overheard him extolling his own deeds, and so sent for the police. (The café on the Boulevard de Magenta where he was apprehended was in consequence itself bombed.) The unrepentant Ravachol became a hero for the revolutionary cause; to admire Ravachol was the perfect means for showing one's contempt for custom. The sordid murders were a little regretted, but did little to tarnish his shining reputation. Ravachol could look like another beautiful soul corrupted by modern life: an editorial in the Anarchist journal *Commonwealth* lamented, 'Down with the accursed system that drives good, brave, capable men full of social feeling, full of love for their fellows like Ravachol, to strife and war with other men.'[111]

However, while the celebration of Ravachol parallels the Surrealists' championing of Berton, it is in the work and deeds of Félix Fénéon that we find the closest precursor to their desires. At a time when Anarchist outrages blasted Paris, and assassinations and attempted assassinations flourished, Fénéon offered up the perfect amalgam of political violence and enigmatic *sangfroid*. Fénéon was an essayist, critic and Anarchist, a dry and dandiacal man of letters in *fin de siècle* Paris. This diffident character was responsible for the latest in the series of explosions. On 4 April 1894, while his acquaintance Émile Henry stood trial for that bomb at the Café Terminus, as an act of solidarity Fénéon deposited a bomb in a flower-pot on the windowsill of the Restaurant Foyot. Having lit the fuse with a cigarette, the anonymous 'author of the outrage' then disappeared into the Parisian night. Other than a pair of waiters, the only man injured was the poet Laurent Tailharde, who was struck in the neck by a fragment of the bomb while his soup was being served. Only a few days before the explosion, at a dinner for young writers, this poet had remarked of the Anarchist outrages, 'Qu'importent les victimes, si le geste est beau?' ('What do the victims matter, if the gesture is beautiful?'). The whirligig of time had brought its revenges; few right-wing papers resisted the opportunity to gloat.[112]

In late June that same year, the French President, Sadi Carnot, was assassinated by a young Anarchist, Caserio. While Caserio awaited execution, a group trial of some thirty Anarchists took place; among them was Fénéon. The police had found detonators and explosives at his apartment. It should have been an open and shut case; in fact, the writer pulled off his own acquittal. Fénéon escaped punishment mainly because of his impeccably discreet court appearance, a triumph of courteous sarcasm.[113]

What was most perplexing to the public at the time was the difficulty of detecting a proper motive for such mayhem. Following the explosion of a bomb in the Rue de Clichy, *The Times* wondered: 'No possible political end can be adduced to justify or explain the detestable acts which have startled us all . . . It is crime for crime's sake.'[114] The last phrase knowingly evoked the mantra of aestheticism, of 'art for art's sake'; ruin had become an aesthetic act.

Miró's attitude, the Surrealists' enthusiasms – all now seem symptoms of a crisis in values. Fénéon stands as the embodiment of that crisis simply because, unlike the others, he translated his thoughts into a pure and gratuitous action. He offers us the whimsy of terrorism, his deed an intervention into the muddle of city life. In later life, Fénéon perfected a new literary form, 'Nouvelles en trois lignes', news stories of three lines, in which events of the day were pithily presented. Compressed into brevity, such anecdotes offered a fleeting impression of violence, the uncontextualised and unmotivated scraps of a senseless world. There was no coherent story – or if there were, it was a mad one. His own aberrant act of terrorism passes into a footnote to greater events, an attempted murder as a fragment of marginalia.

Following on Fénéon and implicit in the Surrealists' and Miró's stance was a new attitude to violence and a new kind of politics too. In a world without traditional values, the only remaining motive for action was impulse: I do this because I want it. To question the legitimacy of this prompting is to offer an insult, a check on the individual's right to act. The only morality is that everyone should be permitted to do all that is permitted. Modern violence grew out of this assertion of the self's wants, its thrill an unwitting confession of emptiness.

The bloodshed of the war that followed Sarajevo habituated a continent to killing. In the south-east of Europe that violence would be a spilling over from the mayhem produced by the simultaneous collapse of the Austro-Hungarian and Ottoman empires. However, events after the war in the heart of Europe, in Spain and Italy and France, would show that the Balkans and the Near East were far from owning a monopoly on carnage. At its heart, as at its peripheries, Europe could not free itself from the bloodshed. Post-war, the most significant advance in the history of assassination was to take place in Germany, as order broke down in the defeated nation. Fittingly, therefore, it was Berlin that was also to act as the location for a murder whose origins lay in the recent war, in the violence of Ottoman history thousands of miles away in the lands of Asia Minor.

10

Necessary Murders

I: A Funeral in Berlin

Who shall heal murder?
LORD BYRON, FROM *CAIN*, 1821

In 1920, on the streets of Berlin, a young man gunned down an Ottoman leader in exile. At first it seemed an especially senseless and indeed insignificant killing, just one more murder after the great bloodshed of the recently ended war. However, this deed was far from senseless: investigation would show that it had its roots in acts of unspeakable violence some five years before. And it was far from insignificant, too: for the act of assassination, the nightmare that provoked it, and the startling response of the legal authorities, all reveal a political and moral collapse that in these decades shook Europe from Dublin to Moscow.

To understand these happenings and that collapse, it is necessary to return for a moment to the disintegrating world of the late nineteenth-century empires. From 1876 to 1909, Sultan Abdülhamid II ruled Turkey as an autocratic reformer, though one who, when opportunity presented itself, could also 'eliminate the Constitutionalists', wiping out the modernising Young Ottoman movement.[1] His similarly brutal treatment of nationalist threats to the integrity of his Ottoman Empire severely damaged his reputation outside Turkey. His empire was anyway breaking up, but the loss of territory in Europe was nothing compared to the danger posed by the emergence of a nationalist consciousness among ethnic Armenians.

Other Christian nationalities (Bulgarians, Serbs, Romanians, Greeks) within the Empire were located outside the territory of Turkey itself; the Armenians were scattered across Asia Minor, the homeland. The Armenians stood as a rival nationality within the nation, and one centred on the border between Turkey and its old rival, Russia, where some Armenians looked for support.[2] However, renewed persecution of Russian Armenians in Tiflis (Tblisi) in 1890 provoked the formation of the socialist and nationalist Armenian Revolutionary Federation (or the 'Dashnaks'). Their aim was to advance Armenian independence from the Ottoman Empire; their methods would be closely modelled on the Russian revolutionaries.[3] For the Turks, these were menacing developments. It was one thing to be forced to acquiesce in the loss of Greece or Bulgaria, and quite another to accept the possibility of an Armenian nation that would mean the dismemberment of the Turkish state.[4]

Therefore Abdülhamid responded brutally. In 1894, in the district of Sasun, Armenians were slaughtered, and in the following two years more massacres occurred, including in Istanbul (in response to Armenian terrorists occupying the Ottoman Bank).[5] At the same time in Crete there were mob killings of Greek Christians. In Liverpool, Gladstone made a speech denouncing the Sultan as 'Abdul the Great Assassin'.[6]

Meanwhile, provoked by other elements of Abdülhamid's oppressive rule, a new movement rose up – the Young Turks. Like the Young Ottomans who came before them, these were liberals, their ranks filled with would-be bureaucrats who had failed to find jobs in the administration. They formed themselves into the Committee of Union and Progress ('Ittihat ve Terakki'), otherwise known as the CUP. In July 1908, a Young Turk revolution led to the restoration of the parliament dissolved in the mid-1870s. In 1909 a counter-revolution followed, one easily defeated by the Young Turks, who on regaining power forced the abdication of Abdülhamid, replacing him with the ineffectual Mohammed V ('that amiable non-entity').[7] In early 1913, the CUP decided to consolidate their authority, and so launched a *coup d'état*; in the mayhem, they assassinated their political rivals, Nazim Pasha, the Minister of War, and Mahmud Şevket Pasha, the Grand Vizier.[8]

In 1908, the Armenians had supported the Young Turks against Abdülhamid, and cheered the CUP on as potential liberators.[9] In exile their mutual opposition to Abdülhamid had made them partners in sedition. In Adana in 1909 massacres that left perhaps as many as 15,000 to 30,000 Armenians dead (the so-called 'Cilician vespers') followed the counter-coup by troops loyal to the old Sultan.[10] This atrocity was only a foretaste of the carnage to come. Although the CUP and the Armenians were nominal allies, deeper divisions remained, and when the unity nurtured by opposition vanished, these rifts emerged. Meanwhile Russia was busy exploiting the Armenian situation as a way of undermining Turkey; the CUP were therefore suspicious of Armenian aims. Moreover, the nationalists among the Armenians were now faced by an imperial government that like them had been inspired by the nationalism of small states. The Balkan wars and the resulting loss of Ottoman territory had led to a new concentration on Turkish nationalism; emulating the ideology of their enemies in the emerging Balkan states, the Young Turks similarly pictured a nation predicated on shared language, culture, education and religion.[11] This definition excluded the Armenians.

One of the dominant leaders of the newly victorious CUP was Talât Pasha (Mehmet Talât). He was born in the province of Edirne (the westernmost part of Turkey) in 1874, the child of a farmer and a gypsy woman.[12] His father's early death ended his hopes of a full army education.[13] Talât's ignominious origins slowed his progress through the bureaucratic ranks; nonetheless, though he began as a worker in the telegraph office, he ended up employed as 'chief clerk in the correspondence division of the Salonika directorate of posts and tele-graphs'.[14] Meanwhile he nurtured his political interests, in the early 1890s joining the Young Turks in Edirne right at the beginning of the movement. In 1896, when the Sultan's police discovered the Young Turks' organisation, he was banished to Salonika. He was still there in 1906 when he founded the 'Ottoman Freedom Society'. At the time of the 1908 revolution, he was the most prominent civilian member of the CUP. After the revolution of 1908, he was appointed Deputy at Adrianople, while also remaining the representative for Edirne in all the CUP's parliaments. He was soon Minister of the Interior.

According to the historian Yves Ternon, Talât was a double man and a consummate liar.[15] Yet Talât was the affable Machiavel of his party, the brightest of all the CUP, and their most skilful politician. He was a brilliant manipulator of events; a tough, witty character, 'the Danton of the Turkish Revolution'.[16] His ultimate desire was to 'Ottomanise' the empire – a nationalist project at heart.[17] In the years leading up to the Great War, he moved towards endorsing the 'Ottomanisation' of Turkish minorities. In 1912, during the Second Balkan War, he was (with Enver Pasha) responsible for the strategy of letting the army push on and retake Edirne, a tactic so successful and so popular that it led to the consolidation of CUP power.[18] In the following *coup d'état*, concerning the assassination of their political enemies, Talât was indirectly involved with Enver Pasha, the soon-to-be war minister, and Djemal Pasha, soon to be appointed minister of public works. He was both physically powerful and rakishly droll. The German ambassador, Johann Heinrich von Bernstorff, who was anyway well disposed towards the Young Turks, found himself hugely impressed by Talât Pasha's unperturbable charm; his elegance was infamous. However, a less indulgent observer might find his quip on being asked about the Armenian question – 'What do you want? The question is settled, there are no more Armenians' – to be more sinister than amusing.[19] At one time Talât was known to be friendly with various Armenians.[20] Yet, as many believed, the 'Armenian massacres which followed the entry of Turkey into the world war were largely his work'.[21] But then, in Bernstorff's view, Talât would pay for his share in the sin against the Armenians with his death.[22]

In 1914, the Ottomans entered the war on the side of Germany, a choice motivated in part by the desire to create a 'greater Turkey' by taking territory from Russia. The Turkish historian (and exile) Taner Akçam sees the advent of war as permitting the CUP to prepare the deportation of the Armenian population from Anatolia – preparations marked by the prompt formation of what was known as the Special Organisation.[23] It was following Turkish military defeat by the Russians at Sarikamiş in December 1914 that the CUP actively determined on the removal of the Armenians.[24] At this freezing Caucasian battle, a whole Turkish army corps had been wiped out (by cold or the enemy) or captured. A division of Armenians, including renegade citizens of the Ottoman Empire, had fought on the Russian side. This provocation presented a remarkable opportunity. In the last days of February 1915, all Armenian soldiers in combat positions were given leave.[25] The order was a prelude to mass murder. Moreover, in April 1915, the declaration of an independent Armenian government followed, one based on Russian soil, but with presumed designs on their fellows in Turkey itself.[26] Inspired by the use of concentration camps by the British in the

Boer War, the CUP decided to gather the Armenians together, either for purposes of control or of extermination. They would attempt to relocate almost the entire Armenian population from the war zone to Zor (according to some historians also a war zone) in the Syrian desert. The CUP considered themselves to be usefully expelling an irritant from the body politic of Turkey.

A mass deportation began; possibly no more than a moving of population was intended. But numerous historians and commentators believe that the chief aim does indeed appear to have been the destruction of all the Armenians. The German missionary Johannes Lepsius estimated that no more than a third of those deported reached their destination.[27]

What happened in Turkey during 1915 remains a subject of marked political and historical controversy; however, it is necessary to address it here, if we are to understand the retribution that followed. The dispute does not turn on the fact that a large number of Armenians died as a direct result of Turkish government policy. What is at stake is the definition of these deaths as genocide, with its implication that the Turkish authorities consciously planned to exterminate the Armenian people. Whatever the facts of the case, there is no doubt that, by the 1920s, it was widely accepted across Europe that large-scale massacres of Armenians had taken place. In one way or another 'a process of deportation . . . became a process of destruction'.[28] In the late 1910s and early 1920s, it was already rumoured that as many as a million had died.[29]

The Turkish government and a majority of Turkish historians, and some European and American historians with Turkish connections, remain convinced that no genocide took place. The Turkish penal code currently makes it illegal to insult Turkish identity; calls for the recognition of the Armenian massacres as genocide are regarded as such an insult. Under this law, a number of academics and writers have been prosecuted. In January 2007, the journalist Hrant Dink was assassinated outside his newspaper's offices; in 2005, he had been given a six-month suspended sentence for writing about the Armenian genocide.

It would be easy to dismiss the Turkish rejection of the genocide label as merely due to reasons of national shame and embarrassment. However, historians have highlighted a number of complexities in the course of events and in their documentation that might for some make an unequivocal use of the word 'genocide' problematic.

Firstly, there is the context of the war. Turkey was fighting on three fronts against Russia in the east and against troops from Britain, France, Australia and New Zealand in the Dardanelles and Mesopotamia. There was the risk of a British advance from Egypt in the south. In the east, Armenians had fought in or alongside the Russian army. Armenian nationalists were tempted by the thought that Russian victory could lead to the fulfilment of their nationalist aspirations. Fears grew that the Armenians within Turkey would rise up, and that they were effectively a 'fifth column' within the country. There were reports of both Ottoman and Russian Armenians participating in army units working with the Russian forces.[30]

It is difficult to ascertain in what numbers Armenians fought against the Turks; while it is correct that some Armenians deserted or joined the Russian side, most did not.[31] After the war, at the Paris Peace Conference, James Gerard, of the American Committee for the Independence of Armenia, declared that without Armenian military support for the Allies the Turks would not have been defeated.[32] However, this claim was very likely influenced by the desire to have the Armenians recognised as co-belligerents, and therefore gain an equal place at the conference table.

Secondly, with the regular army fighting the war on the various fronts, the organisation of the deportations fell to the 'gendarmes', a temporary police militia, ill-disciplined and inexperienced. These fallible guardians created conditions in which people were bound to die, or even enthusiastically joined in when the deportees were attacked by local populations. The temptation to loot proved overwhelming, and the situation similarly presented irresistible opportunities for the fulfilment of private revenges – by the gendarmes and by minor officials.[33]

Thirdly, there had been massacres of Muslims by Armenians.[34] Perhaps these were not only reprisals, but acts of war. Historically speaking, such Christian-led massacres were, to the outside world, an invisible element of the story. For example, in Bulgaria in 1876, a small massacre of Muslims by Christians had led to a large-scale massacre of Christians by Muslims; with the international backing of the Russians this in turn

led to another large-scale massacre of Muslims by Christians. Only the
second of these three massacres provoked European condemnation.
Where Muslims were murdered, few Europeans bothered to protest;
when Muslims killed Christians, however, there were cries of outrage
and eager calls for intervention.

It is also the case that in the Balkans and Near East from at least
the late nineteenth century onwards 'ethnic cleansing' and massacre
were tried and tested tactics for both Christians and Muslims. The
two Balkan wars both saw the widespread murder of civilians, for
instance in largely Muslim Kosovo. In 1914, some Austrians thought
of their war against Serbia as a racial conflict, an attempt to purge a
problem by extermination.[35] The wars between Turkey and Greece
were characterised by atrocities on both sides. As later in the Second
World War in Poland, the Baltic States, Ukraine and Russia, warfare
became all too easily a matter of ethnic conflict, where the liquidation
of civilian populations seemed a desirable or, at least, necessary end.

It will be noted that the first and third 'complexities' merely provide
a context for atrocity, but do little to downgrade genocide. The second
is more persuasive, as, if as important as is claimed, it would suggest
that there was no conscious attempt at extermination. Accounts of
the period by some respected historians, most notably Stanford Shaw,
seek to exonerate the Turks on all counts, and to put the blame on the
Armenians. According to Shaw and others, deportation was an unexcep-
tional wartime practice, many Armenians were exempted, particularly
in the cities (apart from those belonging to 'terrorist' organisations),
and, in his view, given the muddled conditions of wartime, it was hardly
surprising that a few people were killed. Moreover, those marauding the
columns of deportees were not Turks, but rather their long-standing
enemy, the Kurds.[36] In this version of events, when Talât was finally
notified of the mayhem he made attempts to end the butchery and
incompetence. The accusations of a policy of extermination were a
matter of wartime propaganda by the British and, later, the Americans,
and no more worthy of credit than the earlier stories of babies being
tossed on bayonets by German soldiers in Belgium.[37]

Yet there are profound problems with the thesis put forward by Shaw
and other historians sceptical about naming the wartime deportations
as genocide. If the CUP were motivated by strategic reasons, then it

is hard not to feel that besides the untold cost in human life and the damage done to Turkey's international reputation, in some ways the move against the Armenians was counter-productive: depopulating the Armenian districts meant that they could no longer grow food there for the Turkish Army.[38] Besides, if the aim was to remove a potentially hostile native population from the war zone, why were so many Armenians deported from areas of the country where no fighting was taking place? Why the arrest and murder of prominent Armenians in Istanbul itself? Also, is it believable that so many people would die as a result of sporadic, unorganised local attacks, disease and hunger, unless conditions were being intentionally created in order to maximise the number of deaths? For this last reason, the number of Armenian deaths remains central to the argument as to whether or not the CUP intended mass extermination. According to the historian Erik J. Zürcher:

Turkish historians have put the number of deaths as low as 200,000, while the Armenians have sometimes claimed ten times as many. The reason for the discrepancy, propaganda apart, lies in the differing estimates of the number of Armenians who lived in the Empire before the war and of the numbers who emigrated. Between 600,000 and 800,000 deaths seem most likely.[39]

Those historians who debunk the idea of a genocide often exhibit a disturbingly blasé attitude towards the killings themselves. Even their countering the stories of Armenian deaths with the evocation of massacres of Muslims rings hollow, as though the debating point is more important than their sympathy with the unjustly killed.

There are two competing bodies of evidence regarding the massacres: the narratives of eye-witnesses versus government papers. For some, the value of eye-witness accounts is rendered uncertain by fears of bias, the inability of an individual to perceive the overall picture, the distortions produced by confusion and shock; while the government records are tarnished by questions of duplicity, obfuscation, and the fact that the most important documents are burnt or missing (possibly the consequence of officials covering their tracks).[40]

One particular set of documents have acquired a starring role in explorations of the Armenian massacres. These are the so-called Naim–Andonian telegrams, named after 'Naim Bey', apparently an Ottoman government official who is supposed to have given incriminating documents to Aram Andonian, an Armenian journalist who had also worked for the Ottoman administration. The documents consist of a number of telegrams supposedly written by Talât Pasha referring to or directly (or implicitly) ordering the Armenian genocide.[41]

The authenticity of these telegrams is contested. It is plausible that they were concocted by Andonian to use as bargaining counters in the post-war peace negotiations.[42] Several things suggest that they could be counterfeits: they contain flaws of dating; they are printed on the wrong kind of paper for official documents; some signatures seem to be faked; there are mistakes in grammar; and there is the improbability of the documents' survival (especially given their incriminating nature). Moreover, other more benevolent telegrams by Talât were later discovered – though this in itself may be the consequence of a deliberately confusing practice of doubling correspondence. One expert on the subject, Yves Ternon, suggests that the Naim–Andonian documents are flawed, and their authenticity is therefore questionable.[43]

Whatever the validity of these telegrams, Taner Akçam points out that there is enough documentation without using the Andonian documents to show intent of genocide.[44] He also affirms that 'the overall coordination of the Genocide was taken over by Talât Paşa'. German ambassador Paul Wolff Metternich described Talât Pasha as the 'soul of the "Armenian persecution"'.[45]

And so in 1920 on the streets of Berlin, the events that took place in Turkey during the war were revived with new urgency. Here that murder took place, the meaning of which was to be found in the horror of the assassin's life – a horror shared by an entire people. Soghomon Tehlirian was born on 2 April 1897 in Pakarij, but when he was four years old came to Erzincan, a town on the old silk road, on the River Kara, a tributary of the Euphrates, in Eastern Anatolia. Tehlirian's father was originally a merchant in Pakarij; by 1913, he had moved to Serbia to develop his business. Tehlirian remained behind in Erzincan with the rest of his family (he seems to have had two brothers and three sisters). The population of the town was more or less evenly divided between ethnic Armenians and Turks. In 1914, with the outbreak of war, Armenians were conscripted into the Ottoman army; Tehlirian's brother was one of those to join up.[46] In May 1915, the family remaining in Erzincan heard news of the deportations.

Soon afterwards, according to Tehlirian's trial testimony, he and his family were themselves deported along with the entire Armenian population of Erzincan; a report by the American ambassador, Henry Morgenthau, dates the expulsions from Erzincan and Erzeroum to early July 1915.[47] The Armenians were told they were to be moved to Mesopotamia. Once out of town, the column of deportees were robbed by the police. Then soldiers opened fire and the massacre began; in the mayhem, Tehlirian's sister was raped, his younger brother cut down, his mother shot. His father vanished, presumably killed. Tehlirian himself was knocked on the head and fell unconscious.[48] He awoke two days later. His brother's corpse lay across him, his head split open with an axe; there were dead bodies all around.

Independent evidence confirming that the massacre took place comes from eye-witness reports (blaming the Kurds) heard by Henry Morgenthau and also from two Danish Red Cross nurses.[49] These confirm Tehlirian's version of the deportation and the massacre. The Armenians were attacked at Kamakh Boghaz, 'a narrow gorge between two walls of rock', twelve hours' march from Erzincan, where the convoy was caught between the fire of the Kurds and the Turkish gendarmes.[50]

After coming to, Tehlirian stayed with a Kurdish family while his wounds healed, and then made his way south to Persia, with two other Armenian fugitives, going from village to village through the mountains. He went to Tiflis, where for a little over a year he lived in the shop of an Armenian merchant. On hearing in 1916 that Erzincan had been captured by the Russians, he went home, where he found only two Armenian families, both of whom had been forced to convert to Islam. No other Armenians were left alive. There had been 20,000 Armenians in Erzincan. He collapsed, experiencing his first breakdown. He went back to Tiflis where he attended an Armenian school, learning Russian and French. He also bought a German army-surplus automatic pistol.

In February 1919, after the war, Tehlirian left for Constantinople, looking for relatives. Here he read the newspapers and became convinced by them that Talât Pasha had been the architect of the massacres; following a court martial in July 1919 Talât had been condemned to death *in absentia* for the massacres (though the government that convicted him was soon dissolved). After two months, Tehlirian travelled to Salonika, then on to Serbia, then back to Salonika, where he had a second nervous breakdown, and then on, in 1920, to Paris. His mind was foggy and confused; he was unable to settle to anything, or to concentrate.

He spent a year in Paris; while he was there an assassination took place in the city: Essad Pasha, the Albanian leader in exile, was shot as he left the Hotel Continental. His killer, a fellow Albanian called Avni Rustemi, described himself as coming upon Essad Pasha and then being overwhelmed by memories of all the injustices the politician had perpetrated. In the heat of the moment he shot him. Rustemi would in due course be tried and acquitted by a Parisian court. It was an intriguing precedent.

Quitting Paris, Tehlirian then travelled to Geneva in November. He had no real reason to go; he just wanted to see Geneva. By early December 1920, he was in Berlin. Again he had no reason to be there, only the vaguest of intentions of becoming a machinist. But during his travels, in May 1920, an act of Armenian revenge had taken place: the assassination in Tiflis of Khan Khoyski by Aram Yerganian and Misak Garabedian. Soon Tehlirian himself would perform his own act of wild justice.

While Tehlirian wandered, Talât Pasha ran. In 1918, after the Armistice was signed at Mudros between the Ottoman Empire and the Entente powers (Britain, France, and their allies), the wartime leaders of the CUP, including Talât, escaped from Turkey by German submarine. Before fleeing, Talât put in place the beginnings of a resistance movement against the occupying Allied forces.[51] The usurped leaders headed for Odessa, anxious to avoid retribution for their treatment of the Armenians. From here, they would head to Berlin.[52]

There is some evidence that Talât regretted the opprobrium visited on the CUP for their action against the Armenians, while nonetheless believing that they could not have acted otherwise.[53] The new Turkish government was to take a harsher line. In the absence of the old triumvirate of rulers, Djemal, Enver and Talât, a power struggle began between the new Sultan, Mehmet VI, the liberals, the Entente, and the remaining members of the CUP. As we have seen, in the confusion and constant flux of control, in his absence Talât was court-martialled. The courts martial took place in the six months following the Armistice, indicting the leaders and officials of the previous government for crimes related to the deportations and massacres.[54] The aim was in part to pre-empt Allied justice and so influence for the better the deal that Turkey might expect from the forthcoming Paris Peace Conference.[55] The leading CUP politicians, Talât, Enver and Djemal, were sentenced to death.[56]

But by then Talât Pasha was living under an assumed name, Ali Salih Bey, in Berlin, at Hardenbergstrasse, near the zoo.[57] Here Talât met with Aubrey Herbert, a half-blind British adventurer, who had once turned down an invitation from Essad Pasha to be king of Albania. Herbert was on a government mission to sound out the exiled Turk. The runaway had grown gaunt, though his elegance survived his new poverty.[58] He protested his innocence in the matter of the Armenian massacres, while pointing out that the Armenians had provocatively been acting as Russian allies on Turkish soil. In any case, extermination was an impractical solution, and any country attempting it 'cut itself off from civilisation'.[59] Herbert learned that Talât Pasha sought to canvass international Islamic support for Mustafa Kemal's movement in Turkey, aiming by these means to ensure a favourable peace treaty for Turkey, which would be negotiating from a position of strength; yet he also said that he wished for a rapprochement with Britain, and, above all, a strong civilised Turkey, returned to its rightful place as a Great Power.

Nine days later he would be assassinated.[60]

It was late in 1920 when Soghomon Tehlirian also arrived in Berlin, where he registered at the Tiergarten Hotel.[61] Over the next weeks he met up with fellow Armenians: Levon Eftian, Eftian's sister, and Christine Terzibashian and her tobacconist husband. With the help of another young Armenian, Yervaut Apelian, Tehlirian found decent rooms (gas-lit and gas-heated) at Apelian's lodgings at Augsburgerstrasse 51 in Charlottenburg. The landlady, Frau Stellbaum, liked him, considering him a model tenant, 'decent and modest', though somehow more melancholy than the average run of young men. Something seemed to be preoccupying him; he would sit in his room and in the dark play sad songs on a mandolin.

Tehlirian filled his time as best he could. He learnt German with a private tutor, the young Fräulein Beilenson, and went to the cinema and the theatre, and took dancing lessons with Apelian and Eftian. The dancing lessons were meant to cheer him up. However, he remained a dejected youth, timid in approaching young women, thinking more of improving his German than of the possibility of romance.

He was frequently weak and dizzy. Fräulein Beilenson thought how disconsolate he looked. You could tell, she thought, that he had been through a trauma. Once in January, on Erusalemerstrasse near the U-Bahn station, a bank employee had to help him home after he fainted on the street. On another occasion he passed out during his dance class, and lay on the floor, mumbling, trembling, foaming at the mouth. Before such an attack, he would smell again the stench of the corpses.

Alarmed by these symptoms, Tehlirian started seeing Professor Richard Cassirer, a notable expert in neurology and director of the Berliner Poliklinik für Nervenkrank. In Cassirer's opinion, it was the young man's experiences in Turkey during the war which had made him psychotic. He could not erase the impression of the massacre. He was 'enslaved' by an image, his mind taken over by pictures of death.

Once Apelian was reading a book about the wartime massacres, and Tehlirian grabbed the book from his hands, and told him that they should not open old wounds, that they should put the book away and simply have some fun. Yet fun eluded him. There seemed no way he could escape his memories. And then, by chance perhaps, an encounter on the street anyhow brought the past tumbling into the present.

Strolling near the zoo, he passed three men talking Turkish. One mentioned the word 'Pasha', and, startled, Tehlirian looked more closely and saw that one of the men was Talât Pasha. He followed them to a movie theatre. There the Turks parted, one kissing Talât's hand as he left. Tehlirian went into the cinema, and attempted to watch the film, but could see nothing but images of the horror at Erzincan.

Soon afterwards the landlady saw Tehlirian come back, with the effect of a fit upon him; she thought him drunk. He went to his room, and sat very still in the armchair. He often dreamt of his mother, but this time his mother came to him – in a dream or a vision – with a clarity unlike anything he had known before. She told him to avenge their deaths, and kill their enemy. His mother's words determined him; he resolved to dispose of Talât Pasha.

Tehlirian decided to change apartments. He made an excuse to his landlady, telling her that his doctor had warned him that the gas-heater was bad for him, and that he needed sunlight and a room lit by electricity. His new landlady was Frau Dittmann, and his new room was a ground-floor apartment at Hardenbergstrasse 37, the wide thoroughfare near Berlin's zoo. He had remained constant to his desire to commit the murder: the new apartment he found (with the help of the President of the Armenian Students' Association) was opposite Talât's apartment at No. 4.

And here his plans paused as he hesitated. What would it mean to take the life of a human being? He could not do it. He lived on quietly. Still he did not act on his mother's command.

On the morning of 15 March, the maid at Tehlirian's house heard him crying in his room. Frau Dittmann looked in on him, and found him drinking cognac; he had bought the bottle the evening before. It looked dissolute perhaps, drinking in the morning, but he had only taken a small amount, and he promptly switched to tea. Later he was walking about his room, reading, when he looked out of the window and saw across the street Talât Pasha out on his balcony. A little later he watched the Turk come out of his building. It was shortly before 11.00. As Talât Pasha stepped out of his house, Tehlirian thought of his mother. The man responsible for the death of his family was right there. He pulled out his pistol from the trunk where he kept his underwear, put on his hat, ran out of his apartment, and raced down the street. He caught up with Talât by the music school. He crossed the road, came right up close behind Talât, pulled the pistol from his pocket, raised his gun, aiming at the nape of the neck, the space between the overcoat and his hat, pulled the trigger and shot the Turk in the head.[62] Talât fell dead to the ground, a heart attack most probably instantly following the catastrophic wound. A woman fainted. The blood poured onto the pavement from the exit hole above Talât Pasha's eye. Afraid that the bystanders would turn on him, Tehlirian threw the pistol away, and attempted to run. He was brought down nearby on Fasanenstrasse. Just as he had feared, the crowd began to beat him up. One man struck him repeatedly on the head with a key. Tehlirian tried to remonstrate with them, telling them that the man he had killed was a foreigner, and that he was a foreigner, and that the victim was no loss to Germany.

He had killed Talât Pasha, but he was no murderer. His conscience was clear. He was satisfied with his deed.

At the District Court in Berlin, under Justice Lehmberg, Tehlirian was tried on a charge of homicide. A courtroom drawing of Tehlirian reveals a scowling young man in profile: heavy-browed, moustached, his dark hair swept back from a high forehead.[63] There were two translators present (one of them, Kevork Kaloustian, a friend of Tehlirian's). The business of the trial was firstly to establish if he had committed the crime, and secondly to determine if the attack was premeditated; only a premeditated crime was punishable by death. Thirdly, they were to determine if there were extenuating circumstances that made it 'excusable homicide'.

It soon emerged that the trial was to consider matters that went beyond the immediate circumstances of Talât's killing. The court began to explore the nature of the massacres that had, it seemed, transformed Tehlirian into a murderer. Halfway through the trial, the court took evidence from Tehlirian's friend Christine Terzibashian, evidence which was not directly related to the murder of Talât Pasha, but rather concerned its real motive: the Armenian massacres themselves. She was twenty-six years old, an eye-witness to the atrocities. Terrible things were related: mass murders; rapes; foetuses torn from pregnant women. The court responded with distress and uproar. Then there was expert, first-hand evidence concerning the massacres by Doctor Johannes Lepsius and Bishop Balakian. Tehlirian's 'solitary act' began to assume the features of historical justice.

The previously mentioned Naim–Andonian telegrams were to become especially pertinent to Tehlirian's case, as the defence planned to present them as evidence in court, while Andonian himself attended the proceedings. However, the judge, at the district attorney's insistence, did not have them read out, nor did Andonian give evidence.[64] On the surface at least, this was because the issue in court was not whether there had been an attempt to murder all the Armenians, or whether frightful massacres had taken place, or whether, indeed, Talât Pasha was responsible for the killings. The issue was ostensibly whether or not Tehlirian believed that Talât Pasha was responsible, and of that there was no doubt.

The background of the massacres therefore initially entered the testimony of the courtroom so as to provide information regarding extenuating circumstances. Yet, as the horror of the story emerged, evidence was taken simply out of the desire to understand that horror. It was obvious that attention was shifting from Tehlirian's guilt to Tâlat's.

The prosecution was confident that Tâlat's murder was an act of political assassination, and the 'defendant's motives were political hatred and political vengeance'. In the prosecution's eyes, the evidence in court was misleading; in this view there had been no attempt to eradicate the Armenian people, merely a mass deportation undertaken as a legitimate and understandable attempt by the Turkish government to remove from its midst a potentially hostile enemy population. It was presumed that the Armenians had been on the verge of fighting alongside the Russians directly against Turkey itself, in the hope of establishing an independent Armenia. Then, due to the hostility of local populations and the savagery of the 'gendarmes', the deportations had occasioned some sporadic and ad hoc massacres – they were not at all an attempt to murder an entire people.

Meanwhile, using the theories of Gustave Le Bon and Henri Barbusse, the defence argued that the atrocities of the war were the product of forces, of mass compulsions, that had driven people to terrible deeds. Perhaps Tehlirian's deed was the outcome of such a compulsion. Evidence was taken as to the killer's state of mind. There was first of all the question of Tehlirian's fits. These were probably some form of epilepsy. However, the medical witnesses at the trial disagreed over this: one diagnosed classical epilepsy, another that Tehlirian was experiencing 'emotional epilepsy', that is, mental breakdowns caused by the ordeal of having once experienced (and so now continually re-experiencing) the massacre. Otherwise the medical witnesses essentially agreed: there was no question of Tehlirian being insane. He was not mad; he was not intoxicated; he was not deluded. Yet it was also apparent that without the massacres and their appalling effect on his mental and emotional state, there would have been no murder in Berlin.

In court, Professor Cassirer, who had acted as Tehlirian's physician, argued that the man had not acted for revenge or justice, but only under the burden of his mother's imagined order. Regarding the vision of his mother, one doctor who had examined Tehlirian declared that it was no delusion, but a living mental picture: epileptics were sometimes gifted with such visions.

As with earlier assassination trials, the matter turned on the question of free will. The defence's case was that the massacres so deranged Tehlirian that his will was in abeyance; something impelled him to kill. He had been traumatised; he had been orphaned; he had witnessed horrors, and witnessed them still; had smelt the stench of corpses, and smelt them still; he had a form of epilepsy (physical or emotional); he had had typhoid; most likely, he had been drinking; he had strange hallucinations – all added up to a compromised will.

Wilhelm Tell's murder of Albrecht Gessler was invoked in court – the classic Germanic example of the good tyrannicide. According to the defence, Tehlirian was 'the avenger of his people . . . the representative of justice versus brute force . . . of humanity versus inhumanity'.[65] One defence attorney discoursed on the Armenian psyche, in which religion and law, justice and morality were one and the same. Hence his crime was no crime, but rather a cultural phenomenon.[66] With the task of vengeance given to him by the spectre of a dead parent, Tehlirian might even seem a kind of Hamlet. Strangeness and nobility clung to him in equal measure. Though there was no doubt that he had shot Talât down, the conclusion to the trial seemed hardly in doubt.

The evidence given, and the summing-up over, after only an hour the jury delivered their verdict: not guilty. One of the experts, a doctor named Störmer, had suggested that Tehlirian's faith in justice was shattered. Perhaps the not guilty verdict was meant to repair that shattered faith. Tehlirian had killed with impunity; he had been spared in court by a sense of greater justice.

Inevitably other assassinations followed: on 19 July 1921, in Constantinople, Misak Torlakian assassinated Jivanshir, the Minister of the Interior of Azerbaijan (considered responsible for the massacre of Armenians at Baku); on 6 December 1921, in Rome, Arshavir Shirakian killed Said Halim Pasha, the Grand Vizier at the time of the deportations, shooting him through the head while Said Halim took a taxi; on 17 April 1922 in Berlin, Aram Yerganian and Arshavir Shirakian murdered Behaeddin Shakir and Jemal Azmir, two leaders of the 'Special Organisation' that had administered the massacres; in July, Stepan Dzaghigian and others assassinated Djemal Pasha in Tiflis.[67] (A second wave of Armenian assassinations of Turkish diplomats and their families followed in the 1970s and 1980s.)

To the dismay of the Turks, as had happened with Tehlirian, Torlakian, Jivanshir's killer, enjoyed an unexpected reprieve, acquitted by a British court martial, with the judgment confirmed by Sir Charles Harington, the Commander-in-Chief of the allied occupation forces. The mitigating factor was the belief that Torlakian had acted alone and had been crazed by the massacre of his family by the Turks.[68]

This wave of murders casts doubt on the notion, central to the story outlined at the trial, that Tehlirian had no accomplices. Another reading of the events would be that the killings were organised by a network of Armenian revolutionaries (the Armenian Revolutionary Federation, or the Dashnaks); in this view, Tehlirian was no isolated killer, but an agent in an international conspiracy.[69] At least one Turkish writer has suggested that Tehlirian's killing of Talât Pasha was sponsored by the British and Russian secret services, both of whom wanted a weakened Turkey, and so feared the exiled Pasha's influence on international Islamic opinion and hence on the probable outcome of peace negotiations.[70] (It is undoubtedly the case that British officials believed Talât Pasha to be guilty and that he should have been tried and executed by a court of law – though this is by no means the same thing as contriving his extra-judicial murder.[71])

In any case precedents for vengeance had been established. In Paris, on 25 May 1926, Shalom Schwartzbard killed Simon Petlyura, a man responsible for pogroms against the Jews in the Ukraine during 1917–20, in which as many as 100,000 had died.[72] Schwartzbard gave himself up, and when evidence of the atrocities was presented by the defence at his trial, like Tehlirian he was swiftly acquitted.

Tehlirian spent many years in Yugoslavia, and time in Algeria and France, before ending up in America; he died on 23 May 1960 in San Francisco. There remains the clear possibility that Tehlirian's deed was not that of a solitary and grief-stricken man, but a move in an organised campaign of retribution. Its place in such a campaign would make Tehlirian's crime appear quite different, as a premeditated and orchestrated matter. However, the murder's essential nature as the retribution of the weak against the strong would remain unchanged.

Tehlirian's assassination of Talât Pasha was a murder committed in the absence of any international law that could have otherwise effected justice. Tehlirian acted outside the law, because he 'was a member of an ethnic group that did not possess its own state and legal system' and 'there was no tribunal in the world to which [he] could have brought [his] victim'.[73]

Genocides are a form of war, and thrive in wars, which gift ideology with opportunity. Assassinations are expressions of fractured peace. They are solitary gestures, political acts committed by the powerless. Of course, this excludes for the moment political murders performed during *coups d'état*, government purges and state-sponsored killings. The Armenian assassinations were the justice of the helpless. The impotence and inferiority that some Armenian theorists have seen as being one of the two root causes of the genocide were here transmuted into power.[74] The Armenian assassinations differ in this sense from the murders carried out by the Israelis following the Munich Olympics massacre. In that case, a nation behaved like the nationless; in their vendetta against the stateless Palestinians, they mirrored their enemy's tactics.

The historian Robert Melson says we must distinguish between the nationalism of the Young Turks and the nationalism of the Armenians, 'between the views of the perpetrators and those of the victims'.[75] But, leaving aside the horrors of the massacres themselves, if that were possible, what is the difference simply in terms of their nationalism as such? In comparing the Turks and the Armenians, a nationalism with power confronts a nationalism without. On one side stand the Turks with access to the structures of command, military support and police interventions, and on the other, the Armenians with recourse only to assassination, desertion, or the might of another power.

Yet if the Armenians hooked their weakness to the Russians' strength, then the Turks similarly attached themselves to Germany's military vigour. With the Armenian atrocities in mind, after the war this alliance between Turkey and Germany took on the appearance of collusion.

Anxiety regarding the wartime connection to Turkey is one reason why a Berlin court acquitted Tehlirian, an assassin who was so plainly guilty. With the war over, German soldiers, politicians and writers sought to distance themselves from the massacres. The German General Liman von Sanders, who had been put in charge of the Turkish Army at the end of 1913, declared of the Turks that they 'were certainly not alive to the conceptions of European civilisation'.[76] (Within five years of his publishing these words, the National Socialists would have set up Dachau.) Regarding the massacres Sanders affirmed that the Germans, and particularly he himself, were clean.[77]

Such assertions perhaps concealed a murkier past. According to a leading historian of the Armenian genocide, Vahakn Dadrian, the Germans were complicit in the massacres. Germany might have let the atrocities pass, as they thwarted Russian designs on the region, disposed of a presumed hostile internal population, echoed racial prejudice of their own (the Armenians were an 'alien' people, like the Jews), or strengthened Turkey as a power in Asia Minor and the Caucasus, as it retreated from its former European territories.[78] Undoubtedly some Germans 'on the ground' may have participated in the deportation and, on rare occasions, the massacre of Armenians.[79] Otherwise, while some Germans protested against the atrocities, they were constrained by questions of tact in dealing with their ally.[80]

The decision to free Tehlirian answered the question of German guilt. The defence explicitly stated that a not guilty verdict would show the world that Germany had not been an accomplice in the massacres.[81] Tehlirian's acquittal therefore exculpated Germany, which became in retrospect an innocent and warning spectator to genocide. Moreover, the verdict allied the Germans not with the Turks, but on a symbolic level with the Armenians themselves. Both were righteous nationalists; both victims of unjust victors (as Germany stood in relation to the Allies, so Armenia was with Turkey). Finally, the court was enabled implicitly to discredit further the conditions of the Versailles peace treaty. It was a very satisfactory procedure. Even those on the left could feel contented, glad to have seen a blow struck against militarism and a rebuke administered to the unjust.

The astonishment of Tehlirian's acquittal is therefore to be understood not just through its relationship to the horrors committed in Turkey during the war. Rather it belongs with a profusion of political murders committed in Germany at this time. Tehlirian was treated by the court like a Freikorps member: and as such he was exonerated though plainly guilty.

II: A Prelude of Murders

We had fed the heart on fantasies,
The heart's grown brutal from the fare;
More substance in our enmities
Than in our love; oh, honey-bees
Come build in the empty house of the stare.

W. B. YEATS FROM 'MEDITATIONS IN TIME OF CIVIL WAR', 1922

In May 1920, Max Reinhardt's spectacular Berlin production of Shakespeare's *Julius Caesar* could not have been more topical. While Caesar was stabbed on stage and fell step by step down the long stairway leading to his throne, outside Germany descended into a Roman chaos of political killing.[82] At the time, as Reinhardt's innovative theatre itself demonstrated, the Weimar Republic was the fulcrum of modernity, the most 'advanced' nation in Europe.[83] Yet assassinations were this modernity's most telling expression.

Such murders were not confined to Germany. In the early 1920s, across Europe destabilising assassinations flourished. To take only four of the most prominent examples: in 1921 in Madrid Anarchists gunned down the Spanish Prime Minister Eduardo Dato e Iradier; in December 1922, after only five days in office, Gabriel Narutowicz, the President of Poland, was murdered by a right-wing painter in Warsaw's Zachęta National Gallery of Art; in 1923, during a *coup d'état* the Bulgarian Prime Minister, Aleksandar Stamboliyski, was tortured, murdered and decapitated; on 10 June 1924, following impassioned denouncements of Mussolini's tactics of fraud, corruption and intimidation, Giacomo Matteoti, the leader of the United Socialist Party, was kidnapped and murdered – stabbed with a carpenter's file in his chest.[84]

Nonetheless, conditions in Germany were especially extreme. The war and the subsequent dismantling of the monarchy had ruptured the continuity of German political life. A new Social Democratic government endeavoured to create a new order for Germany, but enemies surrounded them and contradiction confounded their attempt. The Weimar Republic was suspected by the Communists and derided by most nationalists and those on the right. Dismay at the monarchy's collapse, despair at German defeat, contempt for the new leaders, suspicion of 'Jewish influence', all combined to enfeeble the new government.[85] The impact of turbulent economic conditions and resentment at the Allied nations' punitive peace terms quickened the collapse of civilised standards. In particular, the trauma of the trenches had erased 'the deep rooted belief in the sacredness of human life'.[86] Both right and left experienced the failure of capitalism, and (as far as some were concerned) the effectiveness of democratic government to manage the unprecedented crisis.[87]

In the midst of this political turmoil, a number of small-scale organisations and parties sprang up. The *Wandervogel* and youth movements of the pre-war period had split by 1919 into myriad marginal left-wing factions, a beleaguered centre, and a substantial nationalist and anti-Communist right. The movements split and re-formed into ever smaller and more disparate factions.[88] Secret societies of the young burgeoned. There were regimental assemblies, rambling groups, professional guilds, officers' clubs.[89] Some were harmless, mystical, or sporty; others variously nurtured an agenda of nationalism, anti-Semitism, imperialism, monarchism and violence.[90] These organisations were not convened for the sake of plotting assassinations, but they became fertile ground for conspiracies.[91] Moreover, influenced perhaps by the example of the Freikorps, some of these new bands began to take on a paramilitary aspect.[92] (The Freikorps were volunteer militia groups set up to combat the Communists during the revolution of 1919. They were ill-disciplined, nationalistic and often vicious, composed in part from those who had not been deemed suitable to enlist earlier in the war.[93])

Clusters of militants were keen to kill for their beliefs. So it was that soon after the collapse signalled by the end of the war, political murder became a frequent occurrence.[94] A wave of violence swept the nation. The typical *Feme* assassin was young, Bavarian and middle-class in origin, and very often had been a junior officer in the last years of the war.[95] The assassins' youth (one of those who killed Rathenau was in his mid-teens, while his co-conspirators were only in their early twenties) itself followed the breakdown in authority.

The murderers offered a parody of *die Feme* justice. The original '*Feme*' courts belonged to the German middle ages and consisted of bands of men who, believing that the country was corrupt, had forged their own secret social realm, a true Germany. Here they made and enforced, usually by death sentence, their own laws (*das Femegericht*).[96]

Tinged by romantic memories of Goethe's *Götz von Berchlingen* (1773), the modern versions of *die Feme* sought to reproduce this clandestine judiciary in 1920s Germany.[97] It was medievalism with machine guns; the members of the *Bünde*, the clubs and organisations that formed the ground of *die Feme*, gazed back to a world that they imagined as the essential roots of the fatherland. The recovery of the archaic and the *völkisch* was for them one defining impulse in the violence that followed.

A '*Femetat*' or a '*Fememord*' therefore was an act of vigilante justice, ordered by a group which saw itself as righteously punishing transgressors against the German nation.[98] At the University of Heidelberg, the statistician Emil Julius Gumbel diligently collected the facts of these murders in a series of books. While most have stated their accuracy to be indisputable, a few have remarked that Gumbel was himself a doctrinaire Marxist and therefore, it is implied, no impartial witness.[99] Later in the 1920s Gumbel himself fell victim to right-wing bullying within the university, after suggesting that German soldiers in the Great War had lost their lives uselessly.[100] Only a public apology saved him from a charge of treason.[101]

Gumbel's most striking accusation was that the courts refrained from punishing assassins from the right. Judges habitually acquitted such men; many did not even face charges. Murderers from the left (there were far fewer of them) were far more liable to receive guilty verdicts; when found guilty, they received far harsher punishment.[102] Between 1919 and the murder of Rathenau in 1922, Germany suffered 376 political assassinations. Of these, according to Gumbel, 354 were undertaken by the right, and 22 by the left. Here it should be pointed out that the very low score of left-wing murders could be evidence of Gumbel's political bias, while the very high score by the right might be down to a vagueness about just what constitutes a political murder.[103] Gumbel's melancholy list of killings made nothing happen. The Minister of Justice, Gustav Radbruch, for the most part confirmed Gumbel's claims, yet not one additional murderer was punished.[104] It is indisputably correct that there were very many killers and that those few on the left were more often convicted and received heavy prison sentences, while those many on the right were very often acquitted or given very light sentences. The reasons for the bias are not hard to find, though it remains incredible that partiality could stretch so far.

The Weimar Republic's judges were appointees from the days of the Wilhelmine Reich.[105] They were middle- and upper-class in origin, and very often conservative, monarchist, nationalist, and anti-Semitic.[106]

Undoubtedly, the murder of Karl Liebknecht and Rosa Luxemburg by members of the Freikorps set the precedent for such unpunished crimes. Liebknecht and Luxemburg were the heads of the Spartakusbund, the most prominent Communist members of an organisation that in late 1918 and the early days of 1919 encouraged (somewhat ineptly) a spontaneous workers' revolt against the centre-left Social Democratic government. Handbills called for the murder of the pair; the right-wing and Social Democratic press joined the chorus of vilification, similarly inciting their assassination.[107] On the evening of 15 January 1919, in Berlin, they were discovered at their hide-out in an apartment in Wilmersdorf, arrested and brought to the Eden Hotel in the city centre.[108] That night, in a room on the first floor, Luxemburg was interrogated.[109] The next day both Luxemburg and Liebknecht were separately taken out and struck hard on the head with a rifle butt. Then they were bundled into a car and driven to the Tiergarten; Liebknecht was murdered in the park itself, while Luxemburg was shot in the back of the car. Near the entrance to the zoo, Luxemburg's body was thrown into the freezing waters of the Landwehr Canal.[110]

Scandalously, most guessed early on that the government had done more than turn a blind eye to the assassinations.[111] After all, Friedrich Ebert, the leader of that government, had 'sold out' to the military and permitted the Freikorps to quash the rebellion with whatever violence was necessary and, above all, to dispose of its leaders.[112] In Berlin at the time of Luxemburg and Liebknecht's murders, the Freikorps were following the orders of the SPD's Gustav Noske, a former butcher.[113] This collusion on the part of the Social Democrats began a process of disillusionment within the left regarding the integrity and good faith of their government.

All those who killed Liebknecht were absolved of the crime. Only a few of Luxemburg's murderers faced retribution: most escaped, one received two years in prison (for attempted manslaughter). Such sentences provided the most feeble of deterrents. Only two months after these murders, a third leader of the Spartakusbund, Leo Jogiches, was shot in the back while under arrest in a Berlin police station.[114]

Such acts were typical of the 'White Terror', blurring the lines between expedient assassination and summary justice.[115]

On 21 February 1919, another prominent politician of the left, Kurt Eisner, the Independent Socialist Minister-President of the Bavarian government, was assassinated.[116] He was shot dead on the street while making his way to the opening of the Landtag (the regional parliament); he was about to offer his resignation.[117] Eisner had been at the head of a revolutionary government that, exploiting the power vacuum created by defeat, had assumed power in the week before the declaration of the Armistice. The months that followed had seen Eisner's political power weaken after elections reduced his party's strength. His murderer was Graf (Count) Anton von Arco-Valley, a young ex-Army officer, then currently a law student in Munich's university. The propaganda value of the act was evident: a son of the Bavarian nobility had dealt with a socialist Berlin Jew.[118] (The fact that Arco-Valley was himself part-Jewish could be safely forgotten.) Eisner's death introduced a period of anarchic instability in Bavaria that led to the brief rule of a Communist (and pro-Bolshevik) administration that April, and then the bloody toppling of left-wing rule by the Freikorps. Many notable Anarchists and Communists were murdered and many more imprisoned. The painful paradox that these right-wing Army units had been called in by a socialist government in Berlin in order to suppress a left-wing revolution in Bavaria further split the left.

Eisner's eminence made his killing exceptionally striking. However, he was only one among many assassinated in Bavaria. Other victims included Max Weinberger, Ernst Lacher, and Georg Graf.[119] In May 1922, Dr Karl Horn, a professor of mathematics and physics, was murdered on Stadelheimerstrasse in Munich.[120] Such instances could be multiplied. Left-wing journalists, academics, lawyers, and bank-workers were singled out, and shot. Twelve workers in the Perlach district of Munich were taken out onto a heap of coal and, one by one, murdered.[121] Perhaps over a thousand people were slaughtered.[122]

The next distinguished target for assassination was Matthias Erzberger. Born in 1875 in Swabia, Erzberger was a devout Catholic who had grown up in a mostly Protestant and Jewish region.[123] During the war, as a member of the Centre Party, he had been in charge of foreign propaganda. From 1919, he was Finance Minister in the new government. In the public mind he was associated with policies of conciliation with the Allies and with democracy; both rendered him a hate-figure to the right.[124] He was frequently singled out for rhetorical abuse in the inflammatory speeches of the rising star of the DAP (German Workers' Party), Adolf Hitler.[125]

Erzberger's position as Finance Minister ended in equivocal disgrace. By means of a series of scathing newspaper pieces, his political nemesis, Karl Helfferich, the leader of the German nationalists, goaded him into fighting a libel trial to save his good name.[126] This proved a catastrophic miscalculation. In court, between January and March 1920, the details of Erzberger's life and political dealings were ruthlessly pored over. He was forced daily to answer Helfferich's numerous and florid accusations, mostly concerning half-truths about the man they were intended to bring down; an atmosphere of guilt began to cling to Erzberger. Erzberger's prosecution team closed the trial with speeches that were in effect indictments of the man they were supposed to be exonerating. These lawyers, like those in the gallery and on the bench, were ideologically opposed to all that Erzberger and the democratic government stood for.[127]

One incident in particular exposes the complicity between the legal system and those who opposed the government. At the end of the first week of the trial, inspired by Helfferich's accusations, a young ex-soldier named Oltwig von Hirschfeld attempted to assassinate Erzberger as he left the court. He fired two shots at the politician; one struck him in the right shoulder, the other ricocheted off a gold watch hanging over his chest. While Helfferich's trial for libel continued, Hirschfeld, his youthful disciple, faced a judge on charges of attempted murder. The court sympathised with the young man's upstanding rigour and baffled virtue. The disbanding of the Army had wrecked his career prospects; his quest to find the people responsible for his own predicament and the nation's troubles had led him, via Helfferich's defamatory articles, to blame Erzberger. Hirschfeld pleaded guilty to an attempt to wound Erzberger, and received a sentence of a mere eighteen months.[128] In April 1921, Hirschfeld was released temporarily from prison on grounds of mental ill-health; he never returned to jail.[129]

Erzberger himself was not to receive so benevolent a verdict. While he was able to prove most of Helfferich's accusations to be libels, he was considered guilty in enough cases (particularly of inappropriately mixing business with politics) to leave his reputation permanently stained. Helfferich was ordered to pay a minimal sum of 300 marks as damages (the figure was so low because the judge deemed that the plaintiff had acted from patriotic motives). Erzberger had no option but to resign.[130]

There followed a period in which Erzberger tried to rehabilitate himself and return to the centre of power. These efforts were to be cruelly cut short. Erzberger had survived, by a kind of fluke, one assassination attempt. He knew the perils inherent in supporting the new republic. There were specific police warnings; he had been advised to carry a revolver and to learn how to use it – something that his Christian beliefs forbade him from doing.[131] He spent July and August 1921 holidaying with his family in the Black Forest. On 26 August they were staying at Bad Griesbach. That day Erzberger went out walking on the Kniebis mountain with a friend, when they were overtaken by two strangers, who drew revolvers and shot the politician at point-blank range. He was hit in the chest and forehead. When Erzberger's friend attempted to intervene he too was shot in the chest. Trying to escape, Erzberger leapt down the slope by the roadside. The assassins fired more shots as Erzberger tried to hide among the pine trees below. He was struck three more times, in the lungs, the stomach and leg. He collapsed and the killers came down to where he lay and, with three more shots, finished him off.[132] The wounded friend crawled and staggered back down the mountain path to the hotel. Finally he came upon a wealthy woman also holidaying at Bad Griesbach. He told her what had taken place up on the mountain. 'How *could* you go walking with a man like Erzberger!' she replied.[133]

While many expressed grief for Erzberger's loss, this woman's retort was characteristic of popular responses to the murder. In considering the two killers' exploit, the Prussian newspaper *Kreuzzeitung* invoked all the customary favourable figures of tyrannicide: Charlotte Corday, Brutus, Wilhelm Tell.[134] With the connivance of members of the Bavarian police, Erzberger's assassins (Heinrich Schulz and Heinrich Tillessen) were allowed to linger for days in Munich before fleeing to Hungary, where the government refused to extradite them. As usual, both were ex-Army officers. At home in Germany, prosecutions against the remaining conspirators either faltered or failed to happen at all.[135] Crowds celebrated the assassination in the streets.[136]

Such reactions were common. When Kurt Eisner's assassin, Count Arco-Valley, had his death sentence commuted to a five-year prison term, a group of left-wing students protested against the injustice. They were roughly handled in front of their university's rector, who failed to intervene. When Max Weber, the celebrated sociologist, spoke out in his turn against the mistreatment of the students, he too became the victim of intimidation.[137] This was despite the fact that Weber was far more sympathetic to Arco-Valley than he had been to Eisner, though he certainly disapproved of the assassin's pardon, a breach of the law that could only ensure that, as he put it, 'Political murders will become the fashion.'[138]

If Erzberger's killing laid bare the pressure that the new republic was under, then the assassination of Walther Rathenau signalled more clearly than any other such murder the untenable strains that democracy faced in post-war Germany.

Rathenau was a political neurotic, exhibiting the conflicts of his position (industrialist and critic of capitalism, Jew and Prussian, superman and businessman, writer and politician) to a largely indifferent public. All who cared to know knew everything about his troubles in following the success of his brilliant father, Emil Rathenau, a self-made millionaire who had founded the electrical company AEG. He took slights to heart, fretting, for instance, that Lloyd George had snubbed him during post-war negotiations at Genoa. Nonetheless his career was a prestigious one. Following a cabinet crisis in late 1921 (brought on by the redrawing by the Allied victors of the frontiers of Upper Silesia), in January 1922 Chancellor Wirth appointed Rathenau as Foreign Minister.[139]

Having pursued his attack on Erzberger in June 1922 in the Reichstag, Helfferich went on the offensive against Rathenau, another old opponent.[140] Rathenau's position rendered him vulnerable to such onslaughts. Anti-Semitism seems to have been one motivation for the nationalists' loathing.[141] In the meeting-halls and beer-cellars, right-wing students and members of the *Bünde* were singing a murderous jingle: '*Knallt ab den Walther Rathenau | Die gottverfluchte Judensau*' ('Pick off [i.e. shoot] Walther Rathenau | The Goddamned Jewish sow').[142] More insidiously, the industrialist Hugo Stinnes's attack on Rathenau as possessing the soul of an alien race ('*eine fremdrassige Seele*') expressed the same prejudice.[143]

Rathenau came back from a conference at Genoa (May 1922) where he had conducted further negotiations concerning German reparations, and had signed the Treaty of Rapallo with the Soviet Union. His policy of fulfilling the conditions of Versailles [*Erfüllungspolitik*] led directly to his murder.[144] Rathenau perceived the danger of the path he was pursuing and, in moments, welcomed it.[145] Both his mother and his friend Albert Einstein warned him that he might pay for his prominence with his life; a priest reported a murder plot that he had learnt of in the confessional.[146] Like others in the administration, he was receiving menacing letters.[147] But it was not just a matter of letters. On 4 June 1922, shortly after his resignation, former Reich President Philipp Scheidemann was assaulted in a wood near Kassel (where Scheidemann was mayor); two men flung prussic acid in the old man's face.[148] Though the plan failed (saved by the low concentration of acid, a fortuitous mountain breeze and the fact that he had scared off his attackers with his revolver), their aim had been to kill.[149] These were dangerous times.

Supporters counselled Rathenau to go to Switzerland and avoid the risks of being 'eliminated' at home. Chancellor Wirth advised him to make sure he travelled with police detectives as security. Rathenau considered these precautions to be cowardly. Perhaps he feared such measures would frighten his elderly mother. Perhaps he felt old, too weary to stave off the threatened blow.[150] In any case, Rathenau was taking precautions of his own: shortly after he was named as Foreign Minister an acquaintance asked him, 'how's it going?', and Rathenau pulled out a Browning revolver, and replied, 'it's going like this!'[151] More than anything Rathenau prized a peculiarly Germanic vision of greatness of soul. There were elements of Nietzschean pride in his self-image, a lonely, self-realising nobility. He could not resist the suspicion that there was something cringing in caring too greatly for his own life. Fear of the coming killing awarded the sneering assassin a premature victory. Better a dead lion than a living dog. He would rather take the blow than cower in expectation of it.

On 23 June 1922, he took the blow.

Not the least of the ironies of the situation is that, according to the historian James Joll, Rathenau's rhetoric resembled at some deeper level that of his killers: one that sought a new beginning and a new purpose for Germany.[152] As Peter Berglar put it, with his passion for Nietzsche and his interest in Spengler, it hardly requires an especial effort to distil from Rathenau's own writings and remarks the mentality of his murderers.[153] His ideal was a lost Prussian form of nobility.[154] One of his assassins, a 25-year-old, blond, blue-eyed ex-Navy officer called Kern, was precisely the kind of man to whom Rathenau was most attracted.[155] One of the witnesses to the coming murder declared of this assassin that he had a healthy open face, an officer's face.[156]

Two young Germans, a seventeen-year-old schoolboy named Hans Stubenrauch, the son of a general, and his psychopathic student friend (and deserter) Willy Günther decided to murder Rathenau. Günther organised a meeting between Stubenrauch and another young student, the same blue-eyed D. Erwin Kern. Kern was a member of Die Organisation Consul, a right-wing group that had emerged from the wreckage of the Kapp Putsch, and that had probably set up the murder of Erzberger.[157] He also had previously served as a naval officer, reaching the rank of Oberleutnant-zur-See. Kern rejected Stubenrauch as too young and too ineffectual, and took over the conspiracy. With a group of other young men Kern schemed to murder Rathenau. The conspirators included Günther, Kern's friend Hermann Fischer, the 21-year-old Ernst Werner Techow, a middle-class youth, and his sixteen-year-old brother, Hans Gerd Techow. (The teenager had been a member of Organisation Consul since he was fifteen.) On 18 June 1922 they met at the apartment where the younger Techow lived with his mother, and plotted their attack. They would follow Rathenau's car in their own car (a blue one lent to them by one Johannes Küchenmeister), and shoot the Foreign Minister as they drove past.[158] Doubting whether they would be accurate enough to hit Rathenau in this way, they went out two days later to suburban Grunewald, the forest at the western edge of Berlin, and there practised shooting among the quiet of the trees. Kern decided to obtain a submachine gun from a rightist ex-sea cadet named Ilsemann (who had been involved in the Kapp Putsch).

The night before the planned murder, while Rathenau dined at the American embassy, the conspirators went out and drank beer, wine and cognac. They discussed the reasons why Rathenau had to die: Rathenau sided with the Bolsheviks; he had submitted to the shame of Versailles; he brought a Jewish influence into Germany.

The next morning, 24 June 1922, Rathenau was late leaving his villa in Grunewald for the office. It was just before 11.00 on a warm Sunday; when at last he and his driver left, they drove out with the top down.[159] The conspirators were waiting in their car on Königsallee, near the corner of Wallotstrasse. Here the road curves in the shape of an S, and cars must slow down. Kern had his submachine gun, Fischer a hand grenade; Ernst Werner Techow would drive. They were dressed in leather coats and caps. Rathenau's driver slowed to negotiate the bend. The conspirators' car bore down on it from behind, pulled alongside and Kern opened fire. Nearby workmen took cover. When Fischer threw his grenade, Rathenau had already sunk lower in his seat, turning on his side, already struck. Rathenau's car ground to a halt on Erdenerstrasse, its driver calling for help. The car with the conspirators sped off. Only then did the grenade explode. The driver was knocked over by the blast and the car jumped. A young girl – by chance a nurse – ran up to help, but it was too late. Rathenau was almost dead; the end would be soon in coming.[160] After the deed was done, Techow went on to his tennis club.[161]

The conspirators were picked up one by one. Kern and Fischer were found by the police at the house of Hans Wilhelm Stein, a writer. Kern was killed in the police gunfire; Fischer shot himself.[162] The others were soon arrested. Letters from prominent politicians, including General Ludendorff and Karl Helfferich, were found in Günther's possession.[163] An accomplice sent a box of pralines, poisoned with arsenic, to Günther in prison. The taken men were to do the honourable thing. Günther shared the pralines with his co-defendants, but though they fell sick they lived to face trial. The older Techow brother was sentenced to fifteen years' penal servitude (*Zuchthaus*) and ten years' loss of civil rights (*Ehrverlust*); his younger brother received four years and one month in prison. Günther earned a penalty of eight years' penal servitude, and ten years' loss of civil rights.[164]

More than any other of '*die Feme*' assassinations, Rathenau's murder shocked Germany.[165] In the Reichstag, Joseph Wirth, the Chancellor, declared: 'There sits the enemy, where Mephisto dribbles his poison into the wounds of the people, there is no doubt this enemy is sitting on the right.'[166] However, some have argued that, in practical terms, the shock soon petered out; it was simply business as usual.[167] In an issue of *Der Welt Spiegel* published the day after Rathenau's funeral, there appeared a page of photographs of the recently assassinated: Liebknecht in silhouette; Rosa Luxemburg; a bespectacled, smiling Kurt Eisner; the murdered Anarchist philosopher Gustav Landauer; a pensive Mathias Erzberger.[168]

Battle-lines hardened. In the Reichstag, Helfferich was taunted as a 'murderer'.[169] Yet in the universities, student groups announced their solidarity with Rathenau's murderers.[170] Einstein quit Germany, declaring that the move would 'take me away from temporarily increased danger'.[171]

Rathenau's death soon acquired the aura of fatalism. His killing appeared to manifest the impossibility of Weimar and democracy. The subtitle of Ernst Schulin's 1979 biography of Rathenau expresses this most clearly, seeing the dead man as a 'representative, critic and sacrifice of his time'.[172] His death was perhaps his greatest political achievement; his assassination was his legacy. In the future he could stand for the suppression of a good Germany, about to go under through the Nazis' onslaught. Dying meant not compromising with the future. He became in the moment of his murder not the equivocal, failing man he had always been, but a brilliant symbol of something valuable and forlorn.

But the violence would not stop with Rathenau. Just over a fortnight after his death, a similar fate nearly overtook his one-time friend, the journalist and writer Maximilian Harden. (Rathenau and Harden had fallen out after the Great War. In 1918 Harden wanted an early peace, while Rathenau's views earned him a reputation as someone who wished to prolong the fighting.[173]) Harden was most famous for his 'outing' in 1907 of prominent homosexuals among the Kaiser's closest advisers and the top ranks of the Army – a tactic with consequences which he himself later saw as leading to the First World War.

On the evening of 3 July 1922, two men attacked Harden just outside his Grunewald home. He was stabbed and struck many times, leaving him with several wounds in the head. He was sixty years old. For fourteen days, he was close to dying. Afterwards, he felt as though his attackers, these lads, had destroyed everything that he had built up over his long career.[174] The two men were soon caught. Anti-Semitic literature was found in their rooms, along with a list of potential murder victims.[175] While clearly motivated by political ideals, the would-be murderers (Walter Ankermann, another ex-Army officer, and Herbert Weichardt) had also been well paid for their task.[176] Harden's Jewishness was allowed to be taken into consideration as a mitigating factor in the crime. The jury decided that the inflammatory nature of Harden's articles also extenuated the attempted murder; the two assassins received minimal prison sentences.

Out of the disorder of the years 1919–24 emerged the conditions in which Nazism prospered. Although distinct from the National Socialists, the killers of *die Feme* would reposition themselves in time as members of the Nazi Party, or find themselves turned into heroes by Hitler's regime. Klintzsch, an ex-Army officer, was at least one of those probably involved in Rathenau's assassination who also had links to Hitler.[177] In November 1923, a failed Nazi *Putsch* saw Hitler put in prison. Symbolically, he displaced from his cell (No. 7) Graf Arco-Valley, the assassin of Eisner, one of the killings that had started it all.[178] When the Nazis assumed power in 1933, Schulz and Tillessen, Erzberger's assassins, returned from 'exile' in Hungary, and were acclaimed as 'Erzberger's judges'.[179] Yet in some cases, the Nazis were ready to honour the victims as well as the perpetrators of assassination: in 1943, by order of Hitler, Talât Pasha's body was exhumed and sent to Istanbul for re-burial.

Writing in a foreword to Gumbel's *Zwei Jahre Mord* (1921), Professor G. F. Nicolai declared that from its beginning assassination had played a vital role in German history.[180] For instance, in the late 1870s and early 1880s there had been a wave of brutal Anarchist-inspired killings. Yet clearly the horrors of *die Feme* were also something unprecedented. How far was *die Feme* a precursor to the violence of the Nazi regime that followed? For a few decades, though the idea is largely unfashionable now, historians talked of Germany pursuing a *Sonderweg*, or special path.[181] In one sense, there was nothing special or *besonders* about the spate of politically motivated murders in Germany. Such killings matched the tactics already employed decades before by Russian Nihilists and international Anarchists, as well as various nationalist movements. The assassins' light sentences were also familiar:

a Russian jury acquitted Vera Zasulich and in the early 1920s there was a wave of amazing courtroom decisions: French juries on occasion freed Anarchist murderers (including Germaine Berton) and, as we have seen, several courts refused to convict Armenian and Ukrainian revengers. Nonetheless, the tacit support of the German legal system, particularly its judges, for the right-wing assassins was, in my reading at least, new. As was happening throughout Europe and Japan, the violence in Germany largely came from the right, a consequence of opposition to the democratic process as such. This opposition united both right and left, and sealed the similarity of their tactics. Like the Anarchists before them, these German killers wished to see the downfall of the rulers, but in the German case only so as to bring on a more authoritarian national government. Undoubtedly the wave of assassinations helped to further a belief that democracy could not function in Germany. Paradoxically the disorder damaged the sitting government more than it did the popularity of the assassins. All those who disliked the Treaty of Versailles, which was at most times a sizeable number of German citizens, could find themselves sympathetic to the murderers. This violence responded to recent events – in particular the education in killing offered by the Western and Eastern Fronts. Only in their own eyes did the right-wing assassins amount to a longer-established, peculiarly German force.

In any case, the havoc produced by *die Feme* was trivial in comparison to the collapse of civilised norms brought in by the Nazis. Yet the modest mayhem practised in Germany between 1919 and 1924 gave a glimpse of the way the world was heading. The Nazis did not exactly legalise assassination; they simply ignored the legal consequences of their acts. On a theoretical level, they redefined the status of the 'legal' itself, which became a purely ideological condition of adherence to Nazi intentions, a matter of the legitimising power to act. When, on 30 June 1934, the Nazis carried out a murderous 'purge' around 400 people were killed. Among them were prominent Nazis and political figures: Ernst Röhm, whose homosexuality had made him a liability, Kurt von Schleicher, a former Reich Chancellor, and Gregor Strasser. The tactics of *die Feme* had become the instrument of the state itself.

Less than a month after that 'night of the long knives', the new politics of assassination received their most disquieting expression so far in Germany's neighbour Austria. Here, in the early 1930s, Chancellor Engelbert Dollfuss tried his 'experiments with state-patriotism', enforcing a Fascist state in order to avoid a Nazi take-over, and then paying the price. Dollfuss had grown up in a family of devoutly Catholic peasant farmers. He was tiny in stature, just 4 foot II inches tall, uncertain of his status in the world: he was born to a single mother, and though she married later, he remained subtly apart from his half-brothers and sister. He saw service in the First World War, leading a machine-gun unit in the mountain fighting against the Italians. Post-war, he pursued conservative Catholic politics, moving from a sentimental pan-Germanism to a growing determination to keep Austria free from German influence. He rose through the ranks, promoting agricultural reform, overseeing the railways, then assuming a position as Minister for Agriculture, before, in May 1932, becoming Chancellor. Despising both Marxists and Nazis, as leader of the Christian-Social Party he steered what seemed a middle course of 'Catholic' fascism, tinged by the legacy of Karl Lueger, reactionary, anti-democratic, acceptably anti-Semitic.[182]

For a time the Christian-Social Party worked with the right-wing paramilitary Heimwehr and other parties such as the Protestant Landbund, but, caught between growing Austrian enthusiasm for the Nazis, a Social Democrat opposition, and the mounting risk of electoral defeat, Dollfuss gave up on party politics altogether and chose dictatorship. He shelved parliament (although during a farcical debate on 4 March 1933, it had in any case shelved itself), clamped down on the press, banned protest and cancelled all further elections. Austria's great generation of writers – including Stefan Zweig and Joseph Roth – headed into exile or, in exile already, expressed their dismay.[183] First, the Communists were banned; next Dollfuss attempted accommodation with Austria's Nazis, but when they proved recalcitrant and greedy, in June 1933 he had them outlawed too.[184] Then, after armed opposition – a four-day civil war that saw fighting on the streets of Linz, Graz, Vienna, and elsewhere – in February 1934 the Social Democrats were banned too.[185] On 30 April 1934, in a special session orchestrated by Dollfuss, the national parliament voted itself out of existence; the next day, Dollfuss promulgated a new constitution in which he effectively granted himself the greatest power in the state. It was the full arrival of *Austrofaschismus*.

Despite this anti-democratic purge, Dollfuss has been seen by some as 'a pioneer of, and martyr to, the cause of a new Austrian patriotism'.[186] It is in the nature of the 1930s that, in C. Day Lewis's words, some should have to 'Defend the bad against the worse'. It is true that Dollfuss briefly and bravely held the line against Hitler's territorial ambitions; that he did so after ordering the firing of artillery against his own people, and closing down or at best suspending the elements of a free state remains his guilt. Most likely he was neither hero nor villain, but simply a man trying to reconcile the irreconcilable, hedged in by threats, and sustained by a religious faith whose political meanings, in this context, pushed him towards intransigent intolerance.

Since the summer of 1932, there had been sporadic but shocking instances of Nazi terrorism across Austria. This localised violence was the visible projection of Austrian Nazi longings that Austria must be absorbed into a greater German movement; on occasion the local Nazis had to be restrained by the Germans lest an ill-disciplined and purposeless move be made. It was clear that without fresh elections to reveal the depth of Nazi support, the local activists were too puny a force to seize power. A premature attempt at an *Anschluss* would very likely end in humiliation.[187] Meanwhile, though Mussolini deemed Dollfuss a tepid fellow Fascist, and Dollfuss resented the Duce's pompous lecturing, the two leaders squared up together in the hope of creating a southern Fascist bulwark against the northern Nazi neighbour.[188]

However, Dollfuss was battling the inevitable. He was being plotted against by Hitler's representative Theo Habicht, the head of the Austrian Nazi Party. On 24 July 1934, with Hitler's lately won permission, even though conditions were not yet fully favourable a Nazi *Putsch* was unleashed.[189] While German involvement was cautious, this was the first time that the Nazis had struck for power outside their own territory.[190] What was intended to be the first blow in a national pro-Nazi revolt fizzled out in an attempt by a couple of hundred men to wrest power from Dollfuss in Vienna. The affair was bloody and short-lived. The plan was brutally simple: they would swoop on the Chancellery and capture the entire Austrian government. On the morning of the *Putsch* various traitors to the conspiracy were busy passing on news of the impending rebellion to anyone who would listen. Word reached Dollfuss, but too late; loaded on lorries, the Nazis drove into the Chancellery through the main gate. They quickly overpowered the guards, who, being there purely for ceremonial show, had in any case no ammunition in their rifles.[191] Alarmed, Dollfuss attempted to flee with an attendant, the faithful secretary, Eduard Hedvicek. The doorkeeper took Dollfuss by the arm and they scurried to find a way out through a side exit. They found the door to their chosen escape route locked. They were attempting to unlock it when behind them a batch of insurrectionists stormed into the room.[192] Their leader, one Otto Planetta, promptly ran up to Dollfuss and shot him twice. The assassination was very likely a spur of the moment impulse, just a mistake. It was in any case the only significant achievement of the coup. Though fighting did spread beyond the capital, the *Putsch* quickly collapsed; Germany was blamed, but could claim innocence.[193] An Austrofascist successor to Dollfuss, Kurt von Schuschnigg, took over; he was still in power four years later, when Hitler drove into Vienna, and annexed the nation to the Nazi cause.

In the period such disorder, of course, went beyond the German-speaking world. In the Soviet Union, political murder had developed into an ongoing political system, one which the Nazis would soon reproduce in their own terms. In Romania, in 1933, an assassin shot down the Premier, Ion Duca; in 1938, the King ordered the murder of the fascist leader Corneliu Codreanu (himself a former assassin). Japan underwent its own political disintegration as a series of high-level assassinations by ultra-nationalists wrecked the chance of establishing a multi-party democracy; between 1931 and 1936 three Japanese prime ministers were murdered. It was such dishonourable and destabilising murders that made the July 1944 plotters hesitate before initiating their own assassination attempt against Hitler.

Such violence in Europe and elsewhere seemed a symptom of democracy's decay. In the post-war era, the continuation of this violence, particularly in the explosion of radical terrorism between the late 1960s and the 1980s, would continue to foster this sense of liberal democracy's failure. The terrorists implied that the old countries of Europe were moribund, and the political assassinations they chose to commit were merely one of the plainer signs of that decline.

Yet in those post-war years the most surprising and telling development in the history of assassination was to be the excess of political murders that would take place in the USA, the international beacon

Claus Schenk Graf von Stauffenberg (*left*), would-be assassin, standing to attention, with Adolf Hitler, his intended victim. Field Marshal Wilhelm Keitel, Hitler's military chief of staff, stands on the right.

After the failed assassination attempt, a German soldier holds up Hitler's bomb-damaged trousers.

Lewis Payne, John Wilkes Booth's co-conspirator, and the would-be assassin of William H. Seward, the Secretary of State.

The young Queen Victoria, the target of many assassination attempts.

Vera Zasulich, Nihilist heroine.

Charles Julius Guiteau, the assassin of President James Garfield.

Henry Clay Frick, industrialist, art collector, and target for an assassination attempt.

Alexander Berkman, Frick's would-be assassin, photographed in 1890.

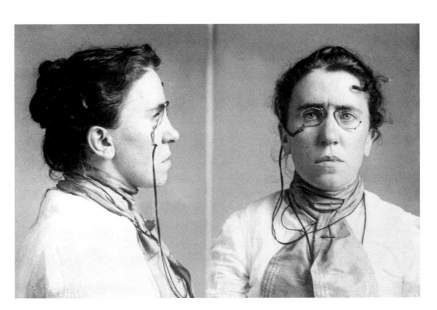

Mug-shots of Emma Goldman, Anarchist thinker, taken in 1901, while she was under arrest on suspicion of complicity in the assassination of President McKinley.

Leon Czolgosz, the assassin of President William McKinley.

From left to right, in a Belgrade park in the spring of 1914, Nedeljko Čabrinović, Milan Ciganović, and Gavrilo Princip, take a break from plotting the assassination of Archduke Franz Ferdinand.

The newspaper headline, on 2 November 1950, the day after two Puerto Rican nationalists attempted to murder President Harry Truman.

FINAL DAILY NEWS 3¢

Vol. 32. No. 112   New York 17, Thursday, November 2, 1950*   96 Main+20 Brooklyn+4 Kings Pages   3 Cents

2 DIE, 3 SHOT AS PAIR TRY TO KILL TRUMAN

—Story on Page 3

Death at Truman's Doorstep. Griselio Torresola [A], one of two men who tried to shoot their way into Blair House in assassination attempt on President Truman, lies dead under hedge outside temporary White House. His gun (arrow) lies in grass. His companion, Oscar Collazo, was wounded. Three White House guards were also wounded (one of them fatally). Despite attempt on his life, Truman went on to memorial service for Sir John Dill at Arlington Cemetery [→].   —Story on page 3

(More pictures of attempted assassination in centerfold)

Cary Grant as Roger Thornhill, apparently caught red-handed after an assassination in New York's UN building in Alfred Hitchcock's *North By Northwest* (1959).

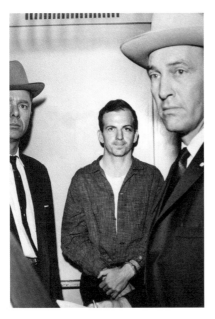

Lee Harvey Oswald, under arrest
for the killing of
President John Fitzgerald Kennedy.

James Earl Ray, the killer of
Martin Luther King (taken some
years before the murder).

Malcolm X, Muslim, radical and
assassination victim.

George Lincoln Rockwell,
the assassinated head of the
American Nazi Party.

Robert Kennedy in the
shadow of JFK.

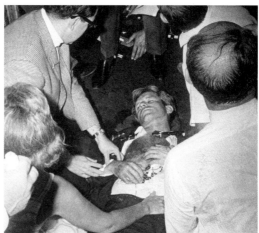

Robert Kennedy, minutes
after being shot by Sirhan
Sirhan, 4 June 1968.

Arthur Bremer, on 15 May
1972, under arrest shortly
after shooting Presidential
candidate, Governor George
Wallace.

Lynette ('Squeaky') Fromme being led into court to face trial for attempting to assassinate President Gerald Ford.

On Monday, 31 March 1981, the moment when John W. Hinckley Jr shot President Ronald Reagan.

of democracy and a country that, for all its economic distresses, had largely and robustly stood above the fray when it came to the political collapse of the 1920s and 1930s. The last part of this book must therefore focus on these dark phenomena.

PART FOUR

Fame and Death in the American Assassination
1950–1981

Celluloid Assassins

She revealed all when discussing future acting roles. 'I'd love to be an assassin. Either that or a lesbian. Maybe both,' she said yesterday. 'Hey, a gay assassin, there's nothing hotter than that.'
'RIHANNA TO GIVE GIRLS A GO?', *THE SUN*, 9 DECEMBER 2009

I: In the Chair

In 1908, Edison declared that 'Hangings, murders and violent deaths in any form should be banned' from the screen.[1] Yet only seven years before, his company had lobbied unsuccessfully to shoot Leon Czolgosz's execution, offering $2,000 for the honour.[2] In one day, short news films could be shot, processed and exhibited in Edison-licensed theatres.[3] The record of such an important moment of public vengeance could hardly be more newsworthy. However, they were turned down, and so chose to re-stage the event themselves.

Edison's interest in the execution was complicated by the fact that he had advised on the introduction of the electric chair, and had performed many of the experiments necessary for its development. The chair had been designed as a humane form of execution; Edison himself disliked capital punishment; though he was proud nonetheless to make use of his knowledge of electricity.[4]

Copyrighted on 9 November 1901, and filmed by Edwin Porter and George S. Fleming, the Edison film opens with 'A Panorama of Auburn Prison', the camera tracking slowly as a steam train passes, and behind the train, the prison walls, and smoking chimneys within. The first electrocution had taken place here over a decade before, with the gruesomely botched putting to death of an axe-murderer, William Kemmler. Shots follow of the prison buildings, the scratchy images of leafless trees; and then we are inside a bare room, with guards on the right, and a prison door on the left, a man standing half-concealed, holding the bars. The four guards march forward, and, while one fumbles with the lock, the others line up against the wall. 'Czolgosz' is led out, and escorted across the screen. The picture fades and returns with men standing around the electric chair, there in the picture's centre. 'Czolgosz' is brought to the chair; strapped in; the wires are checked; and the nod is given. As the power apparently surges through, 'Czolgosz' lifts up sadly from the chair, holds there, and then abruptly slumps back down. The process repeats. And then again. Then the doctors check his heart, and the prisoner is pronounced dead.

Somehow the very brevity of such early films can appear to bypass moral interpretation. There is simply the event itself, silently presented, without comment. And yet such movies were nonetheless infused with meanings. The blankness of the occasion itself was one such message, a human being consigned without comment to death.

Although, to this viewer at least, the film is a gloomy and disgusting one, at the time its effect on audiences appears to have been rather different. As depicted by Edison's men, the apparent painlessness of Czolgosz's death promoted the belief that electrocution was indeed a kindly method of dispatch. The silence of the film furthered this mis-apprehension. Remote and untroubled, the young assassin goes to his modern and scientific death without a scream or a sigh. Designed to replace the spectacle of hanging, the chair nonetheless remained a spectacle, although of a clinical kind.[5] The large audience for the film were no doubt thrilled.[6] Edison believed that film would replace books in education; the representation of such a moment was an education in itself.[7]

For Edison, depicting an execution was nothing unusual. Back in 1895, one of his film-makers, William Heise, produced *The Execution of Mary, Queen of Scots*. This film had, by the skilful use of editing, succeeded in appearing to show Mary's head actually being chopped off.[8] Two years after the Czolgosz film, Edison's company copyrighted a second electrocution film in which, in a cloud of smoke, an unsuspecting circus elephant, Topsy, is impressively executed. (There had been an earlier attempt to electrocute an elephant at the Buffalo Exposition where McKinley had been assassinated.[9]) At a time when executions in America could still be seen in public, the vogue for showing such moments clearly answered to a strong public curiosity. Inspired by the Boxer Rebellion, Siegmund Lubin staged *Beheading the Chinese Prisoner* (1900) in Philadelphia. One year later, while running his movie theatre at the Buffalo Pan-American Exposition, Lubin was a witness when McKinley was murdered.[10] Coincidentally, Edison's film-crew, led by James White, had filmed McKinley at Buffalo; they were lingering outside the Temple of Music when the President was shot inside.[11]

Stagings were not the only way that the public had access to such images: in 1904, the pioneering director Charles Urban shot documentary footage of the beheading of a group of Manchurian bandits; films were made and distributed of hangings, and of the guillotine in action. Urban had also caught magnified images of cheese mites on film; his camera captured the mites and the murders indifferently. Early film was a kind of vaudeville, and for all its pedagogic elements, it was rather the vision of death itself that it traded on. Within the vast range of cinematic material on offer, these films of course offered merely one item on a prodigious menu, at a time when only a few years before, the representation of almost anything on film had been a delight, the whole basis of the pleasure resting in the mechanical illusion of movement, of life.[12]

In 1960, taking *The Execution of Mary, Queen of Scots* as one of his examples, the German film theorist Siegfried Kracauer noted cinema's predilection for scenes of horror and violence, 'its sustained concern with all that is dreadful and off limits'. He confirms that at such moments film indulges a mass appetite for sensation. But he also mitigates the charge by remarking that what is valuable about film is that it should enable us to contemplate such violence without our senses being overwhelmed or our consciousness 'drowned in inner agitation'.[13] Over the century film would indeed contemplate the subject of assassination. However, one consequence of this sustained reflection would be the strengthening of a process that had always dogged such killings: that is, the turning of murder into a mere image.

II: Land Where My Fathers Died

Only a week after Princip fired his gun in Sarajevo, an epic American movie began filming, one which would have at its centre a re-staging of the first great American assassination.[14] Arising out of a tradition of Civil War drama and film, D. W. Griffith's *The Birth of a Nation* (1915) was burdened by a hazy sense of historical re-enactment. At several moments in his film, Griffith cites an historian in his inter-titles (including, to his embarrassment, President Woodrow Wilson). Yet Griffith's representation of the Civil War and the Reconstruction period is hardly a well-balanced one; as the film critic Harry Alan Potamkin put it, the film was 'a vindictive platitude'.[15] Intensely occupied with the transmutation of history into convenient, white supremacist, myth, and notorious for its celebration of the Ku Klux Klan, Griffith troubles to reproduce with punctilious exactitude the settings of his film. The inter-titles inform us that we are about to see 'An Historical Facsimile' of the surrender at Appomattox, or of Lincoln's office, or Ford's Theatre. This desire for outward resemblance affected the casting too, with 'look-alikes' drafted in to play such characters as Charles Sumner. Joseph E. Henabery, the man who played Lincoln, has suggested that if he could have, Griffith would have cast Benjamin Chapin, a well-known Lincoln impersonator, in the role.[16] History becomes a show; it is the details of place that matter, the nuances of expression. However, when it comes to history as narrative, the desire for accuracy falters.

The portrayal of Lincoln is a tightrope act in which the film showily teeters, endeavouring not to fall on either side. Lincoln, the enemy of the noble Confederacy, must also be placed as an unassailably virtuous symbol of the entire United States. The movie resurrects the slur that Lincoln was a tyrant, while simultaneously rendering his life a histrionic sainthood. He overbears the rights of individual states, but also bears the burden of office, thoughtful after the others depart. The Civil War becomes a battle over 'state sovereignty', the issues of slavery or secession largely swept away by sleight of hand. In Joseph Carl Breil's score, the playing of 'America (My Country 'Tis of Thee)' over moments showing Lincoln operating power transcends sectional divides with an image of the whole nation; yet with its (to non-American ears) attenuated echo of the British national anthem, 'God Save the King', and the knowledge that the song had once contained some abolitionist verses, there is also the possibility that an irony is being presented to the American audience.

The moment of Lincoln's assassination is one in which Griffith's racist worldview unravels. After all, Lincoln's murder had exposed the fissures in the imagined American nation, just as Czolgosz's assassination of McKinley had done some thirty-six years later. Now, as an image, the aim is to present a historical tableau that would picture something common to all Americans. A narrative of unity absorbs the crises of dissension. However, the project had to founder, because the disputes that had produced Lincoln's killing remained unresolved. In depicting Lincoln's murder, Griffith was up against the contradiction of his film's political agenda. Lincoln is the sacrificial victim of the moment, treacherously slaughtered; Booth is the pantomime villain, a shady killer stalking his prey. In this scene, the film critic Richard Dyer's suggestion that Griffith lit his heroines so that they should appear as particularly 'white' is also true of Booth (played by Raoul Walsh), his pallor contrasting with Lincoln's darker features.[17] The scene was shot outside, with a mirror's reflected light employed to pick out Booth from the crowd.[18] In this way, the film suggests Booth's otherness, an effect further insisted on by the fact that he is the only character in the film to be shown in extreme close-up.[19] After the shooting Griffith lets us know that the South has lost its 'Greatest Friend'. But Booth was also close kin to the coming Ku Klux Klan, his heinous deed precisely the kind of wild justice that the Klan would perpetrate in the coming decades. Here, at this crossroads moment in the film's structure, a white man murders another white man, and Griffith can do little but skirt over the meanings of this vigilante's act with a beguiling swirl of 'historical accuracy' and manipulative melodrama.

The film knows its own intoxication with the pull of the image, and even sentimentally reflects on it with the dashing Confederate hero falling in love with his Yankee sweetheart (the anaemic Lilian Gish) after seeing – and living with – her photograph. It similarly renders the image of white violence attractive, in ways that were influential in the revival of the Ku Klux Klan.[20]

The true object of assassination in the film is the African-American, who is made to seem both comical and bestial. In the epic of death that is *The Birth of a Nation*, Lincoln dies as a martyr; all the whites die as martyrs. The blacks are simply expunged, put down like rampaging beasts. Black power is Anarchy, a pandemonium of taunts and cruel laughter. The film turns upon an apparently inconsequential sequence of kittens and puppies fighting; this is the way that Griffith chooses to tell us that, like cats and dogs, whites and blacks can never get along.

Such fripperies may seem as though they belong to another order of events than the European assassinations of the same era. Yet, as the next chapters will disclose, the most damaging American assassinations of the next century would owe as much, and sometimes more, to the surface of the Hollywood screen as to an ideological bitterness.

12

The New Frontier

We are living in an Age of Assassination.

HARRISON E. SALISBURY, 1970[1]

The flight . . . would retrace – West to East – America's geography of assassination. Los Angeles. Dallas. Memphis. New York. Kennedy. Kennedy. King. And Malcolm X. I imagined a bloody, crescent-shaped scar on the face of the land, linking the four killer cities.

JACK NEWFIELD, 1969[2]

I: Shooting on Pennsylvania Avenue

During lunchtime on Wednesday 1 November 1950, a bomb exploded at the Puerto Rican government offices in New York. Only an hour later in Washington, DC, in the midday Indian-summer heat, two young Puerto Ricans with a pair of .38 pistols attempted to storm into Blair House, President Truman's temporary home, and there murder the President.[3] A gunfight kicked off between the would-be assassins and the Presidential guards. Two policemen were hit, and a third, Private Leslie Coffelt, was fatally wounded; both the Puerto Ricans were shot down on the steps to the house, one (Griselio Torresola) killed by a bullet bursting through his head from ear to ear, and the other (Oscar Collazo) badly injured. Leslie Coffelt, the dying guard, fired the shot from the ground that brought down Torresola. The assault had been chaotic, badly planned, and amateurish: the two Puerto Ricans had simply advanced on the house, guns blazing, hoping to blast their way in. If they had made it through, they would have found, on the other side of the front door, a guard with a submachine gun waiting for them. Neither man had ever been in Washington before; Oscar Collazo had never fired a gun. It is possible that when the shoot-out began he had not known to remove the safety-catch on his weapon.[4]

The President was inside, preparing to go to Arlington Cemetery to dedicate a bronze monument; half an hour after the killings were done, he kept his appointment.[5] "'A President has to expect these things," he remarked.'[6] Readiness was the key to Truman's understanding of his task as President.[7] However, he had been literally caught napping when the shootings began, and had rushed to the window half-dressed to see what was going on.[8] Truman kept cool throughout the attack; he even had to be forcefully reminded to move out of sight.[9] Later that evening, Margaret Truman, the President's daughter, displayed similar *sangfroid* by singing as scheduled at a concert in Portland, Maine.[10]

The assassins' families were temporarily taken into custody. Both men lived in the Bronx. Collazo appears to have been a hard-working and kindly man.[11] When questioned, he declared that in aiming to murder Truman, they had intended not to kill a man, but to remove a symbol of the system. Their rather fanciful hope was to trigger a revolution in the USA, and thereby gain the necessary conditions for Puerto Rican independence.[12] Collazo was sentenced to the electric chair, though Truman intervened and commuted the penalty to life imprisonment.[13] He was finally released by President Jimmy Carter in September 1979.[14]

It was the first American Presidential assassination attempt since February 1933, when in Miami Giuseppe Zangara had opened fire on Franklin Delano Roosevelt. In the shooting, the Mayor of Chicago, Anton Cermak was badly wounded; some have speculated that he was the real target, and that Zangara was a hit-man for the Chicago Mob. More likely Zangara was just another crazed assassin, a bricklayer troubled by stomach pains, filled with resentment against all those with money and power. Within a week of the shooting, he had been tried and sentenced to eighty years in prison. Shortly afterwards, Cermak died, and Zangara was re-tried on a charge of murder. He was found guilty, and ten days afterwards sent to the electric chair.

In 1948 Truman had visited Puerto Rico, a trip where he had been surprisingly well received. He thought of the place as 'that beautiful island' and would, in time, be proud of giving it a governor, a constitution and home rule.[15] In fact, Puerto Rico was one of the Truman Presidency's few success stories, as his liberal aspirations foundered on the conservative fervour of the times.[16] Truman's instincts were egalitarian; his faith centred on the Sermon on the Mount, on an ideal of fairness. His hope had been to extend self-government on the island, beginning with allowing the native population to elect their own governor, the move matching the international push towards decolonisation.[17] In 1949, Muñoz Marín, the leader of the nationalist PPD (Popular Democratic Party), had been elected. He grasped that the island's economic future depended on the link with capitalist America (a relationship boosted by 'Operation Bootstrap', a policy of tax-breaks and free [that is unregulated] markets to tempt investors). Therefore Muñoz Marín quickly endorsed the view that only a limited independence would be feasible. He pushed for a 'third way' between absolute autonomy and nationhood, a path endorsed in a referendum supporting Public Law 600.[18] The hard-line, but non-violent nationalists of the Puerto Rican Independence Party (PIP) and the revolutionaries led by Albizu Campos boycotted the referendum. On 30 October 1950 a nationalist uprising followed (the latest in a cycle of similar flare-ups of violence).[19] The attempted killing of Truman was probably a key element in the rebellion; there was also an attempt to assassinate Muñoz Marín.[20] The havoc lasted three days, claiming the lives of thirty-two people, but the revolt soon folded, as Communists and nationalists – including Albizu Campos himself – were arrested.[21] A few days later the plans for a referendum on a planned constitution were passed and the National Guard, which had been put on alert, was demobilised.

Symbolically, the assassination attempted by Torresola and Collazo dragged a colonial war back to its centre. For one brief moment, Washington shared the violence in San Juan, forcing Pennsylvania Avenue to recognise its kinship with Puerto Rico.

That violence might have looked like strength, but rather revealed the independence movement's inherent vulnerability. They reached for the gun, as they had no other way of making an impact. While some argue that Puerto Rican culture promoted popular sympathy for bandits and rebels, and that this therefore favoured the revolutionaries, most writers suggest that more importantly Puerto Rico lacked a deep-founded tradition of violent insurrection; in a state where people could draw upon a vibrant political culture, terrorist techniques could not take root.[22] For this reason, the affair was a political cul-de-sac; it led nowhere and soon slipped into the Lethean abyss that drowns much of

American history – particularly that part involving the USA's colonial possessions. The shootings took place during the darkest days of the Korean War, at the start of a nuclear arms race, and during the onset of the McCarthy anti-Communist witch-hunts, and were quickly swept away by these more vital Cold War currents. Besides the looming threat of Russia, these small-island assassins seemed a petty concern.[23] In his *Memoirs*, Truman himself skips over the event, as do even some near-contemporary accounts of his Presidency.[24] In a press conference the day after the shooting, he commented: 'there's no story so far as I am concerned. I was never in danger. The thing I hate about it is the fact that these young men – one of them killed, and two of them badly wounded.'[25] Truman treated his guards (and other workers) with an uncondescending friendliness; a few weeks after the event, when Truman saw a photograph of the murdered guard, he became weepy; the shooting stayed a personal tragedy.[26]

On 1 March 1954, three Puerto Rican nationalists opened fire on congressmen in the House of Representatives; five were wounded. They timed the bloodshed to coincide with the Tenth Inter-American Conference at Caracas.[27] This terrorist outrage was spectacular, and yet once again ultimately feeble. In comparison to Puerto Rican economic dependence on American finance and the island's growing wealth (for some), such vicious acts barely amounted to a gesture.

Meanwhile the life of the American President was becoming routinely menaced: in 1949, the Secret Service dealt with 1,925 reported threats.[28] Some were more than just threats: Margaret Truman writes that in 1947 Palestinians attempted to send her father a letter bomb.[29] In late 1950, for a few weeks after the Puerto Rican shooting, security around Truman remained stringent. The President naturally enough felt hemmed in. On a visit to St Louis he was unable to make his usual walk-about, and in his diary he wrote: 'It's hell to be President of the Greatest Most Powerful Nation on Earth – I'd rather be "first in the Iberian Village".'[30] He also fantasised 'that if I could get my hands on a would-be assassin he'd never try it again. But I guess that's impossible.'[31]

The impact of assassination has depended on the political doctrine of the 'indispensable man' – that one figure commands, manifesting power. To expunge such a figure alters everything; in one moment, a bullet, or bomb removes the embodiment of authority. For quite different reasons, Truman himself was against the doctrine of his own indispensability. As far as he was concerned, power was not about any individual; it resided in the will of a democracy, and the activities of the government did not depend on any single person.[32] Truman's belief strikes at one source of the efficacy of assassination; these killings only matter if the person matters. If the person is no more than a function, or that function's passing incarnation, then murder becomes an aimless act – a symbolic assault upon a symbol. Only in so far as the personality in office seems unique do such killings assume history-changing power. In this way assassinations reproduce a cult of the individual – trusting that the killer is exceptional and the victim irreplaceable.

The shootings outside Blair House had taken place in what was anything but a private spot – the building was right on Pennsylvania Avenue; a couple of thousand office and shop workers and passers-by witnessed the carnage. At first, most thought the sound of the guns was cars backfiring, though veterans of the recent war immediately recognised it for what it was. One witness offered what was to become the classic description of such a violent event:

Mrs. Leslie Lockwood, of Hollywood, Calif., who once worked for a movie studio, was standing alone at the northeast corner of Jackson pl. and Pennsylvania ave. What she saw in front of Blair House across the street, she thought was a movie take.

'I didn't think it was real,' the lady from movieland said. 'Why I've never in my life before seen anybody shoot at anybody.'[33]

It was indeed the event's incongruity that would in time come to seem most pertinent. To the spectators, the colonialist aspects of the moment failed to mean very much. Instead what was left was a lurid thrill, a moment from a *film noir* or some gangster picture, the hero going down in a hail of bullets. One good book dedicated to the telling of the event – Stephen Hunter and John Bainbridge's *American Gunfight* (2005) – cannot dodge the allure of the Weegee-esque image and the Warner Brothers tone. All that was left of this act against the symbol of the Presidency was another set of symbols, of cinematic tropes: the cops and robbers gunfight; the great American shoot-out. Tellingly, Stephen Hunter is both an accomplished writer of hard-boiled fiction and a highly talented movie critic. It is in such worlds that Truman's near-assassination has found its memorial.

II: The New Frontier

It never really came up, but there was no question that Bobby thought of it. We all thought of it when Jack was alive. One evening as we stood in front of the White House, Jackie said, 'What targets we are.' Jack had said it once when we were in an airfield, and we were isolated, and there were throngs way out around us. He looked around and said 'Boy! Aren't we targets!'

    WILLIAM WALTON, 1970[34]

Material furnished by a government seldom satisfies critics or historians, for it lies always under suspicion.

    HENRY ADAMS[35]

Around the time of the Kennedy assassination, an NBC correspondent was interviewed:

I was with Truman every minute everywhere he went during the '48 campaign . . . You sense these things as you are covering. You work closely with the Secret Service, and the routine of covering a President is always that the guy is going to get killed . . . When you cover a President as a photographer, you have three networks and two wire-service photographers usually in a convertible right ahead of the President . . . When you drive into a square or a crowd, you look around at the tops of buildings first and then you shoot a picture of the President. It is a normal feeling, and that is the reason you cover him 24 hours . . . because he is going to be shot. This is where you have all the conflict with the Salingers who say, 'Why not cut it off?' You can't because they can't tell you when. And if he isn't going to get shot, he is going to pick up a baby . . . Who is interested in what the President does 24 hours a day? But you are interested when he gets shot.[36]

This long, patient interest received its reward. President John Fitzgerald Kennedy was shot in Dallas on 22 November 1963.

    The murder took place during a motorcade trip around the city. President Kennedy was in the back of a limousine with his wife beside him. In the second row of seats were Governor John Connally and his wife; the driver and a security man sat in front. In one of the cars behind was Vice President Lyndon B. Johnson and his wife, 'Lady Bird'

Johnson. The limousine turned off Houston Street onto Elm Street; the car was to go on under the triple underpass directly ahead.[37] To the President's left was a grassy knoll, at the top of which, nearest to the underpass, was a wooden fence. At the corner of Houston and Elm was the Texas School Book Depository. Allegedly, from the sixth-floor corner window of this building, an assassin fired at the President. It was 12.30. The shooting lasted between five and six seconds. A bullet struck Kennedy in the throat. Connally turned to see what was happening, when he himself was hit in the torso, the bullet passing through his wrist and striking his thigh. Mrs Connally testified:

I heard a noise, and not being an expert rifleman, I was not aware that it was a rifle. It was just a frightening noise, and it came from the right. I turned over my right shoulder and looked back, and saw the President as he had both hands at his neck . . . and it seemed to me there was – he made no utterance, no cry. I saw no blood, no anything. It was just sort of nothing, the expression on his face, and he just sort of slumped down. Then very soon there was the second that hit John. As the first shot was hit, and I turned to look at the same time, I recall John [her husband, John Connally] saying, 'Oh, no, no, no.' Then there was a second shot, and it hit John, and as he recoiled to the right, just crumpled like a wounded animal to the right, he said, 'My God, they are going to kill us all.'[38]

For some never explained reason, the President's driver slowed the car to around five miles per hour. Just as Mrs Connally described it, another bullet struck the President directly in the head, causing massive damage. (There was also another wound in his upper back, perhaps the exit wound of the bullet that may have passed through his neck.[39]) During the attack, a bystander, James Tague, received a slight wound to the face. The President was rushed to hospital and pronounced dead shortly afterwards. Two hours after the shooting, Lyndon B. Johnson was sworn in as the new President. Jackie Kennedy stood alongside him, the camera that photographed the moment taking care not to show too much of the blood splattered across her pink suit.

Very quickly, based on rather shaky identification, the police issued a description of a man they would like to interview. But there was only ever going to be one suspect: one of the workers in the Texas School Book Depository, a young man named Lee Harvey Oswald. After the shooting Oswald apparently took a bus home, only to go out again, carrying a handgun. For reasons that remain profoundly unclear, on leaving the house Oswald shot a police officer, Patrolman J. D. Tippit, in broad daylight with witnesses scattered around, even though it seems that Tippit had not attempted to apprehend him. Then Oswald went to the movies; in the cinema he was arrested with suspicious ease by the Dallas police force.[40] Only eighty minutes had passed since the assassination.[41]

That Sunday, 24 November 1963, as he was being moved from the Dallas Police Department to the County Jail, Oswald himself was shot by Jack Ruby. 'You son of a bitch,' Ruby was reported as saying, as he pulled the trigger.[42] The murder was broadcast live on television and radio. Oswald died quickly, taken to Parkland Hospital where Kennedy himself had died more or less exactly forty-eight hours before. Ruby was the owner of a 'Big D' strip-joint, 'The Carousel Burlesque', a seedy figure about town with links both to the Mob and the Dallas police force. Ruby had appeared profoundly affected by Kennedy's murder; as a mark of piety, he shut his strip clubs for the weekend.[43] He was observed hanging around the hospital where Kennedy died, and then seen again at the police station where Oswald was held. How Ruby got into the building to kill Oswald remains mysterious. However, given his amiable relations with most of Dallas's police force, it seems not unlikely that someone on the inside let him in through the basement.

Ruby's stated motive for the killing of Oswald was that it was a spontaneous act designed to spare Jacqueline Kennedy the ordeal of testifying at a court case. Later, during the Warren Commission, Ruby appeared to be suggesting to Chief Justice Earl Warren that there was in fact far more to the murder than this, but that he could only say what was going on if Warren would guarantee that he would take him to Washington. During these exchanges Warren proved enormously obtuse, either failing to understand or refusing to grasp Ruby's meaning. Ruby never explained more fully what he had meant. He died of cancer in prison, in 1967, convinced that he had been given the disease by a murderous injection. His death is one of a number that cut short the lives of significant witnesses to the assassination and its aftermath.

Despite the spectacle of American prosperity, it is popularly understood that the shooting of J. F. Kennedy in Dallas inaugurated a period of discord in American political life that was to last for nearly twenty years.[44] Moreover, many have felt that an atmosphere of unease characterised this time of crisis. Why should this be so?

The conspiracy theories around J. F. Kennedy's assassination have multiplied, somehow without much impact. Far-fetched, but, for some, entirely credible speculations gathered, all of which would, if true, mean the complete political and moral bankruptcy of the American state, and yet were merely taken for harmless presumption. Nothing about the events in Dallas is settled, and most assume that nothing can be settled. The Soviets speculated that the murder was part of an ultra-rightist coup; some Americans believed it was a Russian plot.[45] The killing was the work of a solitary gunman; it was the work of pro-war and anti-Communist elements in the government and the 'military-industrial complex'; it was Castro, taking revenge; it was anti-Castro Cuban exiles, taking revenge; it was the CIA; it was the Mafia; it was the Mafia, Castro, Cuban exiles, and the CIA. He was killed by right-wing segregationists; he was killed by left-wing Communists. The President was shot by Oswald; he was shot by his driver. It was about Vietnam; it was about Cuba; it was about Marilyn Monroe.

What matters is not the substance of these mutually exclusive conspiracy theories, it's the way they permeate the real event of the President's murder with the fantastic.[46] The more explanations there are, the more the moment itself appears incomprehensible. In 1975, Anthony Lewis wrote: 'The search for conspiracy . . . only increases the elements of morbidity and paranoia and fantasy in this country . . . It obscures our necessary understanding, all of us, that in this life there is often tragedy without reason.'[47] In the light of conspiracy theory, tragedy becomes a narrative of concealment, where all is unreal, and ultimately only a deceiving, or undeceiving, image. All can now watch Abraham Zapruder's 16-mm amateur film footage of the murder on YouTube.[48]

In part, the event's perceived unreality complemented the optimism that preceded it. Short on actual accomplishment, Kennedy had nonetheless symbolised for many the idea of American potential. The country was already riven over the issue of Civil Rights, and confronted in the shape of the Cold War by a gang of hostile enemies that wished its destruction; the nuclear peril brought to the surface so vividly during the Cuban missile crisis threatened humanity with annihilation.

Yet somehow, and perhaps particularly in the moment of his death, Kennedy could contain a promise. Adlai Stevenson remarked: 'When President Kennedy was assassinated . . . we were all left with a sense of incompleteness.'[49] His death defeated those hopes; in its immediate aftermath only a knowledge of the underlying turmoil seemed to remain. The fear that had been confined to the inner cities and the racist South suddenly spilled over and spread everywhere. No one was safe.

In the case of previous Presidential assassinations, the government had imagined a conspiracy, while the people were sceptical. With Kennedy, these roles were reversed. The belief that the government itself was the conspiratorial agent was new in the history of assassination – though it had American precedents in the Civil War era, the anti-New Deal politics of the 1930s and McCarthyite paranoia.[50] Before the publication of the Warren Report into the assassination, less than a third of Americans believed that Oswald had indeed been a lone gunman.[51] Large numbers of Americans were surprisingly apt to suspect that the CIA or FBI, or even LBJ were involved in the President's murder and its subsequent cover-up. Suspicions had shifted from Anarchist cabals, Reds, Roman Catholics or Jews to Washington, DC.

In the weeks after the attack, Robert Kennedy was troubled by the possibility of there having been a conspiracy, whether by the Cubans or the Chicago Mafia. He even asked John McCone, the Director of Central Intelligence, if the CIA had been behind his brother's murder; McCone assured him they had not.[52] Yet the more the government insisted that Oswald was a 'lone gunman', the more it looked like a stitch-up. Allen Dulles, the former Director of Central Intelligence, began the inquiry into the assassination by pushing the idea that Oswald had worked on his own, even while the CIA sat on evidence that might have wrecked that supposition.[53] In 1964 the Warren Commission concluded that, in shooting the President, Oswald had acted alone. Despite previous doubts, for a while their finding satisfied most in America, although as we have seen there were already many conspiracy theories in play.[54] Even before the Warren Commission had issued its report sceptical voices could be heard in Thomas Buchanan's *Who Killed Kennedy?* or an article on the case by Bertrand Russell.[55] With the report delivered, after initial consensus, cracks began to show, as analysis of the Commission's methods and conclusions began to cast doubt on their validity. Lawyer Mark Lane's book *Rush to Judgment* (1966) was among the first and most significant of these critiques. Lane provided much of the material for the 1973 film *Executive Action*, a work that fused documentary and drama to conjure a persuasive case for conspiracy. However, there were soon many other such attacks – notably that of New Orleans District Attorney Jim Garrison, whose investigation into the murders in Dallas would eventually form the subject of Oliver Stone's movie *JFK* (1991). In March 1975, the screening of the Zapruder film on Geraldo Rivera's television programme *Good Night America* only intensified the questioning.

In response to the increasingly widespread belief that the Warren Commission had fudged the issues, a series of new government investigations began. The Rockefeller Commission attempted to validate the JFK autopsy reports. A United States Senate Select Committee to study Governmental Operations with Respect to Intelligence Activities was set up and produced stunning evidence about government involvement in state-sponsored assassinations. A House Select Committee on Assassinations followed, its aim being the investigation of the murders of JFK, Martin Luther King and Robert F. Kennedy, and the attempted killing of Governor George Wallace. This Committee both endorsed the conclusions of the Warren Commission that Oswald was the man who had shot the President, and yet also declared that someone else had fired a shot during the six seconds in which the President was killed and Governor Connally wounded. This later conclusion arose from recordings of the shooting, which, apparently, clearly reveal four shots being fired; the Warren Commission had asserted that there had only been three shots, all of which had been fired, so they said, by Oswald.[56] If two men had fired, that itself implied conspiracy. However, while the Committee came to no definitive conclusions as to with whom Oswald might have conspired, they did consider it possible that Oswald had been involved with anti-Castro groups, particularly through right-wing activists Guy Bannister and David Ferrie. The Committee ruled out the involvement of any government agency. Many still remained dissatisfied with these conclusions, and the acoustic evidence itself has been both disputed and defended.

Why did the various conspiracy theories take such hold? Firstly, there are the reactions felt by many in response to the absurd randomness of the act. How could such a catastrophe only be the outcome of one man's wickedness? Connected to this was a natural sense of frustration that there was no one to hit back at following the murder. Jack Ruby's shooting of Oswald was not cathartic, but doubly provoking.

However, the clearest and most obvious answer must be that there was much that remained inexplicable, or insufficiently well explained, about the killing. There were other gunshots heard apart from the three supposedly fired by Oswald. There were questions raised about the wounds received by both Kennedy and Governor Connally. There was the improbable speed with which the police settled on Oswald as their sole suspect. There were confused conclusions about fingerprints, discrepancies in the evidence, reports that the third shot had followed on impossibly fast from the second, disputes about the ability of Oswald to hit the President at that range and in so short a time, and so on. Such evidence is compelling, although nothing could be conclusively proved. However, for what it is worth, from a reading of books and the various government inquiries examining the murder, it is the belief of the author of this book that we may well doubt that Oswald could have killed the President acting alone, and even that he shot at the President at all.

The greatest obstacle in the path to accepting the idea of a conspiracy is the assumption that this would make Chief Justice Earl Warren and others on the Warren Commission implicitly guilty of a cover-up. This is especially unlikely as Warren and the Supreme Court in the late 1950s and 1960s had been a force for liberal change, guilty in the eyes of right-wingers of 'judicial activism'; on that basis, the John Birch Society had even initiated a campaign to impeach Earl Warren.[57] However, as Hugh Trevor-Roper argued, Warren's corruption need not be a necessary premise: the Commission may well have been fallible and prejudiced, but for reasons of human incompetence and weakness, rather than deliberate bad intent.[58] With regard to the Commission itself, this 'cock-up' as opposed to 'conspiracy' theory carries a lot of force. The only cover-ups regarding the assassination admitted to by a US government body are those of the FBI and CIA doing their best to conceal the inadequacies of their investigation of Oswald both before and after the shooting and the likelihood that Oswald had been an informer for the FBI.[59] Moreover both agencies hid their involvement in, or knowledge of, plots to assassinate Castro.[60] Whether consciously or not, the Commission does indeed appear to have assumed Oswald's guilt from the outset, and then to have worked towards proving that conclusion in ways that did little justice to the complexity of the evidence.

Perhaps the Commission was beguiled by the culturally resonant portrayal of Oswald as a solitary gunman. The one-volume version of the Warren Report states that Oswald was just another Czolgosz.[61] The picture of Oswald in this official book (one read by several million Americans) was that of an estranged, rootless, deracinated young man. His murder of the President was the culmination of years of 'isolation, frustration and failure'.[62] The myth of the American killer had always been of an outsider, acting out of isolation, disconnected from the lives of others. This image placed Oswald in a tradition. As a recluse given over to violence, the lone assassin belonged with the Western hero, with the private eye, with the runaway.

However, far from exhibiting an alienated purposelessness, Oswald's life seems remarkably packed for someone only twenty-four years old. He was born in New Orleans in 1939, and, brought up by his divorced mother, passed an itinerant childhood and adolescence; he moved house twenty-two times in his first eighteen years. With the family pressed for space, until he was ten years old Lee shared a bed with his mother.[63] His schooling was marked by truancy, sulkiness and his refusal to join in with others' games. In 1953, he saw a psychiatrist, Dr Hartogs, who found that: 'when he asked him whether he prefers the company of boys to that of girls, he answered – "I dislike everybody"'.[64] He joined the Marines, where his training included sharpshooting; opinions differ as to how good a shot he was.[65] The same problems with authority that had marked his school life now troubled his time with the military; he was court-martialled twice. During his spell in the Marines Oswald conveniently took a Russian course, which must have proved helpful when he defected in 1959 to the Soviet Union, hoping to renounce his American citizenship and avow his allegiance to the USSR.[66] He lived in Minsk for a couple of years, marrying a Russian wife, Marina Prusakova, and starting a family.[67] In June 1962 he then returned, with amazing ease, to the United States, with his wife and children.[68] They went to live in Dallas. Here he began to write a memoir of his life in Russia, a literary project that got nowhere. (His mother had also planned to write a book on his defection to Russia.)[69] He flitted through a run of low-skilled jobs, and fell in with various anti-Communist and anti-Castro groups. Simultaneously he became involved with the local Fair Play for Cuba Committee, a pro-Castro group. Two months before the assassination, Oswald apparently took a trip to Mexico City, perhaps to get a visa to travel back to the Soviet Union.[70]

Possibly Oswald attempted a previous assassination: according to the confused testimony of his wife, he had tried and failed to kill Major General Edwin Walker and had wanted to murder Richard Nixon.[71] Walker was a notorious figure on the right, a propagandist for the deranged anti-Communist John Birch Society, and himself not averse to the idea of political violence.[72] In 1963, a sniper did fire at Walker, but whether Oswald was involved remains very unclear.

Indeed, despite the efforts of the Warren Report, much about Oswald remains obscure, not least his intention in killing Kennedy. How could one man, motivated by political aims, both attempt to kill General Walker and President Kennedy? According to his wife, the motive was fame: 'I came to the conclusion that he wanted in any – by any means, good or bad, to get into history.'[73] Oswald succeeded in this aim. He has indeed got into history, and may be imagined to have found it a nightmare from which he can never awaken. His story, his image, and his life have been endlessly examined. This chapter merely represents the latest such retelling; others are doubtless following hot on its heels. However, Oswald's life has become not so much an image of human truth as an absurdity.

For conspiracy theorists, one of their most striking claims is that, on the day of the assassination and in the months before, a number of fake Oswalds circulated around Texas. There is also the strong possibility that one of the most famous photographs of Oswald, showing him holding a rifle, is a forgery.[74] It is already as though Oswald had lost control of his own identity, and that his image was multiplying beyond his control.

Cruelly, the same fate seems to have overtaken Kennedy himself; the substance and beauty of his life lost in a brutal appropriation. The murder stands – particularly in its televised form – as the degradation of beauty, those six seconds of Zapruder's footage exposing not only the stupidity of murder, but also the stupidity of death.

Through media intervention, the Kennedys had become known in a way unlike the family of any previous American President.[75] Although many in America, of course, had disliked Kennedy for political reasons, nonetheless the death was experienced as though it were a personal loss. For most, such a moment transcended party politics. Much of the feeling around the President centred on his ideal nature, especially his supposedly model family relationships: a good father, a good husband, an 'ordinary guy' gifted with the special grace of ordinariness. Although this was considered an electoral liability, for some it was also important that he was a good Catholic.[76] In his mid-forties, he could still represent youth.[77] He was a war hero, whose leadership and personal courage had shown itself after his torpedo boat (*PT-109*) was sunk in the Pacific, where he brought himself to safety and rescued some of his crew.

Yet for some this shining image was already blemished. Kennedy's courage had been less visible in his sidestepping the opportunity to censure Senator Joseph McCarthy in the Senate. To have joined the reprimand against McCarthy would have been a sure vote-loser among his Boston Catholic voters, and, moreover, the Senator for Wisconsin was a family friend – Robert Kennedy had worked on his Permanent Subcommittee on Investigations. The murky associations around Joe Kennedy, his father, as Prohibition-era bootlegger, Hollywood tycoon and unfaithful lover, could also be used to smear the son. Still, in getting elected, the father's money helped more than his reputation did harm. Despite these taints, the 'Kennedy mystique' spread, an atmosphere of the New Frontier and Harvard Yard, hopefulness and good looks, the White House now an American Camelot, as Jackie Kennedy herself described it.[78] That much of this was at best deeply compromised and at worst a deception was not yet widely known. Far from being a King Arthur, Kennedy would come to seem a shop-soiled Sir Lancelot. In time a procession of debunking books exposed the flaws in his character, and after his death he would appear deficient in that dignity considered one of the qualities essential for presidential office.[79] Kennedy once declared that nine of the Ten Commandments were 'derived from nature'; after his death, it became easy to guess which was the tenth.[80]

Influenced perhaps by Richard Neustadt's *Presidential Power* (1960), Kennedy's personal presidency signalled a return to Franklin D.

Roosevelt's centralising use of power; it also marked him out as a 'personal' target for potential assassins, the office subsumed in the individual.[81] It was JFK's intimate relationship with the television screen that most powerfully established this 'personalisation'.[82] The new 35-mm cameras used by photojournalists further changed the press's relationship to the President; their lightness meant they could be carried easily anywhere, and photos snapped. The technology favoured the candid, the off-hand, and, with his effortless grace, Kennedy flourished by such an approach.[83] Particularly new was the live televising of Kennedy's press conferences. These allowed him to show himself at his best, talking off the cuff, responding to journalists. It created a sense of intimacy with the press corps and, more vitally, with the viewer. In a new twist on Roosevelt's radio-broadcast 'fireside chats', the President had become a guest in America's homes.

Though politically speaking it was not their discovery, the Kennedys understood the power of television.[84] The impact of image in the political realm dated back to the contests fought by Truman and Eisenhower, if not before. Already in 1950, David Riesman was writing about 'politics as an object of consumption', the voter supposedly swayed by such ineffable qualities as 'personal magnetism' and glamour.[85] During the 1950s and 1960s, politics seemed newly dominated by what Dorothy Thompson had named 'the cult of personality'; Americans had become 'consumers of politics' and the commodity on sale was the politician's carefully managed public image. 'Greatness' in a politician became a matter of how well they fitted the voters' 'father-image'.[86] Politicians now had to 'project' themselves, impressing their personality on the electorate. With his good looks, Jack Kennedy was made for such a milieu.[87] His presence prophesied a realm where the ultimate ground of presidential power would rest on charm.

Kennedy mastered the new politics, offering charisma to the electorate. His final place in the national consciousness was a symbol of all that was most desirable in the American myth. In terms of solid achievement or foreign policy gains, he left almost nothing for posterity; at best, he founded the Peace Corps. The great legislative triumphs of the period in Civil Rights, Medicaid, environmental laws and social welfare were all down to the much disparaged and untelegenic Lyndon Baines Johnson. In the cruellest interpretation, the single most important impact of JFK's career is that his death handed Johnson the moral force to pass these necessary reforms – laws that Kennedy would have been unlikely to have got through on his own. In foreign policy terms, it was almost certainly his weakness with Khrushchev that prompted the Cuban missile crisis, the solving of which was his only victory. Even that success was not quite what the public perceived it to be, involving as it did the largely hushed-up quid pro quo removal of American missiles from Turkey. Meanwhile Kennedy had already sparked an arms race with the Russians and his policy on Vietnam helped to create the conditions for the disastrous war that followed. There were hints that he would have withdrawn from the conflict had he been re-elected, and then later there were other hints that he was murdered precisely because of this private intention.[88] To imagine that Kennedy could have ended the war presupposes a strength of purpose in him of which there was little evidence in the first years of his presidency, other than the brinkmanship of the missile crisis and (on a much smaller scale) his confrontation with Governor George Wallace over integration. In any case, Kennedy had fatally undermined the Diem regime in South Vietnam with consequences that would likely have precluded such a sudden withdrawal. Otherwise Kennedy inspired and launched the space programme – and that was about all.

Despite this paltry legacy, in the eyes of many Kennedy still stands as a 'great President'. This perception owes more to marketing than delivery. Knowing that his Catholicism would prevent a straightforward Democratic coronation, Kennedy was forced to fight the 1960 election campaign on the basis of his national popularity. He had to win primaries and show his power. It was a new kind of strategy, and it hinged on the retailing of Kennedy. They were going to 'sell Jack like soap flakes'.[89] On 25 September 1960, Kennedy triumphed over Richard Nixon, the Republican candidate, on television; radio listeners were more evenly divided on who they believed had won the debate. Paradoxically it had been Nixon who had supposedly been the first to grasp the centrality of advertising to politics.[90] But on the screen, JFK had looked like a superstar, and the sweating, stubbly Nixon, as one journalist put it, 'a real middle-class uneducated swindler with all the virtues of a seller of fountain-pens in Naples'.[91] The smear in the Democratic poster, 'Would You Buy a Used Car From This Man?'

stuck. The Kennedys' relationship with the press and with television, their youth, their attractiveness, placed them in a position of mediated confidence with the electorate. However, it was the faux intimacy of the television image, the allure of cinema. In 1960, Norman Mailer put it like this:

The Democrats were going to nominate a man who, no matter how serious his political dedication might be, was indisputably and willy nilly going to be seen as a great box office actor . . . Since the First World War Americans have been living a double life, and our history has moved on two rivers, one visible, the other underground; there has been the history of politics which is concrete, factual, practical and unbelievably dull . . . and there is a subterranean river of untapped, ferocious, lonely and romantic desires, that concentration of ecstasy and violence which is the dream life of the nation . . . if elected he would not only be the youngest President ever to be chosen by the voters, he would be the most conventionally attractive young man ever to sit in the White House, and his wife – some would claim it – might be the most beautiful first lady in our history. Of necessity the myth would emerge once more, because America's politics would now be also America's favourite movie, America's first soap opera, America's best seller.[92]

The Kennedys were stars, and John F. Kennedy died on screen. The assassination was an experience broadcast on television; Ruby's murder of Oswald was broadcast live by NBC in the homes of America. Within half an hour of the shooting, 68 per cent of Americans had already heard the news, carried to them by the media.[93] The television set that brought the outside world into the domestic space displayed the horror and the pathos to a nation. All could feel involved; the deed became an image.

As had happened at the Truman shooting, the event was understood from the first by some in the light of fiction and cinema. In Moscow, *Izvestia* declared: 'We have seen a mad detective thriller and we reject it with contempt and anger . . . It was as if a mad film projectionist mixed up cans of film, interlacing the bitter tragedy of the great American nation with a cheap Texas thriller, a detective story and comics.'[94] Closer to home in America, as though they were reviewers, some voiced discontentment that the 'camera could neither expose every intrigue nor control the sequence of episodes':

It was as though they were reviewing a commercial drama, in that they exhibited mild pique or frustration when the 'program' was not to their liking:

'I would like to have seen more of the first of it, when he was shot. They should have a camera on that motorcade, I should think.'

'They could have started the murder scene [sooner], the shooting of Oswald. It looked too fakey to be real. If you had a play . . . usually it [the murder] would be acted out better.'[95]

College students remarked on the event's strangeness:

[It was] like watching a movie in a way. In the sense that there wasn't any connection with you and I really felt no participation in the events . . . like recalling a dream.[96]

In considering the effect of Ruby's televised murder of Oswald on watching children, a professor of political science paused to note the similarity of that moment to the Westerns that children were watching anyway daily on television.[97]

This process was exaggerated and deepened by the fact that an amateur camera-buff, a garment manufacturer named Abraham Zapruder, had picked a spot on the park area north of Elm Street, giving himself a good view of the motorcade. From this position he had filmed the murder itself. The whole sequence was shot using maximum zoom lens.[98] An amateur had caught what the professionals missed. *Life* bought the film, and images from it were published in the magazine.[99] Television executives flew to Dallas to inspect the footage, but decided against broadcasting it. Distinctions were made between showing Oswald murdered on camera, and showing the assassination of Kennedy. Oswald's murder went out live; there was no question of being able to censor the material. However, there was more to it. In one case, Oswald was a man a lot of people would have anyway liked to see shot; in the other, it was the President. The lapse of time between the assassination and the appearance of the film also altered matters; if Zapruder's film had been instantaneously available, it might well have been screened at once. Far more importantly, on a visceral level the shooting of Oswald looks 'clean'; at the moment of being shot, he recoils as though he's been pinched. There's no blood, no guts; it's black and white. The shooting of Kennedy was, on the other hand, a 'whole gory mess'.[100] The saturated colours show everything in an Indian-summer glow. An NBC executive declared: 'About the *Life* film, it wasn't the fact that it was JFK but . . . the inside of a man's brain being outside that was so awful.'[101]

The first screening of the Zapruder footage in 1975 on *Good Night America* began with a string of warnings and disclaimers about the violence on display. It's not for the sensitive; it's not for the queasy; the presenter, Geraldo Rivera, cautions us that it's 'heavy'. At the moment when the head shot hit, and the studio audience gasped, Rivera declared, 'It's the most horrifying thing I've ever seen in the movies.' It was not really Kennedy that people were considering, it was film itself. The sadism of late sixties and seventies cinema had prepared the audience for images that were taboo only twelve years before.[102]

Yet some seven years before, during the Tet Offensive, NBC had screened the public execution of a suspected Viet Cong agent, shot in the head at close range. His executioner was General Nguyen Ngoc Loan, the chief of the South Vietnam National Police. The victim falls to the ground and blood spurts from his head. A photograph of the event by Eddie Adams became an icon of the war; the television footage shocked many, but far less than the equivalent images of Kennedy. For, as far as the public were concerned, the Vietnamese victim was nameless, while Kennedy was Kennedy. It was the conjunction of fame and violence that struck so forcefully.

In the shooting at Dallas a number of events came together; it was an example of what Thomas Hardy termed 'the convergence of the twain'. There had been odd foreshadowings of what was to come. On the night when it was clear that the world had narrowly avoided nuclear war, Kennedy is said to have quipped: 'This is the night to go to the theatre, like Abraham Lincoln.'[103] There had been a previous attempt against JFK's life. In December 1960, the Kennedys had been holidaying in Palm Beach, getting away from the blizzards and snow of the north. While they were there, they were very close to being killed by an old-age-pensioner suicide-bomber, one Richard Pavlick, aged seventy-three. Pavlick had filled his car with dynamite and wiring, and was ready to use himself as a human bomb so as to kill the Kennedys. He hadn't liked the way Kennedy had won the election; it was 'underhand'.[104] Pavlick spent some time stalking the President. He came close to doing the deed just as the Kennedys were leaving church in Palm Beach. But the sight of Jacqueline Kennedy and the couple's two children changed his mind. The police, however, were on to him, alerted to his activities by bizarre postcards that he was sending to a friend. Pavlick was arrested a few days later, and spent six years in an asylum before being released back into the community.

Such craziness reflects a deeper and more damaging decline in American integrity. During the Bay of Pigs crisis, some of the more hawkish members of the Kennedy government had pushed for an air strike against Cuba. Robert Kennedy had apparently dismissed the idea: 'For 175 years we had not been that kind of country. Sunday-morning surprise blows on small nations were not in our tradition . . . We were fighting for something more than survival, and a sneak attack would constitute a betrayal of our heritage, and our ideals.'[105]

Robert Kennedy sounds stirringly confident here about the moral decency at the heart of the American ideal. In 1963 it was precisely this self-definition of America that would begin to unravel. The violence in the South, particularly the murder of Medgar Evers, had threatened it. The killing of John F. Kennedy threw it into crisis. For Dean Acheson, 'the United States looked like the terrorist-racked Congo'; to others the country resembled 'a 'banana republic'.[106] The journalist I. F. Stone asserted:

How many Americans . . . have not assumed – with approval – that the CIA were probably trying to find a way to assassinate Castro? . . . Where the right to kill is so universally accepted, we should not be surprised if our young president was slain. It is not just the ease in obtaining guns, it is the ease of obtaining excuses, that fosters assassination.[107]

Shortly after JFK's funeral, Lyndon Johnson supposedly pointed to a picture of Jean Baptiste Ngo Dinh Diem, the assassinated South Vietnamese President, and remarked: 'We had a hand in killing him . . . Now it's happening here.'[108] In stepping outside acceptable boundaries of political behaviour, the USA had acted just like the petty dictatorships it sought to unseat; in attacking vice, it had become vicious. Writing to Karl Jaspers, Hannah Arendt affirmed that somehow the centre of things had been hurt, and that it seemed as if everything might collapse like a house of cards. The events in Dallas and those early indications that there was something like a cover-up in place reminded her of a police state. An abyss of murderous desire had opened up.[109]

In the 1880s, Secretary Blaine wrote that there was nothing in the murder of either Lincoln or Garfield that was specifically American or that could shame the American form of government:

The assassination of two Presidents . . . while a cause of profound National grief, reflects no dishonor upon popular government. The murder of Lincoln was the maddened and aimless blow of an expiring rebellion. The murder of Garfield was the fatuous impulse of a debauched conscience if not a disordered brain. Neither crime had its origin in the political institutions or its growth in the social organization of the country. Both crimes received the execration of all parties and all sections. In the universal horror which they inspired, in the majestic supremacy of law, which they failed to disturb, may be read the strongest proof of the stability of a Government which is founded upon the rights, fortified by the intelligence, inwrought with the virtues of the people. For as it was said of old, wisdom and knowledge shall be stability, and the work of righteousness shall be peace![110]

It was ringing rhetoric – but one hundred years later, after a sequence of political killings, America itself would feel indicted. On a national level, Kennedy's assassination was a self-inflicted wound.

In a series of interviews designed to assess public reactions to the death, one adolescent in a pool-hall set out his anxieties: 'Well, I think something else will come out in the open like that . . . couldn't say mass assassination, but some sort of mass demonstration where the same thing will happen in key positions all over the United States.'[111] Over the next twenty years something very like the realisation of this fear was indeed to be played out in America.

III: The Accidental Assassin

In American films from the 1950s onwards, anyone can become an assassin, or be taken for one. Killing becomes a curse that might also fall on you. The killer turns out to be the passive victim of a will elsewhere, a sucker whose life falls under others' control. Various fantasies attach to this theme's many versions. One is that anyone might become guilty or be thought to be guilty of the crime of assassination. Surprisingly these films promise that such guilt can offer a kind of redemption, an anonymous life's saving grace. Another theme is that the individual's will is weak and at the mercy of elaborate conspiracies designed to fool the majority. Conspiracy is no longer the revolutionaries' preserve; it is the domain of governments. 'Authority' itself seems to act with the lawlessness and the covert duplicity of an Anarchist, Nihilist or *Feme* cell. In such a scenario, for all its intimations of the possibility of American fascism, an earlier assassination film, Robert Rossen's *All the King's Men* (1949) is quaintly old-fashioned. In this cinematic morality tale adapted from Robert Penn Warren's 1946 novel, the killing of Governor Willie Stark (based on Huey Long) is a simple act of retribution, meagre but comprehensible. The next decades would offer nothing so clear-cut.

Norman Panama and Melvin Frank's medieval comedy *The Court Jester* (1955) was the unlikely place where the new anxieties were first manifested. Danny Kaye plays a hapless Fool who against his will is altered, through the effects of hypnotism, into a remorseless assassin. Of course, the film is daft, but similar tropes would soon be used in edgier material. As we shall soon discover, the new-fangled notion of 'brainwashing' makes an appearance. As well as these more recent fears, the plot's ultimate source was the sleepwalking murderer of Robert Wiene's *Das Cabinet des Dr. Caligari* (1920). Behind that film lay over a century of *unheimlich* tales of somnambulists, the mesmerised and the vampirically controlled. In retrospect, the appropriation of this key film of Germany's *die Feme* era was to prove an unlucky portent for America. The American assassination was about to turn Gothic.

Alfred Hitchcock's *North by Northwest* (1959) presents an intermediate version of the accidental assassin motif.[112] Here Roger Thornhill, played by Cary Grant, is mistaken by enemy spies for an American secret agent, George Kaplan. However, Kaplan does not exist; he is a fictitious decoy created by the American government to distract the enemy's attention from the real double-agent working in their midst. In the course of the film, Thornhill is wrongly thought to have assassinated a high-ranking US diplomat right in the United Nations building. The guilt that attracts to Thornhill with this error actually provides an opportunity. He metamorphoses from a grey-flannel-suited Madison Avenue advertising man with two ex-wives and a singularly close relationship to his mother into a hero at the heart of an adventure, caught up romantically with the beautiful blonde double-agent herself (played by Eva Marie Saint).

The film is a masterpiece of wit and excitement, a visually beguiling exploration of the condition of the actor, an affirmation of modernity's possibilities, and a thrilling statement of a newly defiant individualism and acceptance of love. The Cold War provided the background. Only the year before Boris Pasternak's *Dr Zhivago* had been published in English, and its assertion of the personal life's fragile fulfilment in spite of the demands of history was in the air. Thornhill and Eve Kendall, Cary Grant and Eva Marie Saint, play along with the demands of the government. They are dwarfed figures, lost in an American vastness, belittled by the structures of the state. In the frame Cary Grant in particular dwindles to a tiny figure in huge landscapes: he appears running minutely across the wide-screen, viewed from the dizzy top of the United Nations building, or inconsequential in the dusty fields of the Midwestern prairies. He vanishes among the crowds of Grand Central Station, or blends in with the 'red-cap' porters at Chicago's Union Station. He disappears in public view. There are no 'homes' in the film, only spurious domesticities to hide secret agents, hotel rooms, railway stations and trains, cafeterias, civic spaces. Such absorption into the sterile public zone extended into the production of the film too: 'George Kaplan', the imaginary agent that Thornhill/Grant is forced to play, stays in the same Manhattan hotel where Cary Grant was living during the film's making.

For all its Technicolor glamour, the film conveys national self-doubt. Popular psychological and sociological works of the 1940s and 1950s lamented the decline of American vigour. Having told the nation *How to Win Friends and Influence People* (1937), Dale Carnegie's newest book informed us *How to Stop Worrying and Start Living* (1948). It was precisely the capacity for spontaneous life that seemed in peril. America's nemesis was 'the man in the grey flannel suit', the 'white collar' worker, the 'organisation man', the 'other-directed' member of David Riesman's influential treatise *The Lonely Crowd* (1950). The villain of modern life was the middle class.[113] The new suburbs spread out, the old traditions gone and novel conformities improvised there, a new orthodoxy for the quietly desperate. Of course, there was nothing new in believing the nation was ruined. The Jeremiad, that doleful diagnosis of the contemporary world, was a long-standing American genre. It was the focus of the sociologists' and psychologists' attack that was new. Now the great sin was sameness.

Even President McKinley was a subject of interest again, precisely because he stood on the cusp of this unexpectedly disappointing twentieth-century world. Now he could be taken as the last instance of an 'inner-directed' American President, one who could act, and when he acted did so on the basis of moral certainties.[114] These were now presumed to be forgone, frittered away by a political world founded on indecision and the retailing of glamour. McKinley was imagined as taking power in a 'mood' of 'conscious leadership' in order to pursue a programme based on 'conscious class considerations'. Therefore the 'bullet that killed McKinley marked the end of explicit class leadership'.[115] Czolgosz's assassination ushers in a new age, one deprived of the old certainties.

It was central to the conception of the 'accidental assassin' that it was the ordinary man who was guilty. Indeed his ordinariness was the source of the guilt. He was faceless, unfulfilled, unhappy. Spun out of their dullness, a nation of conformists produced banal mavericks in the form of random murderers, disaffected delinquents, serial killers, and the assassin. The average had won out. Without inner resources, lacking in energy, all they could rely on were their 'social skills', designed to cover their remorseless angst. In 'The Port Huron Statement', Students for a Democratic Society supposed that even the post-war prosperity was merely a glaze over Americans' 'deeply felt anxieties'.[116] 'Other-directed' Americans were educated to be conventional, finding their identity confirmed only in their neighbours' eyes. Workers were thought of as vying for 'status', 'prestige', 'success', an honours system in which existence depended upon the approval granted by others.[117] Mediocrity was highly valued, a sign of a person's place on the level with his fellow players.[118] In what was cast as the American version of Orwellian 'groupthink', it was the team that mattered.[119] The individual had vanished, consumed by the 'personality market'.[120] And now, with the Cold War in progress, this lowest common denominator was uneasily squared off against the differently bland foreign collectivist enemy.

In *North by Northwest*, Cary Grant embodies these anxieties – he is an everyman, constrained by work and alimony payments, and by an international political system that has no interest in the lives of individuals – and also somehow must become the spy he has been mistaken for. Yet he is also Cary Grant, the embodiment of suave style and witty kindliness, the American gentleman, classless and classy. Of course, he is also Archibald Leach, the Bristolian working-class lad with an insane mother who made up the persona of 'Cary Grant' in order to make it big in pictures. This quadruple identity is a paradox that the film seeks to explore. Conformity cannot keep a Cary Grant down; the heroic structures intrinsic to the Hollywood film will not allow it.

Two other things militate against the menace of insignificance found in those sublime moments where Grant is all but lost in the screen's enormity. One is the guilt that follows from the 'assassination'; after the murder, Grant becomes all too visible, all too consequential. Yet by becoming an 'accidental assassin', he opens up the possibility of redemption in his own life. The other is the relationship he forges with Eva Marie Saint. One leads to the other; being thought an assassin brings him romance. Finally, in choosing his love for her over the bullying demands of Cold War politics, the two of them make a space for their own freedom.

John Frankenheimer's *The Manchurian Candidate* (1962) took the scheme of the accidental assassin one stage further, namely in the direction of chaos and hysteria. The film was based on Richard Condon's 1959 novel. It showed a group of American soldiers led by Major Bennet Marco (Frank Sinatra) captured by the enemy (a combination of Russians and Chinese) during the Korean War. They are all brainwashed, and in particular, one of the group, Staff Sergeant Raymond Shaw (Laurence Harvey) is programmed by the Communists to be an assassin. Back in the USA, remembering nothing of their ordeal, bad dreams plague Marco, recalling their time in Manchuria. In particular he senses that something is wrong with Shaw. The Russians put Shaw through a practice assassination in which he kills the newspaper boss who has taken him under his wing. He is then handed over to his 'American operative'. This turns out to be his own mother, played with gorgeously sadistic venom by Angela Lansbury. She is the power behind her husband's, Senator Iselin's, election campaign. Iselin is Shaw's stepfather and a thinly veiled version of Senator Joe McCarthy. Eleanor Shaw Iselin's ultimate aim is to finagle her husband into becoming the Vice Presidential candidate, and then have her son assassinate the Presidential nominee. In fact, Marco breaks Shaw's conditioning down, and Shaw instead assassinates his step-father and mother, before killing himself. Shaw will also kill the love of his life, in a sleepwalked act that is both his own and not his own. Indeed, this somnambulant assassin was to slay precisely those he was closest to – the two soldiers in his platoon he least disliked, his paternally benevolent boss, his father-in-law, his wife, and finally his mother.

While *The Manchurian Candidate* takes over the oedipal anxieties of *North by Northwest*, it replays them as a different kind of Greek tragedy. Raymond Shaw, the programmed assassin, has an Orestes complex; that makes his mother a Clytemnestra, the killer of his father, whom he must murderously avenge. This myth merges guilt between mother and son, controller and controlled, the old and the young. Angela Lansbury even looks like a soured version of Jessie Royce Landis, who had played Cary Grant's mother in *North by Northwest*. (In reality, Landis was only a couple of years older than Grant.) Taking the link between the two films further, just like Cary Grant's Roger Thornhill, Frank Sinatra meets a blonde on a train, in this case a rather off-beam Janet Leigh, fresh from her shower in Hitchcock's *Psycho*.[121]

Images of Abraham Lincoln pervade *The Manchurian Candidate*: we see in turn various bronze busts, a portrait, a fancy-dress costume. Lincoln here stands for his own integrity, for the corrupt appropriation of his nobility by devious politicians, and as the symbol of the assassinated in American life. That last was a role which he was about to lose to JFK, to Martin Luther King and to Bobby Kennedy. John F. Kennedy was a fan of Condon's book. On hearing that a film adaptation would soon be made, he is said to have immediately responded: 'Who's going to play the mother?' (Condon would go on to write *Winter Kills* (1974), a blackly comic novel based on the Kennedy assassination.)

It was the Korean War that introduced the world to the practice of 'brainwashing', though in the 1930s the dramatic confessions of the Moscow show-trials had paved the way. The term derived from the Chinese expression *hsi nao* (literally 'wash brain') and was introduced into the West by the American journalist and Cold Warrior Edward Hunter.[122] In the late 1940s, Hunter had been scandalised by a Soviet film in which a human being was induced to share the same automatic reactions which Pavlov had evoked in dogs.[123] To Hunter, and soon to others, it would seem that the Communists were reducing human beings to the bestial. These fears were realised as Americans learnt of the effects of psychological and physical torture on allied prisoners of war and other 'enemies of the people' in Korea. Before directing *The Manchurian Candidate*, Frankenheimer read as many books on brainwashing as possible; he was naturally interested in its military uses, but also firmly believed that on the broader social level all Americans were being brainwashed.[124]

Following the impact of events in Korea, behaviour and mind control became a recurrent feature in the spy stories and science fiction of the period; scenes where the hero of the tale endeavoured to reclaim the humanity of a processed companion by appealing to memories of loved ones were soon a familiar trope. Such moments belonged to a present that had uncannily started to resemble some unimaginable future. Yet the techniques used in Russia and China were not technological or 'scientific', but rather evidenced the well-established impact of isolation, sleep-deprivation and systematic bullying. Such methods had been practised in much the same ways in the nineteenth century as they were in the 1950s, and indeed would soon be traced back to the Methodists and to the witch trials of the seventeenth century.[125]

A popularised version of Pavlovian behaviourist psychology was behind the idea's contemporary reception. Brainwashing and aversion therapy were both products of the period; in both lay the conviction that the human being was a creature infinitely malleable, a mechanical largely will-less dupe at the mercy of social and biological determinants. This was a period where behaviourist psychology was in the ascendant, whether in the versions promoted by Ivan Pavlov, Edward Lee Thorndike, John B. Watson or B. F. Skinner. It was only a few years since George Orwell's *1984* had dramatised the process by which the state could mould the individual's will. In fact psychologists and propagandists writing on the subject very often invoked Orwell's vision of a debased humanity.[126] The image of the human being as autonomous agent, the initiator of his or her own actions, was lost to a vision of persons conditioned and controlled. The assassin's deed diminished to the quality of an automatic response. In his novel, Condon quotes the Pavlovian psychologist Andrew Salter's remark about 'human fish' swimming about the world, sustaining psychic injuries.[127] The reduction of the human to the animal, along Darwinian lines, was central to Salter's approach and to that of his behaviourist contemporaries.[128]

Nonetheless, some were ready to praise the new techniques, and even to see them as evidence of humanity's freedom to manipulate itself.[129] One professor argued that the lessons learnt by brainwashing could be employed to help old people boost their sense of self-respect.[130] Very often too, such writers on the subject would make links to the sudden transformation of personality found in religious conversions and ceremonies, from Quaker meetings or Voodoo possessions to charismatic Tennessee snake-handlers.[131]

Yet, for most people, it appeared as though 'mass psychoanalysis' was eroding the heart's privacy, that secret self shown to be just another carbon-copy of your neighbour's secrets. Many suspected that modern advertising and marketing borrowed brainwashing techniques. The individual was being 'got at' by corporations and politicians, enlisting his or her support while circumventing his will.[132] Books such as Vance Packard's influential study of psychological manipulation in advertising, *The Hidden Persuaders* (1957) exemplified the new anxiety. (It's worth remembering that in *North by Northwest*, Cary Grant played a Madison Avenue advertising man.) It seemed that consent could be engineered.

The essence of humanity was in question. In *The Hidden Persuaders*, Vance Packard headed one chapter 'The Packaged Soul'; in two separate broadcasts for the BBC, in March 1947, R. H. Stevens talked on 'The Spirit in the Cage', and in January 1953, A. H. Farrar-Hockley, who had himself been a captive in Korean prison-camps, spoke of 'The Spirit in Jeopardy'.[133] In the same year that John Frankenheimer's film appeared, *A Clockwork Orange* was published, with its vision of a hero whose only possibility for free action is violence (unless that too is a behavioural by-product of his youth). Here too the liberty of the individual soul, even in the extreme case of its liberty to choose mayhem, was in jeopardy.

The automatic assassin was one free of responsibility. He was an entirely emptied individual, merely an irresponsible instrument. Drained of will, character dies. The assassin's crimes are not his own; he does what he is told. In a few years, this obedience would look in the eyes of the 'counter-culture' like a fitting symbol for the mind-control they imagined to be at work in the culture at large: their educations, the books they had read, the television they had watched. Particularly, it looked like another form of the obedience that led soldiers to kill in warfare, playing the power games of 'the military-industrial complex'.

The Manchurian Candidate found its home in a cultural milieu of bitter satire: of *The Sweet Smell of Success* and *Dr Strangelove*, *Mad* and *Beyond the Fringe*. In the era of the Cuban missile crisis and the Bay of Pigs, it played as a sinister 'put-on'; from the moment that Kennedy was shot, it looked like prophecy. The coincidences around the film in retrospect became pregnant with significance. The star of the film, Frank Sinatra, was close to John F. Kennedy, close enough to have introduced him to Judith Campbell, a young woman who became the President's mistress; Campbell was also sexually involved with Sam Giancana, boss of the Chicago Mafia.[134] It was through Giancana as intermediary that the US government was working with the Mafia to attempt the assassination of Fidel Castro.[135]

As we shall see was to happen increasingly through the 1960s and 1970s, consequence spilled over from coincidence. All events, however random, seemed to be happening on the same plane, connected and promising an endlessly deferred significance. Angela Lansbury had appeared in *The Court Jester* too, as a spoilt *femme fatale*. Sinatra had already made one film about the assassination of a President, Lewis Allen's glum *Suddenly* (1954), in which he plays Johnny Baron, a psychotic hit-man; there are rumours that Lee Harvey Oswald watched this film a few days before shooting JFK.[136] If Oswald indeed watched the film, it's not hard to imagine its appeal. Citing the murders of Lincoln, Garfield and McKinley, as well as the failed attempt in 1933 by Giuseppe Zangara to shoot Franklin Delano Roosevelt, the movie offers up the assassination of the President as a prize, a grand killing to trump all others. Along the way, Sinatra's anti-hero, by far the most intriguing person on screen, praises the rifle as the ultimate weapon. During the film the question arises whether killing the President is just like killing another man, or murdering a living symbol of something. It intrigues the assassin, but ultimately it's not about ideology; he's not a 'commie', he's an entrepreneur.

In the wake of the murder at Dallas, *The Manchurian Candidate* was withdrawn from exhibition. A reporter rang Richard Condon up to ask him if he felt responsible for the President's killing. Condon told him 'that, with all Americans, I had contributed to form the attitudes of the assassin; and that the assassin, and Americans like him, had contributed to the attitudes which had caused me to write the novel'.[137] Where some felt that Oswald embodied an alien violence, Condon was sure that his origins were closer to home. The American people had been brainwashed into accepting violence and destruction. Yet Condon also pinned Oswald's crime to his aberrant psychology, his resentment that excluded love.[138]

The accidental assassin theme resonated in the post-Kennedy era. What was different about Kennedy's assassination was that no one could make sense of it. The other killings of the early 1960s operated within traditions of the political. They were clearly motivated by long-standing hate. Even when the assassin was insane, the place of the mad could be comprehended. They were extreme, but their extremity made sense. Beginning with John F. Kennedy, assassinations passed beyond the assimilable. Rather than understanding, there was suspicion; rather than certainty, there was only the event itself, replayed over and over, as in Oliver Stone's *JFK*. The murders in Dallas fell into the modernist snare of the incomprehensible, the incommunicable. So it was that the event had to be replayed as a paranoid narrative, the assumption being that there must be a conspiracy behind events that makes them make sense. To illustrate this belief, film-makers seized upon the pre-existing genre of the accidental assassin.

Otherwise the figure of the cold assassin acquired new significance and popularity: Frederick Forsyth's *The Day of the Jackal* (1971) and Fred Zinnemann's 1973 film adaptation of that novel were key works. *The Day of the Jackal* was based on an actual assassination attempt against General De Gaulle; the leader of the attempt was Jean-Marie Bastien-Thiry, his motive being to punish De Gaulle for allowing Algeria's secession. The slippage between real event and film was typical of the time. The Kennedys had sealed a politics infected by film, by the longings of celebrity. In their turn, the political murders that scattered and scarred American life in the 1960s and 1970s seemed to borrow their narrative structure from movies, and indeed a significant proportion of them would be turned into films, fictionalising their unreality.

As we have seen, *North by Northwest* had presented a self that can only come into existence in the moment when it assumes guilt, even a misplaced and fortuitous guilt. In Hitchcock's film, the political seems so all-pervasive, so monolithic, that it requires the romance of being thought a criminal for the average American to gain redemption. This contrasting and interweaving of the personal and the political rendered the film a blueprint for the post-Dallas generation.

For the 'counter-culture' too had its penchant for violence. Michelangelo Antonioni's *Zabriskie Point* (1970) was in effect a remaking of the 'accidental assassin' theme as worked out by Hitchcock. Both were films made by Europeans attempting to sum up, from the outside, the experience of America. Antonioni transferred the story to the student protests and the counter-culture of late 1960s California. Mark, the film's hero, played by Mark Frechette, believes that he has murdered a policeman during a political demonstration. He goes on the run, in a stolen plane (as opposed to Cary Grant in a more humdrum train). In what seems to be an empty desert, he meets a girl, Daria, played by Daria Halprin, the Eva Marie Saint figure. The conjunction of character and actor names repeats the play on Eva Marie Saint/Eve Kendall in *North by Northwest*, and, as in the earlier film, signals that performance will be a theme of the movie. In Antonioni's case, this operates partly through the acting's stilted badness; no one looks like a professional here. The characters are inarticulate, silent; like Cary Grant and Eva Marie Saint, they find themselves by getting lost. Yet once again the most striking point is that the liberation on offer follows an abortive act of political violence.

Fresh from the sentimentally jaded *noir* of *Klute*, Alan J. Pakula's *The Parallax View* (1974) picked up the same theme. The film adapts Loren Singer's 1972 novel. A journalist, Joe Frady (played by Warren Beatty), witnesses the assassination of a Senator, and afterwards tries to connect the murder to the enigmatic Parallax Corporation. Rather than political indignation, it is journalistic ambition that motivates Frady. Meanwhile the assassination's other witnesses are dying one by one, in mysterious circumstances. Investigative commissions that report on 'lone assassins' and then suggest that there is no wider conspiracy are shown to be duplicitous or duped; behind the scenes, the Parallax Corporation arranges the killing of undesirables. Frady believes that they are hiring and training assassins; but in fact they are tracking down stool pigeons, finding violent sociopaths who can be conveniently scapegoated as the conventional mad assassin, while the real killer gets away with it. As Lee Harvey Oswald would put it, they're just 'the patsy'. And the audience is just another 'patsy'; we too take the psychological test that Frady undergoes in his attempt to be accepted by the Corporation.[139] Like him, we are required to ask the question: are we potential killers?

Frady is the 'innocent' man who comes into being by fighting the government, but here his association with the assassin is not a route out of compliance, but another instance of the ultimate victory of threatening forces. The film entraps and beguiles both Frady and the viewer. This is the 'parallax', the distorted view of the title. Paranoia does not confirm the hero's importance (I exist because I am hunted down, as in the 'fraidy cat' pun in his name), but rather turns out to entail his erasure – shot down as he is in the confounded belief that he is himself an assassin; so the film efficiently murders its seemingly indestructible hero.

The script and shooting play along with this ultimate deletion; Frady himself remains an occluded presence – even Beatty's charm cannot invest him with anything substantial enough to be termed a character. The casting of Beatty was a masterstroke. Already well known as politically liberal, his defeat in the film could take on a generational meaning: the 1960s radical finding no place in a cool and empty 1970s.[140] The film's use of modern settings follows and disrupts that of *North by Northwest*; in place of Hitchcock's awe for modernity are shiny, dismal and barren locales. Danger lurks in the everyday world, hidden in the ordinary moment like a bomb on a plane. Characters are shot from a distance (in both senses); voices are low, obscured; faces hard to read. The last assassination victim's words are divorced from his self; a taped speech playing while he stands wordlessly waiting. Often made small by the film's settings, Beatty moves through a wilderness of glass and steel and concrete: Seattle's Space Needle tower; marble offices; the high walkways of conference centres.

In such films as this, the hunted man is the partisan, resisting a government that acts as an occupying power. American government corrupts American ideals. The 'friend' has become the 'enemy'. This sequence of films had appeared in parallel with the assassinations of the 1960s and 1970s. However, as we shall see, that ongoing connection between assassination and film, between murder and its representation, found its celluloid quintessence only a few years later in the relationship between Arthur Bremer and *Taxi Driver*, and between *Taxi Driver* and the shooting of Ronald Reagan.

13

The Hate Bus

I: Probably Dead Men Already

I ask him if he believes in political assassination, and he turns the hard, impassive face and veiled eyes upon me, and says: 'I wouldn't know anything about that.'

ROBERT PENN WARREN INTERVIEWING MALCOLM X IN 1964[1]

When news of Kennedy's shooting came out, people were as likely to feel that Southern racists were behind it as Communists.[2] Such acts of political violence were then familiar in the Southern states of the USA.[3] There had been a move rightwards in the South, including among Democrats themselves. The local Democrats split as the party's liberal and conservative wings began to pull apart. Security was tight around Kennedy at the Dallas visit, mainly because one month earlier Adlai Stevenson, the Ambassador to the United Nations and a leading liberal Democrat, had been struck and spat on there.[4] There was worse being done than spitting: Texas had a higher murder rate than New York; by 1 November 1963, there had already been ninety-eight murders that year in oil-rich Dallas.[5] On the morning of the assassination, the *Dallas Morning News* published a full-page advertisement by 'The American Fact-Finding Committee' 'welcoming' Kennedy to Dallas. The welcome consisted of a succession of leading questions, the implicit meaning of which, in every case, was that Kennedy and his brother were soft on Communism and even that they were traitors.[6] On reading it, Kennedy is reputed to have said, 'We're really in nut country now.'[7]

After the shooting, stories went around that Dallas school children and students had spontaneously applauded the assassination.[8] At least one prominent magazine article explicitly placed the President's murder within the extremity of local conditions, 'the harsh and violent land' of Texas.[9]

The fact that at the time Kennedy's death could be understood within a context of ongoing political violence should put paid to the notion that his murder simply originated a decade of mayhem. Kennedy was about to attempt to push through a Civil Rights bill designed to end 'Jim Crow' laws enforcing segregation in the Southern and Border states. It was a deeply unpopular move, and resistance to the legislation was likely to be fierce.

The segregation laws had remained intact until the early 1950s. Schools, universities, public transport, eating areas, parts of public parks and beaches, water fountains and public toilets were all run on a system where blacks were not permitted to share facilities with whites. Moreover, although African-Americans were nominally eligible to vote, a number of limiting qualifications prevented their doing so. In addition, there was straightforward, or sometimes subtle, intimidation designed to stop black people voting. The injustice of the situation was obvious, but ostensibly unshakeable. It was based on the doctrine that the races should be 'separate, but equal'. In actuality, it enshrined the fundamental inequality of American life – an unfairness that many segregationist whites were happy to use violence to defend. In 1954, the Supreme Court decided in the case of *Brown* v. *Board of Education of Topeka* that racial segregation in public schools was unconstitutional. From then on, the battle was on for integration.

Political violence, in a form determined by racial divisions, already existed as a social fact in the Southern states. This violence was almost exclusively enacted by whites against blacks. There were numerous killings, all politically motivated, in so far as in the Southern states racism was a political matter: in Little Rock, Arkansas, in 1957, a racist crowd attacked nine African-American students hoping to attend a whites-only high school – the riots there drew in Army paratroopers to enforce the law; Emmett Till, a fourteen-year-old from Chicago, was murdered and mutilated in Mississippi in 1955 for flirting with a white woman; in the same year, Rev. George Lee was killed for trying to vote. In 1962, when a black student, James Meredith, enrolled at the University of Mississippi, there was gossip that Ross Barnett, the state's Democratic governor, had given orders for Meredith to be killed; many took the gossip seriously. The university was anyway a long-term stronghold of white supremacy: in 1954, students had honoured Dixie Week with a re-enactment of Lincoln's assassination.[10] At the riot that followed Meredith's admission to the university a French journalist was executed by the mob. (Meredith would in the mid-1960s become a political activist, working for civil rights. As such, in June 1966 he would also be wounded by a would-be assassin, while marching alone from Memphis to Jackson, Mississippi.[11])

However, it was the murder of Medgar Evers in June 1963 that was the clearest sign of the South's political tumult. It was the first of the long list of assassinations and assassination attempts that would scar the 1960s and 1970s. Evers had been head of the NAACP (National Association for the Advancement of Colored People) in Jackson, Mississippi. He was shot on the night that Kennedy made an unusually outspoken Civil Rights speech on national television. The killer, Byron De La Beckwith, a fertiliser salesman and racist, was found and tried. A hung jury led to a retrial, which was also hung. The killer remained free until a third trial in 1994; he died in prison in 2001. Evers's murder enraged African-Americans; there was a riot following his funeral, and talk of a revolution. Martin Luther King attended the burial, but decided it was best not to speak.[12]

Martin Luther King was born in Atlanta in 1929, the son of a pastor of a large African-American church. His father was the son of a sharecropper, but Martin Jr.'s own upbringing was bourgeois. King was under average height, stocky, but determined, and precociously bright. He read, he dated girls (lots of girls), and led the worship at high school.[13] He wanted at first to be a lawyer or a doctor, but then decided that he would be a preacher like his father. King went to Crozier Theological College and then, as a postgraduate, studied philosophy at Boston University, also taking some courses at Harvard. He read Hegel, Heidegger, Sartre, and others. A certain restraint marked his character; it was the quietly rhetorical exposition of theology, rather than passionate emotionalism that distinguished his preaching.[14] He would discourse on *agape* and Christian love in terms as suitable for the lecture hall as the chapel. In time he would even understand segregation in terms that were as much theological as political.[15] An academic career was open to him, but, newly married, in 1954 he chose instead to become a pastor at a mainly middle-class church in Montgomery, Alabama.

A year of quiet obscurity followed, before the Rosa Parks incident drew King into the public eye. Parks had been sitting, as the law required, in the black section of a Montgomery bus. When more white passengers boarded, she was asked to stand up, so the whites could sit, but refused, because, as she put it, 'My feet hurt'. Though an impromptu gesture, she had long thought of the moment when she would refuse to give up her seat to the whites.[16] The police promptly arrested her. The injustice led to protests in the town, focusing on a boycott of the bus service. In its initial stages, Edgar ('Ed') Nixon led the protest, before King was voted in as President of the Montgomery Improvement Association, the group that co-ordinated the campaign.[17] The boycott lasted the year, and in parallel with a legal challenge ended with a decision by the Supreme Court that state and local bus segregation laws were unconstitutional.

Through involvement with the Southern Christian Leadership Conference, King moved to a larger stage. His politics was based on taking Christianity's paradoxes seriously. King advocated self-abnegation, the path of suffering as a means of defeating the racists. An optimism about human nature was at the centre of his philosophy; if confronted by the inhumanity of their own laws, the oppressors would themselves choose justice. In this way, victims would touch their enemies' hearts. Meanwhile African-Americans could enact the moral virtues in their own lives, showing how much they deserved that justice, and how little the white supremacists understood it. It was a theatre of protest, as in public they staged and elicited white hatred and fear.

Although the ethical policy of non-violence was central, passivity was not. King practised and supported boycotts, civil disobedience, marches and protests. Non-violence did not amount to non-engagement; rather it constituted an active rebuke to the daily practice of white rule.[18]

But victory would prove costly and take too long. There had been so many racially motivated explosions in Birmingham, Alabama that the town was nicknamed 'Bombingham'.[19] In 1963, a victory over racial segregation there was won under the leadership of Martin Luther King. This triumph did not come without its costs. On 12 May 1963, segregationists bombed the home of Martin Luther King's brother, A. D. King, and a motel where the protestors had their headquarters. The aim was to kill King; luckily he was in Atlanta at the time.[20] Local blacks responded by rioting, a move towards retaliatory violence that shocked whites, who had long relied on the passivity of the oppressed.[21]

In September of that same year, the racists went further by bombing the Sixteenth Street Baptist Church; four young girls were killed. Violence followed as African-Americans rioted and whites retaliated. At the memorial service for the murdered girls, King insisted that non-violence was still the best route to take.[22] But the policy that had seemed vindicated in Montgomery now looked ragged and insufficiently responsive to the rampant malice of the South.

As G. K. Chesterton had argued in 1936, to be a pacifist on moral grounds was a noble attitude, a sign of stoic independence or faith in higher justice; however, the attitude in itself would not disarm an enemy. The refusal to hit back did not mean that you would not be hit in the first – and second – place. Southern segregationists and racists all over the USA were prepared to strike and even kill. Gandhi in India had relied on the power of shame, in the belief that peaceful tactics of civil disobedience would embarrass an empire. It had worked, though not without violence, in part because the empire in question was apt to be so embarrassed. In the USA, it would take the will of the country as a whole to overrule the laws and customs that enforced segregation. For here the segregationists' sense of the justice of their cause was strong. Moreover, they could both wield the power they had inherited and class themselves as the bullied ones – true Americans browbeaten by liberal Washington.

Of course, as scenes of white violence played on TV screens across America, showing extreme aggression visited on defenceless and un-objectionable crowds, it emerged that King's philosophy was ideally placed to transform majority opinion. White segregationists responded to peaceable protests with eager cruelty. Snarling dogs were set upon children; firemen knocked down demonstrators with water-hoses; police pummelled unresisting men and women with batons. The images were replayed, laying bare the injustice of American life. Men like Birmingham's City Commissioner Eugene (suitably nicknamed 'Bull') Connor should have foreseen that heavy-handed belligerence would prove counter-productive, and help push through the Civil Rights legislation that they dreaded.[23] One can only assume that the desire to attack insolent 'Negroes' was too overpowering.

Yet from the late 1950s onwards King's tactics irritated and perplexed his fellow African-Americans almost as much as they provoked the white segregationists.[24] As the years progressed, he would come under increasing pressure from younger blacks, dismayed at the slowness, meekness and apparent passivity of King's project. Even his essential aim of reconciliation between the races began to look suspiciously like surrender. As instances of white violence multiplied, and resentments about the commonplace occurrences of casual racism mounted, there was small appetite for *agape*.

Martin Luther King's great public rival was Malcolm X. Malcolm X seemed the foil to King: the peaceful versus the violent; the humble versus the proud; the Christian versus the Muslim; the college kid versus the hustler. In the eyes of whites, King represented the upstanding, moral 'Negro', and Malcolm X the vengeful, unpredictable black.[25] In the early 1960s, it was hard to shake the sense that if King's moderate tactics failed, the vision adopted by Malcolm X was the most likely alternative to be taken up by African-Americans. Robert Kennedy reportedly said to journalists: 'If King loses, worse leaders are going to take his place. Look at the black Muslims.'[26]

Both King and Malcolm X had developed rhetorical (and even sartorial) styles that made them ideal for the newspapers, radio and television. Malcolm X's public speeches were punchy and aphoristic; his words lent themselves to what would in time be called 'the soundbite'. King's oratory depended upon the rolling period, the cumulative rhythm, and the Bible-inflected phrases that resonated in the souls of church-going blacks and whites. The speeches themselves possessed a moral and political force. A very few have seen them as packed with clichés that conceal an inner emptiness.[27] The majority view remains that they brought vision to the debate, and allowed for hope within the crisis.

Not all believed. Malcolm X had little time for King's rhetoric or philosophy.[28] He found the idea that African-Americans could protest alongside white liberals ridiculous: 'Who ever heard of angry revolutionists all harmonizing "We Shall Overcome . . . Su-um Da . . ." while tripping and swaying along arm-in-arm with the very people they were supposed to be angrily revolting against?'[29] Yet King's vision was undoubtedly the more popular at the time. A *New York Times* poll among New York's African-Americans, asking who was 'doing the best work for Negroes', showed around three-fourths naming Martin Luther

King and a fifth voting for Roy Wilkins of the NAACP. Only 6 per cent chose Malcolm X.[30]

Yet Malcolm X and Martin Luther King held more in common than their joint destiny as victims of assassination. The distinction between them is real, but masks their shared engagement with American injustice and their mutual desire to end it through direct action. In 1964, the two campaigners seemed closer than anyone had ever expected.[31] However, there would not be time for a full rapprochement.

Moreover, both men were the sons of Christian pastors. Earl Little, Malcolm's father, was a Baptist minister and a dedicated campaigner for Marcus Garvey's visionary Universal Negro Improvement Association. Malcolm Little was born in 1925 in Nebraska. In 1929, in response to Earl Little's Garveyism, the Black Legion (an offshoot of the Ku Klux Klan) burned down the Little family home, by then in Lansing, Michigan. Despite the intimidation, the family remained in the town. Two years later, Earl Little died when he was run over by a trolleybus. Some have seen his death as an accident, but Malcolm was not alone in believing that his father had been murdered by white racists.

Disillusioned by the lack of opportunities for black men, Malcolm Little dropped out of school and moved to Boston. From there he travelled to Harlem, where he hustled and worked for a madam, escorting white clients (men and women) uptown to black prostitutes. He began a love-affair with a white woman, 'Sophia'. The erotics of race were plain, but puzzling. He saw it all: rich old white men, lawyers, politicians, showbusiness people, longing to be whipped by black women; black men desiring white women as trophies of their success; bored white women wanting young black men to ease their ennui or satisfy their lust. In his writing on the subject, there appears a world-weary but baffled curiosity, but one marked by asceticism. This puritanical quality perhaps prepared the ground for his approaching conversion to a particular form of Islam.

Back in Boston, he was arrested for burglary and sentenced to ten years in prison – he served seven years before gaining parole. It was in jail, through his brother Reginald's encouragement, that Malcolm Little was converted by the Nation of Islam, and once he was out of prison became a messenger for the Messenger himself, Elijah Muhammad. The Nation of Islam's beliefs were striking and apt to win over a young man with a history like Malcolm's. The most important element of his new religion was the pride and self-belief it offered to African-Americans. Brought up as he was in a society founded in racism, 'blackness' could seem in itself deviant, ugly and worthless. The teaching of the Nation of Islam instilled a fitting sense of the beauty of black bodies and faces, and the value of their racial identity.[32] Black people became the 'original people', essentially human and dignified. Whiteness was the aberrancy, a late and wicked creation by one Yacub (also Yakub) on the island of Patmos.[33] In metaphor and fact, white people are devils.[34] In a neat variation on Nietzsche's views, Christianity was the religion of the slave-owners, one imposed on slaves, a vast confidence trick designed to reconcile them to their bondage.[35] Life may be hell now, but there was a heaven beyond; that was the lie they had been sold.

The view that white people are devils had the appeal, at least, of explaining the barbarism that represented a great deal of the history of relations between whites and blacks (in the broadest sense of 'blacks'). It explained the empire-building of European nation states, the degradation of Africa, the destruction of the native American peoples, the bombs on Hiroshima and Nagasaki, and, above all, the peculiar institution of slavery in the democratic USA. It also elucidated the ongoing racism and prejudice, institutionalised and personal, which could be experienced in modern-day America.

These truths were revealed by Master Wallace Fard Muhammad, the Teacher, and the Founder of the Nation of Islam. W. F. Muhammad claimed to be both the Messiah and the Mahdi; some have suggested that he was the living incarnation of Allah. There is also some evidence that he might also have been Wallace Dodd, a small-time crook from New Zealand, or Oregon; the Nation of Islam vigorously rebuts this view. His views and divinity were promulgated by Elijah Muhammad (originally Robert Poole), who became the Messenger and effective leader of the Nation of Islam.

There is much in the Nation of Islam's beliefs that strikes an outsider as bizarre. The Nation of Islam bears the same kind of relationship to orthodox Islam as the Mormons do to orthodox Christianity. The faith provides pride, and, more than that, a means for the understanding of the world. It displays many of the cultish concerns that were central to the first half of the twentieth century: a preoccupation with the Masons;

a suspicion (and often more than a suspicion) of Jews;[36] a history of the world based on conspiracy; a parasitic relationship to established religion; Messianic fervour based on the 'charismatic' appeal of a leader; and an understanding of the world based on racial theory.

The Nation of Islam's philosophy depended upon the unmasking of conveniently suppressed truths, in particular, the brutal fact of American slavery and the racism of American society. Black people had been cut off from knowledge of their own history. There were, of course, other truths that Elijah Muhammad and Malcolm could not recognise: for instance the fact that racially speaking (as though such speech makes sense), Jesus was 'Semitic' like the Prophet; and the fact that slavery and a slave trade had been just as endemic in Islamic cultures as in Christian (or indeed as in pre-Christian Greece or Rome).

Yet these views could persuade so intelligent a man as Malcolm X. What mattered most about the Nation of Islam's ideology was its efficacy. It changed lives, reclaimed junkies, and gave many black people hope. How literally Malcolm took the 'devil' idea is hard to tell. He wrote that the term referred to the historical record of white people, rather than to individual whites.[37] At other times, it would seem that he did indeed think of individual whites as devils. Sometimes, it is clear that his faith in the idea is absolute, and pitched to the ardour of his anger. Yet when he calls the hunchbacked white man who officiated at his wedding the 'old devil', can he mean it?[38] In what sense did he believe it? In reading his *Autobiography* and his speeches, the ore of irony embedded in his passionate rhetoric is hard to miss. It is precisely this combination of vehemence and charm that provided the essence of his power on the platform. He smiled often, and more often half-resisted that smile.

Part of Malcolm Little's induction into the Nation of Islam was the changing of his name. Symbolically this action evoked many things. It marked the old self's rejection, and the birth of a new identity. Moreover, it expressed the understanding that the name Little was a lie, a British or white American slave owner's imposition upon his black slaves. It expressed not an identity, but the theft of identity. X was a provisional name for all new Nation of Islam converts; a transitional stage before receiving the Original Name. As Peter Goldman wrote:

To take one's 'X' is to take on a certain mystery, a certain *possibility* of power in the eyes of one's peers and one's enemies; it is to annul one's past and to assert that one has a future. The 'X' said Malcolm, announced what you had been and what you had become: 'Ex-smoker. Ex-drinker. Ex-Christian. Ex-slave.'[39]

X represented the 'unknown factor' of the lost original name; it both pointed to the fact that such a name once existed, and manifested its painful erasure by whites.[40] The curious power of the gesture testifies to a wider sense of identity as unstable and ungrounded among America's blacks – this anxiety being the inevitable product of their history and of discrimination in the present.[41]

The Nation of Islam's political agenda focused on separatism, their aim the creation of an independent state for America's blacks. The Civil Rights movement's hopes for integration appeared a foolish distraction.[42] They were nationalists on behalf of a nation that did not as yet exist. Some have understood the Nation of Islam's philosophy as 'inverted racism'.[43] Uncomfortably enough, their policy gave them something like fellow feeling with white racist groups; in 1961 Malcolm X acted as an emissary on behalf of the Nation of Islam to the Ku Klux Klan, to see if they might help each other in achieving racial separation.[44] George Lincoln Rockwell and the American Nazi Party respected Elijah Muhammad's beliefs; in June 1961 at Washington, DC, and in February 1962 in Chicago, they even shared a platform at Nation of Islam rallies.[45] After leaving the Nation of Islam, Malcolm X exposed their links with white racists such as Rockwell and the Ku Klux Klan.[46] Although it appears that while still a disciple of Elijah Muhammad Malcolm X was happy to talk with the Klan, later he certainly did not partake in the enthusiasm for Rockwell, and is said, by issuing a direct threat in an open telegram, to have ended the American Nazis' involvement in violence against King's Southern integrationists.[47]

Malcolm X scorned King's philosophy of non-violence. The staging of protest was performed by actors who, because they were black, were invisible and inaudible to their white audiences.[48] To him, such a tactic, or such an attitude, was criminal, a delayed solution and therefore a non-solution; no revolution could be made by turning the other cheek.[49] Rather he advocated meeting intimidation with intimidation, attack with attack. You should die for what you believe in, 'But don't die alone. Let your dying be reciprocal. This is what is meant by equality.'[50] It was really only claiming the right of self-defence; but to white ears it sounded threatening, and undoubtedly Malcolm enjoyed the air of threat.[51] The oppression of black people must be countered 'by any means necessary'. That famous phrase should be understood literally, and not merely as a covert way of announcing a programme of violence. Black liberation was the vital goal; if civil disobedience would bring it about, that was good; if violence, then violence was good; if compromise and negotiation, then those methods were the right ones.

Yet above all, Malcolm X strove for the directness of action. Unfortunately, the leadership of the Nation of Islam did not share his appetite for engagement.[52] Consistently, in the early 1960s, Elijah Muhammad shirked confrontation; the weight of support within the movement lay dormant. These circumspect tactics neutralised Malcolm X's potential to change things. While he inveighed against Uncle Toms and tamed 'house Negroes', Martin Luther King's Christian pacifists took the risks.[53] The paradox of the situation was apparent. Malcolm X talked big about violence, but performed no violent act.[54] On the other hand, King, the advocate of non-violence, created dozens of situations in which violence would erupt, as white rage exploded in response to the courageous acts of 'passive' black protestors.[55]

Malcolm X was left making flat-footed expressions of rage. In 1961, Los Angeles policemen shot at a group of black Muslims, killing one. The dead man was a Korean War veteran; he had been unarmed when the police shot him.[56] Malcolm X was grief-stricken and furious, but the philosophy of the Nation of Islam enforced the belief that vengeance belonged to God. Sure enough shortly afterwards news came in that a plane full of white people from Atlanta, Georgia, had crashed at Orly Field in Paris. They were members of the Atlanta Art Association, returning from a once-in-a-lifetime trip to Paris to see paintings. One hundred and thirty were killed. Malcolm X was making a speech when word came through; he turned to the audience and declared: 'I've just heard some good news!'[57] The callousness shocked most Americans. In time, he would regret the statement, but the impulse of the moment was telling.

Elijah Muhammad made him minister of the mosque in Harlem. By the early 1960s, Malcolm was confined to the role of being the

Messenger's mouthpiece; in recognition of the younger man's passionate articulacy, he was promoted to the role of National Spokesman. This was both a shrewd use of significant talents, and also a risky venture. By repute, Elijah Muhammad's presence was intensely charismatic. However, the visual and audio record tells a somewhat different story. He appears, from this distance, an effete and mildly creepy character, dressed in a trademark fez, somewhat resembling Bing Crosby. Meanwhile, Malcolm X's appeal is immediate and obvious. On film he is fast, handsome, engaged, witty and unerringly accurate. In choosing such a position for his up-and-coming lieutenant, Elijah Muhammad created a situation in which envy would predictably arise.

Moreover, Malcolm X was undergoing a similar process to that which had hallowed JFK. The media fell in love with Malcolm X. He was everything that television and the press could desire; they found him 'irresistible'.[58] He was interviewed for discussion programmes, invited time after time to talk on campuses. His looks, his passion, his fluency all rendered him ideal. He was an unusual and therefore a newsworthy voice; a black man speaking in media that had previously found very few places for the USA's African-Americans.

While Elijah Muhammad was forced to watch the younger man become a national media figure, Malcolm X himself was increasingly constrained by the limitations of having to voice another man's ideas. In the early years, this presented no problem. He believed the literal truth of all the Messenger had told him. When Alex Haley began the sequence of interviews that would lead to *The Autobiography of Malcolm X*, Malcolm had a hard time accepting that his own life was really to be the subject of the book. The real focus of interest was Elijah Muhammad, and the philosophy that the older man transmitted.

Yet, as time went on, the task of spokesman became harder to fulfil. One conspicuous failure occurred in the aftermath of Kennedy's assassination. Led astray by the passions of the moment, Malcolm X refused to toe the line, remarking at a public meeting in December 1963 that the President 'never foresaw that the chickens would come home to roost'.[59] The press expressed their horror at the comment, and vilified him as denigrating the dead President. He would say that all he meant was that given the climate of hate and violence in America, it was not surprising that the President had been killed. However, Peter

Goldman suggests: 'the remark about the chickens had got a round of laughter and applause from the faithful and that he had thereupon felt impelled to top himself. "Being an old farm boy myself," he had said, "chickens coming home to roost never did make me sad; they've always made me glad."'[60]

Elijah Muhammad was aghast at his protégé's blunder. He reprimanded Malcolm, and forbade him to speak in public for ninety days. The event would become a ruse for expelling the younger man from the Nation of Islam. However, the precipitating cause was not so much Elijah Muhammad's inability to contain his disciple's fame, as Malcolm X's discovery of the leader's hypocrisy. The supposedly saintly Elijah Muhammad was in fact an ageing lecher, regularly impregnating a succession of teenage secretaries. The result was a number of excommunicated women, all of them mothers to the Messenger's children. Convinced of the women's claims, Malcolm denounced Elijah Muhammad publicly.[61] In doing so, he not only cut his ties, he also signed his own death warrant. Once it had become clear that there was no longer a place for him in the Nation of Islam, one of the first things he did was to buy a rifle.[62]

Though in the end it was nominally Malcolm who made the break, the reality was that he had no other choice. For a moment, it must have seemed as though his world was collapsing. Faith in Elijah Muhammad and his teachings had freed Malcolm from the burdens of his addiction and his history. Now he was once again alone. Yet expulsion was the best thing that had happened to Malcolm X for years. The process of talking through his autobiography with Alex Haley let him recover his own life from the shadow of Elijah Muhammad.[63] Excommunicated from the orthodoxy of the Nation of Islam, he was forced once again to think for himself. The result was the initiation of a process of maturity that saw him acquire an intellectual and moral stature that had only been hinted at in the previous years. He began with a showman's interlude, supporting the young boxer Cassius Clay, a new convert to Islam. In Malcolm X's view, Clay's forthcoming fight against Sonny Liston was to be 'the Cross and the Crescent fighting in a prize ring'.[64]

However, it was a more traditional engagement with Islam that was to inspire the richness of Malcolm X's last year. In April 1964, Malcolm X was one of the very first African-American Muslims to perform the

Hajj, the believer's pilgrimage to Mecca. He came back as El-Hajj Malik El-Shabazz (and still Malcolm X), and was transformed. In particular, he had felt welcomed into a place and a faith that stood genuinely outside racial differences. There had been white pilgrims at Mecca, and he talked and ate with them. Although his just anger, his commitment to black people's right to self-defence and his desire to revolutionise America remained intact, he brought back with him a finer sense of shared humanity.[65] He began to think in terms of human rights; he could value the support of whites in the struggle for freedom.[66] He could even accept an inter-racial relationship, as 'just one human being marrying another human being'.[67] Only eighteen months before, such a statement would have been unthinkable.

He was full of plans and energy. He formed the Organization of Afro-American Unity; he visited Africa and fostered links between America's blacks and their ancestral homelands in that continent; he talked and made things happen. He could see how the struggle in America connected with the struggles of decolonisation around the world.[68] Yet behind it all was the sense that time was running out.

Malcolm X predicted the fate that was coming to him and to King:

The goal has always been the same, with the approaches to it as different as mine and Dr. Martin Luther King's non-violent marching, that dramatizes the brutality and the evil of the white man against defenceless blacks. And in the racial climate of this country today, it is anybody's guess which of the 'extremes' in approach to the black man's problems might *personally* meet a fatal catastrophe first – 'non-violent' Dr. King or so-called 'violent' me.[69]

In a television interview, he declared that he was probably a dead man already. There were many death threats. He had bought that rifle, and let the press know that he had it, and would use it against any uninvited visitor to his house. A rumour was going around that Elijah Muhammad might be assassinated. Malcolm was sceptical.[70] The rumours that Malcolm X himself would be killed were far more widespread and more credible. There were implicit threats and dark insinuations in the Nation of Islam's journal, *Muhammad Speaks*, including some made by the Nation of Islam's next leader, Louis Farrakhan.[71] Malcolm knew that he would not grow old; he would die early as his father had.[72] He talked on camera about how the Nation of

Islam were intending to kill him. It is this strange publicity before the murder that is now so surprising. He told the world that his death was coming; an aura of martyrdom began to suffuse the scene. He told a friend: "'I honestly think they're the only black people in this country who are capable of assassination," he said. "I taught them what they know, so I know what they can do."'[73]

He thought about gaining asylum for his family in an African country, if he were assassinated.[74] It turned out that he was right to worry about his family. In a harrowing replay of his childhood trauma, in the early hours of 14 February 1965 the Nation of Islam fire-bombed Malcolm X's home in Harlem. The building itself was the subject of a dispute between Malcolm X and the Nation of Islam; the house had been a gift while Malcolm was a minister for the movement. Now he had left, they wanted their property back. There were insinuations that Malcolm had burnt down his home himself. However, this is highly unlikely, for the bomb had nearly resulted in the death of his children. Malcolm was both terrified and incensed.

The end was getting closer, and Malcolm knew it, discussing it frequently in the press. On a phone-in show broadcast only a few days after the bombing, a woman caller told Malcolm that 'the Ku Klux Klan should get you'.[75] He told an interviewer for the *New York Times* that he was a marked man. "'This thing with me will be resolved by death and violence."' The interviewer asked why. "'Because I'm me," Malcolm answered.'[76]

The end came on 21 February 1965 during an afternoon meeting at the Audubon Ballroom on West 166th Street in Harlem. Malcolm came out to speak; he was introduced to the audience as 'a man who would give his life for you'.[77] There was a diversion in the crowd, as one man accused another of pickpocketing. Malcolm X tried to calm the situation, but as he was speaking three men approached the platform, armed with guns. He was hit sixteen times, by shotgun pellets and bullets.[78] His wife and children were there in the crowd. He was shot down at 3.22 p.m.; by 3.40, he was dead.

One of the killers, Talmadge Hayer, was himself shot in the thigh and caught at the scene. There is little doubt that the other two murderers were affiliated with the Nation of Islam; Hayer does not seem to have been a Muslim or a member of the Nation of Islam. It remains unclear whether they were hired assassins, or men who had been galvanised by inflammatory reports and speeches in *Muhammad Speaks*. Among Malcolm's supporters, anger was first directed against the Nation of Islam; two days after the assassination, a Harlem mosque was bombed. There were also reports that the killing was drug-related, after Malcolm X had begun a campaign against local dealers.[79] Yet the thought that Malcolm X was assassinated by fellow blacks proved for some unbearable. There was even talk that the Chinese were ultimately responsible.[80] There were white suspects too: the FBI had infiltrated the Nation of Islam, and had been spying on Malcolm X for years; some came to believe that the murder was part of the FBI's COINTELPRO operation, one intended to infiltrate and disrupt radical political groups.[81] Many believed, probably wrongly, that therefore it was the government that was behind the killing.[82] James Baldwin announced that 'the white community would have to share the blame. "Whoever did it," he said, "was formed in the crucible of the Western World, the American Republic."'[83]

Time would reveal Malcolm X as loveable, a hero of the times. For some African-Americans, he became a role-model, a politically faultless saint.[84] Even at the time some of the whites he inveighed against were drawn to him. Journalists wanted to get close to him, to understand. It was part of the secret of his media success, and one of the contradictions of his position. Even when he was espousing extreme violence (as self-defence), his white liberal audiences were more sorrowing than affronted. He manifested both black anger and white guilt. He stood for the fact that the oppression suffered by black people was too long-standing simply to be healed by a condescending, or even a heartfelt, surge of white sympathy. With insinuations of his capacity for violence, he goaded interviewers like Robert Penn Warren.[85] And yet, the lasting response to such tactics was a baffled yearning. If he had lived, he would very likely have in the end achieved, at least outside America and perhaps even there, the easy, guilt-soothing admiration that Nelson Mandela enjoys.

Yet his murder really did leave Malcolm X's task undone, and with no one on the scene with the passion or the ability to do it for him. His aim of politically uniting blacks in America with the new African nation states and other decolonised peoples would falter without him.

Despite the continuing value of Malcolm X as an inspiration to black people and to activists, in this vital sense the murder took him away too soon. This snatching of later promise in death is a feature of all the sixties' assassinations. The Kennedys, King and Malcolm X shared the fact of their relative youth. They all had more to do, and without the intervention of stupidity and cruelty in the form of their assassins, they all had the potential truly to change things.

II: Death of a Clown

Born in 1918 in Illinois, George Lincoln Rockwell, American Nazi, was the son of a vaudeville comedian and a dancer; they divorced when he was six, and he spent the rest of his childhood in Maine, Rhode Island and New Jersey, moving between one parent and the other.[86] He enrolled at Brown University, but dropped out and enlisted in the Navy, with which he fought with distinction as a pilot in both the Second World War and in Korea. Meanwhile his wartime marriage had ended. In the early 1950s, inspired by Senator Joe McCarthy's anti-Communist campaign, he came to his passionate belief in what he termed 'scientific racial idealism' and Hitler.[87]

The next years were marked by attempts to disseminate his philosophy, including as editor of *U. S. Lady*, a magazine for servicemen's wives, and by a sense of professional and personal disarray. He married again, and had another four children (there were three from the first marriage), but in 1959 was once more divorced. He tried out various careers, as commercial artist, management consultant, printer and cartoonist. He was eking out a lonely, makeshift life. But this confusion contrasted with the single-mindedness with which he pursued his white supremacist politics. His family were horrified by his Nazi obsession and pressed for him to see a psychiatrist.[88] Unperturbed, Rockwell advertised, addressed meetings and courted the media's gaze.

He indeed garnered attention, most of it hostile. In his darkest hour, in 1959, Hitler came to him in a vision and inspired him to persevere in his attempts to save America from its racial nightmare.[89] He would stand up for hate. There was a long list of the people Rockwell was against. He abhorred Communists and traitors (including Truman and Eisenhower), especially Jewish Communists and Jewish traitors (the two groups were synonymous), beatniks, uppity Negroes (or, as he called them, 'Coons'), Negro-loving, race-betraying white students and, worst of all, the 'queers'.

In political terms through the 1960s Rockwell and the American Nazi Party were nothing more than a sideshow; nonetheless as media darlings, they imprinted their own gaudy presence. They were ugly characters, but Rockwell had inherited his parents' vaudeville savvy, his tactics mixing showman's swagger with genuine brutality. He knew how to make a splash. Square-jawed, and handsome in a comic-book superhero way (he was all but 6 foot 4), he cultivated the image of an all-American, common-sense kind of bigot, a Nazi you'd be proud to take home to meet your mother. Never one to forgo publicity, Rockwell even attended the peace march to Washington in 1963, organising a 'counter-demonstration' of a few dozen Nazi faithful.[90] A dark counterpart consciously to the Freedom Riders and unwittingly to Ken Kesey's hippy Magic Bus, his 'Hate Bus' toured the South, spreading the good news of racism. In a Canadian television interview, sucking on his trademark pipe and surrounded by his jackbooted henchmen in a set festooned with Nazi flags, Rockwell declared himself to be in the same relation to Hitler as St Paul had been to Jesus Christ. If nothing else, this had panache. At times, the party's programme could seem a Situationist joke: their canine mascot was named 'Gas Chamber'; they released 'hatenanny' singles, racist parodies of the Woody Guthrie folk song.[91] They were exercised as much by Sammy Davis Jnr. (as both black man and Jew) as by 'Martin Luther Coon'. The American Nazi Party were both ludicrous and repellent. For Rockwell's theatrical freakishness masked the fact that the extremity of his views connected to mainstream racism and popular unease about Communists, atheists and African-American unrest. Though he considered George Wallace, the John Birch Society and others insufficiently radical, they were clearly operating in the same spectrum.[92] In 1965, speaking in a college interview at Santa Barbara, Rockwell praised the recently elected Ronald Reagan, Governor of California, observing, 'For a state that could elect Reagan, it'll be ripe for me in a few years.'[93]

If Rockwell was a joke, he was a sick one. He was involved with William Luther Pierce, an anti-Semitic physics professor at Oregon State University. Pierce would go on to write the luridly racist novel *The Turner*

Diaries (1978). This work would in turn influence Timothy McVeigh, who, on 19 April 1995, bombed the Federal Building in Oklahoma City: 168 people lost their lives; nineteen of these were children.

For all his revolutionary zeal, Rockwell was an enthusiastic supporter of the FBI, and did his best to co-operate with the Bureau.[94] On 27 November 1963, after the killing of JFK in Dallas, he even wrote directly to J. Edgar Hoover; they were after all on the same side in the fight against Communism:

Inevitably, however, such an extreme political movement [as the American Nazi Party] attracts irresponsible and lunatic elements who are not welcome, but who force themselves upon the movement and are hard to get rid of. The assassination of the President was, I believe, the work of such a 'nut' on the other side from us . . . Such bloody and violent events tend to generate further violence and bloodshed by deranged and violent people. For this reason, I have made up a list of persons who have made contact of one sort or another with this organization and whom I believe might conceivably become involved in further incidents.[95]

Despite such obsequiously obliging overtures, the FBI remained suspicious of Rockwell, and would attempt, through COINTELPRO, the counter-intelligence programme, to disrupt the American Nazi Party.[96]

Hated by liberal Americans everywhere, Rockwell would in fact be murdered by one of his own. Early in the summer of 1967, there had been a failed attempt to kill him. Shortly afterwards, in August of the same year, Rockwell was assassinated while fetching change for the washing machine at a Laundromat; he had forgotten his bleach.[97]

The assassin was one John Patler, a young, disaffected former fellow Nazi, who had been expelled from the party earlier that year. Perhaps he was dissatisfied with the leadership or prompted by rejection or ambition. Patler may have been acting alone and irrationally, or may – according to some – have been a killer operating as an element in a coup within the party, perhaps one organised by Matt Koehl.

Rockwell's own involvement with violence amounted to little more than badly organised bullying. He spoke publicly of the execution of 'traitors', and downplayed the Holocaust as just such a run of extra-judicial but just executions. Yet the only killings he himself committed were done during his time with the US military. Nevertheless, through the 1960s, his casual provocations intensified the sense of the potential for violence; the rhetoric was ferocious. He stood for extremity and admired other extremists, even those from the other side. In the greater story of American life, his death was a peripheral event. Nonetheless it was one more American assassination. It could easily be paired with Malcolm X's demise, both being the result of internal disputes within an increasingly polarised political sphere. Though few mourned for George Lincoln Rockwell, his death was another sign of the times.

III: The End of King

Although expressed more temperately and with greater sensitivity, King's views about Kennedy's assassination resembled those of Malcolm X. For him too, the murder in Dallas was the manifestation of a climate of hate that involved the whole of America; it was the most visible example of an everyday viciousness. Black people already knew all about assassination: they had the examples of Medgar Evers, William Moore in Alabama, and others to inform them.[98]

Around the time of JFK's assassination, King remained at the forefront of the Civil Rights movement. *Time* made him 'Man of the Year' for 1963. In 1964, he was awarded the Nobel Peace Prize. This was King's apotheosis. He seemed now a saintly figure, and soon acquired some of what is popularly – and wrongly – perceived to be the saint's ineffectuality. Meanwhile President Johnson was amusing close friends with recorded passages of King's adulterous flings, all taped by the FBI.[99] Like others on the right, J. Edgar Hoover judged that King was a Communist agitator, and had therefore decided to do his best to crush him, the tapes being one element in that campaign.[100] Therefore, in early January 1965, the FBI sent such a recording directly to King, with a note that implicitly 'threatened to release the tape recording unless Dr. King committed suicide'. Coretta King, his wife, was the first person to find and listen to the tape, with its recordings of her husband telling dirty jokes and having sex with other women.[101] The accompanying note's intention could justly be considered a perverse form of assassination attempt.

King braved it out, but from now on in any case his influence waned, as new and more strident political forces began to take shape. Partly this followed the segregationists' persisting with violent tactics.

Already, in August 1964, news emerged of the murder of three Civil Rights workers in Mississippi, two of them white, and one black; the whites were shot, but the black man, James Chaney, had been severely beaten before he too was gunned down.[102] Many immediately suspected the local police had killed them; in time, these suspicions were proved correct.

In the summer of 1964, King went to Harlem to join protests there against police brutality. He ended up experiencing antagonism from other blacks who saw him as siding with the forces of white oppression.[103] Though this was new, he was used to violence from whites: he had suffered numerous attacks; his home was bombed, he had been struck, kicked, shot at, and hit with a brick; in 1958, in a New York department store he was stabbed in the chest with a letter-opener by a mentally ill black woman.[104] He had been punched on stage by Roy James, an American Nazi, and he had even been punched on camera at the end of an interview by Jimmy George Robinson, the National States Rights Party leader.[105] There were other narrow escapes. In Montgomery, 1957, dynamite had been found on his porch.[106] There were some who felt that King himself was seeking death, that the logical climax of his non-violence would be to die, like Gandhi, by an assassin's bullet.[107]

Few others were willing to join King in his readiness for a martyr's death. In response to such attacks as the murders in Mississippi, it began to prove increasingly tough to restrain the impulse for self-defence. It was not so much that King was failing as that others were unable to match his vision. The white clergy were in the main indifferent to his cause.[108] And it was not just the whites who were indifferent. Among African-Americans a new rhetoric was on the scene, though it was not mere rhetoric when, in March 1964, Malcolm X declared that 'the Negro has already given up on nonviolence'.[109] A younger generation of activists were emerging, most of them middle-class like King, but more willing than he was to shed 'bourgeois values'. The new emphasis was on 'black power'. Although there were those, such as Bayard Rustin, eager to pursue traditional political paths to justice, as the 1960s reached their end it was the legacy of Malcolm X, rather than King's pacifism that seemed the dominant strain.[110] The precursors of the new belligerence were the Deacons for Defense and Justice, a group of Civil Rights activists from Jonesboro, Louisiana, who had armed themselves as a retort to white racism and black weakness.[111] The policy of non-violence seemed to contradict the experience of African-American protest, where the voicing of love and acceptance by blacks was too readily co-opted by anxious whites as a sign that everything was essentially all right. Peaceful protestors could easily be derided as 'Uncle Toms', more concerned with placating whites than with fighting to end oppression. King himself was not spared the contempt. There were even indications of plans by blacks to assassinate moderate Civil Rights leaders, including Roy Wilkins and Robert Kennedy.[112]

The spread of violence into the 'inner cities' bolstered the feeling that events were leaving King behind. In August 1965 there were riots in the Watts district of Los Angeles, when impoverished African-Americans vented their frustrations, burning down whole areas of the city. Watts was merely a precursor of the anarchy to come: that summer, there were riots in over forty cities; in 1967, there were 164 riots in 128 American cities.[113] Responding to this outbreak of civil unrest, the police, the National Guard, the Army themselves seemed out of control and trigger-happy, all too willing to open fire at an African-American target. Their implementation being flawed, Johnson's Civil Rights reforms had failed to salve the wounds of American life; in any case poverty and hopelessness rendered much of the well-meaning legislation futile. Socially excluded, picked on by the police, bound in poverty, the urban black population had had enough.

But in King's view perhaps the worst discovery was the revelation that such violence worked. Although it unleashed oppression, it also prodded the government into making concessions. After the impact of the non-violent movement, the new turn towards violent unrest showed itself to be just as effective, if not more so.[114]

The shift towards offensive action was signalled by the replacement of John Lewis by Stokely Carmichael as the leader of the Student Non-violent Coordinating Committee (SNCC); in 1969, they would drop the 'Nonviolent' from the name.[115] In 1966, King was first confronted by the move towards 'black power' during the 'Meredith March', where Stokely Carmichael and Willie Ricks and others moved the spirit of the peaceful march towards confrontation.[116]

However, the most significant group were the Black Panthers, led by Huey P. Newton and Bobby Seale; Carmichael was in significant alliance with this movement, whose other prominent members included Eldridge Cleaver, Kathleen Neal Cleaver and Fred Hampton. There were many other such revolutionary groups, many of them also black nationalists, but the Panthers were those with the highest profile; with their berets, leather jackets, sunglasses and guns, they were photogenic enough to appeal to the media. The new activists were well-informed, clear-headed and ready to use extreme terms. They voiced an urgent willingness to resort to violence, although once again such a move was understood as necessary self-defence.[117] In choosing the right to rebel the Panthers were being, of course, essentially American; their printed public statement, 'What We Want, What We Believe' ended with a transcription of the Declaration of Independence.[118] They were indeed a particularly American phenomenon. As H. Rap Brown asserted, violence was a part of American culture, 'as American as cherry pie'. The Panthers were modish, young, ready-made images of stylish aggression for the media. On the political front they embodied the same shift that saw Bob Dylan move from an Okie-imitating Woody Guthrie fan to a dark-sunglassed hipster. Rather than vapid talk about love, the Panthers propounded the thrill of power. Their very presence intimidated whites; they had discovered that the white enemy was after all only a paper tiger, and so learnt the sheer exhilaration of provoking fear.[119] Slogans such as 'Kill, baby, kill' were attention-grabbing, and ultimately cool.

Above all, the Panthers were simultaneously practical people, committed to improving African-Americans' daily lives, and utopian anti-capitalist revolutionaries, intent on destroying white American power. Following Malcolm X, the activists began to understand their position in America as that of a colonised people; as such, their drive for liberation was kin to the anti-colonial wars in Africa and Asia, in the Congo and Vietnam. Their inspiration was Frantz Fanon, not Gandhi.[120]

Yet King was not ready to be left behind. He moved into a Chicago slum, to experience ghetto conditions at first hand. Soon he demonstrated his willingness to push debate forward. He too began to link the oppression in the USA to human rights in general and to specific quarrels elsewhere. In particular, he spoke out against the Vietnam War.[121] In one sense, this was a logical development as, after all, he stood for peace and love. Its effect though was momentous.

As this was King speaking, his words implicitly linked injustices in America to the war abroad. In both cases, some might infer, the bully was the white establishment. Moreover King argued that the government's commitment to the war prevented social improvements at home, miring America in poverty. King's interests were increasingly in justice for the poor, of whatever colour, a shift in perspective that lured some to credit the CIA and FBI accusations that he was a secret Marxist-Leninist.[122]

King's stand against the war merely exacerbated the contempt and hatred that right-wing sections of white America felt for him. King was a marked man, and the end would follow soon. Some have even suspected a conspiracy against him, perhaps one involving the US government.[123] But when death came, its agent was a single man, and a rather unlikely assassin.

James Earl Ray was a conspicuously unsuccessful petty thief and prison drug-dealer (and user).[124] Even he conceded that he was not that smart.[125] He was not that sane either; in 1967, during psychiatric examination in prison, he was declared to be 'severely neurotic', suffering from an 'obsessive compulsive trend'.[126] In 1968, he was on the run from prison, having escaped in the April of the previous year from Missouri State Penitentiary. He was then seven years into a twenty-year sentence for a robbery in St Louis. For the fugitive, the world had changed since he had last been outside; it was now an era of 'peace and love', of 'freaks' and 'straights'. Ray both feared and despised the hippies; later he suspected that it was hippies who informed on him to the FBI.[127]

Evading arrest after breaking out seems to have been one of the few things he ever did well. Growing up in Illinois and Missouri in the Depression years, his childhood had been tough; ashamed of its poverty, when Ray saw the publicity about him after his murder of King, he worried that it made his origins look a little too 'Tobacco Road'.[128] He was shy, inept, rebellious (he was court-martialled during his stint in the Army), friendless, and wayward.

The murder of King was a political crime simply because anything concerning King was political. However, it is difficult to determine whether Ray acted for political motives. He contacted George Wallace's electoral campaign in Los Angeles, in order, according to his own testimony, to provide a cover story; if he were stopped by the police, he would pass himself off as a canvasser. Two of the most important writers on James Earl Ray have suggested that there was more to it than that, and that his commitment to politics may have been passionate and that he was 'obsessed' with Wallace.[129]

While on the run, Ray spent, by his own estimate, about $10,000; he was either financed by drugs money he'd earned selling in prison, or by fellow conspirators. How far Ray was acting alone remains a very open question. For example, considering the hatred and suspicion directed against King by the FBI, some have speculated about their involvement in his murder. King's opposition to the war antagonised powerful figures in the government. Any number of illicit racist groups might have sought King's death. However, why anyone should choose Ray, a small-time crook unused to crimes of violence, for their assassin remains uncertain. Maybe there was no one better they could find. At his trial, the judge declared that the matter was still open to doubt, one of the few moments in the 1960s when the judiciary was as disposed to believe in a conspiracy as the public.

From the Ku Klux Klan to the neo-Nazis, there were undoubtedly many racist and segregationist groups on the right who might have employed someone like Ray to murder King. For instance, there was certainly a St Louis-based plot to induce someone to kill King by offering a $50,000 bounty.[130] Ray had heard reports of this and other perhaps mythical bounties on the head of both King and President Kennedy. Whether or not he made contact with those promising payment, it is probable that his belief that he could make a fortune by killing King, combined with a lifetime's unreflective racism, was all the motivation he needed.[131]

Whether a conspirator or not, Ray's movements in between his prison break and the assassination seem haphazard and meandering. He travelled around Canada, Mexico, and the USA, using, among other names, the pseudonym of Eric Galt. (In London, after the killing, he would go by the name of Ramon George Sneyd.) In order to cure his depression, he let himself be hypnotised by one Reverend Xavier von Koss.[132] In his youth, he had been good-looking in a sullen, skinny James Dean style; on the run, the wrecked version of that young man was still attractive enough to win him the odd romance. He considered setting up in business as a pornographer.[133] In Los Angeles, through the *Free Press* he advertised for married lovers, for oral sex ('Fr. Cult.') and a 'swing session'. He exchanged letters with a number of women, bought a sex manual and some handcuffs, but his approaches came to nothing.[134] He also had plastic surgery on his nose, perhaps in an attempt to alter his appearance and make his recapture more difficult.[135] He was convinced that he would soon be on the FBI's 'Top Ten' list, a fear that was either a delusion of grandeur (he was after all a very petty thief) or an indication that he was already planning, or involved in a conspiracy concerning the murder of King.[136]

In Birmingham, Ray bought a rifle. On 4 April 1968, in the early evening, just after 6 p.m., he shot Martin Luther King, as King left his room at the Lorraine Motel in Memphis.

King was in town helping striking garbage workers. Only five days before, Lyndon Johnson had declared that he would not be seeking re-election; the possibility of political change was in the air. The night before his murder, King delivered a rousing speech that ended with one of his favourite images, of Moses on the mountaintop of Pisgah, seeing the Promised Land that he himself would not enter. After all, there had been a bomb threat on the plane he had taken to the city.[137] He was evoking his own death and the traditions that had long pictured African-Americans as the Jews escaping from Egypt's bondage. Yet despite these sombre forebodings, that next evening he was in playful mood in the motel, fresh from pillow-fighting in his room, and on his way to a dinner with Rev. Billy Kyles.[138] Moments after he left his motel room, the bullet fired by Ray hit him in the jaw, ripped through his mouth and entered his neck, severing his spine; Ray had literally shot out King's power of speech.[139] He was dead within an hour.[140]

That night and the next there were riots across the whole of America; 125 cities were involved. In some cities, notably Chicago, Washington, Baltimore and Kansas, the violence persisted for days. In Washington, the rioting was only ended by the arrival of the military; at the Capitol troops spread out in battle order. Overall, forty-six people died – nearly all of them black.[141]

After the shooting, Ray went on the run, managing (with the help of a series of aliases) to travel, via Montreal and Portugal, as far as London. At a time of outlaw chic, Ray was now a right-wing Clyde Barrow dodging the law. In London he very likely approached the Portuguese Embassy, looking for visas for Angola and Biafra, either to fight as a mercenary or simply as a staging post.[142] He had earlier contacted the John Birch Society to ask them for information about English-speaking African countries; it appears that his primary interest was in emigrating to white-run countries such as Rhodesia or South Africa.[143] Anxious and dejected, Ray rented a room on Cromwell Road, in Earl's Court, later moving on to Pimlico.[144] He was finally captured at London's Heathrow Airport, collapsing into custody almost with relief.[145]

As might be expected, various conspiracy theories clotted around King's death. As we have seen, it was suggested that he was murdered by the FBI, who hated King for being a 'Communist'; by the Communists in the hope of fomenting black rebellion; by white racists purely for reasons of personal hatred; or by more militant African-American radicals fed up with King's pacifist tactics; there was even the possibility that the Mafia were involved. Most of these theories do not stand up to examination. There is no good reason why the Mafia would have killed King, no good reason why black militants would have hired a white racist to kill King. Only the most paranoid could believe that the Communists would have sought to assassinate King. While it is true that the FBI distrusted King, it would seem a counter-productive move to murder him at the moment his influence was waning, and when there were far more militant figures emerging beyond the Civil Rights movement. That Ray could have been mixed up with white racists is the most credible of all these scenarios.[146]

Ray was extradited back to Memphis, where he stood trial, receiving a sentence of ninety-nine years in jail. At first, he had pleaded guilty, but then, three days after the trial's conclusion and his conviction, he promptly repudiated this plea, declared that he was firing his attorney, one Percy Foreman, and asked for a retrial. One of his new lawyers would be J. B. Stoner, a fervent racist who believed that Hitler had been 'too moderate'.[147] Ray's change of mind fuelled speculation that he was in fact an innocent man who had been coerced into pleading guilty in order to obscure any hint of conspiracy in the assassination.[148] Ray himself alleged that both he and his family had been intimidated.[149] However, he had most likely pleaded guilty as part of a bargain with the prosecution, whereby he would, in exchange for co-operation, avoid the electric chair and instead receive a life sentence.[150] In any case, his requests for a retrial were frustrated.

Ray had funded his initial legal defence by securing the involvement of an author named William Bradford Huie, with whom he would collaborate on a book exploring the assassination. Ray supplied Huie with what came to be known as the '20,000 words', a hand-written, befuddled and self-exonerating screed.[151] Though later Ray claimed that his contract with Huie had prejudiced his defence, the writer at first disseminated his alibi. This went as follows: Ray claimed that as early as August 1967, he was pulled slowly into a plot to murder King; in other words, he had been the dupe, the 'patsy', of a conspiracy.[152] That summer he began smuggling packages across the Canadian border for a shadowy underworld figure named 'Raoul'.[153] Ray claimed that all that time therefore 'Raoul' had employed him to sell guns; further, despite his initial guilty plea, Ray would later maintain that it was 'Raoul' and not he who had shot King.[154] In a 1977 television interview with Dan Rather, he also affirmed, and here for once it is hard not to agree with him, that assassination was 'out of his league'. However, Ray's attempts to exonerate himself are full of gaps, inconsistencies and mystifications. As early as 1970, Huie would cast severe doubt on the existence of 'Raoul' and argue that Ray had indeed been a lone assassin.[155]

More recently, evidence seemed to have emerged that corroborated Ray's far-fetched story about 'Raoul'. A certain Glenda Grabow claimed to know a 'Raul' (the name was spelt differently) and cited instances that led her to believe that this man had been involved in the killing of King, and, indeed, of both the Kennedys.[156] This belief that one man was behind all the 1960s assassinations was widespread. In photographs Ray had once tentatively spotted 'Raoul' as one of three mysterious tramps seen near Dealey Plaza on the day that Kennedy was murdered.[157] A 'Raul' was located in New York, who appeared to be the man named by Glenda Grabow; a photograph of the same man was positively identified by Ray himself. However, further investigations demonstrated that it was extremely improbable that the man in New York was in any way connected with King's murder.[158] 'Raoul' returned to the imaginings of Ray's concocted story.

Ever after his conviction, Ray denied that he was King's murderer: 'I wouldn't say I hated King. I do think most preachers are utter phony but I wouldn't consider shooting them'.[159] Through 1977, during the Select Committee's investigation into the 1960s assassinations, James Earl Ray was interviewed again many times concerning his role in King's death.[160] His testimony is strained, obfuscatory and wily; he was as much outraged by the suggestion that he had visited prostitutes as that he had assassinated King.[161] In April 1998, Ray died unrepentant in prison.

Some very little good came of the murder in Memphis: King's death probably helped the passing, a few days later, of the Civil Rights Act, 1968; the government had been poised to water down the bill, but the murder in Memphis provided enough impetus to get the legislation through intact.

The overwhelming impression is of irreparable loss. King had a lover's quarrel with the South. In the eyes of some he died after his work was done, having reached a position where he could no longer meaningfully influence events.[162] This idea neglects to notice the fact that King was still politically developing and considered dangerous enough by white racists to want to have him killed.[163] As part of the wider Civil Rights movement, he had helped to achieve legislation that laid foundations for greater justice in America. Yet, like Malcolm X, his real bequest was his story, an embodiment of honour, justice and love. As with the Kennedys, revelations of adulterous liaisons compromised this legacy for some. For most, such flaws tarnish little of what was great about this man.

For two months, it seemed as though King's death would be the nadir of the degradation of the late 1960s. However, in June 1968 another assassination came that would evoke even more closely the horror at Dallas.

Out from the Shadow

I: The Fire that Fell – the Death of Robert Kennedy

Doom was woven in your nerves, your shirt,
woven in the great clan . . . I miss
you, you out of Plutarch, made by hand –
forever approaching our maturity.

ROBERT LOWELL, 'R.F.K.'[1]

Let us dedicate ourselves to what the Greeks wrote so many years ago:
to tame the savageness of man and to make gentle the life of this world.

ROBERT F. KENNEDY'S EULOGY FOR MARTIN LUTHER KING, 4 APRIL 1968

Robert Kennedy was campaigning in Indianapolis when word came through of King's assassination. A journalist witnessed his reaction to the news: 'Kennedy "seemed to shrink back . . . as though struck physically." He put his hands to his face: "Oh, God. When is this going to stop?"'[2] He went out to break the news to the waiting crowd. He was thoughtful enough to still the audience, and to take the opportunity to express his political faith in compassion and understanding. He told them that he too had lost a brother to an assassin, one who had also been a white man. The next day, he spoke again and reiterated his belief that violence could accomplish nothing in America, except to degrade the nation. In the words of Abraham Lincoln, there could be no appeal from the ballot to the bullet. But, he went on:

Yet we seemingly tolerate a rising level of violence that ignores our common humanity and our claims to civilization alike. We calmly accept newspaper reports of civilian slaughter in far-off lands. We glorify killing on movie and television screens and call it entertainment. We make it easy for men of all shades of sanity to acquire whatever weapons and ammunition they desire . . . violence breeds violence, repression brings retaliation, and only a cleaning of our whole society can remove this sickness from our soul. For there is another kind of violence, slower but just as deadly, destructive as the shot or the bomb in the night. This is the violence of institutions; indifference and inaction and slow decay. This is the violence that afflicts the poor, that poisons relations between men because their skin has different colors.[3]

It was a passionate speech, one legitimated by his brother's assassination. The appeal of his oratory strikes us differently than Martin Luther King's; it's no surprise to learn that one of his favourite poets was Tennyson, or that he was by profession a lawyer. Yet, as with King, sincerity informs the cadences; it is language won from experience. Behind any speech he made lay the shadow of his brother's rhetoric. He had to resist falling into the Kennedy demagoguery; he could not be too eloquent, or too impassioned, without seeming as though he were imitating his brother.

The shadow of JFK was both a burden and an advantage. After Johnson stepped out of the Presidential race, Eugene McCarthy reportedly said: 'Until now Bobby has been running as Jack against Lyndon. Now he's going to have to run as himself against Jack.'[4] Certainly there were many who still hero-worshipped John F. Kennedy, his persona for ever sanctified by his murder. Yet there were plenty who hated the Kennedy family, with their air of privilege and what was deemed the automatic assumption that they should rule. In either case, Robert Kennedy operated at a disadvantage: he was both a pale echo of his golden sibling, and another incarnation of the Kennedy power-lust. He seemed above all a member of a family; his first task was a parody of that which befalls all younger brothers: simply to be himself.

In 1968, there were few politicians so loved and so hated as Robert Kennedy. Hubert Humphrey was a creature of the power-machine, Eugene McCarthy an honourable man; Kennedy was doomed to seem both. Some saw him as irascible and hard. He had made political mistakes: from the early 1960s, Robert Kennedy had not only known that the FBI had long been bugging King, in fact, he failed to end the intrusion, and indeed approved more wire-taps.[5] In 1968, this fact was still a rumour, but one that dogged his campaign and blotted his image. Lyndon B. Johnson loathed him, remarking: 'He skipped the grades where you learn the rules of life.'[6] He could estrange people, put off by some perceived arrogance or his haughty appropriation of the world.

As Saul Bellow wrote: 'His desire was to be continually briefed.' It was a politician's flaw – a grasping for information, for knowing what ought to be known.

Yet, to many, Bobby Kennedy was clearly intensely attractive. He was hero-worshipped, his jokes treasured. He was funny, active, intellectually avid. While making that eulogy for Martin Luther King in Indianapolis, he gave the impression of being well-read enough to quote Aeschylus off the cuff.[7] Above all, he was vulnerable, marked by sadness, and ready to withdraw into himself. It was loveable, this remoteness, this capacity for compassion; it was the terrible gift of his brother's death.[8]

He understood the injustices of American life late, often through his work as Attorney General; his tardy exposure to American racism gave him the exceptional advantage of being able to be shocked. So it was that a one-time confederate of Joseph McCarthy and Southern segregationists joined the Civil Rights camp. He adopted fashionable liberal causes, most notably his support for César Chávez and grape workers in California.[9] In those last four and a half years of his life, he became a gentler, warmer man. These experiences, and the loss of Jack, helped to humanise Robert Kennedy. The very dissociation brought on by grief enriched him.

He was always a 'conviction politician', burdened with the necessary conceit of those who want to change the world. He was pious in his youth, and even considered becoming a priest; in later life, he remained a committed Roman Catholic.[10] In the eyes of critics, he can seem a flawed ascetic – politically rigorous, privately self-indulgent. Their sister's marriage to Peter Lawford introduced the Kennedys to the world of the Rat Pack, though Bobby Kennedy did not take to their swagger and sleaze with anything like his brother's gusto. While relatively young, he was (despite his best intentions) hardly hip: he preferred Bobby Darin's version of 'Blowin' in the Wind' to Bob Dylan's.[11] Yet there were those who doubted that he was always so straight: tales spread that, like his brother, Bobby Kennedy had had an affair with Marilyn Monroe; it was put about that in 1962 his breaking-up with her might have precipitated the actress's death.[12] These adulterous revelations were for now only hints and pool-room chitchat. The public face of Bobby Kennedy reflected just as great a truth. It presented a passion, and a gentleness, that was to lead to his being taken in June 1968 to the brink of ultimate victory.

In early 1968, Robert Kennedy stood on the sideline, refusing to run against Lyndon B. Johnson. His being above the fray irritated those who wanted to see a new Democrat in the White House. For all his domestic successes, Johnson's prosecution of the war in Vietnam was wrong-headed and scandalous.[13] Moves were initiated by, among others, Curtis Gans and the charismatic Allard Lowenstein to start a 'Dump Johnson' campaign. Lowenstein's candidate of choice to oust Johnson was Robert Kennedy. After all, Kennedy had long been critical of the progress of the war; more than that, he was a *Kennedy*. In September 1967, at Hickory Hill, Kennedy's house in Virginia, Lowenstein met with him and did all he could to persuade him to join battle.[14] However, Kennedy hesitated. He worried that he might split the party and feared making a move against LBJ for what might be taken as purely personal motives; their mutual hatred was a subject of national gossip.[15]

Undiscouraged, Lowenstein approached other anti-war Democrats, ending up with Eugene McCarthy, senator for Minnesota, who had abandoned the prospect of becoming a Benedictine monk for wartime military intelligence and then a career in politics.[16] McCarthy was decent and impeccably middle-aged; therefore as a candidate designed to represent student activists, he would not alienate older, more staid voters. Although the senator wanted a scaling down of the war rather than its immediate end, he was still enough of an opponent of Johnson for Lowenstein's purposes. While Kennedy vacillated, McCarthy threw his hat into the ring, and went to the New Hampshire primary and won it. Movie stars such as Paul Newman had come to New Hampshire for McCarthy, but more vitally the students had fallen in behind him; the old liberal looked for a moment like a standard-bearer for youth.[17] And only then, after McCarthy had gained a victory, did Robert Kennedy come out as a candidate for the Democratic nomination. In waiting until McCarthy had already shown that Johnson was susceptible to attack, Robert Kennedy alienated the students who might have been his natural supporters. These were now strongly for McCarthy, who looked a man of principle, whereas Kennedy appeared an opportunist interested only in power. Many were enraged with Kennedy for standing so late and splitting the anti-war vote for what seemed to them trivial reasons of ambition. Even after Kennedy's death, in writing about the campaign, McCarthy could not hide his bitterness.[18]

Those early months of 1968 were spent arduously campaigning. In late March Johnson dropped out of the race, as his opponents' success indicated his own inevitable defeat if he should cling on. In any case, LBJ was dejected, wearied by the war and the civil disturbances at home. Vice President Hubert Humphrey was named as his official successor. Once instrumental in the founding of the Peace Corps, Hubert Humphrey had become as Vice President a mouthpiece for LBJ's ideas and a willing butt for his sarcasm. However, particularly when they concerned Vietnam, those ideas proved a tough sell. He looked hapless: visiting Germany, Humphrey had been threatened by an 'assassination plot' organised by German hippies, where the 'bomb' turned out to be made from custard. Moreover, in the public mind he was too tied to Johnson's policy on Vietnam to seem properly his own man. The mood of the country was for change, and Humphrey failed to appease that mood.

With a show of being above the fray, Humphrey refused to fight the primaries, and painlessly picked up the delegates in the non-primary states. The South was largely his for the taking; faced with the prospect of McCarthy or Kennedy, the Dixie Democrats naturally favoured Humphrey.[19] In states where there was a vote, a majority came out against Humphrey, and against the war. Yet, armed with his pack of delegates, Humphrey still looked set to win the nomination at the Chicago Convention in August.

The struggle between McCarthy and Kennedy soon developed therefore into a battle to see who would oppose Humphrey at Chicago. As we have seen, Kennedy's early reluctance to fight had sabotaged his support among significant sections of the Democrats: McCarthy had the students with him; Kennedy's constituency consisted of African-Americans, Hispanics, native Americans and poor whites.[20] He had as yet apparently failed to convince the white middle class to back him.

However, Robert Kennedy was a charismatic campaigner. He went on the stump, and won the early primaries. Then the run for election stuttered in Oregon, a state where the groups that made up the hard core of his vote were demographically insignificant. Losing Oregon was a set-back, the first electoral loss by any Kennedy for decades. The drive for the nomination suddenly looked shaky; paradoxically, this electoral wobble invigorated the Kennedy will to fight and humanised his public image.[21] The silver spoon had been plucked from his mouth. He came back to California, the next primary in contention, fired up, and against the ropes. Where the fastidious McCarthy stuck to television, Kennedy was on the streets, out among the crowds. His would be a campaign based on contact, on being mauled and manhandled, a rough intimacy.[22] As his own TV adverts made clear, he was 'going to the people'. By the end of the California campaign, he looked tired, his speeches stuttering. Yet his charisma remained. If he could win California, he might still be the man to stop Humphrey.

Kennedy and his entourage spent Monday 3 June campaigning in San Francisco, showing themselves around the city in a convertible. As they were driving through Chinatown in a motorcade, something like shots rang out. Kennedy's wife, Ethel, was distraught, but Kennedy himself managed to keep smiling and waving. Though it had only been firecrackers, inevitably everyone remembered Dallas.[23]

The next day he swam in the Pacific Ocean with his children. In the evening, with John Frankenheimer he drove through the Los Angeles fog up to Wiltshire Boulevard and the Ambassador Hotel. They arrived around 7.30 p.m., and Kennedy settled with friends and family into Suite 511. It was so crowded that for privacy he had to chat to the politician Richard Goodwin in the bathroom.[24] Across the hall in Suite 516 assorted reporters, politicos and donors had gathered. The news was already good: he had swept the board in South Dakota. It was a good omen for California. Although the early results were not encouraging, nevertheless by 10.00 that night, it was apparent that Kennedy had won. He gave an interview to CBS, and was amiably chatty; later he gave another couple of interviews, one for ABC and one for radio. He went back to his hotel room, while the crowd waited impatiently in the Embassy Ballroom. When the victory was definite, he went downstairs to make his acceptance speech. He was hoping that César Chávez would be up there on the platform with him, but, feeling out of place without his wife there, Chávez had already gone home.[25] In a knot of his closest supporters, Kennedy struggled to the platform through a mêlée of journalists. He was smiling; he gave a little 'V for victory' sign, and stood on the podium, while the crowd called out, over and over, 'We want Bobby; we want Kennedy.' The microphones appeared to be down; behind him the cameras flashed. The room was hot, bustling under the chandeliers; girls were wearing campaign boaters, some sitting on others' shoulders to get a better view. He began with various thank-yous, and then with jokes: 'I want to express my gratitude to my dog Freckles, who's been maligned. As Frank Delano Roosevelt said, I don't care what they say about me, but when they start to attack my dog . . . I'm not doing this in any order of importance, but I also want to thank my wife Ethel.' He even jokingly referred to his own reputation as 'ruthless'. He was relaxed, relieved and ultimately inspiring. He spoke against the disenchantment in America and the nation's divisions. And he spoke for the fact that they as a country could work together, and bridge those divisions. 'We can start to work together. We are a great country, an unselfish country, and a compassionate country.'

He was shaking hands as he always did. Often he would come back from a day's campaigning scratched and bruised from the hands of voters. He left the podium to go over to the Colonial Room for a press conference. The party workers began to move around, some to head outside, though most remained in the room. A chant began of 'RFK! RFK!' It petered out, and then another chant began; but this one was ended by screams. Then news of what had happened spread through the crowd, quickly, and the screaming grew louder and spread across the crowded ballroom.

As they left the hall, Kennedy and his entourage walked into a passageway, between the ballroom and the kitchens, and then came out in the kitchen pantry. The room was dishevelled, littered. There was quite a crowd there, with supporters and journalists. Kitchen staff were lined up to meet him, and he shook hands with them as he walked through. There was an instant's hesitation at first – was it balloons popping, or firecrackers? – and then everyone knew what had happened, and confusion broke out: a young man had opened fire. The shots followed one another 'in a fearsome succession'.[26] One of the shots struck Kennedy behind his ear, penetrating into the brain; this would be his death-wound.[27] The youth was immediately restrained by a number of men, including the football player Roosevelt Grier, but he continued firing until his gun was empty of all its eight shots. Then he was on the floor, bundled over by bodies pinning him down, Grier calling out over and over, 'Don't kill him.' No one wanted another Ruby. Five bystanders were also shot, including one who was hit in the head; all survived. There was shouting, sobbing, the room a confusion. A busboy at the hotel, Juan Romero, cradled Kennedy's head in his hands for a moment. Then others rushed up, crowding the body. Kennedy asked, 'Is everybody else all right?'[28] Ethel Kennedy was beside him. As Kennedy lay bleeding on the cement floor, with the panic around him, he asked his wife quietly, 'Am I going to die?' They took photographs of him lying there, spreadeagled in his suit, his head raised a little from the floor. They took photographs too of a distraught Ethel Kennedy, pushing back at bystanders to give her husband room. A Roman Catholic in the crowd had begun to administer the last rites; as he did so, Kennedy looked him in the eyes, and squeezed his hand. Twenty-six hours later at the Hospital of the Good Samaritan, he was pronounced dead.

They flew him to New York, and then he would go south to be buried in Arlington Cemetery. As the train bearing Robert Kennedy's body moved from Manhattan to Washington, DC, in the June heat, all along the route people came out to pay their respects. More accustomed to flying, some on the train felt they were seeing America anew, a nation decrepit, dilapidated and squalid, a place that was strange to them.[29] In Baltimore Station, the crowd sung the 'Battle Hymn of the Republic'.[30] On the platforms, along the sidings, from back gardens, at intersections, the people stood and watched the train going by. Very few took photographs; most just gazed. Some saluted; one man waved a hat; a nun fluttered a white handkerchief. There were flags, the Stars and Stripes; there were hand-painted placards with Bobby Kennedy's name. They kept that strange vigil from Newark down to Maryland, and beyond. Families lined in rows, schoolgirls in uniform, a patient crowd on the Wilmington platform.[31] It was a gesture which for one more moment embodied Kennedy's dream of America breaking down divisions, an expression of a compassionate country.

Even now his murder moves us. John Frankenheimer expressed the views of many when he affirmed that the death of Robert Kennedy deprived the American nation of hope. There was no longer a major political figure active in the field who could transform the nation.[32] There was instead Hubert Humphrey and Richard Milhous Nixon.

The night of 4 June 1968, Richard Nixon certainly believed that he would end up fighting against Bobby Kennedy as the Democratic candidate: 'I believed that Hubert Humphrey had waited too long before declaring his candidacy, and I saw no way a Kennedy juggernaut could be stopped once it had acquired the momentum of a California victory. As I went to bed, I said, "It sure looks like we'll be going against Bobby."'[33] He was wakened the next morning by news of the shooting. Despite Humphrey's apparently commanding position, Nixon's gut feeling about Kennedy's prospects for success was shared by many. Part of the chaos at the Democrats' Chicago Convention that August was prompted by that sense of loss. The probability that Kennedy might have defeated Humphrey, where McCarthy could not, haunted the situation. The assassination wounded both McCarthy and Humphrey; they both looked like second-best. McCarthy observed of the campaign after Bobby's murder that 'It's like a football game without a goal line'.[34] If Kennedy had won the nomination it is entirely possible that he might have gone on to defeat Richard Nixon in the battle for the Presidency. The course of American politics for a generation was therefore altered, once again, by an assassin's bullet.

Sirhan Sirhan, Kennedy's assassin, appeared to come from nowhere. He was a Middle Eastern assassin and few Americans were interested in the Middle East; their eyes were on the ghettoes, the campuses, the jungles of Vietnam. The murder seemed not only tragic, its motivation seemed irrelevant. Yet it offered a perfect illustration of America's fears for itself. Robert Kennedy had been killed at the moment of greatest hope, celebrating a victory that promised a revolt against the Democratic establishment that had betrayed a nation into fighting a largely unwanted war in south-east Asia. Moreover, he had died soothed by the caress of fame: with George Plimpton and famous sportsmen grappling his killer to the ground, with the singer Rosemary Clooney in the ballroom audience, the film director John Frankenheimer upstairs, and the movie-star Robert Vaughn at the funeral. The conjunction of all that was most attractive and glossy about contemporary America and all that was most abject and debased could not have been more forceful. American glory was brought down by its own shadow. And that shadow was a scrawny, insignificant youth, a man whose dreams had extended only as far as a meaningless act of revenge.

Sirhan Bishara Sirhan was a 24-year-old immigrant, a Jordanian Christian born in Jerusalem. As a child he had experienced at first hand the military conflict that saw the creation of the Israeli state and the dispossession of the Palestinians; the family lived through repeated artillery shelling and bombings.[35] As refugees, he and his family moved to the USA, living in California since 1957; unable to adjust to American life, his father returned to Jordan, leaving the family behind him. Sirhan attended high school in Pasadena, and then found small-time jobs as a grocery boy at a health food store, a labourer and clerk. He helped nurse his sister as she struggled with leukemia; she died in 1965.

He did not appear to have a criminal or political past; a preliminary CIA investigation into Sirhan turned up nothing.[36] An enthusiast for learning languages (he had taken both German and Russian at school), his family felt that he might have followed a career as a translator. However, he chose instead to become a trainee jockey and stable boy.[37] A fall from a horse, with a blow to his head, put an end to his ambitions, and also seems to have altered his personality. After the accident, he became solitary and reserved; he developed too an interest in the occult, joining, by mail, the Rosicrucians and reading up on Theosophy.[38] His sister's death nourished this interest; it had inspired him to wonder about the world beyond.[39] As part of his occult preoccupations, he seems to have started practising self-hypnosis. In March 1968, he bought a gun. On 18 May 1968, Sirhan wrote in his notebook, 'R. F. K. must die', repeating the phrase over and over, with variations: 'Robert F. Kennedy must be assassinated. Robert F. Kennedy must be assassinated before 5 June '68.'[40] The date of the murder was the first anniversary of the Six-Day War, in which Israel had defeated a coalition of Arab nations.

After the shooting, there were those who were prepared to take the politics of Sirhan's attack seriously, and even to portray him as 'a good man' if a flawed one. They perceived the assassination as a blow against an American political system that valued Jewish votes over Arab lives.[41] Such accounts described Sirhan unequivocally as a displaced Palestinian. Yet at the same time in the mainstream media the Middle Eastern connection was largely ignored, as the prosecutors and public instead chose to focus on Sirhan's mental state.[42] What seems to have angered Sirhan was Robert Kennedy's support for American-made bombers being provided for the Israeli government. As we have seen, Sirhan and his family had been bombed themselves, the memories of those times a childhood trauma.

However, if placed in the history of assassination, the most striking thing about Sirhan's role as assassin is the fact that he acted without the support of political party, underground group or ideological backing. Rather, in a life of drift, plotting Kennedy's murder gave him a purpose. He was simply enraged, a private individual killing a public man for political reasons. He was not part of a movement; like Oswald, like Ray, he was another example of a new kind of killer whose political motivations appeared insubstantial, unplaced. He belonged not to a group, but to a 'climate' of violence. So it was that Robert Kennedy's death seems to fit so snugly with the other late sixties killings, though each murder was in fact perpetrated for wildly different reasons: a dispute within the black nationalist movement; white anger at the visibility of African-American success; Middle Eastern politics. What linked the killings was not Nihilism, or Anarchism, or a specific political programme; the connection was simply that they were assassinations, and as such manifestations of what was starting to seem a peculiarly American disorder.

On 4 June 1968, Sirhan passed the day casually. In the morning he bought some ammo, two boxes of bullets. He then did some target practice at the San Gabriel Rifle Range. Killing time at Bob's Big Boy diner, he bumped into a friend, challenging him to a game of pool. But the friend wasn't interested, so Sirhan made his way to the Ambassador Hotel, perhaps hoping to join the party there. Usually abstemious, according to his own later testimony on this occasion he downed four Tom Collins cocktails.[43] After this, the evening and the crime itself is a blank to Sirhan. In custody, Sirhan unravelled part of the story out of that blank while under the influence of a hypnotic trance. In this state, he recalled that in the hotel he went looking for a coffee. He met a girl who wanted a coffee too, and he followed her down into the dark pantry. From then on, Sirhan claims to remember almost nothing of what took place that night, just the darkness and some flashes of light, and nothing more.

Sirhan's forgetfulness suggests a self that is somehow not really there. He cannot picture himself writing those incriminating notebooks; he cannot see himself committing the murder. It is this gap in his memory that has kept Sirhan in prison, being taken by parole boards as lack of remorse. Lawrence W. Sloan, the handwriting expert who examined Sirhan's notebooks, declared that 90 per cent of the writing there was undoubtedly that of Sirhan. When asked about the remaining 10 per cent, he suggested 'that the handwriting "indicates a writer who apparently 'experiments' with his writing construction from time to time"'.[44] Similarly, Sirhan may have played with the construction of his personality; his stated motive for joining the Rosicrucians was the sense of how little he knew himself.[45]

Sirhan has pointed to a comparable self-division in Kennedy too, as a politician who pitied America's oppressed blacks, but showed no equivalent sympathy for the similarly oppressed Palestinians. Likewise Sirhan has also expressed his fellow-feeling for Edward Kennedy, who seemingly experienced just such another lapse of self in the moments when he left Mary Jo Kopechne to drown at Chappaquiddick.[46] According to his own account of the matter, the incoherence of self found in Sirhan begins to seem a Kennedy trait.

In January 1969, the case went to trial. Sirhan's lawyers pursued a defence based on diminished capacity on account of the effects of his fall. On 17 April, he was convicted of the first-degree murder of Robert Kennedy; one month later, he was sentenced to death. In California, that penalty would have been carried out in a gas chamber. But in time, due to a change in the law, the sentence was commuted to life imprisonment.

Sirhan's very implausibility as an assassin helped to create a new set of conspiracy theories around this second Kennedy murder. Robert Blair Kaiser offers a particularly compelling version of events, in which all the major assassinations of the period are linked, and Sirhan is said to have killed Kennedy while under the influence of a hypnotic trance.[47] He was in short a Manchurian candidate, but one controlled by American agents. After all, just like the Chinese and Russians, since the early 1950s the Americans had been experimenting in psychological warfare and brainwashing techniques. In 1978, William G. Turner and Jonn G. Christian offered further evidence for this thesis.[48] Is it true, as they argue, that Sirhan was an accidental assassin? There are reasons to doubt it: it is unclear why his controllers (sometimes thought to be the

CIA) should have chosen him. The motive usually given is that it was because Sirhan was so highly susceptible to hypnotism, though it's hard to guess how the CIA would have known this. On the other hand, as we shall soon see, there are inconsistencies in the evidence regarding the shooting itself. As this book goes to press (summer 2012) still in prison for the murder, Sirhan himself continues to imply that his having been brainwashed may be the reason for the murder, and on the basis of this defence he continues to hope to achieve parole.

Sirhan's inability to remember the event has been taken as proof of his brainwashing. It may rather expose another form of self-division, a sense of guilt so great that it refuses to concede its existence. In this understanding of the events, he was not controlled by another, but neither was he fully in control of himself, not through insanity, but through a fragmentation of his identity; he has remarked: 'If I was to accept responsibility for this crime, it would be a hell of a burden to live with – having taken a human life without knowing it.'[49]

So it is that, as with JFK's death, suspicions of conspiracy hang over Robert Kennedy's murder. The doubts regarding the official version depend chiefly on two strands of evidence. Firstly, Sirhan could only have fired at most eight shots, as that was all the ammunition his gun held. Eye-witnesses and, some assert, the evidence of the wounds on the Senator and the five other injured bystanders, to say nothing of the alleged discovery of additional bullets buried in a pantry doorframe, prove, if correct, that there must have been at least nine bullets fired. Moreover, a recently rediscovered audio recording of the shooting, made by Stanislaw Pruszynski, has suggested to some experts the probability of there having been two gunmen in the kitchen pantry of the Ambassador Hotel that night. For some, analysis of the recording suggests that there were indeed more than eight shots fired, perhaps as many as thirteen.[50] Of course, there were ricochets and echoes in the very crowded and noisy room, though Pruszynski no doubt has allowed for these. Secondly, the autopsy performed by Dr Thomas Noguchi found that Kennedy was shot from behind at very close range – perhaps as little as a few inches – in the back of the head.[51] This was the fatal wound. Traces of gunpowder in the hair prove the closeness of the gun. No one present in the pantry at the Ambassador Hotel testified that Sirhan was so close to his victim; all good witnesses placed him at least three feet from Kennedy.

Seen in this light, the evidence for conspiracy appears compelling. Yet there are also good reasons to doubt the doubters. One fatal weakness in this conspiracy theory is simply the circumstances of the shooting. Certainly confusion reigned once the shooting began; however, it stretches belief that, without being noticed in a crowded room, a second shooter could have in effect executed Kennedy at the instant that Sirhan attacked. The coroner, Noguchi, himself believed that Sirhan had acted alone, lunging forward to fire at close range, and then lunging back to fire the remaining shots, though he also agrees that it is impossible to know for certain whether there was in fact a second gunman.[52] Following an interview with Noguchi and thorough investigation of the case, Dan Moldea has presented a plausible scenario whereby the fatal head-wound that killed Kennedy came from the last bullet to hit him, when he was already perhaps falling or had been inadvertently pushed nearer to Sirhan by the reacting crowd, giving Sirhan a close shot at the Senator's head.[53] The estimates of Sirhan's distance from Kennedy are all based on the first shot fired; in the rush of events; it is not disputed that in the muddle of the incident everyone's relative position changed.[54]

However, one reporter, Don Schulman, says that he witnessed one of Kennedy's guards pull out his gun and shoot Kennedy three times. This guard was supposedly Thane Eugene Cesar, who had been hired by the hotel from Ace Security for the night. Cesar was positioned directly behind Kennedy, to the Senator's right; this was precisely the spot from which Dr Noguchi, the physician who performed the autopsy, suggested the fatal shot had been fired. Cesar was by his own admission no fan of the Kennedys, and was opposed to their work for Civil Rights; he voted for George Wallace in the 1968 election. However, none of this presents a strong enough motive for him to commit murder under the eyes of many witnesses. Furthermore no plausible connection between Sirhan and Cesar has been established. Some conspiracy theorists have colourfully imagined a CIA hit-man silently committing the murder, while Sirhan drew the crowd's attention. Whatever happened, Cesar was certainly not such a hit-man. Furthermore, though many suspect Cesar, he was exonerated by polygraph tests.

Then working for the *Daily Mirror*, John Pilger was also in the kitchen pantry, and also believes that there was more than one gunman who fired on Kennedy. He bases this on the fact that the shots continued after Sirhan was restrained; however, a great deal of evidence suggests that Sirhan did in fact keep firing in that position – this was how he came to empty the contents of his revolver. The men restraining him even unsuccessfully attempted to break his finger to prevent his firing again. There were, of course, other people with guns in the kitchen pantry that night; it is possible that one of these people was the second shooter, if such a person existed. It is also distantly possible that the security guards and others pulled their guns out as Sirhan fired, and perhaps fired in response, and perhaps fired wildly; in this unlikely version of events, Kennedy, or one of the bystanders, could have been accidentally shot by one of the men there to protect him.

Elements in the Mafia and organised crime might well have wanted Kennedy killed. Despite the fact that Sirhan may have acquired gambling debts and was often at the racetracks, there is little convincing evidence that could put him in relation to such groups.[55] The same would be true of proposed links to the Teamsters president, James (Jimmy) R. Hoffa, a crooked trade union leader aggressively investigated by Robert Kennedy.[56] The favoured conspiracy theory suggests the involvement of the CIA – the motivation supposedly being annoyance over Cuba, and, more likely perhaps, hard-line anti-Communist anxiety that Kennedy might beat Humphrey at Chicago, and then as President organise a withdrawal from Vietnam. Others have suggested that white racists would have hated Robert Kennedy for his work supporting and enforcing Civil Rights legislation. Most bizarrely, it was even argued that Sirhan was part of an occultist plot, wrapped up with the NOVUS ORDO SECLORUM.[57] In this reading, Sirhan's mail-order Rosicrucianism is the most pertinent piece of evidence against him, suggestive of his being a foot-soldier for the Illuminati.

All these various conspiracy theories once again occlude the stated motive for the assassination: Sirhan's sense of the injustice perpetrated by Israel and its ally, the USA. This ostensible reason for the murder vanishes in the imagined glare of the other home-grown plots. By these means, the killing ceases to be Sirhan's 'political decision'.[58]

Given the fact that Sirhan Sirhan certainly fired his gun at Kennedy, it is difficult to understand any of these American plots drawing in this young Middle Eastern immigrant. Is it imaginable that Cesar and

Sirhan Sirhan conspired together? Or that they were two unknowing elements of a greater conspiracy? It is just as hard to accept that any group of clever conspirators would choose a crowded room packed with witnesses and reporters as an ideal spot for an assassination, especially as campaigning placed Robert Kennedy continually in the public arena in conditions that would have been hugely more favourable for a sniper or even a bomb attack. Above all, it is equally hard to imagine – though not, of course, impossible – that any of these suspected groups would have the power and reach to corrupt the entire LAPD, FBI and CIA in an effort culpably to botch the investigation. For such a conspiracy to have happened, the institutional frame of American life would have to be secretly decayed. It is central to the conspiracy theorists' beliefs that this is precisely the case. In their view, public America has rotted and corrupted itself; they expose the conspiracy in order to revive the corpse.

Perhaps the impact of the 1960s assassinations rather shows instead the resilience of American life. In one sense the two shocks of that spring of 1968 – King's death and Bobby Kennedy's – were intense, and yet sustainable. In the eyes of many, the violent disorder of the period manifested the 'sickness' of American society; however, paradoxically, it also demonstrated its health. Political violence and unrest seemed to grow worse and worse; the atmosphere was one of intense unease; and yet the fabric of social and political life held good.[59] On the surface, this was undoubtedly the case, though many experienced things differently.

Dick Holler's 1968 song 'Abraham, Martin and John' linked the four deaths of Lincoln, JFK, Martin Luther King and Bobby Kennedy. It presents the four men as simple embodiments of goodness who were not allowed to live out their potential. This song commemorates and mourns the worth of an individual life. Similarly the history told in this book is one that is inevitably about individuals; the subject demands it. Assassination implies the centrality of the person, even as it intends their erasure.

Yet, of course, such murders were symptoms of, and emblems for, wider social forces. However, the concept of a 'social force' remains an abstraction unless personified in the lives – and deaths – of particular human beings. The murders transpired within a context of disputes and crises of which they were the gravest manifestations. On one level they were little more than a manifestation. The real problems of America were the poverty, the racism, and the dissatisfaction with 'bourgeois values' which the assassinations themselves only clarified for a moment. As extreme events, the assassinations made actual the everyday crisis of American life.

At the time of King's and Bobby Kennedy's killings, commentators and the bereaved talked of the deaths as arising from a 'culture of violence' – as though these assassinations were merely the most visible element of a culture permeated with violence. Society was 'sick'. There had been similar diagnoses following John F. Kennedy's murder. Oswald's spell in the Soviet Union allowed some to dismiss him as un-American; for others, this ex-Marine living in Texas was as American as they come, his soul 'part of the vast collective soul of America'. So it was that Oswald was understood to have expressed an essentially American violence.[60]

Now rage about Bobby's killing again quickly translated into a sense that America was guilty, or had lost itself. Even before the murder, John Lindsay of *Newsweek* had remarked to Jack Newfield: 'This country is going to kill another Kennedy. And then we won't have a country.'[61] Newfield also recalled, just after the murder, seeing a 'college kid with an RFK peace button . . . screaming, "Fuck this country, fuck this country!"'[62] Newfield concluded his memoir of Robert Kennedy with a note of despair:

Now I realized what makes our generation unique, what defines us apart from those who came before the hopeful winter of 1961, and those who came after the murderous spring of 1968. We are the first generation that learned from experience, in our innocent twenties, that things were really not getting better, that we shall *not* overcome. We felt, by the time we reached thirty, that we had already glimpsed the most compassionate leaders our nation could produce, and they had all been assassinated. And from this time forward, things would get worse: our best political leaders were part of memory now, not hope.[63]

In his address to the nation, made while Robert Kennedy was still dying, President Johnson declared: 'Tonight this Nation faces once again the consequences of lawlessness, hatred and unreason in its midst. It would be wrong, it would be self-deceptive, to ignore the connection between the lawlessness and hatred and this act of violence.' He continued: 'It would be wrong, and just as self-deceptive, to conclude from this act that our country itself is sick . . .'[64] He reassured America that '200 million Americans did not strike down Robert Kennedy last night'. Yet he went on to say that the murder had occurred in 'a climate of extremism, of disrespect for law'.[65] He saw the death as symbolising 'the irrationality that was besieging our nation and the world', of a piece with the murder of the American ambassador in Guatemala or the Soviet repression of the Prague Spring.[66]

And yet it was difficult to elude the accusation of national sickness. When, after Bobby Kennedy's murder, Johnson set up a National Commission on the Causes and Prevention of Violence, its aim was to attempt to understand why America had become so violent.[67] Scenes of random violence were seemingly becoming everyday events. Polls revealed that, more even than the war in Vietnam, Americans were anxious about 'crime and lawlessness' in their own cities.[68] The violence that August at the Democrats' Chicago Convention demonstrated that even the mainstream political system was in meltdown.[69] In New York, Detroit, Los Angeles, Dallas, murder rates spiralled. A recent spate of unrelated mass murders added to the unease, most notably the 1966 shootings by a sniper, Charles Whitman, at the University of Texas, with their resemblances to the murder in Dallas.[70] The assassinations of King and Robert Kennedy threatened the release of Peter Bogdanovich's *Targets* (1968), a film based on Whitman's killings. There was a rash of other random snipers:

In New York an eleven-year-old boy was wounded by a sixteen-year-old one who was practicing target shooting from his family's fifth-floor apartment . . . A sixteen-year-old student set up a sniper's nest in a football stadium and fired some fifteen shots from a rifle into a group of young girls doing gymnastics.

The decade also witnessed the arrival of the random drive-by shooting.[71]

On the day of Kennedy's death, in the *New York Times*, James Reston wrote, echoing Johnson:

Robert F. Kennedy is only the latest victim of a modern world that has turned loose greater forces than it can control . . . There is something in the air of the modern world: a defiance of authority, a contagious irresponsibility, a kind of moral delinquency, no longer restrained by religious or ethical faith.[72]

Ronald Reagan pronounced that the shooting was the result of 'permissiveness'; there were some who felt that this was partly meant to incriminate liberal politicians like Kennedy himself. That fatal night at the Ambassador Hotel, witnesses reported seeing in the aftermath of the murder a girl in a polka-dot dress crying out, 'We shot him!' This perhaps legendary moment has become a key clue for conspiracy theorists; however, if it took place at all, it is more likely to have been a hysterical statement of a generalised American complicity in the crime.[73] Sirhan had pulled the trigger, but a whole culture felt guilty.

What did that guilt entail? Soon after the assassination, the press reported that the strain of violence witnessed at the Ambassador Hotel was something uniquely American, part of a psychology that went back to the frontier and had been popularised in the media. The fact that Sirhan Sirhan was a Jordanian immigrant was once more forgotten in these analyses. The drift of criticism was that this was an American problem, a matter of frustrations concealed by the surface of the country's prosperity. With American self-reliance had come an individualised form of violence, a form whose origins could be found in those same 'social forces'. Similarly, 'Europeans spoke of an underlying social illness that created a climate for violence in the United States.'[74]

Some have pictured the 1960s as a demonised decade, one which conservative politicians and writers have blamed for a collapse in traditional values.[75] What is curious is how far this sense of the decade was present at the time; laments over the imminent demise of the American project proliferate in the era itself. For example, earlier in 1968, Eugene McCarthy had written that what particularly marked the present crisis of American life was the 'disappearance of hope'. There was a sense that 'something is gravely wrong' in America, though what was wrong remained indefinable. The assassinations, the lawlessness of modern life, the arms race, the discontentment of the young, the alienation and simple physical distance from the President provoked by the murder in Dallas, all were said to have contributed to the malaise.[76]

Modern life in America was itself deemed to nourish the spread of crime: 'Part of the existential crisis of our time and fed by the increasing mobility, urbanization, and prosperity of the American scene, it produces more individuals who lack character structures that can resist the increasing temptations to crime.'[77] There was also a new guilty awareness of slavery and the American 'genocide' of the nineteenth century – the hippie identification with the 'Indian' leading to a revival of the noble savage idea. Moreover, there were, as there always had been, and will be, hundreds, even thousands, of daily acts of casual violence, racial violence and crime. And above all, there was the pressure and the broadcasting of the Vietnam War.

Some blamed the shadow of the H-bomb, some poverty and inequality, some the impact of the cruelty in Vietnam. Many blamed the media and the arts, whether on television or in the novel. This broad American social sickness was felt to be especially manifest in television and film (the shocking *Bonnie and Clyde* [1967] had appeared only a year before), as well as being produced by television and film. The influential commentator Frederic Wertham detected a taboo on tenderness in a literary and artistic culture – both highbrow and low-brow – that adored the criminal's existential purity and dwelt on the authenticity of violence.[78] For him, the trends were exemplified in Truman Capote's 'faction' *In Cold Blood* (1966), a study of the murder of a middle-class family in their Kansas home, which uses the methods of the novel to describe the murder of a family by two strangers. Both Capote and critics lingered over the murderers, not the victims; it was the criminal who offered the darkest fascination.[79] There was a thrill in the senselessness of the acts themselves and the lack of reasonable motive in the killers: their madness, their youth, their glamour. Critics picked out Capote's refusal to make moral judgements about the murderers for especial praise. Sirhan had read *In Cold Blood*, where Capote also makes use of the idea of trance to understand the state of mind of killers. In doing so, Capote reaches back to the concerns of Romanticism, and the tropes of Gothic fiction, to Caligari and the sleepwalkers of Dracula. It is possible that Sirhan used his knowledge of Capote's ideas to create his own defence based on hypnotism.[80]

Wertham spoke for many in lamenting the supposed desensitising effects of comic books and television.[81] For Wertham, violence had become a central element in American entertainment. 'While some adults winced, seven-year-old children watched the murder of Lee Harvey Oswald by Jack Ruby with unruffled equanimity. They had seen quick, remorseless killings so often!'[82] The heroes of Westerns were no longer the lawmen but the outlaws. In television plots from the 1950s and 1960s, torture had become acceptable: 'In one study, 78 percent of schoolchildren felt that it is "O.K. for the Lone Ranger and Hopalong Cassidy to beat up outlaws to make them confess".'[83] In the wake of the assassination at Dallas, Jerome Ellison similarly wrote of television as a stimulant to violence in American life, producing an upsurge in murder, suicide and youth crime. He noted that Oswald was a 'horse-opera fan' and 'the vocabulary of the Dallas police was replete with the verbiage of the standard TV western'. In particular, television beguiled its audience with the sense that they too might live out 'the American dream', thereby creating the frustrations that lead to violence when they discover that such dreams are not for them.[84]

Some felt that Sirhan too was a product of the television culture: 'This kid watching TV . . . which is where America lives; it doesn't live anywhere else . . . Sirhan, this nothing, bland, colorless character had come alive because he'd entered television'.[85] The period continued the ongoing cult of celebrity that glorified 'personality' over 'character', elevating the idea of the 'individual' while draining it of any significance other than that of an image. The 1960s killers themselves increasingly seemed not 'individuals', but hollowed out, unmeaning, dull, faceless. In Sirhan's case, his vacuity, his habit of losing himself in the contemplation of others and the belief that he was a 'Manchurian Candidate' all furthered this inanition. Somehow motive had drained away from Sirhan's crime, becoming merely a blunder, crass evidence of the times' random stupidity. Sirhan's killing of Kennedy represented the reversal of the relationship between Frick and Berkman, the conventional and cold versus the idealistic and impassioned. Suddenly the victims manifested human passion and idealism, and the killers seemed emptied of vitality. From JFK onwards, conspiracy replaced political purpose as the motivation for political murder; the murderers themselves were too bland, too null, to have much motivation themselves.

But the victims were more than mere images, more than television celebrities. Each of the sequence of deaths – Evers, JFK, Malcolm X, King, and Bobby Kennedy – strikes us as a goodness erased. The director of a recent film about the second Kennedy assassination, *Bobby* (2006), Emilio Estevez, has described the murder as the death of American decency. What made matters worse was that after death their 'goodness' was erased again, as the compromised nature of the victims' lives emerged – particularly with revelations of their sexual misdemeanours. In each case, a debunking followed the eulogy; the same fate befell JFK, King and Bobby Kennedy. (Malcolm X's Augustinian path from sinner to saint largely reversed this moment of exposure, as he has been 'canonised' since his death.) The earliest biographical responses to Bobby Kennedy are heartfelt tributes: Schlesinger's Kennedy biographies and Jack Newfield's memoir of Bobby Kennedy are both effectively hymns of praise.[86] Newfield praises Robert Kennedy's empathy, imagination, passion and kindliness; but others, such as Gore Vidal, would soon expose his famous ruthlessness, his ambition, his culpable caution, and his willingness as Attorney General to wire-tap. (His brother's decision secretly to record private conversations in the White House as well as to permit FBI bugging would seem of a piece with this.) Newfield celebrates Bobby Kennedy as a man of the people, caught up by the feelings of grape workers and coal miners and ghetto children; others would unmask a patrician condescension which believed that the Presidency ought to be a hereditary office, open exclusively to Kennedys. Newfield envisions a romantic dreamer, a fighter against evil; others denounce a romantic self-deceiver and self-server.[87]

The attacks on the victims' integrity often focused on the public image – that which people felt they had been sold. The Kennedys lived muddled lives, and yet, for all they were tarnished, it remains possible to feel that they *were* men of virtue. Nonetheless the exposure offered by biographers and journalists leaves a doubt. The ultimate impression is of the unknowability of people. Yet the public did indeed feel intimate with the Kennedys, King and Malcolm X. After all, they had seen them so many times, on television and in magazines. Remote in reality, their faces were as familiar as a film star's. This familiarity brought an unbearable poignancy to their deaths; they belonged to the pathos of the photograph. Their passing, complex lives had been appropriated as legend, as surface. Few yet recognised that there was something murderous implicit anyway in this turning of people into appearances. However, just a day before the shooting in Los Angeles, a skewed 'assassination' would take place in New York, where everyone involved was all too aware of the power of the image.

II: Plastic Palace People

Life in this society being, at best, an utter bore and no aspect of society being at all relevant to women, there remains to civic-minded, responsible, thrill-seeking females only to overthrow the government, eliminate the money system, institute complete automation, and destroy the male sex.

VALERIE SOLANAS, OPENING SENTENCE, *SCUM MANIFESTO*, 1968

In 1968, Andy Warhol was, if not the most famous living American artist, certainly the most notorious. His paintings of Campbell's soup cans and Brillo boxes are now respectable icons of art history; in the late 1960s, they remained to most 'bewildering' manifestations of an 'art upheaval'.[88] Warhol's apparent aim was to create, or cultivate, some artwork in each major creative field: in painting; in film; in music (with The Velvet Underground); with a novel (based on the amphetamine-induced ramblings of his 'superstar', Ondine); and even philosophy. To many at the time, these varied projects all seemed evidence of a threateningly vacuous talent.

Born in Pittsburgh in 1928, Warhol belonged to a family of working-class Czechoslovakian Catholic immigrants. In 1949, he moved to New York where he became a commercial artist, providing illustrations for magazines and book covers, and designing shoes. He was also producing paintings, works that chimed with a new movement of American artists: Roy Lichtenstein, Jasper Johns, Robert Rauschenberg. Soon he turned from painting to silk-screen prints, intrigued by the idea of multiples (and attracted by multiple cash payments too). This cottage industry took place at Warhol's Manhattan atelier (at various addresses), named The Factory. People drifted in: assistants, visitors and hangers-on; Warhol himself claimed that he had no idea how it all happened.[89] The scene there was an expression of 1960s gregariousness, and the democracy of the times too; 'everybody got interested in everybody else'.[90] The Factory became the symbol of New York cool, and Warhol above all epitomised that coolness.

Although in his case 'cool's' transcendence of feeling reached a disturbing height, in interviews, and also in person, he was inarticulate, or monosyllabic, or silent. It varied. He remarked that he wanted to be a machine, that he wanted to be plastic.[91] He sent out a look-alike on college lecture tours; it was a joke about mass-production, and the fact that he too was at best an image – a silvery-white wig, sunglasses, an air of amused vacancy, the trademark elements of his style. It was hard to tell whether his infamous lack of affect was evidence of inability, because there was nothing there, or refusal, because there was potentially too much. It was also simply shyness.

In the eyes of most at the time, including his own supporters, Warhol's priority was publicity.[92] In fact, despite his embrace of fame, Warhol was a markedly private man. His homosexuality was apparent to most, yet his relationships were unobtrusive enough for many to believe wrongly that he was in fact frigid. He was also a religious man, a side of his character that was known about, and yet received no obvious expression in his 1960s public persona. He sold the public image, yet retained a hidden life. However, the publicity was necessary, because the art had to be commercial. A wide-eyed, and maybe only a semi-mocking acceptance of contemporary consumer advertising (including the advertising of the personality) was the key to his aesthetic. His art marked the reproduction of the star as an image – Elvis with a gun, the mask of Marilyn Monroe, a weeping Jacqueline Kennedy. And he too, it was to be known, was himself just an image. He refused to be a genius, refused to suffer in a garret, or any other aspect of the romantic artist spiel that had formed around Jackson Pollock and previous generations of doomed artists. Everything would be modern, packaged and clean; he celebrated the mass-produced. His pose was that of the professional maker, tuned in to the interesting. The interesting meant that which everyone knew, and few regarded. Moreover, the range of the interesting included people and practices that, though modern, were most certainly neither packaged nor clean.

Among other things, this meant a preoccupation with violence. In the early 1960s, Andy Warhol began making his screen-prints of car-crashes, suicides and the electric chair. At the beginning of the century, Henry Adams had gazed in sardonic wonder at the destruction unleashed by the new mechanical forces of modern life.[93] Warhol now turned an even blanker gaze on that carnage. When multiplied as screen-prints, these moments of public horror similarly took on the nature of a repetition. Horror became void, and as such seemed somehow even more horrible. Later in the 1960s some of his films, most notably *Vinyl*, a version of Anthony Burgess's *A Clockwork Orange*, would depict scenes of torture.[94] In 1963–4, he had already issued a series of screenprints of a mourning Jackie Kennedy; his film *Since* concerned the assassination of JFK; the actress Mary Woronov played JFK.[95] Questioned concerning the car-crash images in 1971, Mario Amaya suggested: '[Warhol] is an enormously sensitive person, sensitive to the whole society . . . and I think there was a kind of death thing in the air then . . .'[96] It was the same 'climate of violence' that commentators had referred to on the occasion of the two Kennedy assassinations.

Although the idea that Warhol was asexual has been largely discredited, he was, in public at least, merely a voyeur, with a penchant for titillation.[97] After an early interest in the mesmerically boring, the films made by the Factory were increasingly a form of whimsical pornography, at once smutty, static and self-consciously dull. Often, as Warhol himself suggested, they present a pick-up, people just getting acquainted with each other.[98] Warhol was merely the pander to the event. There was something wistful in his avoidance of sex; as he suggestively put it, 'Sex is nostalgia for sex.'[99] His air of absence contained its element of generosity; he was radiantly undemanding company. As such, he attracted the outré and the damaged, who knew that he would indulge their oddity, and perhaps offer some salvation too.[100]

Warhol was a connoisseur of strangeness, a collector of freaks, and in the eyes of the public something of a freak himself. The Factory was a limbo of ambiguity. The various superstars, and other casual drop-ins, took their drugs, had their sexual encounters, and bitched about each other and about Andy. One of the Factory crowd, Billy Name, lived in the Factory's toilet for four years, refusing to come out, while devoting his days and nights to a study of the Cabbala.[101] The hangers-on appeared in Warhol's movies, and were paid, sporadically, by him. Some had private incomes, most came from the street. They were the height of fashion, mainly because they were so thrillingly dangerous. There were transsexuals, drag queens, debutantes, psychotics and guitarists. They enjoyed the distinction of being artists, though for most the only artwork they ever produced was the fabulous inconsequence of their own lives.

For a time, Warhol enjoyed the company of his assembled class. Later in his life, he would upgrade from Taylor Mead to Liza Minnelli, as he left the *demi-monde* and entered the shinier world of up-scale parties.

In the 1960s, he was not so much slumming it as propagandising for
the slum. He was extraordinarily tolerant and ready to accept without
judgement the weirdest behaviour. The astonishing thing is not that
Warhol should have turned cold towards someone like Valerie Solanas,
but rather that he should have become involved with her in the first
place. At first just another oddball hanging on at the fringes of the
party, she would in time aspire to be his assassin.

Valerie Solanas was born on 9 April 1936 in Atlantic City, and grew
up prodigiously bright and precociously sexual. The precocity had been
inflicted on her through abuse by her father. She had a child at fifteen,
a boy who was taken away from her.[102] She majored in psychology
at Maryland University, financing the later stages of her studies by
prostitution. From Maryland she moved, via a fling at post-graduate
study at the University of Minnesota, to New York where, finding a
place in the downtown lesbian community, she hustled for cash and
hawked her literary masterpieces.[103] She had written three self-defining
works: an article for *Cavalier* magazine entitled 'A Young Girl's Primer
on How to Attain to the Leisure Class'; *Up Your Ass*, a play to shock the
bourgeoisie; and her tour de force, the *SCUM Manifesto*. Solanas was
an inventively wayward writer, her shtick being a slide from Victorian
melodrama to the jargon of a streetwise ragamuffin. She relied on the
power of outrage, impolitely saying politely unsayable things. The
Manifesto mixes bar-room patter with a streetwise parody of Betty
Friedan. There is both a utopian strain to her work and a scatological
mischief. Her fundamental problem was having to endure being bored
– even by the bright; she saw through everything.

Written between January and March 1967, the *Manifesto* was to be
the rallying-call for a new revolutionary organisation – SCUM, the
Society for Cutting Up Men. In a later introduction to the work, Vivian
Gornick would compare Solanas to Jonathan Swift, the Marquis de Sade
and Céline.[104] The Swiftian allusion seems most apt; the book reads
like a 1960s version of the 'Modest Proposal', though one where readers
remain perpetually unsure whether she's earnestly advocating outrage,
or only having them on. The *Manifesto* mixes pertinent analysis of
gender relations with scurrilous accusation (men are walking abortions),
incitements to violence with gags. Her experimental work with rats
at Maryland had offered her an explanation for male inadequacy: it

was all down to the Y chromosome; a man was genetically speaking an incomplete woman. Using this insight, she goes on to diagnose the discontents of the 'money–work' culture, and the oppression and unpleasure of heterosexual intercourse.

Her analysis of the confidence trick of 'great art' cannot help but sound, in retrospect, as the first of her assaults on Andy Warhol:

The male 'artistic' aim being, not to communicate (having nothing inside him, he has nothing to say), but to disguise his animalism . . . The vast majority of people, particularly the 'educated ones' . . . are easily conned into believing that obscurity, evasiveness, incomprehensibility, indirectness, ambiguity, and boredom are marks of depth and brilliance . . . How can he who is not capable of life tell us what life is about?[105]

As a reading of most male artists, this is sophomoric; as a reading of Warhol, it is incisive. Her vision of the artist of the future would look rather like Solanas's self-image: 'in a female society the only Art, the only Culture, will be conceited, kookie, funkie females grooving on each other and on everything else in the universe'.[106] Her book is ultimately a work of self-creation, in which she conjures up a version of herself, related to the real, uncomfortable thing, but transformed into something irresistibly desirable – the SCUM female: 'dominant, secure, self-confident, nasty, violent, selfish, independent, proud, thrill-seeking, free-wheeling, arrogant'.[107] In flight from her own sadness, Solanas dreamed up her cool persona.[108]

In the process of creating a proper world for this groovy woman, it will first be necessary to kill all men, except those in SCUM's Men's Auxiliary. The Auxiliary was to be a farrago of gay men ('faggots'), conscientious biologists, 'men who kill men', publishers of Solanas's work, generous men, and 'men who tell it like it is (so far not one ever has)'. The lists of those who are definitely not in the Men's Auxiliary include: lousy singers, breadwinners, landlords, 'Great Artists' (Warhol was well warned), liars and phonies, disc jockeys, double-dealers, flim-flam artists, litterbugs, real estate men, advertisers and censors.[109]

The utopian impulse finds its outlet in a vision of a world where work, disease, death, and men have been banished. Complete automation would remove the burden of work. The necessity for copulation would be replaced by the 'laboratory reproduction of babies'.[110] She advocates a eugenics programme, by which incomplete beings, men, would be prevented; only complete beings, women, need be born.[111] But why stop there? Here she attains her own pinnacle of nihilism: 'Why produce even females? Why should there be future generations? What is their purpose? When aging and death are eliminated, why continue to reproduce? Even if they are not eliminated, why reproduce?'[112] In a way, one cannot help but admire the purity of the extremity here. Solanas had managed to express the caricature version of Anarchism favoured by conservative commentators at the turn of the previous century: the ludicrous longing for the purity of a vacant world.

She advertised for followers in the *Village Voice*. No one answered the call.

A prophet without honour, she lived at the Chelsea Hotel, where she met Maurice Girodias, the publisher of avant-garde erotica and underground classics for his Olympia Press. He found her charmingly naughty, a downtown cliché of a butch lesbian in cap, sweater and workman's coat. She was somehow too sassy for him to take her violent fulminations seriously. Still they were amusing, they were modern, and he sniffed the possibility of a *succès de scandale*. He offered her a contract to publish an autobiographical novel with the Olympia Press.[113]

Girodias was to be only one of her two possible routes to fame and, what she termed 'the groovy world'. The other was Warhol. Solanas first contacted Andy Warhol in an attempt to persuade him to perform her play, *Up Your Ass*. It seemed an ideal way to become famous. Warhol demurred, and Solanas nagged. She became an intermittent and out-of-place presence at the Factory, one more 'creep' among the other creeps passing through.[114] In an effort to appease her, she was invited to appear in one of his films, *I, A Man*, a title that parodied Mac Ahlberg's 'erotic masterpiece' *I, A Woman* (*Jag – en kvinna* [1965]). The film was intended as a sexual odyssey in which a young hero would seduce eight women, one after the other; Solanas played one of the women and subverted the theme. Her bossy persona dominates her scene, which never moves beyond the staircase outside the flat that she shares with her girlfriend. As the *New York Times* reviewer put it: 'he gets short shrift from the sixth, a tough lesbian'.

In late 1967, despite her publishing contract, Solanas was broke and homeless. She pestered Girodias, irritated Warhol, and alienated almost everyone else. To Girodias, she complained that Warhol was exploiting her talents; to Warhol, she complained that Girodias was a thief.[115] She was alternately abrasive and wheedling, and desperate for fame. She appeared on *The Alan Burke Show* on New York's Channel 5. Burke was notorious for inviting guests on to his show merely to goad and insult them. Solanas struck pre-emptively, and began swearing the moment the interview began. Burke bristled, the audience were shocked, and Solanas cursed all the more. The exchange was never aired. In a press interview, she fantasised about vibrant SCUM meetings attended by masochistic men and young pretty women; but there had been no meetings.[116]

By 3 June 1968, Solanas was paranoid, turbulent and desperate. For weeks, there had been reports on television and in the papers of violent student demonstrations in Paris, Rome and Belgrade. Solanas decided to stage a demonstration of her own. On that morning, she went back to her old apartment house, and picked up a bag of laundry from her neighbour. In the laundry were two handguns. Unusually for her, she had make-up on. She wore a fleece-lined winter coat despite the early June Manhattan heat.[117] She went first to Girodias's office, found him away in Montreal (fortunately for him), and so went on to the Factory at Union Square. Her first choice of victim being absent, she naturally fell back on the second. Warhol was also out, so Solanas hung around on 16th Street, going upstairs repeatedly to catch the great man in. Warhol finally showed up mid-afternoon, bumping into one of his assistants, Jed Johnson, on the sidewalk; Solanas joined the gang and walked in with them; all three took the elevator to the Factory together. The place was busy: the film-maker and Warhol collaborator Paul Morrissey was there; the photographer Billy Name was (as usual) in the bathroom; Fred Hughes was at his reception desk; and Mario Amaya, the editor of the London-based *Art and Artists* magazine, was hanging around. Solanas seemed edgy. Warhol spoke on the phone to one of his 'superstars', and while he was talking, Solanas pulled out her gun and shot at him. She missed, and Warhol begged her not to shoot, but she fired anyway, again missing him. Warhol hid under a desk and she strode up and fired into his abdomen at close range. She then shot at Mario Amaya, again missed, and so shot again striking his lower back.[118] He ran and hid in the back room, where Billy Name and

Paul Morrissey joined him, using their weight to stop Solanas getting through the double doors. Left alone with her, Hughes fell to his knees, pleaded his innocence, and talked her into leaving – though just as she was about to go, she changed her mind, came back for one moment, aimed at his head and attempted to fire. The gun jammed. Just then the elevator came up. Again Hughes somehow persuaded her just to go, and she went back into the elevator and left.[119]

Warhol was taken to Columbus Hospital, where he was pronounced clinically dead. Nonetheless, the surgeon, Dr Rossi, persisted in attempting to save the artist's life. He operated, massaging Warhol's heart, and succeeded in resurrecting him.[120] He had been dead for one and a half minutes. When he came to some days later, he heard coverage on the news of Bobby Kennedy's shooting; for a moment, bewildered, he thought that he was in heaven where they had reruns of worldly events:

Right when I was being shot and ever since, I knew that I was watching television. The channels switch, but it's all television . . . When I woke up somewhere – I didn't know it was at the hospital and that Bobby Kennedy had been shot the day after I was – I heard fantasy words about thousands of people being in St Patrick's Cathedral praying and carrying on, and then I heard the word 'Kennedy' and that brought me back to the television world again because then I realized, well, here I was, in pain.[121]

Later, he wrote of the event: 'coming so close to death was really like coming so close to life, because life is nothing'.[122]

Warhol's shooting was meant to be big news; there was an eight-page spread planned for *Life*; and then Bobby Kennedy's murder took all the publicity.[123] Warhol commented afterwards: 'The worst, most cruel review of me that I ever read was the *Time* magazine review of me getting shot.'[124]

Solanas had made no attempt to escape. A few hours after the murder, after rambling around New York, she handed herself in to a policeman at the junction of 42nd Street and Seventh Avenue. She explained that she had shot Warhol as the artist 'had too much control of my life'.[125] Her erratic behaviour led to a psychiatric evaluation, and a spell in Elmshurst Psychiatric Hospital. Once Girodias visited her at Elmshurst, and enquired if she were released, would she shoot him too? 'She answered with a friendly giggle, "You? Oh, no! And I'm over it now, in any case; I don't have to do it again."'[126] Warhol refused to press charges against Solanas, but this forgiving gesture merely further incensed her. Perhaps she sensed indifference behind the generosity. The case went to trial in December, and the judge ordered that she be subject to further psychiatric tests. She was granted bail, and promptly contacted both Girodias and Warhol, threatening both. In January, she was examined by two doctors who diagnosed her as a chronic paranoid schizophrenic.[127] On 25 February 1969, after pleading guilty to assault (she denied that her intention had ever been murder; she merely wanted to catch Warhol's attention), she was sentenced to three years in prison.[128]

Solanas felt that the newspapers misrepresented her and her deed; the *New York Times* described her as an actress, as though one afternoon's work with Andy Warhol outweighed all her writing, and consistently misspelt her name as Solanis. As far as the authorities were concerned, she was simply mad. Yet there were many prepared to take her ideas seriously. Radical feminists in the National Organization for Women and revolutionary hippies in the group Up Against the Wall Motherfucker both endorsed Solanas as a heroine. The latter released a short communiqué which declared that 'Andy Warhol shot by Valerie Solanas. Plastic man vs. the Sweet Assassin' and ended with the words: '*Valerie is ours and the sweet assassin lives.* – SCUM in Exile'.[129] Many years after the event, Solanas would be taken very seriously indeed by some feminist scholars, as though her attempt on Andy Warhol were simultaneously a revolutionary act and an avant-garde artwork.[130] In the spirit of publisher's hyperbole, the Olympia Press's 1970 edition of *SCUM Manifesto* announced on its back cover that: 'This violent, excessive, obnoxious and totally fascinating little book has suddenly become the Charter of all female revolutionaries.' Norman Mailer named her feminism's Robespierre.[131] Charlotte Corday may have been the more fitting comparison. The American critic and essayist Vivian Gornick argued that Solanas represented a visionary epitome of female experience, and a properly livid refusal of all to which women had been forced to submit. Solanas was even supposed to possess Malcolm X's righteous wrath.[132] Solanas's murderousness appeared merely fascinating, its extremism a guarantee of its virtue. This moral confusion was part of a pattern of responses to such crimes in the period. The radical left were predisposed for a while to imagine violence as authentic, edgy and resolutely anti-bourgeois. Solanas's disdain for the polite, the nice and the dignified was of a piece with this. The epitome of such attitudes was to be the praise for Charles Manson, for the Panthers and Weathermen, for the revolutionary groups in Italy and Germany, and for the IRA. However, Solanas was also a ready recipient of such endorsements. Her sexuality, her articulacy, and her – admittedly peripheral – place in the New York underground scene conspired to make her perfect material. In the eyes of some, her act embraced both feminism and art, violence and theatre.

But was it an assassination? Mary Harron who wrote and directed a film about Solanas apparently thinks so; she writes of her: 'Even as a celebrated assassin, she was in the wrong time.'[133] Girodias prefaced his publication of the *SCUM Manifesto* by asserting: 'This little book is my contribution to the study of violence', as though, as Harron suggests, the book 'were a pathological study of an assassin'.[134] Certainly the *Manifesto* had promised that the organisation would be criminal, and would commit murders.[135] However, such statements were poised indeterminately between a threat and a joke. Clearly the act depended upon the perception of Warhol's fame. Mary Harron relates how Jeffrey Gear wrote to Warhol: 'I'm not sure if Valerie would have shot you if Girodias had been as well known as you are.'[136] Warhol himself proposed: 'If I weren't famous, I wouldn't have been shot for being Andy Warhol.'[137]

In fact, the shooting of Warhol marked a turning-point in the chain of American assassinations that ran from Medgar Evers to the attempted killing of Ronald Reagan. From now on, ideology would cease to be anyone's motive; nor was anyone shot out of idealism. Instead the American assassination would be equivocally ideological and at heart insane. It would combine madness, radical politics and the desire for fame. In this sense, Solanas's shooting of Warhol was both politically speaking a non-event, and the mark of a shift in American life.

On her release, Solanas endured over a decade of paranoid fantasies while making others endure a decade of frivolously murderous threats. She planned great books, but wrote nothing; she died of pneumonia in San Francisco in 1988. Warhol meanwhile was never the same again. He became fearful, and his health was permanently damaged: he had to wear a brace or a corset on his scarred body.[138] It is an often-repeated idea in writing about Warhol that he died on that June day in 1968, and that afterwards he was a shadow of the man he had been.[139] The work he produced grew less interesting; he imitated himself. Warhol himself seems to have shared this view, and to have thought of his subsequent life as posthumous. Nonetheless Warhol survived, and lived to saunter serenely through another twenty years of parties, nightclubs and art.

The violence of the 1960s can be viewed as the concomitant of social changes. The Civil Rights movement disturbed the guilty complacency of American life, and for a time that disturbance manifested itself in bloodshed. In this way, most of the killings still made some kind of political sense, even if of the most attenuated kind. The decade that followed would see, in the spirit of Valerie Solanas, the American assassination collapse into an absurd quest for fame.

The Decline of the American Assassination

I: Notes from Underground

If you're a crook you're still considered up-there. You can write books, go on TV, give interviews – you're a big celebrity and nobody even looks down on you because you're a crook. You're still really up there. This is because more than anything people want stars.

ANDY WARHOL, *THE PHILOSOPHY OF ANDY WARHOL*

Although the paranoiacs make the great leaders, it is the resenters who make their best instruments because the resenters, those men with cancer of the psyche, make the great assassins.

RICHARD CONDON, FROM *THE MANCHURIAN CANDIDATE*, 1959

Arthur Bremer feared he was a failure. He wanted to be noticed; without talent of any kind, he realised that one convenient way to grab attention would be to kill someone famous. He was twenty-one years old, a no-hoper unemployed janitor and busboy in Milwaukee. Most of what the public know about him is contained in his published diary, a document of around 120 printed pages, covering six weeks of his life in thirteen entries. In his introduction to the diary, Harding Lemay tells us how like everyone else Arthur Bremer is. Like you and me, he compares the prices of things; like sentimental us, he pauses in wonder at the green grass; just like us too, he wants fame. Why should there be someone like Bremer? It's all, Lemay assures us, because we've been failed by our leaders, gulled by advertising, dulled by TV. 'If everything in our salesman's culture boasts a brand name, what distinguishes the name of Arthur Bremer? Is he expected to exist without a label, inferior to a tube of toothpaste or a can of beer?'[1]

To this reader, the diary rather unveils a personal, but not uncommon, emptiness. It is probable that its roots lay in a troubled childhood, caught between Sylvia Bremer, his irritable, controlling mother and Bill, his weak, easily blamed, emotionally absent father.[2] Other than an unearned world-weariness, there's little to pin Arthur down. His politics are indecipherable; he flips from liberal angst to conservative reaction. His father was a 'Humphrey' man; dad assumed his son felt the same way.[3] In fact, Bremer stalked both Nixon and Humphrey, looking for an opportunity to shoot either man down. He wants to kill George Wallace; he wants to kill George McGovern. He proudly wears his intended victims' campaign badges; he is the man who applauds loudest at the rallies; he even very briefly campaigns for Ronald Reagan.[4]

Bremer had to be somebody; he would 'ACT', and the most obvious type of action was murder.[5] He considered staging a massacre, and one day in February 1972 waited by a bridge over the Milwaukee River, with two guns in his overcoat pocket. But his nerve broke, and he went back home, having accomplished nothing.[6] He was five foot six, plump and worried about it. Afterwards people remembered him, his 'obtrusive' shyness, the something indefinable about him, his blond hair.[7] His fellow students at Milwaukee Technical College judged him, in retrospect at least, a 'weirdo'. 'One said: "We all decided to stay away from him because there was something wrong with him. Whenever he argued, he had a kind of funny smirk on his face. He didn't go into a violent rage – he just had this smirk on his face."'[8] Everything about Bremer's life seemed tawdry; his brother, William, would later be charged with selling phoney weight-reduction courses.[9]

This cut-price quality extends to some of his chosen targets too. Shifty Nixon and slick Wallace were apt choices for Bremer. No American politician of the 1960s and early 1970s drew such venom as Governor George Wallace: it was said that 'Governor Wallace is regarded by the liberal intellectual establishment as the most dangerous man in American political life.'[10]

Born in 1919, George C. Wallace was an Alabama man. His great-grandfather was a Confederate soldier, his grandfather a pious country doctor, and his father a sickly, violent and incompetent wastrel, a failed businessman and farmer whose only successes came in local politics and the numerous knife fights of his youth.[11] His father's failures meant that Wallace grew up poor. However, urged on by their piano-teacher mother, the family were ambitious: one brother became a lawyer, the other a circuit judge. Wallace inherited his father's pugnacity (George Jr. was a good amateur boxer) and his passion for politics. Cornelia Wallace, George Jr.'s second wife, said of her husband, '"if you really want to understand him, just look at this". She held out a photograph of Wallace in a boxing ring, his face grimacing with concentration while he pummelled a blood-covered opponent.'[12] He inveigled his way into a teenage job as a page at the Alabama Senate, and through his boxing skills won a place at the University of Alabama. In World War II, he flew bombers against Japan, and married Lurleen Burns, a girl fresh out of high school. After the war he returned to Alabama, landed himself a job as the state's assistant attorney general, and launched a political career founded on support for 'regular' white people. He worked his way up through the legislature, shaking hands, fighting for causes. Although at this time most considered Wallace a liberal populist, there was one issue on which he belonged firmly on the right. In backing racial 'separatism', Wallace was entirely consistent with his role as man of the people. His dislike of the corporations echoed his contempt for the campaign for civil rights: like the average white Southerner, he suspected both big business and big government. Wallace advocated states' rights against federal rights – in this context a position synonymous with resistance to desegregation.

In 1958, Wallace lost a campaign to become Governor of Alabama to John Patterson, an even more racist candidate who had secured the support of the Ku Klux Klan.[13] When the results came in, Wallace is said to have remarked: 'John Patterson out-nigguhed me.'[14] He would never willingly be outdone on this score again. In 1962, he was elected Governor of Alabama; his inaugural address was written by Asa Carter, 'a professional anti-Semite and hard-line racial terrorist, the organizer of a secret para-military force with the romantic name of the "Original Ku Klux Klan of the Confederacy"'. In 1956, six of Carter's Klan followers had assaulted the singer Nat King Cole; his crime had been performing for a white audience.[15]

In 1963–4, Wallace began to pursue a bid for the Presidency as leader of a third party – the American Independent Party. Alabama law meant that he could not succeed himself as Governor; he dodged the problem by having his wife, Lurleen Wallace, stand as the next Governor; she won by a landslide in 1966. (She was helped by the death of her leading opponent in a plane-crash.) In 1967, when Wallace's campaign began in earnest, the odds were strongly against him. However, the course of events played into his hands. The violence that followed King's death frightened many whites; racist candidates began to fare even better than they had before. Wallace was the chief beneficiary of this fall back to populist conservatism.[16] The murder of Robert Kennedy and the pandemonium at the Democratic Convention in Chicago again fostered a desire among many Americans for a strong leader willing to stand up for social decencies. Soon he was gaining enough ground to worry intellectuals like Hannah Arendt.[17] He spoke for 'the forgotten' white working and lower-middle classes, joining them in their hatred of hippies, their dislike of 'preferential treatment' given to impoverished blacks, their longing for law and order. About the Vietnam War he kept a diplomatic silence, concentrating his attack, in keeping with his populist instincts, on long-haired war protestors. This appeal to political atavism went hand in hand with the use of sophisticated new computer mailing systems that kept him in touch with his core vote. In 1968, Wallace's strength in the South was such that he seriously endangered the possibility of Republican victory; his presence in the race led Nixon to accept the conservative Governor of Maryland, Spiro Agnew, as his running-mate, hoping thus to draw off some of Wallace's votes.[18]

In a potently homespun way, Wallace mastered the media. Funeral-suited, black-haired, he looked like a cross between a Baptist minister and Bela Lugosi. In June 1963, as a publicity stunt he blocked the doorway of the University of Alabama to hinder the first two black students, thereby confirming his credentials as a law-abiding but gutsy opponent of desegregation.[19] In the late 1960s he flew around the country, making barn-storming speeches to eager crowds; at Madison Square Garden, 20,000 people came to hear him, the largest audience for a political speech since FDR.[20] He was a gifted and improvisatory orator, even somehow physically thrilling.[21] Hunter S. Thompson remarked that a Wallace speech was like a 'political "Janis Joplin concert" . . . the bastard had somehow levitated himself and was hovering over us'.[22] Socially conservative, implicitly racist, passionately oratorical, Wallace had all the requisites to appeal to a substantial, disaffected segment of white America.

In '68, the Republicans avoided electoral disaster in the South firstly by pushing the idea that a vote for the third party rewarded the Democrats, and secondly through the gift of some very bad campaign decisions by Wallace. These included, most notably, choosing as his running mate, General Curtis LeMay, a dead-ringer for *Dr Strangelove*'s Bomb-loving General Jack D. Ripper. In May '68 Wallace's wife's death from cancer perhaps further contributed to his failure. Nonetheless, Wallace won a considerable percentage of the vote, enough to encourage him to run again in 1972. Particularly important was the discovery that Wallace's appeal was not limited to the South. Racial tensions in the north presented Wallace with elements in the electorate who felt threatened by the presence of blacks, and who were dismayed at what was seen as the collapse of order and the spurning of traditional moral values.

In June 1970, Wallace fought a dirty fight of racist rage and slurs to regain, at the run-off stage, the governorship in Alabama. He now had the base to run one more time for President. A series of financial scandals then came to light, brought out by a politically motivated investigation by the IRS. Just as things looked worst for Wallace and his allies, a sudden reconciliation with Nixon occurred. Charges were dropped, the investigation discontinued; just one day later, Wallace announced that he would indeed stand as a Presidential candidate in 1972, but would stand as a Democrat. Wallace was no longer a threat to the Republicans; he had become 'the Democrats' problem'.[23]

And the problem turned out to be a huge one. With some snazzy suits and a glamorous new wife, Cornelia (the niece of a former Governor of Alabama, she had once come second in a Miss Alabama contest), Wallace looked a far more attractive prospect than he had in 1968.[24] He dominated the early Democratic primaries, winning a comfortable majority in Florida, and only just losing to a heavy-spending Hubert Humphrey in Pennsylvania and Indiana.[25] He was attracting middle-class voters now, and without shedding his core support. Yet the campaign's religious overtones – there were hymns, testimonies, all the orgiastic piety of the Bible Belt – alienated incredulous journalists from the big cities.[26] At his rallies there was country music and 'barnyard jokes'.[27] His appeal was to American anti-intellectualism, the Forrest Gump mentality that suspected experts, 'pointy-heads', bureaucrats, and

New York dinner-party intellectual snobs.[28] He similarly focused the otherwise diffuse hatred for hippies, welfare scroungers, Weathermen, bra-burners, Communists, campus guerrillas, draft dodgers and blacks. Paradoxically, Arthur Bremer was a typical member of the social group to whom Wallace most appealed: the 'forgotten' blue-collar, white-skinned young American male.[29]

Wallace's status as an outsider greatly benefited his campaign. He appeared as an emissary from an unregarded America, seeming to speak for everyday people, praising the common man.[30] The campaign asserted the potency of the mass against a perceived Washington elite. In this, he was very much of the moment: articles like Peter Schrag's 'The Forgotten American' examined and tacitly honoured the uncared-for white working and lower-middle classes; recent books, such as Richard Scammon and Ben Wattenberg's *The Real Majority* (1970) demonstrated that the typical voter was 'un-young, un-poor, and un-black'.[31] More than any other candidate, Wallace had tuned his pitch to the interests of such voters.

Although Wallace spoke about many policies and topics, there was no doubt that the key issue was busing: that is, the transportation of children in order to enforce a balance of black and white pupils in schools. This was arguably a necessary element in desegregating the education system, but was also a deeply unpopular policy among many whites. Even in Michigan the policy brought the Ku Klux Klan out to protest in the autumn of 1971. For Wallace, it was a gift. The policy manifested what many took as big government's dictatorial attitude; it touched on incipient racism; and it played on white people's fears regarding their children's education. Wallace's stand against busing earned enough support to turn him into a serious threat both within the Democratic Party and to Nixon.[32] His campaign continued to attract votes and to win primaries. At the beginning of May 1972, he came second in Indiana, Wisconsin and Pennsylvania, an unprecedented incursion into the North and Midwest; then, on 8 May, he won in North Carolina; it was a sign that he was unstoppable in the South. Alabama and Tennessee were also his. The momentum of the campaign was with him.

There had always been the fear of 'some nut', as Wallace put it, taking a shot at him.[33] His political career had seen the murders of the

Kennedys, of King, of Medgar Evers, of Rockwell. He was reputedly a scared man; fearful of flying, mindful of being shot. Yet he could not hold back; he was there to win the campaign.

Meanwhile, if fame was the spur, Bremer was wondering if Wallace himself was famous enough to bother killing. Before coming to the decision to take a shot at Wallace, Arthur Bremer had been through a long journey.

That January of 1972, Bremer shaved his long hair. He meant to please his 'girlfriend', Joan Pemrich. She was sixteen years old; they had a few dates, before she broke it off. After the shooting, she was questioned about him. 'He didn't know how to bowl or roller skate,' Pemrich told reporters. 'I don't think he knew how to do anything. He didn't even have a television or a radio in his apartment.' When they had gone out, he'd tried to take her to 'dirty movies'.[34] It was probably 'losing' Joan that prompted his attempt to assassinate a politician. The next day, 13 January, he bought a gun. Bremer's last day of work at the Milwaukee Athletic Club was 16 February. He was about to start out on his mission, travelling to Ottawa to murder Richard Nixon.

In late April, Bremer took his Charter Arms .38, and a Browning 9 mm, and set off on his journey, first of all to New York. According to the testimony of his diary, he forgot his guns on the jet, and had them returned to him by the plane's captain. There in the Big Apple, from his Howard Johnson hotel window, he gazed at a couple kissing in the motel opposite. He wandered the town, purposelessly, his gun with him, plucking up enough courage to approach a 'whore'. He scanned copies of *Screw*, and lingered by brothel doorways. Finally he visited a massage parlour, where he attempted, in vain, to persuade the young masseuse to have sex with him, or, at the least, to take her bikini off. Something about her, some quality of defiance, reminded him of Joan.

He went on to Canada, and spent a discouraging couple of days in Ottawa. One day, in his hotel room, he accidentally fired off his gun, and lay waiting for the police to arrive. They never did. His plan was to enjoy his last few days; but Ottawa wouldn't allow it. It was cold ('longjohn weather'), and hard to find a room, and when he did find one it was a runt. He had shaved off his beard, and his clean-shaven face was strange to him. The snow was still heaped on the sides of the roads; there were rumours that for Nixon's impending visit the piles would be hosed down to clear away possible hiding-places for bombs.[35] The news gave details of the Nixon motorcade. Bremer familiarised himself with the territory, fussing about whether on his big day he should keep his hands in his pockets by the gun, and risk looking suspicious, or keep them in sight, and risk getting frozen. 'Would the assassin get a good view?' he pondered.[36] And then he blew it. The big day came, Nixon drove past, too fast, and was gone before Bremer could do a thing. In the next days, there were other chances, other failures. He went home, and Nixon was still alive. He could not kill a man when he couldn't get near him: 'Can't kill Nixy-boy if you ain't close to him.'[37] But he should have killed him; he should be dead himself. All his efforts had come to nothing. The weather was even colder back in Milwaukee. He must do something. He began considering other victims; finally he settled on Wallace.

It was, to him, a second best, as though he'd failed already in picking such a second-rater for the opportunity of being murdered. Who was Wallace outside the USA? Bremer felt an utter failure. Still, despondently dutiful, he would kill the man. He followed Wallace for weeks, standing loyally among the audience with their straw boaters, clapping on cue, a face in the crowd. On the campaign trail the warmer weather was beautiful, like passing into summer after the chill of Canada and Milwaukee.

He went to a series of Wallace rallies. At Dearborn Youth Center, a young girl, a hippy protestor, joked about taking a shot at the Alabama racist.[38] Bremer could have killed him there, but waited, worried that he might injure two teenage girls in the shooting. On the Saturday, the police in Kalamazoo questioned him, when he was found waiting in his car outside the armoury where Wallace was due to speak. But Bremer managed to persuade them that he was merely after a good seat. Later that day, at the meeting itself, he was photographed wearing glasses and smiling and clapping.

On 15 May, early in the day, Wallace was campaigning at Wheaton Plaza Shopping Center in Maryland. Bremer was there too, watching, with his .38. No opportunity for a shot came up, and that afternoon both Wallace and Bremer moved on to a campaign rally at Laurel Shopping Center, some fourteen miles north of Washington, DC. The fans were out, waving plastic Confederate flags and festooned in straw hats with red, white and blue trimmings. Bremer too had dressed in red, white and blue. The country singer Billy Grammer was there, in cowboy boots, with his electric guitar. The atmosphere was both festive and fraught, the usual mixture at a Wallace event. The Governor was heckled, but that was usual; he made jokes back at them, and inveighed against the Washington establishment, their hypocrisy, their remoteness. It was another campaign day. At one point, the oratory faltered; he had lost his voice. After a moment, he recovered; 'It's been a long campaign,' he told them.[39]

Whenever the crowd applauded, Bremer applauded too. He was wearing a 'Wallace in '72' campaign button. He had failed to get close enough to Nixon to kill him; well, there was nothing remote about Wallace. The Governor took his jacket off, rolled his shirt sleeves up, and went down into the crowd, working his way through the bustling fans, along a rope cordon where the waiting people jostled for a handshake. Bremer was calling 'Hey, George! Hey, George!', trying to get the politician's attention. Those standing by Wallace thought the man was just reaching out to shake hands. And then the months of waiting were over: Bremer opened fire. Wallace was hit several times in the arm, in the stomach, a grievous wound which caused him to lose up to seven pints of blood, and in the chest. Three others were wounded in the shooting, one of them Nicholas Zarvos, a Secret Service officer. Some eight men wrestled Bremer to the ground, roughing him up a little. When he appeared at the magistrate's court late that night, there were bruises on his forehead and blood on the back of his head. Believing that the attack must have been racial, some of Wallace's supporters at the scene laid into a group of African-American youths.

Only seconds after Bremer had fired, a photographer snapped a shot of Cornelia Wallace cradling her husband's body. He lay spread-eagled in his shirt, a dark patch on the material showing where one of the bullets had struck. When she was pulled away from him there was blood smeared on her beige suit. The whole shooting was on film, and was screened that night on national television.

The bullet that had hit Wallace's chest had penetrated to near the backbone, paralysing the Governor from the waist down. The day after the shooting, news came through that he had gained Michigan and Maryland. Wallace had now won five state primaries. It was the highest point of his campaign, an endorsement of his populism made irrelevant by the bullet by his spine. Though in the immediate aftermath both he and his followers were hopeful, his paralysis would effectively force down his Presidential campaign. Cornelia Wallace worked as best she could to keep her husband in the Presidential race. She downplayed the extent of his injuries, presenting him as still a viable candidate.[40] Wallace did fight on, displaying as best he could the verve that had always characterised his political life. However, in the end, he was too sick and too tired to maintain his campaign's momentum. Bremer had ended Wallace's battle either to secure the Democratic nomination or to play kingmaker. On 29 July Wallace officially quit the race. Soon after, at the Democratic Convention, George McGovern won the fight for the candidacy.

There were some who surmised that the limit of Wallace's ambitions would always have been the Miami Democratic Convention; others believed he could have gone all the way to the White House. The intention might have been only to split the Democratic vote; for the GOP, the danger was that he would, after all, have drawn away Republican support and left Nixon vulnerable to the Democrats. No one now will ever know for sure.

The shooting embarrassed the liberals, their contempt for Wallace diverted into an uneasy pity. Political commentators were caught in a double-bind: abhorring both the assassination attempt and Wallace's politics. With the exception of Rockwell, it was the first time in recent years that the victim of such a murder had been a figure from the political right. The Democrats and liberals had become used to seeing their own people killed; it was confusing to have to extend sympathy to the enemy. Fortuitously, he'd been shot by a 'nut'; if an African-American or radical student had fired the gun, the country truly would have been in trouble.

As before, and after, the attack occasioned soul-searching about the American propensity to violence. Extra Secret Service guards watched over all the Presidential campaigners. Assassination was beginning to seem a local custom. Bremer's assault on Wallace joined an increasingly well-rehearsed list of political murders; the very fact that the press grouped together such disparate killings as those of King and Malcolm X, Evers and Rockwell, made them appear connected. Individual acts indicated a shameful pattern; the USA seemed 'infected' by violence. In Europe, despite home-grown problems with political violence, especially in Northern Ireland and Great Britain, Germany and Italy, the phenomenon looked specifically American. Yet in Germany, on the day of Wallace's shooting, the Baader-Meinhoff group exploded a bomb in the car of a judge's wife; miraculously, she survived the blast.

At first Nixon and his team were concerned whether Bremer was from the left or the right; the possibility that he might be a Republican assassin would have wrecked their campaign.[41] When Bremer's home was raided they found among the mess, boxes of bullets, targets for pistol shooting, a comic book depicting famous cartoon figures having sex, old school reports, a Black Panther newspaper, and a diary.[42] The FBI scoured the diary for indications that Bremer might have hinted at an affiliation with Nixon. Instead they found that he had stalked Nixon, and McGovern too, with the intention of killing either of them. The Bureau did its best to conceal the document's existence, until quite certain that it contained nothing incriminating for anyone other than Bremer.[43] However, within a couple of years his diaries would find a publisher.

In those early days after the shooting, Nixon worked hard to display his compassion to the public; wearing television make-up, he turned up at the hospital to visit Wallace.[44] Some doubted Nixon's sincerity. Immediately after the shooting, there were rumours that a second assassin had been at the scene, suspicions focusing on a man supposedly switching licence plates on Bremer's car some time before the attack. This very likely fictive assailant never materialised. But the fact that such rumours so promptly came into being was itself the most significant matter. Paranoia and suspicion were now ready to kick in with each assassination attempt. Brooding over the shooting led Wallace to suspect that he had been the victim of yet another conspiracy. The focus of his suspicions was Nixon himself. As the Watergate scandal unfolded such a conjecture began to seem more and more plausible; might the shooting be part of the administration's dirty tricks campaign?[45] There were rumours that Bremer had been photographed with one of the Watergate conspirators, though the image itself could not be obtained. Nonetheless, in April 1974, Wallace went public with his suspicions.

In December 1973, in the *New York Review of Books*, a review by Gore Vidal of the works of E. Howard Hunt had appeared. The review ended with a consideration of the recently published Arthur Bremer diaries. Succeeding the withering irony directed at the slippery career of Howard Hunt, best-selling novelist, CIA operative and Watergate conspirator, Vidal also insinuates (this side of the libel laws) that Hunt's fine literary works might include the Bremer 'diaries'. Over a year after the shooting, a report had emerged that, on receiving news of the attack on Wallace, Hunt had ordered the raid on Bremer's apartment. The intention was either, as we have seen, to make sure that Bremer was not a Republican supporter, or, in Vidal's view, to implicate Bremer as crazy, or Communist. They planned to create another embodiment of the lone killer myth: 'In a nation that worships psychopaths, the Oswald–Bremer–Sirhan–Ray figure is to the general illness what Robin Hood was to a greener, saner world.'[46] According to Vidal, the diary is too literate, too knowing a text to have been composed by a television-watching, post-Gutenberg, comics-reading, dirty-movie-going nut. He detects the sly hand of a ghost writer, and with it, the trace of a greater conspiracy. The screenwriter Paul Schrader had a similar reaction, noting how odd it was that an ordinary Midwestern guy would talk like the existentialist hero of a Bresson film.[47] Meanwhile Bremer languished in Baltimore County jail's maximum-security block in Towson.

Wallace gave credence to Vidal's argument; perhaps Nixon was behind the shooting; perhaps Nixon's followers had acted on their own initiative. In either case, it struck him as impossible that Bremer could have acted alone. In Bremer's diary, the assassin declares that he has 'a thousand bucks'; but where after all did his money come from?[48] These suspicions were never allayed, but also failed to be taken seriously enough to merit full investigation, although in 1980, the FBI dutifully re-examined Bremer's diary for evidence of conspiracy.[49] In 1992, Wallace's son, George Wallace Jr., again called (in vain) for an investigation into Nixon's role in the assassination attempt.[50]

Wallace won the Governorship of Alabama again in 1974. His platform for a Presidential campaign was still in place, and in 1976 he rejoined the race for the Presidency, though it was a forlorn, almost a nostalgic attempt. At one campaign rally in Wisconsin, some students turned up wearing Arthur Bremer masks, carrying placards declaring,

'Free Artie Bremer'.[51] The protests were both cruel and pointless. Wallace was never again a serious contender. His righteous anger now looked out of place; he had become the object of uneasy compassion. He was crippled, with no feeling below the waist; a chair-lift was installed at the Governor's mansion in Montgomery. Rumours of his wife's infidelity were deflected into the revelation that she had bugged his phone, and so overheard his countless yearningly smutty calls to ex-girlfriends. His political life and his marriage disintegrated into an indelicate shabbiness.

Impotent, frustrated, in constant pain, his life had apparently reached a place of collapse. However, he enjoyed something of a long swan-song, renouncing his racist views (for political advantage his enemies said), marrying again a much younger woman, fund-raising for Troy State University, and enjoying a born-again reprieve: three years before his death, Wallace did the Christian thing and publicly forgave Bremer. He died in 1998, in the midst of the Clinton years, a figure out of time.

In the flow of Gore Vidal's mockery, he remarks of Arthur Bremer's diary: 'no matter who wrote the diary we are dealing with a true author'.[52] By the standards of the day, he's right. The diary is an impressive document, expressively inarticulate, though the enduring impression is of a flat and limited loneliness. On one April day, on eight distinct occasions he almost cries. After failing to murder Nixon, he remarks that in the previous three months he has had one conversation with another human being – the girl in the New York massage parlour. The diary is his letter to the world that never wrote to him. His only other relationships, as they emerge from the diary, are with his intended victims, with whom he grows ever more familiar, as through stalking he moves to the intimacy of assault.

The character that emerges from the diary's pages is part Meursault, part Molesworth. The pathos of the half-educated pervades its pages; Bremer seems, above all things, ineptly young. There's hypochondria – he worries about 'a general weakness in my heart'.[53] 'I am one sick assissin', he remarks.[54] There's existential angst ('I hope my death makes more sense than my life'), literary quotes ('Call me Ismal', 'I Am A Hamlet'), even mangled references to Solzhenitsyn.[55] He enjoys Johnny Cash's murder ballad 'Kate' ('Shot you with my .38, And now I'm doing time'); he watches Kubrick's *A Clockwork Orange*, and imagines himself as madcap Alex ('but without "my brothers" & without any "in and out." Just "a little of the old ultra violence"').[56] Above all, he provides himself with templates, murderous forerunners: John Wilkes Booth, Sirhan Sirhan, Gavrilo Princip.

Coupled with this erudition is an obsessive and sometimes staccato writing style, adorned with inventive misspellings.[57] The blunders convey a weird poetry all their own: the masseuse he visits in New York lights 'incest' to scent the room; all he sees of Nixon is a dark 'shillowet'; his mistaking of 'wo-gees' for 'orgies' is positively Winnie the Pooh. There's 'longe' for 'lounge', 'enteroption' for 'interruption'; he says he has a 'type recorder'; the cops set up 'beracades'; he worries that he'll look like 'a dume lost tourist'. To metamorphose 'gesundheit' into 'gonsunhdit' takes a kind of genius.

His distrust of hippies shines through, and stands in sartorial opposition to his semi-masqueraded straightness. ('They're the new establishment.')[58] He might have got Nixon in Ottawa if it had not been for the lousy peace protestors. He mentions over and over his suits, his ties, his short hair; it's a disguise, a fiction, an inverted rebellion; he looks like a cop, a deserting soldier. He knows that he looks ridiculous.[59] He even misses his second opportunity to kill Nixon because he takes too long adjusting his costume.

There's also the intermittent friction of arousal. Speeding gives him a hard-on; he pictures his murder of Wallace failing to gift the world's television viewers with an erection. With Agla, the recalcitrant masseuse, the moment descends into frustration, a thwarted financial transaction; he's erect, but he's never going to come. He's hindered, he's a dynamic force that's blocked. 'My penis made me do it,' he writes.[60] He could be as big as Gavrilo Princip, but still nothing ever happens.[61] He writes, and writes, but what he really must do is to act.

In court even his defence lawyer pronounced him 'weird'; as he did so, Bremer grinned at the assembled journalists. While he awaited trial, there was a prison riot at the Prince George county jail, where he was now held; yet prison life did not seem to get him down. Bremer's fellow students had talked of him as a smirker. He kept smiling through his first appearance in the magistrate's court, right through the hearing where he pleaded 'not guilty' and on into the trial itself. He was eventually tried, and convicted on a charge of assault with intent to murder; he was also charged with assaulting a Federal officer and interfering with the civil rights of a presidential candidate. The 'not guilty' plea was seriously compromised by the stated intentions to commit an assassination as presented in the diary. He was sent down to fifty-three years in prison, though a few months later the sentence was reduced by ten years. In court, after judgment was passed, he is said to have declared: 'Looking back on my life, I would have liked it if society had protected me from myself.'[62]

As Bremer's diary moves towards its close, the knowledge that he has really nothing to say closes in upon him. The terror of being like Bremer presses on the reader too. What would it be like to live always with this pompous, aggressive, empty voice in one's head? The murderousness looks increasingly suicidal in its intention; he regrets that Michigan lacks the death penalty.[63] Since he is always pressingly conscious that he is a 'failure', it is apt that the shooting itself should have been botched. Yet strangest of all is the permanent sense that there was no reason for his shooting Wallace. This really does seem a murder without a motive. He makes the world share his pain, he insists that attention must be paid; but somehow there is nothing to which we might attend. His boredom prompts him to the killing, but the boredom itself seems as unfathomable as the means he chooses to bring an end to it. The more one looks at the story, the less there is there. 'I dreamed last night,' he writes. 'Forgot it.'[64]

In 1983, the diary itself was put on sale; it was by then a slice of nostalgia. Bremer was released early in November 2007, a mark of the fact that he had proved a model prisoner. He remains on parole, and is under close observation by the authorities. One can only hope for his sake that he has escaped from the state of mind that brought him to shoot down George Wallace.

II: In Their Eyes There's Something Lacking

It reminds me of a maddening undergraduate who used to tell me 'what we need is more meaninglessness'.

DAVID HOLBROOK, 1983

So I asked her, 'How do you feel, as a mother, about the prospect of your child being in that kind of confrontation, a nation in flames?' and she said, 'Let it burn!' And I said, 'What about your own child?' and she said, 'May he light the first match!'

KATHLEEN CLEAVER, INTERVIEWED BY BARBARA WALTERS[65]

While Bremer was essentially an anti-hippy, the greatest potential for political violence looked set to emerge from the counter-culture. That counter-culture could appear both the 'straight world's' antagonist and its double. In his book *It Comes Up Murder*, the conspiracy theorist John Steinbacher unearthed occult leanings in 'hippy culture', from The Doors to free love (in 'troikas'), from *Rosemary's Baby* to Students for a Democratic Society. However, he also detected that same satanic bent in the Carnegie Foundation, the Council on Foreign Relations, trade union leaders, church leaders, civil rights leaders, the Supreme Court and the Federal Reserve Bank. In his view, the same plot that united the dark-hearted hippies suffused the Establishment.[66]

The next American assassination attempt came from a member of the Manson Family, a group on the edge of the late sixties hippy world. As such, the Family shared many of that world's preoccupations: a rejection of the mainstream, faith in unreason and experimentation with communal living. The sixties and seventies counter-culture offered a spectrum of beliefs, yet nonetheless the romanticism of the times coheres all too neatly with the romanticism of assassination.

Since at least Matthew Arnold, writers have lamented the ennui of modern life. Arnold touched on the deadening impact of work, the distraction of modernity, the defeat of ambition, yet provided no resolution for these frustrations. The Anarchists of the turn of the century and the hippies and social radicals of the 1960s shared this discontent, but imagined its political answer. Hippy groups such as the Diggers repeated many of the concerns that had disturbed the pop sociologists of the 1950s; they asked, 'How many weeks would an ad agency require to face-lift the image of the Viet Cong?'[67] Youth – and those on the side of youth – were ready to judge the life created by their parents. The conventional world was deemed criminally bland. Conformism sapped the creative; the standardised flattened out eccentricity. It was the same complaint that had prompted *The Organization Man* or *The Lonely Crowd*, only now, with the war bleeding on in Vietnam, made with a new urgency.

Sex, drugs, rock music and revolution, all signalled ways of apparently shedding the ego. Against the numbness of modern life, spontaneity guaranteed authenticity, the natural expression of the naturally good self. Hippy art aimed at the free-falling, the improvisatory, the inspired. In Theodore Roszak's words, it was an art unmediated by intellect.[68] It was a response to the cult of impulse in Romanticism and to the American stress on the freedom of the individual. Drugs merely eased access to the artless inner core. The problem produced in following the self's natural promptings was an ethical one: what if that self was not naturally good? What if its whims were wicked? The answer to this was an old one: the new authentic self could not be more wicked than the life-denying society that engulfed it. The young shared in the loosening of reality brought on both by hallucinogenic drugs and by the paranoid fantasies of a conspiracy culture; acid altered and therefore relativised the perceived world.[69] Madness itself allured; Jim Morrison, the lead singer of The Doors, declared himself to be interested in 'anything about revolt, disorder, chaos, about activity that appears to have no meaning'.

Yet the fascination with the random masked a deeper fascination with connectedness. In this sense, when discussing the events of the late 1960s in California it is a beguiling game to trace a series of ostensibly random but suggestive connections, such as: on the night of the Halloween Acid Test, some of the Merry Prankster entourage were invited to Anton LaVey's Black Mass; LaVey would later act as technical adviser on Roman Polanski's film, *Rosemary's Baby* (1968); Polanski's wife, Sharon Tate, was killed by Manson's Family, in what was said by some at first to be the work of a rival satanic cult. Strangest of all, in 1968, John Frankenheimer, the director of *The Manchurian Candidate*, was following Robert Kennedy's election campaign, filming promotional material; the senator spent his last night alive at Frankenheimer's house; the director had dinner with Kennedy on the evening of his death, and then he drove the Senator to the Ambassador Hotel where Sirhan Sirhan murdered Bobby; on the CBS newsflash that followed, it was reported that Frankenheimer himself had also been shot.[70]

In her account of the Manson murders, Joan Didion puts it, 'In this light all narrative was sentimental. In this light all connections were equally meaningful and equally senseless.'[71] Coincidence became serendipity. Did it mean anything that on the night Robert Kennedy died, he had supper with friends, including Polanski and Sharon Tate?[72] Or that Vincent Bugliosi, the prosecutor of Charles Manson, worked on a trial where the question of whether Sirhan Sirhan had committed his assassination while under the effects of a hypnotic trance proved central.[73] Another witness in the same trial was Gail Aiken, Arthur Bremer's sister.[74] Then a Congressman, Gerald Ford had been one of the members of the Warren Commission. Jack Ruby was friendly with Santos Trafficante, one of the men involved with the plot to assassinate Castro, but also possibly a double-agent working for Castro.[75] At the time of John Lennon's murder, Ronald Reagan's children were working temporarily with Andy Warhol.[76] Lennon reputedly passed a night with Squeaky Fromme.[77] It is no surprise that Manson scoured the Beatles' lyrics for hidden messages, for such paranoid interpretation was common to many of their fans – including those who believed that their songs and album covers concealed indications that Paul McCartney was in fact dead.[78] And so on, for ever, an endlessly enticing sea of connections, amounting to everything or nothing.

Communal living became a grand social experiment for white middle-class American youth: the Hog Farm, the Merry Pranksters, the Yippies, the Diggers, the Weathermen, the Family. One appeal of such counter-cultural communal life was its concealment, it was a 'great secret life'.[79] The hippies were establishing communities in what they perceived as a 'social vacuum'; even Manson's Family offered a relatedness unavailable elsewhere.[80] The collective stepped in and built up improvised families; they weren't so much escaping worn-out structures as creating the structures for which they yearned. Inevitably the conditions and drives of the parent culture impregnated these communities. With its suggestion of two things in opposition, the very term 'counter-culture' misleads us; rather the two cultures paralleled each other, or were just constituents of one overarching culture.

These utopian experiments reached beyond loneliness. Their ethic of self-sufficiency, however, connected to a renewed fascination with outlaw chic, as witnessed in Arthur Penn's *Bonnie and Clyde* (1967) or the eulogising of the gorgeously anti-establishment Hell's Angels. Jefferson Airplane might have struck a pose of violence in their 1969 song 'We Can Be Together' ('We are obscene, lawless, hideous, dangerous, dirty, violent and young'), but at Altamont, when confronted by the genuine violence of the Hell's Angels who had been hired as 'security' for the concert, they turned out to be as feeble as anyone else.

Violence was hip. In a world characterised by behaviourist conformity, violence retained the character of an act, achieved and authentic. To many it seemed that bloodshed was peculiarly alive. The harsh measures of violence could appear as actions of an instinctual self, a form of relatedness more primal than the compromise of words. In a period where articulacy seemed suspect, to lapse back into the non-verbal power of physical force was mesmerising. The contradiction that the celebration of peace and love was equally central to the youth movements was lost on few.

Violence also possessed the merits of unpredictability. There was no way of knowing where an act of carnage would lead. In a society where one of the chief complaints was the boredom produced by luxury, this was itself a fervid temptation. Mayhem was a 'kick', and many were bewitched by the possibility of enacting the thrills of the movie screen. Violence was Dionysiac, ecstatic; one could lose oneself in it, and many in the period were seriously interested in losing themselves, sloughing off the old ego through music, intoxication, meditation, revolutionary commitment, the passions of the body.

There were other political attractions. If extreme or sudden enough, violence could dissolve the *polis*; it bore the possibility of a return to a state of nature. For those sick of civilised comforts, that was intrinsic to its revolutionary appeal. Whatever else it meant, political violence was a stab at power – for some, a returned blow against the oppressions of the state; for others, a ferocious grabbing of significance.

In particular, the white hippies and the New Left admired the African-American revolutionary groups, especially the Black Panthers, even as they felt guilty at the privileges they as whites, despite themselves, enjoyed. Emissaries from 'the street', the Panthers' perceived capacity for violence was presented as manly after the Christian meekness of King.[81] In November 1969, at a protest meeting in San Francisco, the Black Panther David Hilliard called for Richard Nixon's murder; he was indicted for advocating assassination, but argued that he had merely spoken metaphorically.[82] Meanwhile Eldridge Cleaver had revived the rigours of Nechaev's *Catechism of a Revolutionary*.[83]

Whether or not Nechaev was a direct influence on the most extreme elements in the New Left, they were certainly working in his spirit.[84] Moreover, the Anarchists' sense that government itself was a form of violence re-emerged (if it had ever gone away).[85] The right to punish and wage war remained with the government; violence on the part of the people, including political violence, was vicious and punishable. Prompted by the wickedness of the Vietnam War, student radicals, such as the Weather Underground, chose violence as a fitting response.[86] Vietnam nourished the radical left, yet it is likely that in any case there would have been a move to revolutionary politics, given the worldwide ferment of revolutionary movements and the injustices of American life, particularly with regards to race. The Weather Underground's belief that all American citizens were guilty and therefore deserving of punishment was a return to the 'hard-line' stance of some late-nineteenth-century Anarchists.[87] Although they killed no one, the young terrorists of the Weather Underground were enacting revenge for Vietnam, bringing the war home as partisans in their own country. The Weathermen despised the USA as an imperialist power, imagining themselves to be closer to the freedom fighters of the 'Third World' than to bourgeois America.

The idea of assassination was in the air. These were the years in which Bernard Lewis published his book *The Assassins: A Radical Sect in Islam* (1968); in Donald Cammell and Nic Roeg's film *Performance* (1970), filtered through Nietzsche's *Zur Genealogie der Moral* (1887), Mick Jagger druggily pondered the 'Hashshashin' and the Old Man of the Mountain. In 1969, Jack Newfield wrote: 'within the deepest coils of the New Left, kids talked of sabotage and assassination – "like in France during the Algerian war"'.[88] The new mood dismayed and disconcerted the government. The FBI and the CIA monitored, infiltrated and disrupted student organisations and groups of young radicals. In 1970, a number of meetings took place at the Oval Office. On 5 June, a paper was read which declared: 'We are now confronted with a new and grave crisis in our country – one which we know too little about. Certainly hundreds, perhaps thousands, of Americans – mostly under 30 – are determined to destroy our society.'[89] Charges were brought against six individuals within the anti-war movement ('the Harrisburg Six') that they had planned to kidnap Henry Kissinger.[90] After 4 May 1970 and the shooting of protesting students at Kent State University, Ohio, there were around a thousand student strikes across America. Anything seemed possible.

Some have argued that one of American democracy's strengths is its ability to absorb radical critique.[91] In time, this flexibility defused revolutionary potential; within a few years, hippydom had been commercialised and rendered mainstream. However, the Manson Family was the one expression of the hippy world that was beyond assimilation.

Charles Manson soiled the hippy movement's genuine beauty, its robust and romantic protest, and its few positive and liberal achievements. Born in 1934, Manson spent his childhood passing between a heavy-drinking mother, board school, and young offenders' institutions. He then graduated to a life of petty crime and prison. In March 1967, Manson was released from Terminal Island Penitentiary. He travelled directly to the hippy world's heart, the neighbourhood around Haight-Ashbury in San Francisco. Gifted with a crooner's voice and a musical style that resembled the young hippy singer-songwriters – in the vein of Tim Buckley or Tim Hardin – Manson had hopes of becoming a professional singer. That dream soon ended; if Manson had succeeded in becoming a pop star, there would likely have been no murders. Instead he became a Haight guru, gathering around himself a commune of alienated young women; the young women were then used to attract men to his group. They were the Family. At first, free love, drugs and power over the commune was no doubt Manson's aim; only later did that power expand to include murder.

On 9 August 1969, at 10050 Cielo Drive in Los Angeles, three young women and two young men from the Family butchered Steven Parent, an eighteen-year-old friend of the caretaker's, and then the film-star Sharon Tate (who was eight months pregnant), and her three friends Jay Sebring, Abigail Folger and Voyteck Frykowski. These too were assassinations of a kind. The victims at Cielo Drive had been savagely killed, stabbed, shot, even partially hanged.[92] One of the women who killed Tate was herself a mother of a ten-month-old baby. Sharon Tate's husband was the Polish film director Roman Polanski. Polanski was away in Europe, scouting for locations. When he heard the news he flew back at once to the USA.[93]

The events on Cielo Drive quickly became a matter for public fantasy. Rumours spread. A drugs party or a sex orgy had gone badly wrong. But beyond these rumours that incriminated the victims, a darker fear ran – the invasion of home.

The next night a middle-class couple, Leno and Rosemary LaBianca were similarly butchered and hanged. Legends in blood were daubed on the walls of both murder scenes: 'Pig'; 'Rise'; 'Helter Skelter'. A fork was stuck in Leno LaBianca's abdomen and the word 'War' carved into his chest.

To impressed outsiders, the Manson Family could seem crazily, desirably unworldly. They were a product of those random migrations that characterised the hippy years, of middle-class and lower-middle-class kids dropping out and heading west to Venice Beach and Haight-Ashbury. The young women who joined the Family typically came from broken homes, but that brokenness already looked an everyday American phenomenon. It is their ordinariness that might surprise and move us. How could they have believed Manson's spiel? Yet they did believe it. In killing they were only following orders, though some of Manson's associates refused to kill. Meanwhile the Family offered community and loyalty for those who had experienced little of those things. They renamed themselves or were renamed by Manson, the young women becoming Sadie, Squeaky, Ouisch, Gypsy, Snake – the new names expressing the distance from their old selves. Manson also went under various names, being Jesus, the Devil, Satan, Man's Son, or Soul.[94] While on trial he applied for a credit card; he gave his profession as 'Evangalist [sic]'.[95]

Young teenagers and, it has been suggested, young children took part in the 'orgies' at the Family's home at Spahn Ranch. The 'free sex' at the ranch meant triumph over shame; the murders at Cielo Drive and elsewhere signalled the defeat of disgust. In both instances, long-standing 'inhibitions' were cast off, and a primitive and free self discovered, one free to do whatever Manson wanted it to do. Sex and violence bound them together, asserting the law of the group over the commonplace moral law or the law of the state.

Manson seemingly controlled the Family, the master of all aspects of their lives. In time, the jury that judged their case did all they could think of to avoid giving the death sentence; they believed that the murdering girls had been 'overwhelmingly influenced' by Manson.[96] But that, after all, was precisely the prosecution case. Recognising in Manson something of themselves, the members of the Family willingly gave over their wills to him.[97] He decided who had sex with whom and how they would do it; he directed their drug use, rationing out the pills as he saw fit. He guessed their needs and exposed their fear. He mirrored those who encountered him back on themselves, becoming a looking-glass to their longing for a father, to their fears, their desires, their need to kill.[98] He would tell the court too that he was no more than a reflection of the society that now sought to punish him.

Manson pursued a fantasy of power. The rise of 'leaders' in the New Left and hippy collectives demonstrated the ease with which a charismatic or controlling figure could rise to prominence. When the Merry Pranksters saw the Beatles it was the pop group's domination of the crowd that sparked their interest.[99] This tied in with Jim Morrison's interest in Julian Beck's The Living Theatre and crowd psychology, that soon had him trying to whip up pop concerts into riots. The theatre of insurrection, like the pointless and abortive Days of Rage organised by the Weathermen in Chicago in 1969, exploited the same obsession with mass emotions. A rioting crowd turning to violence offers the same loss of individual identity offered by an orgy or hallucinogenic drugs. Connection to others prompted the self to commit deeds that alone it would have found impossible. In this the Manson murders were of a piece with the My Lai massacre; in both cases, group solidarity submerged the individual conscience, dehumanising the 'others' who were to be killed. The women in the Family belonged to Manson and not to themselves. Manson's megalomaniac charisma was evidence that in a world without authority, power would direct everything.

Within the Family their old selves were 'unprogrammed', and a new self substituted in its place.[100] The old self melted and new connections opened up: 'Under LSD, if it really went right, *Ego* and *Non-Ego* started to merge. Countless things that seemed separate started to merge too.'[101]

Killing also meant discarding the old moral rules, and so standing free in a bare place with your accomplices, the only bearings for the new self found in commitment to the collective.

Manson shared the hippy cult of impulse. In his eyes, whatever he and his Family did was an expression of 'our love'. Hence it lay beyond good and evil. The girls even believed that stabbing Sharon Tate and her friends was an expression of their love; Susan Atkins remarked, 'You have to have a lot of love to do that for people.' There was a kind of antinomianism in this; the Family were the elect and whatever the elect do is right. Manson created a world for himself and his followers where the 'old ego' could perish; all could become 'one'; death was love; love was murder.[102] In Manson's eyes, all human beings were both God and the Devil, and all human beings were part of each other. In this way murder did not matter; you were simply erasing an element of your self.[103] All actions were good, including murder, which merely killed the ego and released the soul. Everything was done for 'love of brother'. Drugs helped the process along, breaking up the shell of self. The paradox of Manson's system was that this destruction of the self went with his own absolute power, his own ego. Though what that ego was remains uncertain: he and his followers saw him as Marx and Lenin, as Hitler, as Jesus Christ, as a scapegoat, as God Himself.

Distanced from their pasts, their identities cracked. The killers were apparently without remorse or guilt; they bragged that they had enjoyed the killings. Such boasts either concealed deep hurt and guilt, or the murderers' values were so removed from those of the judge and jury that they could not even be bothered to mask their indifference. The killers dehumanised their prey; Susan Atkins remarked that to her Sharon Tate was no more than a 'store mannequin'; Tex Watson said that his victims were 'just blobs'.[104]

Although wielding power undoubtedly motivated Manson, there were other, equally irrational reasons for the horror that he unleashed. In writing on Manson, the prosecutor Vincent Bugliosi was intent above all on ascertaining motive. He wished to bring some sense into Manson's seemingly senseless actions. Even if they were mad, their madness had meaning; Manson declared, 'No sense makes sense.' The bizarre nature of the murders meant that the motive itself had to be bizarre.

In prison in the mid-sixties, conversing with black prisoners, Manson had become convinced that a new American revolution was impending. Like J. Edgar Hoover, Manson took the Black Panthers' threat of a bloody American revolution seriously. In fact, he took it seriously enough to wish to precipitate it himself. Race war seemed inevitable, and in the Californian desert he sought a haven where the Family could wait out the cataclysm, breeding a white master-race to take over America. His aim was to order murders that would look as much as possible as though they had been committed by blacks. The more gruesome the killing, the more it would shock the white community. Like most of the 'hippy' community, Manson shared the Panthers' belief that the police were merely the instruments of a tyrannical regime; it was therefore an easy leap for him to have his followers daub in blood the word 'Pig' on the walls where his victims were slaughtered.[105] The deeds' extremity would provoke white reprisals and that in turn would be the catalyst for the revolution.

Mostly unprepossessing themselves, the Family sought to kill the archetypal 1960s Beautiful Person; vicious and obscene fates were imagined for Liz Taylor, Frank Sinatra, Tom Jones, Steve McQueen.[106] Their first victims would include fashionable figures from the world of film and photography; they were assassinating icons of the fabulous jet-set life, icons who were also vulnerable human beings.

The evil expressed in the Tate–LaBianca murders would in time seem devilish even to some of the participants. The group had their connections to Californian satanism; when one of the victims at Cielo Drive had asked Tex Watson who they were and what they were doing, Tex had replied, 'I am the Devil and I'm here to do the Devil's business.'[107] Two of Manson's killers had satanic links: Bobby Beausoleil had starred as Lucifer in Kenneth Anger's film *Lucifer Rising*; Susan Atkins had been involved with Anton LaVey's San Francisco satanists. Manson himself had been peripherally involved with the occult group The Process.[108] There were fantasies that Sharon Tate and her friends had also been involved in 'the occult'; it was remembered that in J. Lee Thompson's *Eye of the Devil* (1966), one of Tate's first roles was playing a young girl practising witchcraft.

Soon after the killings, the murderers were caught stealing cars near a town called Independence. Later a raid took place at the Family's desert home, Spahn Ranch, and the remaining culprits were brought in. At first, no link was made to the Los Angeles murders until Susan Atkins confessed all to a cell-mate.

Quickly the story behind the murders was in the American papers and on American TV. The revelations horrified most, but not all. At a meeting in Flint, Michigan, in December 1969, fresh from the shock of Black Panther Fred Hampton's assassination by the police, the Weathermen celebrated Manson and imagined following him in a campaign of chaotic violence. One of the group's leaders, the young lawyer Bernadine Dohrn, declaimed: 'Dig it; first they killed those pigs, then they ate dinner in the room with them, then they even shoved a fork into pig Tate's stomach. Wild!'[109] The only thing separating this from W. H. Auden's fantasy of the 'necessary murder' was her palpable enjoyment of the carnage. Only days after the Cielo Drive murders, the Weathermen set off their bombs in Chicago. The final desire was to go beyond, to be 'far out'. Extremity charmed them; it was 'for real'. Manson was above all exhilaratingly excessive. The underground paper *Tuesday's Child* named Manson 'Man of the Year'; 1969 was dubbed 'Year of the Fork'. Having fallen in love with Manson's 'cherub face and sparkling eyes', the leading young radical Jerry Rubin visited the killer in prison, so they could 'rap' over revolution.[110]

At the trial, Manson would be eager to show that the Family was after all society's responsibility: 'These children that come at you with knives, they are your children. You taught them, I didn't teach them. I just tried to help them stand up.' Manson depicted himself likewise as the product of American society: 'My father is the jailhouse. My father is your system . . . I am only what you made me. I am only a reflection of you.'[111] The young women killers belonged to the TV generation; Leslie Van Houten would assert that she was influenced 'by the war in Vietnam and TV'; perhaps in an attempt to annoy, Brenda McCann remarked: 'We are what you have made us. We were brought up on your TV. We were brought up watching *Gunsmoke, Have Gun Will Travel, FBI, Combat. Combat* was my favourite show. I never missed *Combat*.'[112]

Appropriately perhaps, Manson's crimes would themselves be quickly understood in cinematic terms; the fact that one of their victims was both a movie-star and the wife of a film director merely quickened the process. Manson wanted Dennis Hopper to play him in any film based on his life.[113] It feels fitting that the Family lived in an abandoned movie-set for Westerns, that is, Spahn's Movie Ranch. In the *LA Herald Examiner*, a reviewer remarked of the 1972 documentary on the Family, *Manson*, that it was 'the horror film to end all horror films, probably the scariest since the original *Dracula*'.[114] The reality of the murders and of the life of the Family had taken on the quality of a fiction.

On 25 January 1971, Charles Manson, Leslie Van Houten, Patricia Krenwinkel and Susan Atkins were found guilty of all the offences with which they had been charged. In October 1971, Charles 'Tex' Watson was similarly found guilty of eight murders. Later Manson was also convicted of the killings of Gary Hinman, a musician, and Donald Shea, a movie stuntman. (Perhaps in an attempt to exonerate Manson, Atkins had also confessed to the killing of Hinman.) Bobby Beausoleil was also convicted of the murder of Gary Hinman. Vincent Bugliosi believes that the Manson Family were in fact responsible for as many as thirty-five murders. All five defendants were sentenced to death; but on 18 February 1972, the California Supreme Court declared the death penalty to be unconstitutional. All those facing the death penalty – including Manson and his accomplices, and Sirhan Sirhan – had their sentences automatically reduced to life imprisonment.

In prison, Manson hooked up with the ultra-racist Aryan Brotherhood; from then on the Manson Family and the Brotherhood would work in close consort.[115] One of the tasks allotted to those female members of the Family still outside prison was to entertain members of the Brotherhood when they were released from jail. Among these nourishing women was the acting leader of the Manson Family on the outside, Lynette 'Squeaky' Fromme. In 1971, she spent three months in prison for feeding a hamburger tainted with a huge dose of LSD to a potential witness against Manson. In November 1972, after the death of a young woman, Lauren Willett, at the house where she was living in Stockton, California, Fromme was arrested but set free for lack of evidence.

Fromme was one of Manson's most loyal followers. She had first met him on the street when she was eighteen years old. Fromme described him as 'a father who knew that it was good to make love'; making love to him felt 'guiltless, like being a baby'.[116] The transparently oedipal nature of her attraction to Manson was commented on at the time; in an unpublished memoir, she described the first time she had sex with Manson:

I felt close to him and layed my hand on his shoulder, wanting daddy to hold me . . . I hoped that he would pursue me or touch me, or rape me or anything good really, yet without me giving up to it. It was a little girl-game I wanted to play. But instead he told me . . . 'You wanted your daddy to hit you, didn't you?' It was so and I nodded. As all daughters, I had wanted all the attention I could get from my daddy.[117]

Her real father was an aeronautical engineer living in Redondo Beach.

Despite her devotion to Manson, on the nights of the murders Fromme remained back at the ranch, while others went out. Was it that Manson believed that, unlike the others, she was no killer? If so, she was about to prove him wrong, by apparently threatening to kill the President of the USA.

* * *

The worry caused by a series of heart attacks among Presidents and Vice Presidents, the threat of nuclear war, and the shock of assassination led to a clarification of the rights of democratic succession. In 1967, the 25th constitutional amendment was passed. If the President was incapacitated or died, power would pass automatically to the Vice President. If the Vice President could not assume power then the office would pass to the Speaker of the House of Representatives, and if he or she was similarly unable to take the role then a President *pro tempore* would be elected from within the Senate by the Senators themselves. In the event of a cataclysm or disaster that prevented this, then Cabinet members in specified order would assume the Presidency. The first man to benefit from the new arrangement would be Gerald Ford, the heir to scheming Richard Nixon.

Ford had never harboured a serious ambition for the Presidency; he more modestly dreamed that one day he might become Speaker of the House.[118] He became Vice President following Spiro Agnew's resignation in disgrace. Nixon picked Ford as a loyalist, a man popular in Congress, and a 'safe pair of hands'. Despite the encroaching flood of Watergate, the prospect of Ford possibly becoming President still seemed remote. That was just as well; Nixon couldn't quite picture unsophisticated Jerry Ford as Presidential material. And yet on 9 August 1974, Ford was inaugurated.

Gerald Ford was a folksy accident-prone ex-football-player famous for tripping on the stairs as he climbed into Air Force One. (Fromme kept a copy of the photograph of his stumble.[119]) He was notoriously ordinary and not especially bright.[120] The all-American Ford appeared reassuringly solid, ploddingly dogged. After sneaky Nixon, the public were eager to believe that the new President was as undesigning as he seemed.[121] Indeed the sense of Ford's goodness emerged partly from the contrast with his predecessor in office. Nixon could not help but look sly and somehow insubstantial; John F. Kennedy was said to have suggested: 'I feel sorry for Nixon, because he does not know who he is, and at each stop he has to decide which Nixon he is at the moment, which must be very exhausting.'[122] Ford on the other hand was simply himself; he may have lacked vision but he liked people.[123]

Ford's term of office was marked by nothing much in particular. Ford's free pardon for Nixon, the dire state of the US economy, seamy revelations about the recent American past, and eye-catching radical violence were the dominant notes of his brief Presidency. With information gleaned from his time on the Warren Commission, Ford had once co-written a book-length portrait of Lee Harvey Oswald; now his time as President would be mired in reports and commissions into the 1960s' baffling assassinations.

Ford himself seemed too innocuous to assassinate. Moreover, despite the murder of King and the attacks on Presidential candidates, there had not really been a serious attack on the President himself since Dallas. In February 1974, in a plan to murder Richard Nixon, Samuel Byck, a mentally disturbed unemployed tyre salesman, attempted to hijack a plane and crash it into the White House. The attempt ended in a shambles, with both pilots shot (one killed) and Byck dispatching himself with a shot to the head. The deed was only one more example of the American chaos, and as such quickly vanished into historical obscurity; in his *Memoirs*, Nixon neglects to mention Byck.

Yet Nixon was obviously a potential victim, guilty as he was of degrading American political life. But who would possibly want to kill

Ford? Yet in September 1975, Ford travelled twice to California; on each occasion a different woman attempted to assassinate him.

In early September, Ford's trip to the west took him first to Portland, Oregon, then down on 4 September to Sacramento. The next morning Ford addressed the party faithful at a breakfast meeting, then went back to his hotel. He then strolled across the park to the Californian state capitol building. His security men gathered around him, some striding ahead; the TV cameramen backed up at the head of the entourage. It was a clear, sunny day. There were many people waiting behind a rope that cordoned off the sidewalk. Ford was smiling, shaking hands, and went to shake the hand of a young woman in a red dress, when he saw that she was raising a gun. She called out, 'The country is a mess! This man is not your President!', but before anything else could happen, the weapon was torn from her hand by a Secret Service agent.[124] It was the Manson Family leader *in absentia*, Lyn 'Squeaky' Fromme. As she was being led away, she called out, 'It didn't go off!' The tone in which these words were uttered would be one major element in her forthcoming trial: was she expressing disappointment, or declaring that there was no need to worry, nothing had really happened?

When she was taken temporarily into custody, Fromme's roommate told the police, 'If the gun had gone off . . . Lyn would have been a true public servant.'[125] The President himself could be no more than that. Only an hour and a half after the incident, Ford went on to deliver his address anyway to the California State Legislature; he deemed it was best just to get on with the day's schedule.[126] The Californian Republicans had wanted 'a presidential crime speech', so he spoke of the rise of violent crime and gun control.[127] (Economic hard times had helped prompt a leap in violent crimes, up 17 per cent between 1973 and 1974.[128]) None of the audience knew that the man making that speech had himself just faced a woman with a gun.

Ford was only out walking because there was perceived to be little threat. The Secret Service were caught off guard, and the shooting laid bare weaknesses in intelligence. In assessing the safety of Ford's Sacramento visit, the Secret Service had checked with an array of local departments and sources; none had apparently mentioned Fromme or the Manson Family – although they knew of her presence in the city.[129] As well as an anonymous threat supposedly from the Symbionese

Liberation Army, there had been two other assassination plans directed at Ford during his visit to Sacramento, one cooked up by a man who boasted that he had once shared a cell with Charles Manson.[130]

Fromme made the front cover of both *Time* and *Newsweek*; if she had sought further publicity for Manson, she had got it, and also an enviable notoriety for herself. Many protested at what was felt to be *Time*'s patronising (at the age of twenty-seven, she was billed as 'The Girl Who Almost Killed Ford') or glamorising approach. Roman Polanski wrote to the magazine, objecting to the cover photograph that showed Fromme 'in all her fresh-faced, tender-lipped vulnerability, gazing dreamily into history . . . Where she may have failed in her attempt to make violence appealing, your cover has not.'[131]

Yet Fromme was not the only person to receive a boost from the incident. The thought that Ford had survived an assassination attempt revivified public affection for the man himself, so damaged by his pardon of Nixon.[132] The incident was felt to repeat uncannily the attack on JFK, coming out of the blue on a sunny Friday.[133] After John Kennedy's death, assassination threats against the President increased by 500 per cent; in the first three weeks of September 1975, there were 320 threats to murder Gerald Ford. In an average month there would be around 100.[134] Thoughts of assassination were imagined as contagious; it was now believed that some three weeks later Fromme's approach to Ford inspired Sara Jane Moore's more aggressive attempt.

On 19 September 1975 Ford flew once again to the West Coast. On 22 September, he was in San Francisco where he addressed a trade union meeting and attended a lunch with the World Affairs Council of Northern California. Later that afternoon, outside the St Francis Hotel in San Francisco, as he stepped from the lobby to the waiting Lincoln Continental, and stopped to wave over to the crowd opposite, Sara Jane Moore fired at the President. Though she was some forty-five feet away, she was a good shot, and would have hit him had she not been jolted by a bystander (one Oliver Sipple). Ford was forced to the ground by his security men, shoved inside the car and driven off.[135]

Initial reports suggested that Moore was known as an energetic member of the local radical underground; she had helped in the distribution of food given by William Randolph Hearst (Patty's father) in answer to the ransom demands of the Symbionese Liberation Army.

That she also befriended the Hearst family showed something of her ability to be on both sides of the game at once. Yet it was soon revealed that, far from being the stereotypical youthful left-wing activist, she was also a professional accountant, the 45-year-old divorced mother of a nine-year-old son, and an FBI informant. As a double-agent, she was a wash-out; she swanked to her radical friends about her FBI connections, was 'compulsively' candid and in love with intrigue. Days before the attempted shooting she had rung the police, requesting that she be taken into custody; she warned that she might start 'testing the system'.[136] On a recent television interview, she has described her motive as being the desire to spark a revolution.

In private as in public, Ford believed that he couldn't 'buckle under to the "crazies"' but had to keep getting out and meeting ordinary Americans.[137] He had to show himself as a man among other men and women. Yet the attacks had demonstrated that touch of common humanity all too negatively. In the case of both Fromme and Moore, it was the President's fear that mattered. When Fromme approached him, he had flinched; when Moore fired at him, his terror was apparent. Of course such responses are only natural; but that was the point, the symbol of American power had been exposed as one mortal man. So it was that reports of the President's later calmness – giving his speech anyway at Sacramento, his commenting blandly on the weather at San Francisco – were so vital; they restored the image of imperturbable authority. Fromme and Moore could only get close to Ford because it was still felt that the President should stage himself for the people. The assassinations subverted that democratic impulse, turning it into a dark reminder.

Was that Fromme's motive? It was hard to discern the truth. She could variously be understood to have raised a gun at Ford to protest the cutting down of redwood trees, on behalf of Charles Manson, or as an act of absurd theatre.[138] In the spirit of Edward Abbey's novel *The Monkey Wrench Gang* (1975), she might seem an environmental activist with a gun. With other members of the Manson Family, she had written letters threatening death to various polluting industrialists.[139] A day after the 'attack' on Ford, her fellow Family member Sandra Good said of Fromme: 'She's a very gentle girl . . . All this monstrousness out here hurts her . . . every day we wake up and think: "How many whales did they kill today?"'[140] Good suggested that she and Fromme were part of an international organisation planning 'to start assassinating Presidents, Vice Presidents and major executives of companies. I'm warning these people they better stop polluting or they're going to die.'[141] During the trial, Fromme threatened further violence unless the Redwood National Park was saved from loggers and polluters.

Some have felt that her main aim was to give Manson and the other imprisoned members of the Family another day in court. Fromme hoped that the Family would be allowed to gather in court and testify, explaining the Tate–LaBianca murders; this suggests that as far as the Family themselves saw it, the explanation understood by the public (the incitement of race war) was not the whole story. What account they might have offered is unclear, though some have speculated about mystical meanings hidden from the unregenerate public.

Recently Fromme has disputed oedipal interpretations of her attack on Ford (partly provoked by the coincidence that when she approached him it appeared on camera – and to the President himself – that the gun was aimed at his groin).[142] Her rebuttals are persuasive. After all, the American press can be imagined as needing a vengeful young woman to embody the anxieties men were feeling about the feminist movement's demands. Both Fromme and Patty Hearst were young women with guns, conceived of as revengers against patriarchy, the older generation blamed for the massacre of American youth in Vietnam, corrupt and emotionally bankrupt like Richard Nixon. It was no accident that the reporters who were most celebrated for unmasking Nixon were youthful. Fromme had been part of a wider group that had committed real, horrible and unjust acts of violence. However, it was as a symbol that she was most captivating, the dreamy daughter envisioned as a lunatic assassin.

In communication with her biographer, Jess Bravin, Fromme has said:

It was too early to put the bullet in the chamber, I did not want to put the bullet in the chamber. I did not want to shoot this guy. He looked like an advertisement, a billboard, unreal . . . when Ford did arrive, I felt I had to go through the motion, took a few steps, raised the gun, and let the rest happen as it did.[143]

This story suggests a more complex set of motives than was allowed for either by the defence or the prosecution; if this account is true, she hesitated between the desire to assassinate Ford and the unexpected realisation that he was too fabricated to kill.

In court, Fromme's defence team wanted to turn her into an 'accidental assassin', a woman whose capacity for judgement was fatally undermined by the lasting effect of her use of drugs (Fromme had reputedly taken LSD 'thousands' of times). However, Fromme was determined to present the deed as her own choice and action, an event staged to garner public attention for environmental issues and for what she believed to be the miscarriages of justice that had put Charles Manson in prison. She claimed her own agency. It was vital to her case that she was not acting on Manson's orders.

During the trial, Fromme attempted to change her plea from 'not guilty' to 'no contest'. It was her way of expressing her belief that the court had no right to judge her. For similar reasons, she would refuse to testify in her own defence. Throughout the trial there were shades of Guiteau, as Fromme acted up, having to be carried into court, disrupting and interrupting, begging that Manson be brought to her, and getting herself thrown out of the courtroom. Later she was removed from the courtroom after leaving her place and advancing on the presiding judge, Thomas J. MacBride. She wanted to make him allow Charles Manson to speak at her trial; her motive after all was to reopen his case. As she was ejected, she menaced the court: 'Lives will be lost . . . It's gonna get bloody if they are not allowed to speak.'[144] Such threats were the most striking element in the Family's public pronouncements; two months before the event in Sacramento, a press release from Fromme and Sandra Good had warned, 'If Nixson's [sic] reality wearing a new face continues to run this country against the law, your homes will be bloodier than the Tate-LaBianca houses and My Lai put together.'[145] She told a Canadian reporter that if his prime minister did not 'stop killing seals and whales . . . he will be assassinated'.[146] There were baleful hints of a company of assassins – the International People's Court of Retribution – formed to wreak revenge on polluters, their wives and the politicians who helped them. She predicted a bloodbath across 'the golf courses and bridge clubs throughout this country'.[147] In court, one Harold Boro (Fromme's 64-year-old lover), who had supplied her with the gun and shown her how to operate it, also told how she had told him that some company executives would have to be killed as an example.[148] It was hard to know how much bravado was in these acts of intimidation; around a hundred members of the Family were still believed to be living free in California. Building on fears of the young and of the hidden underground, such words of warning no doubt rendered the women of the Family terrifying.

A great deal hung on how serious Fromme's intentions had been. In Washington, Ford gave his testimony on videotape. The 'firing hammer was down . . . the barrel slide was uncocked and . . . there was no round in the chamber'; the President himself heard no 'click' as she approached him and could not even recollect whether her finger was on the trigger.[149] The possibility that Fromme had not loaded the weapon properly out of incompetence was weakened by testimony about her familiarity with guns. The prosecution failed to present to the defence a statement by a policeman that he had heard Fromme say, 'It's not loaded anyway.' This statement strongly suggested that she had never intended to do more than frighten the President. However, when questioned in court, the policeman could not properly recollect what Fromme had said. A slip that might have led to the termination of the trial receded in importance.

On 27 November 1975, despite there being considerable evidence that suggested her approaching Ford was nothing more than a hostile gesture, Fromme was found guilty of attempting to assassinate the President. Less than a month later, she was sentenced to life imprisonment; at the hearing she lobbed an apple at a lawyer's head.[150]

While Fromme's arraignment was still in progress, Sara Jane Moore, President Ford's would-be assassin, was found fit to stand trial. In January 1976, she was also sentenced to life imprisonment. Just as both women were appearing in court, another infamous revolutionary woman was also being indicted; the world was watching the trial of Patty Hearst.

In the spring of 1974, the kidnapping of the nineteen-year-old 'newspaper heiress' Patty Hearst played out as a media distraction, the television crews camped outside the Hearst mansion, the cameras scanning the face of her anxious father, playing over and over the messages from his missing daughter, the captive of the 'Symbionese Liberation Army'. (While he was still Vice President, Gerald Ford's daughter Susan had been threatened with kidnap by the same group.[151]) Patty Hearst's messages increasingly betrayed a sympathy with the revolutionaries who held her prisoner, and an irritation, mounting to contempt, for the wealthy family that had raised her. In early March, she was criticising her parents for not doing enough to get her freed; soon she was contemptuous of their attempts to distribute food among the poor (one of the SLA's demands); and then on 3 April, she announced that she would remain with her kidnappers, fighting alongside them in their struggle for revolution. 'I have chosen,' she said, 'to stay and fight.' Just over a fortnight later, during a bank robbery in San Francisco, she was filmed holding a submachine gun. Her family, the FBI and the public wondered if she were a 'reluctant robber', participating under compulsion. She responded with a message to her father, asserting that it was ridiculous to suppose she had become a bank robber against her will, and calling her father 'pig' and 'Adolf'; in later communications, she would refer to 'the pig Hearsts'. Certainly the criminal spree that followed suggested that she was a very willing revolutionary; meanwhile the family clung to the idea that she had been brainwashed.

Two members of the SLA were in prison awaiting trial for their supposed involvement in the assassination of Dr Marcus Foster, an inspiring and good-hearted school superintendent in Oakland, California. The gang had apparently used 'cyanide-tipped' bullets. In the eyes of his assassins, Foster's crime was that he was a black man helping a white government to impose a domineering education system. The cack-handed absurdity of the murder, its pointlessness, its nihilism, would come in time to seem evidence of the SLA's revolutionary authenticity. It was an assassination worthy of Nechaev.

In May 1974, the SLA were cornered by the police in a Los Angeles house. In a shoot-out, televised live to the nation, 150 police surrounded the building, firing into it with tear gas grenades and rifle and automatic fire; the house caught fire and all six occupants were killed. Hearst was elsewhere with the last two remaining SLA revolutionaries; she vowed to fight on. The police assault's well-publicised brutality recruited new members to the SLA, and a second wave of revolutionary transgressions followed, as bombs were planted and banks robbed. In the course of one bank robbery in Carmichael, Sacramento, Myrna Lee Opshal, an innocent mother of four, was murdered.[152]

On 18 September 1975, the police finally caught up with Patty Hearst. She was taken into custody; almost at once, she declared her desire to be taken home to her family. Within days, she was reported as having broken with her fellow revolutionaries; on forms, she altered her official occupation from 'unemployed urban guerrilla' to 'none'. It emerged that she had indeed been 'brainwashed' in a way, and was a sufferer from 'Stockholm Syndrome', whereby captives quickly come to identify with and even love their captors. Held at first in harsh conditions, abused, blindfolded, raped, in fear of her life, Hearst had indeed done her best to comply with her kidnappers and finally fell in love with one of the gang.

The jury at her trial were sceptical about this story; she was found guilty. Before sentencing, the judge ordered further psychiatric tests to be carried out on her. Eventually she was given seven years for her part in the robbing of the San Francisco bank. However, within a few years President Jimmy Carter commuted her sentence, and she was released; in 2001, she was given a full pardon by Bill Clinton.

It seems that Hearst was another 'accidental' terrorist. Her story joined those mythic versions of the brainwashed and temporarily will-less. She presented an image of a malleable self, a woman who could discard her privilege and join the revolution, and then almost as swiftly pick up again the wealthy life she had just forgone. Her compliance involved her will's childlike surrender, adapting her wants to please those of her kidnappers, aiming at simply staying alive. She had adopted the role of revolutionary; she had divided her self.

The Patty Hearst story only deepened the sense of an American maelstrom. While she awaited trial a Puerto Rican independence group bombed Chicago, New York and Washington. It was estimated that of the 131 US police officers killed in 1975, some thirteen were the victims of 'probable guerrilla activity'.[153] Of course, bombs and terrorist activity were just then a worldwide problem. On the day of the Puerto Ricans' explosions, five other cities across the world were bombed; on the day that Lynette Fromme confronted President Ford, a bomb went off at the London Hilton, killing several bystanders and injuring over sixty. The threat of assassination was similarly not confined to American borders; in Japan, to take only one example, there were fears for Emperor Hirohito's life from the 'Red Army'.

In prison, Fromme was interested in hooking up with the Weather Underground, and curious about the exploits of Patty Hearst.[154] In press reports that November, as women with guns, as bandits with mysterious principles, Hearst, Moore and Fromme were routinely linked. All three seemed presages of a new kind of woman – pitiless, unpredictable, incomprehensible within the moral conventions understood by older people. Their anger at 'the system' was palpable, but the anger itself seemed ineffable. Something in America appeared to be breaking apart, and these women were part of the wrecking.

Yet for all their threatening portentousness, the final breakdown that they seemed to herald failed to materialise. Ford carried on, to be replaced in time by the even more homespun, pious and innocuous Jimmy Carter. Their shots had missed or failed even to be fired. While it remains unclear if Moore was making a 'protest' or attempting to murder the President, later statements after her conviction have removed much of the doubt that she had seriously sought Gerald Ford's death.[155] If Fromme had also meant to kill Ford, well, then she blew it. Blowing it was the way that hippy plans mostly ended, like the Merry Pranksters stuck in hot, sticky Mexico, like the Diggers closing down their New York free store after the gangsters came round to offer protection, like *Easy Rider*, like all those radicals pursuing a revolution that failed to arrive.

III: Executive Actions

In the wake of the Watergate scandal, there were moves in Congress, the Senate and the press to examine the workings of the secret state. Scrutiny fell in particular on the CIA. The participation in the Watergate burglary of Howard Hunt, Gore Vidal's favourite ex-CIA clandestine operative, was one ground for suspicion. On 22 December 1974, a piece in the *New York Times* by Seymour Hersh exposed the scale of domestic intelligence and surveillance, including bugging phones and breaking into suspects' homes. Ford ordered an official investigation (the Rockefeller Commission) that would concentrate on abuses by the CIA within the USA, and thus leave the more damaging secrets (the so-called 'family jewels') concerning foreign interventions, particularly assassination plots, secure.[156] However, much had already been given away by the unprompted confessions of William Colby, the current Director of Central Intelligence. Then, on 16 January 1975, attempts by Ford to limit the revelations that might come out foundered on his own unwonted candour: in an 'off-the-record' remark at a press conference, he let slip that the CIA had been involved in assassination attempts.[157] Ford's blundering honesty shook the cat out of the bag.

The two world wars had hastened the end of European authority and signalled the advent of American hegemony. Such power must be protected. In the years after the Truman presidency, the American government showed itself willing to do so by means that would previously have been thought underhand. In most cases, the point of such interventions was to prevent the spread of Communism. A charitable reading would argue that the intention was the nurturing of democratic freedoms; the USA's readiness to co-operate with right-wing dictatorships and undermine elected governments rather shows that the goal was the protection of capitalist markets and the extension of American power and influence. Such action was of course not limited to the United States. Dictatorships and totalitarian regimes were similarly happy to pursue murders outside their borders, and even well-established democracies could also envisage state-sponsored assassination.[158]

This secret violence pursued abroad was investigated in the Church Committee's reports of 1975–6 (United States Senate Select Committee to study Governmental Operations with Respect to Intelligence Activities). Chaired by Senator Frank Church, the committee was set up in January 1975; the public hearings began in September of the same year. Church was rumoured to be harbouring Presidential ambitions; certainly he showed no sign of wanting to contain the harm that his discoveries wrought.[159] The committee's reports were so damaging that they led directly or indirectly to the sacking of Colby, James Schlesinger, the former CIA chief and then Secretary of Defense, and Henry Kissinger as National Security Adviser.[160] Gerald Ford sought to persuade the committee to withhold revelations 'on the subject of assassinations' on the grounds that it would damage American interests and endanger lives.[161] But any attempt at keeping the public in the dark was now futile. Following the release of the Pentagon Papers and the Watergate affair, press investigations of the White House had eroded earlier standards of deference. The assumption was that the public right to know trumped security considerations, especially where the government could be shown to have acted outside the law. On 10 June 1975, Church was interviewed on *The Today Show*, and said that, despite Ford's interventions, his committee would make 'a full disclosure'.[162] Ford had argued that the admissions would put lives at risk; in the eyes of Colby and others, this fear proved to be grounded as they believed that the reports led to the assassination on 23 December 1975 of Richard Welch, the CIA station chief in Athens.

Damaging stories emerged showing that the US government and in particular the CIA had been more or less entangled in plots to assassinate Fidel Castro, Prime Minister Patrice Lumumba of the Congo, the then Chinese Foreign Minister Zhou Enlai, Rafael Trujillo, dictator of the Dominican Republic, and General René Schneider of Chile, and had connived at the murder of President Ngo Dinh Diem only a few weeks before John F. Kennedy himself was shot.[163]

Neither Rafael Trujillo nor Ngo Dinh Diem were themselves above reproach. Only a couple of weeks before the coup that usurped Diem, a telegram from Henry Cabot Lodge, American Ambassador in Saigon, shared Lodge's fears that Diem intended to assassinate him (though expressing such fears was possibly part of Lodge's long-term intention to see the Vietnamese leader ousted).[164] Never enormously popular, Diem had been corrupt, nepotistic and repressive, in particular ordering harsh punishment of the nation's Buddhists. For these reasons, the South Vietnamese both assumed American involvement in the coup and welcomed it.[165] However, although the Americans were on the whole content to have seen it done, the murders of Diem and his brother appear to have been the spontaneous work of the coup leaders themselves.[166]

Once a favoured figure with the USA, Trujillo was himself apt to pursue state assassinations. He helped with a failed plot to assassinate Rómulo Betancourt, the President of Venezuela; in 1956, he also ordered the kidnapping and murder of Jesús de Galíndez, an ex-Dominican resident and then a lecturer at Columbia University.[167] The Americans had lived happily for years with Trujillo's penchant for torture, repression and political murder; in the circumstances of the late 1950s, however, his methods looked likely to provoke instability in the region or even spark a left-wing revolution. Despite new-found CIA eagerness to see Trujillo killed, he was anyway murdered before the USA could get properly involved. American arms had been dispatched to be given to any likely assassin, but were most likely never used.[168] Nonetheless, as with the killing of Diem in Vietnam, the Americans ended up being burdened with the success of an assassination they had wanted, Trujillo's death leading to the brief deployment of thousands of US troops in the Dominican Republic.

It appears that the CIA never directly murdered a foreign leader, the actual killing being sub-contracted out to local assassins. In most cases (the right-wing dictator Trujillo being one exception), the reasons for wanting these leaders dead hinged on their left-wing politics and perceived leanings towards Soviet Russia. The agents were fighting a Cold War, and one they believed themselves to be on the verge of losing. These assassinations were all cooked up in an atmosphere of crisis; the operatives understood such murders to be not only permissible, but righteously justified.[169] Moreover in no instance was an American meant to fire the vital shot. Nonetheless, the basic fact remains: the CIA and the US government had shown themselves willing to intervene violently or to support at a distance violent intervention in the internal affairs of foreign states, including democracies with whom America was nominally at peace. President Eisenhower's parting words on leaving office regarding the danger to democracy posed by the 'unwarranted influence' of the 'military-industrial complex' now looked straightforwardly prophetic.[170]

In view of his words of warning, it is curious that Eisenhower himself might have started the rot. In 1953, Eisenhower approved CIA plans to undermine the pro-Soviet regime in Iran, and allow its replacement by Muhammad Reza Pahlavi, the Shah. In the case of Patrice Lumumba, there were decided implications, although they remained inconclusive, that Eisenhower had either ordered, or grossly hinted at murder.[171] It's possible that these hints were entirely innocent and crassly misinterpreted.[172] The difficulties in proving the charge against Eisenhower in this case existed in all the assassination plots. Given the operations' highly scandalous nature, and indeed their illegality, it proved impossible to find records of direct Presidential orders. Lower down, documents exist. In connection to the ultimate head of the chain of command, things moved by hearsay and rumour, even as they were being embodied in practical moves. It may be that there were no such records higher up because there were no such orders. As likely is the possibility that government officials covered their tracks as best they could. Conversations often proceeded on the basis of hints and innuendoes.[173] Also possible is that individuals in the CIA were working towards the President, attempting to enact decisions based on an assumed knowledge of what they felt he would have wanted.[174] Such interpretations were just as likely to be over-zealously baseless as attentively well-founded. It was a matter of impressions, assumptions and guesses. In any case, in the eyes of the CIA and the White House, the volatile situation in the Congo merited extreme measures; at stake was a possible avenue for Soviet influence in Africa and the loss of access to valuable mineral deposits.[175] As far as the Americans were concerned, Lumumba was not someone with whom they could work.[176] Even after he was dismissed as prime minister, he was still too popular a figure to be allowed to live.[177] Exotically murderous plans were laid, including poisoning Lumumba's toothpaste.[178] In the Congo itself, the plan to kill Lumumba necessarily assumed a cruder shape. It was decided that if an assassination were to take place, it was altogether safer and more fitting if the Congolese themselves could be persuaded to do it. Yet in the end Lumumba was murdered without much reference to the CIA's plots.[179]

In late 1959 and the early months of 1960, the strongest precedent for state-sponsored assassination had been set by the laying of plots against Castro.[180] It is certain that President Eisenhower was aware of the plans to destabilise Castro, but unclear whether he was cognisant of any intention to assassinate him; certainly Allen Dulles, the Director of the CIA knew, and possibly, despite his penchant for undercover operations and his acceptance of the occasional necessity for 'tyrannicide', did not approve of any plan to murder the Cuban leader.[181] Indeed there are clues that Eisenhower was keener than Dulles on the more 'drastic' kind of action.[182] The project was managed at a lower level by Richard M. ('Dick') Bissell, Tracy Barnes and Sheffield Edwards.[183] Just as Kennedy inherited the Bay of Pigs invasion, in early 1961 Bissell and William Harvey renewed the murder plans under Kennedy. At this stage in the Presidency, the Kennedy administration was 'as enthralled by the

Agency's mystique as its predecessor'.[184] The assassination plots were initially tied in with the prospective invasion. Indeed it was felt at first that, without an invasion, murdering Castro made no sense: such a unilateral move might only destabilise the region, and lead to a take-over by some even worse figure – such as his brother Raul, or Che Guevara.[185] After the Bay of Pigs fiasco, the dismissal of Bissell and Allen Dulles signalled a more tempered relationship between the White House and the CIA, leading to a supposedly chastened Agency. Yet the intention to kill Castro would not go away.[186] The revival of the assassination idea can best be understood as a mix of desperation and vengeance.[187]

Precedents were being set that would bear corrupt fruit in Nixon's presidency. Within the highest ranks of the government and the CIA, it began to seem normal that the President would be involved in extreme measures outside the law.[188] In their effort to kill Castro, the CIA even teamed up with the Mafia. In doing so, necessity drove them: the government employed no professional assassins of its own. This was a case where private enterprise was clearly the preferred option; they needed a tough guy, and the reasonable assumption was that the Mafia were the toughest guys around.[189] There are hints that some of the Mafia figures approached by the CIA were as much motivated by American patriotism as by greed or the desire to gain immunity from prosecution.[190] Mostly they seem to have thought of it as a wheeze, and a good way to con the CIA.[191] (The Church Committee would in time declare that 'the United States should not make use of underworld figures for their criminal talents'.[192])

While it remains in doubt whether JFK either knew or approved of the conspiracy against Castro, there is significant evidence that suggests that both he and Bobby Kennedy not only knew something, but indeed were the prime movers in the renewed plots in the months after the Bay of Pigs.[193] Of course, if the President did not know, then the CIA was acting alone and without ultimate authority; therefore for those in the Agency, implicating the Kennedys in their plans might have been a welcome ploy, especially given the Agency's bitterness after the failed invasion. Whatever was going on in private, in November 1961, Jack Kennedy spoke publicly about his belief that the USA could not (not 'should' not) compete with foreign powers in the matter of coups, terror and assassinations.[194] Of course, this explicit statement need not mean that plans in these areas would not continue out of sight. That same month in private at the White House, he discussed plans for 'espionage, sabotage, general disorder' in Cuba.[195] At some point in 1961, it seems that the White House requested the CIA to develop an 'executive action capability', newspeak for assassination.[196] Although, in the opinion of many, Bobby Kennedy was intimately involved with these schemes, his biographer, declares that it was only on 7 May 1962, that Kennedy was first briefed on the assassination plans. Apparently, he was angry and disturbed by the information; given his high-profile campaign against organised crime, the Mafia's involvement particularly dismayed him. Two days later, he ordered that the Department of Justice must be first informed of any such plots.[197] Such an order does not necessarily imply disapproval. As this shows, it is hard to ascertain where the Kennedy brothers stood on the plans to kill Castro; some believe they knew nothing, some that they knew and were outraged, others that they tacitly, or even enthusiastically, approved.[198] On balance there does seem to be significant evidence that the plot against Castro was no rogue secret service conspiracy, but a high-level and determined design.[199]

As the possibility of a direct shot at Castro receded, the government toyed with other more original methods, including, in a touch out of Jacobean tragedy, poisoned Havana cigars.[200] Later there would be a briefly considered design to blow up the Cuban leader while he was snorkelling, by means of an explosive seashell.[201] There was even a proposal to wreck Castro's image by dusting his shoes with a depilatory powder that would cause his beard to fall out.[202] More earnestly, on the day of Kennedy's assassination itself, a CIA agent was meeting a disaffected Cuban in Paris, and supplying him with a poisoned ball-point pen with which to kill Castro.[203]

In an interview on 7 September 1963, Castro had warned, regarding assassination plots against him, that: 'We are prepared to . . . answer in kind.'[204] Given such a statement and these stratagems, Lyndon B. Johnson's privately stated belief that Kennedy's assassination had been a revenge attack by Castro begins to look a little more likely.[205] Johnson is said to have remarked, 'President Kennedy tried to get Castro, but Castro got Kennedy first.' It also appears that LBJ particularly blamed Robert Kennedy for the plots against Castro.[206]

In the view of Kennedy supporter Pete Hamill: 'According to Richard Goodwin and others (I remember discussing this with Robert Kennedy), Jack Kennedy had begun the quiet process of normalising relations with Castro before his death.'[207] If this statement is correct then it certainly represents a remarkable shift in the Kennedys' prevailing attitudes. In the eyes of the administration, and (assuming they knew of the plot) very likely of the Kennedys themselves, assisting Cubans to kill Castro was in all justice an act of tyrannicide, no different than helping the July plotters to murder Hitler. Castro appeared to them an instrument of darkness, the thin end of a Soviet wedge threatening the states of Central America. In the words of Robert McNamara, 'we were hysterical about Cuba'.[208] The impetus was simply the pervasive hatred and fear of Castro throughout the government. According to Richard Helms, 'It was made abundantly clear to everyone involved in the operation that the desire was to get rid of the Castro regime and to get rid of Castro . . . No limitations were put on this injunction.'[209] Moreover, such operations would take place not in the enlightened USA, but in states where the rule of law operated differently and civilised values had no force.[210] The uncomfortable moral paradox unsettling this last belief appears to have been missed by most of those involved.

Assassination presented fewer risks than direct paramilitary action; all it would take was the capture of one CIA operative, and clandestine aid would become public knowledge. In such a situation, there would be only two options: to withdraw ignominiously, or to switch to open warfare.[211] Nonetheless these assassination projects were part of a wider pattern of covert violent intervention in other countries' domestic affairs. In 1976, the Church Committee found that such interventions had been routine, over-zealous and self-defeating.[212] In 1954, a CIA-backed coup led to the ousting of the president in Guatemala; in 1958, America had acted secretly and ineffectively against President Sukarno in Indonesia. There were also scandalous rumours that the USA, through 'the Phoenix program', had been behind the assassination of perhaps as many as 20,000 Vietnamese citizens, suspected of involvement with the secret Viet Cong infrastructure in South Vietnam, though undoubtedly including many innocents.[213] By its very nature, the majority of the programme's targets were, on the surface at least, civilians.[214] Colby's defence on this matter hinged on the notion that these deaths had occurred in combat situations, and particularly while individuals were resisting arrest.[215]

During the Nixon administration, the CIA also involved itself in plots against Salvador Allende, the democratically elected Chilean Socialist leader.[216] The truth about American involvement in Chile appeared in the *New York Times* on the same day that Gerald Ford pardoned Richard Nixon; for many the conjunction of the two events confirmed their belief in government corruption.[217] After US attempts failed to stop Allende being elected, operations were pursued on two levels: one committed to diplomatic pressure including sanctions and the other consisting of a conspiracy to unseat Allende using covert and illegal methods. Less than a decade after the events, Henry Kissinger wrote that, with Nixon's personal involvement, the USA had explored the possibilities of sponsoring a 'constitutional coup' against Allende.[218] The sticking point in plans to prevent Allende assuming power as elected leader of Chile was General René Schneider, the head of the Army, who inconveniently wanted a political rather than a military solution to the problem. Schneider had to go. A kidnapping was therefore arranged, and money and weapons provided to support the venture. In one version of events, at this point both Kissinger and Nixon supposedly resigned themselves to the horror of what they saw as a Communist government on mainland Latin America, and humbly backed away from the thought of a coup. Meanwhile the kidnapping went ahead anyway. The affair was botched, and Schneider ended up being murdered during the struggle to take him. Kissinger was later adamant that the CIA had no direct involvement in the kidnapping, which was undertaken by a right-wing Chilean group under General Roberto Viaux.[219] In his self-absolving memoirs, Nixon both confesses to and excuses financial backing of anti-Communist political parties in the 1970 Chilean election; it is not clear from what he writes whether he admits that help went beyond funding.[220] The Church Committee doubted Nixon's protests of ignorance.[221] Nonetheless they concluded that there had been no intention to murder Schneider. Others have been more sceptical about this conclusion.[222] Despite denials by high-ranking political figures, it is similarly probable that the USA was also directly or indirectly behind the coup that eventually took place in 1973 and that led to Allende's death by gunshot wounds (assassination or suicide).[223]

Many on the radical left believed that within the United States the FBI meanwhile had very likely embarked on a similar – and indeed more fruitfully brutal – pursuit of assassination. The highest-profile such victim was Fred Hampton, a rising star of the Black Panthers, who, during a police raid in December 1969 in Chicago, was shot while sleeping in his bed. In the spring and summer of 1968, the history of the Black Panthers had turned violent. Bobby Seale was arrested for carrying a gun; following a shoot-out with police, Huey Newton was convicted of the murder of a policeman in Oakland; again in Oakland, Eldridge Cleaver and other Black Panthers fought a gun battle with police in which one Panther was killed and several policemen injured; in August 1968, in Los Angeles, depending on whose version is to be believed, either police and Black Panthers fought it out, or the police ambushed a car full of Black Panthers. In either case, three Black Panthers were killed and two policemen wounded.[224] Numerous murders of young blacks by police officers followed, the vast majority of which went unpunished.[225] In the 1970s, documents appeared that indicated FBI involvement in some of these killings.[226] In August 1971, Black Panther George Jackson was murdered in prison, reportedly while attempting to escape; to many in the movement it looked instead to be a state execution.

Certainly, as Seymour Hersh had uncovered, the Bureau was engaged in secretive operations of surveillance and disruption against the Ku Klux Klan, black nationalist groups, including the Black Panthers, and the student movement.[227] Agitators and budding leaders, like Hampton, were specifically targeted. Meanwhile the CIA was itself similarly engaged at home collecting intelligence on the USA's 'Restless Youth', with the hope of proving a connection between student radicals and foreign governments.[228] What such stories showed was that there was something after all in the counter-culture's fear of the government, that truly did set one band of official assassins against the unofficial kind.

16

God's Lonely Men

I: Walking Contradictions

I referred to him as an upright and profoundly sincere man . . . This man is filled with love, and indeed, it cannot be otherwise. A person with no love could not act with such utter self-denial . . . For he is willing to condemn himself to dishonour, general contempt and even to utter oblivion for the sake of the people's liberation. Here lies the *profound, highly courageous* and virginally pure integrity, and with the power of this purity and integrity he crushes us all.

MIKHAIL BAKUNIN ON NECHAEV, 20 JUNE 1870[1]

The violence that appeared on TV news screens during the Vietnam War had soaked into the milieu of cinema too. Sidney Lumet's *Network* (1976) satirised the media's taste for political violence and assassination, marking it down as both a sign of the nation's rising anger and television's need for thrilling images. With Manson, Hearst and Fromme, the politics of revolution dallied with insanity; the TV networks were shown to be busy with the same flirtation. The assassin was both feared and an embodiment of cool. In adapting Joseph Conrad's Congo-based *Heart of Darkness* to the Vietnam of *Apocalypse Now* (1979), Francis Ford Coppola made one vital change to the story: the narrator-figure of the tale, Martin Sheen's 'Willard', now goes in search of Kurtz, not as his relief, but as his 'assassin'. When Willard finally murders Kurtz, he does so accompanied by the Doors' song 'The End', a meandering labyrinth of music that is palpably anti-love and peace, and itself evokes yet another of the era's cool oedipal killers: 'The killer awoke before dawn'.

In the films of the early and mid-1970s, the American self seemed beleaguered, controlled, spied upon. There was the possessed child of *The Exorcist* (1973); the paranoid protagonists of Alan Pakula's films; the pursued driver of Spielberg's *Duel* (1971); the harried victims of the new splatter films, *The Texas Chain Saw Massacre* (1974) or *Halloween* (1978); and the surveillance techniques of Coppola's *The Conversation* (1974). The government began to seem out of control and out to get you: Robert Redford was on the run in *Three Days of the Condor* (1975) or under suspicion in *All the President's Men* (1976). It was paranoia's golden age.

Yet this anxious world seemed a vacant one. The style of the time favoured an alluring emptiness, of figures disconnected in space and people without relation. The cinema screen flattened to the seductive surface, as in Stanley Kubrick's gorgeous *Barry Lyndon* (1975). America was discovering its own loneliness, as divorce rates soared and families separated. As in the 1940s, cinema heroes were once again lonely men, but this time around their isolation looked not so much tough as neurotic. In the figure of the assassin, the killer shared the loneliness that had once belonged to the detective; both hunter and hunted were shy and socially maladroit young men. In *The Conversation*, Harry Caul was a symptom of the times, an eavesdropper fearful of observation by others. In the 1960s and 1970s, loneliness was a newly prevalent psychological worry, solitude itself now seen as a cause of mental illness.[2] This new loneliness drew on an old American theme: no society could ever be good enough for the individual who grows up in it. Killers represented this idea in negative, their rejection of things as they are a petulant shove at a coercive world.

However, more than any other movie, one film from the period would encapsulate the tensions inherent in the American assassin. On 8 February 1976, *Taxi Driver* opened in New York. Its writer, Paul Schrader, was late for the first showing. When he reached the cinema, and saw a huge line of people queuing up to get in, he believed for a moment that the screening had luckily been delayed. He was amazed to discover that the line was for the next, later screening of the film.[3] The cinema was full, and he stood at the back with the film's director, Martin Scorsese, and its producers, Julia and Michael Philips, all of them stunned by the audience's ecstatic reaction to the film.[4] Yet the film had looked like a suicidal enterprise, a story so alienating that it might terminate its director's career. In fact, word of mouth had already sold the movie out; success vindicated everything. Unwittingly the film-makers had produced not merely an analysis of an assassin, but had forged the first link in the chain leading to the latest most serious Presidential assassination attempt.

Taxi Driver was first and foremost Paul Schrader's story. Schrader had followed a path set out by the heroes of the 'Nouvelle Vague', taking the path from critic to film-maker. However, for Schrader the decision to become a film critic had itself been an act of passionate revolt. For a boy growing up in the 1950s and early 1960s in a Dutch Calvinist community in Grand Rapids, Michigan, movie-going was one among a lengthy list of sins. He was in his mid-teens when he saw his first film. For Schrader, the aura of rebellion clung to film, and later at Calvin College, where he was ostensibly training for the ministry, as he sought ways in which to goad authority, film was one of the weapons that came most readily to hand. Schrader appeared then to be on the left: against the war in Vietnam, against the government, against American complacency. Naturally, of course, his mind was still supersaturated by the beliefs that he rejected. From his Christian growing-up, he carried over a fascination with sado-masochistic heroism, a resentful sense of confinement, and the dark energies of what he in retrospect saw as a blood and death cult.[5]

Schrader married a girl he met in college, and wrote for student news-papers. Enthused by a meeting with Pauline Kael, the most powerful film critic of the period, he could also count on her support as a mentor. With her help, he found a place to study film at UCLA, where he caught up on seeing all the great movies he had missed out on during childhood and his teenage years. From here, he found a position at the American Film Institute. A solid academic career stretched out before him. And then, fuelled by the latent anger inspired by his constricted upbringing, everything fell apart. His first marriage ended, and very soon afterwards the affair that had ended it ended too.

It was the late spring of 1972. He spent some months effectively homeless, sleeping on friends' couches, or in his car.[6] He was suicidal, drinking heavily, obsessed with guns and pornography.[7] He was living, in short, like the hero of the script that he was about to create. After a spell in hospital for an operation on a gastric ulcer, he wrote out *Taxi Driver* in around a fortnight.[8]

Taxi Driver presents Travis Bickle, a lonely and socially awkward Vietnam veteran, who takes a job driving cabs in New York. Travis falls in love with a young woman who is working on the Presidential election campaign of Charles Palantine, but his attempts to establish a relationship with her turn out to be futile. He then befriends Iris, an underage prostitute 'owned' by a pimp named Sport (played, at his own request, by Harvey Keitel). Travis tries to assassinate Charles Palantine; however, the attempt fails. Disappointed, he instead decides to 'rescue' Iris, killing Sport, and two other men in the process. The film ends with Travis as an unlikely media hero, admired as someone who has stood up against crime in the city. Yet he is also back where he was. As Schrader put it: '*Taxi Driver* is circular. At the end of the narrative Travis has not been changed, he's been revealed.'[9]

Having finished the script, Schrader loitered in Los Angeles, spending time with movie people, drinking hard, watching the Watergate hearings, playing with guns.[10] The script hung around for a while, gathering interest, while scaring the studios. Brian De Palma considered making it, but decided that it wasn't for him. Instead De Palma introduced Schrader to a good friend, the apprentice director Martin Scorsese. Scorsese was keen to make the film, but the producers, Julia and Michael Philips, who had optioned the story for $1,000, decided that he wasn't yet experienced enough for such a project.[11] (He had at this point only made some student films and a movie for Roger Corman.) With the release of Scorsese's breakthrough film, *Mean Streets* (1973), everything changed: Scorsese was on board to direct the film.

Just four or so years older than Schrader, Martin Scorsese had also grown up in a devoutly religious environment, though in his case this was the Roman Catholic community of Little Italy in New York's Lower East Side; he had at one time nursed an ambition to become a priest. After spending his early years in Queens, he lived on Elizabeth Street, in the Manhattan garment district, where his father was a clothes presser and his mother a seamstress. Although he was a New Yorker, in its own way Scorsese's upbringing was every bit as narrow as Schrader's: when he went to attend film classes at New York University, it was the first time he'd gone so far west and the first time he'd ever talked to blondes.[12] Life may have been confined, but it was decidedly not sheltered. A couple of months before the Kennedy assassination (it is Scorsese himself who makes the link), he was himself nearly involved in a shooting.[13] Short, physically timorous, and asthmatic, Scorsese sought a refuge from the toughness of the neighbourhood in the church and in cinema. Cinema meant passion, beauty, an escape into disturbing dreams.

Like Schrader too, Scorsese had married young, and divorced early. After a period in the New York art-film scene, he travelled to Los Angeles, where he ended up making, for Corman, an exploitation film (*Boxcar Bertha* [1972]). In the early 1970s he was dating Sandy Weintraub, a young woman well connected to the movie business (her father was a producer), and living in a house overlooking the San Fernando Valley, the neighbour, although not yet the peer, of film stars.[14] However, for all the Californian life of ease, like Schrader, Scorsese was drawn to the dark. The story of Travis Bickle, this murderous loser, fascinated the young director; for him the film was to become a labour of love.

There were few doubts about who should play Travis Bickle. In a few short years, Robert De Niro had progressed from being a painfully shy youth to one of the strongest American movie stars. He had grown up in the Lower East Side, not far from Scorsese's home, though De Niro's family were Bohemian artists, a world away from the life of Little Italy. Picked to play an eye-catching part in *Mean Streets*, he was consequently chosen for a role in Francis Ford Coppola's *The Godfather II* (1974). This film in turn led to an invitation to star in Bernardo Bertolucci's *1900* (1976). De Niro was a hot property; it was his modishness that secured a production deal for *Taxi Driver*. In spite of the brilliance of De Niro's performance and his willingness to experience at first hand the life of a New York cabbie, Schrader's desire to imitate the austere style of French film-maker Robert Bresson was sabotaged immediately by the necessity of casting such a film star in the role of Travis.

The Philipses finally overcame the studio's resistance to the project (though David Begelman, president of Columbia Pictures, continued to loathe the script) after Robert De Niro won his Best Supporting Actor Oscar for *Godfather II*, and Scorsese's film *Alice Doesn't Live Here Anymore* brought Ellen Burstyn the Best Actress Oscar.[15] So much success was not to be denied.

For Schrader, it was to be the first of a series of films that would present a male 'existential loner'. A number of influences were at work in the film, particularly Bresson's films and Jean-Paul Sartre's *La Nausée* (1938), which Schrader re-read before writing the script.[16] Both Scorsese and Schrader seem to have thought of Dostoevsky as a point of reference.[17] Closer to home, the film's relationship to John Ford's Western *The Searchers* (1956) is perceptible.[18] Like Ethan Edwards, the hero of Ford's film as played by John Wayne, Travis is a returned soldier, a virulent racist, and a violent outsider doomed to solitude. *Taxi Driver* refers often to the world of the Western, Travis resembling both a 'cowboy' (as Iris's pimp calls him) and, with the Mohawk haircut he adopts at the end of the film, an Indian too.

However, one key influence on the film was the example of Arthur Bremer.[19] In 1972, Schrader was lying in his hospital bed recovering from the operation on his ulcer, when he read the news of Bremer's attack on Wallace.[20] As we have seen he began the writing of the script, only a short while after coming out of hospital. Initially he followed excerpts from Bremer's diary in the press, and these heavily guided the first-person narrative of the film. Later, Schrader read the printed version of the diary, and this perhaps impacted on the film's style and the portrayal of its assassin-hero.[21]

The film was made, relatively quickly, in the sweltering New York summer of 1975. Several times thunderstorms disrupted shooting. The heat was oppressive; Scorsese felt that there was 'an atmosphere at night' that was 'like a seeping kind of virus . . . Many times people threatened us and we had to take off quickly.'[22] New York had become The Great Bad Place; the style of the film was therefore to be aptly what Scorsese has termed 'New York Gothic'. The city sweated and grew grimy. The edginess of the streets was present in the film's makers too; it is possible that it was during filming that Scorsese began to use cocaine.[23]

The story jerks onwards with apparent randomness. Time stutters; the film sometimes decelerates, the slow motion impressing a sense of evil, or disassociation from time, or lostness within a moment. There are Godardian jump-cuts, abrupt fractures of perspective. The unexpected breaks bring us inside Travis's disconnected sense of the world.

For the most part, *Taxi Driver* follows Travis Bickle, allowing us to measure his character, and inviting us to share his perspective. Sometimes Travis steps into his own point of view; in such moments it's unclear whether we are seeing Travis as he sees himself, or reaching towards some more objective understanding of the film's hero. It looks and feels like a bad dream, making plain the dreamlike nature of all film; but as with Bremer's monomaniacal plan, a fantastic purpose invests its haphazardness.[24] Here the fortuitous rules; a million events conglomerate, but to no end. There is no standpoint where the whole life of the city can be seen. The taxi itself becomes a fitting symbol for its random life; as a cab-driver, Travis becomes a man who can connect up the city. The taxi driver unites the urban space, though he does so arbitrarily, taking fares at hazard, unsystematically stitching together the city's boroughs. Travis crosses and recrosses New York (it is made clear that there is nowhere he will not go) in unplanned directions; through countless journeys he threads the unassimilable city.

In the making, the script's rigour collided with the luridly hallucinatory intensity of Scorsese's style.[25] There are the framing opening shots to each sequence, odd moments of stillness and context; but in the main it's an urban style, formed of rapid and disjunctive images: a man drumming on the sidewalk; the fire hydrants spurting; the steam gushing out from the subway; a street-crazy storming by, crying out how he's going to kill some woman. The script aimed at asceticism, but the movie attained rage; Scorsese was too emotional a movie-maker to pull off the desired chill.

In suitably Pauline language, Schrader believed that a film should move towards an 'emotionally blinding moment', a searing experience where viewers are brought up against something greater than themselves. In *Taxi Driver*, this moment must be the massacre that Travis carries out in the New York apartment house where Iris works.

There is no doubt that a significant part of the film's appeal lay in what then seemed the surfeit of its violence.[26] As we have seen, the great films of the mid-to-late 1960s, *Bonnie and Clyde*, *The Wild Bunch*, had made outlaw violence hip. While the young protested against killing people in Vietnam, they fantasised about murder closer to home. Yet even among mid-1970s films, *Taxi Driver* was ostentatiously brutal. While feeling troubled by its moral implications, Scorsese enjoyed screen violence; firearms, and the men who used them, were clearly cool.[27] This film is in love with guns. Scorsese wanted the carnage of the film's conclusion to be ritualistic, a religious experience that would call to mind a Mass.[28] Yet those moments were also meant to have a 'tabloid' look, recalling the flat documentary style of the *Daily News*.[29]

The experience of sharing the longueurs of Travis's tension makes the audience long too for the climax of violent action. The violence of the film's end was artful, a clever construction of camera angles, pacing, and editing. Yet its horrors exceeded the film-maker's intention. The scene was supposed to be a slap in the face for an audience ensnared into identification with a killer. In fact, audiences responded with enthusiastic horror; they were quite content to be complicit with Travis's insane vigilantism. It was an instance of an audience's appetite for bloodshed exceeding the expectation of the artist. A newly sharpened taste for gore was entering the culture.

After all, whether in *Dirty Harry* (1971) or *Death Wish* (1974), the vigilante was a representative of the time. For all the brutality of such figures, they continued to suggest some kind of American ideal. They were independent men, unbowed by social pressures, free of the government; they stood for justice, not law. They represented on an individual level the right of revolution and the power invested in the American people itself. Above all, they were by definition 'vigilant', alive to injustice and to threats against the American ideal.[30] They were part of an all-American urge to aggression. When the National Commission on the Causes and Prevention of Violence reported, its two conclusions were the belief that the number of assassinations corresponded to a society's general level of violence, and that the recent American violence was nothing new. Political violence had a long-standing American tradition.[31] It began with nineteenth-century vigilantism then expanded to include the bloodshed of Reconstruction, labour aggression and anti-labour violence, lynch-mobs, political intimidation, to say nothing of four murdered American Presidents. In this way, American assassinations returned the very centre of political life to the condition of the frontier, the Wild West – a space where law had lapsed or had failed to reach, replaced by vengeance and force.[32]

There was something adolescent in *Taxi Driver*'s angst and anger, and in its itch to resolve life's problems in slasher-movie gore. After all Travis too was, in Schrader's words, 'a little kid playing with guns and acting tough', an idea expressed most forcibly in the famous scene where Travis confronts his reflection as though he were a stranger and aggressor ('Are you talking to me?').[33] The camera is his mirror, as he reflects ourselves back onto us. In childhood and adolescence, inspired by movies, Scorsese too had played the tough-guy before his mirror.[34] The violence in Scorsese's later film *Raging Bull* (1980) would be for its boxer-protagonist a means of making connections to others; there fighting is the inarticulate man's means of articulating his need to relate. But Travis's violence goes nowhere, and connects him to nothing; rather it aims to rob others of their connections, to take Palantine from Betsy, to deny Sport to Iris.

The Motion Picture Association of America threatened the film with an X certificate, something that would have seriously damaged its commercial chances. In order to bring the rating down to an 'R', Scorsese desaturated the film stock used for the massacre scene, thus toning down the crimson blood.[35] Schrader was horrified, but Scorsese rightly realised that the mottled, lifeless look of the desaturated scenes rendered the moment even more disturbing.[36]

Even now the film has the power to shock: Travis's hatred of women and blacks is inescapably apparent, despite Scorsese's attempt to downplay such elements in the original script. In an interview conducted in 1976, Richard Goldstein and Mark Jacobson press Scorsese on his relationship to the film's racism, but he evades a definitive response to their questions.[37] In the massacre at the end of the film, all Travis's victims were originally intended to be African-Americans. In the atmosphere of the mid-1970s it was quickly realised that this would be dangerously provocative. In a gesture of liberal compromise (and in order to give Harvey Keitel a part), it was decided that Iris's pimp should be played by a white man, despite the fact that the huge majority of Manhattan's downtown pimps were black.

More of the misogyny survived into the finished film. The film constantly links Travis's violence to his frustrated sexual drive. Schrader titled one of the chapters of his screenplay 'Foreplay to Gunplay'.[38] Perhaps in an echo of Bremer's virginal fumbling, Travis's relation to women is as incompetently adolescent as his fondness for his .44 Magnum. Caught between the beautiful and angelic Betsy (played with admirable superficiality by Cybill Shepherd) and the twelve-year-old prostitute Iris (Jodie Foster), he turns out in either case to be incapable of an adult relationship. His one proper date with Betsy ends in disaster when he takes her to a 'dirty movie'; he plays it as a blunder, but it is clear that his true intent has been to smear this irreproachable blonde with street slime. This oedipal split of Madonna versus whore carries over into his plans to assassinate Charles Palantine. As Schrader has it: 'He decides to kill the father figure of the girl who rejected him, which of course is a reflection of his own father figure, and when he is thwarted by that he moves on to the pimp, the other father figure.'[39]

Travis's loneliness is entangled in his desire for sex. He cocks his finger like a gun at the copulating couples he regards on screen; he topples the television that shows him the dancing lovers smooching on *American Bandstand*. His interest in pornography turns women into images that can be scrutinised and fantasised, while removing the possibility of actual contact with another person. Written into the idea of the pornographic picture is the woman's simultaneous absence and presence in the room, there, but only as an image. When we watch Travis watching his dirty movies, the film inevitably involves us in his gaze. What are we doing but summoning up violence, while asserting our distance from it? We are complicit with Travis in ways that are bound to unsettle us.

Simultaneously Travis embodies the paradox of the revenger: in attempting to purge the world of its corruption, he himself proves corrupt. This immersion in the corruption of the city potentially imparts more of a social motivation to Travis's lust for mayhem. One striking element in the film is the way in which the whole of New York City looks pent up, and the streets frame a multitude of random acts of violence. Passers-by rage; a store-owner beats a dying thief with a metal rod. At these moments, it seems as if Travis's violence is every-one's possession, something written into city life.

Yet ultimately Travis's rage is his own; it defines him, and marks him out as special. Travis's violence seems inevitable; it moves onwards like an instinctive force. Schrader's script begins with a description of Travis that ends like this: 'As the earth moves towards the sun, Travis Bickle moves towards violence.'[40] There is something loaded about this, and the reader may feel justified in pointing out that the earth does not actually move towards the sun. More importantly, it is an image that makes Travis's violence seem a natural process, and one that is somehow positive (it moves toward the light) and self-destructive (he'll be burned up). The description as a whole is pure American romanticism; the longing for the outsider lingers in its poetic phrases; it's no accident that the script's epigraph quotes Thomas Wolfe.

For all its gloom, the film belonged to a therapeutic culture, that saw action and art as the expression and expulsion of inner promptings. The film embodied Travis's 'acting out'; as it was for Travis himself, the movie was meant to be, for its makers and audiences, an exorcism. While the film might provide such therapy for its audiences, it seems that this was a by-product of the catharsis that it would provide for its makers. Also, to Scorsese's dismay, audiences turned out not to want exorcism so much as performance; far from feeling chastened, viewers were enthralled. Violence's exhilaration was everything; they were electrified, not sobered. Similarly, the efficacy of the 'therapy' for Travis himself remained in doubt.

Yet aggression seemed somehow desirable, or at least preferable to its dangerous repression.[41] A belief spread that murder and assassination were primarily to be understood in psychological terms, even as part of a process of self-realisation. If there were sociological factors at play, then this was only in so far as an individual person can become the scapegoat for society's greater psychological penchant for violence. Some were sceptical about this shift in understanding. Criticising an argument of Colin Wilson, the conservative commentator Frederic Wertham affirmed:

His ideas of psychology are based on a currently fashionable overindividualistic trend of academic psychology which postulates 'self-actualization,' an intense self-assertion, and so-called peak-experiences. Wilson believes that this type of psychology goes to 'the very root of the problem of violence in our society.' In peak-experiences, as they are defined, 'there tends to be a loss even though transient . . . of inhibition . . . control . . . restraint.' 'The peak-experience [is] felt as a . . . self-justifying moment.' This is more or less the same thing juvenile delinquents who had committed violent acts described to me as a thrill. It is disconcerting to see novelists agreeing with them.[42]

In Wilson's view, violence carved a route out of conformity and into life. This was another way of understanding the 'accidental assassin' theme, as the violence of which they are wrongly accused becomes itself a desirable act. Wilson may not have been a centrally important cultural figure, but, for Wertham, his ideas here belong to one dominant strain in the thinking of the 1960s and 1970s:

In Norman Mailer's *An American Dream*, a man's murder of his wife is presented as a positive act in the development of his personality, as a liberation, a catharsis.

After the murder, 'illness' passes away from the murderer. This strikes one as a misunderstanding of psychotherapeutic principles.[43]

Killing no longer seemed a sin, nor assassination a political crime, but both were just a step on the road to fulfilment.

So it was perhaps that the political meanings of *Taxi Driver* were deflected into what its writer, director and star all thought of as a 'personal' expression.[44] Both Schrader and Scorsese saw themselves as outsiders; and Travis Bickle was, after all, the archetypal outsider. For Schrader there had undoubtedly been an autobiographical identification with Travis, and, at one remove therefore, with Bremer. In the published preface to the film script, Schrader declares: 'I was not unlike Travis Bickle: a bundle of tightly wrapped contradictions, driving around, trying but unable to belong.' Later on in the script, Betsy (quoting Kris Kristofferson) describes Travis in strikingly similar terms as 'partly truth, partly fiction, a walking contradiction'.[45] De Niro modelled Travis's wardrobe on Schrader's clothes, using the script-writer's own boots and jacket for the performance.[46]

Scorsese seems to have felt much the same way; it was his credo that the best films were personal statements, made against the odds within an industry dedicated to the manufacture of product. In making the film, Scorsese was also returning to New York, the home ground of his childhood and adolescent loneliness. The fact that Scorsese appears twice in the film reinforces this personal connection. He's first seen sitting outside the campaign office, watching wistfully as the beautiful Betsy passes inside. In a darker mode, he also cast himself in the film as a homicidally jealous jilted husband. He sits in the back of Travis's car, fantasising about shooting his wife in the 'pussy' with a .44 Magnum; significantly his wife's lover is black. Scorsese remarked at the time:

I know this guy Travis. I've had the feelings he has, and those feelings have to be explored, taken out and examined. I know the feeling of rejection that Travis feels, of not being able to make relationships survive. I know the killing feeling, the feeling of really being angry.[47]

Scorsese also remarked: 'I loved Schrader's script so much it was as if I had dreamed it. De Niro felt the same way.'[48] De Niro had intended to write a script about a political assassin at the United Nations building; *Taxi Driver* removed the need to do so.[49] As Scorsese could employ

De Niro as the embodiment of his own grim energies, so Travis himself was a vehicle for all three men's rage.

The bleeding away of politics from *Taxi Driver* derives ultimately from its source in Bremer's attempt to kill Wallace. For Bremer, too, the affair had been a personal crisis, an event from which traditional ideas of politics had been drained. He might after all as easily have shot McGovern as Wallace. Even Oswald's murder of JFK now looked old-fashioned; a new kind of politics had emerged, where assassination was an acting out on a national stage of a personal void. Politics was simply the external domain where a lack of character could be projected; the public sphere was merely the realm of publicity.

The film did not have to be a statement about Vietnam, or social conditions, or the problems of urban life; it was a matter of the individual soul, seeking its own redemption through violence. Travis's self-destruction was something that Scorsese would himself explore in the next few years, as he descended into illness, depression and out-of-control drug use. Such impulses, such themes, had always been close to his heart; in an early short, *The Big Shave* (1967), a young man cuts himself while shaving, but carries on with his razor until his face is a bloody mess. Yet this self-destruction could be seen as political too: Scorsese is said to have thought of that early film as an anti-Vietnam piece.[50] In the late 1960s, Scorsese did participate in some politically engaged work, most notably *Street Scenes* (1970).

Scorsese understood that the anger, the unease about city life, that he, Schrader and De Niro were experiencing was shared by the film's potential audience. It was an urban film for an urban demographic, its style expressing distress at the perceived putrefaction of New York. This was a collective revulsion, a disgust that diagnosed what was then felt to be the rottenness of America itself. Yet, without a coherent political agenda, the film risked seeming merely gratuitously vicious, or indulging in an unappealingly bloody refusal of the modern city.

Though it might be said that social conditions foment Travis's existential crisis, the political context of Bremer's assault drains into frustration about 'relationships'; it truly does seem that for Travis as for Bremer, his penis made him do it. It is a very 1970s movie: the social meaning of the act classified as a matter of 'hang-ups' within the self. Less modishly, the religious meaning with which both Schrader and Scorsese invested Travis – he's a 'false saint', someone on a wrong spiritual path – similarly redefines the assassin's crime.[51]

The film's ending puzzled critics. According to Scorsese, a conclusion in which Travis shoots himself would have been more familiar and comfortable.[52] Instead the film ends with, in order, extreme violence, abject failure, and then the mockery of Travis's apotheosis as a righteous celebrity. The moment clearly satirises the fame awarded to the run of American assassins from Oswald to Lynette Fromme; Schrader himself has remarked that it was Fromme's appearance on the cover of *Newsweek* that prompted the choice of ending. And beneath all runs the suspicion that Travis will explode again.

II: The Death of Harvey Milk

In July 1979, during the 'Address to the Nation', his 'Crisis of Confidence' speech, President Jimmy Carter set out the things that had sapped America's strength; the murders of the Kennedys and of Martin Luther King were the first item on his list.[53] But there had been other, more recent murders. On 27 November 1978, in San Francisco's City Hall, former Supervisor Dan White murdered both Mayor George Moscone and Supervisor Harvey Milk. Recently White had unexpectedly resigned his seat as Supervisor; some days later, he asked to be reappointed. That day, Mayor Moscone was to decide that White would not be offered his former position. White stole into City Hall, with a gun in one pocket, and some rounds of ammunition in the other. He went up to the Mayor's office, and after an argument, shot him dead. White then reloaded his gun, walked across the building to Milk's office, and murdered him.

News had only recently come in from Guyana of the Jonestown massacre, where around 400 members of a San Francisco-based cult, the Peoples Temple, had been persuaded to commit suicide. There would briefly be rumours that assassins from the People's Temple had carried out the killings.[54] The shooting of Harvey Milk and George Moscone added to the sense of unreality. Milk was the leading gay politician in San Francisco, and the USA's first openly gay elected official. After years of tentative diplomacy and slow-moving negotiation by established homosexuals, Milk offered instead an upfront, confrontational approach. He was flamboyant, talented and passionate, an amiable man who had done much to bring together the many minorities of the city – old people and Chinese people as much as gay men and lesbians. A year before he was killed, Milk recorded his will; he knew all too well that he was a likely target for assassination. Despite his manifest good sense the fact that he was both gay and outspoken rendered him a likely victim. Moscone and Milk's murders shocked San Francisco. The night he died a candlelit march honoured Harvey Milk; the silent marchers filled the length and breadth of Market Street all the way down to the Castro.

Milk was a charismatic figure, but his sexuality nonetheless rendered him strange to the majority. Dan White, however, was a politician from a Frank Capra film, square-jawed, clean-cut, simple-minded. He was a veteran, an ex-cop, an ex-firefighter, a regular guy with a wife and kids and money worries. He now found himself in the middle of another kind of script, embroiled with ethnic minorities, gay rights, a shameless and open sexuality. He was in the middle of a new America, and his sense of the fittingness of things seemed outraged.[55] Milk went from accomplishment to accomplishment, while White's own life faltered and stalled. Unable to play the political game, his 'resignation' was a gesture of puerile pique, a sign of his inability to master City Hall. His attempt to regain the position he had lost was forlorn. Depressed, disorientated, furious, he took out his rage on those whose vitality and success made him small.

To those who belonged to minority groups and to the 'counter-culture', Dan White's trial represented the victory of the establishment and the 'moral majority' who oppressed them. It should have been an open and shut case, there being no doubt that White had murdered both Milk and Moscone. Instead the jury's sympathy went out to the troubled White, a man like themselves, honourable but baffled. Dan White was 'good people'. Elaborate psychological evidence suggested that White had killed the two men due to a combination of financial anxiety and depression – signalled by, among other things, an uncharacteristic indulgence in fast food, re-imagined by the media as the notorious 'Twinkie' defence. It may have looked ludicrous, but it worked. White was found guilty of voluntary manslaughter. In January 1984, after five and a half years in prison, White was released on parole; in October 1985, he committed suicide by carbon monoxide poisoning.

III: Second-Hand Lives

If great criminals told the truth – which, being great criminals, they do not –
they would very rarely tell of their struggles against the crime. Their struggles
are towards it.

CHARLES DICKENS, *OUR MUTUAL FRIEND*

Through December 1980, like a morally bankrupt mid-ranking villain
from a spy film, newly released from prison, G. Gordon Liddy, Nixon's
Watergate henchman, was oiling across the country on a lecture tour
of conservative colleges and universities, speaking on stage about
justifiable homicide, and off the cuff about the delightful efficacy of
assassination.[56] It was all, of course, a matter of choosing the appropriate
target.

In New York, on 8 December 1980, John Lennon was murdered
on the threshold of the West 72nd Street entryway of the Dakota
building where he lived. His son was sound asleep in their apartment
seven floors up. Lennon was one of the most talented songwriters of
the sixties and seventies, a rebel who had revolutionised pop culture,
an icon who had encapsulated the hopes of a generation, a symbol
of authenticity in art. He was also one of the most famous people on
earth. His killer was Mark David Chapman, a 25-year-old unemployed
security guard, resident in Hawaii. He had been loitering outside the
Dakota for a couple of days, standing with the celebrity-seekers who
hung out hoping for a glimpse or a word with Lennon. That Monday,
he spent much of the day outside the building. When Lennon and
his wife, Yoko Ono, had left some hours before, he had asked for an
autograph. Lennon generously signed and dated the copy of his latest
album, which Chapman was carrying. Some five hours later, after an
evening in a recording studio, Lennon and Ono returned. They passed
Chapman, who called out for Lennon and then fired five shots into his
back and shoulder. Lennon died in the back of a police car on the way
to hospital.

Vigils were held all around the world. In Moscow, a spontaneous
gathering by Beatles fans unsettled the state police. Chapman's first
lawyer, Herbert J. Adlerberg, bowed out of the case after death threats
were made against him. Everyone wanted to know why the killer had

done it. Reporters surrounded his father's house, but there was nothing he could tell them. The man who shot John Lennon seemed a different person from the son he knew.[57] Earlier that November, Chapman had spent a weekend in Atlanta, where he had seemed depressed, but none of his old school-friends could say why. In time, some would suspect that Lennon was the victim of powerful forces in the USA, perhaps including the CIA.[58] The fact that the US government had indeed pursued a vendetta against Lennon in his radical years in the early 1970s lent a little weight to this otherwise unlikely theory. The more probable reason is in many ways more disturbing.

Chapman was plump, broody, bespectacled, married. He came from Georgia, an average student who had played in a teenage rock band; he had always liked the Beatles. At first Chapman pleaded not guilty – presumably his defence was to be insanity; later in the proceedings, after receiving a command from God, he changed his plea to guilty. On 24 August 1981, Chapman was sentenced to twenty years to life for Lennon's murder. After the verdict was given, he read out a section from J. D. Salinger's novel of adolescent confusion, *The Catcher in the Rye* (1951). It was through an enraptured reading of that book that the idea to murder Lennon came to him. He suddenly realised that he was just like Holden Caulfield – more than that, he actually was Holden Caulfield. This was the assassin as lost boy, as the wised-up outsider, alienated and American. He would kill Lennon because he understood him to be, as Salinger's book termed it, a 'phoney'. His phoniness derived from his wealth and fame, a man who asked us to imagine 'no possessions' while being himself hugely rich. Mark Chapman had imagined too: he imagined himself as Holden Caulfield, as Travis Bickle; he imagined himself as famous; he imagined that he should kill a star.

It is a paradox that Chapman's assessment of Lennon as a counterfeit character should coincide with his own dearth of self. With the Anarchists and Nihilists, the assassin had been a 'good person' pushed into violence, according to their own sense of things by the injustices of the society in which they lived. For Chapman, and the other assassins of the 1970s and early 1980s, their criminal acts enunciated nothing. They were walking absences, bodies holding an identity that did not fully exist. Chapman was another man without a self: on his last day of work, he signed himself out as 'John Lennon'.

Based on Chapman's own words, Andrew Piddington's film *The Killing of John Lennon* (2008) opens with Chapman quoting Travis Bickle. The parallels and quotes from *Taxi Driver* do not end there. When he finally shoots his Beatle, he remarks, 'It was like a movie. It was like I was in a movie'. In time, Chapman's life seems a quote, his actions another's. His self gets lost between three romantic orphans: Caulfield, Bickle and Lennon himself. Piddington's film enacts the same failing, itself being a reconstruction of a real event, an affair of stand-ins and replacements, speaking another's real words, doubling events in their 'original locations'.

Chapman shot Lennon so as to acquire his fame. His back-up plan was to murder Jackie Onassis, George C. Scott or Johnny Carson, just so long as they were famous enough. To kill JFK's widow would have had particular impact. It was better to win renown as an idiotic killer than never to be known at all. At the end of Woody Allen's recent film *Stardust Memories* (1980), a fan stalks his hero, only to shoot him in the stomach at the movie's end; 'I'm your greatest fan,' he tells him. Love of the American star clearly contained large reserves of resentment and rage. That Lennon should have been killed on account of his fame was rendered all the more ludicrous by the fact that he himself had always presented an equivocal but undeniable scepticism about its meanings. For all the pampered life of a hugely wealthy recluse, he knew still that he was just a man who had written some songs. He was the first to debunk and question the Beatles myth.[59] He had used his fame as best he could to try to create political change, to bring peace. Although those attempts undoubtedly carried some measure of self-regard, they also showed his willingness to appear a fool in pursuit of nobler ends. More than any other pop star of his generation, he turned his stardom to account and made a small difference.

Warhol had also been shot because he was famous. But Warhol represented the celebrity as remote, chilly, unknowable; contrariwise Lennon was an element in the biographies of millions. The shock of Lennon's death was deepened by this shared sense of intimacy with him. People felt that they knew Lennon; he was familiar from films and concerts, from media interviews and countless photographs, from biographies – like that of Hunter Davies – published in his lifetime, and, above all, from the songs themselves. In the heyday of the Beatles,

Lennon had come to dislike songs that presented characters as a fiction; instead he sought increasingly in his own art to find the authenticity of self-expression.[60] His art laid him bare. So it was that his fans knew of his abandonment as a child by both mother and father, of his upbringing with his Aunt Mimi, of his mother's death in a road accident. More than any other major pop artist of the period, Lennon's music exposed the man.

That sense of loss was shared by one young man, drifting across America, a Beatles fan who could not understand how the world could carry on now Lennon was dead. That man was John W. Hinckley Jr. In three months he would attempt to assassinate the President of the United States.

IV: American Lives

There was another screening [of *Taxi Driver*] in L.A. at the Directors Guild. Julia [Philips] bumped into Towne and Bert Schneider coming out of the screening, thought they didn't like the movie, but neither would say so. Five years later, after John Hinckley, apparently under the influence of *Taxi Driver*, shot Reagan, Julia again ran into Schneider. 'See, it wasn't such a bad movie,' she said, smiling. He replied, 'If it was really great he would've killed him.'[61]

After waking up in the recovery room, Ronnie wrote, echoing W. C. Fields, 'All in all, I'd rather be in Philadelphia'. . . The notes showed me that despite the harm done to his body, Ronnie's outlook was strong. 'Can we rewrite this scene beginning at the time I left the hotel?' he asked.[62]

It was Monday 31 March 1981, coming up to 2.30, and he was fidgeting by the Florida Avenue entrance of the Washington Hilton, catching the attention of a police lieutenant who stopped again and again to stare over at him. He jostled with reporters too, complaining that the press were always getting in the way, before finding a place among the TV cameras. It drizzled, off and on, and the sidewalk was damp.[63] His speech inside finished, President Reagan came out of the hotel, flanked by security men, acknowledging the few onlookers across the street and the small crowd of pressmen on the sidewalk beside him. For a moment, one man watching in the crowd asked himself the question 'Should I do this or not?'[64] A journalist shouted to the President, and as he stood by the waiting limousine, Reagan raised his arm to wave. It was then that the assassin crouched and fired – six shots flashing out in a couple of seconds. The assassin was no more than ten feet away. Reagan heard what sounded like a 'small fluttering sound, *pop, pop, pop*', looked suddenly serious, as though unable to believe what was happening, and then sagged; in that moment he was bundled into the car by Jerry Parr, one of his Secret Service agents; as they went down to get into the car one of the bullets ricocheted off the limousine and struck the President under his arm.[65] The shot felt like an 'unbelievably painful' blow in his upper back; Reagan didn't yet know that he'd been shot, but thought the pain had come from Parr falling onto him, so as to cover him from further shots.[66] In the same flurry of bullets, three other men were hit: James S. Brady, Reagan's press secretary, was struck above the left eye, the bullet passing through his skull; Thomas K. Delahanty, a police officer, was shot in the neck; and Timothy J. McCarthy, a Secret Service agent was hit in the torso – he had courageously taken a bullet for the President.[67] The gunman kept pulling the trigger, even though the gun was empty.[68] There was what looked like a chaos of shouts, screams and scuffles, though in fact the Secret Service men had launched their much rehearsed protective routine – interposing themselves between the gunman and the President, making sure that Reagan was got away as quickly as possible from the scene, and within no more than a second grabbing the gunman himself, piling on top of him and holding him down on the sidewalk. The news cameras recorded everything; within half an hour all three major networks were running film of the shooting.[69]

While the other wounded men lay being given first aid on the sidewalk, and the Secret Service agents huddled around the assassin, pulling him to a police car, Reagan was in the limousine, 'sat up on the edge of the seat almost paralyzed by pain'. Then he put up his hand to his mouth and coughed, and looked down to see a handful of frothy blood.[70] It was only then that they realised that the damage was serious. On Parr's instructions, the car changed direction from the White House direct to the George Washington University Hospital.[71] Reagan carried on coughing up blood, filling first his own handkerchief, and then Jerry

Parr's; it was hard to breathe too; as Reagan pithily put it: 'Getting shot hurts.'[72]

Chapman's bullet had passed through the President's armpit and then been deflected off one of his ribs. By good fortune, although it pierced Reagan's left lung by about three inches, and though the lung had partly collapsed, it did little serious damage.[73] Although on the surface the wound was slight, Reagan had lost a lot of blood, and if he had gone into shock he might have died.[74] Both at the time and afterwards, he appears to have been most concerned about the brand new suit he was wearing, one that was cut off his body using scissors before the operation began.[75]

On hearing the news, Vice President George Bush flew back at once from Texas. As second-in-command, he knew that he would have to take charge. However, with Reagan in hospital, and Bush in the air, Secretary of State Alexander Haig decided that it was up to him to hold the reins of power. Besides, it was believed that invoking the 25th Amendment would unduly alarm the public.[76] That afternoon, a clearly anxious Haig held a press conference in the White House briefing room where, clutching the lectern, his voice unsteady, he informed the media that he was in control.[77] He looked anything but. It was a serious miscalculation, an attempt to show strength that looked either desperate or greedy; the 25th Amendment had set out the order of succession just for such a moment as this, and there was no way that Haig should have assumed power or declared himself to be the one in charge. For a while, the government rallied around him, but his days were numbered, and the following year Haig left office.[78]

It was quickly ascertained that the would-be assassin was John W. Hinckley Jr., the plump blond-haired, 25-year-old son of a Denver oil executive. He was the youngest child of a 'fine Christian family', apparently a rather ordinary and typical young American.[79] But why had he tried to kill the President?

On taking office, Jimmy Carter had looked 'like a miniature, blonde Lincoln'.[80] By the end of his unlucky, tortured Presidency, few would have made the same comparison. At least Carter would not share Lincoln's fate. There had been at least one unavailing attempt on Carter's life, after Raymond Lee Harvey was arrested in Los Angeles.

He was carrying a starting pistol; however, despite vague indications of a plot, nothing was proved, and charges were dropped. Yet, as it turned out, the man who eventually shot Reagan had spent time 'psyching' himself up to murder Carter.

There was something pepperish and petulant in Carter's attempts at action. He had looked meek and been tough, squaring up to the Soviet Union over Afghanistan, and instigating a disastrous mission to set free American hostages in the embassy in Teheran. Sadly neither helped much, and he could not shake his ineffectual public image. He was lucky even to have gained the re-nomination. Given such an incumbent, almost any Republican might have won the 1980 election; as it was, the ex-Hollywood movie actor Ronald Reagan secured (with 51 per cent of the vote) what looked like a landslide in the electoral college.

Myths that Reagan had been voted into power by 'the Moral Majority' were indeed merely myths.[81] Yet undoubtedly conservatism was triumphant again, though the movement that brought Reagan to the White House had begun far back in the 1968 election campaign, with Wallace and Nixon. Attracted by his anti-Washington stance, some of Wallace's followers now voted for Reagan.[82] Reagan appealed to the same constituency – though without the taint of racism.

Reagan imagined an America prosperous, self-confident, free. He offered himself as an embodied nostalgia, his age itself (he was sixty-nine when he assumed office, the oldest man ever to be elected President) acting as a charm, allowing him to stand for the virtue of the Great Generation. It was a backward glance, one that passed over the compromises of the seventies and the divisions of the sixties. He passed on a dream of the future, pregnant with an image of the past. He was, above all, the representative of old Hollywood. In the month before the shooting, his diaries are full of meetings with Mickey Rooney, Ann Miller, Jerry Lewis, Liz Taylor. His very inadequacies – his slightly puzzled air as he muffed the answers in press conferences – only added to the sense of his old-world allure.

For all his contradictions, he benefited from the vigour of the single vision, the force of a heart-held truth. Above all, he exuded a chipper vim, the gusto of an old man from a Dickens novel. The Brylcreemed black hair defied the passing years.[83] It was not easy for all to see that this hearty fellow was also an ideologue intent on rolling back the liberal advances of the last twenty years. And while advertised as the dream of the ordinary Joe, all the profits were in fact to be bestowed on the long-resentful rich.

Apart from its dangerously contradictory economics, its staunch fear and hatred of 'the Reds', its dewy-eyed heartlessness, its sentimental approval of an apple-pie America split by a widening rift between rich and poor, Reaganism was mostly a matter of beautiful slogans. 'It's morning again in America', voters were told in 1984, and the brief puff of feeling contained in that hopeful, if vapid, message was, for many, enough.

Reagan was a conviction politician ready to alter his policies when they worked out badly – though all the time advertising this change in plan as evidence of stern commitment to what he had always believed. Though insisting on his consistency, and without ever losing his admiration for Franklin D. Roosevelt, he had already shifted from being a Democrat voter to the darling of the right-wing Republicans; he had gone from being a union man to a politician whose policies would put hundreds of thousands of Americans out of work.[84] The consistent element in his career was his contempt for communism, and for what he saw as its manifestations in the United States; after all he believed he had witnessed a communist plot to conquer Hollywood.[85] We can now see that Reagan was a highly effective President, and (among others) responsible for the West's winning the Cold War. Yet some have believed that Reagan was not so much a complex individual as a smoothed-out figurehead, built up from his own deepest wishes and those of his electorate. Certainly he met each challenge with a rhetoric that, purely by the power of speech, transformed disaster into imminent victory. In some ways his image did little credit to his truly held beliefs; seen as a trigger-happy war-lover, he in fact loathed nuclear weapons, and very likely would never have launched a nuclear attack, even if Russia had fired first.[86] Flawed, inadequate, contradictory, he proffered a simulacrum of American decency. Although he has been depicted as vacuous and his ideas as dangerous, he nonetheless seemed to tender a route back to a forsaken American dignity.

A couple of days after the shooting, Reagan woke up to see his wife sitting by his bedside; he wrote her a note: 'I'm still alive, aren't I?'[87]

Reagan was the only American President to survive being injured in an assassination attempt. The media were led to believe that Reagan's recovery was smoother than in fact it was; but even with this smoke-screen, his recovery was remarkable. Far from degrading him, or revealing his vulnerability, the shooting only increased Reagan's stature. He emerged from the attempt by Hinckley appearing a stronger, nobler, more heroic and, above all, more loveable figure. He is also the only President to have introduced the note of comedy into assassination: right after the shooting, as he was being wheeled in for surgery, he pulled up his oxygen mask, his face pale and his lips caked with blood, and told his wife, 'Honey, I forgot to duck.'[88] (He was quoting 'Jack Dempsey's lines to his wife the night he was beaten by Gene Tunney for the heavyweight championship'.[89]) That remark did what no other victim in this book was able to do: it laughed off the assassin. He winked at one of his advisers as he sped past on a hospital trolley and even joked with a surgeon just before he went under, saying that he just wanted to make sure they were all Republicans.[90] If his humour had sometimes looked staged, here there was no doubt that the wit and pluck were natural to him.[91] Although no one then knew it, even more impressively, while struggling for breath with a collapsed lung, Reagan had paused to pray for the young man who had shot him: 'Isn't that the meaning of the lost sheep? We are all God's children & therefore equally beloved by him. I began to pray for his soul and that he would find his way back to the fold.'[92]

Moreover the Reagan assassination attempt was unusual in that it seemed to provoke no conspiracy theory, no rumours of a second shooter, no alternative history. The FBI published a report denying all evidence of an assassination plot and, for once, everyone believed it.[93]

Following Hinckley's attempt, there were fears that (so soon after the murder of John Lennon) the post-election mood of optimism would be shattered. Reagan's appeal had seemed to some to be no more than a matter of mood-changing, the long defeat of the seventies countered by a retreat to a more confident America. But Reagan's cheerfulness, his courage under fire, transcended that bleak moment; the movie actor had become a genuine hero; he was back at work at the White House within a fortnight of the shooting. More than that, despite chest pains and difficulties breathing, he had even walked into the hospital, wounded as he was. If he had remembered to duck, he would only have looked like another Gerald Ford. In fact, beyond these nebulous impacts, the shooting may even have boosted the President in concrete political terms.

Just minutes before Hinckley's attack, Reagan had been giving a speech to an audience from the Building Trades Council of the AFL-CIO, informing them, among other things, that the recent surge in violent crime was the result of government straying from its basic principles, and not protecting citizens, but instead running their lives. He left the room to a standing ovation.[94] He had come into office promising to free Americans from their own government. Indirectly Hinckley might have helped him to achieve this aim.

Reagan's first days in office were marked by a striking energy. He made a few gestures limiting American involvement in making the world a better place (such as pulling out of UNESCO, or cancelling the Law of the Seas Treaty so as to do his bit for businessmen eager to exploit the oceans). But his big project was to make good on his campaign promises and put an end to 'big government'; as he said in his inaugural address, 'government is not the solution to our problem; government is the problem'.[95] A plan was put forward proposing a huge cut both in income tax and the federal budget. It was a bold and contradictory initiative, one that sought to cut government spending, while simultaneously paving the way for the biggest-ever peacetime defence spending. Government would shrink to let the Pentagon expand. Tax cuts would leave the Treasury in trouble, but, it was believed, the shortfall would be made good by the benefits of 'supply-side economics', as the entrepreneurial spirit of America flourished. It was a paradoxical stance and one that would mean that this simple fiscal conservative would see the budget deficit more than double between 1981 and 1989. In time America's rocketing defence spending would bring down an ailing Soviet Union, unable to keep up. It should have bankrupted America too, and would have done so if the attractions of the US dollar and the power and magnitude of the American economy hadn't also been in the picture.

With the Republican-controlled Senate on his side, Reagan's hopes were high; he trusted that he would get the budget past the Democratic majority in the House with the support of that declining breed, the conservative Southern Democrats. Whether his expectations would have been realised remains unknown, although even as things were, the proposals were advancing through Congress. It is possible that the Democrats might yet have rallied against them and dragged a few social programmes from the wreckage, but, as it turned out, Hinckley's bullet pushed the package through; few could vote against a heroically injured, newly elected President.[96] On 28 April 1981, a plucky and apparently fit President gave a televised address to the nation; soon after, the budget was passed. 'Reaganomics' had been given a kick-start, aided in some measure by an assassin's bullet.

It is fitting that one response to the shooting was that that year's Academy Awards ceremony was postponed for twenty-four hours; the event was to begin with a videotaped message from the wounded ex-movie star himself. The last time the Oscars had been postponed was right after Martin Luther King was killed. On the night itself, *Ordinary People* won Best Picture.

Otherwise the shooting prompted the customary calls for greater gun control, and the customary defence of the right to bear arms, led, of course, by the National Rifle Association. At that time in America, someone was murdered with a gun every forty-eight minutes – amounting to around 10,000 gun-related murders per year. Reagan had been in New York when Lennon was shot. Asked if he believed that gun control was the way to prevent murders like Lennon's, he offered instead his own solution: if someone committed a crime while in possession of a handgun, the judge should add five to fifteen years to the prison sentence. His tough words were somewhat undermined a few days later, when Nancy Reagan revealed that she kept a handgun in a drawer beside her bed.[97]

Born in 1955, in Ardmore, Oklahoma, John W. Hinckley, Jr., had grown up in Dallas; he was by most reports an unremarkable kid, shy but well-enough liked. He was his parents' third child, and although as loved as any of them, somewhat in the shadow of his beautiful sister and practical brother.[98] An elementary school sports-field-star and, for a couple of years, his junior-high class president, he appeared set to follow in the footsteps of his successful parents and siblings.[99] However, later at high school things started to go wrong. He withdrew from others, though the real problems emerged with the transition to college. His studies at Texas Tech University were fitful (he was majoring in Business Administration – his father's idea); he would drop out, drop back in, finding it hard to settle to things.[100] Apart from some time in a pizza restaurant, some menial work as a busboy at a supper club, and one week working with *The Rocky Mountain News*, he never really held down a good job. Although amiable enough at high school, he acquired a reputation as an isolated character.[101] He seemed to lack a sense of purpose, eating only fast food, playing guitar and dreaming of becoming a rockstar. He dropped out of college and moved to Hollywood in order to be near the music publishers that he hoped would buy his songs; after his apartment was burgled, this attempt at independence crashed and he ended up living on the streets, writing to mum and dad to bale him out.[102] What his parents did not know was that this was the moment when their son would become obsessed with the movie *Taxi Driver*, going to see it some fifteen times.[103] With their help, he lived on there in L.A. for a while, trying to get a job to tide him over, waiting to become famous. He invented a girlfriend, 'Lynn Collins', largely based on Cybill Shepherd's character, Betsy, in *Taxi Driver*. When he finally came home, he was wearing a combat jacket, in the style of Travis Bickle.

He became irascible, unpredictable; he was intrigued by the American Nazi Party, though the extent of his involvement with it is uncertain; after the shooting there were rumours, later denied, that in 1978, he might have gone on a march in St Louis commemorating the birth of George Lincoln Rockwell. He would later invent a fictitious right-wing party, the 'American Front', of which he was National Director, and sole member.[104] In August 1979, at a pawn shop, Hinckley bought his first gun. That Christmas he remained alone, unable to face the contact with his family; he had started taking anti-depressants and Valium. On his fast food diet, he got fatter, going from 165 pounds in his first year at college to 230 pounds in February 1980.[105] In early 1980, he photographed himself holding a gun to his temple, *à la* Travis Bickle; later that year he would allegedly several times play 'Russian roulette'.[106]

In the summer of 1980, he began seeing a psychologist, presenting the moment as a new start to his mum and dad. He now wanted to become a writer, and persuaded his parents to loan him money so that he could enrol on a creative writing course at Yale. But he had no intention of taking any course; he was going to Yale to be close to Jodie Foster; after seeing her in *Taxi Driver*, his life now revolved around his obsession with its teenage star. In October 1980, Hinckley was arrested by the police at Nashville airport; he had in his possession three pistols, some handcuffs and about fifty rounds of ammunition. Jimmy Carter had spent part of that same day in the city, speaking at the Grand Old Opry; Hinckley had been at the airport when Carter was passing through. He had already been stalking Carter, and on 2 October 1980 had been in the crowd with him at Dayton Conference Center, getting so close that he could have shaken the President's hand.[107] He was flirting with the possibility of becoming an assassin, steeling himself for that leap into the unknown. In terrible poems, he praised the gun's 'pornographic power'.[108] He researched assassination, reading 'true crime' books, including Robert Kaiser's *R.F.K. Must Die!* He began to drift around the country, flying from place to place, staying sometimes with his parents, or in Lubbock, Texas, or hanging around the set of Jodie Foster's latest movie, *Carny*, or later wandering up to New Haven to be close to her.[109] At his trial, in the prosecution's closing speech, the attorney remarked that there were 'probably enough miles there to qualify for the 10,000 Mile Club'.[110]

In October 1980, he came home. Hinckley's family were, as Reagan put it, 'completely crushed by the "sickness" of their son'.[111] He told his family nothing about the arrest in Nashville, though soon afterwards he took an overdose of Surmontil, his prescribed anti-depressant. This possibly spurious suicide attempt led Hinckley's mum and dad to pay for regular visits to Dr Hopper, a local psychiatrist. (He would take another overdose, while awaiting trial, and later attempted to hang himself.[112]) Though in the therapy session on election day Hinckley mentioned Foster, he concealed almost all of his preoccupation with *Taxi Driver* and his love for its star.[113] He travelled to Washington where he stalked Ronald Reagan, and had himself photographed outside Ford's Theatre.[114] In December, he went to New York and joined the crowds mourning the death of John Lennon; in February 1981, he would several times visit the Dakota building where Lennon had been assassinated. He played with the idea of killing himself on the same spot. His thoughts seemed to sway indiscriminately from assassination to suicide, as though the acts were somehow equivalent.[115] He thought about staging a mass murder too, on the Yale campus or in the US Senate.[116] He went around Washington, contemplating what he might do.[117] In March, he went back to Colorado. His dad picked him up at the airport, but said that he would have to stay at the YMCA. Hinckley slept at motels in town, in one of which he registered as Mr J. Travis.[118] He watched television; he read; to raise money he sold his typewriter, some of his records and some of his collection of guns. He then told his parents that he would try one more time to go to Hollywood and become famous. His mum drove him to the airport; neither spoke; both knew that it was the end of their relationship.[119]

He spent a day in Hollywood, and then took the bus to Washington, DC. He put up at the Park Central Hotel. It was 29 March 1981. He was worn out from the ride, and spent his time watching TV. The next morning, he went out for breakfast at a fast food restaurant, bought the *Washington Star* and found in it Reagan's itinerary for the day; he decided to go to the Hilton and assassinate Reagan. He showered, took some Valium, wrote one last letter to Jodie Foster, and left with his .22 pistol, a 'Saturday Night Special' loaded with six Devastator bullets.[120] At Hinckley's hotel room after the shooting, the FBI found a Band-Aid box with a hijacking note, a John Lennon calendar, and the following unmailed letter addressed to Jodie Foster,[121] imploring her:

There is a definite possibility that I will be killed in my attempt to get Reagan. It is for this very reason that I am writing you this letter now . . .

I feel very good about the fact you at least know my name and how I feel about you. And by hanging around your dormitory I've come to realize that I'm the topic of more than a little conversation, however full of ridicule it may be. At least you know that I'll always love you.

Jodie, I would abandon this idea of getting Reagan in a second if I could only win your heart and live out the rest of my life with you, whether it be in total obscurity or whatever. I will admit to you that the reason I'm going ahead with this attempt now is because I just cannot wait any longer to impress you. I've got to do something now to make you understand in no uncertain terms that I am doing all of this for your sake. By sacrificing my freedom and possibly my life I hope to change your mind about me. This letter is being written an hour before I leave for the Hilton Hotel.

Jodie, I'm asking you to please look into your heart and at least give me the chance with this historical deed to gain your respect and love.[122]

Also in the hotel room were his prescription drugs, his clothes, some paperbacks (including *The Catcher in the Rye*), a postcard of Ronald and Nancy Reagan, on which Hinckley had written that he and Jodie Foster would one day occupy the White House ('Until then, please do your best to remain a virgin'), and a picture of Napoleon ripped from an art-book, under which he had written: 'Napoleon and Josephine / John and Jodie'.[123] Already he was planning that if he failed to assassinate Reagan, he would travel on to New Haven and either shoot himself there or murder Foster and then kill himself.[124] He would just see how things panned out.

As a student, Jodie Foster did her best to shrug off her own stardom and be anonymous, refusing interviews and asking in private life that she be called Alicia, her birth name.[125] In 1980, she had enrolled at Yale University, intent on getting a good education, and, as yet, uncertain as to whether she ought to continue with her acting career.[126] According to her brother, as a six-year-old child Foster had been shocked and disturbed by the assassinations of Martin Luther King and Bobby Kennedy, and indeed by the violence of the 1960s in general.[127] In this she shared something with Hinckley (who, after all, had been living in Dallas when JFK was shot) and with most of her generation. But, in most other ways, Foster's life was very unlike that of the average American. She had been a child actor; at the age of three, she was already appearing in advertisements for Coppertone suntan lotion.[128] She was pursuing a career as a child actor, one which might have ended up with her being sidelined as a performer in children's films and television, had she (or her mother) not made a conscious decision to work in movies for adults. No film was more adult than *Taxi Driver*. In many ways, the casting of Foster in that film as the young prostitute, Iris, was an unlikely move. Foster was, after all, a very good girl. But she had already worked with Scorsese on *Alice Doesn't Live Here Anymore*, playing a streetwise shoplifting kid. Nonetheless the casting had been controversial and, again in her brother's account, Foster was even made the subject of psychological profiling to make sure that she was emotionally mature enough for the role.[129]

When she had played the role of the prostitute in *Taxi Driver*, Jodie Foster had been only twelve years old. She had been nominated for Best Supporting Actress. Shortly before the Oscars ceremony, Scorsese received an anonymous letter warning him that if 'little Jodie' won the Oscar, he would be killed.[130] Foster did not win, and the incident was temporarily forgotten, until later events brought it back to mind. Her role was of the kind most likely to encourage rescue fantasies, just as it had for Travis himself, her childlike vulnerability, her poignant attempts at being kooky, the fact that she only seemed to engage with older men.

With the discovery of the incriminating letter in his hotel room, the link between Hinckley's assassination attempt and the cinema was quickly established. On the night of the shooting the FBI interviewed Paul Schrader about Hinckley. The day after the shooting it was reported that it was in particular Foster's role in *Taxi Driver* that had inspired Hinckley's love. Hinckley, it was said, 'may have been living out the role of the taxi driver'.[131] Hinckley remarked of the shooting itself, 'I felt like I was walking into a movie.'[132] In his despair, he saw himself in Travis Bickle, consciously adopting aspects of that character's history and performance so as to make himself feel 'more competent, more able, more effective in life'.[133] By consciously playing out a movie character he endowed himself with some purpose and discovered some meaning in his own life, doubled as it now was with the life that Bickle had led up there on the screen.

Many commentators pointed out the discrepancy between virile, attractive Robert De Niro and the plump, gawky, besuited Hinckley. If a battle between youth and age had underlain the revolutionary spirit of the Vietnam years, then the new assassin (Bremer, Chapman, Hinckley) was someone young who by his very 'squareness', his inability to be hip, resembled the grown-up 'straight world'. Yet Hinckley's social awkwardness, his lack of style, did indeed resonate with Travis Bickle's position outside the world of cool. In *Taxi Driver*, it's the pimps and the prostitutes who are fashionable; Travis could stand for the failure of many to adapt themselves to the essentially Californian 'beautiful people' ideal that dominated American film, fashion and music in the seventies. Hinckley had tried to fit in to the music scene; when that failed, he fell back on being Travis Bickle.

Ronald Reagan never saw *Taxi Driver*.[134] As he didn't like movies with 'naughty words' in them, it's just as well.[135] In the eyes of some, *Taxi Driver* itself was tainted with guilt. At the trial's close, the jury viewed the film, as evidence in criminal proceedings.[136] Schrader was clear that Hinckley's misuse of the movie should be no grounds for censorship. Such men were simply mad, and even the most innocuous of images could stimulate their fantasies. In inspiring Hinckley to attempt murder, *Taxi Driver* laid bare the fundamental instability of all representations of crime, the way that any provocative image might indeed provoke. And the film had not just offered Hinckley a fictional role model in the shape of Travis Bickle, it had also displayed to him a real girl with whom he could fall in love, an American teenager, an undergraduate at Yale – Jodie Foster.

Silent and taciturn in real life, Hinckley could release himself in writing to Jodie Foster, pouring out his feelings in prose. She was in receipt of a host of letters, postcards, love poems from Hinckley, mostly adoring, some also threatening.[137] He phoned her twice at Yale, endeavouring to flirt with her and get close; she did all she could think of to put him off. He doted on her and was clearly also contemplating her murder.[138] When she got more letters at the beginning of March, she passed them on to the Dean.

By means of the murder Hinckley hoped to establish a 'mystical union' with Foster.[139] Shooting Reagan was 'romantic', a gesture born of an impossible love. To others that love seemed unreal, rancorous and perverse. He declared that he didn't want to hurt her (itself a worrying thing to have to insist on), but also that 'I think I'd rather just see her not, not on earth, than being with other guys . . .'[140] But in his own mind, shooting Reagan, his own suicide, even her murder, were all undoubtedly beautiful gestures born from their *Liebestod*, a forlorn union of desire and death. He was 'suffering' from a delusion about what he might achieve in a relationship with Foster. On a more mundane level, he was simply attempting to win her attention: 'To impress her, almost to traumatize her. That is the best word. To link myself with her for almost the rest of history, if you want to go that far.'[141] In that sense, Foster was the target he shot at, Foster the person he planned to assassinate. He had very little concern for the impact on Reagan himself, or on his friends and family, or on the political life of the nation.[142] Shooting Reagan was a vicious approach to her, its aim to shock her out of her distance and her stardom, and to barge in to the sacred aura of her fame. Unable to share love, they would at least share notoriety. For by shooting Reagan he did enforce a relationship with her, just as earlier his nagging presence, his stalking, had been an aggressive means to push himself into contact. It was the idea of reciprocity that was delusional, the belief that Foster must share his feeling, seeing even in her rejections of him signs of her true, concealed interest. According to government witnesses, Hinckley knew, however, that his love for her was unrequited; her being unattainable merely added to her attraction.[143] He clearly had a great deal of frustrated love in him, something that would open out into affection with cats or his sister's young baby.[144] Vulnerable himself, he perhaps sought to care for Foster's imagined vulnerability; in one poem, he compared himself to the Elephant Man, marking himself out as an outsider, a 'doomed creature' who 'would kill for someone to love'.[145]

Almost as soon as Hinckley was arrested, Foster was troubled by another stalker, one Edward Richardson, a young gardener who, just as easily as Hinckley had done, tracked her down to her dorm room in Yale. He planned to assassinate her while she performed on stage in a college play, but lost his nerve, went home and phoned the college to say that he had planted a bomb in her dorm. His one demand was Hinckley's prompt release. Fortunately he was arrested while on his way, as he claimed, to attempt the assassination of Reagan.[146]

Foster responded to the situation with grace and an understandable desire to maintain something of her privacy. Shocked by events, and perhaps anxious concerning their effect on her career, in the December 1981 issue of *Esquire*, Foster published an article on her relation to Hinckley, entitled 'Why Me?' She was using the media to lament the fact that the media had doubled her identity. Sold on the basis of her sexuality from a young age, growing up with herself as an image on film, she was aware now of how there were effectively two Jodie Fosters – the one that existed in public, and with whom Hinckley and her other stalker had become obsessed – and another, hidden from view, private, unremarked. The article in which she questioned the effects of her fame was published because she was famous, but then she had only entered Hinckley's fantasies because of her fame. She was trapped in a hall of mirrors, and her attempt to control the situation in order to preserve some dignity for herself (and consequently hold on to the possibility of continued work) was probably the best that could have been done.

The National Commission on the Causes and Prevention of Violence had reported that the typical American assassin 'evidenced serious mental illness'.[147] Hinckley looked no exception; he showed clear signs of mental disturbance, and in the eyes of the psychological experts for the defence was psychotic, a 'borderline personality', even schizophrenic (whether suffering from 'process schizophrenia' or 'simple schizophrenia'): unable to experience common emotional responses, in retreat from reality, depressed, suicidal, and unable to work or form relationships.[148] The experts for the prosecution, however, thought him merely a sufferer from the milder mental illnesses of 'dysthymic disorder' (so-called 'sad mood disorder'), narcissistic personality disorder, or a 'schizoid personality disorder'. In short, the experts could not agree, and Hinckley's case would reopen the debates about crime and mental illness that back in the nineteenth century had formed around Guiteau or the M'Naughton case.[149]

After the Second World War, the District of Columbia had abandoned the M'Naghten Rules and briefly experimented with the 'Durham Test' (named after the opinion given by Judge David Bazelon in the 1954 case *Monte Durham* v. *United States*). By this test, the key question was whether the accused was suffering from a mental illness and if the crime was the product of that illness. The test revived the nineteenth-century writer Isaac Ray's understanding of mental illness and crime, though the concept of a mental 'disease' as used by Ray had by and large vanished from the clinical literature.[150] As time showed that causation – the certainty that the act had indeed been produced by the illness – proved too difficult to establish, in 1972 the Washington courts, like the rest of the USA, adopted the Brawner Rule (named after an acquitted defendant, Archie Brawner), as set out in the American Law Institute Model Penal Code.[151] This test adapted M'Naghten, asserting that the court had to prove that the accused had at the time of the crime 'substantial capacity to appreciate the wrongfulness of his conduct or to conform his conduct to the requirements of the law'. The word 'appreciate' was a key change, as it moved beyond mere cognitive understanding of the difference between right and wrong and towards an affective comprehension of the meaning of a criminal act. The test also allowed for a defendant operating under 'irresistible impulse', unable to control his or her actions.[152] Could Hinckley have conformed to the requirements of the law? Regarding Hinckley's case, the key psychological issue was whether he was 'psychotic' and therefore unable properly to test reality and to know what was real or not; delusions and hallucinations were standard symptoms, as well as the inability to control one's own behaviour.[153] Someone suffering from psychosis would of course fail the American Law Institute Test, and therefore have to be acquitted on grounds of insanity. The ancient idea that 'madmen' suffered the 'misfortune of the deed' would apply, and in this case Hinckley would be just as much of a victim as Reagan, or Foster.[154]

Having weighed all the evidence, on 21 June 1982 the jury acquitted Hinckley on account of insanity. Reagan himself did not seem that troubled by the verdict, simply remarking in his diary: 'Yesterday Hinckley was found innocent by reason of insanity. Quite an uproar has been created.'[155] This was typically understated; in fact, the verdict led to a public outcry that forced significant changes in American legal practice. Many believed that in being committed to St Elizabeth's Hospital, rather than to prison, Hinckley had been let off; conservative journalists asserted that psychiatry was an expression of a liberal ideology that enabled criminals simply to get away with it.[156] There was a feeling that the rich – such as Hinckley's father – could pay for elaborate psychiatric evidence that was denied to the poor; on hearing of the acquittal, the wounded Secret Service agent, Timothy McCarthy remarked: 'well, that's what money will do for you'.[157] There were suspicions that Hinckley was 'malingering' and had set out to deceive the defence psychiatrists.[158] Some believed that the court had failed to define mental disease properly, or that Hinckley's 'mental illness' in fact amounted to no more than personality disorders (such as might very likely afflict the great majority of America's violent criminals).[159] In any case, the political pressure for changes in the law was immense.

Prompted by dismay at Hinckley's acquittal, the states of Idaho, Utah and Montana abolished the insanity plea as a separate plea in criminal trials.[160] There were calls to do so elsewhere, and many states enacted changes limiting the defence, adding a new verdict of 'guilty but mentally ill', or shifting the burden of proof to the defendant.[161] New legislation was proposed that would 'restore the balance between the forces of law and the forces of lawlessness'.[162]

Just as with the nineteenth-century cases, the arguments regarding Hinckley's guilt or innocence depended on whether or not he was mentally ill, whether he had chosen to kill, and whether he knew that his choice was wrong. To what extent was the act Hinckley's own? As so often in its history, the question of assassination had raised the ownership of a deed. In considering this, the prosecution concentrated its attention on the day of the assassination attempt itself, exposing Hinckley's apparently rational and premeditated behaviour, his doubts and hesitations, his power to choose to shoot. The defence team instead offered the jury a view of Hinckley's life, bringing to light the fractured biography of a clearly troubled man.[163] For one, responsibility was the assent of a moment; for the other, mental illness was embedded in a private history. Some thinkers might dispute the notion of responsibility as such (it implies free will), and with it the idea of guilt or innocence, these being in their eyes only codes of social utilitarianism.[164] What impact the current psychological model based on genetics will have on such old-fashioned notions as 'guilt' remains to be seen. In the era of 'propaganda by the deed', assassination had once seemed an assertion of the assassin's will on behalf of an ideal. Now, as in the movies, the self seemed will-less, entranced, guided by obsessions outside its control. More recently some have held the view that a senseless action, having no utilitarian end or evolutionary motive, must at least belong to the actor. Yet, in considering the disturbances of Bremer, Chapman and Hinckley, the trials of the 1970s and 1980s demonstrated that there was no act less free than a mad one.

In any case, volition (the 'substantial capacity to conform his conduct to the requirements of the law') looked increasingly shaky as a legal category; the American Psychiatric Association recommended that the concept of volition be removed, and instead courts should simply focus on the accused's ability to understand or not the wrongfulness of their act. In 1984, among other changes, the Federal Insanity Law Reform Act limited the insanity defence to those whose mental illness was judged to be severe and removed 'the volitional part of the defense'.[165] It also placed, in matters of insanity, the burden of proof on the defendant (who from now on had to prove him or herself to be suffering from a 'severe mental disease').[166]

After several suicide attempts, a long process of therapy, and the slow decline of a continuing interest in Foster and other iconic American criminals (apparently he once sought the address of Charles Manson), at the time of writing, Hinckley is still in hospital, though moving gradually towards full freedom.[167] Reagan had long ago expressed the wish that Hinckley ('a mixed-up young man from a fine family') would get well as he himself had recovered.[168] It remains to be seen if that wish has finally been granted.

In relationship to state-sponsored violence once again the Reaganite contradictions reigned. In December 1981, Reagan signed Executive Order 12333, forbidding all government employees from engaging in, or conspiring to engage in, assassination.[169] From now on, it seemed, state-sponsored assassination would be something foreigners did: there was, for instance, a plot by Colonel Qaddafi to murder Reagan.[170] The President's Executive Order was a public gesture towards the re-establishment of American rectitude. The USA would once again for ever stand as a shining city upon a hill. (None yet had heard particularly of Guantanamo Bay, or at all of 'special rendition' or Abu Ghraib.) Yet under Reagan, the USA's interventionist foreign policy flourished. A CIA document giving instructions on tactics, including assassination, has been discovered.[171] Image and reality were again at odds.

However, it was the private assassin who caught the world's attention. In the period after Hinckley's attempt, assassination spread like a virus. It was very likely a virus borne by the newspapers and television; the media attention loaded on each killing or attempted killing provided ample motivation for the next. On 13 May 1981, in St Peter's Square in the Vatican City, the Pope was shot four times by a sniper; in Cairo, on 6 October 1981, President Anwar El Sadat of Egypt was murdered, gunned down by a whole squad of assassins during a military parade; on 14 September 1982, in Beirut, after less than a month in office, the Lebanese President, Bachir Gemayel, was murdered in a bomb blast. The attempted assassination of the Pope looked especially mysterious; it seems that Reagan believed that the KGB were behind it.[172] Later in 1981, Chapman's and Hinckley's notoriety inspired an English teenager, Marcus Sarjeant, to fire some blanks at the Queen during the Trooping of the Colour. Obsessed with assassination, his motive, he told the court, was that 'I wanted to be somebody. I wanted to be famous.'[173]

Guiteau had confronted his contemporaries with someone who could not grasp the distinction between right and wrong; although he passed the test and was executed, the M'Naghten Rules were made for someone like him. Yet Hinckley and Bremer and the other mad assassins of the period presented instead an extreme version of tendencies that many could recognise as endemic within Western society. Zasulich, Berkman and Princip fought for a cause; Hinckley had no cause to fight for, just an atomised pursuit of fame. When Hinckley shot Reagan, there were at that time some 400 people monitored in the United States as serious potential assassins, and another 25,000 filed as a lesser risk. Hinckley was on neither list.[174] How many other potential killers were out there?

James W. Clarke has traced a shift in the nature of the American assassin. Before 1963, these were either rational political extremists (Booth, Czolgosz, or Oscar Collazo and Griselio Torresola) or 'utterly insane' (Guiteau or John Schrank, who wounded Theodore Roosevelt in the 1912 election campaign). Since 1963, in his view six of the eight attacks on political figures had been carried out by sane, but emotionally damaged individuals (Oswald, Bremer, Byck, Fromme, Moore and Hinckley). He excludes both James Earl Ray and Sirhan Sirhan from this group.[175] These six killers of the television age were sociopaths aggressively in search of recognition and acceptance otherwise missing from their lives. Conscience does not seem to operate in them; they would kill out of a surplus of frustrated rage. Clarke traces the reasons for this rage to childhood experience: in Hinckley's case caught between a fearful, clinging mother and a distant, dissatisfied father. It is a difficult task to speculate on the complexities of a family's life together, yet Clarke's characterisation of the Hinckleys' domestic problems is confessedly borne out in the parents' account of their relationship with their youngest son. Clarke blames the parents, but the parents had already blamed themselves. If Clarke is right, Bremer and Hinckley and the others acted out the fury engendered by their private childhood experience in the public realm. That public world, the world of politics and the Presidency, seemed just another fantasised place, akin to the dreams offered by television or cinema. And then they too would be on TV, their invisible life finally receiving its deification as an image. There they could transform themselves as on a stage, making themselves into something else. The only prop required was a gun.

The famous victim was both unknown and intensely familiar, suitable therefore as a surrogate for an anger elsewhere, both a stranger and an icon of authority, both the father of the nation and all fathers. It should be no surprise to anyone that the President may exist as a type of father-figure.[176] The National Commission on the Causes and Prevention of Violence had traced the desire to kill a President to oedipal fantasies, a totem and taboo-like parricide.[177] Moreover the centrality of the symbol of the Presidency in American life meant that it was all the more available as the site for transferred hatreds of 'father, brother, sister, or mother'.[178] One of Hinckley's short stories was a textbook example of an oedipal hostility:

'Son of a Gun Collector,' Hinckley's favorite of his stories, tracks a show-down between father and son. Against orders, the son touches his father's prized gun; the father disciplines the son; the son touches the gun again; the father rages; the son shoots his father and says, 'Don't worry, Mama . . . From now on, I'll be the man in the house.'[179]

In the course of this book, the assassins have moved (as we all have) from a culture organised around the concept of character, a life in time, a human biography with chronology and development and choices, to a new kind of personality, instant and consuming, vacant, and violent. And so this book has turned from John Wilkes Booth or Sergei Nechaev, decayed romantic heroes and figures who belong in a nineteenth-century novel, characters for Dostoevsky or Melville, to Mark Chapman or John Hinckley, empty men confined to their emptiness.

That emptiness sought to fill itself with fame. Over the period covered by this book, newspaper reports and magazine essays began to assert with increasing frequency the idea that many modern assassins killed not for political motives, but for public attention. What such commentators failed to notice was that these murderers were also in fact prescient forerunners, prematurely aware that the political sphere was itself fast dwindling to a place of gestures, a world of demagoguery and celebrity. It was for this reason that in the post-war period assassination became such a feature of American political life. More than anywhere else the USA married a cult of individualism and personal success to existences of struggle and anonymity. The resulting frustrations led to a peculiarly American version of 'propaganda by the deed': that is, propaganda for the self.

So this history of assassination in Europe and America from Lincoln to Reagan comes to its necessarily bathetic end. The political killing that had once been an individualistic sacrifice of the self now was fully manifest in a public murder concerned only with entirely illusory private passions. A man shot the President because he had fallen in love with a movie image. Yet this neat version of events must recognise too the fact that the idealistic killers of the past had also loved images, inspired by novels and romance, and that mad personal concerns were ever a factor in such public murders. Perhaps all that can be affirmed is that assassination is murder wrapped in fame, and so must bear the traces of fame's contradictions. Only the state that killed secretly was immune to its glamour.

Making an Ending

Finally, brethren, whatsoever things are true, whatsoever things are honest, whatsoever things are pure, whatsoever things are lovely, whatsoever things are of good report; if there be any virtue, and if there be any praise, think on these things.

PHILIPPIANS 4: 8

On 21 March 1981, only ten days before he himself was shot, Ronald Reagan went to Ford's Theatre for a benefit performance. In his diary, he wrote: 'Our 1st visit – there is a definite feeling when you see the flag draped Presidential Box where Booth shot Lincoln'.[1] Chronologically speaking, this book began with Lincoln, a President shot by an actor in a theatre. It is fitting that it should end with Reagan, a President who had been an actor shot to impress an actress.

It is fitting, because that reversal suggests something of the cultural distance travelled between the 1860s and the 1980s. For centuries, assassinations were understood morally, although that morality was one ambiguously divided between Roman virtue and Christian respect for all human lives. Assassins operated in a confused ethical space, but could defend their actions.

Regarding Manson and Fromme, Sirhan and Bremer, Chapman and Hinckley, the assassin's deed now looked simply like their deed, personal to them, and legitimised by nothing more than their personality. Indifferent to reproof, there is little sense that they even comprehended the right of a court to punish them. They did what they wanted to do. Worldly achievement meant popularity, an adolescent marker of success in life; there are few less popular than Bremer or Chapman. Celebrity was just another version of social triumph on a broader stage – *Newsweek* or *Time* rather than the high-school yearbook. Deprived of attention from others that might have shored up their sense of self, they resorted to extreme measures to be noticed at all. Killing would mark their 'difference', the shtick that would pluck them from the anonymous mass. Presidents could seem no more than celebrities too, the deference due to them just a peculiar branch of that envying, cruel fascination that characterises our relation to the star. Killing such a figure automatically endowed the murderer with their victim's fame. Shooting Reagan was no different from shooting Warhol or Lennon; politics had become a subdivision of stardom.

Assassination is not just the murder of a public figure for the reason that they are a public figure; it is a public death. Otherwise death has become a private, even an invisible process. Assassination makes dying violently shared, torn into the open. Such violence is really only akin to the car-crash, that other form of public death immortalised by Andy Warhol. Only in war does death occur so often in the open and among unfamiliar others. In assassination, as in the post-war mass murders, a ghastly death such as that experienced in war explodes the customarily peaceful civil space.

In American terms – in a world away from the Old World's poisonings and palace coups – the arena of the assassin was a shared space. A stranger commits an assassination; their anonymity is the ground of their action, ending it one of their motives. It is fitting therefore that the fate of a public death was also shared by so many of the assassins in this book, from the public hanging of the Lincoln assassins and Guiteau, the staged filming of Czolgosz's electrocution, to the televised murder of Lee Harvey Oswald.

In the later nineteenth century, one of the key elements in the new importance of assassination was the commodification of the story as 'news'. Assassination was particularly suited to the circulating economy of news; such stories were after all ideally immediate, violent and sensational. Their instantaneous nature, their being truly an event, made them fit a medium whose attention was always given to the sudden. As such, assassination's worth as propaganda became obvious to all. Like the terrorist bomb, assassination exposes and stages pain. But unlike the bomb, it is based on familiarity. The victims are recognised, and therefore an element in our public narrative. They are not anonymous casualties, but the known, understood, loved, admired, hated figures of the public world.

The Russian film-maker Aleksandr Sokurov has argued that there should be no representation of murder in film. One feature of assassination's history is the process by which, from Lincoln's death onwards, these public deaths were received as images, the event transformed into pictures. After the killing of JFK, the American assassinations offer to researchers a series of murders on film or in photographs. And where they weren't filmed, they have since been staged or turned into cinematic or television narrative. In researching this book it has been a help and a sorrow to discover that most of the later shootings – from the death of King Alexander I of Yugoslavia to Ronald Reagan – are all available on YouTube, where they have been viewed hundreds of thousands of times, those deaths and maimings rendered as shared images.

The exposure of death in assassination ties in with another shared interest of several of the killers in this book: that is, in a greater openness about sexual matters. So it is perhaps that the hidden sex lives of the victims have themselves become a matter of public speculation. This fascination with making sex public matches the interest in pornography, the representation of sex on film, shared by many in the last chapters of this book (James Earl Ray, Warhol, Bremer, the Manson family, *Taxi Driver*, Chapman). When Hinckley extolled the 'pornographic power' of the gun, he was saying no more than Bremer had already said, or than *Taxi Driver* had speculatively enacted: combining the violence of pornography with the pornography of violence. The semi-legendary art-school movie that edited together the Zapruder footage of JFK's murder with shots from a 'blue movie' was only making explicit what the assassins themselves had already stated to be true.

Fame was the measure of the assassins' desire. They won Warhol's 'fifteen minutes', but discovered that in becoming public property they had thrown away their selves. In assassination as in other aspects of modern life, the need for renown has led people to accept notoriety at the cost of their own degradation. They would rather be noticed and demeaned than not be noticed at all. Reading of Oswald, Bremer or Chapman, one senses how becoming a murderer debases the self. It is an act of power that renders the actor disgusting; hence the grubbiness and dreariness, the dullness of these later killers. Perhaps they wished to soil their victims likewise.

Certainly assassination pictures physical vulnerability in the political figure who is its victim. It exposes a bare humanness of pain and renders the viscera in us visible. This is something apparently humiliating, and intended to be such. But it may also be thought to be despite itself ennobling; a reminder of the human in the office is to show us the purely human nature of their achievement.

Unhappily this demeaning of the victim by the violence was matched in another sphere by the post-war debunking of political reputations. American Presidents – especially Lincoln – had once been glorified as objects of national reverence and respect. They symbolised a democratic nobility, that peculiarly American form of greatness that embraces the ordinary. Lincoln was an everyman, someone that all might aspire to resemble. In recent decades, the inconsistencies and disappointments of Lincoln's position have been again brought to light. On the subject of race, Lincoln, with his schemes for solving the African-American problem by reverse colonisation, looked suspect.[2] Like the slave-holding writers of the Constitution, his fame began to be tainted. To take more recent examples, the besmirching of the Kennedys, of Martin Luther King and Malcolm X (particularly in relation to their sexual lives) has resulted from a shift in biographical practice, foreshadowed by James Froude's biography of Carlyle, and strengthened in the 1910s by Lytton Strachey and others, a method that exposed flaws and lingered over contradictions. The dead martyrs remained martyrs to some; to others, they now stood for hypocrisy and corruption. Naturally this feeling about the illustrious dead is not altogether new. After all most of the victims of assassination in this book were killed because they were contentious; it was because Lincoln was already viewed as a bad man that Booth shot him. In the case of Lincoln or JFK our disabused view returns us to the contemporary disputes of their careers. For, despite all the platitudes, American politics has often been a hostile and aggressive business. One can trace a typical progress in the history of reputations. A divisive figure is assassinated, and in the moment of their death is instantly re-imagined as a martyr; they gain the halo of the legendary; and then return to contention and dispute, while still being available for those who need models of integrity and goodness. (In JFK's case, this was a much speeded-up process.)

With moral suspicion comes political suspicion. Fears about conspiracy arrived with the debunking. There were many factors at work:

most particularly the belief that concepts of truth could no longer be applied to historical narrative (it was merely a partial tale like any other). The official version sold to us was most suspect of all. If truth did exist, it would be a dark matter – something concealed from the eyes of us mugs.

The conspiracy theory digs out a depth under the shallow event, framing a story from the hidden elements in the public image. That narrative is sketched out only in its traces, but remains essentially secret, though decodable, making the public act a visible manifestation of a veiled plot. One of the oddities of conspiracy theories is their plausibility. One thing connects to another; like a private eye, the theorist unravels a concealed thread. Closed cases again become mysteries, and then join the path to greater mysteries, leaping from clue to clue. In the end, someone like myself, who really does not want to consider himself a believer in such tales, nonetheless comes half to believe. Yet it is good to guard oneself against too easy an enchantment. Both the film *RFK Must Die!* and Dan Moldea's book on the assassination of Robert Kennedy raise the beguiling possibility of conspiracy – and then turn on themselves and deny what they hitherto have suggested.[3] Recently, Martin Scorsese has returned obliquely to the themes of *Taxi Driver*. *Shutter Island* (2010) suggests a parable of American paranoia, set in the cultural moment when that paranoia truly set in: the years that saw the creation of the CIA and the hardening battle-lines of the Cold War. The film closes with the realisation that far worse than any conspiracy is the possibility of our own evil, our own complicity with the darkness. What conspiracies may stave off is the thought of our own involvement in the violence.

Nonetheless conspiracy theories serve their purpose as a belated balm to soothe that startling initial experience of shock. For shock is the medium of all assassinations. Assassinations lay bare the contingency of life; they are the archetypal event. They jolt us with a self-inflicted wound, for very rarely have the assassinations in this book been a matter of foreign interference. In terms of American history, assassination was an American product and an American problem.

In reading and hearing the immediate American responses to Hinckley's assassination attempt one catches, through the professions of horror and outrage, a downbeat world-weariness. You hear the litany of responses, that even the journalists know will sound tired, the jaded reaction to yet another American assassination. The same complaints about the lack of gun control, the same hand-wringing over American violence, the same wearied reassurance about the stability of American democracy. The press reports bring Booth and Guiteau, Czolgosz and Oswald back to the public's eye. Parallels are drawn, comparisons fashioned.

Yet the responses feel exhausted, as though in the path from Dallas to the Washington Hilton some capacity for genuine outrage has been beaten out of us. Writing about Hinckley's assault on Reagan, one columnist titled his piece 'Once Again'; an Amtrak stewardess declared, 'I feel like I felt when President Kennedy was shot, and I was in seventh grade'; Mayor Koch added, 'Anything that I or anyone else could say would just be a cliché. It's been said before and it is true – what a horror. When will it stop?'[4] Hinckley's attack looked like just another in an unending series of mad assassinations.

Since Valerie Solanas, American assassination has seemed tied up with the death of passionate belief in ideologies, and its replacement by narcissistic self-concern. Outside the USA, that has been far from the case. Elsewhere assassinations in the vein of the Nihilists and Anarchists, driven by belief and wrapped up in a dismissal of the self, are far from being an outmoded practice; this American journey does not present the whole story. Elsewhere political passion continued to motivate such killings. Another route would take us from Phoenix Park to the seaside village of Mullaghmore, County Sligo, where on 27 August 1979, Lord Louis Mountbatten was blown up while out at sea on his boat, *Shadow V*. With him were killed two teenage boys, Nicholas Knatchbull and Paul Maxwell, and the 83-year-old Dowager Lady Patricia Brabourne. That same day, beside Carlingford Lough, a convoy of soldiers from the Parachute Regiment were ambushed, hit by first one bomb, then sniper fire, and then (as the rescue party arrived) struck by a further blast. Eighteen men were killed; it was the paratroopers' bloodiest day since the battle for Arnhem.[5] A Republican newspaper, *An Phoblacht*, crowed, 'I.R.A. Make Britain Pay'.[6]

In some ways, such murders were business as usual, a reprise of Nihilist tactics with shades of terrorism as vendetta. Yet even here a newly modern vacuity underlay the deed. Mountbatten was very likely chosen for no better reason than his fame, as war hero, the Supreme Allied Commander in South East Asia in the last years of the war, and, as the last Viceroy of India, the man who had overseen the hand-over of power to an independent India. Yet he was now an old man, an icon of Englishness both aristocratic and modern; good-looking, conceited, ambitious, adored, he was the nearest the Royal Family came to movie-star-style allure. He seemed invested with trans-Atlantic glamour rather than seedy, tweedy British post-war decline.[7] His assassination accomplished nothing; if Mountbatten was linked to Britain's 'sentimental, Imperialist heart' (as an IRA bulletin put it), he was in fact connected to the compromised, yet noblest elements of Britain's behaviour to its former colonial lands.[8] His killing encouraged a newly elected Margaret Thatcher to seek closer security ties with Dublin and to demonstrate her opposition to republicanism, but the reaction was, in IRA eyes, disappointingly temperate.[9] In Roy Foster's excellent history of modern Ireland, the killing (one among so many) receives no mention. Moreover, regarding his own death, some have speculated that Mountbatten might have welcomed the manner of his ending – quick, attention-grabbing, somehow heroic.[10]

The IRA's assassination attempts continued: an abortive attempt to blow up Geoffrey Howe in Belgium; a mortar attack on 10 Downing Street; and, most spectacular of all, on 12 October 1984, during the Conservative Party Conference an attempt to murder the Prime Minister and much of her Cabinet with a bomb at the Grand Hotel in Brighton – five were killed, and thirty more injured. Yet the nihilism, or vicious pragmatism of the terrorists was perhaps shared by the British government, who were rumoured to be secretly operating a 'shoot to kill' policy (as some believe was witnessed at Loughgall, Drumnakilly and Gibraltar) that effectively meant state assassination of political enemies.[11] Though a horrible emptiness infects all these pointless murders, there can be little doubt that they were truly political killings. Fame was vital to the meaning of such deeds, but it was not the vital impetus.

In an American context, many have long dreaded another assass-ination attempt. There were particular worries that the most likely victim would be the first black President of the USA. On 10 February 2007, Barack Obama announced his candidacy for President on the steps of the Illinois statehouse, a consciously resonant gesture designed to evoke memories of Abraham Lincoln. Later, after his election, Obama likewise followed Lincoln's train journey to the White House. This identification with one assassinated politician chimed in with the public's perception of him then as resembling another, the young, gifted and cruelly murdered JFK. Understood twice over in relation to great American lives cut short, it proved inevitable that anxieties should form concerning the possibility of Obama's assassination. There were many public expressions of that fear: a Princeton Professor of Politics, Melissa Harris-Perry, talked of anxieties among African-Americans about Obama's safety; in February 2008, Doris Lessing predicted that Obama would be assassinated if he became President. Lessing's remark was part of an endorsement of Hillary Clinton's candidacy; Clinton herself would unfortunately suggest that she ought to stay in the Presidential race as unforeseen events, such as an assassination, might alter her chances. Infamously, in May 2008, Liz Trotta, a guest on a Fox News show, joked about someone 'knocking off' Obama.

No doubt there have been countless threats screened by the Secret Service, and there have been a couple of more serious incidents. In August 2008, an extreme right-wing conspiracy was uncovered that had aimed to assassinate Obama while he accepted the nomination for Presidential candidate at the Democratic Convention in Denver; a sniper was meant to shoot him as he appeared on national TV. In the autumn of 2008 there was one clownishly wicked plot put together by a couple of Tennessee skinhead Nazis, who constructed together a malevolent fantasy in which they would assassinate Obama at the end of a mass-murder spree designed to kill as many African-Americans as possible. The two were arrested before they started. In November 2011, one Oscar Ramiro Ortega-Hernandez, a young man from Idaho, was arrested after rifle shots were fired at the White House; he is currently awaiting trial. (The President was away in California at the time.) With shades of James Hadfield, the alleged gunman is apparently obsessed with the Apocalypse. Fortunately nothing more professional has materialised. And yet, in the first years of Obama's Presidency, the spirit of contempt and rage was once again strongly an element in American political life. The hatred and suspicion directed against the President during the passing of the healthcare reforms was intense. In this atmosphere an assassination attempt would have surprised few. Nonetheless, when a blow did come, it came – of course – entirely unexpectedly.

* * *

In the nine years that I was writing this book, every month or so I would hear of another assassination somewhere in the world. Some were the product of liberation movements; some were organised by dictatorial states. Many were connected to 'radical Islam', carried out by figures of illiberal dissent, enemies of the secular modern state. We were sometimes reminded that the very word 'assassin' derived from the Islamic world. However, involved as I was in the lives of Goldman and Berkman, of Tehlirian and Princip, of Nechaev and Zasulich, I could not help but be struck by other echoes. The bombers and assassins of the last decade offered at least a family resemblance to the romantic anti-bourgeois figures of the 'heroic' era of Western assassination.

And then in the weeks when I was completing a final draft of this book, the news was dominated by stories of assassination. In Lebanon, Hezbollah pulled out of the government in protest at the possibility that members of their organisation were about to be indicted by a United Nations tribunal for the assassination in 2005 of the former Prime Minister Rafik Hariri. As the month progressed, Hezbollah used the accusations (by most accounts true) in order to bring in a new government more favourable to themselves.

On 4 January 2011, at the Kohsar Market in Islamabad, inspired by the teachings of a Sunni Muslim cleric, Qari Hanif, one Mumtaz Qadri assassinated the Punjab Governor, Salman Taseer, firing twenty-seven bullets into him at close range. Qadri was Taseer's bodyguard. Having shot his charge, he stood and calmly awaited arrest. Taseer's crime was being a moderate, and above all for campaigning for the repeal of Pakistan's blasphemy law. He had bravely challenged extremism, tendering a rational, humane voice; his murder was meant to extinguish that voice. In particular, he had protested against the sentencing to death of a mother-of-five, Asia Bibi, a Christian condemned for the crime of insulting the Prophet Muhammad. Many mourned Taseer. Yet, while there was no doubt about Qadri's guilt, or the treachery that he had performed, for many Pakistanis the assassin became a hero, a man who should be blessed for the assassination he had committed. Lawyers fought to be the one to defend him and outside the court showered the smiling assassin with rose petals; the policemen guarding him posted adoring videos of their captive on YouTube; in January 2012, prominent clerics and Islamists demonstrated in Lahore demanding Qadri's release. Other liberals received death threats, most notably Sherry Rehman, a former federal minister; just as I was writing this, news came in that Shahbaz Bahtti, the Pakistani Minister for Religious Minorities, had been assassinated. A Christian, Bahtti had also stood out against the nation's blasphemy laws; only one of his fellow ministers from the ruling Pakistan Peoples Party attended his funeral. In 2009, there had been other similar assassinations: a prominent cleric who spoke out against suicide bombers was himself murdered by a suicide bomber. It seemed as though the shades of the *Feme* murders in Weimar had been evoked. The significance of these events was clear; assassination was still a tool used by the extreme to enforce social and political change.

The killings in Lebanon and Pakistan had been committed out of passion and ideology, out of faith and 'righteous' rage. However the story that received the most attention in that January of 2011 was something quite different.

On a Saturday morning, 9 January 2011, in Tucson a young man, Jared Loughner, was stopped by police for running a red light. As he was not wanted on any warrants, he was let off with a verbal warning. He drove on to a Safeway supermarket, where in the parking lot an open-invitation meeting with constituents ('Congress on Your Corner') was being held by the local Congresswoman, Gabrielle Giffords. It was just after 10 a.m. Loughner joined the crowd and then pulled out a semi-automatic gun and opened fire at Giffords from a couple of feet away, striking her in the head. She was clearly his main target but he emptied the thirty-three bullets in the clip indiscriminately; he murdered six people, among them Judge John Roll, Arizona's chief federal judge, and a nine-year-old girl, Christina Taylor Green. Christina had been born on 11 September 2001, the day the World Trade Center was attacked by Al Qaeda. One of the other people killed, Dorwan Stoddard, died while shielding his injured wife from the assassin's bullets. In addition to the fatalities, fourteen people were wounded. Several people managed to restrain Loughner while he was trying to reload.

In his police mugshot, Loughner appeared grinning, his head and eyebrows shaved. He was assigned a lawyer, Judy Clarke, who had previously defended Ted Kaczynski (the 'Unabomber'), and one of the 9/11 conspirators. While I'm writing this, Loughner is still awaiting trial; he seems at present another killer in the mode of Bremer and Chapman. By many accounts a long-haired, shy but sweet high school student, it appears that he began a slow descent into mental illness in his late teens. Having dropped out of high school, he had been suspended from his local community college over a number of bizarre and threatening incidents, and rejected by the Army for drug use. He was described as a pot-smoking loner, given to oddball political theorising and posting weird messages on chat-room sites (including the conspiracy theorist site 'Above Top Secret'), YouTube and MySpace; he fretted about the gold standard and the government control of grammar. Though quickly seen as a right-wing killer in the vein of James Earl Ray and Timothy McVeigh, the Oklahoma bomber, he could find it in himself to admire both Karl Marx and Adolf Hitler. In the months before the attack, his behaviour had become increasingly menacing. It seems that in 2007 he had once before made contact with Giffords at another public event, asking her an incomprehensible question that he believed she had failed to answer. She courteously wrote to him with a fuller reply; he scrawled 'Die, bitch' on the letter.

At the time of the shooting, Giffords was forty years old, a rising star in the Democratic Party, and the first Jewish representative from Arizona. She had recently seen off a strong attack by the local Tea Party candidate. She indeed represented everything that the Tea Party despised: she had voted for Obama's healthcare reforms; she supports green energy, especially solar power (as makes good sense in a state like Arizona); but worst of all, she backs immigration reform. After the healthcare vote, someone smashed the windows at her office. The event at the Safeway supermarket was one of many organised by her team each year, known as she was for her energy and her commitment to engaging with local people.

Meantime Ms Giffords's husband, Mark Kelly and his twin brother, Scott Kelly were orbiting the earth, on board the International Space Station. Scott Kelly broadcast to the world: 'I look out of the window and see a very beautiful planet that looks very inviting and peaceful;

unfortunately, it is not. These days we're constantly reminded of the unspeakable acts of violence and damage we can inflict upon one another, not just with our actions but also with our words'. As of now, Ms Giffords is recovering; in August 2011 she was well enough to return to Congress to vote for the raising of the American national debt limit (although she has since stepped down to concentrate on her recovery).

As Kelly's words indicated, the debates produced by the shooting rapidly focused on gun control (Loughner was, after all, a disturbed young man able to buy a Glock 19 semi-automatic), but more intriguingly on the possibility that Loughner had expressed in real violence the divisive, furious and hostile political style of the new Tea Party Republicans. In particular, attention fell upon Sarah Palin's electioneering material in which key constituencies (including Ms Giffords's) were targeted using cross-hairs. The intention had been to suggest that the Republicans meant business, that they had those seats in their sights, and probably to evoke Palin's reputation as pro-gun and an amateur hunter. In the wake of the massacre, they looked downright sinister. One of Palin's slogans had been 'Don't retreat, reload'.

Congress cancelled all business for a week, thus putting off a planned vote organised by Republicans and designed to begin the repeal of Obama's healthcare legislation – the law that had first sparked the Tea Party movement. Some pointed out that Judge Roll, murdered by Loughner, was a conservative Republican, but had gone to the supermarket that day to show his support for Giffords, a 'blue dog', moderate Democrat. In the heat of debate, the question of gun control slipped out of view. It was pointed out that Giffords also owned guns. It might be argued that all over the world there are lonely, angry, mentally ill young men who spend too much time on the internet; there are few civilised countries where they can go out and purchase a semi-automatic gun over the counter at a sporting-goods store. Yet later in 2011, the massacre of young people at a socialist summer camp on an island in Norway by a mentally unstable right-wing gunman showed that this was far from being a uniquely American phenomenon.

Obama began his Presidency looking like a potential assassin's victim; at the end of 2011, he himself authorised an assassination. Regarding the murder in Yemen of the US-born terrorist Anwar al-Awlaki (a man who was deemed to be a threat to US interests and the safety of its citizens), Obama asserted the right of the state to assassinate, without due process of law, any US citizen who was its known enemy. Such killings could be carried out purely on the President's approval. This was despite the fact that such drastic action contravened 'an executive order banning assassinations, a federal law against murder, protections in the Bill of Rights, and various strictures in the international laws of war'.[12] The consolidation of such potentially tyrannous powers seals for this moment the recent history of assassination: on one side the deranged and deracinated individual like Jared Loughner, on the other – after all the scandals and select committees of the 1970s – the approval by a supposedly liberal President, for pragmatic reasons, of the right to assassinate.

This book has traced the decline of the Western assassin. It has depicted three broad kinds of assassin. There are the mad, who can only be pitied. There are those who kill for a romantic dream, whether a greater Serbia or an Islamic caliphate, an imagined homeland or a historical fantasy; these are the lost, the consumers of illusion. And then, finally, in a few instances, we find those who chose assassination to redress an injustice elsewhere – Zasulich, Tehlirian, Bonhoeffer. Here perhaps, as Hannah Arendt termed it, 'only the violence of this goodness is adequate to the depraved power of evil'.[13] At least, these are the few assassins who may lay claim to our compassion and even admiration. It will be apparent to most that since World War II, the first two kinds of assassin have dominated.

Up to Stauffenberg, even the most vicious assassins performed their deeds for ends they perceived as noble. They were enthused by a fire for justice. Alexander Berkman was perhaps more vivid, more alive, than the man he sought to kill. In the post-war period, in America certainly, the assassin dwindles into vague banality. Heroism has emptied out of him. The relationship of the assassin to power has also altered. With the Anarchists and Nihilists, the Armenian avengers and the July plotters, the powerless struck a blow against power. In post-war America, the shooting merely announced the gun's authority. The run of assassinations from Oswald to Hinckley echoes the post-war school-shooting and mass-murder phenomenon – massacres committed by the dullest person in the university, school or workplace. The cowardice of such shootings is obvious to all but their perpetrators; the tables are turned, but the power resides in the gun, and not in the individual;

the armed bully shooting the unarmed innocents. Such killings occupy much of the same moral realm as the post-war assassinations, just an acted-out nihilism, a murderous gesture by the trivial. Even George Wallace was a better man than his assailant.

With the assassin, not just madness but idiocy itself intrudes into history; he is the vicious jester, reminding the noble of the limit to their greatness. Into the biographies of good and creative people encroach the lives of ludicrous believers – self-righteous, self-obsessed, absurdly certain. In writing a novel that played with the story of Sergei Nechaev, the prototype for the modern revolutionary 'terrorist', Dostoevsky came to an aesthetic conclusion that may seem at first surprising: he realised that in essence the fanatical killer, the political assassin, is funny. They believe themselves to be tragic heroes, but their natural environment is comedic; the ludicrous lies deep in the existential vacuum in which such 'heroes' move.

Sadly it appears that the history of assassination has a long future. These blows will continue, for as long as human beings are given to violence. Education will not solve the problem, only universal justice and contentment. Few are expecting their imminent arrival.

Recently, some psychologists and sociologists have put forward the idea that violence is 'situational'.[14] For these academics, violence arises out of contexts of conflict. People are not good or evil; situations are conducive to producing cruelty, or not. Such an understanding might work for some of the stories this book has explored: for the murder of Abraham Lincoln, the violence at Homestead, and even the shooting of Martin Luther King. What this theory leaves hanging is the question of responsibility for setting up such situations, for the ways in which they might arise. As with behaviourist reflections on the subject, situational accounts of violence omit the possibility of individual decision, the fact that a person might will the bad.

Since at least the early 1800s, authors have desired to understand and humanise the 'villain', to comprehend and explain wickedness. All too often, this can look like condoning chaos or forgiving cruelty. This book too aims at moral sympathy; though it may have failed it aspires to comprehend all its characters, even the worst. Though sympathy is distinct from approval, I have sometimes wondered whether it might have more usefully established a plea for moral judgement, for the right to judge others.

Were the killers in this book assassins or tyrant-slayers? That question comes down to this: were the governments of Europe and America from the 1860s to the 1980s good sources of authority or bad? To the anarchist there is no good authority, but to an outsider to their ideology, it does matter whether those politicians, those victims, were democratic representatives or misguided criminals. Over that time, the real enemies were industrialism and unjust and wicked regimes; it was these that wrecked lives by injustice, by poverty, by senseless wars. In relation to this, what is the moral significance of killing an honourable President like McKinley, a good man like Martin Luther King? What benefit is gained by trying to understand their killers?

What does it mean then to write even so limited a history of assassination? How can one talk sensitively and responsibly enough about the lives of others? About the violence they have done or the violence that was done to them?

In writing this book and re-reading it many times, it has borne down on me how hard it is to elude the delightful tension of mayhem. I abhor the violence that I have described, and yet feel its abrupt narrative kick. Moreover there broods over the subject a glum awareness of the instrumentality of human lives – people becoming instruments of rule, killed by instrumental weapons, by individuals who make themselves instruments of revolution. In doing harm to others, the most idealistic assassins blinkered their own imaginations. They shot or stabbed only political or economic selves; yet, to paraphrase the Second World War poet Keith Douglas, death that had the politician singled did the lover mortal hurt.

My ultimate aim in this book has been to explore and manifest our tainted relationship to the violent. Despite my wishes, it may be one more instance of that odd and disreputable love affair between the literary and civilised and the perpetrators of political violence. Cinema and literature boast many instances of works that futilely sought to protest at violence by representing it. Their works are most often co-opted by those with a taste for extremity. In the last 150 years, the relation of art and beauty to violence has become especially fraught. Art may contain and represent wrong, depending as it often must on the oppressive frame of society, while also offering an antidote to brutality, particularly by engendering imaginative sympathy.

This could not be a book just about the practice of violence. What is vital in the portrayal of a specifically political violence is the conjunction of righteousness and murder, of compassion and carnage. Contextualising assassination means relating the crime to an injustice elsewhere; for example behind the horrible attack on an industrialist such as Henry Clay Frick lies the suffering engendered by capitalist greed. The moral cloudiness of such situations is our problem, one belonging to the grey area of our pampered and inadequate pity. Within that pity yearns our hunger for violence and retribution, our desire to see things (the social, the city) smashed. These stories of assassination necessarily touch our desire for devastation, even as their close analysis involves our baffled empathy.

Considering what I have just said of unconscious or even conscious approval, it should also be pointed out that the majority of citizens appear to have been justly repulsed by the outrages that this book describes. Obviously some, including some intellectuals, sighingly condoned, connived at, celebrated, or even joined in the havoc. It is those few people who form the subject of this book. It should be said from the first that theirs was an eccentric and unusual reaction. However, I want to propose that even among those who appeared to condemn the acts, the violence itself possessed a strange appeal. It is at least possible to suggest that some of the public horror at the acts of violence mingled with a kind of admiration, even a fascination with the criminal, the conspirator, the 'blond assassin'. This mingled response is not true just in the sphere of assassination, but in other modes of violence; behind it lingers the heroic Romantic Satan.

Finally it hits me that I have been engaged in the story of the enforcing of pain. Assassinations make us share in our vulnerability – the power of the gun exposing the weakness of power, the weakness of us all – and yet they also show the durability of the institutions and the society that establishes that authority. Walter Benjamin's angel of history hurtled backwards through time, his face turned towards the past, his eyes fixed in horror at the barbarism that spread out behind him.[15] Yet amidst the catastrophe of human wickedness continue the traces of art and creativity, of kindness and generosity. I trust that in the midst of the destruction and disorder that I have described, in what is finally a record of human iniquity, some affirming flame might have occasionally shone out. To me, at least, that flame is visible in the absolving resignation of Lucy Cavendish and in the lights of the candles on Castro Street; in Alexander Berkman's and Emma Goldman's tortuous path from fanaticism to humanity; in Zasulich's and Tehlirian's quest for rectitude and recompense; in the ineradicable nobility of Abraham Lincoln or Martin Luther King; in the hopes still manifest in the Kennedys and Malcolm X. It is even there, perhaps, in our tentative pity for the blundering of Booth or M'Naghten, for the wrongheaded idealism of Czolgosz or Fromme. But certainly, it would blaze out in the example of Stauffenberg and Bonhoeffer and George Bell, good men prepared to take on disgrace and sin for the sake of justice. I think of Ronald Reagan, and even George Wallace, publicly forgiving the men who shot them. Above all, I think of Bobby Kennedy, in the midst of mayhem and fury, even as he was dying, present enough to forget himself to ask about another man. If nothing else, this history may at least indicate the complexity of human experience, and our capacity for resilience and even a somewhat puzzled hope.

For this book wishes to make a stand on the absolute value of a human life. To adapt W. H. Auden on reading classic works, history is one of our few means of breaking bread with the dead. The history book wants to resurrect departed spirits, not as a real return and meeting, but as a conjuration, as imagined between the writer and the reader, making the figures of the past new again. These events once happened. However ragged, however broken, storytelling itself protests against the erasure of the killings, though it knows that life was always more complex and open than even a story can allow. Nonetheless such fables may amount to a reparative act. The desperation and nihilism of murder extinguishes identity, both that of its victim and of the perpetrator; it commits its crime against life itself. It is my hope that this book will run counter to that crime, and those killings, by summoning up the vanished presences of all those who appear in its tales, not merely as ghosts, or revenants, but as traces of the multifaceted and various people that they once were. Such an enterprise is doomed and naïve. And yet it has been my experience in researching and writing this book to be so haunted, aware of those lost lives that were sometime here.

Notes

PREFACE

1 'A distinguished psychiatrist and contributor to the Commission [that is, the American 'National Commission on the Causes and Prevention of Violence' (1970)], Dr. Lawrence Z. Freedman, has suggested that in some senses, with the possible exception of the attack upon President Truman, there have been no political assassination attempts directed at the President of the United States. The attacks are viewed as products of mental illness with no direct political content' (Kirkham, 1970: 2).
2 Jowitt, 1977: 142.
3 In passing it should be noted that chronology was very important to the history of assassination, as each unique story added a model for latecomers. Assassinations provoked further assassinations, a pattern that also seems to hold good for other forms of violence.

INTRODUCTION: A Justifiable Killing

1 Schulthess, 2008: 83.
2 Finker, 1977: 13–14, 20; Hoffmann, 1998: 11–13, 15.
3 Roon, 1979: 178; see Hamerow, 1997, for an account that lays bare the initial National Socialist sympathies of many among the conservative and church resistance.
4 Finker, 1977: 67.
5 Kramarz, 1965: 24–32; Finker, 1977: 25–7; Hoffmann, 1998: 15–16.
6 Gay, 1968: 49.
7 Roon, 1971: 269; Klemperer, 1992: 377.
8 Hamerow, 1997: 224–5, 315–16; Hoffmann, 1998: 61–2.
9 Wolf, 1966: 252.
10 Paraphrased from a reported conversation with his wife, in Kramarz, 1965: 201.
11 Hamerow, 1997: 285.
12 'Der Putsch wurde unternommen in vollen Bewußtsein sehr geringer Erfolgschancen' (Wolf, 1966: 254).
13 Klemperer, 1992: 198.
14 Messerschmidt, 1986: 76–8; Hamerow, 1997: 349–50. 'Das Attentat muß erfolgen . . . Sollte es nicht gelingen, so muß trotzdem in Berlin gehandelt werden. Denn es kommt nicht mehr auf den praktischen Zweck an, sondern darauf, daß der deutsche Widerstand vor der Welt und vor der Geschichte den entscheidenden Wurf gewagt hat' (Stauffenberg, quoted in Wolf, 1966: 254).
15 Hamerow, 1997: 364–6.

16 Hoffmann, 1988: 127–8.

17 Klemperer, 1992: 20.

18 Hamerow, 1997: 313.

19 Hoffmann, 1988: 106–7.

20 Ibid.: 108.

21 Scheurig, 1982: 236; Hoffmann, 1988: 110.

22 Hamerow, 1997: 312–13.

23 Klemperer, 1992: 378.

24 Messerschmidt, 1986: 76.

25 Hitler quoted in Kramarz, 1965: 145.

26 Hoffmann, 1998: 85.

27 Ueberschär, 2006: 15.

28 Ueberschär, 2006, 15, 26.

29 Kramarz, 1965: 204.

30 Ibid.: 204.

31 'Es lebe das heilige Deutschland', quoted in Finker, 1977: 341.

32 Hamerow, 1997: 374–5.

33 Hoffmann, 1988: 125.

34 Roon, 1971: 275; Hoffmann, 1988: 125.

35 Klemperer, 1982: 153.

36 See also Hamerow, 1997: 367, 373. The letter is quoted at greater length, with a slightly different translation, in Roon, 1971: 385.

37 Goerdeler is reputed to have proposed a Jewish state on Madagascar (Arendt, 1985: 581); he was undoubtedly interested in the mass emigration of Europe's Jews to Palestine (Hamerow, 1997: 229). See also the letters between Hannah Arendt and Karl Jaspers (Arendt, 1985, letters 351 and 378).

38 The impact of the case of Hans and Sophie Scholl is already visible in Pechel, 1947: 96–104.

39 See Minister of Defence Kai-Ewe von Hassel in 1964, quoted in Finker, 1977: 400.

40 See the discussion of responses to the *attentat* in the post-war period in Ueberschär, 2006, 182–214.

41 Hans-Bernd von Haeften was the brother of Werner von Haeften, the man who assisted Stauffenberg with the assassination attempt. Werner's brother had severe misgivings about the ethics of an assassination attempt (see Roon, 1971: 273).

42 Wolf, 1966: 252; Klemperer, 1982: 153.

43 While suspicious of the early responses to Nazism by most of the eminent men associated with the resistance, Theodore Hamerow sets Bonhoeffer aside as the 'only well-known member of the ecclesiastical resistance who from the outset criticized the regime's racial program, openly, repeatedly, and consistently' (1997: 161).

44 Bethge, 1984: 121–3.

45 Norden, 1986: 130.

46 Klemperer, 1992: 40.

47 Ibid.: 41.

48 Klemperer, 1982: 154.

49 King's College London, Liddell Hart Centre for Military Archives, LH1/58/74, 'An Impression of George Bell, Bishop of Chichester', 11 December 1945.

50 'Do not mistake my meaning. I am convinced that if Hitler were to win this war it would make the very notion of such an appeal an impossible thing; and it would mean

the domination of a huge area of the world by a ruthless anti-Christianity. Therefore, we must resist Hitler's powerful onslaught with all our strength, and do our utmost to defeat him in battle' (from a speech given at the Stoll Theatre by George Bell, 10 May 1941 in Lambeth Palace Library, Sword of the Spirit Papers, MS3418, ff 67–73, p. 3).

51 Bell, 1946: 51, 64, 76.

52 Letter from George Bell to William Temple, Archbishop of Canterbury, 26 February 1944: 'If this [saturation bombing] is really defensible are you not inevitably led to the adoption of the principle that the end justifies the means, and that anything – poison gas or anything else you like to mention – is justifiable if it is going to secure military victory?' (Lambeth Palace Library, William Temple Papers 57, ff 164).

53 Thorpe, 2003: 446; Jasper, 1967: 262; see transcript of the programme, a paper by Professor D. M. MacKinnon, 13 November 1967, in King's College London, Liddell Hart Military Archives, LH1/58/193.

54 Bell, 1946: 145, 189–90.

55 As evidenced by the publication of his letters to Gerhard Leibholz and Alphons Koechlin (Bethge and Jasper, 1974; Lindt, 1969).

56 Bell, 1946: 165; Jasper, 1967: 267.

57 Klemperer, 1992: 283; Müller, 1990: 279.

58 Bell, 1946: 167–8.

59 Jasper, 1967: 267–8. It is a matter of debate just how coherent and free of prejudice the plan put forward by Schönfeld was regarding the position of the Jews; Bell seems to have interpreted this aspect of the plan more generously than it perhaps deserved (Müller, 1990: 280).

60 Bethge and Jasper, 1974: 57.

61 Bonhoeffer, 1970: 157, 336.

62 Bell, 1946: 169; Jasper, 1967: 269.

63 Bell, 1946: 171.

64 Bell, 1946: 172. '"Wir wollen der Buße nicht entfliehen. Unsere Handlung muß als ein Sühneakt verstanden werden"' (quoted in Hammelsbeck, 1959: 32). 'Ein Sühneakt' might be better translated as 'an act of atonement' or 'act of expiation' rather than as 'act of repentance' as Bell has it.

65 Bell, 1946: 175.

66 Jasper, 1967: 270.

67 Bethge and Jasper, 1974: 57–8.

68 Bell, 1946: 74–5.

69 See for instance, his letter to Captain Liddell Hart, 25 September 1942, in King's College London, Liddell Hart Military Archives, LH1/58/26.

70 Eden, 1965: 333.

71 Letter to Eden from George Bell, 25 July 1942, in Bethge and Jasper, 1974: 64.

72 James, 1986: 282.

73 Klemperer, 1992: 278–9.

74 Kettenacker, 2002: 25.

75 Eden, 1965: 464.

76 Lambeth Palace Library, Bell Papers 39, ff 358.

77 Hamerow, 1997: 356–8.

78 Klemperer, 1992: 387.

79 James, 1986: 284.

80 Lambeth Palace Library, George Bell Papers 39, 404.

81 *Daily Mail*, 5 June 1957.

CHAPTER 1: A Murder at the Theatre

1 The details of this opening section are taken from the testimony of Lieutenant Colonel Everton J. Conger, one of the men who captured Booth, and also from contemporary press accounts derived from interviews with Conger and his Lieutenant Baker (extracts from the *New York Times* in *The Times*, Friday 12 May 1865: 5). See also Herold and Pitman, 1954: 93.

2 From information quoted in the *New York Times* and printed verbatim in *The Times*, Friday 12 May 1865: 5).

3 Lattimer, 1980: 69; see also testimony of Willie Jett in Herold and Pitman, 1954: 91.

4 From the *American Encyclopedia*, quoted in *The Times*, 27 April 1865: 7.

5 Kolchin, 1995: 82, 94.

6 There is a lovely oval photographic portrait of Mary Ann Holmes, owned by the Handy Studios, Washington, DC, reproduced in Kimmel, 1969.

7 Farjeon, 1938: 18.

8 Burlingame, 2008: Vol. 2, 815.

9 Farjeon, 1938: 14.

10 Bates, 1929b: 452.

11 Edwin Booth quoted in Burlingame, 2008: Vol. 2, 814.

12 Booth Clarke, 1938: 73.

13 The Freudian reading of the murder – that Booth hated his father and so killed Lincoln – has very little to recommend it. Moreover by marginalising conscious motive, it diminishes the impact of the political and cultural meanings of the crime.

14 Clara Morris quoted in Hatchett, 1983: 138.

15 Samples, 1982: 130.

16 Ibid.: 129–31.

17 Deusen, 1967: 413. Lincoln was a fan of John Wilkes Booth's actor brother, Edwin. There are a couple of invitations extant asking Lincoln to attend a performance by Edwin Booth (The Abraham Lincoln Papers, Letters from Leonard Grover to Abraham Lincoln, 20 and 25 February 1864), online at http://memory.loc.gov/ammem/alhtml/malhome.html (accessed 27 March 2010). That spring of 1864, Lincoln and Seward enthusiastically saw Edwin Booth play Hamlet, Richard III, Brutus, and Shylock, and he dined with Seward and his family (Goodwin, 2009: 612–13). In New York, in 1864–5, he played Hamlet for a hundred nights.

   After the assassination, the theatrical profession publicly endeavoured to cleanse themselves of any taint derived from their association with Booth. See 'At a Meeting of the Members of the Theatrical Profession' and 'A Card' from John Ford in *American and Commercial Advertiser* (Baltimore), 19 April 1865: 1.

18 Booth, 1997: 148.

19 Booth had been conspiring with Arnold and O'Laughlen since August 1864. See Booth, 1997: 120.

20 Kauffman, 2004: 155.

21 Quoted in *The Times*, 4 May 1865: 7.

22 As remarked upon in Fanny Seward's diary, 13 April 1865: 181–2, in the William H. Seward Papers, online at http://www.library.rochester.edu (accessed 20 March 2010).

23 To Mary Ann Holmes Booth, Washington, DC, 14 April 1865 (quoted in Rhodehamel and Taper, 1997: 144–5).

24 Kimmel, 1969: 215.

25 Ibid.

26 Hatchett, 1983: 52–3.

27 Bates, 1929a: 449.

28 Wilson, 1929: 94–5.

29 Bryan, 1940: 116.

30 Kimmel, 1969: 216.

31 Booth, 1997: 146.

32 Hanchett, 1983: 82.

33 A modern biographer describes him as a 'complicated and occasionally devious person' (Taylor, 1991: x).

34 Goodwin, 2009: 29–30.

35 Adams, 1999: 90–1.

36 Paraphrased from Kunhardt, 1965: 25.

37 Booth, 1997: 150, 151.

38 Ibid.: 147.

39 McPherson, 1998: 56, 98–9.

40 Adams, 1999: 87.

41 Booth, 1997: 148.

42 Ibid.: 149–50. He quotes Shakespeare, *Julius Caesar*, II. i: 169–71.

43 Ibid.: 154.

44 Kunhardt, 1965: 35–7.

45 Bryan, 1940: 154. Also spelt Taltavall.

46 Seward, 1916: 255.

47 From 'The Freedman's Monument To Abraham Lincoln: An Address Delivered in Washington, D.C., on 14 April 1876', in Douglass, 1991: 436.

48 With echoes of Adolf Eichmann in our mind, Lincoln's interest in establishing a colony for African-Americans now looks deeply suspect; however, from the 1810s (and the foundation of the American Colonization Society in 1817) to 1830, this was seen as a respectable and pragmatic solution to American problems. Lincoln was unusual in persisting with the idea so long after it had been discredited in the eyes of most abolitionists (Jones, 1995: 170). Further to contextualise Lincoln's interest in this idea, it should also be pointed out that some American blacks were themselves engaged with the idea of emigration (Kolchin, 1995: 84–5).

49 McPherson, 1998: 769.

50 Burlingame, 2008: Vol. 2, 778.

51 McPherson, 1998: 846.

52 Burlingame, 2008: Vol. 2, 789–90.

53 Ibid.: Vol. 2: 799–800.

54 Quoted from the testimony of Lewis Powell (Paine) to Thomas T. Eckert in Burlingame, 2008: Vol. 2, 803.

55 There are a number of previous invitations to Ford's Theatre preserved in the Abraham Lincoln Papers.

56 Burlingame, 2008, Vol. 2: 807, 808–9.

57 Charles Warwick, quoted in Booth Clarke, 1938: 164.

58 The Abraham Lincoln Papers, letter from James S. Knox to Knox, 15 April 1865: 1,

online at http://memory.loc.gov/ammem/alhtml/malhome.html (accessed 27 March 2010); Burlingame, 2008: Vol. 2, 810.

59 Testimony of Peter Taltavul and John E. Buckingham in Herold and Pitman, 1954: 72–3.

60 The Abraham Lincoln Papers, letter from James S. Knox to Knox, 15 April 1865: 2, online at http://memory.loc.gov/ammem/alhtml/malhome.html (accessed 27 March 2010).

61 Kunhardt, 1965: 29.

62 Testimony of Captain Theodore McGowan in Herold and Pitman, 1954: 78; testimony of James P. Ferguson in Herold and Pitman, 1954: 76; also Ferguson's statement as printed in the *Richmond Times*, Vol. 1, No. 1, 21 April 1865: 2.

63 Kauffman, 2004: 225; testimony of Major Henry R. Rathbone in Herold and Pitman, 1954: 78.

64 It is not certain what Booth said in the box, but Major Rathbone heard it as 'freedom' (Hatchett, 1983: 56).

65 Testimony of Major Henry R. Rathbone in Herold and Pitman, 1954: 78. Rathbone married Clara Harris, but in 1894, went mad and murdered her (Booth, 1997: 156).

66 Although other witnesses disagree as to what Booth said at this moment, according to Booth's own writing, he cried out '*Sic semper tyrannis*' before he shot the President (Booth, 1997: 154). One eye-witness, positioned in a stalls seat just below the President's box, believed that he had heard Booth shout, '*Sic semper tyrannis*, the South is avenged' (The Abraham Lincoln Papers, letter from James S. Knox to Knox, 15 April 1865: 2, online at http://memory.loc.gov/ammem/alhtml/malhome.html [accessed 27 March 2010]).

67 Testimony of Joseph B. Stewart in Herold and Pitman, 1954: 79–80.

68 The Abraham Lincoln Papers, letter from James S. Knox to Knox, 15 April 1865: 3, online at http://memory.loc.gov/ammem/alhtml/malhome.html (accessed 27 March 2010).

69 Taylor, 1991: 240; Fanny Seward's diary, dated 5 April 1865: 173–4, in the William H. Seward Papers, online at http://www.library.rochester.edu (accessed 20 March 2010).

70 See Fanny Seward's diary, dated 14 April 1865, but composed some weeks later, on pages 182–3, in the William H. Seward Papers, online at http://www.library.rochester.edu (accessed 20 March 2010).

71 The description of Paine's voice comes from the wanted posters. The source of information in these derives from witnesses who knew Paine at first hand. See Turner, 1982: 194.

72 Testimony of William Bell in Herold and Pitman, 1954: 154.

73 See Fanny Seward's diary, dated 14 April 1865, but composed some weeks later, on pages 183–4, in the William H. Seward Papers, online at http://www.library.rochester.edu (accessed 20 March 2010).

74 Seward, 1916: 258; testimony of William Bell in Herold and Pitman, 1954: 154.

75 It is also equally possible that Robinson opened the door, and was injured by Paine, before the attacker struck Fanny Seward. Fanny's testimony is confused, and there are details of the attack that she could not remember. Kauffman, 2004: 23; Lattimer, 1980: 362.

76 From Fanny Seward's diary account of the events, dated 14 April 1865, but composed some weeks later, on pages 185–6, in the William H. Seward Papers, online at http://www.library.rochester.edu (accessed 20 March 2010).

77 Testimony of Major Augustus H. Seward from Herold and Pitman, 1954: 156.

78 The Abraham Lincoln Papers, letter from James S. Knox to Knox, 15 April 1865: 4, online at http://memory.loc.gov/ammem/alhtml/malhome.html (accessed 27 March 2010).

79 From a telegram by W. H. Seward, presumably sent in the early hours of 15 April 1865 (but dated, very likely wrongly, 16 (?) April 1865) in the William H. Seward Papers, at Rare Books and Special Collections, University of Rochester, New York, online at http://www.library.rochester.edu (accessed 20 March 2010).

80 From Fanny Seward's diary account of the events, dated 14 April 1865, but composed some weeks later, on pages 188–9, in the William H. Seward Papers, online at http://www.library.rochester.edu (accessed 20 March 2010).

81 Seward, 1916: 261–2.

82 Testimony of William Bell in Herold and Pitman, 1954: 155.

83 Tidwell, 1988: 437–8.

84 The Sun (Baltimore, Maryland), 20 April 1865: 1.

85 From the testimony of Major Augustus H. Seward in Herold and Pitman, 1954: 157.

86 From the testimony of Thomas A. Jones in Booth Clarke, 1938: 172.

87 Weckesser, 1991: 34.

88 From the testimony of William Williams, including the hearsay evidence of Dr Samuel Mudd, in Herold and Pitman, 1954: 89.

89 Tidwell, 1988: 5.

90 From the testimony of Thomas A. Jones in Booth Clarke, 1938: 173.

91 Booth, 1997: 154–5.

92 J. L. Magee, 'Satan tempting Booth to the Murder of the President' (Philadelphia, Pennsylvania: 1865), found in the Alfred Whital Stern Collection of Lincolniana housed at the Rare Book and Special Collections Division of the Library of Congress, Washington, DC, online at http://memory.loc.gov/ammem/collections/stern-lincoln/ (accessed 26 March 2010).

93 Tidwell, 1988: 6–7.

94 Testimony of Willie Jett in Herold and Pitman, 1954: 90–1.

95 Testimony of Everton J. Conger in Herold and Pitman, 1954: 91. In press reports, it is stated that prior to reaching Jett, the pursuing cavalry had questioned another black man, who said that he'd seen two men of the same description earlier that day on the porch at Richard Garrett's farm. However, it is hard to see why, if they had information already as to the fugitives' whereabouts, they still needed to use Jett.

96 This detail derives from contemporary press accounts (quoted from the New York Times and printed verbatim in The Times, Friday 12 May 1865: 5) and is absent from the courtroom testimony of Everton J. Conger – although Conger does declare that he threatened the man with hanging 'from one of those locust trees' (Herold and Pitman, 1954: 91).

97 From the testimony of Everton J. Conger in Herold and Pitman, 1954: 92.

98 Apparently in the eighteen months before the assassination, the quality of Booth's voice had begun to deteriorate, becoming 'hoarse and weak' (Kirkham, 1970: 63). However, there is other evidence, such as the accounts of this moment that suggest that it nonetheless remained stronger than most.

99 From a report quoted from the New York Times and printed verbatim in The Times, Friday 12 May 1865: 5.

100 From the testimony of Everton J. Conger in Herold and Pitman, 1954: 92.

101 Lattimer, 1980: 59, 61. There is a dispute as to whether or not Booth in fact shot himself. It seems from the evidence presented by Lattimer and others that he did not. That the issue is a contested one is typical of the Lincoln assassination story, where practically every incident is the subject of debate. I have attempted to steer a middle course through the competing accounts. However, where such a path is impossible, I have exercised my judgement, and gone with the most plausible version of events, one that mostly coincides with the majority view.

102 For a while there was some confusion as to which Hale daughter Booth was 'engaged' to; at one time, Lucy's sister, Elizabeth ('Bessie') Hale was believed to be the woman.

103 These last details derive from a press account of Booth's death in *The Times*, 12 May 1865: 5.

104 Bancroft, 1900: Vol. 1, 418.

105 This was despite the fact that President Andrew Jackson had narrowly escaped assassination at the hand of Richard Lawrence, a madman.

106 Such as, for example, from The Abraham Lincoln Papers, letters from Frederic Bates to Abraham Lincoln, Tuesday 10 November 1863 and from Seymour Ketchum to Abraham Lincoln, Wednesday 2 November 1864, online at http://memory.loc.gov/ ammem/alhtml/malhome.html (accessed 27 March 2010).

107 The Abraham Lincoln Papers, letter from John K. Smith to Abraham Lincoln, Monday 24 December 1860, online at http://memory.loc.gov/ammem/alhtml/malhome.html (accessed 27 March 2010).

108 For instance, The Abraham Lincoln Papers, the letter from Thomas Langford to Abraham Lincoln, Wednesday 23 November 1864, online at http://memory.loc.gov/ ammem/alhtml/malhome.html (accessed 27 March 2010).

109 Whitman, 1887: 68.

110 Burlingame, 2008: Vol. 2, 808.

111 Ibid.: Vol. 2, 807–8.

112 From 'Death of Abraham Lincoln', a lecture delivered in New York, 14 April 1879, in Philadelphia in 1880, and in Boston in 1881, in Whitman, 1982: 1039.

113 The Abraham Lincoln Papers, [Charles P. Stone], Thursday 21 February 1861: 1–2 (Memorandum pertaining to danger in Baltimore), online at http://memory.loc.gov/ ammem/alhtml/malhome.html (accessed 24 March 2010).

114 Burlingame, 2008: Vol. 2, 32.

115 Burlingame, 2008: Vol. 2, 34.

116 Goodwin, 2009: 311.

117 The Abraham Lincoln Papers, letter from Edwin V. Sumner to John G. Nicolay, Monday 7 January 1861: 1, online at http://memory.loc.gov/ammem/alhtml/malhome .html (accessed 27 March 2010).

118 Burlingame, 2008: Vol. 2, 812.

119 Letter in the Abraham Lincoln Papers, from Nathaniel P. Banks to William H. Seward, Tuesday 9 July 1861: 2, online at http://memory.loc.gov/ammem/alhtml/malhome. html (accessed 27 March 2010).

120 Malamud, 2009: 24–5.

121 McPherson, 1998: 783.

122 Image entitled 'Theory. Practice. Effect', found in the Alfred Whital Stern Collection of Lincolniana housed at the Rare Book and Special Collections Division of the Library of Congress, Washington, DC, online at http://memory.loc.gov/ammem/ collections/stern-lincoln/ (accessed 26 March 2010).

123 Hanchett, 1983: 60.

124 Castel, 1999: 201. Castel, Quantrill's foremost biographer, doubts the likelihood of this particular assassination plan.

125 McPherson, 1998: 786.

126 Quoted in Burlingame, 2008: Vol. 2, 546.

127 McPherson, 1998: 788.

128 Burlingame, 2008: Vol. 1, 418.

129 Jones, 1995: 206.

130 See 'The Assassination and Its Lessons: An Address Delivered in Washington, DC, on 13 February 1866', in Douglass, 1991: 115.

131 McPherson, 1998: 150–1.

132 Ibid.: 200.

133 Jones, 1995: 197.

134 Zinn, 2003: 186; see also Brown quoted in Emerson, 2000: 795: 'Better that a whole generation of men, women and children should pass away by a violent death than that one word of either [the Golden Rule and the Declaration of Independence] should be violated in this country.'

135 Reynolds, 2006: 292.

136 Oates, 1970: 318; McPherson, 1998: 203.

137 Foner, 1988: 427–8.

138 On the attitude of the police and courts to Klan violence, see Foner, 1988: 434–5.

139 Hanchett, 1983: 63.

140 Ibid.: 86.

141 Kauffman, 2004: xxv.

142 Turner, 1982: 155–6.

143 Booth, 1997: 156.

144 Turner, 1982: 144–6.

145 Hanchett, 1983: 68.

146 Turner, 1982: 47; Hanchett, 1983: 59–60.

147 Hanchett, 1983: 72–3, 64.

148 *Union*, 1865: 1, 3.

149 Hanchett, 1983: 79–81.

150 Andrew, 1995: 23–4.

151 Hanchett, 1983: 84.

152 Speech by Mr Doster in Herold and Pitman, 1954: 161.

153 Testimony of Dr Charles H. Nichols, in Herold and Pitman, 1954: 161–2.

154 From questions addressed and answered and the judge's intervention during the testimony of Dr Charles H. Nichols, in Herold and Pitman, 1954: 164.

155 Turner, 1982: 194.

156 Kunhardt, 1965: 199.

157 Lattimer, 1980: 118.

158 Kunhardt, 1965: 204–15. As well as the photographs taken at the scene, there are a number of illustrated prints of the execution. (There are a couple of examples in the Alfred Whital Stern Collection of Lincolniana housed at the Rare Book and Special Collections Division of the Library of Congress.)

159 Williams, 1966: 303. See also Jones, 1995: 218–19.

160 McPherson, 1998: 854.

161 See 'The Assassination and Its Lessons: An Address Delivered in Washington, D.C.,

on 13 February 1866', in Douglass, 1991: 109–10.

162 It is curious that one response to the crime appears to have been that it was a rumour designed to make money for speculators on the stock exchange. The telegraph had both increased the efficiency and power of newspapers and enabled the interconnection of financial markets across the country (McPherson, 1998: 12, 190).

163 *The Times*, 29 April 1865: 9.

164 Advertising poster printed for a performance on 31 July 1866 in Clinton, found in the Alfred Whital Stern Collection of Lincolniana housed at the Rare Book and Special Collections Division of the Library of Congress, Washington, DC, online at http://memory.loc.gov/ammem/collections/stern-lincoln/ (accessed 26 March 2010).

165 http://memory.loc.gov/cgi-bin/query/D?scsmbib:59:./temp/~ammem_sV7V (accessed 28 March 2010).

166 Letter from Whitman to William Michael Rossetti, in Hindus, 1971: 128.

167 See John Burroughs, 'Walt Whitman and His *Drum-Taps*', from *Galaxy*, Vol. 2, printed 1 December 1866, in Price, 1996: 129–30.

168 From 'Death of Abraham Lincoln', a lecture delivered in New York, 14 April 1879, in Philadelphia in 1880, and in Boston in 1881, in Whitman, 1982: 1045.

169 Whitman, 1887: 106–7.

170 Ibid.: 100. The 20th Amendment to the Constitution, passed in 1933, moved the date of the inauguration of a new President from March to 20 January.

171 Milkis, 2008: 167.

172 On Whitman's anxiety regarding the anonymity of the Civil War dead, see M. Wynn Thomas, 'Fratricide and Brotherly Love: Whitman and the Civil War', in Greenspan, 1995: 37.

173 Burlingame, 2008: Vol. 2, 820.

174 Ibid.: 828–9.

175 From *Specimen Days* in Whitman, 1982: 770.

176 Grant and Tolstoy, quoted in Goodwin, 2009: 747.

177 McPherson, 1998: 790.

178 See Turner, 1982.

179 Kauffman, 2004: 80; Randall, 1929: 237.

180 Randall, 1929: 236, 248.

181 Milkis, 2008: 169.

182 Ibid.: 155.

183 Adams, 1999: 113.

184 Ruskin, 1987: 75.

185 Randall, 1929: 240.

186 See Malamud, 2009.

187 McPherson, 1998: 804.

188 Randall, 1929: 241.

189 McPherson, 1998: 560, 721, 517, 596–7, 494.

190 Ibid.: 359.

191 Ibid.: 585, 821.

192 *The Times*, 6 June 1867: 11.

193 Ibid.

194 'Assassination of Abraham Lincoln', 1866: 385. Ravaillac killed Henri IV of France; Orsini failed in an attempt against Napoleon III.

195 'Assassination of Abraham Lincoln', 1866: 119.

196 From the *Gazette de France*, 30 April 1865, quoted in 'Assassination of Abraham Lincoln', 1866: 121.

197 From 'The Assassination and Its Lessons: An Address Delivered in Washington, D.C., on 13 February 1866', in Douglass, 1991: 108.

198 Kimmel, 1969: 214; Turner, 1982: 97.

199 Adams, 1999: 178.

200 An undated poster printed in Lansing, Michigan, headed 'Assassination of Abraham Lincoln. The pursuit, capture, death and burial of J. Wilkes Booth', found in the Alfred Whital Stern Collection of Lincolniana housed at the Rare Book and Special Collections Division of the Library of Congress, Washington, DC, online at http://memory.loc.gov/ammem/collections/stern-lincoln/ (accessed 25 March 2010).

201 *The Times*, 10 July 1865: 10.

CHAPTER 2: Enemies of This World

1 Riasanovsky, 2000: 370–1.

2 Engel, 2006: 316.

3 Kropotkin, 1905: 103.

4 See Chubarov, 1999: 84–6.

5 Or so Dmitry Pisarev argued. See, for instance, Pipes, 1974: 271.

6 See the *OED* definition of 'nihilist', noun and adjective.

7 Venturi, 2001: 326–7.

8 Ibid.: 331. Chernyshevksy is himself a key figure in the Nihilist pantheon. A radical sent to prison in the early 1860s, he came to stand in the mind of many as an exemplary figure of integrity and resistance. As it was designed to do, his novel provided a role model for the revolutionary, the 'new man'.

9 Seth, 1966: 28.

10 Ibid.: 30.

11 In the Russian calendar, the date was 4 April; in the Western calendar, it was 17 April. It seems that Karakozov missed due to the intervention of a peasant, Kommissarov, who was standing beside him in the crowd. As a reward, the Tsar elevated Kommissarov to the rank of nobleman (*The Times*, 23 April 1866: 10).

12 Venturi, 2001: 347.

13 Moss, 2005: 36. Shuvalov would himself be assassinated in 1905; Daly, 2006: 638.

14 Quoted in Venturi, 2001: 361. Nechaev appears to have wished to follow Karakozov's lead, including naturally the practice of assassination, though it is possible that for a time at least the supposed target of such plans did not include the Tsar (see Pomper, April 1974: 126), though later it certainly did (ibid., 132–4).

15 Quoted in Venturi, 2001: 359.

16 Cochrane, 1977: 11.

17 Venturi, 2001: 360.

18 Cochrane, 1977: 10–14.

19 'Let not our veneration for Milton forbid us to look with some degree of merriment on great promises and small performance – on the man who hastens home because his countrymen are contending for their liberty, and, when he reaches the scene of action, vapours away his patriotism in a private boarding-school' (Johnson, n.d.: Vol. 1, 62).

20 Cochrane, 1977: 26–7.

21 Cochrane, 1977: 51. Venturi declares that Nechaev wrote the *Programme* in collaboration with Tkachev alone (Venturi, 2001: 361).

22 Cochrane, 1977: 52.

23 Venturi, 2001: 362.

24 McClellan, 1979: 36.

25 Quoted in Marshall, 1993: 270.

26 Herzen, paraphrased in Marshall, 1993: 264.

27 See Hamburg, 2006: 129.

28 McClellan, 1979: 33.

29 Venturi, 2001: 59.

30 McClellan, 1979: 35.

31 Frank, 1995: 439.

32 Pomper, 1970: 98. It seems credible that Nechaev and Bakunin were lovers, given the background facts (or rumours) of Bakunin's impotence with women, Nechaev's intense relationships with older men, including his schoolmaster, and his failed attempts to have sustained relationships with women. It also makes psychological sense given the emotional, political and intellectual needs of the two men. Bakunin's later accusations that Nechaev set out to seduce young women in order to bring them onto his side may itself be evidence not of Nechaev's simple heterosexuality, but of a sexual tension and jealousy between the two men. After all, had Nechaev not already seduced Bakunin? On the other hand, there is no tangible evidence whatsoever for a sexual liaison, and the intensity of the relationship (including the sense that Bakunin may have been in love with Nechaev) can be adequately explained without needing to assume that their relationship became physical or 'romantic'. The argument that if Bakunin had been Nechaev's lover, Nechaev would have used that fact as means to blackmail the older man does not carry much weight. Such blackmail would also have had the effect of incriminating himself, though it would seem that Nechaev did indeed set out to blackmail Bakunin over something.

33 Kelly, 1982: 270.

34 McClellan, 1979: 38.

35 Frank, 1995: 400.

36 This title is the one most commonly used, although in fact the original pamphlet had no title at all (Cochrane, 1977: 200). For a complete English translation of the text see Dmytryshyn, 1967: 241–7.

37 This is to simplify a complex matter. The manner of the collaboration and the relative input of the two men are very difficult to determine. Critics of Bakunin credit him with a great deal of the *Catechism*; supporters put the blame on Nechaev. Whatever the process of composition, Bakunin certainly knew and approved the contents of the whole pamphlet, and certain of the paragraphs reveal their origin in his thinking.

38 Paraphrased from Venturi, 2001: 365–7. The paragraphs condensed here are almost certainly Nechaev's; the more constructive vision provided by the end of the *Catechism* is most likely by Bakunin.

39 Marshall, 1993: 284.

40 Pomper, 1970: 97.

41 Venturi, 2001: 356.

42 The student found out, and took back the money; afterwards he married the Likhutins' sister and ended up becoming Minister of Finance (Venturi, 2001: 378).

43 Ibid.: 380.

44 Offord, 1999: 68–9.

45 The freeing of many of the accused led to a tightening of the process by which political criminals were tried. See Daly, 2006: 638.

46 Quoted in Venturi, 2001: 377.

47 Kelly, 1982: 270.

48 Ibid.: 268.

49 Cochrane, 1977: 204.

50 Naarden, 1992: 55.

51 Paraphrased from Frank, 1995: 439–42.

52 McClellan, 1979: 78.

53 Venturi, 2001: 381.

54 Frank, 1995: 443.

55 Berlin, 1995: 191.

56 Quoted in Feuer, 1984: 24. Marx's relationship to political violence changed over the years, and is, overall, difficult to determine. Bruno Naarden writes: 'he admired the Irish freedom fighters, who were also an inspiring model for the Russian terrorists. The Russian scholar Kovalevsky was visiting Marx in 1878 when the news of the failure of Dr Nobiling's attack on the German emperor reached him. "Marx reacted to this report by cursing the unsuccessful terrorist, explaining that there was only one thing to expect from his criminal attempt to accelerate the course of events – new reprisals against the socialists"' (Naarden, 1992: 69–70). See also Hamburg, 2006: 130.

57 Frank, 1995: 448.

58 Hillyar, 2000: 38.

59 Ibid.: 40–1.

60 Teaching was becoming increasingly an occupation for women, attracting the independently minded and those with a social conscience. See Engel, 2006: 317.

61 Engel, 1975: 74.

62 Broido, 1977: 147.

63 Bergman, 1983: 27–8.

64 Chubarov, 1999: 96.

65 *The Times*, 30 January 1877: 8.

66 *The Times*, 2 January 1877: 6.

67 Seth, 1966: 53–4; Pomper, 1970: 135.

68 Bergman, 1983: 36–7.

69 Zasulich certainly shared her intentions with Maria Kolenkina, who was meant to commit a simultaneous assassination, but it is also possible that she disclosed details of her plans to other members of Land and Freedom. See Bergman, 1983: 37.

70 Quoted in *The Times*, 22 April 1878: 8.

71 Engel, 1975: 79.

72 Siljak, 2008: 1–4, 11–12.

73 Engel, 1975: 84.

74 See Baberowski, 2006.

75 Siljak, 2008: 221–2.

76 Bergman, 1983: 47.

77 Ibid.: 51.

78 Paraphrased from Broido, 1977: 151.

79 Bergman, 1983: 51–2.

80 Baberowski, 2006: 364.

81 Stepniak, 1883: 117–18.

82 Ibid.: 121.

83 Ibid.: 120.

84 For Zasulich's relationship with the Anarchists see Cahm, 1989: 108–9.

85 Hillyar, 2000: 44–5; Engel, 1975: 93.

86 Naarden, 1992: 91.

87 Pomper, 1970: 136.

88 Kravchinskii is the real name of Stepniak.

89 'The Father of Russian Terrorism', by 'A Correspondent', *The Times*, 2 February 1884: 7.

90 Cochrane, 1977: xii; Venturi, 2001: 387–8.

91 From the testimony of Vera Figner, translated in Engel, 1975: 44–6.

92 Riasonovsky, 2000: 384.

93 Hamburg, 2006: 116–17.

94 From 'The Programme of the "People's Will" Group', 1 January 1880, quoted in Vernadsky, 1972: 664, and also in Dmytryshyn, 1967: 247–51.

95 Chubarov, 1999: 98.

96 Daly, 2006: 639.

97 Pipes, 1974: 302.

98 Engel and Rosenthal, 1975: 53–4.

99 Chubarov, 1999: 83.

100 See 'Letter from The Revolutionary Committee of Narodnaia Volia to Alexander III, March 22, 1881', in Dmytryshyn, 1967: 251–5.

101 Chubarov, 1999: 98.

CHAPTER 3: The Praise of Murder

1 Cahm, 1989: 109.

2 Hayman, 1980: 329–30.

3 'mein Attentat auf zwei Jahrtausende Widernatur und Menschenschändung' (Nietzsche, 1999: 313); translation from Nietzsche, 1979: 81.

4 'Von diesen vier Attentaten hatte das erste einen ausserordentlichen Erfolg' (Nietzsche, 1999: 317).

5 For his aristocratic contempt for Anarchism, see Nietzsche, 1974, section 370 – although Nietzsche seems to have felt some kinship with the individualist Anarchist philosopher Max Stirner: 'Sie beweisen, dass ich kein "Hans der Träumer" war, dass es mir Vergnügen macht, den Degen zu ziehn' (Nietzsche, 1999: 316); 'Ich bin kein Mensch, ich bin Dynamit' (Nietzsche, 1999: 365).

6 Quoted in Hayman, 1980: 334.

7 'He once said that he really had it in for morality but had to force himself to always turn back to its underlying relations until he could no longer stand it and made the leap to the aesthetic. This leap gave him great relief, the feeling of having finished with morality, of having re-valued it' (recollections of Ida Overbeck in Gilman, 1987: 105–6).

8 *The Times*, 16 March 1881: 9.

9 From the translation of the article read out in court by the Attorney General, filed in National Archives: CRIM 12/82.

10 Carlson, 1972: 254.

11 Ibid.: 173.

12 Ibid.: 127–9.

13 Ibid.: 181.

14 That is the *Kommunistischer-Arbeiterbildungsverein*.

15 Trautmann, 1980: 41–2.

16 Naarden, 1992: 73.

17 Trautmann, 1980: 44.

18 From the testimony of PC Ward, filed in National Archives: CRIM 12/82.

19 *The Times*, 20 June 1881: 6.

20 *The Times*, 2 April 1881: 12.

21 Jowitt, 1977: Vol. 1, 142.

22 The use of speeches from Shakespeare's *Julius Caesar* as evidence in favour of
    tyrannicide produced, in court, an intriguing literary discussion, in which both the
    Attorney General and the Lord Chief Justice pointed out that people in Shakespeare's
    plays speak in character, and therefore that we can never infer Shakespeare's own views
    of any matter.

23 HO 451/102541/X36450 – Report by E. R. Henry, Assistant Commissioner, Scotland
    Yard on Anarchists to Home Office – 7 January 1902.

24 *The Times*, 20 June 1881: 6.

25 Trautmann, 1980: 69.

26 Oliver, 1983: 1; Vizetelly, 1911: 37–8.

27 Blind, January 1894: 140.

28 Bakunin, quoted in Woodcock, 1963: 11.

29 Marshall, 1993: 346.

30 Oliver, 1983: 10, vii, 15.

31 Vizetelly, 1911: 70.

32 Oliver, 1983: 10.

33 Oliver, 1983: 15–16; Carlson, 1972: 250.

34 Woodcock, 1963: 243.

35 Oliver, 1983: 13.

36 Ibid.: 13.

37 Marshall, 1993: 446.

38 Cahm, 1989: 76.

39 Marshall, 1993: 449.

40 Cahm, 1989: 83–4.

41 *The Times*, 28 April 1879: 5.

42 Stoddart, 1986: 131.

43 Ibid.: 136.

44 Ibid.: 130.

45 Marshall, 1993: 342–3.

46 Quoted in Cahm, 1989: 131.

47 Regarding Guillaume, see Carlson, 1972: 249. In his *Memoirs*, Kropotkin makes very
    brief mention of his visit to the conference (Kropotkin, 1989: 407).

48 Wilde, 1979: 216.

49 Quoted in Woodcock and Avakumović, 1950: 225.

50 Cahm, 1989: 92 and *passim*.

51 See an interesting article and editorial on Brousse and Blanqui in *The Times*, 28 April
    1879: 5, 11. For the influence of Reclus on Kropotkin, see Cahm, 1989: 131–2.

52 Cahm, 1989: 94–5.

53 Ibid.: 104.

54 Hulse, 1970: 53.

55 Kropotkin, 1886: 7.

56 As witness his interest in the case of the would-be republican regicide Giovanni Passanante (Cahm, 1989: 119–20).

57 Cahm, 1989: 320.

58 Woodcock, 1963: 241. Though the word 'moral' was used in a qualified sense: 'que le mot morale employé dans les considérants n'est pas employé dans le sens que lui donne la bourgeoisie, mais dans ce sens que la société actuelle, ayant pour base l'immoralité, ce sera l'abolition de celle-ci, par tous les moyens, qui nous amènera à la moralité' (quoted in Maitron, 1992: 11).

59 Cahm, 1989: 156–7.

60 Oliver, 1983: 16.

61 Cahm's phrase – from Cahm, 1989: 159.

62 From a Berlin newspaper, quoted in Blind, January 1894: 151.

CHAPTER 4: Insanity Rules

1 At the time of the trial of Charles Guiteau for the murder of President Garfield, an American physician wrote:

'Moral insanity as a defense for capital crime is an importation from the mother-country, being an invention of the brilliant genius of Erskine, and by him successfully applied in the defense of Hadfield for an attempt on the life of George the Third, eighty years ago. It was again used with success by Sir John Campbell and Sir Thomas Wilde, in the case of Oxford for shooting at Queen Victoria, forty years later; and again in the McNaughton case, for the murder of Mr. Drummond, private secretary of Sir Robert Peel, mistaking him for Sir Robert himself, by Mr. Cockbourne, afterward Chief-justice of England' (Elwell et al., 1882: 1).

Little of this was strictly true; but that it was believed to be so is of interest. The defence had been used, however, in the trial of Lewis Paine for the attempted assassination of Seward.

2 Sir Roger Ormrod, in West and Walk, 1977: 4.

3 West and Walk, 1977: 93, 100.

4 Walker, 1968: 52.

5 Harrison, 1979: 210.

6 Winslow, 1843: 19.

7 Everest, 1887: 25; Eigen, 1995: 48.

8 William Orange, entry on 'Criminal Responsibility', in Tuke, 1892: Vol. 1, 300.

9 Quen, 1969: 1221.

10 Sir Roger Ormrod, in West and Walk, 1977: 5.

11 Winslow, 1843: 2.

12 Keeton, 1961: 38–9.

13 Walker, 1968: 76.

14 Keeton, 1961: 57; Walker, 1968: 80–1; Harrison, 1979: 210; Moran, January 1985: 37.

15 Moran, January 1985: 35–7.

16 Gray, 1963: 455.

17 PRO 30/29/6/11; Treherne, 1909: 198; Gray, 1963: 455.

18 Gray, 1963: 456.

19 Treherne, 1909: 199.

20 Walker, 1968: 186.

21 Treherne, 1909: 194.

22 Lord Holland, quoted in Treherne, 1909: 196; Gray, 1963: 459.

23 PRO 30/29/6/11.

24 *The Times*, 16 May 1812: 2.

25 Everest, 1887: 31–2.

26 *The Times*, 19 May 1812: 3.

27 Buckle, 1926a: 265.

28 Buckle, 1926b: 266.

29 *Royal Movements*, 1883: 58–9.

30 Davey, 1897: 89.

31 *The Times*, 11 June 1840: 4.

32 Quoted in Woodham-Smith, 1972: 212; Benson, 1987: 41.

33 *The Times*, 12 June 1840: 6.

34 However, this may just be a family legend: no member of Millais's family was called as a witness at Oxford's trial, although many other bystanders did testify (Millais, 1899: 20–1).

35 PRO 30/43/25/7.

36 *The Times*, 11 June 1840: 4.

37 Police report 14 June 1840, MEPO 3/17.

38 Wallis, 1892: 504–5; *Royal Movements*, 1883: 139; Wallis, 1892: 535 and 537.

39 Letter from Edward Oxford, 19 June 1840, MEPO 3/17.

40 Letter 13 June 1840 – MEPO 3/17.

41 MEPO 3/17, another letter written 13 June 1840.

42 *The Times*, 23 June 1840: 6.

43 For a transcript of the trial, see Wallis, 1892: 497–556.

44 Wallis, 1892: 528–31; *The Times*, 13 June 1840: 6.

45 Testimony of Hodgkin, in Wallis, 1892: 538–9.

46 Wallis, 1892: 539–40.

47 Wallis, 1892: 554.

48 Davey, 1897: 124. This information on Oxford's later fate probably derives either from *Royal Movements*, 1883: 142, or from what appears to be its original source in an article in *Vanity Fair*, March 1882.

49 *Royal Movements*, 1883: 173.

50 *The Times*, 31 May 1842: 5.

51 Letter to the King of the Belgians, from Windsor Castle, 6 June 1842, quoted in Benson and Esher, 1907: Vol. 1, 503.

52 *The Times*, 18 June 1842: 7.

53 Weintraub, 1997: 134–5; Benson and Esher, 1907: Vol. 1, 509.

54 MEPO 3/19A.

55 Walker, 1968: 187.

56 Peel, 1860: 312–13; Gash, 1976: 265–83.

57 *The Times*, 4 March 1848: 5.

58 Wallis, 1892: 852.

59 Wallis, 1892: 853.

60 *The Times*, 4 March 1843: 5.

61 William Orange, entry on 'Criminal Responsibility', in Tuke, 1892: Vol. 1, 297.

62 Wallis, 1892: 856–7.

63 Ray, 1838: 19–20.

64 Walker, 1968: 104.

65 Finkel, 1988: 27.

66 Ray, 1838: 33.

67 Wallis, 1892: 879.

68 Cockburn quotes the authority of Baron Hume (Wallis, 1892: 888).

69 Wallis, 1892: 899.

70 Ibid.: 894.

71 Ibid.: 894.

72 Ibid.: 917.

73 West and Walk, 1977: 95. More particularly, M'Naughton might be thought to be suffering from a 'monomania of suspicion', a condition elucidated in 1852 by Charles Lasègue (Victor Parant, entry on 'Persecution, Mania of', in Tuke, 1892: Vol. 2, 925).

74 Moran, 1981.

75 There are a number of possible spellings of M'Naughton's name: he was called either McNaughten or McNaughton in the asylum reports and M'Naughton in the trial transcripts, though the rules bear the name M'Naghten. These are just some of the more prominent spellings. I have decided to refer to 'M'Naughton' when discussing the man himself, and to M'Naghten when referring to the rules.

76 Wallis, 1892: 848.

77 Ibid.: 848.

78 Everest, 1887: 44–5.

79 See Low, 1986: 11–14.

80 Ibid.: 14–17.

81 Clyne, 1973: 20.

82 William Orange, entry on 'Criminal Responsibility', in Tuke, 1892: Vol. 1, 313; Goldstein, 1967: 212–13; Mackay, 1995: 96.

83 Quoted in Finkel, 1988: x; *The Lancet*'s leading article from 18 March 1843 is transcribed by Alexander Walk, in West and Walk, 1977: 113–15. The same *Lancet* article also implies that the execution of Bellingham had deterred assassins, and voices some scepticism about the supposed insanity of Oxford.

84 MEPO 3/19 B; letter from Queen Victoria to the King of the Belgians, 22 May 1849, in Benson and Esher, 1907: Vol. 3, 261–2.

85 *The Times*, 28 June 1850: 5.

86 Buckle, 1928: 267.

87 Quoted in White, 2000: 20.

88 Ibid.: 22.

89 Letter from Treasury Lawyers, 14 April 1882 in HO 144/95/A1281/15.

90 See, for instance, Adams, 1882.

91 Hibbert, 2000: 423.

92 Ibid.: 420–1.

93 Quoted in White, 2000: 61.

94 Dated 20 April 1882, in Buckle, 1928: 269–70.

95 White, 2000: 12.

96 Quoted in White, 2000: 66; the British courts returned to the original wording with

the passing of the Criminal Procedure (Insanity) Act, 1964 (White, 2000: 1); see also A. Wood Renton, entry on 'Criminal Cases, Summary of Practice as to Plea of Insanity', in Tuke, 1892: Vol. 1, 292.

97 See Sikes, 1881.

98 Ibid.: 157.

99 Crapol, 2000: 62; Jones, 1995: 353.

100 It was not until the ratification of the 22nd Amendment in 1951 that a third-term presidency became unconstitutional.

101 *Washington Post*, 3 July 1881: 1; Guiteau, 1882: 120.

102 Guiteau, 1882: 121.

103 Ibid.: 149.

104 Peskin, 1978: 583.

105 On the day of the shooting, ignorant of what had happened that morning, she visited the *Washington Post* with an advertisement seeking the apprehension of Charles Guiteau: he had absconded without paying his six weeks' worth of rent (*Washington Post*, 3 July 1881: 1).

106 Peskin, 1999b: 715; Guiteau, 1882: 116–17.

107 Guiteau, 1882: 117.

108 Ogilvie, 1881: 106.

109 Quoted in *New York Times*, 3 July 1881: 1.

110 Guiteau, 1882: 125–6, 135–6.

111 Peskin, 1978: 591.

112 Guiteau, 1882: 119.

113 Ogilvie, 1881: 105.

114 Guiteau, 1882: 140.

115 Ibid.: 137, 141.

116 Ibid.: 149.

117 *Washington Post*, 3 July 1881: 1.

118 *Washington Post*, 4 July 1881.

119 *New York Times*, 3 July 1881: 1.

120 Clark, 1993: 145.

121 Peskin, 1978: 600.

122 *The Times*, 21 September 1881: 5.

123 Extract from the Queen's Journal – Balmoral, 20 September 1881, quoted in Buckle, 1928: 240. Lowell was the American ambassador to the UK.

124 Buckle, 1928: 240.

125 *Washington Post*, 4 July 1881.

126 *New York Times*, 12 October 1908.

127 *Washington Post*, 2 December 1881.

128 An editorial comment from the British press remarks: 'Guiteau's confession teaches us one thing. It shows that directly you leave off calling an ugly thing by an ugly name the mind loses some sense of its foulness ... Guiteau, you will note, does not call his attack on the President a "murder" or even an "assassination." These are shocking words. So he speaks of the act as one of "removing" his victim' (from *Funny Folks* (London), Saturday 22 October 1881: 330). The connection with the later practice of Nazi, Soviet and more recent governments will be obvious to most.

129 Guiteau, 1882: 136.

130 Beard, 1882: 21–2.

131 Edmunds, 1882: 226.

132 Quoted in *Funny Folks*, Saturday 17 December 1881: 394.

133 *Funny Folks*, Saturday 24 December 1881: 406; *Judy* (London), Wednesday 25 January 1882: 46.

134 Guiteau, 1882: 1536–7.

135 Clark, 1993: 128.

136 *Washington Post*, 25 November 1881.

137 Though Scoville did not put the matter in these terms. Indeed given his family involvement with the prisoner, he seems to have been rather dispassionate about his approach to the case (see 'A Talk With Mr Scoville', *New York Times*, 5 October 1881: 5).

138 Moran, 1981; Moran, 1985: 37–9.

139 *The Times*, 4 April 1882, issue 30472: 6.

140 The belief that Guiteau was a 'rejected placeman' spread quickly. See the array of comments collected in 'The Press on the Attempted Assassination of President Garfield', *Pall Mall Gazette* (London), 4 July 1881, issue 5103, and 'The Irish in America', *Friend of India & Statesman* (Calcutta), 26 September 1881: 1008: 'Guiteau's act was so obviously a result of the present pernicious system that even the professional politicians lacked the courage to say a single additional word in favor of it, lest they should be suspected of palliating the crime which had thrown a nation into mourning'.

141 Rosenberg, 1968: ix.

142 Caplan, 1984: 31.

143 Rosenberg, 1968: 53.

144 Channing, 1902: 16–17.

145 Quoted in *Sporting Times* (London), Saturday 6 August 1881: 7.

146 Walker, 1968: 89; John B. Chapin, entry on 'America', in Tuke, 1892: Vol. 1, 89.

147 Paraphrased from Kirkham, 1970: 89–90.

148 John B. Chapin, in Tuke, 1892: Vol. 1, 90.

149 Rosenberg, 1968: 54.

150 Ibid.: 55.

151 Clark, 1993: 136.

152 *The Times*, 20 December 1881: 9.

153 See Rosenberg, 1968.

154 Evidence of Dr Fordyce Barker, quoted in the *Washington Post*, 19 December 1881; also from the evidence of Walter Kempster, superintendent at the Northern Hospital for the Insane in Wisconsin (Guiteau, 1882: 1540).

155 Savage, 1881: 153.

156 Tuke, 1891: 116.

157 Ellis, 1882: 11–17; Beard, 1882: 16–18.

158 Rosenberg, 1968: 57.

159 Essay by Dr Charles Folsom, included in Ellis, 1882: 34.

160 Charles Folsom in Ellis, 1882: 37–8.

161 See Elwell et al., 1882: 2; quote from *The Lancet* from Elwell et al., 1882: 8.

162 This argument derives from the ideas presented in Mackay, 1995: 81–6.

163 Ray, 1838: 36–7.

164 Fingarette and Hasse, 1979: 223.

165 Adams, 1931: 166.

166 *The Times*, 1 July 1882: 7.

167 Ibid.

CHAPTER 5: A Killing in the Park

1 Buckle, 1926a: 466.
2 Short, 1979: 9; Foster, 1989: 394.
3 Kee, 2000: 347.
4 *The Times*, 14 December 1867: 6.
5 Buckle, 1926a: 478.
6 Ibid.: 479.
7 Ibid.: 480.
8 Ibid.: 484.
9 Ibid.
10 Eversley, 1912: 82.
11 *Davitt*, 1890: 338. The spy Major Henri Le Caron (more correctly, and prosaically, known as Thomas Billis Beach) recorded that a couple of years later, Parnell told him that 'he had long since ceased to believe that anything but the force of arms would accomplish the final redemption of Ireland' (Le Caron, 1893: 175). This claim has been much disputed, as it would make Parnell's attempts to change things by constitutional means futile, hypocritical or intentionally deceptive. In the late 1880s, letters forged by Richard Pigott, a blackmailer, were printed in *The Times* in an attempt to besmirch Parnell's reputation and expose him as a proponent of violence. Le Caron offered impressive evidence at the subsequent government investigation into the matter, but no direct link between Parnell and terrorist tactics was proved.
12 *The Times*, 19 May 1868: 5.
13 The article was reprinted in *The Times*, 4 March 1872: 8.
14 Ibid.
15 Buckle, 1926b: 199.
16 Ibid.: 201.
17 Cannadine, 1996: 56.
18 Eversley, 1912: 98.
19 Foster, 1989: 293.
20 Paraphrased from Eversley, 1912: 116.
21 Morley, 1903: 49.
22 *The Times*, Wednesday 29 September 1880: 8.
23 *Annual Register*, 1881: 97.
24 Ibid.: 104.
25 Or, at least, so it was reported in *The Times*, Thursday 30 September 1880: 6.
26 Buckle, 1928: 222–3.
27 As reported by Patrick McIntyre, an Ulster policeman in London, in 'Scotland Yard. Its Mysteries and Methods', *Reynold's Newspaper*, Sunday 10 March 1895.
28 As quoted in Adams, 1903: 564; O'Donovan Rossa, 2004: 389–90.
29 McGee, 2007: 81–2.
30 Ibid.
31 Kenny, 2007: 290.
32 Murphy, 1980: 111.
33 'The Irish in America', *Friend of India & Statesman* (Calcutta), Monday 26 September 1881: 1008.
34 Reported in the *Bristol Mercury and Daily Post*, 16 September 1881, and also in *Trewman's Exeter Flying Post or Plymouth and Cornish Advertiser* (Exeter), 21 September 1881.

35 *Hampshire Telegraph and Sussex Chronicle* (Portsmouth), 26 October 1881.

36 Reported in *The Times*, 14 January 1881: 10.

37 Stamped 30 March 1881 (HO 144/1537/1).

38 Evidence of Henri Le Caron, at the Special Commission into 'Parnellism and Crime', as reported in *The Times*, 6 February 1889: 6. Le Caron refers to communications within the movement from the later months of 1880.

39 Quoted in Cole, 1984: 117.

40 *The Times*, 16 August 1881: 9.

41 Matthew, 1990: xlv.

42 Morley, 1903: 49.

43 There are strong arguments for considering that in effect the Land Act of 1881 met the tenants' demands in such a way that it signalled the beginning of the end of the power of the Irish land-owning aristocracy (see Cannadine, 1996: 104). The literature of lament for the 'great houses' would consequently begin in earnest over the next decades, ranging from the fiction of Elizabeth Bowen to the poems of W. B. Yeats.

44 On the popular character of the agitation see McGee, 2007: 66.

45 Buckle, 1928: 244.

46 In his 1968 book on the Phoenix Park tragedy, Tom Corfe declares that there are only two sources of information on the Invincibles: the memoir by Patrick Tynan (1894) and contemporary evidence derived from the trials of 1883. He asserts that both sources are compromised and should be taken sceptically. It is in fact best to say that a great deal of what occurred in the Phoenix Park conspiracy is lost to certain knowledge. The confessions used in the trial might naturally be viewed with suspicion. And Tynan's book, certainly, is an odd and self-serving affair. Its writing and publication were probably financed by money provided by the Conservative and Liberal Unionist Party, and covertly passed to Tynan through the auspices of the Home Office (PRO 30/60/13/3). They did so knowing the book would contain both a description of the Phoenix Park murders (they really are the centre of the account) 'and an adverse chapter on Gladstone's Home Rule Bill which could be used politically to show what the extreme party in Irish politics thought of Gladstone's Home Rule Bill' (request for expenses from T. D. Farrall, 3 August 1904, PRO 30/60/13/3). If these documents are taken at face value, they undoubtedly smear Tynan's work. Nonetheless, though I have treated a great deal of the more contentious material in their accounts with scepticism, much of the circumstantial details that Carey confessed and Tynan remembered seem logical, convincing and, in the circumstances, likely. The fact that the information was useful to the British government should not necessarily invalidate it.

47 Corfe, 1968: 138.

48 McGee, 2007: 95–6. Paul Bew quotes Henri Le Caron in a document owned by Peter Rowan, in which Le Caron reports that Luke Dillon had declared that money intended for the Land League had been paid to 'the assassins of Burke and Cavendish, although he doubts if Parnell knew of the affair beforehand, prior to the act, although he says Egan declares that Parnell did know and would neither countenance nor discountenance the perpetration of the act' (Bew, 2007: 336).

49 Carey's statement, HO/144/98/A16380C.

50 Tynan, 1894: 285, 294.

51 Corfe, 1968: 143.

52 Maume, May 1995: 364; Bew, 2007: 335.

53 McGee, 2007: 94–5.

54 Falkiner, 1901: 466–7.

55 Hammond, 1938: 252; McCarthy, 1884: 188. Disputes exist about the actual numbers, and not everyone arrested went to prison, but there is no doubt that the figure of the imprisoned is a high one, at least 600 and perhaps just over a thousand.

56 Hammond, 1938: 253; Bew, 1980: 55.

57 Tynan, 1894: 393.

58 *Annual Register*, 1883: 187.

59 *The Times*, 4 April 1882: 6.

60 *Annual Register*, 1883: 185.

61 Kee, 2000: 381.

62 Corfe, 1968: 157.

63 *The Times*, Tuesday 4 April 1882: 10.

64 Jennings, 1887: 87. Jennings was a political antagonist of Gladstone.

65 Bew, 2007: 332.

66 For the harsher view of Gladstone again see Jennings, 1887: 70ff.

67 Bew, 2007: 330.

68 Hammond, 1938: 263–4, 272.

69 Carey's statement, HO/144/98/A16380C.

70 Bew, 1980: 56–7.

71 O'Brien, 1898: 345.

72 Shannon, 1999: 294.

73 Buckle, 1928: 281.

74 Bew, 2007: 335.

75 Maume, May 1995: 363–4, 367–8. Maume finds Quinn a reliable witness, but has more doubts about Sheridan (see 369).

76 Maume, May 1995: 369; Bew, 2007: 335.

77 O'Donnell, 1910: Vol. 2, 131.

78 Matthew, 1990: 247.

79 Lucy, 1886: 236; Buckle, 1928: 276.

80 Lucy, 1886: 232.

81 O'Brien, 1898: 348. Cowper had in fact been replaced by Spencer before Forster's resignation (Buckle, 1928: 270–4).

82 Jenkins, 1958: 152. It seems unclear if the job was offered both to Porter, as Cavendish believed, and also to Cavendish's older brother, Lord Hartington, or, as Jenkins states, only to Hartington. In either case, Cavendish was not the first choice, though he was still picked over more obviously suitable men. Cavendish suggested that the post go to his brother, but the suggestion was not taken up.

83 Eversley, 1912: 213–14.

84 Eversley, 1912: 214.

85 Bailey, 1927: Vol. 1, 228.

86 Bailey, 1927: Vol. 2, 303.

87 Ibid.: 305.

88 Ibid.: 307.

89 Ibid.: 306–7.

90 Quoted and adapted from Bailey, 1927: Vol. 2, 310.

91 *Irish Times*, Saturday 6 May 1882.

92 'The Man About Town', *County Gentleman: Sporting Gazette and Agricultural Journal* (London), Saturday 6 May 1882: 477.

93 Bailey, 1927: Vol. 1, 314.

94 Brooke, 1981: 59; Matthew, 1990: 252.

95 Carey's statement, HO/144/98/A16380C.

96 Tynan, 1894: 400.

97 Eversley, 1912: 215.

98 O'Brien, 1898: 354.

99 Carey's statement, HO/144/98/A16380C.

100 *The Times*, Monday 19 February 1883: 6.

101 Carey's statement, HO/144/98/A16380C; *Illustrated London News*, 17 February 1883.

102 *Irish Times*, Tuesday 9 May 1882.

103 *Illustrated London News*, 17 February 1883, reports the testimony of Michael Kavanagh that the two men were arm in arm. The same information is given in a letter from Spencer to Gladstone, 7 May 1882, Add.Ms.44308f.217.

104 Again according to Kavanagh's testimony, Brady went from Cavendish to Burke, and gave each in turn their death blow (*Illustrated London News*, 17 February 1883). However, the boy witness, Samuel Jacob, only saw him dispatch Burke; only Burke's throat was severed.

105 Letter from Spencer to Gladstone, 7 May 1882, Add.Ms.44308f.217.

106 Short, 1979: 75–6.

107 O'Brien, 1898: 356.

108 Anderson, 1906: 102.

109 Buckle, 1928: 283.

110 Shannon, 1999: 296 – though Shannon imports a note of scepticism about the veracity of the rumour.

111 Matthew, 1990: 253.

112 Bailey, 1927: Vol. 2, 318.

113 Morley, 1903: 69–70.

114 From the Masterman Papers, material relating to Lady Cavendish at Special Collections, University of Birmingham Library, CFGM 46/3/4: 37.

115 *Annual Register*, 1883: 63–4.

116 Matthew, 1990: 255.

117 Lucy, 1886: 240; Hammond, 1938: 286.

118 Morley, 1903: 69.

119 *The Times*, Thursday 11 May 1882: 6.

120 *Punch* (London), Saturday 13 May 1882: 220.

121 O'Brien, 1898: 357; see also Davitt, 1890: 330–1.

122 McCarthy, 1884: 204; *The Times*, Monday 8 May 1882: 11.

123 For an account of how *The Times* employed government archives and false witnesses to frame Parnell, see O'Callaghan, 2004: 50–4.

124 O'Brien, 1898: 374.

125 See the anecdote on receiving the news on landing in New York in Adams, 1903: 563.

126 Anderson, 1906: 102–3.

127 O'Brien, 1898: 356.

128 McCarthy, 1884: 273.

129 *Belfast News-Letter*, 2nd edn, 8 May 1882.

130 *Ipswich Journal*, 22 July 1882.

131 *Birmingham Daily Post and Journal*, 8 May 1882; *Daily News*, 10 May 1882.

132 See, for instance, *Daily News* (London), 8 May 1882.

133 *Freeman's Journal and Daily Commercial Advertiser* (Dublin), 20 March 1883; *The Times*, 9 May 1882: 6.

134 Short, 1979: 116, 218–19; Adams, 1903: 565.

135 Ellis, 1882.

136 Hammond, 1938: 284; *The Times*, 13 May 1882: 7.

137 Morley, 1903: 69.

138 Davitt, 1890: 351.

139 The quotation comes from a letter to *The Times*, signed 'An Old Whig', 10 May 1882: 5.

140 Matthew, 1990: cxxii.

141 Bew, 1980: 59; Bew, 2007: 337.

142 Matthew, 1995: 203–4.

143 Buckle, 1928: 287.

144 Buckle, 1928: 287.

145 Davitt, 1890: 350.

146 Quoted in Graham, 1998: 7.

147 Morley, 1903: 68.

148 McCarthy, 1884: 202.

149 Trautmann, 1980: 64.

150 See letters relating to Most's treatment in prison in HO 144/77/A3385.

151 Trautmann, 1980: 65.

152 Quoted in *The Times*, 18 May 1882: 11.

153 Letter from Charles Maw, 2 March 1882, in HO 144/A14281/1.

154 See Trautmann, 1980: 71.

155 McCarthy, 1884: 222–3.

156 Venezuelan Consul to Earl Granville, 24 July 1882 (HO 144/98/A16380); *Annual Register*, 1883: 31–2.

157 From 'Scotland Yard', one of a series of articles by Patrick McIntyre, in *Reynold's Newspaper*, Sunday 31 March 1895; see also *Annual Register*, 1884: 193ff.

158 It is, however, possible that both she and her husband were involved in the conspiracy, and are therefore the only, or at least only significant, link between the Invincibles and Parnell. See Corfe, 1968: 137. However, such a connection does not by any means prove that Parnell knew of the plans for the assassinations.

159 On evidence supplied by Peter Johnstone in HO 144/113/A25251.

160 Letter from British Consulate, 23 March 1883, HO 144/113/A25251.

161 HO 144/98/A16380C. He had fled to the USA via France (Maume, May 1995: 365). In a secret memorandum dated 29 January 1884, Robert Anderson refers to Sheridan as 'Sheridan of the "Kilmainham Treaty"' (HO 144/1537/1).

162 HO 144/113.

163 Bew, 2007: 355, 357; Maume, May 1995: 365.

164 PRO 30/60/16.

165 See note 46 to this chapter.

166 *The Times*, 16 September 1896: 7.

167 *The Times*, 16 September 1896: 7; *New York Times*, 22 September 1896: 5; *New York Times*, 4 October 1896: 5.

168 Letter from Balfour, 1896?, PRO 30/60/16.

169 Letter to Balfour from the Law Room, Dublin Castle, 22 September, PRo 30/60/16.

170 *Davitt*, 1890: 352.

171 Testimony of Thomas Francis Carey in CRIM 1/19/4.

172 *The Times*, 2 August 1883: 7.

173 Testimony of James Parish, Thomas Jones and Thomas Francis Carey in CRIM 1/19/4.

174 Testimony of Margaret Carey in CRIM 1/19/4.

175 The paper in question might have been either the *Freeman's Journal* or the *Weekly Freeman*.

176 *The Times*, 1 December 1883: 10.

177 Testimony of James Parish and of Thomas Jones in CRIM 1/19/4; the Careys were travelling steerage, one consequence of which was that men and women slept separately in communal single-sex cabins.

178 Testimony of James Parish and of Thomas Jones in CRIM 1/19/4. An entirely different and very likely erroneous account of the shooting is given in *Reynold's Newspaper*, Sunday 31 March, 1895.

179 Testimony of Thomas Francis Carey in CRIM 1/19/4.

180 By her own testimony she said 'You shot my husband' (CRIM 1/19/4).

181 Testimony of Thomas Jones and Thomas Francis Carey in CRIM 1/19/4. Thomas Jones heard 'I didn't do it'; Thomas Francis Carey and Margaret said that they had heard 'I was sent to do it', though under cross-examination young Carey changed his mind and said that he had either heard 'I didn't do it' or 'I had to do it'. Neither Carey's son nor his wife caught what Mary Gallagher said to O'Donnell.

182 Testimony of Frederick Ensor, district surgeon at Port Elizabeth in CRIM 1/19/4.

183 Testimony of John Cherry, Chief Inspector of Police at Port Elizabeth in CRIM 1/19/4.

184 *The Times*, Wednesday 1 August 1883: 7.

185 *Reynold's Newspaper*, Sunday 31 March 1895.

186 Patrick McIntyre, 'Scotland Yard. Its Mysteries and Methods', *Reynold's Newspaper*, Sunday 17 March 1895.

187 From *The Citizen* (Chicago), 22 December 1883 in HO 144/1/1537/1.

188 McCarthy, 1884: 281–2; Vizetelly, 1911: 85.

189 *The Times*, 15 August 1887: 6; 16 August 1887: 3; 18 August 1887: 3; 18 August 1887: 7.

190 See, for instance, 'The Dynamite Danger', *The Spectator*, 24 March 1883: 382–3; 'The Fear of Dynamite', *The Spectator*, 14 April 1883: 477–8; and 'Dynamite', *Cornhill Magazine* (London: Smith, Elder & Co., 1884): Vol. 3, 273–91.

191 'The Dynamite Plot', *Saturday Review*, Vol. 55, 14 April 1883: 1.

192 Adams, 1931: 163–4.

CHAPTER 6: Frick's Gallery

1 These opening paragraphs derive from the account of the incident given in Burton J. Hendrick, 'shooting of Henry Clay Frick', Berkman Papers, B104, IISH. Some supplementary details are drawn from Sanger, 1998, and one particular fact, the striking of the assailant with a hammer, is here, a little prematurely, brought in from Berkman's own account. See note 66, below, for more details on the sources for the description of the shooting of Frick.

2 Sanger, 1998: 201.

3 Ibid., 210.

4 The eldest was a boy, Childs; the younger girl, Helen, was born in 1888.

5 Josephson, 1962: 260–1.

6 Sanger, 2001: 9.

7 Ibid.

8 Ibid.: 23.

9 In a letter, after hearing news of the death of her brother, Goldman writes: 'dearest, I have no pleasant recollections about my brother Herman. In our childhood he only caused me many beatings for pranks he had committed and had shoved on me' (letter from Emma Goldman to 'Emmchen', February 1935, Berkman Papers, B359, IISH).

10 'Emma Goldman in Law's Grasp', *Chicago Daily Tribune*, 11 September 1901: 3, IISH, EG Papers, Reel 47, 880623019.

11 Passenger Manifest, 29 December 1885, Goldman Papers, IISH, Reel 56, 870706000.

12 Examination of Emma Goldman before Board of Special Inquiry, government transcript, Bureau of Immigration, Department of Commerce and Labor, 8 April 1908, IISH, EG Papers, Reel 56, 830214014.

13 Ibid.

14 EG Papers, FBI Files for Emma Goldman's Deportation Proceedings, report by F. M. Sturgis, for 2–5 December 1919.

15 'Emma Goldman in Law's Grasp', *Chicago Daily Tribune*, 11 September 1901: 3, IISH, EG Papers, Reel 47, 880623019.

16 The German-born John Peter Altgeld would soon afterwards become the Democratic Governor of Illinois, in which position he would resist the successful attempt by President Cleveland to put a violent end to the 1894 Pullman strike (Jones, 1995: 314; Milkis, 2008: 199). That neutral body of men, the Supreme Court, found that the President had behaved entirely constitutionally (Zinn, 2003: 260).

17 Goldman, 1931: Vol. 1, 42.

18 Ibid.: 5–6.

19 Berkman, 1926: 236–7.

20 Carlson, 1972: 254–5.

21 Ibid.: 267.

22 Goldman, 1931: Vol. 1, 6.

23 Berkman, outline of 'An Enemy of Society. Autobiography of Alexander Berkman', November 1932, Berkman Papers, B218, IISH.

24 Ibid.

25 Berkman suggests that this move was enforced upon them because of anti-Semitic regulations operating in the capital (Berkman, outline of 'An Enemy of Society. Autobiography of Alexander Berkman', November 1932, Berkman Papers, B218, IISH).

26 Letter 25 June 1897, EG to Augustin Hamon, IISH, EG Papers, Reel 1, 890128064.

27 Berkman, 'Women I Have Known', Berkman Papers, B237, IISH.

28 Berkman, outline of 'An Enemy of Society. Autobiography of Alexander Berkman', November 1932, Berkman Papers, B218, IISH.

29 Berkman, 'Women I Have Known', Berkman Papers, B237, IISH.

30 Letter 25 June 1897, EG to Augustin Hamon, IISH, EG Papers, Reel 1, 890128064.

31 Berkman, 1926: 56.

32 'He told me about the famous Russian revolutionary catechism that demanded of the true revolutionist that he give up home, parents, sweetheart, children, everything dear to one's being. He agreed with it absolutely and he was determined to allow nothing to stand in the way' (Goldman, 1931: Vol. 1, 46).

33 Letter 25 June 1897, EG to Augustin Hamon, IISH, EG Papers, Reel 1, 890128064.

34 Goldman, 1931: Vol. 1, 43.

35 Berkman, 1926: 201–3.

36 See Josiah Strong, 'Why America is Particularly Vulnerable to Socialism' (1885), in Davis, 1971: 169–76.

37 Examination of Emma Goldman before Board of Special Inquiry, government transcript, Bureau of Immigration, Department of Commerce and Labor, 8 April 1908, IISH, EG Papers, Reel 56, 830214014: 7.

38 They longed to bring Kropotkin over from his new home in London to speak at a meeting of the Jewish Anarchists at Orchard Hall, and began saving money, from the very little that they earned, so they could do so. But Kropotkin could not come, as he was too poor to pay for himself, and unwilling to be paid for by his comrades. See 'Reminiscences of Peter Kropotkin', January 1922, Berkman Papers, B180, IISH.

39 Zinn, 2003: 254.

40 Josephson, 1962: 45–6, 37, 41; Jones, 1995: 305.

41 Zinn, 2003: 255.

42 Phillips, 2002: 36, 39–40.

43 Carnegie, June 1889; Josephson, 1962: 105–6.

44 Williams, 1966: 350; Zinn, 2003: 261.

45 Jones, 1995: 306.

46 Williams, 1966: 325.

47 Green, 1987: 23–37.

48 *The Commonweal*, 19 March 1892.

49 Sanger, 1998: 169.

50 Warren, 1996: 64–5.

51 McPherson, 1998: 361.

52 *The Times*, Thursday 7 July 1892: 5.

53 Berkman, 1926: 1.

54 Berkman, 'Autobiographische Skizzen', in Berkman Papers, B96: 10, IISH. Translated by the author.

55 Ibid.: 10–11.

56 Ibid.: 11–12.

57 Goldman, 1931: Vol. 1, 31.

58 Berkman, 1926: 9–10.

59 Letter 25 June 1897, EG to Augustin Hamon, IISH, EG Papers, Reel 1, 890128064.

60 Berkman, 1926: 180.

61 Ibid.: 5–6.

62 '"I won't call employers despots, I won't call them tyrants," remarked one steelworker, "but the term capitalist is sort of synonymous and will do as well"', quoted in Williams, 1966: 315.

63 Berkman, 1926: 7.

64 Ibid.: 7–8.

65 In *History of the Great American Fortunes*, the following is quoted from 'The Pittsburg Survey': 'One-third of all who die in Pittsburg, die without having anything to say about it. That is, they die under five years of age. One-fourth of all who die, die without having anything to say about anything. That is, they die under one year of age. Most of these deaths are preventable, being the outcome of conditions which, humanly speaking, have no right to exist' (Myers, 1936: 618).

66 Berkman, 1926: 33–5. Berkman's account should be compared with the one which opens this chapter, which is drawn from sources close to Frick. The discrepancies between the two versions of events are all of interest, and mostly unresolvable. Frick's

friends and family assert his courage and Berkman's heinousness. In contrast to Frick's supposed 'cowardice', Berkman stresses his iron will. Berkman's version omits the firing of the second bullet that wounded Frick, something which certainly happened. Perhaps the shooting of the man at close range while he was on the ground was too distressing, or compromising, for him to recall. Goldman believed that the dagger was to be poisoned; Berkman himself makes no mention of this.

67 'A Convict's Memoirs', Berkman Papers, B161, IISH.

68 'Berkman Had Nitro-Glycerin in his Mouth', 24 September 1901, unidentified newspaper clipping, Berkman Papers, B101, IISH.

69 Berkman, 1926: 69.

70 Ibid.: 45.

71 Ibid.: 48.

72 Ibid.: 55.

73 Ibid.: 57.

74 Ibid.: 59.

75 Ibid.: 66.

76 Goldman, 1931: Vol. 1, 91–5.

77 Carlson, 1972: 279.

78 Oerter's political career would see him imprisoned for possession of explosives; he later became the Social Democrat prime minister of Brunswick in 1920–1, before ending up in his last years as a Nazi.

79 This last incident is a paraphrased version of Interview, etc, 'Anarchy's Den', *The World*, Thursday 28 July 1892, IISH, EG Papers, Reel 47, 881014019.

80 'Who Will Thrash Mr. Most?', *The World*, Friday 29 July 1892: 3, IISH, EG Papers, Reel 47, 881014020.

81 Interview etc., 'Anarchy's Den', *The World*, Thursday 28 July 1892, IISH, EG Papers, Reel 47, 881014019.

82 'Who Will Thrash Mr. Most?', *The World*, Friday 29 July 1892: 3, IISH, EG Papers, Reel 47, 881014020.

83 'Wild Anarchist Talk', *New York Times*, 2 August 1892, IISH, EG Papers, Reel 47.

84 'They Talked a Great Deal', unidentified newspaper, 2 August 1892, IISH, EG Papers, Reel 47.

85 'Wild Anarchist Talk', *New York Times*, 2 August 1892, IISH, EG Papers, Reel 47.

86 *The Commonweal*, Saturday 30 July 1892: Vol. 7, No. 324: 1.

87 Josephson, 1962: 371.

88 Ward, 1999: xxii.

89 Berkman, 1926: 59–60.

90 *The Nation*, 28 July 1892: Vol. 55, No. 1413: 60.

91 Goldman, 1931: Vol. 1, 105–6.

92 Berkman, 1926: 100–3.

CHAPTER 7: The Years Between

1 Examination of Emma Goldman before Board of Special Inquiry, government transcript, Bureau of Immigration, Department of Commerce and Labor, 8 April 1908, IISH, EG Papers, Reel 56, 830214014: 1. The Government, Secret Service and FBI papers on Goldman generally spell Goldman's husband's name as 'Kersner', as

here; however Goldman herself writes of him as Kershner. They had never divorced, because, it was rumoured, Kershner had always remained in love with Goldman.

2 Josephson, 1962: 418–20.

3 Garland, June 1894; Warren, 1996: 111–12.

4 Vizetelly, 1911: 189.

5 James, 1987: 34.

6 Berkman, 'Statement', 7 October 1919, IISH, Berkman Papers, B118.

7 Sanger, 1998: 201–3.

8 Berkman, 1926: 108–9.

9 These notes were however written much later, most likely on Sunday 27 March 1904, IISH, Berkman Papers, B94.

10 Alexander Berkman to Emma Goldman, Western Penitentiary, 19 October 1892, IISH, Berkman Papers, B95.

11 Berkman, 1926: 141.

12 Ibid.: 133.

13 Ibid.: 183–4.

14 Ibid.: 221.

15 Berkman, 'Eine americanische gerichts-Farce', IISH, Berkman Papers, B96.

16 Ibid.

17 Either Berkman's ability to calculate was as poor as his aim with a gun, or he was trying to convey how time shuffled on in prison; there are 31,536,000 seconds in a year.

18 Berkman, 1926: 234.

19 Berkman, 1926: 263. Berkman certainly contemplated homosexual intercourse in prison, and very likely did more than that. In a handwritten review of his sexual life, composed in 1932 or afterwards, he wrote: 'In Prison – boys or girls?' (Berkman, 'Women I Have Known', IISH, Berkman Papers, B237). An undated letter from Edward Carpenter to Berkman shows the kind of interest a homosexual, or 'Uranian', could take in Berkman's *Prison Memoirs*: 'There are in your book cameos describing how romantic friendships may be and are formed & sustained even in the midst of the most depressing & dispiriting conditions' (IISH, Berkman Papers, B12).

20 IISH, Berkman Papers, B93.

21 Ibid.

22 'Random Thoughts, Original and Otherwise', IISH, Berkman Papers, B115.

23 Ibid.

24 Berkman, 1926: 342.

25 'Reminiscences of Peter Kropotkin', January 1922, IISH, Berkman Papers, B180.

26 Berkman, 1926: 399.

27 Goldman, 1931: Vol. 1, 111.

28 Letter from Emma Goldman, to *The Firebrand* (Portland: Oregon), 21 July 1895, IISH, EG Papers, Reel 1, 87111700.

29 'Nellie Bly Again', *The World*, 17 September 1893, IISH, EG Papers, Reel 47.

30 'Only the Moral Law', *The World*, 7 October 1893, IISH, EG Papers, Reel 47.

31 *People of New York* v. *Emma Goldman*, trial transcript, 4 October 1893, Goldman Papers, IISH, Reel 56, 870508001.

32 'Emma Goldman's Beliefs', *New York Daily Tribune*, 7 October 1893, IISH, EG Papers, Reel 47, 880722003.

33 Goldman, 1931: Vol. 1, 146.

34 'Emma Goldman in London', *Liberty*, October 1895, Vol. 2, No. 22: 173–4, IISH, EG

Papers, Reel 47, 880805006.

35 'A Woman Anarchist', *Pittsburg[h] Leader*, 22 November 1896, IISH, EG Papers, Reel 47.

36 'Joy at the Death of Canovas', *New York Times*, 17 August 1897, IISH, EG Papers, Reel 47; 'Anarchy in Spain and in New York', *The World*, 17 August 1897, IISH, EG Papers, Reel 47.

37 Goldman, 1931: Vol. 1, 190.

38 'Anarchy in Spain and in New York', *The World*, 17 August 1897, IISH, EG Papers, Reel 47.

39 'Anarchy Her Theme', *St Louis Post-Dispatch*, 17 October 1897, IISH, EG Papers, Reel 47.

40 'Emma Goldman, Anarchist', *San Francisco Call*, 27 April 1898, IISH, EG Papers, Reel 47.

41 *The Times*, 19 September 1898: 4.

42 *The World* (New York), 18 September 1898, IISH, EG Papers, Reel 1, 891207004.

43 'Her Comrades Rebuke Emma Goldman', *New York Tribune*, 23 August 1897, IISH, EG Papers, Reel 47.

44 See letter from Benjamin Tucker, *Liberty*, 7 December 1898: 8, IISH, EG papers, Reel 1, 900103002.

CHAPTER 8: Shooting the President

1 'Miss Emma Goldman, in my opinion, is – how does one say it in French – an apostle, yes, an apostle.' The American dancer Loie Fuller, in an interview with *Le Figaro*, 25 September 1901, IISH, EG Papers, Reel 67, 910620036.

2 'Defends Acts of Bomb Throwers', *Cleveland Plain Dealer*, 6 May 1901, IISH, EG Papers, Reel 47, 890221000.

3 Goldman, 1931: Vol. 1, 290–1.

4 Ibid.: 291.

5 Drinnon, 1982: 71.

6 Paraphrased from Goldman, 1931: Vol. 1, 292.

7 Goldman, 1931: Vol. 1, 292–5.

8 Adams, 1999: 297.

9 Ibid.: 312.

10 On the popular supposition that Hanna controlled McKinley, as though he were 'a monkey on a string', see Morgan, 1963: 185. The origins of the image appear to have been the cartoons of Homer Davenport as drawn for William Randolph Hearst's *New York Journal*; Hearst was a consistent critic of McKinley (Russell, 1976: 1). Herman H. Kohlsatt remarked 'that Hanna's attitude toward McKinley was "always that of a big, bashful boy toward the girl he loves," a story that Hanna liked and repeated' (ibid.).

11 Green, 1987: 45.

12 Williams, 1966: 335, 360–1.

13 Jones, 1964, 103; Russell, 1976: 12, 15, 21.

14 Russell, 1976: 18.

15 Glad, 1964: 96–7.

16 Rauchway, 2003: 33.

17 Jones, 1995: 363–4; Milkis, 2008: 200–1.

18 John T. Flynn from *Scribner's* (1936), quoted in Russell, 1976: 18.

19 White, 1946: 335.

20 After William Howard Taft hesitated to accept a post in the Commission for the Philippines, on the grounds that the USA should not be in control of those islands, 'McKinley reportedly answered, "You don't want them any less than I do, but we have got them and in dealing with them I think I can trust the man who didn't want them better than the man who did"' (Graubard, 2009: 129).

21 Russell, 1976: 35; 'Adams knew no one in the United States fit to manage these matters in the face of a hostile Europe, and had no candidate to propose; but he was shocked beyond all restraints of expression to learn that the President meant to put Senator John Sherman in the State Department to make a place for Mr. Hanna in the Senate . . . John Sherman, otherwise admirably fitted for the place, a friendly influence of nearly forty years, was notoriously feeble and quite senile, so that the intrigue seemed to Adams the betrayal of an old friend as well as that of the State Department' (Adams, 1999: 298).

22 Malone, 1946: XV, 138.

23 Kipling, 1987: 105. The Upper's name was John D. Long.

24 Malone, 1946: XV, 137.

25 Quoted in Milkis, 2008: 210.

26 Morgan, 1963: 517.

27 Barry, 1901: 5.

28 Fine, 1955: 777.

29 'the city and Exposition officials had arranged for city policemen, Exposition guards, Pinkerton detectives, and a small detachment of artillerymen to assist the Secret Service in guarding the President' (Sherman, November 1983: 1–2).

30 *Annual Report*, 1902: 1.

31 Leech, 1959: 586.

32 Day, 1901: 428–35.

33 Thomas Edison's company filmed the President's speech and the Exposition; some of the visual references in this chapter refer to images preserved in these films. The film of the speech was copyrighted on 11 September 1901 while the President lay wounded, but apparently on the road to recovery.

34 Barry, 1901: 8.

35 Johns, 1970: 90.

36 'Czolgosz Trial', 1901: 10.

37 Barry, 1901: 10.

38 Johns, 1970: 89–90.

39 'Czolgosz Trial', 1901: 76.

40 Ibid.: 96.

41 Ibid.: 71, 82, 91, 96.

42 Barry, 1901: 22; Johns, 1970: 89. In some accounts of this moment, it is Geary, a detective, who pulls Czolgosz down and Parker who punches him. See, for instance, Johns, 1970: 94. 'Czolgosz Trial', 1901: 71.

43 'Czolgosz Trial', 1901: 51, 56.

44 When his autopsy was conducted his nose still showed the impact of the blow (Spitzka, 1902: 387).

45 'Czolgosz Trial', 1901: 101.

46 Ibid.: 50, 55.

47 'Latest Intelligence', *The Times*, Saturday 7 September 1901: 5.

48 Barry, 1901: 25.

49 'Czolgosz Trial', 1901: 101.

50 Ibid.: 51.

51 Wilson, 1901: 207.

52 'Czolgosz Trial', 1901: 30.

53 Ibid.: 77.

54 'Official Report', 1901: 271.

55 'Czolgosz Trial', 1901: 21.

56 Wilson, 1901: 209.

57 Park, 1914: 376.

58 Parmenter, 1901: 205–6.

59 'Official Report', 1901: 275.

60 Wilson, 1901: 212; Park, 1914: 379.

61 Wilson, 1901: 212.

62 'Official Report', 1901: 275. This information is drawn from remarks made by the leading surgeon in the operation, Dr Matthew D. Mann.

63 Park, 1914: 377–8.

64 The bullet was never found, not even at the President's autopsy, which was ended prematurely out of respect for the dead man. See 'Official Report', 1901: 287.

65 Abbott, 2008: 82.

66 Johns, 1970: 96; 'Czolgosz Trial', 1901: 108.

67 'Emma Goldman, High Priestess of Anarchy, Whose Speeches Inspired Czolgosz to his Crime', *Chicago Daily Tribune*, 8 September 1901, IISH, EG Papers, Reel 47.

68 *Annual Report*, 1902: 2; it is also claimed that he told them that he was born in Alpena, Michigan, in 1873, and then moved to Detroit when he was five (Channing, 1902: 259). Elsewhere in his article, Channing quotes an interview with Czolgosz's family, in which the order of the Czolgosz family residences is given as follows: 'They lived in the following places in Michigan: Detroit City seven years, Rogers City six months, Alpena five years, Posen five years, Natrona near Pittsburg, Pa, nearly two years' (Channing, 1902: 237). For more detail on Czolgosz's birthplace and other family matters see note 138, below.

69 *Annual Report*, 1902: 2; 'Latest Intelligence', *The Times*, Saturday 7 September 1901: 5; 'Czolgosz Trial', 1901: 103, 108.

70 'Czolgosz Trial', 1901: 59. In his excellent book on the case, Rauchway notes that the evidence regarding the interrogation of Czolgosz is questionable. There are perhaps as many as six hours unaccounted for from Czolgosz's arrest to the signing of the statement in the presence of Quackenbush and Penney, and therefore suspicions may arise that some of the assassin's testimony was suppressed, concocted or beaten out of him (Rauchway, 2003: 29–32).

71 Testimony of James Quackenbush, 'Czolgosz Trial', 1901: 63.

72 'Trial of Czolgosz', *The Times*, Wednesday 25 September 1901: 3; 'Czolgosz Trial', 1901: 64.

73 IISH, EG Papers, Department of Justice letter signed by agent M. F. Blackman, October 1919.

74 'Czolgosz Trial', 1901: 61.

75 *Annual Report*, 1902: 2.

76 MacDonald, 1902: 379–80; Spitzka, 1902: 389.

77 Channing, 1902: 258.

78 Rauchway, 2003: 42.

79 Drinnon, 1982: 71.

80 Ibid.

81 Thomas I. Porter, Daily Report of Agent, Secret Service, Chicago District, 17 September 1901, IISH, EG Papers, Reel 56, 850401040.

82 'Latest Intelligence', *The Times*, Monday 9 September 1901: 3.

83 *Annual Report*, 1902: 4.

84 Some reports say no one visited him that day but his wife.

85 Park, 1914: 379.

86 'Latest Intelligence', *The Times*, Wednesday 11 September 1901: 3.

87 John E. Murphy, Daily Report of Agent, Secret Service, St Louis District, 9 September 1901, IISH, EG Papers, Reel 56, 850401031.

88 Thomas I. Porter, Daily Report of Agent, Secret Service, Chicago District, 10 September 1901: 1, IISH, EG Papers, Reel 56, 850401036.

89 Ibid.: 2.

90 Goldman, 1931: Vol. 1, 297.

91 Ibid.: 298–9.

92 Schuettler had been active in the investigations following the Haymarket bomb, and had helped the New York police find Adoph Luetgert, a Chicago sausage manufacturer who murdered his wife and then dissolved her in acid in his factory. Schuettler later became Chief of the Chicago Police Department (Herman F. Schuettler, 'How Anarchy Should be Watched', *Chicago Sunday Tribune*, 15 September 1901: 13; 'Luetgert Case in New York', *New York Times*, 4 August 1897: 3; 'Chicago Police Chief Schuettler', *New York Times*, 23 August 1918: 9).

93 Goldman, 1931: Vol. 1, 299–300.

94 'Latest Intelligence', *The Times*, Wednesday 11 September 1901: 3.

95 'Emma Goldman in Jail Charged With Conspiracy', *The World*, 11 September 1901, IISH, EG Papers, Reel 47, 890118004.

96 Goldman, 1931: Vol. 1, 300.

97 'Emma Goldman in Law's Grasp', *Chicago Daily Tribune*, 11 September 1901, IISH, EG Papers, Reel 47, 880623019.

98 Ibid.

99 Photograph of Emma Goldman, September 1901?, IISH, EG Papers, Reel 56, 810807029; photographs of Emma Goldman, September 1901, IISH, EG Papers, Reel 56, 830214083.

100 Police Record of Emma Goldman, printed in the New York *World*, 15 September 1901, IISH, EG Papers, Reel 56, 881012019.

101 'Czolgosz Trial', 1901: 110–11. Rauchway presents a friend of Czolgosz's from Cleveland named Nowak, a printer, who confronted his 'old friend' in a prison visit; this man also appears to have joined in the police investigation, and even to have taken part, as we see here, in the questioning of Goldman in Chicago – unless there was another Nowak, a policeman, in the story (Rauchway, 2003: 25–6). To add to the confusion around this matter, Czolgosz's landlord at the time of the shooting was also named (John) Nowak.

102 'Emma Goldman in Law's Grasp', *Chicago Daily Tribune*, 11 September 1901: 3, IISH, EG Papers, Reel 47, 880623019.

103 Goldman, 1931: Vol. 1, 271–2.

104 'Emma Goldman in Law's Grasp', *Chicago Daily Tribune*, 11 September 1901: 3, IISH, EG Papers, Reel 47, 880623019.

105 Ibid.

106 George W. Hazen, Daily Report of Agent, Secret Service, San Francisco District, 23 September 1901, IISH, EG Papers, Reel 56, 850401029.

107 Thomas I. Porter, Daily Report of Agent, Secret Service, Chicago District, 17 September 1901, IISH, EG Papers, Reel 56, 850401040.

108 William J. Flynn, Daily Report of Agent, Secret Service, New York District, 17 September 1901, IISH, EG Papers, Reel 56, 850401018.

109 John E. Murphy, Daily Report of Agent, Secret Service, St Louis District, 19 September 1901, IISH, EG Papers, Reel 56, 850401033.

110 Goldman, 1931: Vol. 1, 302.

111 Hearst had been attacking McKinley on the basis that he himself would run for President come the next election.

112 Goldman, 1931: Vol. 1, 306.

113 'Emma Goldman in Law's Grasp', *Chicago Daily Tribune*, 11 September 1901: 1, IISH, EG Papers, Reel 47, 880623019.

114 Goldman, 1931: Vol. 1, 301.

115 'Government to Put the Reds Behind Bars', *The World*, 11 September 1901: 1, IISH, EG Papers, Reel 47, 890118004.

116 'Latest Intelligence', *The Times*, Wednesday 11 September 1901: 3.

117 Goldman, 1931: Vol. 1, 313.

118 See, for instance, 'Assassination of President McKinley', 1901: 226–8.

119 'Roosevelt's View of Czolgosz's Crime', *The World*, 11 September 1901: 1, IISH, EG Papers, Reel 47, 890118004.

120 Paine, 1917: 2, 715–16.

121 Fine, 1955: 785–6.

122 Trautmann, 1980: 214.

123 Morton, 1992: 38; IISH, EG Papers, FBI files relating to deportation proceedings against Goldman, report by Agent V. P. Crighton, Buffalo, NY, 18 October 1919.

124 This information is drawn from 'Official Report', 1901: 277–84 and Wilson, 1901: 222–4.

125 Morris, 2001: 3.

126 Johns, 1970: 157.

127 Wilson, 1901: 207.

128 White, 1946: 336. His wife and one of his physicians heard his last words to be those of the hymn 'Nearer, My God, to Thee' (Johns, 1970: 162).

129 Parmenter, 1901: 224–5.

130 Leech, 1959: 601; Morris, 2001: 7.

131 Milkis, 2008: 210.

132 Adams, 1999: 349.

133 *Annual Report*, 1902: 4.

134 Adams, 1999: 307.

135 Barry, 1901: 16.

136 Morton, 1992: 39.

137 'Czolgosz Trial', 1901: 69.

138 The Census information regarding Czolgosz's birthplace is doubtful. In the 1880 United States Federal Census, for District 7, Alpena, Michigan, on 10–11 June 1880,

the family records for the 'Chandgas' family match closely but not exactly with what is known of Leon Czolgosz's family. Here one 'Louis Chandgas' might be a garbled version of Leon Czolgosz. His place of birth is given as 'Michigan'. The 1900 United States Federal Census, for District 229 [Warrensville], Cuyohoga, Ohio, on 9–11 June 1900, gives information regarding a 'Czolgaez' family. We know that the Czolgosz family were living in this area, and the details again fit some of what we know about the Czolgoszes, though with intriguing discrepancies concerning some family names and dates. Here Leon's birthplace is given as Ohio, while all the siblings listed here are said to have been born in Michigan. (Leon was certainly the first of his family to have been born in the United States.)

Equally confused is the matter of Leon's parents' birthplace; in 1880 for the Chandgas family, it is listed in both cases as Poland; in 1900 for the Czolgaez family, in both cases as Germany. This may be because only the second of these families is actually the Czolgosz family, or, as likely, it reflects the slippery nature of national identity in the east of Europe at this time: outside the census records, Czolgosz's father is described in contemporary sources as being both Prussian and Polish. Some respondents to the Census recorded their place of birth as being 'Poland Ger[many]' or 'Poland Russ[ia]'. Leon Czolgosz himself is cited as describing his mother as German and his father as Polish. If the Chandgas family are the Czolgoszes, then the adoption of that new name either records the inability of the census-taker to understand the 'unpronounceable' Polish, or the desire of new immigrants to Americanise themselves.

139 Information derived from 1900 United States Federal Census, for District 229, Cuyohoga, Ohio, 9–11 June 1900.

140 Ibid.; Leech, 1959: 592–3.

141 Channing, 1902: 245–6, 251, 240.

142 Channing, 1902: 241–3; Leech, 1959: 593.

143 Channing, 1902: 240.

144 Leech, 1959: 593.

145 'When asked why he took the name of Nieman, he said because it was his mother's name. Later he said his own mother's name was Niebock, which in German was Nieman' (Channing, 1902: 259).

146 Thomas I. Porter, Daily Report of Agent, Secret Service, Chicago District, 17 September 1901, IISH, EG Papers, Reel 56, 850401040.

147 'Czolgosz Trial', 1901: 59–60, 105.

148 Johns, 1970: 90.

149 Accounts vary as to whether Jim Parker was before or behind Czolgosz in the line to meet the President.

150 Johns, 1970: 90–4.

151 'Czolgosz Trial', 1901: 76.

152 Goldman, 1931: Vol. 1, 307.

153 From Emma Goldman, 'The Tragedy at Buffalo', reprinted from *Free Society*, October 1901, in *Mother Earth*, Vol. 1, No. 8 (October 1906): 11, IISH, EG Papers, Reel 47, 890419011.

154 Goldman, 1931: Vol. 1, 313.

155 Emma Goldman, 'The Tragedy at Buffalo', reprinted from *Free Society*, October 1901, in *Mother Earth*, Vol. 1, No. 8 (October 1906): 13, IISH, EG Papers, Reel 47, 890419011.

156 Ibid.

157 Emma Goldman, 'Excerpt from Lecture, "Anarchism is not Necessarily Violence"', police transcript, 6 January 1907, IISH, EG Papers, Reel 47, 891002001.

158 Emma Goldman, 'The Tragedy at Buffalo', reprinted from *Free Society*, October 1901, in *Mother Earth*, Vol. 1, No. 8 (October 1906): 14, IISH, EG Papers, Reel 47, 890419011.

159 Ibid.

160 Ibid.

161 Trautmann, 1980: 213; Drinnon, 1982: 73.

162 Trautmann, 1980: 225–6.

163 'Muth Knows, but Cannot Give Proof', unidentified newspaper clipping, Berkman Papers, B101, IISH.

164 Dr B. Rubin, Letter to E. D. Crumpacker, House of Representatives, in the Records of the Department of Justice, 11 September 1901, IISH, EG Papers, Reel 56, 810813013.

165 Berkman, 1926: 413–17.

166 See Ward, 1999: xxiii.

167 'Czolgosz Trial', 1901: 4. 'The law is so merciful of the rights of its citizens that it will not permit a man to plead guilty of the high crime of murder, so that even after he had conceded his guilt in this case, it was incumbent upon the court to insist that the trial should proceed, and that the People should establish, beyond a reasonable doubt, that the defendant was guilty of the crime charged against him' – speech of defence counsel, Loran Lewis, 'Czolgosz Trial', 1901: 114.

168 'Czolgosz Trial', 1901: 60–1, 106.

169 MacDonald, 1902: 370–1, 383–4.

170 MacDonald, 1902: 378–82. In the next volume of the same journal where MacDonald published his conclusions, Walter Channing, a doctor, expressed his doubts about Czolgosz's supposed sanity. However, he did so by such convincing methods as expressing his subjective opinion of the assassin's photograph ('The general impression is at first sight pleasant, but finally leaves an impression of introspection and cynicalness'), his father's eccentric manner and appearance, his acting 'queerly' for a number of years, his being 'bashful', his eating alone, and the fact that his maternal aunt was insane (Channing, 1902: 235–7, 261–5). He was a '*solitaire*' and 'prone to mysticism' (ibid., 266–7).

171 Rauchway, 2003: 24–5, 47–50; 'Czolgosz Trial', 1901: 114–18. Hugh Brogan dismisses Czolgosz 'as a lunatic of the Booth and Guiteau type' (Brogan, 1999: 449); in fact, his motives seem more gnomic than lunatic.

172 MacDonald, 1902: 371, 374.

173 Johns, 1970: 237.

174 'Czolgosz Trial', 1901: 135–6.

175 Johns, 1970: 240.

176 'Latest Intelligence', *The Times*, Tuesday 10 September 1901: 3. Attacks on McKinley in the press were fairly common, but the most vituperative were those of Ambrose Bierce. In 1900, following the assassination of William Goebel, the newly elected Governor of Kentucky, Bierce wrote the following lines for the *New York Journal* (printed February 1900): 'The bullet that pierced Goebel's breast | Can not be found in all the West; | Good reason, it is speeding here | To stretch McKinley on his bier' (O'Connor, 1967: 255–6).

177 Lombroso, 1897: 380.

178 Lombroso, 1902: 165.

179 Lombroso, 1897: 385.

180 Giddings, December 1892: 723.

181 Ellis, 1910: 1–2.

182 Ibid.: 412.

183 Ibid.: 413–14.

184 Ibid.: 417.

185 Emma Goldman, 'In Justice to Leon Szolgosz [*sic*]', *Mother Earth*, Vol. 4, No. 8 (October 1909): 240, IISH, EG Papers, Reel 47, 840514068.

186 Emma Goldman, 'As to "Crammers of Furnaces"', *Mother Earth*, Vol. 1, No. 10 (December 1906): 21, IISH, EG Papers, Reel 47, 890420000.

187 Emma Goldman, 'Excerpt from Lecture, "Anarchism is not Necessarily Violence"', police transcript, 6 January 1907 in IISH, EG Papers, Reel 47, 891002001.

188 Emma Goldman, 'As to "Crammers of Furnaces"', *Mother Earth*, Vol. 1, No. 10 (December 1906): 22–3, IISH, EG Papers, Reel 47, 890420000.

189 MacDonald, 1902: 375–6; 'Execution of Czolgosz', *The Times*, Wednesday 30 October 1901: 3.

190 Spitzka, 1902: 386–7. Spitzka was an enthusiast for electrocution; he wrote the article on the subject for the *Encyclopedia Britannica*, 11th edn (Essig, 2003: 278).

191 Spitzka, 1902: 388. The left ear of the resulting cast broke off during the drive out from Auburn.

192 Ibid.: 391, 397.

193 *New York Times*, 30 October 1901: 5; Trautmann, 1980: 240.

194 'I'm an Anarchist, says A. Berkman', unidentified newspaper clipping, Sunday 2 July 1905, IISH, Berkman Papers, B101.

195 Alexander Berkman, outline of 'An Enemy of Society. Autobiography of Alexander Berkman', November 1932, IISH, Berkman Papers, B218. A statement appeared in *Mother Earth* informing the readers that there was 'little truth' in the story of Berkman's disappearance and kidnapping: 'People never realize that there are worse things in human life than merely external forces. But what made it impossible for our friend to continue his tour lies in the terrible contrast of solitary confinement, enforced silence and monotony and the rush and hurry of our daily lives' (Emma Goldman, 'To the Readers of Mother Earth', *Mother Earth*, Vol. 1, No. 9 (November 1906): 55, IISH, EG Papers, Reel 47, 890419013).

196 Letter from Voltairine de Cleyre to Alexander Berkman, 517 Randolph Street, 7 August 1906, IISH, Berkman Papers, B13.

197 Alexander Berkman, outline of 'An Enemy of Society. Autobiography of Alexander Berkman', November 1932, IISH, Berkman Papers, B218.

198 'Berkman Says He Isn't Here to Do Any Violence', newspaper clipping, November 1914?, IISH, Berkman Papers, B111.

199 Emma Goldman, 1908, *What I Believe* (New York: Mother Earth Pub. Ass'n): 13–14, IISH, EG Papers, Reel 47, 821022000.

200 Emma Goldman, 1911, *The Psychology of Political Violence* (New York: Mother Earth Pub. Ass'n): 1, IISH, EG Papers, Reel 47, 830420007.

201 Emma Goldman, 'Alexander Berkman', *Mother Earth*, Vol. 1, No. 3 (May 1906), IISH, EG Papers, Reel 47, 890419005.

202 Harry Boland to Alexander Berkman, 1912, Berkman Papers, B159, IISH.

203 Letter from 'Jack and Annie', 1912, IISH, Berkman Papers, B159.

204 'Summer Resort', *Denver Post*, 14 February 1915: 8, IISH, Berkman Papers, B111.

205 Berkman, 'Statement by Alexander Berkman, on his release from the United States Penitentiary, at Atlanta, Ga., October 1st 1919', IISH, Berkman Papers, B117.

206 Alexander Berkman to 'Mac', 18 January 1922, IISH, Berkman Papers, B14.

207 Letter from Emma Goldman to Ordway Tead, 17 October 1932, IISH, Berkman Papers, B356.

208 Emma Goldman to Alexander Berkman, Berlin, 3 March 1932, IISH, Berkman Papers, B28.

209 IISH, Berkman Papers, B28.

210 IISH, Berkman Papers, B30.

211 Letter from Emma Goldman to Emmy Eckstein, 20 July 1929, IISH, Berkman Papers, B358.

212 Report of 'Le Directeur de la Police d'Etat', 3 July 1936, IISH, Berkman Papers, B91.

213 Gary L. Doebler to IISH, IISH, Berkman Papers, B104.

214 'The World Better Off', *Weirton, West Virginia Times,* 7 July 1936, IISH, Berkman Papers, B104.

215 'Anarchist Who Tried to Kill Steel Baron 44 Years Ago Suicides', *Kane Republican,* 2 July 1936, IISH, Berkman Papers, B104.

216 'Anarchists', *Sandusky Register,* 14 July 1936, IISH, Berkman Papers, B104.

217 Heffernan, 2004: E3.

CHAPTER 9: Choosing the Most Terrible

A note on the sources for this chapter:

Along with other secondary material, the section on Gavrilo Princip relies in particular on three sources: Luigi Albertini's masterly account of the origins of the First World War; the courtroom testimony as edited and translated into French by Mousset; and Dr Martin Pappenheim's notes on his interviews with Gavrilo Princip in prison. The latter two sources are in some ways compromised. Princip's courtroom comments were sometimes disingenuous, and he certainly picked his words in order to avoid incriminating his fellow conspirators. Pappenheim's psychiatric notes were recorded in extraordinary circumstances, with Princip wounded from beatings, recently suicidal and in solitary confinement. The interviews were conducted in German, a language which was not Princip's mother-tongue. However, as providing the best access we have to Princip's motives and beliefs, and as a way to enable us to hear (at one remove) Princip's voice, both the trial reports and the psychiatric notes remain invaluable.

  1 Brook-Shepherd, 1984: 61.

  2 See Mazower, 2002.

  3 Okey, 2001: 362.

  4 Taylor, 1971: 455.

  5 During this war, King George I of Greece was assassinated by Alexandros Schinas, an Anarchist, who himself died while in police custody, having jumped from, or been shoved out of, an upper-storey window.

  6 Quoted in MacKenzie, 1995: 10.

  7 Woolf, 1956: 88–9; MacKenzie, 1995: 22.

  8 Okey, 2001: 366.

  9 Okey, 2001: 361.

10 Albertini, 1953: 22.

11 Woolf, 1956: 90.

12 Cassels, 1984: 121.

13 MacKenzie, 1995: 39.

14 See Albertini, 1953: 13–14.

15 Albertini, 1953: 15; Okey, 2001: 366.

16 Brook-Shepherd, 1984: 109–11.

17 Stone, 1985: 324.

18 Albertini, 1953: 18.

19 Albertini, 1953: 5; Cassels, 1984: 111.

20 Quoted in Cassels, 1984: 162.

21 Keegan, 2000: 16.

22 Cassels, 1984: 161.

23 Jovan Jovanović quoted in Albertini, 1953: 21.

24 Cassels, 1984: 115.

25 Mousset, 1930: 152.

26 Pappenheim, 1926: 11.

27 'Je suis fils de paysan et je sais ce qui se passe au village; c'est pour cela qui j'ai voulu me venger et je ne regrette rien' (testimony of Princip, in Mousset, 1930: 130).

28 Pappenheim, 1926: 11–12.

29 R. P.'s commentary in Pappenheim, 1926: 20.

30 Testimony of Princip, in Mousset, 1930: 147; also 'Sprachen von anarchistischen Flugschriften die zu Attenat aufgereizt haben' [spoke of Anarchist pamphlets which provoked him to (commit) the assassination]; 'Denkt heute anders, den soziale Revolution sei in ganz Europa möglich, da Sache verändern' (Pappenheim, 1926: 12).

31 Albertini, 1953: 50. 'Il a été mon premier modèle. Lorsque j'avais 17 ans, je passais souvent des nuits entières près de sa tombe. Je réfléchissais à notre misérable situation et je méditais sur lui. C'est là que je me suis decidé à l'attentat' (testimony of Princip, in Mousset, 1930: 151).

32 Pappenheim, 1926: 12. This sense of not having fought for their country motivated others in the conspiracy.

33 'Schon vorher Attentate, die Attentäter waren wie Heroen für unsere Jugend' (Pappenheim, 1926: 13).

34 Pappenheim, 1926: 13.

35 Testimony of Princip, in Mousset, 1930: 116, 150–1.

36 Ibid.: 114, 146.

37 Ibid.: 134.

38 *The Times*, 29 June 1914: 8; Cassels, 1984: 145.

39 Okey, 2001: 365.

40 Testimony of Princip and Čabrinović in Mousset, 1930: 117, 150–1.

41 Pappenheim, 1926: 15.

42 Testimony of Grabež in Mousset, 1930: 157.

43 For Ilić's recruitment, see Pappenheim, 1926: 15. The term 'nationalist' used in this chapter is in some ways misleading. Princip and the others were not supporters of the nation state Serbia; rather they saw Serbia as playing the equivalent role that Piedmont had played in Italian nationalism: that is, as the home of free Serbs it could be used as the base from which a homeland for all '*les Yugoslaves*' could be formed (testimony of Princip, in Mousset, 1930: 116). Far from being partisans for Serbia, Princip envisioned

a union of the southern Slav peoples, the Serbs, Croats and Slovenes (Pappenheim, 1926: 13).

44 Albertini, 1953: 76–8.
45 MacKenzie, 1995: 11.
46 Gilfond, 1975: 58.
47 From a description of Dimitrijević by the Serbian diplomat M. Bogičević, quoted in Albertini, 1953: 28–9.
48 Albertini, 1953: 81–2.
49 'Il aurait entravé, comme future souverain, notre union en réalisant certaines réformes qui seraient évidemment allées à l'encontre de nos intérêts' (testimony of Princip, in Mousset, 1930: 131).
50 Testimony of Princip, in Mousset, 1930: 117–18.
51 Cassels, 1984: 148.
52 From the Bildarchiv in the Österreichische Nationalbibliothek, and reproduced in Cassels, 1984.
53 Testimony of Princip, in Mousset, 1930: 148.
54 Albertini, 1953: 49.
55 Quoted in Cassels, 1984: 156.
56 Albertini, 1953: 46.
57 As reported in *The Times*, 29 June 1914: 8.
58 Albertini, 1953: 47.
59 Ibid.: 46.
60 'L'automobile arriva et j'entendis l'explosion de la bombe; je savais que cela venait de l'un des nôtres, mais j'ignorais duquel. La foule se mit à courir, et moi aussi je courus un peu; les automobiles avaient stoppé. Je pensais que tout était fini et je vis que l'on emmenait Cabrinovic. L'idée me vint alors de le tuer pour que l'affaire en restât là, puis je me serais tué à mon tour. Mais je renonçai à cette intention en voyant les automobiles poursuivre leur chemin' (testimony of Princip, in Mousset, 1930: 129).
61 Testimony of Princip, in Mousset, 1930: 129.
62 Testimony of Princip, in Mousset, 1930: 129–30.
63 Quoted in Albertini, 1953: 37–8.
64 Remak, 1959: 187.
65 Ibid.: 192.
66 Testimony of Princip, in Mousset, 1930: 130.
67 Introduction by R. P. to Pappenheim, 1926: 6.
68 Pappenheim, 1926: 12.
69 Keegan, 2000: 7–8.
70 Quoted in Albertini, 1953: 51.
71 From introduction by R. P., quoting the testimony of Dr Martin Pappenheim, Princip's prison psychiatrist: 'Die Nachrichten über das Golgotha seines Volkes wirkten auf ihn vernichtend. Er tröstete sich damit, daß auch ohne sein Attentat der Weltkrieg ausgebrochen wäre'; R. P. also reports, 'Er bereute nichts' (Pappenheim, 1926: 6).
72 Pappenheim, 1926: 14.
73 Quoted in Albertini, 1953: 52.
74 As reported in *The Times*, 3 July 1914: 7.
75 *The Times*, 29 June 1914: 8.
76 Albertini discusses this possibility but dismisses it, saying instead that very likely in the press of events, the Austrians simply forgot about the existence of the Black Hand

(Albertini, 1953: 65–6).

77 It was rumoured that Nikola Pašić, prime minister of Serbia, knew of the plot, and so warned the Austrians ineffectually through the Minister to Vienna, Jovan Jovanović. Far from showing complicity, this would be evidence of a Serbian governmental attempt to help the Austrians. However, the rumour was apparently started by Jovanović himself, someone whom some historians have deemed a less than credible witness (Taylor, 1971: 520). In Seton-Watson's correspondence with Jovanović, the Serbian makes it clear that there was no specific warning given to the Austrians, which if it had existed would have gone to the highest levels, and not, as the rather more general warning did, to Bilinksi. On the other hand, there is elusive and possibly erroneous evidence of a cipher telegram being sent to the Serbian embassy in Vienna ordering Jovanović to give a warming (Seton-Watson, 1976: Vol. 2, 123–4).

78 Albertini, 1953: 70.

79 MacKenzie, 1995: 2.

80 See Seton-Watson, 1926. Of this book, Seton-Watson wrote that his aim was to blame Austrian and German plans laid before 23 July 1914 for the onset of the war, and to exculpate, as far as possible, Serbia (letter to Jovan Jovanović, 7 November 1924), in Seton-Watson, 1976: Vol. 2, 119; letter to Jovan Jovanović, 4 December 1924: Vol. 2, 121–2).

81 Keegan, 2000: 56–8.

82 The plan was also redundant, imagining a successful dual frontal attack, and requiring immediate outright victory: a purely defensive plan would have worked far better.

83 Stone, 1985: 282.

84 Quoted in Tuchman, 1966: 422.

85 Stone, 1985: 288.

86 Goldberg, 1962: 460–1.

87 On the Parisian demonstrations see Gallo, 1984: 571.

88 Gallo, 1984: 574.

89 In Le Figaro littéraire, 28 January 1965, quoted in Guillemin, 1966: 224. Guillemin adds that Villain's antipathy for Jaurès was created by the right-wing press; he also addresses the rumour that Villain was paid by the Russian embassy in Paris (224); the Ambassador, Alexander Isvolsky was a long-standing opponent of Jaurès. Other authors have been more sceptical about the possibility of such a conspiracy (Gallo, 1984: 588).

90 Rabaut, 1971: 538, 541.

91 Rabaut, 1984: 110, 111–15; Gallo, 1984: 579.

92 Gallo, 1984: 587.

93 Rabaut, 1984: 8.

94 As reported in The Times, 5 August 1914: 5. At the same time in Germany, Kaiser Wilhelm II was saying, 'I do not see parties any more; I see only Germans' (quoted in Taylor, 1971: 529).

95 Rabaut, 1984: 106–8.

96 Interview with E. Tériade in L'intransigeant (Paris), 7 April 1930: 5, quoted in Miró, 1987: 314. In French, assassiner can also mean simply 'to murder'.

97 Interview with Francisco Melgar in Abora, 1931, in Miró, 1987: 116, 117.

98 Miró sought to create an art 'absolutely detached from the outer world' (Joan Miró, Letter to Michel, 10 August 1924, in Miró, 1987: 86).

99 From 'A Conversation with Joan Miró' by Francesc Trabal, in La Publicitat (Barcelona),

14 July 1928, in Miró, 1987: 95.

100 From 'A Conversation with Joan Miró' by Francesc Trabal, in *La Publictat* (Barcelona), 14 July 1928, in Miró, 1987: 96; from a 'Statement' in *Minotaure* (Paris), December 1933, in Miró, 1987: 122.

101 From a 'Statement' published in *Variétés* in 1929, in Miró, 1987: 108.

102 Quoted in Wertham, 1966: 342.

103 'L'acte surréaliste le plus simple consiste, revolvers aux poings, à descendre dans la rue et à tirer au hazard, tant qu'on peut, dans la foule. Qui n'a pas eu, au moins une fois, envie d'en finir de la sorte avec le petit système d'avilissement et de crétinisation en vigueur a sa place toute marquée dans cette foule, ventre à hauteur de canon' (Breton, 1930: 12). For Breton's qualifications see the same page, and especially his long note on the matter (ibid., 85–6).

104 Goll, 1925: 28–9.

105 Auclair, 1954: 617. On the centrality of Jaurès to the case see Goll, 1925: 58–60.

106 Eburne, 2008: 76–7, 80–1.

107 Goll, 1925: 27, 22, 7, 29.

108 Eburne, 2008: 90.

109 Ades, 2001: 175–6.

110 From *The Times*, 11 December 1983: 9.

111 *Commonwealth*, 23 July 1892: 2.

112 *The Times*, 6 April 1894: 5.

113 'Pas la moindre trace d'insolence, mais plutôt de la timidité dans le ton de Fénéon. Il semble qu'il hésite à chaque fois, comme s'il cherchait d'abord la réponse la plus modeste mais la plus juste' (Paulhan, 1998: 42).

114 *The Times*, 29 March 1892: 5.

CHAPTER 10: Necessary Murders

A note on the sources for this chapter:

The section on Tehlirian again relies on trial proceedings. Some have questioned the reliability of the evidence presented in court. Certainly it does appear that a certain line of enquiry was pursued in the courtroom, one that excluded other credible interpretations of Tehlirian's crime (including the possibility that he was an Armenian agent). Nonetheless, if treated with caution, the testimony presented is invaluable in providing an image of the events in Berlin and Turkey. Other problems with the veracity of sources for this chapter are discussed in the main text itself or in the individual notes.

1 Shaw, 2000: Vol. 5, 32.

2 Melson, 1992: 138–9.

3 Laqueur, 2002: 43; Kirkham, 1970: 556.

4 Lewis, 2002: 356.

5 Zürcher, 2004: 83; Kinross, 2003: 559–63.

6 Kinross, 2003: 565.

7 So described in Seton-Watson, 1917: 137.

8 Djemal, 1922: 34–6 (a rather exculpatory account); Zürcher, 2004: 107–8.

9 Davison, 1990: 181; Melson, 1992: 156.

10 See Djemal, 1922: 329–36, an oddly defensive report by someone who was himself not

responsible for the massacres – Djemal blames the Armenians, and mitigates Turkish guilt. His view that the massacres were a response to an Armenian uprising has found support among some historians, most notably Erickson, 2001: 96. For other accounts see Davison, 1990: 181; Lewis, 2002: 216, mentions the massacres, but does not give a figure for the number of deaths. See also Melson, 1992: 156. Melson gives a figure of 15,000 to 20,000 deaths; the historian Vahakn N. Dadrian says 25,000 (Dadrian, 2003: 182).

11 'It was only in the later nineteenth century that Turkish nationalism started up in its modern sense. The example was Balkan' (Stone, 2003: xvi).

12 While arguing that none of the leading members of the CUP were fully Turkish, Seton-Watson describes Talât as 'an Islamised Bulgarian gypsy' (Seton-Watson, 1917: 136).

13 Shaw, 1977: 299.

14 Lewis, 2002: 205, 226.

15 Ternon, 1989: 133, 135.

16 Kinross, 2003: 600; quoted in Lewis, 2002: 226.

17 Lewis, 2002: 218.

18 Shaw, 1977: 297.

19 Bernstorff, 1936: 126–7.

20 These friends included Vartkes Effendi. See 'The Late Talaat Pasha', *The Times*, 17 March 1921: 11.

21 'Talaat's Career', *The Times*, 16 March 1921: 11.

22 Bernstorff, 1936: 130.

23 Akçam, 2004: 158–60.

24 Akçam, 2004: 164; '. . . even if the Ottoman government as such was not involved in genocide, an inner circle within the Committee of Union and Progress under the direction of Talât wanted to "solve" the Eastern Question by the extermination of the Armenians and that it used the relocation as a cloak for this policy. A number of provincial party chiefs assisted in this extermination, which was organised through the Teşkilât-i Mahsusa under the direction of its political director (and CUP central committee member) Bahaeddin Şakir' (Zürcher, 2004: 116).

25 Hofmann, 1994: 23.

26 Keegan, 2000: 223.

27 Paraphrased from Hofmann, 1994: 25.

28 Dadrian, 1986: 311.

29 See, for instance, 'A Million Christians Massacred', *The Times*, 13 December 1921: 5.

30 Shaw, 2000: Vol. 1, 57. In a longer view of Armenian–Turkish relations, Djemal Pasha anyway traced their breakdown to Russian political influence (Djemal, 1922: 313ff).

31 Melson, 1992: 158–9.

32 Shaw, 2000: Vol. 2, 378–9.

33 Sanders, 1928: 157.

34 Ibid.: 157.

35 Mazower, 2002: 118.

36 Violence against Armenians had long been linked to the settlement of the Kurds (Donald Quartaert, in İnalcik, 1994: 877).

37 Shaw, 2000: Vol. 1, 57–9. A great deal of this 'propaganda' was written by the historian Arnold Toynbee in the form of the book *The Treatment of the Armenians in the Ottoman Empire, 1915–16* (1916). Shaw describes how Toynbee told him in a private conversation

that this wartime book was pure propaganda, but ignores the fact that while Toynbee softened some of the judgements made in that book, and came to a complex and intelligent understanding of the situation in Turkey in 1915, nonetheless he continued to write of the massacres of 1915–16 as a genocide. (For example, Toynbee, 1923: 265–6, in a book felt, by Greeks at least, to be markedly pro-Turkish [Melas, 1922].) Over forty years later, Toynbee wrote: 'In Turkey, however, in 1915, the Ottoman Armenian deportees were not only robbed; the deportations were deliberately conducted with a brutality that was calculated to take the maximum toll of lives en route. This was the C.U.P.'s crime; and my study of it left an impression on my mind that was not effaced by the still more cold-blooded genocide, on a far larger scale, that was committed during the Second World War by the Nazis' (Toynbee, 1967: 241–2).

38 Sanders, 1928: 156–7.

39 Zürcher, 2004: 115.

40 Ibid.: 115–16.

41 Dadrian, 1986: 314.

42 With an eye on international politics, French and English translations of the Andonian documents were published in the immediate post-war period. In the introduction to the English edition, Viscount Gladstone writes: 'We are about to make a Treaty with the governing Turk reeking of deeds surpassing in magnitude and vileness the most imaginative pictures of hell ever conceived' (Andonian, 1920: vii). For a sustained and persuasive attack on the authenticity of the documents see Orel, 1986.

43 Ternon, 1999. Ternon also notes the creepy modernity of the telegrams, with their euphemisms for massacre, their frank and barbaric consent (Ternon, 1989: 23).

44 Akçam, 2006: 4–5.

45 Akçam, 2004: 174. The Metternich quote comes from a report made on 7 November 1915.

46 According to a website devoted to critiquing, and indeed denying the idea that there ever was an Armenian genocide, at this point in 1914 Tehlirian joined the Russian troops, and thereafter a murder squad, or Dashnak group, which carried out many massacres against Turkish civilians. These activities were part of his transformation into a 'professional hit man'. If true, none of this emerged in the Berlin courtroom. See online at http://www.tallarmeniantale.com/samantha-power-hell.htm (accessed 15 March 2008).

47 Sarafian, 1995: 12–13. Later historians have dated the massacres in early June 1915 (Walker, 1980: 212).

48 It is possible to detect inconsistencies in Tehlirian's testimony: was Tehlirian's father in Erzincan or Serbia? Did Tehlirian even have sisters? The evidence regarding these issues is highly confused and to some therefore suspicious. At his trial, it was accepted that Tehlirian's family were present at the massacre, but the prosecution suggested that the atrocity was perpetrated by Kurdish bandits who attacked both the Armenians and the soldiers.

49 Sarafian, 1995: 12–13; Sarafian, 2000: 276–84: 'Statement by Two Red Cross Nurses of Danish Nationality, Formerly in the Service of the German Military Mission at Erzeroum; Communicated by a Swiss Gentleman of Geneva' (statement made by Flora A. Wedel Yarlesberg, a Danish nurse – told to M. Léopold Favre). Original – copy of German report, Schuchardt to German Foreign Office communication dated Frankfurt, 21 August 1915, Auswärtiges Amt – Politisches Archiv, Türkei 183/38, A24724 [Sarafian, 2000: 276]).

50 Sarafian, 2000: 277.

51 Shaw, 1977: 340.

52 Zürcher, 2004: 135.

53 See as quoted in Shaw, 2000: Vol. 1, 61–3; the Turkish-speaking reader is referred to Rauf Orbay, *Cehennenm Değirmeni: Siyasi Haturalarum* (2 vols, Istanbul, 1995), I, 44–5; Djemal Kutay, ed., *Osmanlidan Cumhuriyete, Yüzyıhmızda Bir İnsanımız Hüseyin Rauf Orbay (1881–1964)* (5 vols, Istanbul, 1992), I, 49 – though these are two sources that I have not been able to consult myself.

54 Dadrian, 1986: 325.

55 Akçam, 2006: 3.

56 Hovannisian, 1999: 161.

57 'Talaat Pasha Murdered', *The Times*, 16 March 1921: 12.

58 Herbert, 1924: 308.

59 Herbert, 1924: 309. On page 323, Talât repeats the defence that the action against the Armenians had been provoked by their fighting on the side of the Russians. During the war itself, Herbert had earlier received a letter from Talât Pasha declaring that he was not responsible for the Armenian massacres, and that he could prove his innocence (Herbert, 1924: 307–8).

60 Ibid.: 310, 312–28.

61 The details regarding Tehlirian's time in Berlin derive from the translated transcript of his trial, available online at http://www.cilicia.com/armo_tehlirian.html (accessed 20 February 2008).

62 Talât was usually pictured wearing a fez, as in, for example, *Volk und Zeit: Bilder zum Vorwärts*, 27 March 1921: 3.

63 See *Berliner Illustrirte Zeitung*, 12 June 1921: 355.

64 Orel, 1986: 18–19.

65 http://www.cilicia.com/armo_tehlirian.html: 81–2 (accessed 20 February 2008).

66 Ibid.

67 Walker, 1980: 344. Walker is unequivocal that Tehlirian acted as one of a Dashnak network of assassins codenamed 'Nemesis'.

68 *The Times*, 12 November 1921: 9.

69 See, for instance, *Armenian Allegations*, 1987: 10, and Walker, 1980: 344–5.

70 Öke, 1988: 269.

71 Nassibian, 1984: 116.

72 Arendt, 1977: 265.

73 Arendt, 1977: 266. Though, as we have seen, Talât had in fact been condemned to death by a military court.

74 Adalian, 1995: 6–7.

75 Melson, 1992: 154.

76 Sanders, 1928: 157.

77 Ibid.: 157–8.

78 Dadrian, 2003: 250, 252, 254, 257–9.

79 Hofmann, 1994: 30; Akçam, 2006: 6–7.

80 Hofmann, 1994: 30.

81 http://www.cilicia.com/armo_tehlirian.html: 100 (accessed 20 February 2008).

82 Sayler, 1968: 13.

83 Laqueur, 1974: 183. It can persuasively be argued that 1900–39 European art, philosophy, physics, film, music, architecture and literature were substantially fostered by German

speakers, just before – and even during – that culture's entire moral collapse.

84 Mazower, 2002: 129.
85 Laqueur, 1974: 5–6.
86 'Der Krieg hat die tief wurzelnde Auffassung von der Heiligkeit der menschlichen Lebens zerstört' (Gumbel, 1929: 23). See also Bookbinder, 1996: 101.
87 Gumbel, 1929: 23–5.
88 See Laqueur, 1962: 144ff.
89 Gumbel, 1922: 132.
90 Kessler, 1923: 360.
91 Gumbel, 1922: 126.
92 Laqueur, 1962: 164.
93 Bookbinder, 1996: 30–1.
94 Kessler, 1923: 356.
95 Bookbinder, 1996: 105.
96 Ibid.: 102.
97 Pagel, 1935: 9.
98 See Gumbel, 1929: 17–19.
99 Gay, 1968: 23; Felix, 1971: 163.
100 Even university life had become more violent. Those teaching in the universities were, in the main, anti-republican (Laqueur, 1974: 183). Those few professors espousing left-wing views were apt to find their lectures degeneratng into right-wing-inspired riots. However, more significant than the students' turbulent protests was the tepid disciplinary response or even the tacit connivance of the university authorities (Ringer, 1969: 215).
101 Ringer, 1969: 217.
102 Gumbel, 1922: 73–81.
103 Gumbel, 1929: 22; Felix, 1971: 163.
104 Möller, 2004: 188.
105 Gay, 1968: 21.
106 Bookbinder, 1996: 112.
107 Nettl, 1966: Vol. 2, 769; Laschitza, 2000: 617.
108 Laschitza, 2000: 620.
109 Nettl, 1966: Vol. 2, 772–3.
110 Gumbel, 1922: 10–11.
111 Arendt, 1968: 34–5.
112 Nettl, 1966: Vol. 2, 769–70. Nettl states that the SPD did not go so far as to order the murder of Liebknecht and Luxemburg (774); other biographers disagree (Laschitza, 2000: 620).
113 Ettinger, 1986: 243; Nettl, 1966: Vol. 2, 773–4; Evans, 1996: 487.
114 Arendt, 1968: 47.
115 Evans, 1996: 521–3.
116 Kershaw, 1999: 112.
117 Möller, 2004: 127; Evans, 1996: 488.
118 Winkler, 1993: 76.
119 Gumbel, 1922: 29–30.
120 Ibid.: 38.
121 Ibid.: 40–1.
122 Evans, 1996: 488.

123 Epstein, 1959: 3.

124 Gumbel, 1929: 53.

125 Kershaw, 1999: 145.

126 In one speech Helfferich proclaimed, 'Issue and person are simply not to be distinguished in the case of Erzberger', an invitation to consider that assassination might therefore be a solution to the problem; on Helfferich's campaign against Erzberger see Felix, 1971: 164.

127 Epstein, 1959: 353–5.

128 Ibid.: 357–9.

129 Gumbel, 1922: 70.

130 Epstein, 1959: 367.

131 Ibid.: 384.

132 Ibid.: 386.

133 Ibid.: 386–7.

134 *Kreuzzeitung*, 28 August 1921, quoted in Epstein, 1959: 388.

135 Gay, 1968: 22.

136 Ibid.: 160.

137 Ringer, 1969: 215–16; Weber, 1975: 673.

138 Weber, 1975: 672–3.

139 Gay, 1968: 160.

140 Kessler, 1923: 357; Federn-Kohlhaas, 1927: 243.

141 Bernstorff, 1936: 207–9.

142 Kessler, 1923: 356; Gay, 1968: 161. It is tempting to speculate that other than the exigencies of rhyme, the common insulting term '*Sau*' here implicitly alludes to Rathenau's homosexuality.

143 Joll, 1967: 45.

144 Ibid.: 53.

145 Ibid.: 48.

146 Stern, 2001: 193–4; Felix, 1971: 168.

147 Kessler, 1923: 353.

148 Sabrow, 1994: 56–8.

149 Ibid.: 58.

150 These last sentences are in effect translations from Federn-Kohlhaas, 1927: 247.

151 'Als ich, kurz nach seiner Ernennung zum Außenminister, zum erstenmal mit dem üblichen "Guten Tag, wie geht's?" sein Arbeitszimmer in der Wilhelmstraße betrat, griff er rückwärts in die Hosentasche, zog einen Browning heraus und antwortete: "So geht's!"' (Kessler, 1923: 353).

152 See Joll, 1967: 53, where he quotes the words of Ernst-Werner Techow.

153 This is a rough translation of Berglar, 1970: 88.

154 Sabrow, 1998: 39.

155 Kessler, 1923: 359; Stern, 2001: 195.

156 Kessler, 1923: 366.

157 Like most secret societies, it is hard to determine the nature, extent and programme of Die Organisation Consul; see Gumbel, 1929: 52–3; Stern, March 1963: 20–32; Sabrow, 1994: 27–9. Sabrow describes the group as the orderers or clients (*die Auftraggeber*) for the Erzberger killing (1994: 49).

158 Gumbel, 1922: 71; Kessler, 1923.

159 Felix, 1971: 172; Sabrow, 1994: 86.

160 Kessler, 1923: 365–8.

161 Gumbel, 1922: 72.

162 Ibid.

163 Bookbinder, 1996: 110.

164 Gumbel, 1922: 72.

165 Sabrow, 1994: 7; Sabrow, 1998: 27.

166 Quoted in translation in Bookbinder, 1996: 106.

167 The event is typically downplayed by Felix (1971: 174).

168 *Der Welt Spiegel*, Sunday 2 July 1922.

169 Schulin, 1979: 135.

170 Laqueur, 1974: 193.

171 Pais, 1982: 317.

172 Schulin, 1979.

173 Pogge von Strandmann, 1985: 233, n. 1.

174 Harden, 1963: 244.

175 Gumbel, 1922: 141.

176 See the wonderful courtroom speech made by Harden – a masterpiece of impassioned irony (Harden, 1963: 244–52). Ankermann had been an Oberleutnant. Weichardt was on parole (*Bewährungsfrist*) for the accidental shooting of a little girl. The two men received 25,000 marks from a go-between, most likely from the Deutschvölkische Partei, via Wilhelm Grenz, a bookseller (Gumbel, 1929: 63; 'Munich Group Hired Harden Assailants', *New York Times*, 9 July 1922).

177 Kershaw, 1999: 174.

178 Ibid.: 211.

179 Epstein, 1959: 389. After the end of the Second World War, in late 1946, both men were tried and sentenced for the murder. Both were released on parole ten years later in 1956.

180 Gumbel, 1921: 3.

181 A version of the thesis of a *Sonderweg* has recently been revived by the highly respected German historian Heinrich August Winkler in *Germany: The Long Road West* (Oxford: OUP, 2008).

182 Brook-Shepherd, 1961: 60–2, gives a rosy picture of what he sees as Lueger's benign influence; Arendt, 1975: 44, 108, and Kitchen, 1980: 36–7, offer a more measured assessment of Lueger's combination of nationalism, conservatism, anti-intellectualism and anti-Semitism. Hitler was a tempered admirer of Lueger (Kershaw, 1999: 34–5). Brook-Shepherd's view is of a piece with his broadly celebratory account of Dollfuss.

183 Alfred Pfoser and Gerhard Renner, '"Ein Toter führt uns an!" Anmerkungen zur kulturellen Situation im Austrofaschismus', in Tálos and Neugebauer, 1984: 226–7.

184 Kitchen, 1980: 70–1.

185 See Kitchen, 1980: 202–31; Lewis, 1991: 199–201.

186 Kindermann, 1984: ix.

187 Gehl, 1963: 90; Carsten, 1986: 203.

188 On Mussolini's doubts about Dollfuss see Gehl, 1963: 69, and Kitchen, 1980: 151–2; on Dollfuss's distaste for Mussolini see, for instance, Gehl, 1963: 71.

189 At this point, eager to keep in with Mussolini, Hitler was more circumspect regarding Austria than were the Nazis on the ground. Hitler's 'consent' was really won by a kind of trick, whereby Habicht persuaded Hitler that the Austrian armed forces were ready to force Dollfuss's government to accept an *Anschluss* or be overthrown; in that event, Habicht asked Hitler, should the local Nazis support or restrain the move? Hitler

answered that if the armed forces made a move, the Party should support them. For Habicht, that was the green light to start the coup (Ross, 1966: 235–6; Kershaw, 1999: 523). In reality, there were no significant plans for insurrection among the Austrian armed forces.

190 On Hitler's knowledge of the coup, see Anton Hoch and Hermann Weiss, quoted in Kindermann, 1984: 192, and Gehl, 1963: 96–7.

191 Brook-Shepherd, 1961: 253–4.

192 Dollfuss, 1994: 330–1; testimony of Hedvicek, Dollfuss's doorkeeper, quoted in Kindermann, 1984: 193–4.

193 Carsten, 1986: 213–14.

CHAPTER 11: Celluloid Assassins

1 From *Variety*, 20 June 1908: 12.

2 Harding, 1996: 63.

3 Musser, 1995: 31.

4 Moran, 2002: 102. Though in relation to the electric chair his knowledge may in fact have been a bit shaky (Ibid.: 178).

5 Essig, 2003: 291.

6 Ibid.: 279.

7 Edison, 1948: 65, 112–13.

8 Musser, 1995: 22; Harding, 1996: 63. Mary was played by Robert Thomae.

9 Essig, 2003: 336.

10 Eckhardt, 1998: 34. Though according to Musser (1995: 32), Lubin had left the USA in July 1901, following a judgment against him passed by the US Circuit Court on infringement of Thomas Edison's patents.

11 Musser, 1995: 32.

12 On Edison's purported interest in 'illusion' and 'commercial, living picture art' see Baldwin, 2001: 274–5.

13 Kracauer, 1960: 57–8.

14 Stokes, 2007: 208.

15 From Harry Alan Potamkin, '"A" in the Art of the Movie and Kino' (1931), in Lopate, 2006: 49.

16 Stokes, 2007: 88, 174.

17 See Dyer, 1996.

18 Stokes, 2007: 96.

19 Ibid.: 103.

20 Ibid.: 232–5.

CHAPTER 12: The New Frontier

1 Kirkham, 1970: xx.

2 Newfield, 1969: 302.

3 The Trumans lived at Blair House from 21 November 1948 to 27 March 1952, while the White House was being renovated (Hamby, 1995: 468).

4 Donovan, 1982: 294.

5 The monument was to be dedicated to Field Marshal Sir John Dill.

6 Truman, 1973: 488.

7 'Within the first few months I discovered that being a President is like riding a tiger. A man has to keep riding or be swallowed. The fantastically crowded nine months of 1945 taught me that a President either is constantly on top of events or, if he hesitates, events will soon be on top of him' (Truman, 1956: 13).

8 McCullough, 1992: 809.

9 Hamby, 1995: 471.

10 Truman, 1973: 488–9.

11 Kirkham, 1970: 74.

12 Donovan, 1982: 292.

13 McCullough, 1992: 812.

14 Ferrell, 1980: 197.

15 Ferrell, 1980: 250.

16 McCoy, 1984: 295.

17 Tugwell, 1947: xviii. However, Truman drew the line at allowing Spanish to be the language of instruction in Puerto Rican schools (Morris, 1995: 42).

18 Carr, 1984: 75–8.

19 Most notably the events of 1936 when an American policeman, Francis Riggs, had been murdered by nationalists, and the Palm Sunday massacre at Ponce in 1937, when police opened fire on marching nationalists, killing seventeen, and wounding over a hundred (Christopulos, 1974: 140–2).

20 Praeger, 1995: 47.

21 Carr, 1984: 167; Praeger, 1995: 47–8.

22 Guerra, 1998: 170ff. She examines literary treatments of such bandits and outlaws, and demonstrates the ambiguities present in their representation. On the lack of a tradition of insurrection see, for example, Lewis, 1974: 468.

23 On Truman and the build-up of the Cold War in the period see, for instance, Pollard, 1989.

24 For instance Hillman, 1952, and Bernstein, 1966.

25 Truman Papers, 1965: 278.

26 McCullough, 1992: 808; Hamby, 1995: 470; McCoy, 1984: 242.

27 Hanson, 1955: 6.

28 Washington Post, Thursday 2 November 1950: 6.

29 Truman, 1973: 489–90.

30 Ferrell, 1980: 198.

31 Ibid.: 199.

32 Hillman, 1952: 13.

33 Washington Post, Thursday 2 November 1950: 2.

34 Interview with William Walton, in Stein, 1970: 291.

35 Adams, 1999: 228.

36 Quoted in Greenberg, 1965: 77–8.

37 Kurtz, 1982: 196.

38 Quoted from the Report of the President's Commission on the Assassination of President John Kennedy (Warren Commission Report), Vol. IV: 147 in Lane, 1966: 72.

39 I am indebted here to much of the literature on the assassination, but particularly to the excellent photographs in Lifton, 1980 – although I think it unlikely that Lifton is correct in holding that as part of a cover-up the wounds to the body of the President were significantly altered.

40 Hannah Arendt was one of those who believed that there must be something behind the speed with which Oswald was discovered to be the assassin (Arendt, 1985: 569–70).

41 Knight, 2007: 3.

42 Report on Jack Ruby shooting Lee Harvey Oswald, Central Intelligence Agency, in *Declassified Documents Reference System* (Farmington Hills, Michigan: Gale, 2008).

43 Mailer, 1995: 733.

44 'Although political violence in the United States obviously did not begin with the death of President Kennedy in 1963, the last half-dozen years have produced a plethora of racial riots, student demonstrations, and assassinations – enough to prompt some to term the United States a sick society' (Havens, 1970: 1–2).

45 On the Soviets' belief, see Memo on 'Reaction of Soviet and Communist Party Officials to the Assassination of President John F. Kennedy', 1 December 1966, Federal Bureau of Investigation, in *Declassified Documents Reference System*, Document Number: CK3100487004 (Farmington Hills, Michigan: Gale, 2008).

46 'The assassination of President John F. Kennedy unleashed a swarm of wild theories of conspiracy; many had nothing to do with ideological conflict, but were simply ingenious responses to the unexplained discrepancies connected with the shocking event' (Davis, 1971: 339).

47 Quoted in Schlesinger, 1978: 617.

48 Zapruder had an 8-mm Bell and Howell zoom-lens camera, but was using 16-mm film. See Memorandum by Special Agent in Charge in J. Edgar Hoover, 5 December 1963, Federal Bureau of Investigation, in *Declassified Documents Reference System*, Document Number: CK3100386400 (Farmington Hills, Michigan: Gale, 2008).

49 Quoted in Ross, 1966: 57.

50 Davis, 1971: 263–4.

51 Knight, 2007: 65.

52 Shesol, 1997: 130. However, Schlesinger suggests that McCone did not always know 'what his own Agency was up to'; as a devout Catholic, McCone was too likely to disapprove – and so he was kept deliberately in the dark (1978: 489–90). He also records that, in a private conversation, RFK told him that McCone believed 'there were two people involved in the shooting' (616).

Robert Kennedy's eventual acquiescence regarding the conclusions of the Warren Commission was taken by many as proof that they were indeed correct. See Memorandum by T. J. Jenkins to J. B. Adams, 17 July 1975, Federal Bureau of Investigation, Document Number: CK3100388073, in *Declassified Documents Reference System* (Farmington Hills, Michigan: Gale, 2008): 3–4: 'Nevertheless, the Commission and its defenders were eager to interpret Robert Kennedy's silence as an endorsement of the Warren Report.'

53 Andrew, 1995: 311–12. Although Dulles knew of the plots to kill Castro, and the involvement of the Mafia in those plots, he held back all this information. See *Final Report*, v. Though the Commission finally decided to endorse the lone gunman theory, during the enquiry there had been dissension on this matter within the Commission, with some strongly doubting the 'single bullet' theory (Bird, 1992: 564–5).

54 For a time, the Warren Report allayed the fears of many regarding a conspiracy in the killing; after its publication, 87 per cent accepted that Oswald had acted alone (Knight, 2007: 65).

55 Knight, 2007: 77.

56 See the typically clear account in Knight, 2007: 70–1.

57 Jones, 1995: 552–3; from Lisa McGirr, 'Piety and Property: Conservatism and Right-Wing Movements in the Twentieth Century', in Chafe, 2008: 365.

58 Trevor-Roper, 1966: 15–17.

59 See Memorandum by T. J. Jenkins to J. B. Adams, 17 July 1975, Federal Bureau of Investigation, in *Declassified Documents Reference System*, Document Number: CK3100388073 (Farmington Hills, Michigan: Gale, 2008); Grose, 1995: 545–6.

60 *Final Report*, 1976: v, 3–6; 'For reasons of bureaucratic self-preservation, the CIA and the FBI thus found themselves in the ironic position of denying any possibility of Cuban or Soviet implication' (Schlesinger, 1978: 614–16).

61 In the 'Introduction' by Harrison E. Salisbury, in *Warren Report*, 1964: xxviii.

62 *Warren Report*, 1964: xxxi.

63 Oswald, 1967: 41.

64 Ibid.: 56–7, 59.

65 Grose, 1995: 550.

66 'Chronology of Information on Lee Harvey Oswald', Department of State, in *Declassified Documents Reference System*, Document Number: CK3100388073 (Farmington Hills, Michigan: Gale, 2008): 2.

67 See Visa Application of Marina Nicholaevna (née Prusakova), 22 November 1963, Department of State, in *Declassified Documents Reference System* (Farmington Hills, Michigan: Gale, 2008).

68 *Warren Report*, 1964: 236–9.

69 Oswald, 1967: 120.

70 Weiner, 2008: 257–9.

71 Lane, 1966: 308 and 310; *Warren Report*, 1964: 175–6.

72 Rorabaugh, 2002: 100.

73 Quoted from the *Report of the President's Commission on the Assassination of President John Kennedy (Warren Commission Report)*, Vol. V: 607 in Lane, 1966: 313.

74 For example, see Joesten, 1964: 121–2, 87–91.

75 See Greenberg, 1965.

76 Graubard, 2009: 410; James D. Barber in Greenberg, 1965: 114–16.

77 On the marketing of Kennedy as 'youthful' in the 1960 election campaign see Hugh Sidey, in Goodman, 2006: 11.

78 For a discussion of this topic see Toscano, 1975.

79 Reeves, 1991: 6–7.

80 Schlesinger, 1965: 107.

81 Milkis, 2008: 323.

82 Ibid.: 326–7.

83 Hugh Sidey in Goodman, 2006: 9–10.

84 Schlesinger, 1965: 736; Toscano, 1975: 19.

85 Riesman, 1950: 212–16.

86 Packard, 1957: 185–6.

87 Hugh Sidey in Goodman, 2006: 9.

88 See, for instance, a reported conversation between Bobby Kennedy and Pete Hamill, in an essay by Hamill, in Eppridge, 2008: 12; Milkis, 2008: 331; but above all, John Newman's book *JFK and Vietnam* (1992), and Howard Jones, *Death of a Generation* (2003). The belief that JFK was killed over Vietnam is essentially the thesis of Oliver Stone's movie *JFK* (1991).

89 Quoted in Rorabaugh, 2002: 11.

90 Packard, 1957: 191.

91 Quoted, not in relation to the television debates, in Rorabaugh, 2002: 7. Paradoxically, Nixon's first notable public success had been through the manipulation of television, that is his famous 'Checkers' speech in which he denied allegations that he had been supplied by secret electoral funds (Graubard, 2009: 473).

92 Mailer, November 1960: 122–3.

93 Knight, 2007: 9.

94 Quoted in *The Times*, 27 November 1963: 11.

95 William A. Mindak and Gerald D. Hursh quoting members of the public, in Greenberg, 1965: 135–6.

96 Quoted by Fred I. Greenstein, in Greenberg, 1965: 226.

97 Roberta S. Siegel in Greenberg, 1965: 217.

98 Zapruder filmed the assassination from in front of a wooden fence on one side of Dealey Plaza. He is reported to have affirmed that the shots came from behind him (Lane, 1966: 41). See also Memorandum by Special Agent in Charge in J. Edgar Hoover, 5 December 1963, Federal Bureau of Investigation, in *Declassified Documents Reference System*, Document Number: CK3100386400 (Farmington Hills, Michigan: Gale, 2008).

99 Greenberg, 1965: 11.

100 Ruth Leeds Love, quoting an unnamed ABC executive, in Greenberg, 1965: 83.

101 Quoted by Ruth Leeds Love, in Greenberg, 1965: 84.

102 Of course, many in the television audience had witnessed scenes of equal violence in actuality, not least as military personnel in Europe or the Pacific, in Korea, or Vietnam.

103 Schlesinger, 1965: 830.

104 *New York Times*, 17 December 1960. Pavlick's belief that Kennedy had stolen the election by chicanery was much shared, with Republicans claiming electoral irregularities in Texas and Illinois (Graubard, 2009: 413). Kennedy won by the tiny margin of 0.1 per cent of the vote (Jones, 1995: 544).

105 Schlesinger, 1965: 807.

106 Rorabaugh, 2002: 225; Arendt, 1985: 537.

107 Quoted in Shesol, 1997: 125.

108 Hammer, 1987: 309; see also Holland, 2004: 236, 229. Johnson continued to believe that there had been a conspiracy involved in Kennedy's assassination, and may even have believed that the CIA were involved in it (Bird, 1992: 566). Given the operational fragmentation of the CIA from the late 1950s onwards, such a supposition is not as far-fetched as some might believe; elements within the greater CIA began to act with increasing autonomy, not necessarily informing other wings of the agency or even their bosses higher up (Grose, 1995: 497).

109 'einen Abgrund von möglicher Gewaltsamkeit und reiner Mordlust' (Arendt, 1985: 570, 574). In the first instance, she is quoting her partner's words, though with obvious agreement. From early on, Arendt doubted the possibility that Oswald was the President's assassin (see letter 354 in Arendt, 1985).

110 Blaine, 1884: 2, 676.

111 Quoted by James D. Barber, in Greenberg, 1965: 121.

112 My reading of this film is much indebted to Cavell, 2009, an excellent essay which I first read in the book *Themes Out of School* (1984).

113 As Riesman puts it, 'other direction is becoming the typical character of the "new"

middle class – the bureaucrat, the salaried employee in business etc.' (1950: 21).

114 Riesman, 1950: 240.

115 Ibid.: 236–7.

116 Quoted in Chafe, 2008: 82.

117 Mills, 1956: 239ff.

118 Whyte, 1960: 190ff.

119 Packard, 1957: 201.

120 Mills, 1956: 182–8.

121 Armstrong (2008: 89–90) argues that the film owes much to other Hitchcock films, notably *Foreign Correspondent* (1940), *Spellbound* (1945), both versions of *The Man Who Knew Too Much* (1934; 1956), and *Psycho* (1960).

122 Hunter, 1951: 4; Brown, 1963: 253; Schein, 1971: 16.

123 Hunter, 1956: 23.

124 Quoted in Pratley, 1969: 100.

125 Hunter, 1956: 12–13; Brown, 1963: 267–8; Edgar H. Schein, 'The Chinese Indoctrination Program for Prisoners of War: A Study of Attempted "Brainwashing"', in Karlins, 1972: 106–41.

126 See, for instance, Sargant, 1957: 180; Packard, 1957: 5; and the reported words of Dr José M. R. Delgado, a researcher into the brain, in Karlins, 1972: 2.

127 Condon, 2004: 48; he's quoting Salter, 1952: 40.

128 For instance, Salter, 1952: v, 1–2, 34–5 etc., and Salter even goes so far as to affirm, 'We are meat in which habits have taken up residence' (36). Salter was a passionate opponent of Freud and a pioneer in the development of behavioural therapies; he believed that many psychological problems were caused by inhibition.

129 Karlins, 1972: 5–11.

130 Brown, 1963: 284.

131 For instance the discussion of religious conversion and 'techniques', in Sargant, 1957; also the account of religious authority in relation to Communist power, in Brown, 1963: 290–1.

132 Ibid.: 268–9.

133 Both cited in Sargant, 1957: 191; 227.

134 See Exner, 1977. Campbell became Kennedy's mistress before he had been elected President, and was involved with Kennedy before she became Sam Giancana's mistress. See also Kelley, 1986: 293–4.

135 Marcus, 2002: 66. In the initial report of the Church Committee, Campbell is euphemistically referred to as 'a close friend of the President' (*Alleged Assassination Plots*, 1975: 129). It's clear from the record that Hoover put a stop to this friendship (*Alleged Assassination Plots*, 1975: 130).

136 Kelley, 1986: 358.

137 Condon, December 1963: 449.

138 Ibid.: 449–50.

139 'So I designed this kind of free-association test sequence from still photos and about the viewer's reaction to images of mother, father, and country. It is designed to rip you into a kind of frenzy of rage if you are one of the people who have been left out of society and to see if you are one of the ones who have been unwanted, one of the tragic people who are the unknowns of society, people society doesn't care about' (Alan J. Pakula quoted in Emery, 2002: 100).

140 Brown, 2005: 126.

CHAPTER 13: The Hate Bus

1 Warren, 1965: 260.

2 For example, Arendt, 1985: 569 – from letter 342, Karl Jaspers to Hannah Arendt (22 November 1963).

3 As described, for instance, by Harrison E. Salisbury, writing in Greenberg, 1965: 40.

4 Schlesinger, 1965: 1020–1.

5 Ibid.: 1022.

6 Ibid.: 1024; the advertisement is partly reproduced in Joesten, 1964: 169.

7 Quoted in Lane, 1966: 248.

8 Schlesinger, 1970: 1027; Arendt, 1985: 574. On the cheering of some high school students, see Tim Hewat's *World in Action* documentary, *Dallas* (broadcast 3 December 1963).

9 See McGee, December 1963: 428. Then an associate professor of sociology at the University of Texas, McGee blames the murder on Texan culture: its moral absolutism; the habit of personal violence; the proliferation of firearms (he estimates that half the male students and a third of the female students at his university carry a gun); the political respectability of the radical right; and the nonexistence of a radical left.

10 Paraphrased from Rorabaugh, 2002: 87.

11 Williams, 1970: 93.

12 Rorabaugh, 2002: 114.

13 Tallmer, 1970: 3–4.

14 Baldwin, 1970: 91.

15 Bosmajian, 1970: 136–7.

16 Havens, 1970: 65; Garrow, 2004: 12.

17 Bennett, 1970: 14; White, 1996.

18 Hill, 2004: 6.

19 Rorabaugh, 2002: 106.

20 Williams, 1970: 179; Garrow, 2004: 260.

21 Schlesinger, 1978: 330.

22 Williams, 1970: 57.

23 See Cleghorn, 1970: 113–14; Halberstam, 1970: 193–4.

24 Baldwin, 1970: 98–9.

25 Wolfenstein, 1981: 355.

26 Quoted in Rorabaugh, 2002: 110.

27 As, for instance, Meier, 1970: 147.

28 Goldman, 1973: 229–30.

29 Malcolm X, 1965: 284.

30 Paraphrased from Alex Haley's epilogue to Malcolm X, 1965: 418–19. According to an informant for John A. Williams, King was rather vain about being voted top (1970: 189).

31 Williams, 1970: 77.

32 And also their cultural identity; see Warren, 1965: 252–3.

33 Goldman, 1973: 39.

34 Ibid.: 33–4.

35 For instance, Malcolm X, 1965: 244, and the interview with Malcolm X in Lomax, 1962: 171–2.

36 For some of his complex responses to the Jews, see, for instance, Malcolm X, 1965: 280–1 and 286–7, and the interview with Malcolm X in Lomax, 1963: 172–3.

37 Malcolm X, 1965: 269.

38 Interview with Malcolm X, in Lomax, 1963: 172–5; Malcolm X, 1965: 234.

39 Goldman, 1973: 46.

40 Wolfenstein, 1981: 19.

41 Ibid.: 261–2.

42 Interview with Malcolm X, in Lomax, 1976: 172.

43 Indeed some have characterised Malcolm X himself as 'racist'. In the spring of 1964, he stated, 'Once I was a racist – yes. But now I have turned my direction away from anything that's racist' (Warren, 1965: 263). An ambivalent observer of Malcolm X, Robert Penn Warren, comments, 'At the same time, Malcolm X must be aware that the basic appeal he has is not merely his incorruptibility or his origin in the lower depths; it inheres in his racism, his celebration of blackness, his promise of vengeance' (Warren, 1965: 264). On 14 February 1965, in response to such attacks, Malcolm X declared: 'I am not a racist in any form whatsoever. I don't believe in any form of racism. I don't believe in any form of discrimination or segregation. I believe in Islam' (Breitman, 1965: 162).

44 Dyson, 1995: 135.

45 Schmaltz, 1999: 119–20. A photo by Eve Arnold shows Rockwell in Nazi uniform at a Nation of Islam meeting. The image can be seen online at http://static.wikipedia .org/new/wikipedia/en/articles/r/o/c/Image-Rockwell_at_Nation_of_Islam_Rally. jpg_f3e3.html (accessed 21 September 2008).

46 Perry, 1991: 358. Rockwell appears to have esteemed Malcolm X (Schmaltz, 1999: 202, 242–3), though on occasion he put down the young black's superiority to his being largely of 'white blood'.

47 On Malcolm X's speech to the Klan see Perry, 1991: 358; for the telegram itself, see Breitman, 1965: 201, and Goldman, 1973: 228. Perry remarks that the telegram was actually intended for Jimmy George Robinson, the National States Rights Party leader, but was directed by his staff to Rockwell by mistake (1991: 349–50).

48 Wolfenstein, 1981: 326–7.

49 Malcolm X, 1965: 372–3; interview with Malcolm X by A. B. Spellman, in Breitman, 1970: 8–9.

50 Breitman, 1965: 33.

51 Goldman, 1973: 73–4.

52 Wolfenstein, 1981: 271–2; Dyson, 1995: 11.

53 On the idea that King's non-violent resistance was by no means passive, see Cone, 1991: 303.

54 'But Malcolm X has, in fact, never had any associations with actual violence in behalf of the Negro cause. He has always, by happy accident or clever design, been somewhere else' (Warren, 1965: 264).

55 See Perry, 1991: 348.

56 Goldman, 1973: 97.

57 Malcolm X, 1965: 398.

58 Goldman, 1973: 63.

59 Quoted in Rorabaugh, 2002: 28.

60 Goldman, 1973: 119.

61 Warren, 1965: 250.

62 Goldman, 1973: 131.

63 Wolfenstein, 1981: 37, 285–7.

64 Malcolm X, 1965: 311.
65 Regarding Malcolm X's interest in the Mau Mau revolt in Kenya, see Goldman, 1973: 228.
66 Goldman, 1973: 224–5.
67 Malcolm X, 1965: 425; also in Breitman, 1965: 197.
68 Wolfenstein, 1981: 316.
69 Malcolm X, 1965: 384.
70 Goldman, 1973: 203.
71 Dyson, 1995: 141–2.
72 Goldman, 1973: 238; Perry, 1991: 357.
73 Quoted in Goldman, 1973: 247.
74 Goldman, 1973: 256.
75 Breitman, 1965: 184.
76 Goldman, 1973: 266.
77 Perry, 1991: 365.
78 Malcolm X, 1965: 434.
79 Perry, 1991: 371–2.
80 Malcolm X, 1965: 441.
81 See Breitman, 1976: 167ff.
82 Goldman, 1973: 359–60, though Goldman himself does not believe that the government were behind the killing; see also Breitman, 1976: 49–60, 77, 156–9, 167ff.
83 Warren, 1965: 267.
84 Goldman, 1973: 378.
85 Warren, 1965: 261.
86 Simonelli, 1999: 5–9.
87 Ibid.: 21.
88 Ibid.: 12–13; Schmaltz, 1999: 39.
89 Schmaltz, 1999: 41.
90 Williams, 1970: 64.
91 On Gas Chamber, see Schmaltz, 1999: 190; on the hatenanny songs, Schmaltz, 1999: 227–9.
92 Dobratz, 1997: 57.
93 Quoted in Schmaltz, 1999: 318.
94 Schmaltz, 1999: 135.
95 Letter from George Lincoln Rockwell to J. Edgar Hoover, 27 November 1963, in *Declassified Documents Reference System*, Document Number: CK3100386032 (Farmington Hills, Michigan: Gale, 2008).
96 Schmaltz, 1999: 226–7, 243–5.
97 See Simonelli, 1999: 181–2; Schmaltz, 1999: 324, 331–2.
98 Quoting Martin Luther King's *Why We Can't Wait* (1964), in Williams, 1970: 66.
99 Andrew, 1995: 311. The aim of the wiretapping used against King was ostensibly to prove a connection between him and Communist agents (Schlesinger, 1978: 272). Schlesinger suggests that Bobby Kennedy authorised the tapping with extreme reluctance, and then only for 'defensive purposes' (360). However, the FBI pursued a vendetta against King, whom they considered a dangerous and subversive radical. His very eloquence was suspicious (*Final Report*, 1976: II, 11). Hoover seems to have been driven by a vivid hatred of King (*Final Report*, 1976: III, 154–7).
100 See 'Communist Influence in Racial Matters – A Current Analysis', Federal Bureau of

Investigation report, 10 April 1967, Document Number: CK3100519130 (Farmington Hills, Michigan: Gale, 2008). On King as Communist, see for example, Medford Evans, 'Civil Rights Myths and Communist Realities' (1963), in Davis, 1971: 322–3; on a slightly different tack: 'ominous as the violence excited by the infamous Martin Luther King and other criminals engaged in inciting race war with the approval and even, it is said, the active co-operation of the White House' (Revilo P. Oliver, 'Marxmanship in Dallas', in Davis, 1971: 343).

101 *Final Report*, 1976: II, 11; III, 158–60; Garrow, 2004: 372–4.

102 Malcolm X discusses the incident in a riposte to a 'non-violent heckler', in Breitman, 1965: 209.

103 Williams, 1970: 191–2.

104 Frank, 1972: 413–14; Garrow, 2004: 109–10.

105 Schmaltz, 1999: 167; Perry, 1991: 349.

106 Tallmer, 1970: 2.

107 Williams, 1970: 66.

108 Ibid.: 57.

109 Interview with Malcolm X by A. B. Spellman, in Breitman, 1970: 11.

110 Goldman, 1973: 384.

111 See Hill, 2004.

112 *New York Times*, 22 June 1967: 1, 25, quoted in Deburg, 1992: 168. *New York Times*, 6 June 1968: 18. These assassinations were not planned by Black Panthers, but by another African-American group of activists, the Revolutionary Action Movement (Wolfe, 1970: 64).

113 Lomax, 1968: 161–2; LaFeber, 2005: 75.

114 Lomax, 1968: 190.

115 Jones, 1995: 553.

116 'The creative tension they [i.e. King, Carmichael, and Floyd McKissick, director of the Congress of Racial Equality] induced along the highway was second only to the tension that was developing among the triumvirate itself . . . the three men became absorbed in a debilitating argument over the basic philosophy that would undermine the civil rights movement from that point forward' (Lomax, 1968: 120–1); Garrow, 2004: 482–4.

117 Deburg, 1992: 19.

118 Quoted in Chafe, 2008: 150.

119 Wolfe, 1970: 119–20.

120 Lomax, 1968: 163.

121 At Riverside Church, New York, on 4 April 1967, one year to the day before his assassination, King spoke out against the war.

122 LaFeber, 2005: 72–3.

123 Young, 1996: 472.

124 Posner, 1998: 132–3.

125 Select Committee on Assassinations, 1979: XII, 42, 145. In prison, Ray's IQ was measured as a middling 105 (McMillan, 1976: 213).

126 Quoted in McMillan, 1976: 217–18, and Posner, 1998: 142.

127 See, for example, his testimony in Select Committee on Assassinations, 1979: X, 114; on his suspicions of being informed on by some hippy girls ('I would think that the hippies would be sympthic [sic] to people like King'), see *Select Committee on Assassinations*, 1979: XII, 146.

128 Huie, 1970: 147.
129 Select Committee on Assassinations, 1979: III, 48; X, 51–3; Huie, 1970: 73–4; McMillan, 1976: 278–9.
130 Select Committee on Assassinations, 1979: XIII, 245.
131 Select Committee on Assassinations, 1979: XIII, 245–9. Most of the evidence on this matter came from Ray's fellow convicts and therefore was viewed circumspectly by the Select Committee. See also Posner, 1998: 135–7, 334.
132 Select Committee on Assassinations, 1979: XII, 84–7; Posner, 1998: 208–9.
133 McMillan, 1976: 252.
134 Posner, 1998: 210–11.
135 Select Committee on Assassinations, 1979: XII, 37, 40–1, 144, 148. As the number of references here shows, Ray worried that people might misinterpret his reasons for having plastic surgery, largely due to George McMillan's representation of the surgery as connected to Ray's personality problems, and a belief (imparted by Dr Maxwell Maltz's book *Psychocybernetics*) that he could cure his emotional scars by altering his face (McMillan, 1976: 272–4). On other scores too, Ray seems to have been especially irritated by McMillan's depiction of him.
136 Posner, 1998: 213–14.
137 Lomax, 1968: 196; Garrow, 2004: 619.
138 Young, 1996: 464; Pepper, 1995: 28.
139 Abernathy, 1970: 223.
140 Kurtz, 1982: 179.
141 See 'Racial Developments and disturbances throughout the U.S. in protest of the assassination of Martin Luther King Jr.', in cables sent by the Federal Bureau of Investigation, 5 April 1968, Document Number: CK3100091790 (Farmington Hills, Mich.: Gale, 2008); Havens, 1970: 70.
142 Select Committee on Assassinations, 1979: III, 252; XII, 27.
143 Select Committee on Assassinations, 1979: XII, 96; XIII, 251–6.
144 Huie, 1970: 152–3.
145 Ibid.: 155.
146 Though not, most likely, the Ku Klux Klan, despite the fact that earlier in the 1960s they had plotted King's murder (Huie, 1970: 20–1; Frank, 1972: 414).
147 Posner, 1998: 254–5.
148 'An analysis of the guilty plea entered by James Earl Ray: criminal court of Shelby County, Tenn., March 10, 1969', in Select Committee on Assassinations, 1979: XIII, 217–40.
149 Ibid., 222.
150 Ibid., 219.
151 Select Committee on Assassinations, 1979: XII.
152 Baxter Smith, in Breitman, 1976: 170.
153 Posner, 1998: 59–60.
154 See, for instance, Select Committee on Assassinations, 1979: X, 127.
155 See Huie, 1970.
156 The story is set out in Pepper, 1995.
157 See for instance, Huie, 1970: 89–90; Posner, 1998: 297.
158 Posner, 1998: 299–300.
159 Select Committee on Assassinations, 1979: XII, 43.
160 Select Committee on Assassinations, 1979: IX, X and XI.

161 Select Committee on Assassinations, 1979: XII, 43–5.
162 James Meredith quoted in Williams, 1970: 17.
163 Williams, 1970: 164.

CHAPTER 14: Out from the Shadow

1 Lowell, 1970: 197. Lowell had given a copy of Plutarch to Jacqueline Kennedy, and then found that Robert Kennedy had borrowed it (Schlesinger, 1978: 820). 'Bobby seemed so much younger than he actually was. His death seemed like the death of one's own adolescence' (interview with Robert Lowell, in Stein, 1970: 341).
2 John L. Lindsay of *Newsweek*, quoted in Schlesinger, 1978: 874.
3 Quoted in Newfield, 1969: 249.
4 Quoted by Victor S. Navasky, in 'The Haunting of Robert Kennedy', *New York Times Magazine*, 2 June 1968: 78.
5 Williams, 1970: 184–5.
6 Quoted in Rorabaugh, 2002: 9. On Johnson's admiration for JFK, and his hatred for Robert Kennedy, see also Califano, 1991: 294–7.
7 Newfield, 1969: 247; he had been introduced (or re-introduced) to the meanings of Greek drama by Jacqueline Kennedy's present of Edith Hamilton's *The Greek Way*, shortly after his brother's murder. Both the widow and the brother used the ideas in the book as a means to find consolation regarding John F. Kennedy's death (Schlesinger, 1978: 617–18). See also Schlesinger interviewed in Stein, 1970: 145–6.
8 'You know, he's the only one of those people – of all the people who were associated with John F. Kennedy – he's the only one who grew or went on living after he died' (interview with Adam Walinsky, in Stein, 1970: 147).
9 He even attended mass with Chávez (Solberg, 1984: 338).
10 Newfield, 1969: 44–5.
11 Ibid.: 283.
12 See Summers, 1985: 287–97, 348–56. For a more sceptical account of Kennedy's involvement, see Noguchi, 1983: 75–7, and Thomas, 2000: 191–4, 428–9. In tapes recorded during sessions with her psychiatrist, Monroe talks of her affairs with both Kennedy brothers (Thomas, 2000: 192–4). Thomas is skeptical about the truthfulness of these rumours, and uncharitably doubtful about Monroe's veracity, as a 'sick and drug-ridden' woman, a 'borderline paranoid who abused drugs and alcohol' (192–3).
13 Among others, Walter LaFeber has argued that it was Johnson's attempt simultaneously to pursue reform at home and war in Vietnam that undid him (LaFeber, 2005).
14 Evans, 2000: 349.
15 For a while, McCarthy could make use of this much-publicised antipathy, presenting himself as a candidate motivated by higher impulses than dislike (Eisele, 1972: 308–9).
16 McCarthy himself understandably downplays Lowenstein's role in his decision to run, and states that he had already decided to run before meeting Lowenstein (McCarthy, 1969: 53, 58–9).
17 LaFeber, 2005: 41.
18 Although in the circumstances an attack on Kennedy would have been impossible, it is not hard to detect the veiled contempt in such moments as, for instance, McCarthy, 1969: 163, 164–5, 171.
19 Solberg, 1984: 336–7.

20 Newfield, 1969: 271.

21 Ibid.: 272.

22 Solberg, 1984: 338. See also interviews with Robert Lowell and Tom Wicker, in Stein, 1970: 304–5.

23 Schlesinger, 1978: 912.

24 Interview with Richard Goodwin, in Stein, 1970: 332.

25 Interview with Dolores Huerta, in Stein, 1970: 334.

26 Interview with George Plimpton, in Stein, 1970: 335. According to one witness, Kennedy apparently backed up against the freezers, and Sirhan stepped up and shot him again in the head at point-blank range (Evidence of Boris Yaro, quoted by Mel Ayton, 'The Robert Kennedy Assassination: Unraveling the Conspiracy Theories', online at http://crimemagazine.com/05/robertkennedy,0508–5.htm, posted 8 May 2005).

27 Evans, 2000: 391.

28 It has also been suggested that he more particularly asked, 'Is Paul all right?', referring to Paul Schrade who also had been shot in the head (Moldea, 1995: 311).

29 Interview with John Kenneth Galbraith, in Stein, 1970: 288.

30 Interview with Gillian Walker, in Stein, 1970: 330.

31 This paragraph is a response to Bill Eppridge and Paul Fusco's evocative photographs of the crowds who watched the train pass by (see Fusco, 2000, Fusco, 2008 and Eppridge, 2008).

32 Quoted in Pratley, 1969: 220. 'A country can't afford to lose, you know, three men like Robert Kennedy and John F. Kennedy and Martin King. It takes too long to build people like that' (interview with the Reverend Andrew J. Young in Stein, 1970: 342).

33 Nixon, 1978: 305.

34 'After the convention, even the most loyal McCarthy supporters, like Murray Kempton, John Kenneth Galbraith, and Jeremy Larner, acknowledged that Robert Kennedy, had he lived, would have been nominated that bloody week in that armed city' (Newfield, 1969: 293). For the impact on Humphrey and McCarthy, and the source for the McCarthy quote, see also Solberg, 1984: 339–40.

35 Kaiser, 1970: 305–6.

36 'CIA conducts preliminary search of background information on Sirhan Bishara Sirhan', 6 June 1968, in *Declassified Documents Reference System* (Farmington Hills, Michigan: Gale, 2008).

37 Moldea, 1995: 101–5.

38 Ibid.: 107.

39 Ibid.: 297.

40 Facsimile on page 9 of illustrations, in Turner, 1978.

41 Mehdi, 1968: 5.

42 Yet on 31 May 1968, there had been a recent assassination attempt on the Christian ex-President of Lebanon Camille Chamoun. Chamoun had brought American forces to the country in 1958, in order to help suppress a pro-Communist Muslim revolt. The LAPD did naturally consider international connections to the shooting, for instance investigating an Iranian Kennedy campaign worker (Moldea, 1995: 111–12).

43 Other witnesses have doubted that he was drunk (Moldea, 1995: 324–5).

44 Ibid.: 108.

45 Ibid.: 106.

46 Interview with Sirhan Sirhan, in Ibid.: 301.

47 The same argument has also been put forward, albeit tentatively, in Shane Sullivan's documentary film *RFK Must Die* (2007).

48 Turner, 1978: 110, 194, 206.

49 Interview with Sirhan Sirhan, in Moldea, 1995: 301.

50 See the television programme, *Conspiracy Test: The RFK Assassination*, broadcast on the Discovery Times Channel, 6 June 2007.

51 Traces of gunpowder found in hairs shaved from the back of Kennedy's head suggested a shot had been fired 'within *inches* of the head' (Noguchi, 1983: 101). Noguchi found several fresh wounds on Kennedy's body: two were under his right armpit; the fatal bullet 'had entered the skull an inch to the left of Kennedy's right ear, in what is known as the mastoid region, and shattered' (Ibid.: 99–100).

52 Ibid.: 105–6, 108.

53 This description of chaotic movements is conveyed also by the fact that Thane Eugene Cesar also took a tumble in the confusion of the shooting (Kaiser, 1970: 26). Also confirming Moldea's theory is Freddy Plimpton's statement that the first bullet hit Kennedy in the arm (Kaiser, 1970: 26).

54 Moldea, 1995: 312–13.

55 Greil Marcus records a rumour that Sirhan once worked as one of Jack Ruby's minor employees, carrying drugs for him, though he gives no source for this information (Marcus, 2002: 32).

56 At various times, Hoffa had threatened the life of Robert Kennedy in response to the Attorney General's legal campaign against him (Moldea, 1995: 117–18).

57 See Steinbacher, 1968.

58 Mehdi, 1968: 31.

59 Havens, 1970: 73.

60 See editorial, 'The American Condition', *The Nation*, 21 December 1963, Vol. 197, No. 21 (New York: The Nation Company): 425.

61 Newfield, 1969: 286.

62 Ibid.: 300.

63 Ibid.: 304.

64 Quoted in Shesol, 1997: 455.

65 Califano, 1991: 298.

66 Johnson, 1971: 543.

67 Califano, 1991: 298.

68 LaFeber, 2005: 29.

69 'Many of the 89 million Americans watching the appalling spectacle of violence on their television screens that night exclaimed: "The Democrats are finished"' (Solberg, 1984: 365).

70 Clarke, 1990: 94.

71 Wertham, 1966: 273–4.

72 *New York Times*, 6 June 1968: 20.

73 The only other possibility is that after carrying out a highly secret and well-organised conspiracy to assassinate a Presidential candidate, one of the central members of that conspiracy immediately popped outside and confessed all to passers-by.

74 *New York Times*, 6 June 1968: 25.

75 See, for instance, Marwick, 1998: 8–9.

76 McCarthy, 1968: 17–19.

77 Abraham Goldstein summarising the beliefs of others, in Goldstein, 1967: 21.

78 Wertham, 1966: 340–2.
79 Ibid.: 7.
80 Mel Ayton, 'The Robert Kennedy Assassination: Unraveling the Conspiracy Theories', online at http://crimemagazine.com/05/robertkennedy,0508–5.htm, posted 8 May 2005.
81 His most famous text on this subject is *Seduction of the Innocent* (1955); he returned to the theme in Wertham, 1966: 195ff.
82 Wertham, 1966: 210.
83 Ibid.: 211.
84 Ellison, December 1963: 433–4.
85 Interview with Robert Scheer, in Stein, 1970: 339–40. The end of all of Dan Moldea's investigations into the murder of Kennedy was the realisation that Sirhan's 'unilateral motive consisted of nothing more than his desire to prove to himself and those who knew him that he still had his nerve. He wanted everyone to know his name and be forced to recognize him' (Moldea, 1995: 323).
86 Schlesinger declares his own 'bias' or sympathy for Kennedy (Schlesinger, 1978: xiii).
87 Newfield, 1969: 47–8, 69.
88 Quoting the *New York Times*' assessment of Warhol's standing on the day following his shooting, 4 June 1968: 1.
89 Warhol, 2007: 24.
90 Ibid.: 25.
91 Malanga, 2002: 93.
92 See interview with Gerard Malanga, in Wilcock, 1971: 11.
93 Adams, 1999: 412.
94 Kostenbaum, 2001: 82–3.
95 Ibid.: 125.
96 Mario Amaya, interviewed in Wilcock, 1971: 104.
97 Interviews with Ondine, Andreas Brown and Truman Capote, in Stein, 1982: 209, 216–17.
98 Warhol, 2007: 48.
99 Ibid.: 53.
100 See interview with Truman Capote, in Stein, 1982: 239.
101 Interviews with Paul Morrissey and Ondine, in Stein, 1982: 205.
102 Watson, 2003: 36.
103 Harron, 1996: xv.
104 Gornick, 1970: xv.
105 Solanas, 1970: 27–8, 29.
106 Ibid.: 29.
107 Ibid.: 40.
108 Mary Harron reports that Solanas's psychiatrist felt that: 'though she makes strenuous efforts to present herself as a hard, tough, cynical misanthrope, Miss Solanas is actually a very frightened and depressed child' (1996: xxvi).
109 Solanas, 1970: 44–5.
110 Ibid.: 38.
111 Ibid.
112 Ibid.: 39.
113 Girodias, 1970: viii–ix.
114 Mario Amaya, quoted in Wilcock, 1971: 105.

115 Girodias, 1970: x.

116 Watson, 2003: 353–4.

117 *New York Times*, 5 June 1968; Harron, 1996: xxv.

118 Mario Amaya, interviewed in Wilcock, 1971: 105.

119 Watson, 2003: 380–1; *New York Times*, 5 June 1968.

120 Watson, 2003: 382.

121 Warhol, 2007: 91.

122 Ibid.: 12.

123 Interview with David Bourdon, in Stein, 1982: 292–4.

124 Warhol, 2007: 78.

125 *New York Times*, 4 June 1968: 36.

126 Girodias, 1970: xii.

127 Watson, 2003: 395.

128 Ibid.: 396.

129 Ibid.: 385–6.

130 Ibid.: 425.

131 'Beyond Linda Phelps was Valerie Solanis [*sic*], even as Robespierre was beyond Rousseau' (Mailer, 1971: 55). Later in this book, Mailer figuratively compares Kate Millet to a hired assassin (96–7).

132 Gornick, 1970: xv–xvii, xxiv–xxvi.

133 Harron, 1996: x.

134 Girodias, 1970: xii; Harron, 1996: xxviii.

135 Solanas, 1970: 47–8.

136 Harron, 1996: xxvii.

137 Warhol, 2007: 78.

138 Interview with Ronnie Tavel in Wilcock, 1971: 55; interview with Maura Moynihan in O'Connor, 1996: 149, 151; Kostenbaum, 2001: 131.

139 'Andy died when Valerie Solanas shot him. He's just somebody to have at your dinner table now. Charming, but he's the ghost of a genius, a walking ghost' (interview with Taylor Mead, in Stein, 1982: 294).

CHAPTER 15: The Decline of the American Assassination

1 Lemay, 1973: 7.

2 Clarke, 1990: 86–7.

3 Quoted in *The Times*, Wednesday 17 May 1972: 7.

4 Marcus, 2002: 32.

5 Bremer, 1973: 29.

6 Carter, 1995: 422.

7 Quoted in the *Washington Post*, Wednesday 17 May 1972: A1 and A11.

8 Quoted in *The Times*, Wednesday 17 May 1972: 7.

9 *New York Times*, Wednesday 24 May 1972: 35.

10 Kurland, 1972: 3.

11 Ibid.: 4–5.

12 From Dan Carter, *From George Wallace to Newt Gringrich: Race in the Conservative Counterrevolution, 1963–1994* (1996), in Chafe, 2008: 352.

13 Kurland, 1972: 14.

14 Kurland, 1972: 15; Dobratz, 1997: 227.

15 From Dan Carter, *From George Wallace to Newt Gringrich: Race in the Conservative Counterrevolution, 1963–1994* (1996), in Chafe, 2008: 337–8.

16 Havens, 1970: 71–2.

17 Arendt, 1975: 716.

18 Carter, 1992: 27, 30; Jones, 1995: 557. In effect, Nixon appealed to the same kind of voters as Wallace, the 'forgotten Americans' (Graubard, 2009: 479).

19 See Robert Drew's documentary film *Crisis* (1963). The film's three protagonists are John F. Kennedy, Robert Kennedy and George Wallace; in time all three would be the victims of assassins.

20 Carter, 1992: 29.

21 Rohler, 2004: 72.

22 Quoted in Dan Carter, *From George Wallace to Newt Gringrich: Race in the Conservative Counterrevolution, 1963–1994* (1996), in Chafe, 2008: 349.

23 Carter, 1992: 42–3.

24 Carter, 1995: 415, 417; Rohler, 2004: 69.

25 Carter, 1992: 43.

26 Carter, 1995: 424.

27 *The Times*, 25 March 1972: 6.

28 'Pointy-heads' was Wallace's favoured term for the Washington bureaucrats.

29 See Peter Schrag, quoted in Chafe, 2008: 296; also Dan Carter, *From George Wallace to Newt Gringrich: Race in the Conservative Counterrevolution, 1963–1994* (1996), in Chafe, 2008: 353.

30 Rohler, 2004: 69; *The Times*, 19 January 1971: 6. His slogan was 'people power'.

31 Schrag's piece was first printed in *Harper's Magazine* in 1969, reprinted in Chafe, 2008: 287–99; Scammon, quoted in *The Times*, 12 September 1970: 12.

32 Rohler, 2004: 69–70.

33 Quoted in *Washington Post*, Tuesday 16 May 1972: A10.

34 Quoted in *The Times*, Wednesday 17 May 1972: 7.

35 Bremer, 1973: 63–70.

36 Ibid.: 71.

37 Ibid.: 90.

38 Ibid.: 127.

39 Quoted in *Washington Post*, Tuesday 16 May 1972: A12.

40 Carter, 1995: 446.

41 Carter, 1995: 441; there have since been unsubstantiated reports that Nixon schemed to have George McGovern campaign material planted at Bremer's apartment, in order to incriminate the Democrat candidate (Irvin Molotsky, 'Article Says Nixon Schemed to Tie Foe to Wallace Attack', *New York Times*, 7 December 1992).

42 Quoted in *Washington Post*, Tuesday 16 May 1972: A13.

43 Carter, 1995: 444.

44 Ibid.: 445.

45 Ibid.: 452.

46 Vidal, 1973: 18.

47 Taubin, 2000: 10.

48 Bremer, 1973: 28; Carter, 1995: 453.

49 *The Times*, Saturday 30 August 1980: 5.

50 *New York Times*, 14 December 1992.

51 *The Times*, Thursday 1 April 1977: 9.

52 Vidal, 1973: 18.

53 Bremer, 1973: 107.

54 Ibid.: 121.

55 Ibid.: 106, 105, 51, 26.

56 Ibid.: 104.

57 It is possible that Bremer was dyslexic.

58 Bremer, 1973: 75.

59 Ibid.: 66.

60 Ibid.: 117.

61 Ibid.: 98.

62 Quoted in 'Editor's Note', Ibid.: 142.

63 Ibid.: 114.

64 Ibid.: 122.

65 Tom Wolfe quoting Barbara Walters interviewing Kathleen Cleaver, in Wolfe, 1970: 72–3.

66 Steinbacher, 1968: 51–3.

67 From 'Trip Without a Ticket' by The Diggers, quoted in Chafe, 2008: 278.

68 Roszak, 1969: 128.

69 Varon, 2004: 104–5.

70 Turner, 1978: xiii; Marcus, 2002: 69–70; Armstrong, 2008: 27. To complete the circle of connections, Frankenheimer would end up making a bio-pic, *George Wallace* (1997), a portrait of the Alabama governor and survivor of an assassination attempt. A young Angelina Jolie played Wallace's second wife, Cornelia.

71 Didion, 1990: 44.

72 Turner, 1978: xiii.

73 Ibid.: 246–50.

74 Ibid.: 265.

75 Schlesinger, 1978: 483.

76 Warhol, 1989: 346–8.

77 Marcus, 2002: 32.

78 MacDonald, 1998: 273–5.

79 Wolfe, 1989: 74.

80 'These were children who grew up cut loose from the web of cousins and great-aunts and family doctors and lifelong neighbors who had traditionally suggested and enforced the society's values. They are children who have moved around a lot, *San Jose, Chula Vista, here*. They are less in rebellion against the society than ignorant of it, able only to feed back certain of its most publicized self-doubts, Vietnam, Saran-Wrap, diet pills, the Bomb' (Didion, 1993: 123).

81 Wolfe, 1970: 8.

82 Varon, 2004: 163.

83 Marshall, 1993: 283.

84 Varon, 2004: 189.

85 'Governments attempt to monopolize violence and generally succeed in legitimizing it' (Havens, 1970: 1).

86 See Varon, 2004.

87 The Weather Underground made a bow to their late-nineteenth-century forebears by blowing up the statue dedicated to the Chicago policemen killed in the Haymarket bombing.

88 Newfield, 1969: 176.
89 Quoted in *Final Report*, 1976: III, 936.
90 Graubard, 2009: 490.
91 Kirkham, 1970: 8–9.
92 Noguchi, 1983: 127–9.
93 Biskind, 1998: 78.
95 Bugliosi, 1974: 175.
95 See the reproduction of the application form in Bugliosi, 1974.
96 *The Times*, 31 March 1971: 6.
97 Bugliosi, 1974: 441–2.
98 Ibid.: 391, 415.
99 Wolfe, 1989: 183.
100 Bugliosi, 1974: 367.
101 Wolfe, 1989: 128.
102 Bugliosi, 1974: 135.
103 *The Times*, 6 December 1969: 4; Bugliosi, 1974: 179, 181.
104 Bugliosi, 1974: 430, 465.
105 On the Black Panthers' attitude to the police see Deburg, 1992: 158.
106 Bugliosi, 1974: 371–2.
107 Ibid.: 177.
108 Ibid.: 470–3.
109 Varon, 2004: 151, 160.
110 Bugliosi, 1974: 221–2.
111 Ibid.: 389.
112 Brenda McCann was the alias for Nancy Pitman; here she is speaking in Robert Hendrickson's film *Manson* (1973).
113 Biskind, 1998: 79.
114 Quoted on the sleeve of the promotional DVD version of the film.
115 Bugliosi, 1974: 479.
116 *The Times*, 4 February 1971: 8.
117 Quoted in *Time*, Vol. 106, No. 11, 15 September 1975: 12.
118 Gerald Ford, 1979: 77.
119 Schapsmeier, 1989: 205–6; Bravin, 1998: 407.
120 See the sympathetic but damning assessment of Ford's character in Reeves, 1975: 116–19.
121 Greene, 1995: 34–5.
122 Quoted in Rorabaugh, 2002: 7.
123 Greene, 1995: 191.
124 Gerald Ford, 1979: 309–10.
125 Bravin, 1998: 233.
126 *Ford Papers*, 1977: 1348.
127 Casserly, 1977: 154.
128 Mieczkowski, 2005: 174.
129 White House memo, 'Secret Service interim report on the attempted assassination of President Ford', 11 September 1975, in *Declassified Documents Reference System*, Document Number: CK3100069257 (Farmington Hills, Michigan: Gale, 2008).
130 Bravin, 1998: 219–20.
131 Ibid.: 271–2.
132 Ibid.: 248.

133 *Time*, Vol. 106, No. 11, 15 September 1975: 8.

134 *The Times*, 31 March 1981: 1; *The Times*, 1 October 1975: 1; *Time*, Vol. 106, No. 11, 15 September 1975: 18.

135 *The Times*, 23 September 1975: 1; *The Times*, 16 January 1976: 1; Gerald Ford, 1979: 310–12; Betty Ford, 1979: 236.

136 *The Times*, 23 September 1975: 1; *The Times*, 24 September 1975: 1, 5.

137 Casserly, 1977: 167, 180–1.

138 *The Times*, 3 November 1975: 6.

139 From the speech in court of Catherine Share ('Gypsy'), 17 March 1971: 'We are all in a gas chamber right here in L.A., a slow-acting one. The air is going away from us in every city. There is going to be no more air, and no more water, and the food you are eating is poisoning you. There is going to be no more earth, no more trees. Man, especially white man, is killing the earth' (Bugliosi, 1974: 423).

140 Quoted in *The Times*, 8 September 1975: 4.

141 *Time*, Vol. 106, No. 11, 15 September 1975: 11.

142 Bravin, 1998: 409.

143 Ibid.: 409.

144 *The Times*, 8 November 1975: 4; Bravin, 1998: 327.

145 *Time*, Vol. 106, No. 11, 15 September 1975: 9.

146 Quoted in Bravin, 1998: 239.

147 Bravin, 1998: 259–60.

148 *The Times*, 12 November 1975: 7.

149 Quoted testimony of a Secret Service agent, *The Times*, 13 November 1975: 7; evidence of Gerald Ford in *The Times*, 15 November 1975: 4.

150 *The Times*, 18 December 1975: 6.

151 Betty Ford, 1979: 153.

152 Hearst, 1982: 333.

153 *The Times*, 28 October 1975: 12.

154 Hearst, 1982: 369, 436–7; Bravin, 1998: 337.

155 Bravin, 1998: 285.

156 Colby, 1978: 398–9; Gerald Ford, 1979: 229–30.

157 On Colby's sincerity, see Colby, 1978: 400.

158 In the mid-1950s in Britain, Anthony Eden had been poised to sanction the murder of Gamal Abdul Nasser (Graubard, 2009: 383).

159 Although hardly an impartial commentator, see Gerald Ford, 1979: 265.

160 Gerald Ford, 1979: 324–6.

161 See, for instance, a letter from President Ford to the Select Committee on Intelligence Activities, 31 October 1975, in *Declassified Documents Reference System*, Document Number: CK3100092320–3 (Farmington Hills, Michigan: Gale, 2008).

162 A CIA transcript of the interview with Senator Frank Church on *The Today Show*, 10 June 1975, in *Declassified Documents Reference System* (Farmington Hills, Michigan: Gale, 2008).

163 For Zhou Enlai, see Ambrose, 1981: 297–8. For Lumumba, see *Alleged Assassination Plots*, 1975: 13–70. The Americans do not seem to have so much directly assisted in the coup as to have conspicuously stood back from interfering in it (Hammer, 1987: 309), though that certainly amounts to complicity, effectively giving the coup leaders their blessing (Jones, 2003: 425–6, 433). Regarding the killing of Diem, it has been argued that Kennedy knew of American involvement in this action, and indeed it

seems that he made efforts to warn the Vietnamese leader of the danger that he was in (Reeves, 1991: 409). There are tales of the President's horror on hearing the news of Diem's murder, despite his foreknowledge of the coup (Hammer, 1987: 300–1; Jones, 2003: 425). In the rather partial account of Jack Newfield, that author asks Robert Kennedy 'whether "the American government had anything to do with the overthrow of Diem,"' and RFK 'replied enigmatically, after a pregnant silence, "Not in Washington"' (Newfield, 1969: 117–18). In a significant move (given the stated views of Gore Vidal), E. Howard Hunt forged telegrams that incriminated JFK in the assassination of Diem and attempted to sell them to *Life* magazine; however, the slur was quickly discovered (Carter, 1995: 442). Kennedy spoke of his guilt regarding Diem's death, but these statements were perhaps not so much a confession as the scrupulous expression of anxiety over his indirect involvement (Dallek, 2003: 683).

164 Telegram from Ambassador Henry Cabot Lodge to Secretary of State Dean Rusk, 10 October 1963, in *Declassified Documents Reference System*, Document Number: CK3100195472/CK3100195473 (Farmington Hills, Michigan: Gale, 2008). Lodge ends by implying that any attempt to assassinate him will lead to massive American retribution.

165 Jones, 2003: 424–5, 427; Jacobs, 2006: 178.

166 Hammer, 1987: 300 (though JFK's horrified reaction to the coup was a notable exception to the general sense of satisfaction); Jones, 2003: 429; Jacobs, 2006: 180.

167 Atkins, 1972: 108–10, 69–74.

168 Srodes, 1999: 543; Blum, 2003: 176; Weiner, 2008: 198–9.

169 *Alleged Assassination Plots*, 1975: 264–7.

170 See Dwight D. Eisenhower's 'Farewell Address', reprinted in Chafe, 2008: 34.

171 'The chain of events revealed by the documents and testimony is strong enough to permit a reasonable inference that the plot to assassinate Lumumba was authorised by President Eisenhower. Nevertheless, there is enough countervailing testimony by Eisenhower Administration officials and enough ambiguity and lack of clarity in the records of high-level policy meetings to preclude the Committee from making a finding that the President intended an assassination effort against Lumumba' (*Alleged Assassination Plots*, 1975: 51); shortly after publication of the report, friends of Eisenhower pressed for this statement to be rescinded – on reflection, the Church Committee stuck to their initial judgement (Ambrose, 1981: 294–5); see also Grose, 1995: 502.

172 Schlesinger, 1978: 485.

173 'When asked by the Chairman why, in this context, persons within the Agency talked "in riddles to one another," Bissell replied that: "I think there was a reluctance to spread even on an oral record some aspects of the operation"' (*Alleged Assassination Plots*, 1975: 95).

174 Grose, 1995: 505–6.

175 Ambrose, 1981: 293–4; Grose, 1995: 500–1.

176 Ambrose, 1981: 300.

177 Blum, 2003: 158.

178 Sullivan III, 2008: 83.

179 Grose, 1995: 503–4.

180 Graubard, 2009: 395–6.

181 *Alleged Assassination Plots*, 1975: 91–2; Reeves, 1991: 259; Andrew, 1995: 251; Grose, 1995: 493–4, 496; 'In a public speech after the war [Dulles] had said, "Assassination

may be the only means left of overthrowing a modern tyrant"' (Grose, 1995: 501).

182 Andrew, 1995: 251–2.

183 Cline, 1976: 186.

184 Wilford, 2008: 233.

185 Schlesinger, 1978: 454, 483, 486.

186 Wilford, 2008: 233–4.

187 'But in 1963, with invasion absolutely excluded, with the anti-Castro policy drastically modified and with the White House drifting toward accommodation, assassination had no logic at all' (Schlesinger, 1978: 546).

188 Milkis, 2008: 328.

189 David W. Belin's interview with former CIA official, James P. O'Connell on matters pertaining to an alleged plot to assassinate Fidel Castro, 17 May 1975, in *Declassified Documents Reference System* (Farmington Hills, Michigan: Gale, 2008); Andrew, 1995: 252; 'Edwards and the Support Chief decided to rely on Robert A. Mahen to recruit someone "tough enough" to handle the job' (*Alleged Assassination Plots*, 1975: 74).

190 On the appeal to the Mafia's patriotism, see David W. Belin's interview with former CIA official James P. O'Connell on matters pertaining to an alleged plot to assassinate Fidel Castro, 17 May 1975, in *Declassified Documents Reference System* (Farmington Hills, Michigan: Gale, 2008): 5–6.

191 Schlesinger, 1978: 484.

192 *Alleged Assassination Plots*, 1975: 259.

193 See, for instance, Freedman, 2000: 151, and on the Kennedys as the instigators of the continued assassination plans see Srodes, 1999: 545–6 and Weiner, 2008: 209 ('In November 1961, in the greatest secrecy, John and Bobby Kennedy created a new planning cell for covert action, the Special Group (Augmented). It was RFK's outfit, and it had one mission: eliminating Castro') and also Weiner, 2008: 214–15 ('The Kennedy White House twice had ordered the CIA to create an assassination squad . . . in 1975, Richard Bissell said those orders had come from national security adviser McGeorge Bundy and Bundy's aide Walt Rostow, and that the president's men "would not have given such encouragement unless they were confident that it would meet with the president's approval"').

Though admittedly a partisan for the Kennedys, on the other hand Arthur M. Schlesinger seems adamant that neither brother knew anything of the plans to kill the Cuban leader (1978: 488). Yet at other points in his narrative, he suggests that John F. Kennedy was under pressure to accept assassination as an option, though he intensely disapproved of the plan (492–3, 497). He also plainly states that Robert Kennedy was told of the plot involving Giancana on 7 May 1962 (493–4), and points out that nonetheless RFK persisted in his plan to prosecute Giancana (496). He takes this as evidence of RFK's disapproval of the assassination plot itself. He concludes: 'I too find the idea incredible that these two men, so filled with love of life and so conscious of the ironies of history, could thus deny all the values and purposes that animated their existence' (498). Unfortunately, and probably unfairly, Schlesinger's willingness to exonerate the Kennedys in most matters compromises his powerful case for their innocence here. Later, for instance, he argues that Marilyn Monroe's interest in Robert Kennedy was one of 'the fantasies of her last summer'. He definitely implies that this was all it was, and thereby acquits RFK of having had an affair with her (591). Schlesinger's gullibility or naïveté regarding the possibility of an affair with Monroe may make us wonder about his assertions elsewhere.

194 Freedman, 2000: 152.

195 Beschloss, 1991: 375.

196 Testimony of McGeorge Bundy before the Commission on CIA Activities Within the U.S., 7 April 1975, in *Declassified Documents Reference System*, Document Number: CK3100088659 (Farmington Hills, Michigan: Gale, 2008); Weiner, 2008: 209.

197 Shesol, 1997: 129; Weiner suggests that it was not the assassination that was news to RFK, merely the fact of the Mafia's involvement, and that he did nothing to stop the assassination plans (2008: 215). During the 1960 election campaign there were rumours that either Mayor Richard Daley or the Mafia had helped Kennedy win the vote in Chicago (Graubard, 2009: 476).

198 Shesol, 1997: 129; on Robert Kennedy's impatience to have Castro assassinated, see Srodes, 1999: 544.

199 Cline, 1976: 188–9; Powers, 1979: 154–5; Reeves, 1991: 259–61; Andrew, 1995: 263, 274.

200 *Alleged Assassination Plots*, 1975: 73.

201 Andrew, 1995: 275.

202 *Alleged Assassination Plots*, 1975: 72.

203 Ibid.: 88–9.

204 Quoted in Shesol, 1997: 126.

205 Holland, 2004: 426–7. The idea that Castro was behind the assassination was presented to Johnson in a conversation held on 29 November 1963: '[Senator Richard] Russell dismissed suspicions of Soviet involvement but started to add, "I wouldn't be surprised if Castro" – Johnson cut him off. "Okay, okay, that's what we want to know"' (Grose, 1995: 542). Regarding this conversation see also Holland, 2004: 201; Weiner, 2008: 260, 313–14. He may well have cut Russell off because he was dismissing the idea, or otherwise because he felt the force of the notion, but did not wish to hear details. In a conversation in February 1967, Johnson remarked that he had been presented with a story whereby Castro hired Oswald as revenge for the abortive assassination attempts directed against himself (Holland, 2004: 395–6). Yet, Johnson could, at times, express official doubt about such stories; the next month, in conversation with Senator Connally, he listened to a version of the same story, and then effectively dismissed it (Holland, 2004: 405–7).

206 See *New York Times*, 25 June 1976 quoted in Powers, 1979: 157. He also seems to have suggested that, given the murders of Trujillo and Diem, Kennedy's assassination was 'divine retribution' (Schlesinger, 1978: 649). (Actually, the USA's part in these two murders was somewhat tenuous.) Johnson also appears to have given credence to the idea that the CIA was involved in Kennedy's murder (Bird, 1992: 566). See also Califano, 1991: 295.

207 Hamill, 2007: 531.

208 *Alleged Assassination Plots*, 1975: 142n.

209 Richard Helms quoted giving evidence to the Church Committee in Shesol, 1997: 129; see also Weiner, 2008: 212 ('The overthrow of Castro was "the top priority in the United States Government," Bobby Kennedy told [the new CIA director, John] McCone on January 19, 1962').

210 Andrew, 1995: 421.

211 Cline, 1976: 182.

212 *Final Report*, 1976: I, 425.

213 The facts are contested. One American participant in the Phoenix programme declines to accept the claim that it was set up as 'an indiscriminate counterterror weapon that

was ruthlessly employed by us and the South Vietnamese against a defenceless rural peasantry' and that many of the victims were 'innocent civilians' (Herrington, 1997: 196).

214 Valentine, 1990: 13.

215 Colby, 1978: 270–2. Colby's denials that Phoenix pursued a policy of assassination are clearly open to charges of self-exoneration.

216 *Alleged Assassination Plots*, 1975: 227–46; Kissinger, 1979: 658–60, 666–78.

217 Graubard, 2009: 515. Though some believe it is unfair to see Ford's pardon of Nixon as cunning (see Casserly, 1977: 39).

218 Kissinger, 1979: 674.

219 Kissinger, 1979: 676.

220 Nixon, 1978: 489–90.

221 *Final Report*, 1976: IV, 122–3.

222 Hitchens, 2001: 64–6.

223 Sullivan III, 2008: 141. For the denials see Kissinger, 1982: 374–413.

224 Kirkham, 1970: 356–7.

225 Zinn, 2003: 462–3.

226 Baxter Smith, in Breitman, 1976: 168.

227 *Final Report*, 1976: II, 86–9, III, 185–224.

228 *Final Report*, 1976: II, 101; III, 697.

CHAPTER 16: God's Lonely Men

1 Cochrane, 1977: v.

2 Brown, 1963: 33.

3 Jackson, 2004: 120.

4 Biskind, 1998: 313.

5 Jackson, 2004: 5.

6 Ibid.: 111.

7 Ibid.: 117.

8 Biskind, 1998: 290.

9 Schrader, 2002: viii.

10 Biskind, 1998: 240–1, 293.

11 Ibid.: 246.

12 Brunette, 1999: 54.

13 Christie, 2003: 9.

14 Biskind, 1998: 294.

15 Brunette, 1999: 49–50; Biskind, 1998: 296; Taubin, 2000: 12.

16 Jackson, 2004: 116.

17 Christie, 2003: 62; Biskind, 1998: 295.

18 Christie, 2003: 66.

19 Christie, 2003: 53, 62; Biskind, 1998: 295; Taubin, 2000: 10.

20 Taubin, 2000: 10.

21 Immediately following Reagan's shooting, Schrader asserted that his script was complete before he read Bremer's diaries (*New York Times*, 1 April 1981: A19).

22 Christie, 2003: 54, 60.

23 Biskind, 1998: 300.

24 Christie, 2003: 54.
25 Taubin, 2000: 18.
26 Jackson, 2004: 116.
27 Christie, 2003: 32.
28 Brunette, 1999: 61.
29 Christie, 2003: 63 and 66.
30 Kirkham, 1970: 292–3.
31 Ibid.: 13, 294.
32 Given the very small number of assassinations in Australia and Canada, two other countries with a myth of the frontier, some have cast doubt on this cultural element in American assassination (see Murray C. Havens, 'Assassination in Australia', in Kirkham, 1970: 722–3).
33 Jackson, 2004: 119.
34 Christie, 2003: 42.
35 Brunette, 1999: 55.
36 Biskind, 1998: 307.
37 Brunette, 1999: 61–3; Taubin, 2000: 16–17.
38 Schrader, 2002: 66.
39 Jackson, 2004: 119.
40 Schrader, 2002: 5.
41 Brown, 1963: 154.
42 Wertham, 1966: 348–9.
43 Ibid.: 346.
44 Jackson, 2004: 120.
45 Schrader, 2002: vii, 40.
46 Biskind, 1998: 299.
47 Brunette, 1999: 56.
48 Ibid.: 132, 183.
49 Christie, 2003: 62; Biskind, 1998: 295.
50 Christie, 2003: 26.
51 Brunette, 1999: 131.
52 Brunette, 1999: 60.
53 Quoted in Chafe, 1979: 329.
54 Shilts, 1982: 271.
55 Ibid.: 310.
56 'Meanwhile, the talk in Liddy's group was turning to one of his favourite subjects, assassination . . . "You don't assassinate people as an act of revenge", he mused. "It's a preventive thing . . . if Jane Fonda had done in the Second World War what she did in the Vietnam era she would have been shot or electrocuted." It has been documented how Liddy, at one stage in his career, recommended the assassination of Jack Anderson, an investigative journalist, but was over-ruled by higher authority' (Michael Leapman, 'Today's American Hero', *The Times*, 15 December 1980: 12).
57 *New York Times*, 11 December, 1980: B3.
58 Coleman, 2000: 56–61.
59 Ibid.: 370, 577.
60 MacDonald, 1998: 210–11.
61 Biskind, 1998: 313.
62 Reagan, 1989: 11.

63 Testimony of Dr Park Elliott Dietz, in Low, 1986: 83.

64 Ibid.: 63; cross-examination of Dr William T. Carpenter, Jr., in Low, 1986: 68.

65 Reagan, 1990: 259, 262; Reagan, 2007: 303. When the bullet was removed it was 'darkened by the paint on the limousine' (Reagan, 1990: 262).

66 Reagan, 2007: 12.

67 On McCarthy's bravery, see Reagan, 1990: 262. Of the three men who were shot, McCarthy made a full recovery, Delahanty recovered but suffered a permanent disability in his left arm, while Brady, the most seriously injured, was confined to a wheelchair and suffered slurring in his speech. Brady has since become a persuasive and dynamic campaigner for gun control.

68 Reagan, 1989: 17.

69 *New York Times*, 31 March 1981: A6.

70 Reagan, 1990: 260.

71 A decision that very likely saved Reagan's life (Reagan, 1989: 18; Morris, 2000: 429).

72 Reagan, 2007: 12.

73 From 'Excerpts From Transcript of Briefing on Wounds of President and Two Others', the statement of Dr Dennis S. O'Leary, *New York Times*, 31 March 1981: A7.

74 Reagan, 1989: 5. 'I started taking notes . . . "Doctors believe bleeding to death. Can't find a wound. 'Think we're going to lose him' [one doctor said]" . . . The entry hole from the bullet was so tiny that the emergency room crew had trouble finding it' (Speakes, 1988: 6).

75 Reagan, 1990: 259–60. Nancy Reagan appears to have shared his concern for this new suit (Reagan, 1989: 6).

76 Speakes, 1988: 9.

77 *New York Times*, 31 March 1981: A5. 'Haig's image never recovered from the events of March 30' (Speakes, 1988: 11).

78 In the weeks before the assassination attempt, Haig had in any case been irritated by what he perceived as encroachments on his patch, and had talked about resignation (Reagan, 2007: 11).

79 *New York Times*, 31 March 1981: A2.

80 Cooke, 2008: 261.

81 See E. J. Dionne, 'The Religious Right and the New Republican Party', in Chafe, 2008: 376.

82 Schapsmeier, 1989: 209.

83 Reagan seems to have especially worried that people thought he dyed his hair (Reagan, 1989: 11–12; Speakes, 1988: 102–3).

84 Leuchtenberg, 1983: 209–32. In his autobiography, Reagan accepts that, although intellectually a conservative Republican by 1960, he remained nominally a Democrat for a further two years; though he also flourishes that old excuse, 'I'm not so sure *I* changed as much as the parties changed' (Reagan, 1990: 134).

85 'The Communist plan for Hollywood was remarkably simple. It was merely to take over the motion picture business' (Reagan, 1981: 162).

86 Reagan, 1990: 257–8; Morris, 2000: 659–60.

87 Reagan, 1989: 9.

88 Ibid.: 6.

89 Reagan, 1990: 260.

90 *The Times*, 31 March 1981: 1; 'Excerpts From Transcript of Briefing on Wounds of President and Two Others', the statement of Dr Dennis S. O'Leary, *New York Times*,

31 March 1981: A7; Reagan, 1989: 7; Reagan, 1990: 261.

91 *New York Times*, 1 April 1981: A18.

92 Reagan, 2007: 12. As further evidence of Reagan's capacity for fellow-feeling, it seems that his darkest moment in hospital was when he guessed the extent of James Brady's injuries (Reagan, 2004: 551). In his diary Reagan modestly mentions none of the jokes he made while in distress.

93 *The Times*, 27 July 1981: 6.

94 *New York Times*, 31 March 1981: A6. That 'standing ovation' may be poetic licence, or was otherwise given in a spirit of obligation: Reagan himself remembered that he had not been 'riotously received – I think most of the audience were Democrats' (Reagan, 1990: 259). The day after the shooting it was revealed that in the previous twelve months, violent crime had risen by 13 per cent (*New York Times*, 1 April 1981: A1). Particularly worrying – including to Reagan himself – were the murders of over twenty black children in Atlanta (Reagan, 2007: 8).

95 Quoted in Houck, 1993: 177.

96 Graubard, 2009: 559.

97 *New York Times*, 11 December 1980: A34; *The Times*, 15 December 1980: 4. Despite this, after the shooting, Nancy Reagan changed her views on gun control (Reagan, 1989: 19). Her autobiography begins with an account of her husband being shot, and she remarks: 'I expected that the memory of the shooting would fade with time, but it never has' (20).

98 Clarke, 1990: 60–1.

99 Ewing, 2006: 91–2. 'A neighbour said of Mr and Mrs Hinckley's relationship with their son: "They only talked about him in the way parents would when they hoped their individualist [son] would come round and be one of the gang"' (*The Times*, 1 April 1981: 7).

100 Hinckley, 1985: 68.

101 *New York Times*, 31 March 1981: A2.

102 Hinckley, 1985: 84–7.

103 Low, 1986: 23.

104 Caplan, 1984: 35–6.

105 'Closing Argument by Mr. Fuller for the Defense', in Low, 1986: 96.

106 'Closing Argument by Mr. Fuller for the Defense', in Low, 1986: 95; Low, 1986: 24. As there were no other witnesses to these games of Russian roulette, there is some doubt as to whether Hinckley actually did this, or merely fantasised that he had done so, or simply invented the incidents in order to convince the authorities that he had been mad (Ibid.: 29).

107 Ewing, 2006: 38; testimony of Dr William T. Carpenter, Jr., in Low, 1986: 65.

108 Quoted in ibid.: 91.

109 Foster, 1997: 122.

110 'Closing Argument by Mr. Adelman for the Government', in Low, 1986: 87.

111 Reagan, 2007: 13. Reagan had been contacted by Billy Graham, who knew the Hinckleys.

112 *The Times*, 28 May 1981: 6; *The Times*, 18 November 1981: 7.

113 He does appear to have made an attempt to alert his psychiatrist to his obsession, but Hopper dismissed the revelation as just a typical infatuation with a movie star ('Closing Argument by Mr. Fuller for the Defense', in Low, 1986: 97); see also Ewing, 1984: 40.

114 Ewing, 1984: 40.

115 Low, 1986: 26.

116 Clarke, 1990: 93.

117 Testimony of Dr William T. Carpenter, Jr., in Low, 1986: 68.

118 Ewing, 1984: 41.

119 Low, 1986: 27.

120 Testimony and cross-examination of Dr William T. Carpenter, Jr., in Low, 1986: 30–1, 70. A Devastator bullet is designed to explode on impact; fortunately the bullet that hit Reagan failed to do so (Reagan, 1989: 5); Speakes, 1988: 10.

121 Ewing, 1984: 42.

122 *New York Times*, 1 April 1981: A1; the text of the letter is quoted in Hinckley, 1985: 169.

123 Ewing, 1984: 42–3; Hinckley, 1985: 170.

124 Testimony of Dr William T. Carpenter, Jr., in Low, 1986: 32.

125 Foster, 1997: 125.

126 Hollinger, 2006: 142.

127 Foster, 1997: 66–8.

128 Hollinger, 2006: 141.

129 Foster, 1997: 100.

130 Biskind, 1998: 333. 'At the same time, Scorsese was also receiving death threats from members of the Manson family, after he had been asked to play Manson in a made-for-TV movie, *Helter Skelter*' (*ibid.*).

131 *New York Times*, 1 April 1981: A1.

132 Quoted in Taubin, 2000: 9.

133 Testimony of Dr William T. Carpenter, Jr., in Low, 1986: 56.

134 Reagan, 1990: 263.

135 Though he disliked swearing in films and 'seldom uses any curse words stronger than "hell" or "damn"' (Speakes, 1988: 103), according to some who knew him, Reagan 'could cuss as well as James Baker in male company' (Morris, 2000: 427).

136 'Closing Argument by Mr. Fuller for the Defense', in Low, 1986: 95; Clarke, 1990: 57–8.

137 Foster, 1997: 122.

138 Ibid.: 136–7.

139 'He had, by then, come to believe that the only salvation that he had, the only way he could extricate himself from this life was through union with her. He had come to believe that a union with her was in some sense ordained, that he was being propelled in that direction' (Testimony of Dr William T. Carpenter, Jr., in Low, 1986: 34).

140 From Hinckley's tape-recorded New Year monologue of 1981, quoted in 'Closing Argument by Mr. Fuller for the Defense', in Low, 1986: 98.

141 Hinckley quoted in the testimony of Dr Park Elliott Dietz, in Low, 1986: 44.

142 Testimony of Dr William T. Carpenter, Jr., in Low, 1986: 54.

143 Testimony of Dr Park Elliott Dietz, in Low, 1986: 40–1.

144 Hinckley, 1985: 104.

145 Ewing, 1984: 46; Hinckley, 1985: 197.

146 *The Times*, 9 April 1981: 7; Foster, 1997: 138–9.

147 Kirkham, 1970: xliv.

148 Low, 1986: 27–8.

149 Finkel, 1988: ix.

150 Caplan, 1984: 21; Low, 1986: 21. For Isaac Ray, see Chapter 4.

151 Low, 1986: 20; Clarke, 1990: 50.

152 Caplan, 1984: 24.

153 Low, 1986: 20–1.

154 Walker, 1968: 27.

155 Reagan, 2007: 90.

156 Ewing, 2006: 98.

157 *The Times*, 23 June 1982: 6. On CBS, Dan Rather told the nation: 'money talks, and in the Hinckley case money yelled and banged on the table and won the day. The cleverest lawyers were hired, the most expensive psychiatrists. The Hinckleys committed a considerable part of their considerable wealth to the case, and when it was over, the victorious defense attorney smiled and said, "Another day, another dollar"' (Noonan, 1990: 29).

158 On the 'malingering' issue, see Clarke, 1990: 53–6.

159 Low, 1986: 118.

160 Geis, January 1985: 73.

161 Low, 1986: 126–7; Mackay, 1995: 118–21.

162 Finkel, 1988: x.

163 Low, 1986: 121.

164 Clyne, 1973: 92–3.

165 Low, 1986: 127–30.

166 Ewing, 2006: 99.

167 Ibid.: 100.

168 Reagan, 1990: 263.

169 http://www.archives.gov/federal-register/codification/executive-order/12333.html (accessed 15 January 2011).

170 Andrew, 1995: 464.

171 Sullivan III, 2008: 177.

172 Andrew, 1995: 463.

173 *The Times*, 15 September 1981: 30.

174 *New York Times*, 31 March 1981: A2.

175 Clarke, 1990: 81ff.

176 Paul B. Sheatsley and Jacob J. Feldman, in Greenberg, 1965: 170–1. They are writing in the context of the assassination of JFK, and immediately go on to say that such parental feelings probably did not operate for most in so young a President.

177 Kirkham, 1970: 92–3.

178 Ibid.: 131–2.

179 Ewing, 1984: 44.

CONCLUSION: Making an Ending

1 Reagan, 1990: 254; Reagan, 2007: 10.

2 Much as he had to Frederick Douglass – see 'The Freedman's Monument To Abraham Lincoln: An Address Delivered in Washington, D.C., on 14 April 1876', in Douglass, 1991: 427–40.

3 Moldea, 1995: 307.

4 *New York Times*, 1 April 1981: A31; *New York Times*, 31 March 1981: A5.

5 Taylor, 1997: 228.

6 Hanley, 2010: 190.

7 Smith, 2010: 302.

8 Ziegler, 1985: 699.

9 Bew, 2007: 525–6; Moloney, 2002: 176. In March 1979, the Conservative spokesman on Northern Ireland, Airey Neave, had been assassinated in an underground Westminster car park (Bell, 1980: 443).

10 Hough, 1981: 287; Ziegler, 1985: 700.

11 Taylor, 1997: 268; Moloney, 2002: 329–30; Hanley, 2010: 199.

12 Charlie Savage, 'Secret U.S. Memo Made Legal Case to Kill a Citizen', *New York Times*, 8 October 2011.

13 Arendt, 1990: 84.

14 As argued by, for instance, Philip Zimbardo, the psychologist behind the Stanford Prison Experiment, in Zimbardo, 2007), and also in Collins, 2008).

15 Benjamin, 1977: 255.

Works Consulted

UNPUBLISHED SOURCES AND ARCHIVAL MATERIAL

At British Library, London: Gladstone Papers (Add.Ms.44308); Viscount Gladstone Papers, British Library (Add.Mss.46067). Also on CD-Rom, items from the Declassified Documents Reference System and the Lexis-Nexis Congressional Hearings Digital Collection

At International Institute of Social History, Amsterdam: Papers of Alexander Berkman; The Emma Goldman Papers, A Microfilm Edition, edited by Candace Falk, Ronald J. Zboray and Daniel Cornford, with Alice Hall (Government Documents Editor) (Alexandria, VA, and Cambridge, UK: Chadwyck-Healey); papers of Alfred Marsh (4328.1, files 174–229); correspondence from Prince Peter Kropotkin; Kropotkin Papers

At the National Archives, Kew, London: papers relating to: Johann Most (CRIM 12/82; HO 144/77/A3385); Phoenix Park Murders (HO 144/98/A16380; HO 144/98/A16380B; HO 144/98/A16380C; HO 144/113/A25251; PRO 30/60/16; PRO 30/60/13/3; T 13105/83; HO 144/113; CRIM 1/19/4); Papers of Sir Robert Anderson (HO 144/1537/1); Assassination attempts on Queen Victoria (MEPO 3/17; HO 144/95/A14281; HO 45/2568; MEPO3/19A; MEPO 3/19B); the assassination of Spencer Perceval (PRO 30/29/6/11; PRO 30/43/25)

At Lambeth Palace Library: the William Temple papers; Sword of the Spirit archives; the George Bell papers

At the Liddell Hart Centre for Military Archives, King's College London: correspondence between Liddell Hart and George Bell

At Special Collections, University of Birmingham Library, from the Masterman Papers, material relating to Lady Cavendish (CFGM 46/3/4)

WEBSITES, ONLINE AND DATABASE MATERIAL CONSULTED IN THE WRITING OF THIS BOOK

The following sites were all up and running during the writing of this book; the dates on which the online material was consulted will be found in the relevant notes.

The Alfred Whital Stern Collection of Lincolniana housed at the Rare Book and Special Collections Division of the Library of Congress, Washington, DC, online at http://memory.loc.gov/ammem/collections/stern-lincoln/

The Abraham Lincoln Papers at the Library of Congress, Washington, DC, online at http://memory.loc.gov/ammem/alhtml/malhome.html

The William H. Seward Papers, including 'Lincoln and his Circle', at the Rare Books and
    Special Collections, University of Rochester, New York, and also materials available
    online at http://www.library.rochester.edu
The transcripts of Leon Czolgosz's trial are available as a pdf file from http://www.eriebar.
    org/pr_ed_brochures.asp
http://freenet.buffalo.edu/bah/h/mckinley.html – page by Chuck LaChiusa, *History of
    Buffalo: President William McKinley in Buffalo, NY*. This includes access to the Annual
    *Report of the Board of Police of the City of Buffalo, for the Year Ending December 31,
    1901* and Richard H. Barry, *The True Story of the Assassination of President McKinley at
    Buffalo* (Buffalo, NY: Robert Allan Reid, 1901)
http://ublib.buffalo.edu/hsl/resources/guides/mckinley.html – another very impressive
    website, prepared by Linda Lohr and Sharon Gray, with access online to various
    contemporary articles on the McKinley assassination – all listed individually in the
    bibliography below. The site also contains a useful article on Leon Czolgosz, 'Lights
    Out in the City of Light: Anarchy and Assassination at the Pan-American Exposition',
    online at http://ublib.buffalo.edu/hsl/exhibits/panam/law/czolgosz.html
Michigan State University Libraries, Vincent Voice Library, has recordings of McKinley's
    speeches at http://www.lib.msu.edu/cs/branches/vvl/presidents/mckinley.html
    and of a news report on the shooting of Ronald Reagan at http://vvl.lib.msu.edu/
    showfindingaid.cfm?findaidid=ReaganR
http://www.whitehouse.gov/history/presidents/wm25.html is the official White House
    online biography of William McKinley
There are early films available of President McKinley and of his funeral at the Library of
    Congress website: http://rs6.loc.gov/papr/mckhome.html
McKinley's writings can be found through Project Gutenberg at http://www.gutenberg.
    org/author/William_McKinley
Copies of the telegrams allegedly sent by Talât Pasha can be found online at http://www.
    firstworldwar.com/source/armenia_talaatorders.html
At the same source is an extract of Lord Bryce's 'British Government Report on the
    Armenian Massacres of April–December 1915': http://firstworldwar.com/source/
    brycereport_armenia.htm
Also on this site is an extract from the 'Memoirs and Diaries' of Dr Martin Niepage at
    http://firstworldwar.com/diaries/armenianmassacres.htm
The transcript of the trial of Soghomon Tehlirian, translated from German, is available
    online at http://www.cilicia.com/armo_tehlirian.html. See also below under Yeghiayan,
    Vartkes
The entire Warren Commission report can be read online at www.historymatters.com
    and the subsequent revisions made by the House Select Committee on Assassinations
    and a huge array of other Kennedy assassination related material can be found online
    at www.archives.gov/research/jfk
Declassified FBI files can be read in CD-Rom form in the *Declassified Documents
    Reference System* (Farmington Hills, Michigan: Gale, 2008)
Mel Ayton, 'The Robert Kennedy Assassination: Unraveling the Conspiracy Theories',
    online at http://crimemagazine.com/05/robertkennedy,0508-5.htm – posted 8 May
    2005

OTHER SOURCES

In addition, I also consulted a number of contemporary news reports and interviews stored on YouTube. I have decided not to list this material individually as it would take up too much space, but those who are interested will quickly find relevant footage under the obvious key-words. However, to give one example, the first screening of the Zapruder film can be seen online at http://www.youtube.com/watch?v=4DwKK4rkeEM.

I have also decided not to list references to newspaper cuttings in the bibliography, as these are all fully set out in the notes. However, the *19th Century British Library Newspapers* (managed by Gale Cengage), *Nineteenth Century UK Periodicals* (Gale Group) databases and *The Times Digital Archive* (Gale Cengage) have been an invaluable source (if used warily) in the research of this book, as have the paper and microfiche copies at the British Library's Colindale Newspaper Library.

PRIMARY AND SECONDARY READING

Abernathy, Ralph (1970) 'Our Lives Were Filled with the Action', in *Martin Luther King Jr. A Profile*, ed. C. Eric Lincoln (New York: Hill & Wang): 219–22

Abbott, Philip (2008) *Accidental Presidents: Death, Assassination, Resignation, and Democratic Succession* (New York & Basingstoke: Palgrave Macmillan)

Adalian, Rouben Paul (1995) *Remembering and Understanding the Armenian Genocide* (Yerevan, Armenia: National Commission of the Republic of Armenia on the 80th Commemoration of the Armenian Genocide)

Adamic, Louis (1931) *Dynamite: The Story of Class Violence in America* (New York: Viking)

Adams, Coker (1882) *Protect the Queen. A Sermon Preached at Saham Toney, Norfolk, March 12, 1882* (London: James Parker)

Adams, Henry (1999) *The Education of Henry Adams* (1906), ed. Ira B. Nadel (Oxford: Oxford University Press [OUP])

Adams, H. L. (1931) *C.I.D. Behind the Scenes at Scotland Yard* (London: Sampson Low, Marston)

Adams, Jad (2003) 'Striking a Blow for Freedom', *History Today*, Vol. 53, No. 9 (London: Longman): 18–19

Adams, William Edwin (1903) *Memoirs of a Social Atom*, 2 vols (London: Hutchinsion)

Ades, Dawn (2001) 'Surrealism, Male-Female', in *Surrealism, Desire Unbound*, ed. Jennifer Mundy (London: Tate Publishing): 170–201

Akçam, Taner (1994) 'Wir Türken und die Armenier. Plädoyer für die Auseinander-setzung mit dem Massenmord', in *Armenier und Armenien – Heimat und Exil*, ed. Tessa Hofmann (Hamburg: Rowohlt Taschenbuch): 33–43

Akçam, Taner (2004) *From Empire to Republic: Turkish Nationalism and the Armenian Genocide* (London & New York: Zed Books)

Akçam, Taner (2006) *A Shameful Act: The Armenian Genocide and the Question of Turkish Responsibility* (1999), trans. Paul Bessemer (New York: Metropolitan Books)

Albertini, Luigi (1953) *The Origins of the War of 1914*, trans. and ed. Isabella M. Massey, Vol. 2 (London & New York: OUP)

Alleged Assassination Plots (1975) *Alleged Assassination Plots Involving Foreign Leaders. An Interim Report of the Select Committee to Study Governmental Operations with Respect to Intelligence Activities*, United States Senate (Washington, DC: US Government Printing Office)

Almira, José and G. Stoyan (1927) *Le Déclic de Sarajevo* (Paris: Éditions Radot)

Altman, Peter, Heinz Brüdigam, Barbara Mausbach-Bromberger and Max Oppenheimer (1975) *Der deutsche antifaschistische Widerstand 1933–1945 in Bildern und Dokumenten* (Frankfurt: Röderberg)

Ambrose, Stephen E. (1981) *Ike's Spies: Eisenhower and the Espionage Establishment*, with Richard H. Immerman, research associate (Garden City, NY: Doubleday)

Anarchist Response, The (no date) *The Anarchist Response to War and Labor Violence in 1914. Rebecca Edelsohn, Alexander Berkman, Anti-Militarism, Free Speech and Hunger Strikes* (London & Berkeley, CA: Kate Sharpley Library)

Anderson, Margaret (1930) *My Thirty Years' War* (London: Knopf)

Anderson, Sir Robert (1906) *Sidelights on the Home Rule Movement* (London: John Murray)

Andonian, Aram (1920) ['Compiler'], *The Memoirs of Naim Bey*, with an introduction by Viscount Gladstone (London: Hodder & Stoughton)

Andrew, Christopher (1995) *For the President's Eyes Only: Secret Intelligence and the American Presidency from Washington to Bush* (New York: HarperCollins)

Annual Register, The (1881) *The Annual Register: A Review of Public Events at Home and Abroad, for the Year 1880* (London: Rivingtons)

Annual Register, The (1882) *The Annual Register: A Review of Public Events at Home and Abroad, for the Year 1881* (London: Rivingtons)

Annual Register, The (1883) *The Annual Register: A Review of Public Events at Home and Abroad, for the Year 1882* (London: Rivingtons)

Annual Register, The (1884) *The Annual Register: A Review of Public Events at Home and Abroad, for the Year 1883* (London: Rivingtons)

Annual Register, The (1895) *The Annual Register, A Review of Public Events at Home and Abroad for the Year 1894* (London: Longmans, Green)

Annual Report (1902) *Annual Report of the Board of Police of the City of Buffalo, for the Year Ending December 31, 1901* (Buffalo, NY: The Wenbourne-Sumner Co.)

Archer, Stephen M. (1999a) 'John Wilkes Booth', in *American National Biography*, Vol. 3 (New York & Oxford: OUP): 194–6

Archer, Stephen M. (1999b) 'Junius Brutus Booth', in *American National Biography*, Vol. 3 (New York & Oxford: OUP): 196–7

Arendt, Hannah (1968) *Men in Dark Times* (San Diego, New York & London: Harcourt Brace)

Arendt, Hannah (1975) *The Origins of Totalitarianism* (1951), new edn (New York: Harcourt Brace Jovanovich)

Arendt, Hannah (1977) *Eichmann in Jerusalem* (1965) (Harmondsworth: Penguin)

Arendt, Hannah (1990) *On Revolution* (1965) (London: Penguin)

Arendt, Hannah and Karl Jaspers (1985) *Hannah Arendt–Karl Jaspers Briefwechsel, 1926–1969* (Munich & Zurich: Piper)

Armenian Allegations (1987) *Armenian Allegations: Myth and Reality. A Handbook of Facts and Documents*, compiled and edited by The Assembly of Turkish American Associations (Washington, DC)

Armstrong, Stephen B. (2008) *Pictures About Extremes: The Films of John Frankenheimer* (Jefferson, NC, & London: McFarland)

Assassination of Abraham Lincoln (1866) *The Assassination of Abraham Lincoln, Late President of the United States of America, and the Attempted Assassination of William H.*

Seward, Secretary of State, and Frederick W. Seward, Assistant Secretary, on the evening of the 14th of April, 1865 (Washington: Government Printing Office)

'Assassination of President McKinley' (1901) 'The Assassination of President McKinley', *The Buffalo Medical Journal*, Vol. 57, No. 3 (Buffalo, NY): 226–32

Atkins, G. Pope and Larman C. Wilson (1972) *The United States and the Trujillo Regime* (New Brunswick, NJ: Rutgers University Press [UP])

Auclair, Marcelle (1954) *La vie de Jean Jaurès* (Paris: Éditions du Seuil)

Baberowski, Jorg (2006) 'Law, the Judicial System and the Legal Profession', in *The Cambridge History of Russia. Volume II, Imperial Russia, 1689–1917*, ed. Dominic Lieven (Cambridge: Cambridge University Press [CUP]): 344–68

Bailey, John, ed. (1927) *The Diary of Lady Frederick Cavendish*, 2 vols (London: John Murray)

Baldwin, James (1970) 'The Highroad to Destiny', in *Martin Luther King Jr. A Profile*, ed. C. Eric Lincoln (New York: Hill & Wang): 90–112

Baldwin, Neil (2001) *Edison: Inventing the Century* (1995) (Chicago: Chicago UP)

Ball, T. Frederick (1886) *Scenes and Incidents of Her Life and Reign* (London: S. W. Partridge)

Bancroft, Frederic (1900) *The Life of William H. Seward*, 2 vols (New York & London: Harper & Brothers)

Barry, Richard H. (1901) *The True Story of the Assassination of President McKinley at Buffalo* (Buffalo, NY: Robert Allan Reid)

Bates, Ernest Sutherland (1929a) 'John Wilkes Booth', in *Dictionary of American Biography*, ed. Allen Johnson, Vol. 2 (New York: Scribner's): 448–52

Bates, Ernest Sutherland (1929b) 'Junius Brutus Booth', in *Dictionary of American Biography*, ed. Allen Johnson, Vol. 2 (New York: Scribner's): 452–4

Beard, George M. (1882) *The Case of Guiteau – A Psychological Study*, reprinted from the *Journal of Nervous and Mental Disease*, Vol. 9, No. 1 (January 1882)

Bell, George (1946) *The Church and Humanity (1939–1946)* (London: Longmans, Green)

Bell, J. Bowyer (1980) *The Secret Army: The IRA 1916–1979* (Cambridge, MA: MIT Press)

Benjamin, Walter (1977) *Illuminationen: Ausgewählte Schriften* (Frankfurt: Suhrkamp)

Bennett, Lerone (1970) 'When the Man and the Hour Are Met', in *Martin Luther King Jr. A Profile*, ed. C. Eric Lincoln (New York: Hill & Wang): 7–39

Benson, Arthur Christopher and Viscount Esher, eds (1907) *The Letters of Queen Victoria: A Selection from Her Majesty's Correspondence Between the Years 1837 and 1861*, 3 vols (Vol. 1: 1837–43; Vol. 2: 1844–53; Vol. 3: 1854–61) (London: John Murray)

Benson, E. F. (1987) *Queen Victoria* (1935) (London: Chatto & Windus)

Berglar, Peter (1970) *Walther Rathenau: Seine Zeit, sein Werk, seine Persönlichkeit* (Bremen: Schünemann Universitätsverlag)

Bergman, Jay (1983) *Vera Zasulich. A Biography* (Stanford, CA: Stanford UP)

Berkman, Alexander (1926) *Prison Memoirs of an Anarchist* (1912), with an introduction by Edward Carpenter (London: C. W. Daniel)

Berlin, Isaiah (1995) *Karl Marx* (1939) (London: Fontana)

Bernstein, Barton J. and Allen J. Matusow, eds (1966) *The Truman Administration: A Documentary History* (New York & London: Harper & Row)

Bernstein, Eduard (1921) *My Years of Exile: Reminiscences of a Socialist*, trans. Bernard Miall (London: Leonard Parsons)

Bernstorff, Graf Johann Heinrich von (1936) *Errinnerungen und Briefe* (Zurich: Polygraphischer)

Beschloss, Michael R. (1991) *Kennedy v. Khrushchev: The Crisis Years, 1960–63* (London: Faber and Faber)

Bethge, Eberhard and Renate, eds (1984) *Letzte Briefe im Widerstand. Aus dem Kreis der Familie Bonhoeffer* (Munich: Chr. Kaiser)

Bethge, Eberhard and Ronald C. D. Jasper, eds (1974) *An der Schwelle zum gespaltenen Europa. Der Briefwechsel zwischen George Bell und Gerhard Leibholz, 1939–1951* (Stuttgart: Kreuz)

Bew, Paul (1980) *C. S. Parnell* (Dublin: Gill & Macmillan)

Bew, Paul (2007) *Ireland: The Politics of Enmity, 1789–2006* (Oxford: OUP)

Bird, Kai (1992) *The Chairman: John J. McCloy, The Making of the American Establishment* (New York: Simon & Schuster)

Bishop, Patrick and Eamonn Mallie (1987) *The Provisional IRA* (London: Heinemann)

Biskind, Peter (1998) *Easy Riders, Raging Bulls: How the Sex 'n' Drugs 'n' Rock 'n' Roll Generation Saved Hollywood* (London: Bloomsbury)

Blaine, James G. (1884) *Twenty Years of Congress: From Lincoln to Garfield. With a Review of the Events Which Led to the Political Revolution of 1860*, 2 vols (Norwich, CT: Henry Bill)

Blind, Karl (January 1894) 'The Rise and Development of Anarchism', *Contemporary Review*, Vol. 65 (London: Isbister): 140–52

Blum, William (2003) *Killing Hope: US Military and CIA Interventions Since World War II*, rev. and expanded edn (London: Zed Books)

Bonhoeffer, Dietrich (1970) *Widerstand und Ergebung: Briege und Aufzeichnungen aus der Haft*, ed. Eberhard Bethge (Munich: Chr. Kaiser)

Bonhoeffer, Dietrich (1974) *Tagebücher – Briefe – Dokumente, 1923–1945*, ed. Eberhard Bethge (Munich: Chr. Kaiser)

Bookbinder, Paul (1996) *Weimar Germany: The Republic of the Reasonable* (Manchester & New York: Manchester UP)

Booth Clarke, Asia (1938) *The Unlocked Book. A Memoir of John Wilkes Booth by his Sister Asia Booth Clarke*, with a foreword by Eleanor Farjeon (London: Faber and Faber)

Booth, John Wilkes (1997) *'Right or Wrong, God Judge Me'. The Writings of John Wilkes Booth*, eds John Rhodehamel and Louise Taper (Urbana & Chicago: Univ. of Illinois Press)

Bosmajian, Haig (1970) 'The Letter from Birmingham Jail', in *Martin Luther King Jr. A Profile*, ed. C. Eric Lincoln (New York: Hill & Wang): 128–43

Bravin, Jess (1998) *Squeaky. The Life and Times of Lynette Alice Fromme* (1997) (New York: St Martins Press)

Breitman, George, ed. (1965) *Malcolm X Speaks: Selected Speeches and Statements* (London: Secker & Warburg)

Breitman, George, ed. (1970) *By Any Means Necessary: Speeches, Interviews and a Letter by Malcolm X* (New York: Pathfinder Press)

Breitman, George, Herman Porter and Baxter Smith (1976) *The Assassination of Malcolm X*, ed. with an introduction by Malik Miah (New York: Pathfinder Press)

Bremer, Arthur H. (1973) *An Assassin's Diary*, with an introduction by Harding Lemay (New York: Harper's Magazine Press)

Breton, André (1930) *Seconde Manifeste du surréalisme* (Paris: Éditions Kra)

Brogan, Hugh (1999) *The Penguin History of the USA* (London: Penguin)

Broido, Vera (1977) *Apostles into Terrorists. Women and the Revolutionary Movement in the Russia of Alexander II* (New York: Viking)

Brook-Shepherd, Gordon (1961) *Dollfuss* (London: Macmillan)

Brook-Shepherd, Gordon (1984) *Victims At Sarajevo: The Romance and Tragedy of Franz Ferdinand and Sophie* (London: Harvill)

Brooke, John and Mary Sorenson, eds (1981) *W. E. Gladstone. IV: Autobiographical Memoranda 1868–1894* (London: Her Majesty's Stationery Office)

Brown, J. A. C. (1963) *Techniques of Persuasion: From Propaganda to Brainwashing* (Harmondsworth: Penguin)

Brown, Jared (2005) *Alan J. Pakula: His Films and His Life* (New York: Back Stage Books)

Brunette, Peter, ed. (1999) *Martin Scorsese: Interviews* (Jackson, MS: Univ. of Mississippi Press)

Bryan, George S. (1940) *The Great American Myth* (New York: Carrick & Evans)

Buckle, George Earle, ed. (1926a) *The Letters of Queen Victoria. A Selection from Her Majesty's Correspondence and Journal Between the Years 1862 and 1885*, Second Series, *Vol. 1: 1862–1869* (London: John Murray)

Buckle, George Earle, ed. (1926b) *The Letters of Queen Victoria. A Selection from Her Majesty's Correspondence and Journal Between the Years 1862 and 1885*, Second Series, *Vol. 2: 1870–1878* (London: John Murray)

Buckle, George Earle, ed. (1928) *The Letters of Queen Victoria. A Selection from Her Majesty's Correspondence and Journal Between the Years 1862 and 1885*, Second Series, *Vol. 3: 1879–1885* (London: John Murray)

Bugliosi, Vincent and Curt Gentry (1974) *The Manson Murders: An Investigation into Motive* (London: Bodley Head)

Burlingame, Michael (2008) *Abraham Lincoln: A Life*, 2 vols (Baltimore: Johns Hopkins UP)

Butler, Leslie (2004) 'Dead President and Progressive Reform', *Reviews in American History*, Vol. 32, No. 3: 399–406

Cahm, Caroline (1989) *Kropotkin and the Rise of Revolutionary Anarchism 1872–1886* (Cambridge: CUP)

Califano, Joseph A. (1991) *The Triumph and Tragedy of Lyndon Johnson: The White House Years* (New York: Simon & Schuster)

Cannadine, David (1996) *The Decline and Fall of the British Aristocracy* (1990) (Basingstoke & Oxford: Papermac)

Caplan, Lincoln (1984) *The Insanity Defense and the Trial of John W. Hinckley, Jr.* (Boston: David R. Godine)

Carlson, Andrew R. (1972) *Anarchism in Germany. Vol. I: The Early Movement* (Metuchen, NJ: Scarecrow Press)

Carnegie, Andrew (June 1889) 'Wealth', *North American Review*, Vol. 148, No. 391 (New York): 653–65

Carr, Edward Hallett (1933) *The Romantic Exiles: A Nineteenth-Century Portrait Gallery* (London: Victor Gollancz)

Carr, E. H. (1937) *Michael Bakunin* (London: Macmillan)

Carr, Raymond (1984) *Puerto Rico: A Colonial Experiment* (New York: Random House)

Carsten, F. L. (1986) *The First Austrian Republic, 1918–1938: A Study Based on British and Austrian Documents* (Aldershot: Gower/Maurice Temple Smith)

Carter, Dan T. (1992) *George Wallace, Richard Nixon, and the Transformation of American Politics* (Waco, TX: Markham Press Fund)

Carter, Dan T. (1995) *The Politics of Rage: George Wallace, the Origins of the New Conservatism, and the Transformation of American Politics* (New York: Simon & Schuster)

Cassels, Lavender (1984) *The Archduke and the Assassin: Sarajevo, June 28th 1914* (London: Frederick Muller)

Casserly, John J. (1977) *The Ford White House: The Diary of a Speechwriter* (Boulder, CO: Colorado Associated UP)

Castel, Albert (1999) *William Clarke Quantrill: His Life and Times* (1962) (Norman, OK: Univ. of Oklahoma Press)

Cavell, Stanley (2009) 'North by Northwest', in *A Hitchcock Reader*, eds Marshall Deutelbaum and Leland Poague, 2nd edn (Oxford: Wiley-Blackwell): 250–63

Chafe, William H., Harvard Sitkoff and Beth Bailey (2008) *A History of Our Time: Readings on Postwar America* (New York & Oxford: OUP)

Channing, Walter (January 1902) 'The Mental Status of Czolgosz, the Assassin of President McKinley', *American Journal of Insanity*, Vol. 59 (Baltimore: Johns Hopkins Press): 233–78

Chesterton, G. K. (1986) *Heretics, Orthodoxy, The Blatchford Controversies*, Vol. 1 of *The Collected Works of G. K. Chesterton*, ed. David Dooley (San Francisco: Ignatius Press)

Christie, Ian and David Thompson, eds (2003) *Scorsese on Scorsese* (London: Faber and Faber)

Christopulos, Diane (1974) 'Puerto Rico in the Twentieth Century: A Historical Survey', in *Puerto Rico and Puerto Ricans: Studies in History and Society*, eds Adalberto López and James Petras (New York: John Wiley): 123–63

Chubarov, Alexander (1999) *The Fragile Empire. A History of Imperial Russia* (New York: Continuum)

Clark, James A. (1993) *The Murder of James A. Garfield. The President's Last Days and the Trial and Execution of His Assassin* (Jefferson, NC, & London: McFarland)

Clarke, James W. (1990) *On Being Mad or Merely Angry: John W. Hinckley, Jr., and Other Dangerous People* (Princeton: Princeton UP)

Cleghorn, Reese (1970) 'Crowned with Crises', in *Martin Luther King Jr. A Profile*, ed. C. Eric Lincoln (New York: Hill & Wang): 113–27

Cline, Ray S. (1976) *Secrets, Spies and Scholars: Blueprint of the Essential CIA* (Washington, DC: Acropolis Books)

Clyne, Peter (1973) *Guilty but Insane. Anglo-American Attitudes to Insanity and Criminal Guilt* (London: Nelson)

Cochrane, Stephen T. (1977) *The Collaboration of Nečaev, Ogarev and Bakunin in 1869, Nečaev's Early Years* (Giessen: Wilhelm Schmitz)

Colby, William and Peter Forbath (1978) *Honorable Men: My Life in the CIA* (New York: Simon & Schuster)

Cole, J. A. (1984) *Prince of Spies: Henri Le Caron* (London: Faber and Faber)

Coleman, Ray (2000) *Lennon: The Definitive Biography* (London: Pan Books)

Collins, Randall (2008) *Violence: A Micro-Sociological Theory* (Princeton, NJ: Princeton UP)

Condon, Richard (December 1963) '"Manchurian Candidate" in Dallas', *The Nation*, Vol. 197, No. 22 (New York: The Nation Associates): 449–51

Condon, Richard (2004) *The Manchurian Candidate* (1959) (New York: Pan Books)

Cone, James H. (1991) *Martin & Malcolm & America* (Maryknoll, NY: Orbis Books)

Cooke, Alistair (2008) *Reporting America: The Life of the Nation, 1946–2004*, with an introduction and commentary by Susan Cooke Kittredge (London: Allen Lane)

Corder, Percy and H. C. G. Matthew (2004) 'Robert Spence Watson', in *Oxford Dictionary of National Biography*, Vol. 57 (Oxford: OUP): 657–8

Corfe, Tom (1968) *The Phoenix Park Murders. Conflict, Compromise and Tragedy in Ireland, 1879–1882* (London: Hodder & Stoughton)

Cragoe, Matthew (2004) 'Henry Austin Bruce, first Baron Aberdare (1815–1895)', in *Oxford Dictionary of National Biography*, Vol. 8 (Oxford: OUP): 298–302

Crapol, Edward P. (2000) *James G. Blaine. Architect of Empire* (Wilmington, DE: Scholarly Resources)

Crick, Bernard (1974) *Crime, Rape and Gin. Reflections on Contemporary Attitudes to Violence, Pornography and Addiction* (London: Elek/Pemberton)

Crofts, Daniel W. (1999) 'William Henry Seward', in *American National Biography*, Vol. 19 (New York & Oxford: OUP): 676–81

'Czolgosz Trial' (1901) 'The People of the State of New York against Leon Czolgosz', online at http://www.eriebar.org/pr_ed_brochures.asp

Dadrian, Vahakn N. (1986) 'The Naim-Andonian Documents on the World War I Destruction of Ottoman Armenians: The Anatomy of a Genocide', *International Journal of Middle East Studies*, Vol. 18, No. 3 (Cambridge: CUP): 311–60

Dadrian, Vahakn N. (2003) *The History of the Armenian Genocide: Ethnic Conflict from the Balkans to Anatolia to the Caucasus* (1996), revised edn (New York & Oxford: Berghahn Books)

Dallek, Robert (2003) *John F. Kennedy: An Unfinished Life, 1917–1963* (London: Allen Lane)

Daly, Jonathan (2006) 'Police and Revolutionaries', in *The Cambridge History of Russia. Volume II, Imperial Russia, 1689–1917*, ed. Dominic Lieven (Cambridge: CUP): 637–54

Daly, Mary E. (2003) 'Nationalism, Sentiment and Economics: Relations between Ireland and Irish America in the Postwar Years', in *New Directions in Irish-American History*, ed. Kevin Kenny (Madison, WI: Univ. of Wisconsin Press): 263–79

Davey, Richard (1897) *Victoria, Queen and Empress* (London: Roxburghe Press)

Davies, Hunter (1985) *The Beatles* (1968) (London: Arrow House)

Davis, David Brion, ed. (1971) *The Fear of Conspiracy: Images of Un-American Subversion from the Revolution to the Present* (Ithaca, NY, & London: Cornell UP)

Davison, Roderic H. (1990) *Essays in Ottoman and Turkish History, 1774–1923: The Impact of the West* (Austin, TX: Univ. of Texas Press)

Davitt (1890) *Speech Delivered by Michael Davitt in Defence of the Land League* (London: Kegan Paul, Trench, Trübner)

Day, Holman F. (1901) 'Three Pilgrims at the "Pan"', *Everybody's Magazine*, Vol. 5, No. 26 (New York: John Wanamaker): 427–39

Deburg, William L. Van (1992) *New Day in Babylon: The Black Power Movement and American Culture, 1965–1975* (Chicago & London: Univ. of Chicago Press)

Deusen, Glyndon G. Van (1967) *William Henry Seward* (New York: OUP)

Dickens, Charles (1911) *Reprinted Pieces* (London: Chapman & Hall)

Didion, Joan (1990) *The White Album* (1979) (New York: Farrar, Straus & Giroux)

Didion, Joan (1993) *Slouching Towards Bethlehem* (1969) (London: Flamingo)

Djemal, Ahmed (Pascha) (1922) *Erinnerungen eines türkischen Staatsmanne* (Munich: Drei Masken)

Dmytryshyn, Basil, ed. (1967) *Imperial Russia. A Source Book, 1700–1917* (New York, Chicago, etc.: Holt, Rinehart & Winston)

Dobratz, Betty A. and Stephanie L. Shanks-Meile (1997) *'White Power, White Pride!' The White Separatist Movement in the United States* (New York: Twayne Publishers)

Dollfuss, Eva (1994) *Mein Vater: Hitlers erstes Opfer* (Vienna & Munich: Almathea)

Donovan, Robert J. (1982) *Tumultuous Years: The Presidency of Harry S. Truman 1949–1953* (New York & London: W. W. Norton)

Dostoevsky, Fyodor (1971) *The Devils* (1871), trans. with an introduction by David Magarshack (Harmondsworth: Penguin)

Dostoevsky, Fyodor (1990) *Complete Letters*, ed. and trans. David A. Lowe, Vol. 3 (Ann Arbor, MI: Ardis Publishers)

Douglass, Frederick (1991) *The Frederick Douglass Papers. Series One: Speeches, Debates, and Interviews. Volume 4: 1854–80*, eds John W. Blassingame and John R. McKivigan (New Haven & London: Yale UP)

Doyle, David Noel and Owen Dudley Edwards, eds (1980) *America and Ireland, 1776– 1976. The American Identity and the Irish Connection* (Westport, CT: Greenwood Press)

Drinnon, Richard (1982) *Rebel in Paradise: A Biography of Emma Goldman* (1961) (Chicago & London: Univ. of Chicago Press)

Dryzhakova, Elena (1980) 'Dostoevsky, Chernyshevsky, and the Rejection of Nihilism in 1890', in *Oxford Slavonic Papers*, eds J. L. I. Fennell, A. E. Pennington and I. P. Foote, New Series, Vol. 13 (Oxford: Clarendon Press): 58–79

Dyer, Richard (1996) 'Into the Light: The Whiteness of the South in *The Birth of a Nation*', in *Dixie Debates: Perspectives on Southern Cultures*, eds Richard H. King and Helen Taylor (London: Pluto Press): 165–76

Dyson, Michael Eric (1995) *Making Malcolm: The Myth and Meaning of Malcolm X* (New York & Oxford: OUP)

Eburne, Jonathan P. (2008) *Surrealism and the Art of Crime* (Ithaca, NY, & London: Cornell UP)

Eckhardt, Joseph P. (1998) *The King of the Movies: Film Pioneer Siegmund Lubin* (London: Associated University Presses; Madison, NJ: Fairleigh Dickinson UP)

Eden, Sir Anthony, the Rt. Hon The Earl of Avon (1965) *The Eden Memoirs: The Reckoning* (London: Cassell)

Edison, Thomas Alva (1948) *The Diary and Sundry Observations of Thomas Alva Edison*, ed. Dagobert D. Runes (New York: Philosophical Library)

Editor's Miscellany (1901) 'Editor's Miscellany: Nurses who Cared for the President', *American Journal of Nursing*, Vol. 2, No. 1: 1

Edmunds, George F. (1882) 'The Conduct of the Guiteau Trial', *North American Review*, Vol. 134, No. 304 (New York: No. 30 Lafayette Place): 221–31

Eigen, Joel Peter (1995) *Witnessing Insanity: Madness and Mad-Doctors in the English Court* (New Haven & London: Yale UP)

Einstein, Albert (2002) *The Collected Papers of Albert Einstein: The Berlin Years: Writings, 1918–1921*, Vol. 7, eds Michel Janssen, Robert Schulmann, Jósef Illy, Christoph Lehner and Diana Kormos Buchwald (Princeton, NJ: Princeton UP)

Einstein, Albert (2006) *The Collected Papers of Albert Einstein: The Berlin Years: Correspondence, May–December 1920 and Supplementary Correspondence, 1909–1920*, Vol. 10, eds Diana Kormos Buchwald, Tilman Sauer, Ze'e Rosenkranz, Jósef Illy, and Virginia Iris Holmes (Princeton, NJ: Princeton UP)

Eisele, Albert (1972) *Almost to the Presidency: A Biography of Two American Politicians* (Blue Earth, MN: The Piper Company)

Ellis, Havelock (1890) *The Criminal* (London: Walter Scott)

Ellis, Havelock (1901) *The Criminal*, 3rd edn (London: Walter Scott)

Ellis, Havelock (1910) *The Criminal*, 4th edn (London: Walter Scott)

Ellis, Rowland (1882) *The Dublin Tragedy Viewed By the Light of the Sanctuary. A Sermon Preached in the Parish Church of Hawarden on Sunday Morning, May 14th, 1882* (Chester: Phillipson & Golder)

Ellison, Jerome (December 1963) 'Stimulant to Violence', *The Nation*, 21 December 1963, Vol. 197, No. 21 (New York: The Nation Company): 433–6

Elwell, J. J., George M. Beard, E. C. Senguin, J. S. Jewell, Charles Folsom (1882) 'The Moral Responsibility of the Insane', *North American Review*, Vol. 134, No. 302 (New York: No. 30 Lafayette Place): 1–39

Emerson, Ralph Waldo (2000) *The Essential Writings of Ralph Waldo Emerson* (New York: Random House)

Emery, Robert J. (2002) *The Directors – Take Two* (New York: Allworth Press)

Engel, Barbara Alpern (2006) 'Women, the Family and Public Life', in *The Cambridge History of Russia. Volume II, Imperial Russia, 1689–1917*, ed. Dominic Lieven (Cambridge: CUP): 306–25

Engel, Barbara Alpern and Clifford N. Rosenthal, eds (1975) *Five Sisters: Women Against the Tsar* (London: Weidenfeld & Nicolson)

Eppridge, Bill (2008) *A Time It Was: Bobby Kennedy in the Sixties*, with an essay by Pete Hamill (New York: Abrams)

Epstein, Klaus (1959) *Matthias Erzberger and the Dilemma of German Democracy* (Princeton, NJ: Princeton UP)

Erickson, Edward J. (2001) *Ordered to Die: A History of the Ottoman Army in the First World War* (Westport, CT: Greenwood)

Essig, Mark (2003) *Edison and the Electric Chair* (Stroud: Sutton Publishing)

Ettinger, Elżbieta (1986) *Rosa Luxemburg: A Life* (Boston: Beacon Press)

'European Explosions, The' (28 April 1892) 'The European Explosions', *The Nation*, Vol. 54, No. 1400 (New York: Evening Post Publishing): 317–18

Evans, Richard J. (1996) *Rituals of Retribution: Capital Punishment in Germany, 1600–1987* (Oxford: OUP)

Evans-Gordon, Major W. (1903) *The Alien Immigrant* (London: William Heinemann)

Everest, Lancelot Feilding (1887) *The Defence of Insanity in Criminal Cases* (London: Stevens & Sons)

Eversley, Lord (1912) *Gladstone and Ireland. The Irish Policy of Parliament from 1850–1894* (London: Methuen)

Ewing, Charles Patrick and Joseph T. McCann (2006) *Minds on Trial: Great Cases in Law and Psychology* (Oxford: OUP)

Exner, Judith (1977) *My Story*, as told to Ovid Demaris (New York: Grove Press)

Falk, Candace, Ronald J. Zboray, Alice Hall, Stephen Cole and Daniel Cornford, eds (1990–1) *The Emma Goldman Papers* (Alexandra, VA, & Cambridge, UK: Chadwyck-Healey)

Falkiner, C. Litton (1901) *The Phoenix Park: Its Origin and Early History, with some Notices of its Royal and Viceregal Residences* (Dublin: Dublin UP)

Farjeon, Eleanor (1938) 'Foreword' to *The Unlocked Book. A Memoir of John Wilkes Booth by his Sister Asia Booth Clarke* (London: Faber and Faber)

Federn-Kohlhaas, Etta (1927) *Walther Rathenau: Sein Leben und Wirken* (Dresden: Carl Reissner)

Felix, David (1971) *Walther Rathenau and the Weimar Republic: The Politics of Reparations* (Baltimore & London: Johns Hopkins Press)

Fénéon, Félix (1970) *Oeuvres plus que complètes*, ed. Joan U. Halperin, Vol. 2 (Geneva: Librairie Droz)

Ferrell, Robert H., ed. (1980) *Off the Record: The Private Papers of Harry S. Truman* (New York: Harper & Row)

Feuer, Lewis, ed. (1984) *Karl Marx and Friedrich Engels. Basic Writings on Politics and Philosophy* (1959) (London: Fontana/Collins)

Final Report (1976) *Foreign and Military Intelligence. Final Report of the Select Committee to Study Governmental Operations with Respect to Intelligence Activities, United States Senate*, 6 vols (Washington, DC: US Government Printing Office)

Fine, Sidney (1955) 'Anarchism and the Assassination of McKinley', *The American Historical Review*, Vol. 60, No. 4: 777–99

Fingarette, Herbert and Ann Fingarette Hasse (1979) *Mental Disabilities and Criminal Responsibility* (Berkeley, CA: Univ. of California Press)

Finkel, Norman J. (1988) *Insanity on Trial* (New York & London: Plenum Press)

Finker, Kurt (1977) *Stauffenberg und der 20. Juli 1944* (Cologne: Pahl-Rugenstein)

Foner, Eric (1988) *Reconstruction: America's Unfinished Revolution, 1863–1877* (New York: Harper & Row)

Foner, Philip S. (1969) *The Autobiographies of the Haymarket Martyrs* (New York: Humanities Press)

Ford, Betty, with Chris Chase (1979) *The Times of My Life* (London: W. H. Allen)

Ford, Gerald (1979) *A Time to Heal: The Autobiography of Gerald Ford* (London: W. H. Allen)

Ford Papers (1977) *Public Papers of the Presidents of the United States: Gerald R. Ford. Containing the Public Messages, Speeches, and Statements of the President. 1975. Book II – July 21 to December 31, 1975* (Washington, DC: US Government Printing Office)

Foster, Buddy and Leon Wagener (1997) *Foster Child: A Biography of Jodie Foster* (London: Heinemann)

Foster, R. F. (1989) *Modern Ireland, 1600–1972* (1988) (London: Penguin)

Frank, Gerold (1972) *An American Death: The True Story of the Assassination of Dr. Martin Luther King, Jr. and the Greatest Manhunt of Our Time* (Garden City, NY: Doubleday)

Frank, Joseph (1995) *Dostoevsky: The Miraculous Years 1865–1871* (London: Robson Books)

Freedman, Lawrence (2000) *Kennedy's Wars: Berlin, Cuba, Laos, and Vietnam* (Oxford: OUP)

Frick, Helen Clay (1959) *My Father, Henry Clay Frick* (as told to Mary O'Hara), reprinted from 1959 article, without publication date for the reprint (New York: Frick Art & Historical Center)

'From A Revolutionary Point of View' (26 January 1885) 'From A Revolutionary Point of View', *Pall Mall Gazette*, Vol. 41, No. 6201: 1–2

Fusco, Paul (2000) *RFK Funeral Train* (New York: Umbrage Editions)

Fusco, Paul (2008) *RFK* (New York: Aperture)

Gallo, Max (1984) *Le Grand Jaurès* (Paris: Éditions Robert Laffont)

Ganz, Marie (1919) *Rebels. Into Anarchy and Out Again* (New York: Dodd, Mead)

Garland, Hamlin (June 1894) 'Homestead and Its Perilous Trades', *McClure's Magazine*, Vol. 3, No. 1 (New York)

Garraty, John A. and Mark C. Carnes, eds (1999) *American National Biography*, 24 vols (New York & Oxford: OUP)

Garrow, David J. (2004) *Bearing the Cross: Martin Luther King and the Southern Christian Leadership Conference* (1986) (New York: Perennial Classics)

Gash, Norman (1976) *Peel* (London & New York: Longman)

Gay, Peter (1968) *Weimar Culture: The Outsider as Insider* (Harmondsworth: Penguin)

Gehl, Jürgen (1963) *Austria, Germany, and the Anschluss, 1931–1938*, foreword by Alan Bullock (London: OUP)

Geis, Gilbert and Robert F. Meier (January, 1985) 'Abolition of the Insanity Plea in Idaho: A Case Study', in *The Insanity Defence*, a special issue of *The Annals of the American Academy of Political and Social Science*, ed. Richard Moran (Beverly Hills, CA: Sage Publications): 72–83

Giddings, Franklin H. (December 1892) 'Review of C. Lombroso and R. Lasch', *Le Crime Politique et les Révolutions*, Vol. 7, No. 4 (New York, Boston & Chicago: Ginn): 721–3

Gilfond, Henry (1975) *The Black Hand at Sarajevo* (Indianapolis & New York: Bobbs-Merrill)

Gilman, Sander L., ed. (1987) *Conversations with Nietzsche: A Life in the Words of His Contemporaries*, trans. David J. Parent (New York & Oxford: OUP)

Girodias, Maurice (1970) 'Publisher's Preface', to Valerie Solanas, *Scum Manifesto* (1968) (New York: Olympia Press): vii–xiii

Glad, Paul W. (1964) *McKinley, Bryan and the People* (Philadelphia & New York: J. B. Lippincott)

Goldberg, Harvey (1962) *The Life of Jean Jaurès* (Madison, WI: Univ. of Wisconsin Press)

Goldman, Emma (1931) *Living My Life*, 2 vols (New York: Knopf)

Goldman, Peter (1973) *The Death and Life of Malcolm X* (New York: Harper & Row)

Goldstein, Abraham (1967) *The Insanity Defense* (New Haven & London: Yale UP)

Goll, Ivan (1925) *Germaine Berton: die rote Jungfrau* (Berlin: Verlag die Schmeide)

Goodman, Jon (2006) *The Kennedy Mystique: Creating Camelot*, with commentary by Hugh Sidey, Letitia Baldrige, Robert Dallek and Barbara Baker Burrows (Washington, DC: National Geographic)

Goodwin, Doris Kearns (2009) *Team of Rivals: The Political Genius of Abraham Lincoln* (2005) (London: Penguin)

Goring, Charles (1919) *The English Convict*, abridged edn with an introduction by Karl Pearson (London: Her Majesty's Stationery Office)

Gornick, Vivian (1970) 'Introduction', to Valerie Solanas, *Scum Manifesto* (New York: Olympia Press)

Gosnell, Harold F. (1980) *Truman's Crises: A Political Biography of Harry S. Truman* (Westport, CT, & London: Greenwood Press)

Graham, Colin (1998) 'Colonial Violence, Imitation and Form: Samuel Ferguson and The Phoenix Park Murders', in *Irish Encounters: Poetry, Politics and Prose since 1880*, ed. Neil Sammells and Alan Marshall (Bath: Sulis Press): 5–15

Graml, Hermann, ed. (1982) *Widerstand im Dritten Reich: Probleme, Ereignisse, Gestalten* (Frankfurt am Main: Fischer Taschenbuch)

Graubard, Stephen (2009) *The Presidents. The Transformation of the American Presidency from Theodore Roosevelt to Barack Obama* (London: Penguin)

Gray, Denis (1963) *Spencer Perceval: The Evangelical Prime Minister, 1762–1812* (Manchester: Manchester UP)

Green, David (1987) *Shaping Political Consciousness: The Language of Politics in America from McKinley to Reagan* (Ithaca, NY, & London: Cornell UP)

Greenberg, Bradley and Edwin B. Parker, eds (1965) *The Kennedy Assassination and the American Public: Social Communication in Crisis* (Stanford, CA: Stanford UP)

Greene, John Robert (1995) *The Presidency of Gerald Ford* (Lawrence, KA: UP of Kansas)

Greenspan, Ezra, ed. (1995) *The Cambridge Companion to Walt Whitman* (Cambridge: CUP)

Grose, Peter (1995) *Gentleman Spy: The Life of Allen Dulles* (Boston & New York: Houghton Mifflin)

Grossman, Leonid (1974) *Dostoevsky: A Biography*, trans. Mary Mackler (1965) (London: Allen Lane)

Guerra, Lillian (1998) *Popular Expression and National Identity in Puerto Rico* (Gainesville, Tallahassee, etc., FL: UP of Florida)

Guillemin, Henri (1966) *L'Arrière-Pensée de Jaurès* (Paris: Gallimard)

Guiteau (1882) *Report of the Proceedings in the Case of the United States vs. Charles J. Guiteau. Tried in the Supreme Court of the District of Columbia, Holding a Criminal Term, and Beginning November 14, 1881*, 3 vols (Washington, DC: Government Printing Office)

Gumbel, Emil Julius (1921) *Zwei Jahre Mord*, with a foreword by G. F. Nicolai (Berlin: Verlag Neues Vaterland)

Gumbel, Emil Julius (1922) *Vier Jahre politischer Mord* (Berlin & Fichtenau: Verlag der neuen Gesellschaft)

Gumbel, Emil Julius (1929) *Verräter verfallen der feme: Opfer / Mörder / Richter, 1919–1929* (Berlin: Malik-Verlag)

Halberstam, David (1970) 'When "Civil Rights" and "Peace" Join Forces', in *Martin Luther King Jr. A Profile*, ed. C. Eric Lincoln (New York: Hill & Wang): 187–211

Halperin, Joan Ungersma (1988) *Félix Fénéon, Aesthete & Anarchist in Fin-de-Siècle Paris* (New Haven & London: Yale UP)

Hamburg, Gary M. (2006) 'Russian Political Thought, 1700–1917', in *The Cambridge History of Russia. Volume II, Imperial Russia, 1689–1917*, ed. Dominic Lieven (Cambridge: CUP): 116–42

Hamby, Alonzo L. (1995) *Man of the People: A Life of Harry S. Truman* (New York & Oxford: OUP)

Hamer, David (2004) 'John Morley, Viscount Morley of Buckland (1838–1923)', in *Oxford Dictionary of National Biography*, Vol. 39 (Oxford: OUP): 226–34

Hamerow, Theodore S. (1997) *On the Road to the Wolf's Lair: German Resistance to Hitler* (Cambridge, MA: Belknap Press of Harvard UP)

Hamill, Pete (2007) 'Once We Were Kings', in *Making the Irish American. History and Heritage of the Irish in the United States*, eds J. L. Lee and Miriam R. Casey (New York & London: New York UP): 526–34

Hammelsbeck, Oskar (1959) 'Dietrich Bonhoeffer', in *Männer des Glaubens im deutschen Widerstand*, by Robert Rafael Geis and Oskar Simmel (Munich: Ner-Tamid)

Hammer, Ellen J. (1987) *A Death in November: America in Vietnam, 1963* (New York: E. P. Dutton)

Hammond, J. L. (1938) *Gladstone and the Irish Nation* (London: Longmans, Green)

Hanchett, William (1983) *The Lincoln Murder Conspiracies* (Urbana & Chicago: Univ. of Illinois Press)

Hanley, Brian (2010) *The IRA: A Documentary History 1916–2005* (Dublin: Gill & Macmillan)

Hanson, Earl Parker (1955) *Transformation: The Story of Modern Puerto Rico* (New York: Simon & Schuster)

Hapgood, Hutchins (1972) *A Victorian in the Modern World* (1937), with an introduction by Robert Allen Skotheim (Seattle & London: Univ. of Washington Press)

Hardcastle, Mary Scarlett, ed. (1881) *Life of John, Lord Campbell*, 2 vols (London: John Murray)

Harden, Maximilian (1963) *Köpfe: Portäts, Briefe und Dokumente* (Hamburg: Rütten & Loening)

Harding, Colin and Simon Popple (1996) *In the Kingdom of Shadows. A Companion to Early Cinema* (London: Cygnus Arts; Cranbury, NJ: Fairleigh Dickinson UP)

Harrison, John Fletcher Clews (1979) *The Second Coming: Popular Millenarianism, 1780–1850* (London: Routledge & Kegan Paul)

Harron, Mary (1996) 'Introduction', to *I Shot Andy Warhol*, script by Mary Harron and Daniel Minahan (London: Bloomsbury): vii–xxxi

Hart, W. C. (1906) *Confessions of an Anarchist* (London: E. Grant Harris)

Hatchett, William (1983) *The Lincoln Murder Conspiracies* (Urbana & Chicago: Univ. of Illinois Press)

Havel, Hippolyte (1911) 'Emma Goldman', in *Anarchism and Other Essays*, by Emma Goldman (New York: Mother Earth Publishing Association): 5–44

Havens, Murray Clark, Carl Leiden and Karl M. Schmitt (1970) *The Politics of Assassination* (Englewood Cliffs, NJ: Prentice-Hall)

Hayman, Ronald (1980) *Nietzsche: A Critical Life* (London: Weidenfeld & Nicolson)

Hearst, Patricia Campbell, with Alvin Moscow (1982) *Every Secret Thing* (London: Methuen)

Heffernan, Virginia (2004) 'Anarchist, Revolutionary and Eccentric', *New York Times*, 12 April 2004: E3

Herbert, Auberon (May 1894) 'The Ethics of Dynamite', *Contemporary Review*, Vol. 65 (London: Isbister): 667–87

Herbert, Aubrey (1924) *Ben Kendim: A Record of Eastern Travel*, ed. Desmond McCarthy (London: Hutchinson)

Herbert, Robert L. and Eugenia W. Herbert (November 1960) 'Artists and Anarchism: Unpublished Letters of Pissarro, Signac and others – I', *Burlington Magazine*, Vol. 102, No. 692 (London): 473–82

Herbert, Robert L. and Eugenia W. Herbert (December 1960) 'Artists and Anarchism: Unpublished Letters of Pissarro, Signac and others – II', *Burlington Magazine*, Vol. 102, No. 693 (London): 517–22

Herold, David E. and Benn Pitman, eds (1954) *The Assassination of President Lincoln and The Trial of the Conspirators* (New York: Funk & Wagnalls)

Herrington, Stuart A. (1997) *Stalking the Vietcong: Inside Operation Phoenix: A Personal Account* (1982) (Novato, CA: Presidio Press)

Herzen, Alexander (1927) *My Past and Thoughts. The Memoirs of Alexander Herzen*, trans. Constance Garnett, Vol. 6 (London: Chatto & Windus)

Hibbert, Christopher, ed. (1984) *Queen Victoria in Her Letters and Journals* (London: John Murray)

Hibbert, Christopher (2000) *Queen Victoria, A Personal History* (London: HarperCollins)

Hill, Lance (2004) *The Deacons for Defense: Armed Resistance and the Civil Rights Movement* (Chapel Hill, NC, & London: Univ. of North Carolina Press)

Hillman, William (1952) *Mr. President: The First Publication From the Personal Diaries, Private Letters, Papers and Revealing Interviews of Harry S. Truman* (New York: Farrar, Straus & Young)

Hillyar, Anna and Jane McDermid (2000) *Revolutionary Women in Russia, 1870–1917* (Manchester & New York: Manchester UP)

Hinckley, Jack and Jo Ann, with Elizabeth Sherrill (1985) *Breaking Points* (London: Hodder & Stoughton)

Hindus, Milton, ed. (1971) *Walt Whitman: The Critical Heritage* (London: Routledge & Kegan Paul)

Hitchens, Christopher (2001) *The Trial of Henry Kissinger* (London & New York: Verso)

Hofmann, Tessa, ed. (1994) *Armenier und Armenien – Heimat und Exil* (Hamburg: Rowohlt Taschenbuch)

Hofmann, Tessa (1994) 'Verfolgung und Völkermord. Armenien zwischen 1877 und 1922', in *Armenier und Armenien – Heimat und Exil*, ed. Tessa Hofmann (Hamburg: Rowohlt Taschenbuch): 15–32

Hoffmann, Peter (1988) *German Resistance to Hitler* (Cambridge, MA, & London: Harvard UP)

Hoffmann, Peter (1998) *Stauffenberg und der 20. Juli 1944* (Munich: C. H. Beck)

Hogan, Michael J. (1998) *A Cross of Iron: Harry S. Truman and the Origins of the National Security State, 1945–1954* (Cambridge: CUP)

Holland, Max, ed. (2004) *The Kennedy Assassination Tapes* (New York: Knopf)

Hollinger, Karen (2006) *The Actress: Hollywood Acting and the Female Star* (New York & London: Routledge)

Houck, Davis W. and Amos Kiewe, eds (1993) *Actor, Ideologue, Politician: The Public Speeches of Ronald Reagan* (Westport, CT: Greenwood Press)

Hough, Richard (1981) *Mountbatten* (New York: Random House)

Hovannisian, Richard G. (1999) 'L'Hydre à quatre têtes du négationnisme: negation, rationalization, relativisation, banalisation', in *L'Actualité du Génocide des Arméniens* (Paris: Edipol): 143–76

Huie, William Bradford (1970) *He Slew the Dreamer: My Search, with James Earl Ray for the truth about the Murder of Martin Luther King* (London: W. H. Allen)

Hulse, James W. (1970) *Revolutionists in London. A Study of Five Unorthodox Socialists* (Oxford: Clarendon Press)

Hunter, Edward (1951) *Brainwashing in Red China: The Calculated Destruction of Men's Minds* (New York: Vanguard Press)

Hunter, Edward (1956) *Brainwashing: The Story of Men Who Defied It* (New York: Farrar, Straus & Cudahy)

Hunter, Stephen and John Bainbridge, Jr. (2005) *American Gunfight: The Plot to Kill President Truman – and the Shoot-out That Stopped It* (New York: Simon & Schuster)

İnalcik, Halil and Donald Quataert, eds (1994) *An Economic and Social History of the Ottoman Empire, 1300–1914* (Cambridge: CUP)

'Ivanoff' (January 1894) 'Anarchists: Their Methods and Organisation', *The New Review*, Vol. 10, No. 56 (London: William Heinemann): 9–16

Jackson, Kevin, ed. (2004) *Schrader on Schrader & Other Writings*, rev. edn (London: Faber and Faber)

Jacobs, Seth (2006) *Cold War Mandarin: Ngo Dinh Diem and the Origins of America's War in Vietnam, 1950–1963* (Lanham, MD: Rowman & Littlefield)

James, Henry (1987) *The Princess Casamassima* (1886), ed. Derek Brewer with notes by Patricia Crick (Harmondsworth: Penguin)

James, Robert Rhodes (1986) *Anthony Eden* (London: Weidenfeld & Nicolson)

Jasper, Ronald C. D. (1967) *George Bell, Bishop of Chichester* (London: OUP)

Jenkins, Roy (1958) *Sir Charles Dilke. A Victorian Tragedy* (London: Collins)

Jennings, Louis J. (1887) *Mr Gladstone. A Study* (Edinburgh & London: William Blackwood)

Joesten, Joachim (1964) *Oswald: Assassin or Fall Guy?* (New York: Marzani & Munsell)

Johns, A. Wesley (1970) *The Man Who Shot McKinley* (South Brunswick & New York: A. S. Barnes)

Johnson, Lyndon Baines (1971) *The Vantage Point: Perspectives of the Presidency, 1963–1969* (New York: Holt, Rinehart & Winston)

Johnson, Samuel (no date) *Lives of the English Poets*, 2 vols (London: J. M. Dent & Sons)

Joll, James (1964) *The Anarchists* (London: Eyre & Spottiswoode)

Joll, James (1967) 'Prophet ohne Wirkung', in *Walther Rathenau Tagebuch 1907–1922*, ed. Hartmut Pogge von Strandmann, trans. Nora Pogge (Düsseldorf: Droste): 15–53

Jones, Howard (2003) *Death of a Generation: How the Assassinations of Diem and JFK Prolonged the Vietnam War* (New York: OUP)

Jones, Malcolm (2002) 'Dostoevskii and Religion', in *The Cambridge Companion to Dostoevskii*, ed. W. J. Leatherbarrow (Cambridge: CUP): 148–74

Jones, Maldwyn (1995) *The Limits of Liberty: American History, 1607–1992*, 2nd edn (Oxford & New York: OUP)

Jones, Stanley (1964) *The Presidential Election of 1896* (Madison, WI: Wisconsin UP)

Josephson, Matthew (1962) *The Robber Barons: The Great American Capitalists, 1861–1901* (1934) (London: Eyre & Spottiswoode)

Jowitt, William Allen, Earl and Clifford Walsh and John Burke (1977) *Jowitt's Dictionary of English Law*, 2nd edn, 2 vols (London: Sweet & Maxwell)

Kaiser, Robert Blair (1970) *'R.F.K. Must Die!' A History of the Robert Kennedy Assassination and Its Aftermath* (New York: E. P. Dutton)

Kaplan, Justin (1967) *Mr. Clemens and Mark Twain* (London: Jonathan Cape)

Karlins, Marvin and Lewis M. Andrews, eds (1972) *Man Controlled: Readings in the Psychology of Behavior Control* (New York: Free Press)

Kauffman, Michael W. (2004) *American Brutus: John Wilkes Booth and the Lincoln Conspiracies* (New York: Random House)

Kebabian, John S. (1970) *The Haymarket Affair and the Trial of the Chicago Anarchists 1886* (New York: H. P. Kraus)

Kee, Robert (2000) *The Green Flag. A History of Irish Nationalism* (1972) (London: Penguin)

Keegan, John (2000) *The First World War* (1998) (New York: Vintage)

Keeton, G. W. (1961) *Guilty But Insane* (London: MacDonald)

Kelley, Kitty (1986) *His Way: The Unauthorized Biography of Frank Sinatra* (London: Bantam)

Kelly, Aileen (1982) *Mikhail Bakunin: A Study in the Psychology and Politics of Utopianism* (Oxford: Clarendon Press)

Kenny, Kevin, ed. (2003) *New Directions in Irish-American History* (Madison, WI: Univ. of Wisconsin Press)

Kenny, Kevin (2007) 'American-Irish Nationalism', in *Making the Irish American. History and Heritage of the Irish in the United States*, eds J. L. Lee and Miriam R. Casey (New York & London: New York UP): 289–301

Kershaw, Ian (1999) *Hitler, 1889–1936: Hubris* (1998) (London: Penguin)

Kessler, Harry Graf (1923) *Walther Rathenau: Sein Leben und sein Werk* (Berlin-Grunewald: Verlagsanstalt Hermann Klemm)

Kettenacker, Lothar (2002) 'Der deutsche Widerstand aus britischer Sicht', in *Der deutsche Widerstand gegen Hitler: Wahrnehmung und Wertung in Europa und den USA*, ed. Gerd R. Ueberschär (Darmstadt: Wissenschaftlich Buchgesselschaft): 25–38

Kimmel, Stanley (1969) *The Mad Booths of Maryland*, 2nd edn (New York, Dover)

Kindermann, Gottfried-Karl (1984) *Hitler's Defeat in Austria, 1933–1934: Europe's First Containment of Nazi Expansionism*, trans. Sonia Brough and David Taylor (London: C. Hurst & David Taylor)

Kinross, Lord (2003) *The Ottoman Empire*, introduction and addenda to the select bibliography by Norman Stone (1977) (Bath: Folio Society)

Kipling, Rudyard (1987) *Something of Myself* (1936), ed. Robert Hampson, with an introduction by Richard Holmes (London: Penguin)

Kirkham, James F., Sheldon G. Levy and William J. Crotty (1970) *Assassination and Political Violence: A Staff Report to the National Commission on the Causes and Prevention of Violence*, introduction by Harrison E. Salisbury (New York: Bantam Matrix)

Kissinger, Henry (1979) *White House Years* (Boston & Toronto: Little, Brown)

Kissinger, Henry (1982) *Years of Upheaval* (Boston & Toronto: Little, Brown)

Kitchen, Martin (1980) *The Coming of Austrian Fascism* (Montreal: McGill-Queen's UP)

Klemperer, Klemens von (1982) 'Glaube, Religion, Kirche und der deutsche Widerstand gegen den Nationalsozialismus', in *Widerstand im Dritten Reich: Probleme, Ereignisse, Gestalten*, ed. Hermann Graml (Frankfurt am Main: Fischer Taschenbuch): 140–56

Klemperer, Klemens von (1992) *German Resistance Against Hitler: The Search for Allies Abroad, 1938–1945* (Oxford: Clarendon Press)

Knight, Peter (2007) *The Kennedy Assassination* (Edinburgh: Edinburgh UP)

Kolchin, Peter (1995) *American Slavery* (1993) (London: Penguin)

Korolenko, V. G. (1972) *The History of My Contemporary*, trans. and abridged by Neil Parsons (London: OUP)

Kostenbaum, Wayne (2001) *Andy Warhol* (London: Weidenfeld & Nicolson)

Kracauer, Siegfried (1960) *Nature of Film. The Redemption of Physical Reality* (London: Dennis Dobson)

Kracauer, Siegfried (2004) *From Caligari to Hitler: A Psychological History of the German Film*, rev. and expanded edn (1947) (Princeton, NJ, & Oxford: Princeton UP)

Kramarz, Joachim (1965) *Claus Graf Stauffenberg, 15. November 1907–20. Juli 1944, Das Leben eines Offiziers* (Frankfurt am Main: Bernard & Graefe)

Kropotkin, Peter ['Pierre'] (1886a) *Law and Authority. An Anarchist Essay* (London: International Publishing)

Kropotkin, Peter ['Pierre'] (1886b) *The Place of Anarchism in Socialistic Evolution* (*An Address delivered in Paris*) (London: International Publishing)

Kropotkin, Peter ['Pierre'] (1886c) *War!* [from *Paroles d'un Revolté*] (London: International Publishing)

Kropotkin, P. (1905) *Russian Literature* [*Ideals and Realities*] (London: Duckworth)

Kropotkin, 'Prince' (1909) *The Terror In Russia. An Appeal to the British Nation.* (London: Methuen)

Kropotkin, Peter (1989) *Memoirs of a Revolutionist* (1899), with an introduction by George Woodcock (Montreal: Black Rose Books)

Kunhardt, Dorothy Meserve and Philip B. Kunhardt Jr. (1965) *Twenty Days. A Narrative in Text and Pictures of the Assassination of Abraham Lincoln and the Twenty Days that Followed – the Nation in Mourning, the Long Trip Home to Springfield* (New York: Harper & Row)

Kurland, Gerald (1972) *George Wallace: Southern Governor and Presidential Candidate* (Charlotteville, NY: SamHar Press)

Kurtz, Michael L. (1982) *Crime of the Century: The Kennedy Assassination from a Historian's Perspective* (Knoxville, TN: Univ. of Tennessee Press)

LaFeber, Walter (1999) 'Frederick William Seward', in *American National Biography*, Vol. 19 (New York & Oxford: OUP): 674–5

LaFeber, Walter (2005) *The Deadly Bet: LBJ, Vietnam, and the 1968 Election* (Lanham, MD: Rowman & Littlefield)

Lane, Mark (1966) *Rush to Judgment. A Critique of the Warren Commission's Inquiry into the Murders of President John F. Kennedy, Officer J. D. Tippit and Lee Harvey Oswald* (London: Bodley Head)

Laqueur, Walter Z. (1962) *Young Germany: A History of the German Youth Movement* (New York: Basic Books)

Laqueur, Walter (1974) *Weimar: A Cultural History 1918–1933* (London: Weidenfeld & Nicolson)

Laqueur, Walter (2002) *A History of Terrorism* (New Brunswick & London: Transaction Publishers)

Laschitza, Annelies (2000) *Im Lebensrausch, trotz alledem Rosa Luxemburg* (Berlin: Aufbau Taschenbuch)

Lattimer, John K. (1980) *Kennedy and Lincoln. Medical and Ballistic Comparisons of Their Assassinations* (New York & London: Harcourt Brace Jovanovich)

Laughton, John Knox (1898) *Memoirs of the Life and Correspondence of Henry Reeve, C.B., D.C.L.*, Vol. 2 (London: Longmans, Green)

Leatherbarrow, W. J., ed. (1999) *Dostoevsky's* The Devils*: A Critical Companion* (Evanston, IL: Northwestern UP)

Leatherbarrow, W. J., ed. (2002) *The Cambridge Companion to Dostoevskii* (Cambridge: CUP)

Le Caron, Henri (1893) *Twenty-Five Years in the Secret Service: The Recollections of a Spy* (London: William Heinemann)

Ledger, Sally and Roger Luckhurst, eds (2000) *The Fin de Siècle. A Reader in Cultural History, c. 1880–1900* (Oxford: OUP)

Lee, J. L. and Miriam R. Casey, eds (2007) *Making the Irish American. History and Heritage of the Irish in the United States* (New York & London: New York UP)

Leech, Margaret (1959) *In the Days of McKinley* (New York: Harper Brothers)

Lemay, Harding (1973) 'Introduction', to Arthur H. Bremer, *An Assassin's Diary* (New York: Harper's Magazine Press)

Leuchtenburg, William E. (1983) *In the Shadow of FDR: From Harry Truman to Ronald Reagan* (Ithaca, NY: Cornell UP)

Lewis, Bernard (2002) *The Emergence of Modern Turkey*, 3rd edn (New York & Oxford: OUP)

Lewis, Gordon K. (1974) 'Puerto Rico: Towards a New Consciousness', in *Puerto Rico and Puerto Ricans: Studies in History and Society*, eds Adalberto López and James Petras (New York: John Wiley): 455–70

Lewis, Jill (1991) *Fascism and the Working Class in Austria, 1918–1934: The Failure of Labour in the First Republic* (New York & Oxford: Berg)

Lieven, Dominic, ed. (2006) *The Cambridge History of Russia. Volume II, Imperial Russia, 1689–1917* (Cambridge: CUP)

Lifton, David S. (1980) *Best Evidence: Disguise and Deception in the Assassination of John F. Kennedy* (New York: Macmillan)

Lincoln, C. Eric, ed. (1970) *Martin Luther King, Jr. A Profile* (New York: Hill & Wang)

Lindt, Andreas, ed. (1969) *George Bell, Alphons Koechlin: Briefwechsel 1933–1954* (Zürich: EVZ-Verlag)

Lomax, Louis E. (1962) *The Negro Revolt* (New York and Evanston: Harper & Row)

Lomax, Louis E. (1963) *When the Word Is Given . . .* (New York: New American Library)

Lomax, Louis E. (1968) *To Kill A Black Man* (Los Angeles: Holloway House)

Lombroso, Cesare (1897) 'Criminal Anthropology', in *Twentieth Century Practice. An International Encyclopedia of Modern Medical Science*, ed. Thomas L. Stedman, Vol. 12 (London: Sampson Low, Marston): 369–423

Lombroso, Cesare (1902) 'Anarchy', *Everybody's Magazine*, Vol. 6, No. 2, trans. Lionel Strachey (New York: John Wanamaker): 165–8

Lombroso, Cesare and Guglielmo Ferrero (2004) *Criminal Woman, the Prostitute, and the Normal Woman* (1893), trans. with an introduction by Nicole Hahn Rafter and Mary Gibson (Durham & London: Duke UP)

Lopate, Phillip, ed. (2006) *American Movie Critics. An Anthology From the Silents Until Now* (Washington, DC: Library of America)

Low, Peter W., John Calvin Jeffries, Jr. and Richard J. Bonnie (1986) *The Trial of John W. Hinckley, Jr.: A Case Study in the Insanity Defense* (Mineola, NY: Foundation Press)

Lowell, Robert (1970) *Notebook* (London: Faber and Faber)

Lucy, Henry W. (1886) *A Diary of Two Parliaments* (London: Cassell)

McCaffrey, Lawrence J. (1980) 'A Profile of Irish America', in *America and Ireland, 1776–1976. The American Identity and the Irish Connection*, eds David Noel Doyle and Owen Dudley Edwards (Westport, CT: Greenwood Press): 81–91

McCarthy, Eugene (1968) *First Things First: New Priorities for America* (New York: New American Library)

McCarthy, Eugene (1969) *The Year of the People* (New York: Doubleday)

McCarthy, Justin Huntly (1884) *England Under Gladstone, 1880–1884* (London: Chatto & Windus)

McCarthy, Justin (1903) *Portraits of the Sixties* (London: T. Fisher Unwin)

McClellan, Woodford (1979) *Revolutionary Exiles: The Russians in the First International and the Paris Commune* (London: Frank Cass)

McCorkle, John and O. S. Barton (1992) *Three Years With Quantrill* (1914), with notes by Albert Castel and commentary by Herman Hattaway (Norman, OK: Univ. of Oklahoma Press)

McCoy, Donald R. (1984) *The Presidency of Harry S. Truman* (Lawrence, KA: UP of Kansas)

McCullough, David (1992) *Truman* (New York: Simon & Schuster)

MacDonald, Carlos (January 1902) 'The Trial, Execution, Autopsy and Mental Status of Leon F. Czolgosz, Alias Fred Nieman, the Assassin of President McKinley', *The American Journal of Insanity*, Vol. 58, No. 3 (Baltimore: Johns Hopkins Press): 369–86

MacDonald, Ian (1998) *Revolution in the Head: The Beatles' Records and the Sixties* (London: Pimlico)

McEldowney, John (1993) 'Miscarriages of Justice? The Phoenix Park Murders, 1882', *Criminal Justice History, An International Annual*, Vol. 14 (Westport, CT, & London: Greenwood Press): 143–9

McGee, Reece (December 1963) 'The Roots of the Agony', *The Nation*, 21 December 1963, Vol. 197, No. 21 (New York: The Nation Company): 427–33

McGee, Owen (2007) *The IRB: The Irish Republican Brotherhood from the Land League to Sinn Féin* (2005) (Dublin: Four Courts Press)

Mackay, John Henry (1891) *The Anarchists. A Picture of Civilization at the Close of the Nineteenth Century*, trans. George Schumm, with a portrait of the author and a study of his works by Gabriele Reuter (Boston: Benjamin R. Tucker)

Mackay, R. D. (1995) *Mental Condition Defences in the Criminal Law* (Oxford: Clarendon Press)

MacKenzie, David (1995) *The 'Black Hand' on Trial, Salonika, 1917* (Boulder, CO: East European Monographs)

McMillan, George (1976) *The Making of an Assassin: The Life of James Earl Ray* (Boston & Toronto: Little, Brown)

McPherson, James (1998) *Battle Cry of Freedom: The Civil War Era* (Oxford: OUP)

Mailer, Norman (November 1960) 'Superman Comes to the Supermart', *Esquire*, Vol. 54, No. 5 (New York: Esquire): 199–227

Mailer, Norman (1971) *The Prisoner of Sex* (Boston & Toronto: Little, Brown)

Mailer, Norman (1995) *Oswald's Tale. An American Mystery* (New York: Random House)

Maitron, Jean (1992) *Ravachol et les anarchistes* (1964) (Paris: Gallimard)

Majendie, Sir Vivian Dering (1902) *Guide Book to the Explosives Act, 1875*, 11th edn (London: His Majesty's Stationery Office)

Malamud, Margaret (2009) *Ancient Rome and Modern America* (Chichester: Wiley-Blackwell)

Malanga, Gerard (2002) *Archiving Warhol: An Illustrated History* (Washington, DC: Creation Books)

Malcolm X and Alex Haley (1965) *The Autobiography of Malcolm X* (New York: Grove Press)

Malone, Dumas, ed. (1946) *Dictionary of American Biography*, vols 7, 11 & 15 (New York: Scribner's)

Marcus, Greil (2002) *The Manchurian Candidate* (London: British Film Institute)

Marsh, Margaret (1981) *Anarchist Women 1870–1920* (Philadelphia: Temple UP)

Marshall, Peter (1993) *Demanding the Impossible. A History of Anarchism* (1992) (London: Fontana)

Martin, Theodore (1879) *The Life of His Royal Highness The Prince Consort*, Vol. 4 (London: Smith, Elder)

Marwick, Arthur (1998) *The Sixties: Cultural Revolutions in Britain, France, Italy, and the United States* (Oxford: OUP)

Matthew, H. C. G., ed. (1990) *The Gladstone Diaries with Cabinet Minutes and Prime-Ministerial Correspondence*, Vol. 10 (Oxford: Clarendon Press)

Matthew, H. C. G. (1995) *Gladstone, 1875–1898* (Oxford: Clarendon Press)

Matthew, H. C. G. (2004a) 'Herbert John Gladstone, Viscount Gladstone (1854–1930)', in *Oxford Dictionary of National Biography*, Vol. 22 (Oxford: OUP): 377–80

Matthew, H. C. G. (2004b) '[John] Arthur Godley, first Baron Kilbracken (1847–1932)', in *Oxford Dictionary of National Biography*, Vol. 22 (Oxford: OUP): 582–3

Maume, Patrick (May 1995) 'Parnell and the I.R.B. Oath', *Irish Historical Studies*, Vol. 29, No. 115 (Antrim: W. & G. Baird): 363–70

Mazower, Mark (2002) *The Balkans: A Short History* (New York: Random House)

Mehdi, M. T. (1968) *Kennedy and Sirhan: Why?*, with a foreword by Gibran Khalil Gibran (New York: New World Press)

Meier, August (1970) 'The Conservative Militant', in *Martin Luther King Jr. A Profile*, ed. C. Eric Lincoln (New York: Hill & Wang): 144–56

Melas, G. (1922) *The Turk As He Is* (London: A. Probsthain)

Melson, Robert (1992) *Revolution and Genocide. On the Origins of the Armenian Genocide and the Holocaust* (Chicago & London: Univ. of Chicago Press)

Messerschmidt, Manfred (1986) 'Motivationen der nationalkonservativen Opposition seit 1940', in *Der deutsche Widerstand, 1933–1945*, ed. Klaus-Jürgen Müller (Paderborn & Munich: Ferdinand Schöningh): 60–78

Mieczkowski, Yanek (2005) *Gerald Ford and the Challenges of the 1970s* (Lexington, KY: UP of Kentucky)

Milkis, Sidney M. and Michael Nelson (2008) *The American Presidency: Origins and Development*, 5th edn (Washington, DC: CQ Press)

Millais, John Guille (1899) *The Life and Letters of Sir John Everett Millais*, Vol. 1 (London: Methuen)

Mills, C. Wright (1956) *White Collar: The American Middle Classes* (1951) (New York: OUP)

Miró, Joan (1987) *Selected Writings and Interviews*, ed. Margit Rowell, trans. from the French by Paul Auster, trans. from the Spanish and Catalan by Patricia Matthews (London: Thames & Hudson)

Moldea, Dan E. (1995) *The Killing of Robert Kennedy: An Investigation of Motive, Means and Opportunity* (New York: W. W. Norton)

Möller, Horst (2004) *Die Weimarer Republik: eine unvollendete Demokratie*, rev. and expanded edn (Munich: Deutscher Taschenbuch)

Moloney, Ed (2002) *A Secret History of the IRA* (London: Penguin)

Moore-Anderson, A. P. (1919) *Sir Robert Anderson, K.C.B., LL.D.* (London: Morgan & Scott)

Moran, Richard (1981) *Knowing Right from Wrong: The Insanity Defence of Daniel M'Naghten* (New York: Free Press)

Moran, Richard (January 1985) 'The Modern Foundation for the Insanity Defence: The Cases of James Hadfield (1800) and Daniel McNaughtan (1843)', in *The Insanity Defence*, a special issue of *The Annals of the American Academy of Political and Social Science*, ed. Richard Moran (Beverly Hills, CA: Sage Publictations): 31–42

Moran, Richard (2002) *Executioner's Current. Thomas Edison, George Westinghouse, and the Invention of the Electric Chair* (New York: Knopf)

Morgan, H. Wayne (1963) *William McKinley and his America* (Syracuse, NY: Syracuse UP)

Morley, John (1903) *The Life of William Ewart Gladstone*, Vol. 3 (London: Macmillan)

Morley, John, Viscount (1917) *Recollections* (London: Macmillan)

Morris, Dan and Inez Morris (1974) *Who Was Who in American Politics* (New York: Hawthorn Books)

Morris, Edmund (2000) *Dutch: A Memoir of Ronald Reagan* (1999) (London: HarperCollins)

Morris, Edmund (2001) *Theodore Rex* (New York: Random House)

Morris, Nancy (1995) *Puerto Rico: Culture, Politics and Identity* (Westport, CT, & London: Praeger)

Morton, Marian J. (1992) *Emma Goldman and the American Left: 'Nowhere at Home'* (New York: Twayne)

Moss, Walter (2005) *A History of Russia*, 2nd edn, Vol. 2 (London: Anthem Press)

Mount, Graeme S., with Mark Gauthier (2006) *895 Days That Changed the World* (Montreal: Black Rose Books)

Mousset, Albert, ed. (1930) *L'Attentat de Sarajevo: Documents inédits et textes intégral des sténogrammes du procès* (Paris: Payot)

Müller, Christine-Ruth (1990) *Dietrich Bonhoeffers Kampf gegen die nationalsozialistische Verfolgung und Vernichtung der Juden* (Munich: Chr. Kaiser)

Müller, Jan-Werner (2003) *A Dangerous Mind. Carl Schmitt in Post-War European Thought* (New Haven & London: Yale UP)

Müller, Klaus-Jürgen, ed. (1986) *Der deutsche Widerstand, 1933–1945* (Paderborn & Munich: Ferdinand Schöningh)

Murphy, John A. (1980) 'The Influence of America on Irish Nationalism', in *America and Ireland, 1776–1976. The American Identity and the Irish Connection*, eds David Noel Doyle and Owen Dudley Edwards (Westport, CT: Greenwood Press): 105–15

Murray, Donald (1901) 'The Automatic Age. Electrical Marvels and Mechanical Triumphs at the Pan-American Exhibition', *Everybody's Magazine*, Vol. 5, No. 26 (New York: John Wanamaker): 387–404

Musser, Charles (1995) *Thomas Edison and His Kinetographic Motion Pictures* (New Brunswick, NJ: Rutgers UP)

Myers, Gustavus (1936) *History of the Great American Fortunes* (New York: Modern Library)

Naarden, Bruno (1992) *Socialist Europe and Revolutionary Russia: Perception and Prejudice 1848–1923* (Cambridge: CUP)

Naayem, J. ['Naim Bey'] (1920) *Les Assyro-Chaldéens et les Arméniens massacres par les Turcs* (Paris: Bloud & Gay)

Nassibian, Akaby (1984) *Britain and the Armenian Question 1915–1923* (New York: St Martin's Press)

Nataf, André (1986) *La Vie quotidienne des anarchistes en France, 1880–1910* (Paris: Hachette)

Nelson, Bruce C. (1988) *Beyond the Martyrs: A Social History of Chicago's Anarchists, 1870–1900* (New Brunswick & London: Rutgers UP)

Nettl, J. P. (1966) *Rosa Luxemburg*, 2 vols (London: OUP)

Nevins, Allan (1960) *The War for the Union: Volume II War Becomes Revolution, 1862–3* (New York: Scribner's)

Newfield, Jack (1969) *Robert Kennedy. A Memoir* (New York: E. P. Dutton)

Newman, John (1992) *JFK and Vietnam: Deception, Intrigue, and the Struggle for Power* (New York: Warner)

Nietzsche, Friedrich (1974) *The Gay Science*, trans. Walter Kaufmann (New York: Vintage)

Nietzsche, Friedrich (1979) *Ecce Homo*, trans. with an introduction by R. J. Hollingdale (Harmondsworth: Penguin)

Nietzsche, Friedrich (1999) *Der Fall Wagner; Götzen-Dämmerung; Der Antichrist; Ecce Homo; Dionysos-Dithyramben; Nietzsche contra Wagner*, eds Giorgio Colli and Mazzino Montinari (Munich: Deutscher Taschenbuch)

Nixon, Richard (1978) *R. N. The Memoirs of Richard Nixon* (London: Sidgwick & Jackson)

Noguchi, Thomas T., with Joseph DiMona (1983) *Coroner* (New York: Simon & Schuster)

Noonan, Peggy (1990) *What I Saw at the Revolution: A Political Life in the Reagan Era* (New York: Random House)

Norden, Günther van (1986) 'Widerstand in deutschen Protestantismus, 1933–1945', in *Der deutsche Widerstand, 1933–1945*, ed. Klaus-Jürgen Müller (Paderborn & Munich: Ferdinand Schöningh): 108–34

Oates, Stephen B. (1970) *To Purge This Land with Blood: A Biography of John Brown* (New York: Harper & Row)

O'Brien, Barry (1898) *The Life of Charles Stewart Parnell, 1846–1891* (London: Smith, Elder)

O'Callaghan, Margaret (2004) 'New Ways of Looking at the State Apparatus and the State Archive', *Proceedings of the Royal Irish Academy*, Vol. 104C, No. 2 (Dublin: Royal Irish Academy): 50–4

O'Connor, John and Benjamin Liu (1996) *Unseen Warhol* (New York: Rizzoli)

O'Connor, Richard (1967) *Ambrose Bierce: A Biography* (Boston & Toronto: Little, Brown)

O'Donnell, Frank Hugh (1910) *A History of the Irish Parliamentary Party. Volume II: Parnell and the Lieutenants, Complicity and Betrayal, with an Epilogue to the Present Day* (London: Longmans, Green)

O'Donovan Rossa, Jeremiah (2004) *Rossa's Recollections 1838–1898. Memoirs of an Irish Revolutionary* (1896–8) (Guilford, CT: Lyons Press)

'Official Report' (1901) 'The Official Report on the Case of President McKinley', *Buffalo Medical Journal*, Vol. 57, No. 3 (Buffalo, NY): 271–93

Offord, D. C. (1999) '*The Devils* in the Context of Contemporary Russian Thought and Politics', in *Dostoevsky's* The Devils: *A Critical Companion*, ed. W. J. Leatherbarrow (Evanston, IL: Northwestern UP): 63–99

Ogilvie, J. S. (1881) *History of the Assassination of James A. Garfield* (New York: J. S. Ogilvie)

Öke, Mim Kemal (1988) *The Armenian Question 1914–1923* (Nicosia: K. Rustem & Brother)

Okey, Robin (2001) *The Habsburg Monarchy c. 1765–1918: From Enlightenment to Eclipse* (Basingstoke: Macmillan)

Oliver, Hermia (1983) *The International Anarchist Movement in Late Victorian London* (London & Canberra, Croom Helm; New York: St Martins Press)

Orel, Şinasi and Süreyya Yuca (1986) *The Talât Pasha 'Telegrams': Historical Fact or Armenian Fiction* (Nicosia: K. Rustem & Brother)

Oswald, Robert L., Myrick and Barbara Land (1967) *Lee: A Portrait of Lee Harvey Oswald by His Brother* (New York: Coward-McCann)

Packard, Vance (1957) *The Hidden Persuaders* (New York: David McKay)

Pagel, Karl (1935) *Die Feme des deutschen mittelalters* (Leipzig: Bibliographische Institut)

Paine, Albert Bigelow (1912) *Mark Twain, A Biography. The Personal and Literary Life of Samuel Langhorne Clemens*, 3 vols (New York & London: Harper & Brothers)

Paine, Albert Bigelow (1917) *Mark Twain's Letters. Arranged with Comment*, 2 vols (New York: Harper & Brothers)

Painter, Nell Irvin (2008) *Standing at Armageddon: The United States, 1877–1919* (New York & London: W. W. Norton)

Pais, Abraham (1982) *'Subtle is the Lord . . .': The Science and the Life of Albert Einstein* (Oxford: Clarendon Press)

Pappenheim, Martin (1926) *Gavrilo Princips Bekenntnisse. Zwei Manuskripte Princips. Aufzeichnungen seines Gefängnispsychiaters Dr. Pappenheim aus Gesprächen von Feber bis June 1916 über das Attentat, Princips Leben und seine politischen und sozialen Anschauungen*, with an introduction and commentary by 'R. P.' (Vienna: Rudolf Lechner & Sohn)

Pares, Bernard (1931) *My Russian Memoirs* (London: Jonathan Cape)

Park, Roswell (1914) 'Reminiscences of McKinley Week', *Selected Papers Surgical and Scientific* (Buffalo, NY: Julian Park): 375–81

Parmenter, John (1901) 'The Surgery in President McKinley's Case', *Buffalo Medical Journal*, Vol. 57, No. 2 (Buffalo, NY): 205–6. Found at http://ublib.buffalo.edu/hsl/resources/guides/mckinley.html

Paulhan, Jean (1998) *F. F. ou le Critique* (1945) (Paris: Éditions Claire Paulhan)

Pechel, Rudolf (1947) *Deutscher Widerstand* (Erlenbach-Zürich: Eugen Rentsch)

Peel, Sir Lawrence (1860) *A Sketch of the Life and Character of Sir Robert Peel* (London: Longman, Green, Longman, & Roberts)

Pepper, William F. (1995) *Orders to Kill: The Truth Behind the Murder of Martin Luther King* (New York: Carroll & Graf)

Perkins, Dexter (1935a) 'Frederick William Seward', in *Dictionary of American Biography*, ed. Dumas Malone, Vol. 16 (New York: Scribner's): 612–13

Perkins, Dexter (1935b) 'William Henry Seward', in *Dictionary of American Biography*, ed. Dumas Malone, Vol. 16 (New York: Scribner's): 615–21

Perris, G. H. (1905) *Russia in Revolution* (London: Chapman & Hall)

Perry, Bruce (1991) *Malcolm: The Life of a Man Who Changed Black America* (Barrytown, NY: Station Hill Press)

Peskin, Allan (1978) *Garfield* (Kent State University, OH: Kent State UP)

Peskin, Allan (1999a) 'James Abram Garfield', in *American National Biography*, eds John A. Garraty and Mark C. Carnes, Vol. 8 (New York & Oxford: OUP): 715–17

Peskin, Allan (1999b) 'Charles Julius Guiteau', in *American National Biography*, eds John A. Garraty and Mark C. Carnes, Vol. 9 (New York & Oxford: OUP): 715–16

Phillips, Kevin (2002) *Wealth and Democracy. A Political History of the American Rich* (New York: Broadway Books)

Pipes, Richard (1974) *Russia Under the Old Regime* (London: Weidenfeld & Nicolson)

Pogge von Strandmann, Hartmut, ed. (1967) *Walther Rathenau Tagebuch 1907–1922* (Düsseldorf: Droste)

Pogge von Strandmann, Hartmut, ed. (1985) *Walther Rathenau: Industrialist, Banker, Intellectual, and Politician. Notes and Diaries 1907–1922*, trans. Harmut and Hilary Pogge von Strandmann, and Caroline Pinder-Cracraft (Oxford: Clarendon Press)

Pollard, Robert A. (1989) 'The National Security State Reconsidered: Truman and Economic Containment, 1945–1950', in *The Truman Presidency*, ed. Michael J. Lacey (Woodrow Wilson International Center for Scholars & Cambridge: CUP): 205–34

Pomper, Philip (1970) *The Russian Revolutionary Intelligentsia* (New York: Thomas Y. Crowell)

Pomper, Philip (April 1974) 'Nechaev and Tsaricide', *Russian Review*, Vol. 33, No. 2 (Stanford CA: Russian Review Inc.): 123–38

Posner, Gerald (1998) *Killing the Dream: James Earl Ray and the Assassination of Martin Luther King, Jr.* (New York: Random House)

Powers, Thomas (1979) *The Man Who Kept the Secrets: Richard Helms & the CIA* (New York: Knopf)

Pratley, Gerald (1969) *The Cinema of John Frankenheimer* (London: A Zwemmer; New York: A. S. Barnes)

Price, Kenneth M., ed. (1996) *Walt Whitman: The Contemporary Reviews* (Cambridge: CUP)

Proudhon, P. J. (1886) *The Malthusians*, trans. Benjamin Tucker (London: International Publishing)

Quen, J. M. (1969) 'James Hadfield and Medical Jurisprudence of Insanity', *New York State Journal of Medicine*, Vol. 69 (Lake Success, NY: New York State Medical Association): 1221–6

Rabaut, Jean (1971) *Jaurès* (Paris: Librairie Académique Perrin)

Rabaut, Jean (1984) *Jaurès Assassine* (Brussels: Editions Complexe)

Radzinowicz, Sir Leon and Roger Hood (1986) *A History of English Criminal Law and Its Administration from 1750*: Volume 5: *The Emergence of Penal Policy* (London: Stevens & Sons)

Randall, James G. (1929) 'Lincoln in the Role of Dictator', in *The South Atlantic Quarterly*, eds William K. Boyd and William H. Wannamaker, Vol. 28, No. 3 (Durham, NC): 236–52

Rathenau, Walther (2006) *Briefe. Teilband 2: 1914–1922*, eds Alexander Jaser, Clemens Picht and Ernst Schulin (Düsseldorf: Droste)

Rauchway, Eric (2003) *Murdering McKinley: The Making of Theodore Roosevelt's America* (New York: Hill & Wang)

Ray, Isaac (1838) *A Treatise on the Medical Jurisprudence of Insanity* (Boston: Charles C. Little & James Brown)

Raym, Agatha, ed. (1998) *The Gladstone–Granville Correspondence* (1952), with a supplementary introduction by H. C. G. Matthew (Cambridge: CUP)

Reagan, Nancy, with William Novak (1989) *My Turn: The Memoirs of Nancy Reagan* (New York: Random House)

Reagan, Ronald, with Richard G. Hubler (1981) *My Early Life or Where's the Rest of Me* (1965) (London: Sidgwick & Jackson)

Reagan, Ronald (1990) *An American Life* (New York: Simon & Schuster)

Reagan, Ronald (2004) *Reagan: A Life in Letters*, ed. with an introduction and commentary by Kiron K. Skinner, Annelise Anderson and Martin Anderson (2003) (New York: Free Press)

Reagan, Ronald (2007) *The Reagan Diaries*, ed. Douglas Brinkley (New York: HarperCollins)

Reeves, Richard (1975) *A Ford, Not a Lincoln* (New York & London: Harcourt Brace Jovanovich)

Reeves, Thomas C. (1991) *A Question of Character: A Life of John F. Kennedy* (New York: Free Press)

Remak, Joachim (1959) *Sarajevo: The Story of a Political Murder* (London: Weidenfeld & Nicolson)

Report of the Physicians (1901) 'Report of the Physicians who Attended President McKinley', *Buffalo Medical Journal*, Vol. 57, No. 4 (Buffalo, NY): 295–6

Reynolds, David S. (2006) *John Brown, Abolitionist: The Man Who Killed Slavery, Sparked the Civil War, and Seeded Civil Rights* (New York: Knopf)

Rhodehamel, John and Louise Taper, eds (1997) *'Right or Wrong, God Judge Me.' The Writings of John Wilkes Booth* (Urbana & Chicago: Univ. of Illinois Press)

Riasanovsky, Nicholas V. (2000) *A History of Russia*, 6th edn (New York & Oxford: OUP)

Richards, Francis, ed. (1905) *At Scotland Yard. Being the Experiences during Twenty-Seven Years' Service of John Sweeney* (London: Alexander Moring)

Riesman, David (1950) *The Lonely Crowd: A Study of the Changing American Character* (New Haven, CT: Yale UP)

Ringer, Fritz K. (1969) *The Decline of the German Mandarins: The German Academic Community, 1890–1933* (Cambridge, MA: Harvard UP)

Roediger, Dave and Franklin Rosemont, eds (1986) *Haymarket Scrapbook* (Chicago: Charles H. Kerr)

Rohler, Lloyd (2004) *George Wallace: Conservative Populist* (Westport, CT: Praeger)

Roon, Ger van (1971) *German Resistance to Hitler: Count von Moltke and the Kreisau Circle*, trans. Peter Ludlow (1967) (London: Van Nostrand Reinhold)

Roon, Ger van (1979) *Widerstand im Dritten Reich*, trans. Marga E. Baumer-Thierfelder (1968) (Munich: Oscar Beck)

Rorabaugh, W. J. (2002) *Kennedy and the Promise of the Sixties* (Cambridge: CUP)

Rosenberg, Charles E. (1968) *The Trial of the Assassin Guiteau. Psychiatry and Law in the Gilded Age* (Chicago & London: Univ. of Chicago Press)

Ross, Dieter (1966) *Hitler und Dollfuss: Die deutsche Österreich-Politik 1933–1934* (Hamburg: Leibniz-Verlag)

Ross, Lillian (1966) *Adlai Stevenson* (Philadelphia & New York: J. B. Lippincott)

Roszak, Theodore (1969) *The Making of a Counter-Culture: Reflections on a Technocratic Society and Its Youthful Opposition* (Garden City, NY: Doubleday)

Royal Movements (1883) *A Diary of Royal Movements and of Personal Events and Incidents in the Life and Reign of Her Most Gracious Majesty Queen Victoria*, Vol. 1 (London: Elliot Stock)

Ruskin, John and Charles Eliot Norton (1987) *The Correspondence of John Ruskin and Charles Eliot Norton*, eds John Lewis Bradley and Ian Ousby (Cambridge: CUP)

Russell, Francis (1976) *The President Makers. From Mark Hanna to Joseph P. Kennedy* (Boston/Toronto: Little, Brown)

Sabrow, Martin (1994) *Der Rathenaumord: Rekonstruction einer Verschwörung gegen die Republik von Weimar* (Munich: R. Oldenburg)

Sabrow, Martin (1998) *Die Macht der Mythen: Walther Rathenau im öffentlichen Gedächtnis* (Berlin: Verlag das Arsenal)

Salter, Andrew (1952) *Conditioned Reflex Therapy: The Direct Approach to the Reconstruction of Personality* (1949) (London: George Allen & Unwin)

Samples, Gordon (1982) *Lust for Fame: The Stage Career of John Wilkes Booth* (Jefferson, NC, & London: McFarland)

Sanders, Liman von (1928) *Five Years in Turkey*, trans. from the 1920 German edn (Annapolis: Williams & Wilkins)

Sanger, Martha Frick Symington (1998) *Henry Clay Frick* (New York, London & Paris: Abbeville Press)

Sanger, Martha Frick Symington (2001) *The Henry Clay Frick Houses* (New York: Monacelli Press)

Sarafian, Ara, ed. (1995) *United States Official Documents on the Armenian Genocide: Vol. III The Central Lands* (Watertown, MA: Armenian Review)

Sarafian, Ara, ed. (2000) *The Treatment of Armenians in the Ottoman Empire, 1915–1916*, written by James Bryce and Arnold Toynbee (Princeton, NJ: Gomidas Institute)

Sargant, William (1957) *Battle for the Mind: A Physiology of Conversion and Brain-Washing* (London: Heinemann)

Savage, George H. (1881) 'Moral Insanity', *The Journal of Medical Science*, eds D. Hack Tuke and George H. Savage, Vol. 27, No. 82 (London: J. & A. Churchill): 147–55

Sayler, Oliver M., ed. (1968) *Max Reinhardt and His Theatre* (1924), trans. Mariele S. Gudernatsch (New York & London: Benjamin Blom)

Schapsmeier, Edward L. and Frederick H. (1989) *Gerald R. Ford's Date with Destiny* (New York: Peter Lang)

Schein, Edgar, with Inge Schneier and Curtis H. Barker (1971) *Coercive Persuasion: A Socio-psychological Analysis of the "Brainwashing" of American Civilian Prisoners by the Chinese Communists* (1961) (New York: W. W. Norton)

Scheuerman, William E. (1999) *Carl Schmitt. The End of Law* (Lanham, Boulder, New York, Oxford: Rowman & Littlefield)

Scheurig, Bodo (1982) 'Henning von Tresckow', in *Widerstand im Dritten Reich: Probleme, Ereignisse, Gestalten*, ed. Hermann Graml (Frankfurt am Main: Fischer Taschenbuch): 140–56

Schlesinger, Arthur M. (1965) *A Thousand Days: John F. Kennedy in the White House* (Boston & Cambridge, MA: Houghton Mifflin & Riverside Press)

Schlesinger, Arthur M. (1978) *Robert Kennedy and His Times* (Boston: Houghton Mifflin)

Schmaltz, William H. (1999) *Hate: George Lincoln Rockwell and the American Nazi Party* (Washington, DC, & London: Brassey's)

Schmidt, Regin (2000) *Red Scare. FBI and the Origins of Anticommunism in the United States, 1919–1943* (Copenhagen: Museum Tusculanum Press)

Schrader, Paul (2002) *Collected Screenplays: Volume I – Taxi Driver, American Gigolo, Light Sleeper* (London: Faber and Faber)

Schroers, Rolf (1961) *Der Partisan. Ein Beitrag zur politischen Anthropologie* (Cologne & Berlin: Kiepenheuer & Witsch)

Schulin, Ernst (1979) *Walther Rathenau: Repräsentant, Kritiker und Opfer seiner Zeit* (Zurich & Frankfurt: Musterschmidt Göttingen)

Schulthess, Konstanze von (2008) *Nina Schenk Gräfin von Stauffenberg: Ein Porträt* (Munich: Piper)

Select Committee on Assassinations (1979) *Investigation of the Assassination of Martin Luther King, Jr.: Hearings and Appendices to Hearings Before the Select Committee on Assassinations of the U. S. House of Representatives, Ninety-Fifth Congress, Second Session* (Washington, DC: US Government Printing Office) consulted in CD-Rom form in the Lexis-Nexis Congressional Hearings Digital Collection

Seth, Ronald (1966) *The Russian Terrorists: The Story of the Narodniki* (London: Barrie & Rockliff)

Seton-Watson, R. W. (1917) *The Rise of Nationality in the Balkans* (London: Constable)

Seton-Watson, R. W. (1926) *Sarajevo: A Study of the Origins of the Great War* (London: Hutchinson)

Seton-Watson, R. W. (1976) *R. W. Seton-Watson and the Yugoslavs: Correspondence 1906–1941*, eds Hugh Seton-Watson, Christopher Seton-Watson et al., 2 vols (Zagreb: Univ. of Zagreb)

Seward, Frederick W. (1916) *Reminiscences of a War-Time Statesman and Diplomat, 1830–1915* (London: G. P. Putnam's Sons)

Seward, William H. (1873) *William H. Seward's Travels Around the World*, ed. Olive Risley Seward (New York: D. Appleton)

Seymour, Henry (1895) *The Monomaniacs: A Fable In Finance* (London: W. Reeves)

Shannon, Richard (1999) *Gladstone: Heroic Minister, 1865–1898* (London: Allen Lane)

Shaw, Stanford J. and Ezel Kural Shaw (1977) *History of the Ottoman Empire and Modern Turkey. Vol. II. Reform, Revolution, and Republic: The Rise of Modern Turkey, 1808–1975* (Cambridge: CUP)

Shaw, Stanford J. (2000) *From Empire to Republic: The Turkish War of National Liberation 1918–23, A Documentary Study*, 5 vols (Ankara: Türk Tarih Kurum Basimevi)

Sherman, Richard B. (November 1983) 'Presidential Protection during the Progressive Era: The Aftermath of the McKinley Assassination', *Historian*, Vol. 46, No. 1 (Tampa, FL): 1–20

Shesol, Jeff (1997) *Mutual Contempt: Lyndon Johnson, Robert Kennedy, and the Feud that Defined a Decade* (New York & London: W. W. Norton)

Shilts, Randy (1982) *The Mayor of Castro Street: The Life and Times of Harvey Milk* (New York: St Martin's Press)

Short, K. R. M. (1979) *The Dynamite War: Irish-American Bombers in Victorian Britain* (Dublin: Gill & Macmillan)

Sikes, Wirt (1881) *Studies of Assassination* (London: Sampson, Low, Marston, Searle, & Rivington)

Siljak, Ana (2008) *Angel of Vengeance: 'The Girl Assassin,' the Governor of St. Petersburg, and Russia's Revolutionary World* (New York: St Martin's Press)

Simmel, Georg (2000) 'The Metropolis and Mental Life' (1903), in *The Fin de Siècle. A Reader in Cultural History, c. 1880–1900*, eds Sally Ledger and Roger Luckhurst (Oxford: OUP): 61–6

Simonelli, Frederick J. (1999) *American Fuehrer: George Lincoln Rockwell and the American Nazi Party* (Urbana & Chicago: Univ. of Illinois Press)

Simpson, H. B. (July 1896) 'Crime and Punishment', *Contemporary Review*, Vol. 70 (London: Isbister): 91–108

Slater, Michael, ed. (1996) *Dickens' Journalism. 'The Amusements of the People' and other Papers: Reports, Essays and Reviews 1834–51* (London: J. M. Dent)

Smith, Adrian (2010) *Mountbatten: Apprentice War Lord* (London: I. B. Tauris)

Smith, David Frederick (2004) 'Sir George Grey, second baronet (1799–1882)', in *Oxford Dictionary of National Biography*, Vol. 23 (Oxford: OUP): 839–41

Solanas, Valerie (1970) *SCUM Manifesto* (1968) (New York: Olympia Press)

Solberg, Carl (1984) *Hubert Humphrey: A Biography* (New York & London: W. W. Norton)

Speakes, Larry, with Robert Pack (1988) *Speaking Out: The Reagan Presidency from Inside the White House* (New York: Scribner's)

Spetter, Allan Burton (1999) 'James Gillespie Blaine', in *American National Biography*, ed. John A. Garraty and Mark C. Carnes, Vol. 2 (New York & Oxford: OUP): 902–6

Spitzka, Edward Anthony (January 1902) 'The Post-Mortem Examination of Leon Czolgosz, the Assassin of President McKinley', *The American Journal of Insanity*, Vol. 58, No. 3 (Baltimore: Johns Hopkins Press): 386–404

Srodes, James (1999) *Allen Dulles, Master of Spies* (Washington, DC: Regnery)

Stavrianos, L. S. (1963) *The Balkans 1815–1914* (New York: Holt, Rinehart & Winston)

Steele, David (2004) 'James Howard Harris, third earl of Malmesbury (1807–1889)', in *Oxford Dictionary of National Biography*, Vol. 25 (Oxford: OUP): 434–9

Steele, E. D. (1991) *Palmerston and Liberalism, 1855–1865* (Cambridge: CUP)

Stein, Jean (1970) *American Journey: The Times of Robert Kennedy*, ed. George Plimpton (New York: Harcourt Brace Jovanovich)

Stein, Jean and George Plimpton, eds (1982) *Edie: American Girl* (New York: Grove Press)

Steinbacher, John (1968) *The Man, The Mysticism, The Murder* (Los Angeles: Impact)

Stepniak, S. (1883) *Underground Russia. Revolutionary Profiles and Sketches from Life* (London: Smith, Elder)

Stern, Fritz (2001) *Einstein's German World* (1999) (London: Penguin)

Stern, Howard (March 1963) 'The *Organisation Consul*', *Journal of Modern History*, Vol. 35, No. 1 (Chicago: Univ. of Chicago Press): 20–32

Stoddart, D. R. (1986) *On Geography and its History* (Oxford: Blackwell)

Stokes, Melvyn (2007) *D. W. Griffith's* The Birth of a Nation. *A History of 'The Most Controversial Picture of All Time'* (Oxford: OUP)

Stone, Norman (1985) *Europe Transformed, 1879–1919* (1983) (London: HarperCollins)

Stone, Norman (2003) 'Introduction', to Lord Kinross, *The Ottoman Empire* (Bath: Folio Society): vii–xxiii

Strachey, Lytton (1928) *Queen Victoria* (1922) (London: Chatto & Windus)

Stutfield, Hugh E. M. (2000) 'Tommyrotics' (1895), in *The Fin de Siècle. A Reader in Cultural History, c. 1880–1900*, eds Sally Ledger and Roger Luckhurst (Oxford: OUP): 120–6

Sullivan III, Michael J. (2008) *American Adventurism Abroad: Invasions, Interventions and Regime Changes Since World War II*, rev. and expanded edn (Oxford: Blackwell)

Summers, Anthony (1985) *Goddess: The Secret Lives of Marilyn Monroe* (London: Victor Gollancz)

Tallmer, Jerry (1970) 'A Man With A Hard Head', in *Martin Luther King Jr. A Profile*, ed. C. Eric Lincoln (New York: Hill & Wang): 1–6

Tálos, Emmerich and Wolfgang Neugebauer, eds (1984) *'Austrofaschismus': Beiträge über Politik, Ökonomie und Kultur 1934–1938* (Vienna: Verlag für Gesellschaftskritik)

Taubin, Amy (2000) *Taxi Driver* (London: British Film Institute)

Taylor, A. J. P. (1948) *The Habsburg Monarchy 1809–1918* (London: Hamish Hamilton)

Taylor, A. J. P. (1971) *The Struggle for Mastery in Europe, 1848–1918* (1954) (Oxford: OUP)

Taylor, John M. (1991) *William Henry Seward: Lincoln's Right Hand* (Washington & London: Brassey's)

Taylor, Peter (1997) *Provos: The IRA and Sinn Fein* (London: Bloomsbury)

Ternon, Yves (1989) *Enquête sur la négation d'un genocide* (Paris: Éditions Parenthèses)

Ternon, Yves (1999) 'La qualité de la prevue: A propos des documents Andonian et de la petite phrase d'Hitler', in *L'actualité du génocide des Arméniens*, ed. Hrayr Henry Ayvazian (Paris: Edipol): 135–42

Theoharis, Athan G. (2004) *The FBI & American Democracy* (Lawrence, KA: UP of Kansas)

Thomas, Benjamin (1953) *Abraham Lincoln* (London: Eyre & Spottiswoode)

Thomas, Evan (2000) *Robert Kennedy: His Life* (New York: Simon & Schuster)

Thorpe, D. R. (2003) *Eden: The Life and Times of Anthony Eden, First Earl of Avon, 1897–1977* (London: Chatto & Windus)

Tidwell, William A., James O. Hall and David Winfred Gaddy (1988) *Come Retribution: The Confederate Secret Service and the Assassination of Lincoln* (Jackson, MS, & London: UP of Mississippi)

Tollemache, Lionel (1898) *Talks with Mr. Gladstone* (New York: Longmans, Green)

Toscano, Vincent Lawrence (1975) *Since Dallas: Images of John F. Kennedy in Popular and Scholarly Literature, 1963–1973* (PhD thesis for State Univ. of New York at Albany)

Toynbee, Arnold J. (1923) *The Western Question in Greece and Turkey. A Study in the Contact of Civilisations* (London: Constable)

Toynbee, Arnold J. (1967) *Acquaintances* (London: OUP)

Trautmann, Frederic (1980) *The Voice of Terror: A Biography of Johann Most* (Westport, CT, & London: Greenwood Press)

Treherne, Philip (1909) *The Right Honourable Spencer Perceval* (London: T. Fisher Unwin)

Trevor-Roper, Hugh (1966) 'Introduction', to Mark Lane, *Rush to Judgment. A Critique of the Warren Commission's Inquiry into the Murders of President John F. Kennedy, Officer J. D. Tippit and Lee Harvey Oswald* (London: Bodley Head)

Truman, Harry S. (1956) *Memoirs*, Vol. 2 (New York: Signet Books)

Truman Papers (1965) *Public Papers of the Presidents of the United States. Harry S. Truman. Containing the Public Messages, Speeches, and Statements of the President. 1950* (Washington, DC: US Government Printing Office)

Truman, Margaret (1973) *Harry S. Truman* (New York: William Morrow)

Tuchman, Barbara (1966) *The Proud Tower: A Portrait of the World Before the War, 1890–1914* (London: Hamish Hamilton)

Tugwell, Rexford Guy (1947) *The Stricken Land: The Story of Puerto Rico* (New York: Doubleday)

Tuke, Daniel Hack (1882) *Chapters in the History of the Insane in the British Isles* (London: Kegan Paul, Trench)

Tuke, Daniel Hack (1891) *Prichard and Symonds In Especial Relation to Mental Science with Chapters on Moral Insanity* (London: J. & A. Churchill)

Tuke, Daniel Hack, ed. (1892) *A Dictionary of Psychological Medicine, Giving the Definition, Etymology and Synonyms of the Terms Used in Medical Psychology with the Symptoms, Treatment, and Pathology of Insanity and the Laws of Lunacy in Great Britain and Ireland*, 2 vols (London: J. & A. Churchill)

Tunney, Thomas (1919) *Throttled! The Detection of the German and Anarchist Bomb Plotters*, as told to Paul Merrick Hollister (Boston: Small, Maynard)

Turner, Thomas Reed (1982) *Beware the People Weeping: Public Opinion and the Assassination of Abraham Lincoln* (Baton Rouge & London: Louisiana State UP)

Turner, William W. and Jonn G. Christian (1978) *The Assassination of Robert F. Kennedy: A Searching Look at the Conspiracy and the Cover-up 1968–1978* (New York: Random House)

Tynan, P. J. P. (1894) *The National Invincibles and their Times* (New York: Irish National Invincible Publishing)

Tyndall, John (1887) *Mr Gladstone and Home Rule* (Edinburgh & London: William Blackwood)

Ueberschär, Gerd R., ed. (2002) *Der deutsche Widerstand gegen Hitler: Wahrnehmung und Wertung in Europa und den USA* (Darmstadt: Wissenschaftliche Buchgesselschaft)

Ueberschär, Gerd R. (2006) *Stauffenberg und das Attentat vom 20. Juli 1944* (Frankfurt am Main: Fischer Taschenbuch)

Union (1865) *Jeff's Last Proclamation* (Burlington, Vermont: H. L. Story)

Valentine, Douglas (1990) *The Phoenix Program* (New York: William Morrow)

Varon, Jeremy (2004) *Bringing the War Home: The Weather Underground, The Red Army Faction, and Revolutionary Violence in the Sixties and Seventies* (Berkeley & Los Angeles: Univ. of California Press)

Veblen, Thorstein (2007) *The Theory of the Leisure Class* (1899), ed. with an introduction by Martha Banta (Oxford: OUP)

Venturi, Franco (2001) *Roots of Revolution. A History of the Populist and Socialist Movements in 19th Century Russia* (1960), trans. Frances Haskel with an introduction by Isaiah Berlin, rev. edn (with a rev. introduction by Venturi, 'Russian Populism' [1982]) (London: Phoenix Press)

Vernadsky, George and Ralph T. Fisher, eds (1972) *A Source Book for Russian History from Early Times to 1917. Volume 3: Alexander II to the February Revolution* (New Haven & London: Yale UP)

Vidal, Gore (1973) 'The Art and Arts of E. Howard Hunt', *New York Review of Books*, Vol. 20, No. 20 (New York): 6–19

Vizetelly, Ernest Alfred (1911) *The Anarchists, Their Faith and their Record Including Sidelights on the Royal and Other Personages Who Have Been Assassinated* (London: John Lane, The Bodley Head)

Volwiler, Albert T., ed. (1940) *The Correspondence Between Benjamin Harrison and James G. Blaine, 1882–1893* (Philadelphia: American Philosophical Society)

Walker, Christopher J. (1980) *Armenia: The Survival of a Nation* (London: Croom Helm)

Walker, Nigel (1968) *Crime and Insanity in England*, Vol. 1 (Edinburgh: Univ. of Edinburgh Press)

Wallis, John E. P. (1892) *Reports of State Trials. New Series. Volume IV. 1839–1843* (London: Her Majesty's Stationery Office)

Ward, John William (1999) 'Introduction' (1970) in *Prison Memoirs of an Anarchist*, Alexander Berkman (1912) (New York: New York Review of Books): ix–xxviii

Warhol, Andy (1989) *The Andy Warhol Diaries*, ed. Pat Hackett (New York: Warner)

Warhol, Andy (2007) *The Philosophy of Andy Warhol (From A to B and Back Again)* (1975) (London: Penguin)

Warren Report (1964) *Report of the Warren Commission on the Assassination of President Kennedy*, with an introduction by Harrison E. Salisbury and additional material prepared by the *New York Times* (New York: Bantam)

Warren, Kenneth (1996) *Triumphant Capitalism, Henry Clay Frick and the Industrial Transformation of America* (Pittsburgh, PA: Univ. of Pittsburgh Press)

Warren, Robert Penn (1965) *Who Speaks for the Negro?* (New York: Random House)

Wasiolek, Edward, ed. (1968) *The Notebooks for The Possessed* (Chicago & London: Univ. of Chicago Press)

Watson, Steven (2003) *Factory Made: Warhol and the Sixties* (New York: Pantheon Books)

Weber, Marianne (1975) *Max Weber: A Biography*, trans. Harry Zohn (New York & London: John Wiley)

Weckesser, Elden C. (1991) *His Name Was Mudd: The Life of Dr Samuel A. Mudd Who Treated the Fleeing John Wilkes Booth* (Jefferson, NC, & London: McFarland)

Weiner, Tim (2008) *Legacy of Ashes: The History of the CIA* (2007) (London: Penguin)

Weintraub, Stanley (1997) *Albert: Uncrowned King* (London: John Murray)

Weintraub, Stanley (2004) 'George Earle Buckle (1854–1935)', in *Oxford Dictionary of National Biography*, Vol. 8 (Oxford: OUP): 525–7

Wertham, Frederic (1966) *A Sign for Cain: An Exploration of Human Violence* (New York: Macmillan)

West, Donald J. and Alexander Walk, eds (1977) *Daniel McNaughton. His Trial and the Aftermath* (Ashford, Kent: Gaskell Books)

Westall, William (17 January 1885) 'A Defence of Prince Krapotkin and Co.', *Pall Mall Gazette*, Vol. 41, No. 6194: 2

Wharton, J. J. S. (1841) *Criminal Jurisprudence Considered in Relation to Man's Responsibility: Repudiating Mr. M. B. Sampson's Phrenological Theory, and His Philosophy of Insanity* (London: A. Maxwell)

Whibley, Charles (May 1900) 'Musings Without Method', *Blackwood's Edinburgh Magazine*, Vol. 167 (Edinburgh: William Blackwood): 688–94

Whibley, Charles (September 1900) 'Musings Without Method', *Blackwood's Edinburgh Magazine*, Vol. 168 (Edinburgh: William Blackwood): 402–4

Whibley, Charles (July 1906) 'Musings Without Method', *Blackwood's Edinburgh Magazine*, Vol. 180 (Edinburgh: William Blackwood): 128–31

White, John (1996) '"Nixon *Was* The One": Edgar Daniel Nixon, the MIA and the Montgomery Bus Boycott', in *The Making of Martin Luther King and the Civil Rights Movement*, eds Brian Ward and Tony Badger (New York: New York UP): 45–63

White, Stephen (2000) *What Queen Victoria Saw: Roderick Maclean and the Trial of Lunatics Act, 1883* (Chichester, England: Barry Rose Law Publishers)

White, William Allen (1946) *The Autobiography of William Allen White* (New York: Macmillan)

Whitman, Walt (1887) *Specimen Days in America* (London: Walter Scott)

Whitman, Walt (1982) *Complete Poetry and Collected Prose* (New York: Library of America)

Whyte, William H. (1960) *The Organization Man* (1956) (Harmondsworth: Penguin)

Wieczynski, Joseph L., ed. (1981) *The Modern Encyclopedia of Russian and Soviet History*, Vol. 24 (Gulf Breeze, FL: Academic International Press)

Wilcock, John (interviewer and editor) (1971) *The Autobiography and Sex Life of Andy Warhol by John Wilcock and a cast of thousands* (New York: Other Scene)

Wilde, Oscar (1979) *Selected Letters of Oscar Wilde*, ed. Rupert Hart-Davis (Oxford: OUP)

Wilford, Hugh (2008) *The Mighty Wurlitzer: How the CIA Played America* (Cambridge, MA: Harvard UP)

Williams, John A. (1970) *The King God Didn't Save* (New York: Coward-McCann)

Williams, William Appleman (1966) *The Contours of American History* (1961) (Chicago: Quadrangle Books)

Wilson, Francis (1929) *John Wilkes Booth. Fact and Fiction of Lincoln's Assassination* (Boston & New York: Houghton Mifflin)

Wilson, N. W. (1901) 'Details of President McKinley's Case', *Buffalo Medical Journal*, Vol. 57, No. 2 (Buffalo, NY): 207–25

Winkler, Heinrich August (1993) *Weimar, 1918–1933: Die Geschichte der ersten deutschen Demokratie* (München: C. H. Beck)

Winslow, Forbes (1843) *The Plea of Insanity in Criminal Cases* (London: H. Renshaw)

Winslow, Forbes (1854) 'On Medico-Legal Evidence in Cases of Insanity', in his *Lettsomian Lectures on Insanity* (London: John Churchill): 82–158

Wolf, Ernst (1966) 'Zum Verhältnis der politischen und moralischen Motive in der deutschen Widerstandsbewegung', in *Der deutsche Widerstand gegen Hitler: Vier historisch-kritische Studien von Hermann Graml, Hans Mommsen, Hans Joachim Reichhardt und Ernst Wolf*, eds Walter Schmitthener and Hans Buchheim (Cologne & Berlin: Kiepenheuer & Witsch): 215–55

Wolfe, Tom (1970) *Radical Chic & Mau-Mauing the Flak Catchers* (New York: Farrar, Straus & Giroux)

Wolfe, Tom (1989) *The Electric Kool-Aid Acid Test* (1968) (London: Black Swan)

Wolfenstein, Eugene Victor (1981) *The Victims of Democracy: Malcolm X and the Black Revolution* (Berkeley, Los Angeles & London: Univ. of California Press)

Woodcock, George and Ivan Avakumović (1950) *The Anarchist Prince: A Biographical Study of Peter Kropotkin* (London & New York: T. V. Broadman)

Woodcock, George (1963) *Anarchism. A History of Libertarian Ideas and Movements* (1962) (Harmondsworth: Penguin)

Woodham-Smith, Cecil (1972) *Queen Victoria. Her Life and Times, 1819–1861* (London: Hamish Hamilton)

Woolf, Robert Lee (1956) *The Balkans in Our Time* (Cambridge, MA: Harvard UP)

Woronov, Mary (1995) *Swimming Underground: My Years in the Warhol Factory* (London: Serpent's Tail)

Yarmolinsky, Avraham (1971) *Dostoevsky, Works and Days* (New York: Funk & Wagnalls)

Yeghiayan, Vartkes (trans.) (1985) *The Case of Solomon Tehlirian* (Los Angeles: ARF Varantian Gomideh)

Young, Andrew (1996) *An Easy Burden: The Civil Rights Movement and the Transformation of America* (New York: HarperCollins)

Young, G. M. (1944) *Mr. Gladstone* (Oxford: Clarendon Press)

'Z' (January 1894) 'Anarchists: Their Methods and Organisation', *New Review*, Vol. 10, No. 56 (London: William Heinemann): 1–9

Zeisler, Ernest Bloomfield (1956) *The Haymarket Riot* (Chicago: Alexander J. Isaacs)

Ziegler, Philip (1985) *Mountbatten: The Official Biography* (London: Collins)

Zimbardo, Philip (2007) *The Lucifer Effect: How Good People Turn Evil* (New York: Random House)

Zinn, Howard (2003) *A People's History of the United States* (New York: HarperPerennial)

Zürcher, Erik J. (2004) *Turkey. A Modern History*, rev. edn (London & New York: I. B. Tauris)

FILMOGRAPHY

The following films are either referred to in the text or were helpful in forming my understanding of the subjects they discuss.

Allen, Lewis (1954) *Suddenly*

Antonioni, Michelangelo (1970) *Zabriskie Point*

Bate, Peter (1994) *Charles Manson: The Man Who Killed the Sixties*

Coppola, Francis Ford (1974) *The Conversation*

Coppola, Francis Ford (1979) *Apocalypse Now*

Davis, Peter (1974) *Hearts and Minds*

Drew, Robert (1960) *Primary*

Drew, Robert (1963) *Crisis: Behind a Presidential Commitment*

Edison, Thomas (producer) (1901) *Execution of Czolgosz With Panorama of Auburn Prison*

Ehrlich, Judith and Rick Goldsmith (2009) *The Most Dangerous Man in America: Daniel Ellsberg and the Pentagon Papers*

Epstein, Robert and Richard Schmeichen (1984) *The Times of Harvey Milk*

Estevez, Emilio (2006) *Bobby*

Frank, Melvin and Norman Panama (1956) *The Court Jester*

Frankenheimer, John (1962) *The Manchurian Candidate*

Green, Sam and Bill Siegel (2002) *The Weather Underground*

Griffith, D. W. (1915) *The Birth of a Nation*

Harron, Mary (1996) *I Shot Andy Warhol*

Hendrickson, Robert and Laurence Merrick (producers and directors) (1972) *Manson*

Hitchcock, Alfred (1959) *North by Northwest*

Kopple, Barbara (1976) *Harlan County U.S.A.*

Leaf, David and John Scheinfeld (2006) *The U.S. vs. John Lennon*

Lee, Spike (1992) *Malcolm X*

Lumet, Sidney (1976) *Network*

Mekas, Jonas and Andrew Solt (2000) *Gimme Some Truth: The Making of John Lennon's Imagine Album*

Miller, David (1973) *Executive Action*

Mueller, Niels (2004) *The Assassination of Richard Nixon*

O'Sullivan, Shane (2007) *RFK Must Die: The Assassination of Robert Kennedy*

Pakula, Alan J. (1974) *The Parallax View*

Pakula, Alan J. (1976) *All the President's Men*

Piddington, Andrew (2006) *The Killing of John Lennon*

Range, Gabriel (2006) *The Assassination of George W. Bush*

Rossen, Robert (1949) *All the King's Men*

Scorsese, Martin (1976) *Taxi Driver*

Scorsese, Martin (2010) *Shutter Island*

Stone, Oliver (1991) *JFK*

Stone, Robert (2004) *Neverland: The Rise and Fall of the Symbionese Liberation Army* (released on DVD as *Guerilla: The Taking of Patty Hearst*)

Van Sant, Gus (2008) *Milk*

Workman, Chuck (1990) *Superstar: The Life and Times of Andy Warhol*

Zinnemann, Fred (1973) *The Day of the Jackal*

Also fascinating to see are the following *World in Action* documentaries (available on DVD from Network).

Hewat, Tim (executive producer) (3 Dec. 1963) *Dallas* (a report on the city in the wake of JFK's assassination)

Valentine, Alex (executive Producer) (23 Feb. 1965) *Malcolm X*

Moser, Brian (producer) and David Plowright (executive producer) (11 Dec. 1967) *End of a Revolution* (on the death of Che Guevara)

Fontaine, Dick (producer) (27 Sept. 1971) *Death of a Revolutionary* (on the death of George Jackson)

Clark, Malcolm and Michael Ryan (producers) (3 Oct. 1977) *The Life and Death of Steve Biko*

Index